THE CAMBRIDGE HISTORY OF AFRICA

Volume 5
from *c.* 1790 to *c.* 1870

edited by
JOHN E. FLINT

CAMBRIDGE UNIVERSITY PRESS
CAMBRIDGE
LONDON · NEW YORK · MELBOURNE

Published by the Syndics of the Cambridge University Press
The Pitt Building, Trumpington Street, Cambridge CB2 1RP
Bentley House, 200 Euston Road, London NW1 2DB
32 East 57th Street, New York, NY 10022, USA
296 Beaconsfield Parade, Middle Park, Melbourne 3206, Australia

© Cambridge University Press 1976

Library of Congress catalogue card number: 76–2261

ISBN: 0 521 20701 0

First published 1976

Printed in Great Britain
at the
University Printing House, Cambridge
(Harry Myers, University Printer)

THE CAMBRIDGE HISTORY
OF AFRICA

General Editors: J. D. FAGE and ROLAND OLIVER

Volume 5
from *c.* 1790 to *c.* 1870

THE CAMBRIDGE HISTORY OF AFRICA

CONTENTS

CONTENTS

MAPS

PREFACE

In the English-speaking world, the Cambridge histories have since the beginning of the century set the pattern for multi-volume works of history, with chapters written by experts on a particular topic, and unified by the guiding hand of volume editors of senior standing. *The Cambridge Modern History*, planned by Lord Acton, appeared in sixteen volumes between 1902 and 1912. It was followed by *The Cambridge Ancient History, The Cambridge Medieval History, The Cambridge History of English Literature*, and Cambridge Histories of India, of Poland, and of the British Empire. The original *Modern History* has now been replaced by *The New Cambridge Modern History* in twelve volumes, and *The Cambridge Economic History of Europe* is now being completed. Other Cambridge Histories recently undertaken include a history of Islam, of Arabic literature, of the Bible treated as a central document of and influence on Western civilization, and of Iran and China.

It was during the later 1950s that the Syndics of the Cambridge University Press first began to explore the possibility of embarking on a Cambridge History of Africa. But they were then advised that the time was not yet ripe. The serious appraisal of the past of Africa by historians and archaeologists had hardly been undertaken before 1948, the year when universities first began to appear in increasing numbers in the vast reach of the African continent south of the Sahara and north of the Limpopo, and the time too when universities outside Africa first began to take some notice of its history. It was impressed upon the Syndics that the most urgent need of such a young, but also very rapidly advancing branch of historical studies, was a journal of international standing through which the results of ongoing research might be disseminated. In 1960, therefore, the Cambridge University Press launched *The Journal of African History*, which gradually demonstrated the amount of work being undertaken to establish the past of Africa as an integrated whole rather than – as it had usually been viewed before – as the story of a series of incursions into the continent by peoples coming from outside, from the Mediterranean basin, the Near East or western Europe. This movement will of course continue and develop further, but the increasing facilities available for its publication soon began to demonstrate a need to assess both what had been done, and what still needed to be done, in the light of some general historical perspective for the continent.

The Syndics therefore returned to their original charge, and in 1966 the founding editors of *The Journal of African History* accepted a commission to become the general editors of a *Cambridge History of Africa*. They found it a daunting task to draw up a plan for a co-operative work covering a history which was in active process of exploration by scholars of many nations, scattered over a fair part of the globe, and of many disciplines – linguists, anthropologists, geographers and botanists, for example, as well as historians and archaeologists.

It was thought that the greatest problems were likely to arise with the earliest and latest periods: the earliest, because so much would depend on the results of long-term archaeological investigation, and the latest, because of the rapid changes in historical perspective that were occurring as a consequence of the ending of colonial rule in Africa. Initially, therefore, only five volumes were planned, of which the first, Africa before *c.* 500 BC, based entirely upon archaeological sources (and edited by an archaeologist), would be the last to appear, while of the others – dealing with the periods of approximately 500 BC to AD 1050, 1050–1600, 1600–1790, and 1790–1870 – it was expected that they would appear in an order inverse to their chronology. In the event, Professor Flint's volume 5 was overtaken by Professor Gray's volume 4, but there is every likelihood that volumes 3, 2 and 1 will appear in that order. The General Editors decreed that only after these volumes were well under way would an attempt be made to plan for the period after *c.* 1875. Nine years later, it can be said that three further volumes have been planned, and that it is hoped that these will appear at regular intervals following the publication of volume 1.

When they started their work, the general editors quickly came to the conclusion that the most practicable plan for getting out the first five volumes within a reasonable period of time was likely to be the simplest and most straightforward. The direction of each volume was therefore entrusted to a volume editor who, in addition to having made a substantial contribution to the understanding of the period in question, was a man with whom the general editors were in close touch. Within a volume, the aim was to keep the number of contributors to a minimum. Each of them was asked to essay a broad survey of a particular area or theme with which he was familiar for the whole of the period covered by the volume. In this survey, his purpose should be to take account not only of all relevant research done, or still in progress, but also of the gaps in knowledge. These he should try to fill by new thinking of his own, whether based on new work on the available sources or on interpolations from congruent research.

It should be remembered that the plan for these first five volumes was drawn up nearly a decade ago, when little or no research had been done on many important topics, and before many of today's younger scholars – not least those who now fill posts in the departments of history and archaeology in the universities and research institutes in Africa itself – had made their own deep penetrations into such areas of ignorance. Two things follow from this. If the general editors had drawn up their plan in the 1970s rather than the 1960s, the shape might well have been very different, perhaps with a larger number of more specialized, shorter chapters, each centred on a smaller area, period or theme, to the understanding of which the contributor would have made his own individual contribution. Indeed, the last three volumes seem likely to be composed more on such lines. Secondly, the sheer volume of new research that has been published since the contributors for the first five volumes accepted their commissions has often led them to undertake very substantial revisions in their work as it progressed from draft to draft, thus protracting the length of time originally envisaged for the preparation of these volumes.

But histories are meant to be read, and not simply to be continually rewritten and modified by their authors and editors. Volume 5 of *The Cambridge History of Africa* now joins volume 4 for public use and appraisal, together with the promise that six further volumes will follow at more or less regular intervals.

J. D. FAGE
ROLAND OLIVER

May 1976

INTRODUCTION

This volume is concerned with a period of African history which has traditionally been defined by events emanating from Europe. The year 1790 roughly marks the beginnings of the effective impact of the British anti-slavery movement on West Africa, where the freed slave colony of Sierra Leone was already struggling to establish itself. Protestant missionary enterprise in West and South Africa had begun. In 1795 the British first occupied the Cape of Good Hope, while three years later Napoleon's occupation of Egypt launched the movement of 'modernization' in North Africa. In succeeding decades the impact of European traders, missionaries and consuls increasingly began to affect the internal social, political and economic balances within African societies. The choice of 1870 as the terminal date for this volume is obviously dictated by the beginnings of the European scramble for African territory which will be a major theme of volume 6. The period can thus be considered as one dominated by the theme of Africa's growing contact with Europe, as a time of slow penetration and preparation by Europeans for the coming of partition and colonial rule.

Such a perspective, however, offers a somewhat irrelevant pattern for the history of the continent as a whole. Though Bantu in South Africa, or Arabs in Algeria, felt the direct impact of European settler colonization, elsewhere in the continent the vast mass of Africans rarely saw a European, and Europe influenced their lives only indirectly or at second-hand, except for those who lived in coastal areas where there was a direct European presence. If African history in this period is to be viewed in a perspective of external impact, then that of the Arabs and Islam, rather than that of the Europeans and Christianity, must be judged the more formidable. The intermingling of the Arab-Muslim world with African culture along the frontiers of contact between north and tropical Africa was an ancient theme of African history, but after 1790 Islamic expansion became dynamic and aggressive throughout the West African savanna, across to the Nile valley, into Ethiopia and the Somali country, and down the East African coast. Egypt presented the threat of open colonial conquest to the peoples of the Nile valley and the Red Sea littoral, and by the 1870s was attempting to expand along the Somali coast, into Ethiopia, and to the shores of Lake Victoria. The

Fulani erupted as a conquering Muslim race of empire-builders in the West African savanna. The decision of Sayyid Sa'īd to move his state from Oman to Zanzibar was a stage in the creation of a vast network of commercial penetration in East Africa, whose repercussions would be felt deep into the Congo basin, north to Lake Victoria and south to Malawi. Whether Arabs in East Africa might have transformed their commercial empire into political hegemony is a question made purely speculative by the European intervention of the 1880s. The Egyptian threat collapsed with the financial bankruptcy of Turkey and Egypt in the mid-1870s. The success of the jihads of the western savanna, however, indicated that stable and viable political regimes, using Islamic political concepts, could work successfully among African peoples. Even more important in the long term was the way in which the penetration of Islam developed mixed Islamic-African cultures from the west African savanna to the Swahili coast, and penetrated substantially into areas of traditionally strong African politics such as Bunyoro and Buganda, or the Yoruba and Asante. A wide belt of peoples by 1870 were brought closer to the Muslim world than the Christian, representing bridging cultures between Arab and Black Africa. European contact in the period produced nothing on this scale, though the Cape Coloured group in South Africa, or the 'Creoles' of Sierra Leone or Liberia were comparable, though far less numerous, communities.

An Islamic perspective, however, though less 'external' to Africa than the European one, provides frameworks only for certain regions of Africa, and is irrelevant for most of southern Africa and the western Congo basin, while in the West African rain forest Islam was peripheral in this period. The ideal perspective for a volume of this kind would be a pan-African one developed from advanced historical research, in which the available sources had been exhaustively examined to the point where the historical events of the period had become an accepted corpus of 'facts', as in European history. Unfortunately African history is still in its infancy, despite the wealth of detail to be found in the chapters which follow. Some day it will become possible to range over the continent using historical typologies of states and societies which will have provided us with new regional patterns drawn from African history instead of from the geographical regions used in this volume. Some of these historical regions are already clear. The West African savanna is one used in a subsequent chapter. The rise of the Zulu and the *mfecane* created a new historical region linking Zulu, Lesotho, Ndebele, Barotse and the Ngoni of Malawi and Tanzania in a pattern spanning South, Central and East Africa. Likewise the Lwo-Nilotic states stretch from the Shilluk to northern Tanzania. With a deeper and firmer corpus of knowledge, it might be possible to consider groups of states which together seem to form types. Morocco, Ethiopia, Buganda, Zulu, Barotse and others might be seen as showing a pattern of developing centralization, evolving royal bureaucracies, standing armies and external expansion. Other families of states fragmented and dissolved into near-chaos in the same period under many of the same stresses, states like those of the Wolof, Yoruba, Lunda-Luba and Ovimbundu. If such types could be firmly established, comparative analysis would then become possible, but the present state of African historical research is not sufficiently advanced to permit the confident comparison of types of states or historical regions.

In the planning of this volume a perspective drawn from the observation of European or Islamic activities has been rejected. A perspective based on historical regions created by African activities, or on comparisons between types of states and societies, seemed premature, for the reasons outlined above. Instead it was decided to construct this volume, like others in the Cambridge History, as a series of studies of geographical regions, each of which spans the entire period, with certain themes, such as the activities of Africans overseas and the impact of Europeans, to be dealt with in separate chapters. A broad division of Africa into cultural regions has been attempted, with the Maghrib, Egypt and the Nile valley, Ethiopia and the Horn, East Africa from the Lakes to the Indian Ocean, West Africa forest and savanna, Congo and Central Africa, Madagascar and southern Africa considered separately through the entire period of the volume.

The evident danger in such an approach is that the history of Africa might disappear from view in a plethora of regional histories. This possibility was judged a lesser evil than that of imposing a thematic structure based on the impact of external forces. In the event, as this volume took shape, it became apparent that the effect of the regional approach was to expose similarities as well as to delineate differences, and to suggest that there are some common themes in African history in its last phase before the imposition of colonial rule. Some of these themes appear more significant than, and do not always noticeably result from, contact with Europe or Islam.

In African political history the most outstanding phenomenon of the period was the creation of states bearing many of the attributes of nationalism. The concept of the nation and nationalism in Africa has,

3

because of recent political history, come to take on peculiar meanings. We are accustomed to regard the leaders of the movement against colonial rule, and the post-colonial élite of independent Africa, as the first movement of African nationalism, because they couched their political demands in terms drawn from European nationalist thought. But contemporary African nationalists are men striving to create nations, or to strengthen recently developed concepts of loyalty to political units created after 1880 by European partition. In contra-distinction, loyalties to pre-colonial political units or societies are des-cribed (often with a certain contempt) as 'tribalism', whereas in reality such feelings express loyalties to a common language, common forms of social organization and a sense of belonging to a wide community which in European history would be characterized as nationalism. Many of these so-called tribes number millions of people and are larger than the smaller nationalities of Europe. Contemporary 'tribalism' may thus be regarded as the survival of pre-colonial sentiments of African forms of nationality. It would be more accurate to describe groups such as the Asante, Zulu, Ganda or Hausa-Fulani as nations, at least when dis-cussing African history before the colonial partition.

Many of these pre-colonial nations were the result of centuries of development, based on common language and culture, and were mature before 1790. Monarchical institutions expressing a political theory which claimed that the king was descended from divine ances-tors who were the 'fathers' of the society had done much to develop loyalty and solidarity in the nation. The Luba and Lunda kingdoms of West-Central Africa, the Oyo empire and the Benin kingdom in Nigeria, the rule of the *mais* in Bornu, or the regimes in the interlacustrine states such as Rwanda, Buganda and Bunyoro, are examples of such develop-ments over several centuries. Asante and Dahomey were more recent examples of monarchies founded more on principles of *realpolitik*, which nevertheless strove to weld their peoples together with a sense of national identity. In the period after 1790 most of these states faced severe internal and external problems. A few, like Dahomey, Asante and Bornu, survived intact and strengthened by 1870, but most ex-perienced shrinkage of territory or severe internal upheavals.

After 1790 many areas of Africa experienced political ferment in which new types of states emerged which were both nationalistic and expansionist. They varied greatly from region to region, but all dis-played a common tendency not merely to form a community with common language into a state, but to use new forms of political authority and new military techniques to absorb and 'nationalize' other peoples of different languages and culture. Hitherto African nations had been built on pre-existing foundations of common language and feelings of kinship. The ancient empires of sub-Saharan Africa, like Mali and Songhay, were controlled by linguistic minorities which did little to impose their culture on the masses, and were content to rule subject peoples by indirect means as tributary nations. There now appeared assimilative states and empires which strove to absorb conquered and subjected peoples directly into the language and culture of the ruling group.

The nineteenth century was the age of European nationalism, and it is tempting to postulate an influence from Europe upon the African nation-builders. This can be traced in special cases, but the evidence will not support a theory of generalized European influence in all these phenomena. European pressures were important in North Africa. Napoleon's conquest of Egypt, and the penetration thereafter of British and French capital and technology in Egypt, Tunis and Tripoli, with the added threat posed by the French conquest of Algeria after 1830, all worked a ferment in North African Islamic thought. The efforts of North African rulers to secure their dynastic independence from Turkey, coupled with their failure to introduce controls which would make European finance and technology produce social benefits, produced movements of reform and discontent. In Egypt the rule of the Khedives, and the failure of their attempts to build a vast empire in the Sudan, Ethiopia and the Horn, led to the cry of 'Egypt for the Egyptians' and a nationalist movement among the army officers by the 1870s. European influence also played its part in the expansion of the Malagasy kingdom of Merina. Radama I consciously admired Napoleon, introduced European techniques and training into his army, employed a Jamaican, a Frenchman and an Englishman as generals, and brought missionaries to run schools and workshops. After his death in 1828 a long period of 'reaction' characterized by hostility to European influences was followed by a second opening of the country to Europe in 1861 under Radama II. Much weaker and more indirect European influence may have played some part in the renaissance of Ethiopia in the nineteenth century.

But the creation of the Zulu monarchy and the large number of Nguni-speaking states in southern, central and eastern Africa, the welding together of new nations such as the Sotho kingdom of Moshoeshoe or the new kingdoms of the Congo basin, the development of the increasingly homogeneous Hausa-Fulani culture in the

Sokoto caliphate cannot be explained, even partially, by a theory of imitation of European models. Moreover, where direct European influence through missionaries, traders and consuls was strongest, as on the West African coast, this seems to have weakened rather than strengthened the building of national loyalties around language groups. English- or French-speaking Africans looked to colonial units as the bases for 'modern' types of nationality, wider than traditional language groups and built upon newly forming 'national' classes which would replace clan and lineage loyalties. The 'Creoles' of Freetown, the African clergy of Bishop Crowther's Niger Mission, or the early educated élites of Lagos, Dakar and Accra were the forerunners of the twentieth-century nationalist politicians, and like them were unwilling to identify African nationality with African languages.

The most outstanding examples of African nation-building after 1790 took place in southern Africa. Shaka's meteoric career transformed the Zulu from a petty clan of the Nguni into a fully developed nationality – so much so that the clan gave its name to the Zulu language. The military system of age regiments which made this possible was itself the instrument for assimilating conquered males and making them Zulu. In turn the Zulu spawned the new Nguni-speaking nations, which used the same regimental system and ideas of kingship developed by Shaka. Defeated rivals created new states in their retreat from Shaka's warriors, as did Sobhuza in Swaziland, or Shoshangane in Gaza. Seceding generals like Mzilikazi made new nations such as the Ndebele. In trying to stem the Zulu advance, non-Nguni welded new nations from refugee bands, the outstanding example being Moshoeshoe's Sotho. It is perhaps no coincidence that Lesotho and Swaziland are among the handful of pre-colonial African nation-states which have emerged autonomous and intact into the post-colonial period.

Elsewhere nation-building in Africa after 1790 was a less self-conscious process, developing from dynastic, religious, territorial or economic ambitions. The renaissance of Ethiopia was a remarkable achievement of the period; in 1790 scarcely to be considered as a unit and torn by rivalries of virtually independent princes, Ethiopia by 1870 was a revived nation soon to defeat Egyptian invasion. Later it would not only escape partition, but itself become one of the partitioning powers. Though in reality an empire of many nations, rulers like Tewodros and Yohannes gave Ethiopia a concept of revival which drew strength from a long historical tradition and from the existence of the Christian Church as a single Ethiopian institution. Shoans, Tigreans, and even portions of the Galla, as well as the ruling Amhara, increasingly developed a sense of Ethiopian patriotism. This was to present the Egyptian and later Italian invaders with a unified and vibrant resistance such as few African states could mount.

Islam in the West African savanna, like Christianity in Ethiopia, could serve as an alternative to ethnicity and as an ideology for the state. In the jihads of the Fulani reformers, the ideal was the elevation of Muslims to office, and the creation of Muslim polities and Muslim culture. In the initial stages of these movements, the Fulani seemed to regard themselves as a ruling class, but had this alone been their goal the result would have been the creation of multi-ethnic empires which reduced the nationalities to tributary status, as in ancient Mali or Songhay. Instead Fulani dominance was used to control the processes of reform, and this was interpreted as the appointment of Muslims to administer the state. The empire of al-Ḥājj 'Umar remained a Fulani conquest state, and developed little sense of nationality. In the Sokoto caliphate, however, the nineteenth century was a period in which Islamic political ideas replaced traditional Hausa political loyalties. Fulani intermarried extensively with the Hausa, and by 1870 a Fulani-Hausa culture, loyal to the regime, had come into existence. Even this is an understatement which masks more complex achievements, for large numbers of Yoruba, Nupe, Gwari and a multiplicity of smaller ethnic groups came into the caliphate and began to accept its citizenship proudly. The Hausa themselves were not a 'tribe', but a culture, divided politically before the jihad into warring states. After 1800 'becoming Hausa' was a widespread phenomenon within the Sokoto caliphate. Thus a kind of northern Nigerian nation existed in the Sokoto empire by 1870. This would not merely survive, but strengthen and develop itself during the British colonial regime, and in modern Nigeria occupy the position of a powerful pre-colonial nationality.

Whether historical connections between all these phenomena can be perceived is a somewhat speculative proposition. The Fulani jihads and the *Mfecane* in southern Africa seem worlds apart. It can be argued that the nineteenth century saw an African, or perhaps an Arab-African, pre-partition of Africa, nipped in the bud by the European scramble after 1880. But this concept is more mystical than concrete.

More closely related to the evidence is the view that state-formation was stimulated by the development of trade and commerce, and particularly by the elaboration of long distance trade routes. In this respect there was in 1790 an evident and marked contrast between West Africa and Bantu Africa. In West Africa long distance trade was of ancient origin, and had been elaborated and expanded over many centuries. The trade had fostered an artisan class of gold, iron and silver smiths, cloth weavers and dyers, tanners and leather workers, clustered in urban centres which may have originated as market places. Commercial entrepreneurs were also an established and long-standing element in the social structure. The long history of complex and highly organized states and empires in West Africa is closely bound up with their strategic control of long distance trade routes, their command of the major sources of production of the trade items, their desire to tax and organize traders and markets, and to provide them with security and conditions for peaceful commerce. In Bantu Africa, by contrast, long distance trade was absent in most places, and small-scale where it existed in 1790. With the exception of the gold mines of the Mutapa kingdom, and places such as Bunyoro with useful salt and iron deposits, Bantu Africa had little to offer long distance traders until the demand for slaves and ivory made its appearance after 1790.

Trading activity, trade routes, the number and size of markets, and development of professional traders and artisans underwent a remarkable expansion after 1790 in all parts of tropical Africa. In West Africa this took place upon an established base, and before 1870 it would seem that while traditional trades and routes (except for the Atlantic slave trade) held their own or expanded, the new European demands for palm oil and other tropical produce created a larger scale of economic activity and a widening of routes and markets. In general West African peoples were well able to satisfy these new demands, and to make the political adjustments which were needed. In Bantu Africa, as the authors of the chapters dealing with this area show, the impact was more fundamental, and its effects more violent and far-reaching, precisely because Bantu Africa lacked the basic structures built in West Africa over many centuries. Moreover the trade of Bantu Africa was more narrowly based on a single wasting asset, ivory, the source of which might be controlled for twenty years or so by a state, which would then have to adjust itself to command a middleman position dominating more remote suppliers, or perhaps lose the trade altogether.

In all the interior parts of the continent, Africans after 1790 began building complex trading networks to supply the demand from Europeans or Arabs on the coasts for palm oil, ivory, slaves and other exports, and to take goods from the coasts to supply the inland peoples with newly acquired wants, cheaper manufactured goods, guns and firearms. These developments gave the opportunity to peoples who were strategically placed across developing trade routes to tax trade and give protection of markets and routes in return. Traders would be attracted to large efficient states, like the Sokoto caliphate, which were capable of ensuring peaceful conditions for commerce. Markets could become embryonic urban centres, attracting the state's administrative attentions. Fortified royal camps would naturally attract traders looking for a secure place to buy and sell. Contact with foreigners, rarely European, sometimes Arab, but generally stranger Africans, led to the exchange of ideas, as well as of goods, and to political and military innovations.

The roots of the partition of Africa may be seen, with benefit of hindsight, in the period covered by this volume. If the larger effects of European and Arab trading demand were indirect, they began to display substantial erosions of African sovereignty, especially in coastal areas. The creation of the Zanzibar empire entailed true colonization by Arab settlers on Zanzibar and Pemba islands and in the mainland coastal strip, with the reduction of substantial numbers of Africans to slave labour status in a colonial plantation economy. Egyptian expansion foreshadowed the later endeavours of European powers, employing the paraphernalia of governors and colonial bureaucracies, and proclaiming the imperialist morality of the 'civilizing mission'. The efforts of African state-builders indicated the beginning of the end of African ethnic particularism.

The direct European partition of Africa also began towards the end of the eighteenth century, but as a slow process, quite unlike the scramble for African territory which erupted after about 1880. There is considerable irony in the process of European colonial expansion in Africa. In the seventeenth and eighteenth centuries, the Atlantic slave trade grew to form an essential element underpinning the European imperial systems, without which the Caribbean or mainland American plantation colonies could not have been developed or maintained. But formal imperial rule in West Africa proved unnecessary, for African middlemen supplied the demand for slave labour with efficiency and despatch. The legacy of the slave trade was a string of European forts and castles on the West African coast. It was the emergence of anti-slave trade sentiments in Europe and North America which brought the establishment of colonies in West Africa, designed to serve aggressive attempts to force legitimate trade by political and naval pressures. Freetown was the first British colony of settlement in Africa. Later,

Liberia and Libreville were American and French equivalents. The difficulties of expanding legitimate commerce, and the moral righteousness with which the British in particular pursued it, led to a steady erosion of African sovereignty along the West African coast. This was seldom as formal as the British annexation of Lagos in 1861, but generally took the form of diplomatic intervention, sometimes backed by naval and military threats, in the internal affairs of recalcitrant African states. In this way the Fante and other peoples of southern Ghana fell gradually into quasi-colonial dependence on the British after 1828, the French pushed their influence up the Senega vallley, while the British created mixed courts and interfered in succession disputes in the states of the Niger delta.

In South Africa there were signs by the 1770s that the Dutch settler population had outgrown its simple status as a provision ground for Dutch shipping on its way to India. The British occupation of the Cape, made permanent in 1814, introduced humanitarian pressures and the missionary factor, judicial reforms, and the abolition of slavery in 1833. The response was the Great Trek, which partitioned African lands among the Boer republics of the Transvaal and Orange Free state, established the new British colony of Natal, and left a temporary balance of power between Bantu, Boer and Briton which would last until the age of diamonds and gold.

North Africa also experienced substantial growth of direct European influence after 1790 in the shape of the French conquest of Algeria, which at first sight appears an analogous counterpart to Britain's advance in South Africa. It was, however, an aberration, caused and maintained by internal pressures within France, and thus failed to provoke a scramble for North African territory. Instead, Egypt, Tunis and Tripoli were penetrated by European finance. These states were attempting to 'modernize', but by the 1870s the results had proved disastrous, and widespread bankruptcy set the scene for the imposition of European political control in the 1880s.

The Algerian conquests, the expansion of white settlement in South Africa and the colonial enclaves in West Africa were in themselves substantial additions to the British and French colonial empires, but their impact on the African continent was by no means a dominant theme of its history before 1870. The period covered in this volume must be seen overall as the last phase of African pre-colonial history. The wider impact of Europe was its indirect influence, especially on the development of interior trade and trade routes. The rapid industrialization of

Britain, and the somewhat slower development in western Europe, created an energetic demand for vegetable oils, ivory, gold, dyestuffs, cotton and other tropical products. The massive British cotton industry and the expansion of the metal trades also gave rise to a new emphasis on the tropical African as a potential consumer of manufactures. The African response to these developments was massive, and there was scarcely a part of the continent which did not at some time after 1790 and before 1870 find itself able to procure European goods in return for African produce by trading with African intermediaries who formed part of a chain of trade reaching ultimately to Arab or European traders on or near the coasts. This process, which carried with it the introduction of firearms deep into the interior, brought with it much violence, social dislocation and political change. But the response was made; Africans had begun to participate in a world-wide economy and had started to make the cultural, social and political adjustments which this made necessary. Still in 1870 the scope and nature of these changes, except in a few colonial territories, were matters for African decision and initiative.

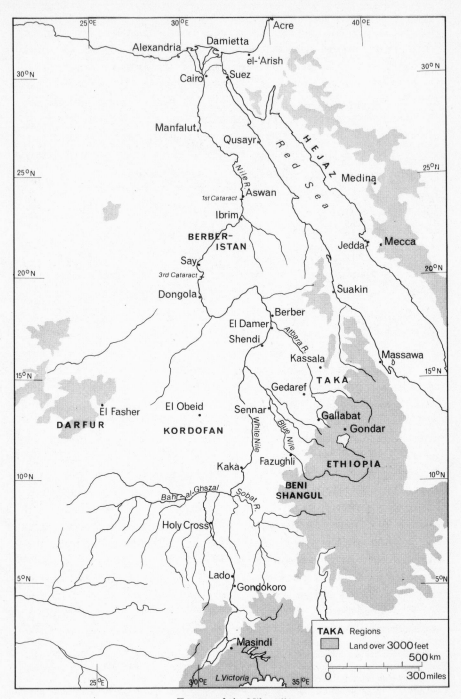

1 Egypt and the Nile valley

CHAPTER 1

EGYPT AND THE NILE VALLEY

EGYPT AND THE NILE VALLEY IN THE LATE
EIGHTEENTH CENTURY

In the last decade of the eighteenth century, the political condition of Egypt and the Nilotic Sudan was not far removed from anarchy. Egypt was still, as it had been since 1517, a province of the Ottoman Empire, but it was no longer under the effective control of the sultan. Since the early seventeenth century, the power of the Ottoman viceroy had been eroded until he was no more than a figurehead. The country was dominated by a military élite composed of the officers of the Ottoman garrison-corps (especially the Janissaries) and a group of grandees, the beys, most of whom were members of Mamluk households,[1] and were of Circassian, Bosniak or other alien origin. The whole political structure was deeply riven by faction. By the middle of the eighteenth century, a group known as the Qāzdughliyya, after the Mamluk household which formed its nucleus, had triumphed over their rivals, only to split up into competing personal factions. Between 1760 and 1772, the most capable and ruthless of the Qāzdughlī leaders, *Bulut Kapan* 'Alī Bey (often called *al-Kabīr*, 'the Great'), established a kind of dictatorship. After he had been overthrown, and eventually killed (in 1773), the primacy in Egypt passed to his own former *mamlūk*, Muḥammad Bey Abu'l-Dhahab, whose death in 1775 was followed by a revival of faction-fighting. After many vicissitudes, including an Ottoman expedition in 1786–7 intended to restore the sultan's control over Egypt, the ultimate victors in this contest were two men, Ibrāhīm Bey and Murād Bey, who established a somewhat uneasy duumvirate. The country meanwhile was reduced to a pitiable state. Agriculture was ruined by the unconscionable exactions of the duumvirs. A series of popular revolts took place in Cairo, during which the '*ulamā*' (the religious scholars and jurists) began to play a politically active part. The few European traders, of whom the most important were the French, suffered from the extortions of the beys. Egypt in 1798 was a divided

---

[1] A *mamlūk* was a male slave (usually in this period from the Caucasus or Georgia) who was imported into Egypt, converted to Islam, trained as a horse-soldier and emancipated. The Mamluk households were companies of retainers recruited in this way by military officers and other notables, many of whom were themselves of *mamlūk* origin. See further, *Cambridge History of Africa*, **4**, ch. 1, pp. 14–20.

and enfeebled country. The Ottoman sultan, Selīm III, lacked the means to reintegrate it in his empire, while there was no one in Egypt itself capable of establishing a strong, autonomous administration.

The traditional southern frontier of Egypt lay at the First Cataract of the Nile, just above Aswan. Beyond this point, and as far as the Third Cataract, lay the territory of Lower Nubia, known to the Ottomans as Berberistan, the land of the Barābra. This was technically a part of the Ottoman Empire, although neither the sultan nor the viceroy exercised any power there. A family of hereditary *kāshifs* (administrative officers) held political authority in the region, while the three fortresses of Aswan, Ibrim and Say were occupied by the light-skinned descendants of their original Bosniak garrisons.

Beyond the Third Cataract lay the dominions of the Funj, a negroid clan, who had in the sixteenth century established a high-kingship over the territories of the main and Blue Niles as far as the Ethiopian marches, and had extended their authority to the White Nile and even, at times, into Kordofan. By the late eighteenth century, the power of the Funj sultan was no more than nominal. In 1761–2 a military coup d'état had brought about the deposition of the last effective sultan, Bādī IV, and the manager of the plot, Shaykh Muḥammad Abū Likaylik, installed himself as regent. While he lived, the territories he controlled were well administered, but after his death in 1776 or 1777, factional strife in his family hastened the disintegration of the Funj sultanate. The regents, who belonged to an ethnic group known as the Hamaj, were reduced to being masters of Sennar, the old capital of the Funj, and a certain amount of territory on both banks of the Blue Nile. Ironically, the last and one of the best of the Hamaj regents, Muḥammad walad ʿAdlān, was murdered early in 1821, when the invading troops of Muḥammad ʿAlī Pasha were already advancing on Sennar.

Out of the decline of the Funj high-kingship a number of tribal states had emerged. One of these was that of the Jaʿaliyyūn, who lived (mainly as sedentaries) on the main Nile south of the confluence of the Atbara. Their tribal capital was Shendi, and their ruler during the two decades preceding the Turco-Egyptian conquest was Makk (i.e. King) Nimr. John Lewis Burckhardt, who visited Shendi in 1814, describes it as being a prosperous commercial metropolis, lying at a crossroads of routes. At the northern tip of Nimr's kingdom lay the religious centre of El Damer, which had grown up around the holy family of the Majādhīb. These were the leaders of an indigenous branch of the Sufi order of the Shādhiliyya, and their prestige safeguarded the passage of

caravans to Shendi, and even across the desert to the Ottoman port of
Suakin. Farther to the north, where the Nile makes its great swing
westwards, was the country of the Shāyqiyya, a warrior tribal confederacy, which had thrown off subordination to the Funj high-king in
the seventeenth century. They were the terror of their neighbours up
and down the main Nile, until in 1812 refugee Mamluks from Egypt
(headed by the aged Ibrāhīm Bey) established an encampment (in
Turkish *ordu*, whence the Sudanese name, al-'Urḍī, for their settlement)
at the site which today is known as Dongola.

Another Muslim Sudanese sultanate, that of Darfur, had developed
more or less contemporaneously with that of the Funj. Until the later
eighteenth century, it had been preoccupied with relations with its
western neighbour, the sultanate of Wadai, but Sultan Muḥammad
Tayrāb (d. 1787) carried out the conquest of Kordofan, previously a
dependency of Sennar. Under his successor, Sultan 'Abd al-Raḥmān
al-Rashīd (d. 1800 or 1801), Darfur was at the height of its power. There
was a prosperous trade with Egypt and the Nilotic Sudan. Bonaparte,
when in Egypt, wrote to 'Abd al-Raḥmān for slaves to train as soldiers.
The English traveller, W. G. Browne, visited Darfur in 1793–6, and
saw the sultan. A much fuller account of Darfur was given by the Arab,
Muḥammad ibn 'Umar al-Tūnusī, who spent eight years in the country
under the next sultan, Muḥammad Faḍl. It was during the reign of
Muḥammad Faḍl that the Turco-Egyptian forces of Muḥammad 'Alī
made an unsuccessful attempt to conquer Darfur.

THE FRENCH OCCUPATION AND THE PERIOD OF ANARCHY, 1798–1805

Until the last quarter of the eighteenth century, Egypt did not feel the
direct impact of developments beyond the borders of the Ottoman
Empire. The factional struggles, the meteoric careers of the military
grandees, took place in a territory which (considering its role in earlier
and later history) seemed curiously remote. But throughout the
eighteenth century, the Ottoman power, which protected the turbulent
and refractory despots of Egypt, was failing. Since the Treaty of Carlo-
witz in 1699, the Habsburgs had pushed the frontier in Europe steadily
eastwards. Still more ominous for Egypt was the war of 1768–74, when
a Russian fleet cruising in the eastern Mediterranean demonstrated that
the Ottoman flank had indeed been turned. Russian interest in the area
continued in the following years.

It was, however, not Russia but revolutionary France which was to end the isolation of Egypt. French interest in the eastern Mediterranean lands went back to the time of the Crusades, and during the seventeenth and eighteenth centuries various schemes had been put forward for occupying Egypt. During the French Revolutionary War, such projects acquired a topical urgency. Bonaparte, after his successful campaign against the Austrians in Italy in 1797, considered and rejected a project for the invasion of England. The conquest of Egypt seemed a more feasible alternative, and from Egypt British trade with India could be threatened. Even an invasion of India did not seem wholly beyond the bounds of possibility. But Egypt was seen not only as a strategic necessity, but as a field for colonization and enlightenment. When the French expeditionary force sailed in May 1798, the troops were accompanied by a remarkable body of scholars and scientists, the savants whose researches were to lay the foundations of present-day knowledge of Egypt in ancient and more recent times.

Revolutionary France was at this time at peace with the Ottoman Empire, and both Bonaparte and his government were at pains to demonstrate that no derogation of the sultan's sovereignty over Egypt was intended. The invasion was represented in a proclamation as being directed solely against the beys. Bonaparte represented himself to the Egyptians as bringing just and legitimate government, democracy and careers open to talent.

When this proclamation was issued, the French had landed, on 1 July 1798, and had taken Alexandria. Murād led an expeditionary force down the Rosetta branch of the Nile, but he was defeated by the invaders, and fell back towards the capital. Ibrāhīm Bey prudently waited in Cairo to see the outcome. Murād, defeated again on 21 July at Inbaba opposite Cairo (the miscalled Battle of the Pyramids), fled to the traditional refuge of Upper Egypt, while Ibrāhīm and the Ottoman viceroy made their way to the east of the delta. Bonaparte entered Cairo on 25 July.

He was still far from being the master of Egypt. Both Ibrāhīm and Murād refused to negotiate. The former was defeated by Bonaparte at al-Ṣāliḥiyya on 11 August, and withdrew to Syria, where he was given asylum by Aḥmad al-Jazzār in his virtually autonomous pashalik of Acre. An expedition was sent against Murād in Upper Egypt. At this juncture a calamity befell the French: the naval force which had brought them to Egypt, and which secured their line of communications with France, was virtually annihilated by Nelson, in Aboukir bay (the so-called Battle of the Nile), on 1 August. Once this became known in Istanbul, the Ottoman government, which had long been anxious about French intentions in Egypt, declared war on the Republic.

Bonaparte, although isolated in a country only partly under his control, did not lose heart. Threatened by the advance of al-Jazzār and Ibrāhīm Bey to the frontiers of Egypt in the winter of 1798, he determined to strike at them before their local forces were strengthened by the Ottoman Empire and Britain. The Syrian campaign began in February 1799. Although initially successful, it came to a halt at the walls of Acre, where al-Jazzār was helped by two allies: the British naval officer, Sir Sidney Smith, who captured Bonaparte's siege artillery at sea; and the plague, which caused fearful losses in the French camp. The siege was raised, and Bonaparte re-entered Cairo on 14 June 1799.

When Bonaparte first landed, as we have seen, he sought the co-operation of the Egyptians against the Mamluk grandees, and during the early weeks of the occupation he made some attempt to conciliate Muslim opinion and to win collaborators. He showed a politic sympathy for Islam and cultivated the society of the 'ulamā'. At the same time he organized new consultative institutions, the divans, by means of which the notables might be associated with the French military administration. The chief of these, the Divan of Cairo, consisted of nine members belonging to the 'ulamā': others were set up in the four sub-provinces of Lower Egypt at that time under French control. These were established directly after the taking of Cairo; rather later, in September, he summoned a General Divan consisting of deputies nominated by the French commanders in the various parts of Egypt.

The divans formed at most a channel of communication between the Egyptians and the new military élite which had displaced the Mamluks. In their brief and disturbed existence, there was not sufficient time for them to establish themselves as vehicles of political education, still less as organs for the expression of the popular will. Even as sounding-boards of public opinion, they were seriously defective: the French seemed to have had no idea how completely they were alienated from the mass of their subjects when, on 21 October 1798, an insurrection broke out in Cairo. At root this was a popular rising, resembling those which had flared out at intervals through the previous twelve years, and it was caused by unpopular fiscal and administrative methods. It was also a reaction against alien rule – not really nationalist in content, but rather traditionalist, since the French were seen as meddling innovators, who were destroying the settled Islamic way of life. This aspect of the revolt was reinforced by Ottoman propaganda, which denounced the French as atheists, and summoned the Egyptians to a holy war. The rising's centre was in the mosque of al-Azhar. Although the French were taken by surprise, they acted quickly and decisively. Al-Azhar was bombarded, and by nightfall of the second day the revolt was over. Cairo settled down in sullen acquiescence once again.

Thus, by the summer of 1799, when Bonaparte returned from Syria, his position in Egypt was precarious. The Ottomans took the offensive, and landed an expeditionary force by Aboukir. On 21 July, however, Bonaparte attacked and destroyed their bridgehead. This was his last important act in Egypt. Informed of the situation in France from newspapers sent by Sir Sidney Smith, he determined to return, and on 22 August slipped away from Alexandria with a very small entourage. He left in such secrecy that it was only after his departure that Kléber, his successor, learnt that he had been appointed to command the army of occupation.

Kléber had been put in charge of a failing and bankrupt enterprise, from which he sought to extricate himself and the troops under his command. In January 1800, he concluded with the Ottomans, under the auspices of Sir Sidney Smith, the Convention of el-'Arish, which provided for the evacuation of the French from Egypt. But the agreement was disavowed by the British government, and Kléber, who was preparing for evacuation, had to secure his position by defeating an Ottoman force at the battle of Heliopolis (20 March 1800) and by suppressing another, and much more prolonged, revolt in Cairo.

On 14 June, Kléber was assassinated by a Syrian Muslim, and the command devolved upon General Menou, a man of administrative rather than military abilities, who had been converted to Islam and married an Egyptian girl. He was confident of holding Egypt as a French possession, but the British and Ottoman governments were determined to oust him. In March, 1801, a British force landed at Aboukir, followed soon after by Ottoman troops. Another Ottoman army entered Egypt from Palestine. In July, a force from India disembarked at the Red Sea port of Qusayr. The French garrison at Cairo had already capitulated: that of Alexandria under Menou's command did so at the end of August. The French occupation of Egypt had lasted a little over three years.

Although French domination had been so brief, and although French hopes, whether of colonial exploitation or of enlightened regeneration, had so quickly been disappointed, this short period marked a turning-point in the history of Egypt. Its long isolation was at an end, and the country was to assume its modern position at the strategic and diplomatic centre of the Middle East. A century of almost uninterrupted Anglo-French contention for influence in, and control over, Egypt began. At a different level, the French occupation was decisive in that it ended for ever the ascendancy of the Mamluks. Of the two men who had held the highest power before the coming of Bonaparte, Murād Bey, fearing a restoration of Ottoman rule, had in 1800 made his peace with Kléber, but died of plague in the following year. Ibrāhīm Bey, now somewhat superannuated, returned to Egypt in the company of the Ottomans. He was to survive until 1816 when, as a refugee from Muḥammad ʿAlī Pasha, he died in Nubia.

The withdrawal of the French left a power-vacuum in Egypt, and the history of the ensuing years is confused and anarchic, as various groups and individuals struggled for the upper hand. The British government, now awake to the strategic and commercial importance of Egypt, wished to recognize Ottoman sovereignty, but was at the same time favourable to a restoration of the Mamluk regime, which might be more compliant to British wishes. In March 1803, however, Britain's troops were evacuated in accordance with the Treaty of Amiens, and her government was thus deprived of any effective influence in Egypt. The Ottomans, on the other hand, under the vigorous and modernizing Sultan Selīm III (1789–1807), were determined to seize this opportunity of breaking Mamluk power, and of bringing the province under the effective control of a viceroy. The Mamluks, for their part, hoped to regain their ascendancy, but as ever they were hopelessly divided. Apart from Ibrāhīm Bey, their rival leaders were two members of Murād's Mamluk household, ʿUthmān Bey al-Bardīsī and Muḥammad Bey al-Alfī. A new factor in the military and political situation was a contingent of Albanian troops, forming part of the Ottoman army of occupation. Under its leader, Ṭāhir Pasha, and his lieutenant, Muḥammad ʿAlī Bey (later Pasha), it was virtually an autonomous force, throwing its weight now on one side, now on the other, in the kaleidoscopic shifts of power.

It soon became clear that the attempt by the Ottomans to restore the authority of the viceroy would not succeed. Muḥammad Khusraw Pasha, who was installed in 1802, was driven out of Cairo by Ṭāhir Pasha in the following year. Although Ṭāhir was assassinated shortly afterwards, Khusraw failed to regain his position, but was blockaded in Damietta by a combined force of Albanians under Muḥammad ʿAlī and Mamluks under al-Bardīsī, and made prisoner. His successor as viceroy lacked the military strength to establish himself in Egypt, and after intrigues with both the Albanians and the Mamluks, was put to death in January 1804. The next viceroy, Khūrshīd Pasha, showed a determination to rule strongly, but this inevitably aroused the opposition of the military grandees, while his fiscal levies caused discontent among the population, coming as they did after many years of instability and extortion.

This was the situation which in 1805 terminated in the downfall of Khūrshīd and the appointment of Muḥammad 'Alī as viceroy. Muḥammad 'Alī was born in 1769 at Kavalla in Macedonia, the son of a commander of irregular troops. He came to Egypt with a locally levied contingent in 1801, and rapidly rose to be second-in-command of the Albanians. When Ṭāhir Pasha was assassinated in May 1803, Muḥammad 'Alī succeeded him. In the events of 1805, however, Muḥammad 'Alī did not owe his ultimate success entirely to his own political skill, nor yet to the Albanians, who were by no means unanimous in his support. An important part was played by the mobilization in Muḥammad 'Alī's favour of the civilian artisan population of Cairo, who acted for a few vital weeks as a revolutionary army.

The organizer of the revolution was a certain 'Umar Makram, an obscure adventurer from Upper Egypt, who had assisted Ibrāhīm and Murād in 1791. In 1793, presumably as a reward for his services, he was appointed *naqīb al-Ashrāf*, the head of the Ashrāf, or alleged descendants of the Prophet, who formed a sort of hereditary aristocracy. During the French occupation, he went into exile, but subsequently he returned to Cairo, where he acquired, by means that are not now clear, enormous influence in the poorer quarters. In spite of his association with the religious leadership, he was not, strictly speaking, a member of the *'ulamā'*, who were also involved in the revolution, but a demagogue who concerted their actions with that of the populace and of Muḥammad 'Alī's military supporters. It is this deliberate political management which distinguishes the events of 1805 from the sporadic risings of the previous twenty years.

The first phase of the revolution was a popular insurrection, touched off by resentment at the quartering of irregular troops and the incessant demand for financial contributions. On 1 May 1805 the *'ulamā'* of al-Azhar suspended teaching, and ordered the shops to close. The viceroy, meeting 'Umar Makram at the house of the rector of al-Azhar, was stoned and insulted by youths in the crowd. On 11 May, the house of the chief judge became the rendezvous of the *'ulamā'* and of the

Cairo mob, which demonstrated against the viceroy, shouting anti-Ottoman slogans. A council summoned by the chief judge drew up a petition stating the popular complaints, and demanded an immediate reply from the viceroy. This was not forthcoming, and on 12 May, after another assembly at the chief judge's house, the notables went to Muḥammad ʿAlī, and announced the necessity of deposing Khūrshīd Pasha from office. They declared their determination to have him as viceroy. After some hesitation he agreed, was invested by ʿUmar Makram and the rector of al-Azhar, and was proclaimed in the city. One may speculate as to how far the whole episode had been contrived by ʿUmar Makram and Muḥammad ʿAlī in collusion: certainly it fell out very conveniently for Muḥammad ʿAlī, who on 9 May had been invested by Khūrshīd as governor of Jedda – an appointment which would have removed him from the Egyptian scene.

Whether stage-managed or not, the popular insurrection had ended unprecedentedly in the deposition of a viceroy. But Khūrshīd Pasha was not prepared to accept deposition by *fallāḥīn* (as he phrased it), and announced that he would remain in the Citadel until he received the sultan's command. The second phase of the revolution now began, with Khūrshīd blockaded in the Citadel. The regular military forces were divided, and an important section of the Albanians remained with Khūrshīd. On 18 May ʿUmar Makram alerted the mob. A night-watch was set up, barricades were erected, and firing began between the two parties, in the Citadel and town respectively. During the next few days, the popular forces from the working-class quarters emerged into greater prominence and began to develop into a kind of militia.

Discussions began on 24 May between ʿUmar Makram and the Albanian leaders opposed to Muḥammad ʿAlī. After an exchange of recriminations, the meeting broke up fruitlessly. During the three days of negotiations, the Citadel had been reprovisioned, thus prolonging the blockade. On 4 June, the regular troops who had been supporting Muḥammad ʿAlī demanded pay, which he was unable to give them, and deserted their posts. The civilian militia now took over the whole burden of the blockade, and also were repeatedly engaged in street-fighting with the malcontent troops. The most prominent of the popular leaders was a greengrocer named Ḥajjāj, coming from the Rumayla, a working-class quarter in the south of the city.

The prolonged and successful defence of the Citadel by Khūrshīd Pasha was rendered fruitless when, on 9 July, a messenger arrived from Istanbul with an imperial order for the appointment of Muḥammad

'Alī as viceroy. Realizing that he was impotent to intervene in Egypt, the sultan had deferred to the accomplished fact. The envoy was greeted by a great assembly of the populace, headed by Ḥajjāj. Although Khūrshīd held out until his deposition was confirmed by the sultan, and did not leave the Citadel until 6 August, the revolution was now accomplished, and the liquidation of the popular forces began. On 12 July, the 'ulamā', whose acts on 1 May had inaugurated the insurrection, felt that the time had come to withdraw. They decided to proclaim the re-establishment of public security, the re-opening of shops, and the resumption of teaching. Going to Muḥammad 'Alī Pasha, they declared him responsible for the government. This attempt to end the revolution was by no means agreeable to the populace of Cairo, who looked to 'Umar Makram for leadership, while reviling the 'ulamā' who had abandoned them. For several days there was tension in the city, and armed affrays occurred between civilians and troops. But Muḥammad 'Alī was steadily strengthening his hold. He was master of Cairo, although not yet of Egypt as a whole. The military base of his power was untrustworthy, and Sultan Selīm III wished to bring Egypt under his own control, not to legitimate the authority of a local despot. France and Britain were still at war, and Egypt might again become involved in their strategic dispositions.

THE RULE OF MUḤAMMAD 'ALĪ, 1805–48

The circumstances in which Muḥammad 'Alī thus found himself at the beginning of his viceroyalty determined the political aims of the rest of his career. His overriding purpose was to secure domination in Egypt for himself and his family against both internal and external threats. To achieve this, he carried out far-reaching military, administrative and economic changes, and undertook the creation of an empire in Arabia, the Sudan and Syria. He has rightly been called 'the founder of modern Egypt', but his objectives were personal and dynastic. In this respect, he was the last and most successful of the local despots who emerged in the declining days of the Ottoman sultanate.

The most immediate danger to Muḥammad 'Alī in the years immediately following his assumption of power came from his opponents and potential opponents within Egypt. One of the most conspicuous of these was 'Umar Makram, who in 1809 was sent into exile. 'Umar Makram's importance had rested on his alliance with two very different groups – the artisans of Cairo, and the 'ulamā' of al-Azhar. After the accession of Muḥammad ʿAlī, the mob ceased to play a part in events, while the *ʿulamā* never formed a united and politically conscious party under ʿUmar Makram's leadership. It was thus possible for Muḥammad ʿAlī to play on internal rivalries in order to eliminate ʿUmar Makram and other leaders, and to reduce the *ʿulamā* to what had been (before the late eighteenth century) their habitual condition of subservience. The economic basis of their independence was undermined by changes which Muḥammad ʿAlī introduced into the system of landownership. Estates held in trust for religious purposes, and paying a very low rate of tax, were first registered and then confiscated. Thus by about the end of Muḥammad ʿAlī's first decade as viceroy, the *ʿulamā*, leaderless, divided and disendowed, had become dependents of the administration.

More formidable as opponents were the survivors of the Mamluks, who had arms in their hands, landed revenues and a long tradition of rule in Egypt. Muḥammad ʿAlī countered them, as he did the *ʿulamā*, by eliminating their leaders and expropriating their lands. Neither aim was easily achieved, and for several years Mamluk leaders were virtually independent war-lords in many parts of Egypt, especially in the south. In March 1811, Muḥammad ʿAlī hoodwinked many of the Mamluks into attending a celebration in the Citadel of Cairo. On leaving, they were massacred. A proscription in the provinces ensued, and in 1812 the last remnant of the Mamluks of Upper Egypt fled southwards beyond the Third Cataract to the territory of Dongola. Here they established a camp, and began to recruit slave-troops. The extirpation of the Mamluks in Egypt was followed by the abolition of the tax-farms which they had exploited and which had given them actual, if not legal, control of most of the cultivable land of Egypt. By 1815 this process was completed. Muḥammad ʿAlī had thereby resumed into his own hand the estates which were the primary source of revenue.

The weakening of the *ʿulamā*, the elimination of the Mamluks, and the confiscation of the land marked the first stage in Muḥammad ʿAlī's consolidation of his power in Egypt. The second stage was one of territorial expansion, and of confrontation between Muḥammad ʿAlī on the one hand, and the Ottoman sultan and European powers on the other.

The thirty years from 1811 to 1841 were dominated by Muḥammad ʿAlī's wars. Between 1811 and 1818, at the request of Sultan Maḥmūd II (1808–39), he undertook a campaign against the Wahhābī rigorists, who, under the leadership of the house of Saʿūd, had expanded their rule from central Arabia into the Hejaz, and held the holy cities of

Mecca and Medina. By 1813 the Hejaz had been reconquered. In the second phase of the war, between 1816 and 1818, Ibrāhīm Pasha, Muḥammad 'Alī's eldest son, penetrated Najd, the Wahhābī heartland, and took the Sa'ūdī capital. As a consequence of the war, Muḥammad 'Alī's rule was extended over much of Arabia, as far east as the Persian Gulf and as far south as the Yemen.

Muḥammad 'Alī's second war, the conquest of the Nilotic Sudan, was undertaken on his own account, to dislodge the Mamluk remnant, and, by acquiring Sennar and Darfur, to gain control of the main arteries of the slave trade supplying Egypt, as well as the fabled gold of those regions. Two armies were sent out. The first under another of Muḥammad 'Alī's sons, Ismā'īl Kāmil Pasha, advanced from Aswan in the summer of 1820 through Lower Nubia and into the former dominions of the Funj sultanate. The Mamluks were driven out of the Dongola region, and finally disappeared from history. The Shāyqiyya alone among the riverain tribes resisted the invaders. Lacking firearms, they were quickly defeated, and swung over to become loyal followers of the new rulers. In June 1821 Sennar was reached, and Bādī VI, the last Funj sultan, made his submission. Meanwhile a second army, commanded by Muḥammad 'Alī's son-in-law, Muḥammad Bey Khusraw (usually called the *Defterdār*, his official title), had struck south-westwards from the Nile into Kordofan, at that time ruled by a governor from the sultan of Darfur. Here again the local warriors failed to withstand artillery and firearms, and Kordofan was conquered. The *Defterdār*, however, was unable to pursue the invasion of Darfur itself, which remained independent for more than fifty years more.

In the years following the conquest of the Sudan, Muḥammad 'Alī Pasha organized a new army, based on western models (see below, pp. 25–6), and it was with this force at his disposal that he was again called upon by Maḥmūd II. The sultan was having little success in his attempts to suppress the Greek revolt, which had begun in 1821, and in 1822 he asked Muḥammad 'Alī to intervene in Crete. By 1824 Crete had been reduced to submission, and then Muḥammad 'Alī, again at the sultan's request, sent an expeditionary force, under Ibrāhīm Pasha, to the Greek mainland. Here he was both successful and unsparing – so much so that in 1827 Prussia, Great Britain and France agreed to enforce an armistice by a naval blockade. The immediate consequence was a clash with the Ottoman and Egyptian fleets at the battle of Navarino, the imposition of a settlement, and the evacuation of Ibrāhīm and his forces.

The outcome of the Greek War had been a severe setback for

Muḥammad ʿAlī: his fleet had been destroyed, and the military successes achieved by Ibrāhīm had been cancelled by political failure. Nevertheless, within a few years, he undertook the most spectacular of his wars, the invasion of Ottoman Syria, in October 1831. Beginning as a dispute between Muḥammad ʿAlī and his rival the governor of Acre, the war quickly developed into a full-scale confrontation between the viceroy of Egypt and the Ottoman sultan, whose forces were defeated by Ibrāhīm Pasha at Konya in Anatolia. Muḥammad ʿAlī at this point restrained Ibrāhīm from advancing on Istanbul, and by the convention of Kütahya (1833) withdrew his troops from Anatolia. The Syrian provinces, however, remained in his possession, and were governed by Ibrāhīm. In 1839 an Ottoman army invading Syria was defeated. This event, followed within a few days by the death of Maḥmūd II, seemed to presage the subversion of the Ottoman Empire, and once again the European powers (except France) intervened against Muḥammad ʿAlī. Ibrāhīm was forced to evacuate Syria in 1840, and the Arabian possessions could no longer be held. Nevertheless, within Egypt itself, Muḥammad ʿAlī remained powerful, and the new sultan, Abdülmecid, reluctantly granted him the country as an hereditary domain in 1841. The Sudanese provinces were conceded to him only for life – although neither then nor later was any attempt made by an Ottoman sultan to detach them.

The middle decades of Muḥammad ʿAlī's viceroyalty were also a time of military, administrative and economic reconstruction, all intended to strengthen his position. The army was central to his designs. His motley and turbulent troops were of diverse origins, most important among them being the Albanians, who had accompanied him to Egypt and had helped to raise him to power. They were impatient of discipline, and broke out in revolt when, in 1815, he attempted to reorganize them as a regular army. He therefore resolved to construct a new force in which the name of *Niẓām-i jedīd* ('the new organization') is given. Following the precedent of many earlier Muslim rulers, he determined to use slaves as most likely to be loyal and dependent upon him. The officer-corps consisted of his own *mamlūks*, trained in European drill by former officers of Napoleonic armies, whose careers had been terminated by the ending of the wars in Europe. The rank and file were black slaves obtained in the Sudan. Muḥammad ʿAlī's conquests there had given his officials access to the traditional hunting-grounds for slaves among the pagan tribes beyond the frontier of Islam. In addition, the punitive taxes which were levied by the new administration on the free Muslim Sudanese resulted in the surrender of slaves to the government, since the Sudan had no indigenous coinage and was lacking in currency. The slave-recruits were taken to Manfalut in Upper Egypt, where their training began in 1823.

The plan was nevertheless not wholly successful, since there was a very high mortality among the slave-soldiers, and Muḥammad ʿAlī realized that he would have to find another and more reliable source of recruits. Acting on the advice of the French consul-general, he began to conscript the Egyptian peasantry. The conscription, unpopular in itself, was carried out with great brutality and was an important factor in producing agrarian unrest (see below, pp. 29–30). Although in 1835 Muḥammad ʿAlī sought to extend the conscription to the Sudanese provinces, he dropped the project on hearing of the violent reaction it was expected to provoke. Instead, a fresh levy of recruits was made from slaves held by the Sudanese.

The creation of an army organized and trained according to western models entailed the development of a range of ancillary educational and technical institutions. These included schools of cavalry, artillery and engineering, a medical school (founded in 1827) and a school of languages, the function of which was to provide Turkish and Arabic translations of works required for the training of the new military and administrative élite. After 1837 a number of 'preparatory schools' were founded to feed the higher schools. Since about 1822, a government printing press had been established at Bulaq, a suburb of Cairo, and an official gazette first appeared in 1828. In the development of these institutions, expatriates (especially Frenchmen and Italians) played an important part, but contact with the west was also maintained through the sending of 'educational missions' to France and other European countries. Over 200 students were thus sent abroad between 1826 and 1847. The military reorganization was in this way the starting-point of a cultural reorientation which continued throughout the century after Muḥammad ʿAlī's death.

Muḥammad ʿAlī reasserted the long-forgotten authority of the viceroy, but to make that authority effective he had to reconstruct the administrative machinery. Here he was essentially an improviser, devising expedients to suit changing circumstances, not proceeding consistently according to a preconceived plan. Nevertheless the principles on which he acted were clear throughout. He wished to substitute a centralized administration, wholly dependent upon his autocracy, for the anarchy in which he came to power. By the end of his reign he had largely succeeded. He had created an administration which in outward form resembled that of a European state. At the centre were government departments headed by officials with quasi-ministerial functions. An official hierarchy governed the provinces and their subdivisions, but in strict subordination to the instructions received from the centre. A thriving bureaucracy underpinned the work of the departmental and provincial officials. With the destruction of the old system of rewards – largely tax-farms of one kind or another – the way was clear for the establishment of a salaried governmental service, and although salaries did not end corruption, they increased the dependence of the officials upon the viceroy as their paymaster. The administration of the Sudan developed concurrently with that of Egypt. The conquered territories, divided into four provinces (Dongola, Berber, Sennar and Kordofan), were controlled at first by military officers. Between 1826 and 1833, however, they were united under a single governor (*mudīr*), 'Alī Khūrshīd Pasha, under whom the rudiments of a civil administration, a fiscal bureaucracy and an Islamic judiciary developed. A similar grouping of provinces into larger units under *mudīrs* was taking place at the same time in Egypt. In 1835, however, the special status of the governor of the Sudan was reflected in his new title of *ḥükümdār*, usually translated 'governor-general'.

Muhammad 'Alī's family played an important part in the new administrative, as in the new military organization. His close relatives were perhaps the only persons whom he trusted completely, and so he appointed them to supreme commands in the army and to high office in the government. In both these respects, Ibrāhīm was his right-hand man, and appropriately, if very briefly, succeeded him as viceroy in 1848. Next in importance to the viceregal family were the 'Turks', i.e. the Turkish-speaking immigrants, Albanians, Circassians and others, who had come into Egypt (sometimes as *mamlūks*) from other parts of the Ottoman Empire. They were the regular officers and held the chief executive posts in the administration. This predominance of Turkish-speaking officials characterized the administration of the Sudan also, where the regime was known as *al-Turkiyya*. In both Egypt and the Sudan, however, the bureaucracy was largely staffed by Arabic-speaking natives of the country, while the Copts had virtually a monopoly of the fiscal departments – in this connection it is noteworthy that Muhammad 'Alī sent forty Coptic clerks to work in the Sudan in 1839. On the fringe of the official hierarchy were the headmen (Arabic sing., *'umda*) of the villages, whose importance increased under Muhammad

'Alī. In 1833, Muḥammad 'Alī began to eliminate the Turks from the lower grades of the official hierarchy in Egypt, and to replace them with Egyptians of this class. Although this policy was unpopular, not least with the peasants (who found the new officials both less accessible and more extortionate than the Turks), and was partly abandoned in 1841, it prepared the way, with conscription, for increasing Egyptian participation in the government of the country.

These military and administrative changes, the employment of salaried troops and officials, as well as the series of foreign wars fought by Muḥammad 'Alī's forces, necessitated in turn a reconstruction of the financial bases of government. This he accomplished in three ways, by reorganizing the land-tax, by developing a system of monopolies, and by exploiting new sources of wealth. By expropriating the beneficiaries of religious trusts and the tax-farmers, Muḥammad 'Alī brought the fiscal administration into direct contact with the cultivators, while a cadastral survey and reclassification of cultivable land in 1813–14 gave the government an accurate picture of the agrarian resources of Egypt for the first time in three centuries. Certain lands were, however, exempt from the payment of tax: in particular members of the viceregal family and officials were allowed (even encouraged) to build up large tax-free estates, partly as a means of securing their loyalty to the regime.

The system of monopolies developed out of the very profitable export of corn, mainly to the British and their allies, in 1810 and 1811. The corn represented taxes paid in kind. This was the starting-point both of governmental control of export trade and of government direction of agriculture. From 1819 the viceroy monopolized the export of virtually all Egyptian products, and the monopoly was subsequently extended to the produce of the Sudan. Long-staple cotton, introduced into Egypt from the Sudan in 1821, became for some years an important article of export, although a decline in its quality ensued. The monopolies were much resented by the European merchant community in both Egypt and the Sudan, and pressure was constantly brought on Muḥammad 'Alī to abolish them. The convention of Balta Liman (1838) between Britain and the Ottoman Empire, which established free trade between the two parties, could not be applied to Egypt until 1841, when Muḥammad 'Alī's power had been broken. Even then, in spite of formally undertaking to execute the Convention, Muḥammad 'Alī fought a long delaying action. As late as 1846 he obtained from the sultan the lease of the two Red Sea ports of Suakin and Massawa, thereby closing one route by which the produce of the Sudan might evade his control.

The new sources of wealth which Muḥammad ʿAlī exploited were the products of his conquests. His invasion of the Sudan was partly undertaken, as we have seen, in order to acquire the gold in which the land was supposed to be rich. Here he was disappointed, although some Sudanese products, notably gum, cattle and camels, made a contribution to the economy of his empire. The Yemen provided coffee, and the timber of Lebanon supplied a most serious deficiency in the resources of a ruler who was aiming at naval power, while silk was an important article of export to Europe. Muḥammad ʿAlī, who had monopolized the domestic textile manufacture of Egypt, endeavoured to industrialize it in the years following 1817. Although factories were built, machinery bought, and European workmen brought to Egypt from Italy and France, the experiment was premature and failed.

The changes outlined above were productive of important social consequences. The old neo-Mamluk ruling élite, with its allies, the officers of the Ottoman garrison in Egypt, greatly enfeebled by the French occupation and the ensuing anarchy, was finally evicted from power and largely extirpated. Its place was taken by a new official and landed aristocracy, headed by the Turco-Circassian entourage of the viceregal family. The *'ulamā'*, their economic independence ended, declined in prestige. Two developments of Muḥammad ʿAlī's reign foreshadowed the diminution of their social importance. The new schools and training institutions which he founded ended their monopoly of the means of education. Furthermore, the content of the traditional Islamic curriculum was an inappropriate preparation for a career in a country undergoing modernization. The development of westernized education lapsed for a time after Muḥammad ʿAlī's death, and its social consequences did not become fully apparent until the second half of the century. The *'ulamā'* had a second traditional function; as jurists in the Holy Law of Islam, they staffed the *Sharīʿa* courts. But during the reign of Muḥammad ʿAlī, both the scope of the Holy Law and the competence of the Islamic courts were restricted (as indeed they had been by previous Muslim governments) by administrative regulations. A series of these, issued between 1830 and 1845, formed a body of penal legislation, dealing with offences committed by peasants. An administrative court, to try high officials, was set up in 1842, and commercial courts in 1845, while provincial governors exercised criminal justice.

The changes introduced by Muḥammad ʿAlī weighed most heavily on the common people, especially the Egyptian peasantry. They were accustomed to extortionate taxation and corrupt administration, but these familiar incidents of life were accompanied by a breaking of the traditional mould and the imposition of the new and heavy burden of conscription. The reaction of the peasants showed itself in two ways. The first was by revolt against the government. Peasant unrest seems to have been widespread, but usually to have dissipated itself without serious consequences. Sometimes, however, the peasants found a leader and won some local successes. This happened on three occasions between 1820 and 1824 in Upper Egypt. In each case the leader was named Aḥmad, although apparently three different individuals were involved. The leaders introduced some degree of organization among their followers, and plundered the local government storehouses and the tax-collectors. It is very significant that two of these risings show traces of millenarianism: the leader in 1822–3 was called 'the Mahdi', while in that of 1824 the leader 'declared that he had been sent by God and His Prophet to end the vexations from which the Egyptian people suffered and to punish Muḥammad 'Alī for introducing innovations which were contrary to the dogma of Islām'.[1] The phenomenon of agrarian unrest was sufficiently serious to be noticed in Muḥammad 'Alī's penal legislation.

The second way in which the peasants reacted to intolerable conditions was by flight. Some refugees made their way to other villages, or to the towns. Alexandria especially acted as a magnet, and a *bidonville* of mud huts grew up to shelter the refugee families. This migration was (together with the conscription) a factor in rural depopulation and a decrease in cultivation. In 1831 and subsequent years, Muḥammad 'Alī compelled the refugees to evacuate their settlements, and sent them back to their villages under armed convoy. The peasants who escaped to Palestine, some thousands in number, were not so easy to recapture. They were not returned by 'Abdallāh Pasha, the governor of Acre, but given holdings of land, and exempted from taxation for three years. This episode served Muḥammad 'Alī as a pretext for his invasion of Syria in 1831.

The same phenomena of revolt and flight appeared in the Sudan. Although there was no resistance to the Turco-Egyptian conquest as such, except by the Shāyqiyya and the Fūrāwī governor of Kordofan, the heavy taxation which was immediately imposed produced a revolt among the Ja'aliyyūn and, in the northern part of the Gezira, between

[1] Helen Anne B. Rivlin, *The agricultural policy of Muḥammad 'Alī in Egypt* (Cambridge, Mass., 1961), 201–2.

the White and Blue Niles. The rising began with the murder of Ismā'īl Kāmil Pasha, late in 1822: it was rigorously suppressed by the *Defterdār* in the following year. Thereafter there was no general Sudanese rising for nearly sixty years, until the outbreak of the Mahdia in 1881. There was, however, extensive migration from the regions controlled by the Turco-Egyptian regime. The harshness of the *Defterdār*, and of his successor, 'Uthmān Bey the Circassian, created a problem of depopulation in the cultivable riverain lands. A more conciliatory policy was followed by the next commander-in-chief, Maḥū Bey, and by 'Alī Khūrshīd, who, as we have seen, became the first governor-general of the Sudan. In consultation with a Sudanese notable, Shaykh 'Abd al-Qādir walad al-Zayn, a member of an old religious family, Khūrshīd offered amnesties to the refugees, who had fled to the hilly country in the marches of Ethiopia. Exemption from taxation was granted to the notables and religious leaders (*fakīs*), and many of the emigrants returned.

The refugee problem was one of several factors which produced tension in the frontier districts of the Egyptian Sudan and Ethiopia in the time of Muḥammad 'Alī. Between the two countries there was no defined boundary. The rulers of Ethiopia had in the past intervened in the politics of the Funj sultanate, and on occasion claimed a suzerainty which was resisted. At the time of the Turco-Egyptian conquest, however, the authority of the Ethiopian emperor was non-existent, and it was the great lords of the frontier districts who had effective power. Turco-Egyptian pressure began to make itself felt in the time of 'Alī Khūrshīd Pasha, and his successor as governor-general, Aḥmad Pasha Abū Widān (1838–43). It was applied in three areas: the upper Blue Nile, the territory of Fazughli and Beni Shangul; the central sector between Gedaref and Gondar; and the northern sector lying between Taka and Massawa.

The Fazughli and Beni Shangul area, which had been tributary to the Funj sultanate, interested Muḥammad 'Alī as being rich in gold. Ismā'īl Kāmil Pasha went there in the winter of 1821–2, and imposed a levy of gold on its merchants. In 1836 reports of rich mineral deposits in the region were forwarded to the viceroy by 'Alī Khūrshīd. This was the time when Muḥammad 'Alī's empire was at its height, and his economic resources were severely taxed. He sent European mining engineers to prospect the region, and in spite of his age (he was in his seventieth year) he made an arduous journey to Fazughli in the winter of 1838–9. But the outcome was disappointing, since the alluvial gold was not present in economic quantities. Although the area around Fazughli was again prospected at the end of Muḥammad ʿAlī's reign, it was to attain notoriety as a penal settlement, not as a boom town.

The central sector of the Ethiopian–Sudanese frontier region was otherwise important. The district of al-ʿAṭīsh, east of Gedaref, had given asylum to many Sudanese refugees in the early years of Turco-Egyptian rule. Many of them, as we have seen, had returned to the riverain lands, but the area was still a magnet to those who sought to evade taxation. The region also sheltered the former ruler of Shendi, the Jaʿalī chief, Makk Nimr, who had caused Ismāʿīl Kāmil to be assassinated in 1822, and had subsequently fled with his family and followers. He had obtained the protection of one of the Ethiopian march-lords, and established a small predatory frontier principality. This unsettlement along the border disturbed the current of trade between Ethiopia and the Sudan. An important route ran through the frontier-town of Gallabat, which was populated by a colony of Takārīr, i.e. Muslims from the western *Bilād al-Sūdān*. Their shaykh submitted to ʿAlī Khūrshīd in 1832. The instability in this region came to a head in 1837, when a Turco-Egyptian force, commanded by the district officer of Gedaref, advanced towards Gondar, but was heavily defeated by the Ethiopian march-lord, Kinfu, at the battle of Wad Kaltabu. ʿAlī Khūrshīd Pasha, fearing the reassertion of Ethiopian power in the frontier-districts, appealed to Muḥammad ʿAlī for reinforcements, and advanced to the threatened sector. These developments alarmed the European powers, especially the British, who apprehended a Turco-Egyptian conquest of Ethiopia. Under British pressure, the campaign was suspended.

In the following year, ʿAlī Khūrshīd was replaced as governor-general by Aḥmad Pasha Abū Widān, a son-in-law of Muḥammad ʿAlī. He withdrew most of the forces from the Gondar sector, but (after Muḥammad ʿAlī's visit to Fazughli) carried out operations in Taka to the north. This region was inhabited by the nomadic, Hamitic-speaking Hadendowa, whose territory ʿAlī Khūrshīd had unsuccessfully raided in 1831–2. Although Abū Widān's expedition in 1840 failed to reduce the Hadendowa to submission, he captured a number of their chiefs, and established a new military and administrative centre, around which grew up the town of Kassala. This extension of Turco-Egyptian power to the east may have been intended as a step towards linking the Sudanese hinterland with the port of Massawa, at that time under Muḥammad ʿAlī's control. Massawa however reverted to the Ottomans in the settlement of 1841, although, as noted earlier, it was leased to the viceroy in 1846.[1]

In the governor-generalship of Abū Widān, an event of the utmost importance for the history of the Sudan (and indeed of Egypt also) took place. This was the penetration of the upper White Nile. Since the sixteenth century, the frontier of Arabic speech and of islamization had remained stable, on the southern fringe of the Funj and Darfur sultanates. Beyond this was the land of the negro tribes, who might be raided and enslaved, but had not been conquered. On the White Nile itself, the cohesive and bellicose Shilluk, navigating the river in their reed canoes, not only held the Arabs and Funj at bay, but on occasion made devastating raids as far as the junction with the Blue Nile. The Turco-Egyptian invaders, with their superior organization and fire-arms, and their hunger for slaves, soon tried to break through to the south. In 1827, ʿAlī Khūrshīd, advancing overland from the Blue Nile, cut through the Dinka country to the river Sobat. In 1830 he made a river expedition against the Shilluk, and penetrated as far as the confluence of the Sobat. But the real credit for opening the way up the White Nile belongs to the Turkish sailor, Salīm Qabūdān, who made three expeditions between 1839 and 1842 and reached the country of the Bari tribe, near the present site of Juba. The consequences of this break-through were to become apparent in the next two decades.

THE REIGNS OF ʿABBĀS I AND SAʿĪD, 1848–62

After 1841 a good deal of Muḥammad ʿAlī's energy left him, although he was still capable of spurts of activity. But by 1848 he had fallen into senility. The sultan formally appointed Ibrāhīm viceroy, but in a few weeks Ibrāhīm was dead before his father. The short reigns of the two succeeding viceroys ʿAbbās Ḥilmī I (1848–54) and Muḥammad Saʿīd (1854–63), who were respectively the eldest grandson and the youngest surviving son of Muḥammad ʿAlī Pasha, have sometimes been seen as a time of intermission and relaxation of effort. This is not entirely correct. The diminishing force of administration had already become evident in the last years of Muḥammad ʿAlī's reign, after the collapse of his empire in Syria and Arabia. Furthermore although ʿAbbās was a traditionalist in outlook, and unsympathetic to many of Muḥammad ʿAlī's westernizing projects, he was by no means an ignorant reac-

[1] A more extensive treatment of these events, considered from the Ethiopian side, occurs in ch. 2, pp. 56–7 and 62–5.

tionary. He had already had administrative experience before he became viceroy, and he was as anxious as other rulers of his dynasty to maintain the special status of the viceroy of Egypt.

This determination inevitably led to another clash with the Ottoman government, which since the death of Sultan Maḥmūd II had been developing its own programme of reforms, known as the *Tanẓīmāt*. These had in many respects been anticipated in Egypt. Hence when, in 1851, the sultan's government endeavoured to compel the viceroy to apply in Egypt the new Ottoman penal code, 'Abbās put up a firm resistance, particularly since, under the new regulation, he would lose his prescriptive right to impose the death-sentence without reference to Istanbul. In 1852, a compromise was reached, by which the new code was to be introduced into Egypt, but 'Abbās was to retain temporary and limited powers in capital cases. The Ottoman code was never, in fact, implemented during his reign, but was used as the basis of an Egyptian code, promulgated early in the reign of Sa'īd.

'Abbās had been stiffened in his resistance by the diplomatic support of Great Britain. In his reaction against westernization, he had also turned against the French, who had been its principal agents and representatives in Muḥammad 'Alī's time, but, since some external helper was necessary, he had swung towards the British. Since Bonaparte's expedition, the British government had been nervously aware of the importance of Egypt as a stage on the route to India and the Far East. For some time, however, nothing was done to realize its potentialities, and the initiative was taken, in the end, not by the government, but by an individual, Thomas Waghorn, who, having demonstrated the advantages of the Mediterranean–Red Sea route for the transmission of mail between Britain and India, organized the 'Overland Route' for transit across the desert between Cairo and Suez. Already during Muḥammad 'Alī's reign, proposals had been put forward for linking Alexandria, Cairo and Suez by railway, but the old viceroy, fearing the growth of British influence, had never granted a concession. In 1851, 'Abbās signed a contract for the construction of a railway between Alexandria and Cairo by Robert Stephenson. This intensified the tension already existing over the *Tanẓīmāt* question, since the Ottoman government asserted that the previous approval of the sultan was necessary. With Palmerston's support, however, 'Abbās succeeded in maintaining his position, and the sultan sanctioned the project. The railway so begun was not completed until 1856, after Sa'īd's accession.

It was continued from Cairo to Suez in 1858. Subsequently the railway was extended up the Nile valley to Aswan.

The problem of relations between the viceroy and his suzerain, which had arisen in connection with the railway contract, reappeared in a more acute form when, in 1854, Muḥammad Sa'īd Pasha granted his old friend, Ferdinand de Lesseps, formerly French consul-general in Egypt, a concession for the construction of a maritime canal from the Mediterranean to the Red Sea across the isthmus of Suez. The concession marked the first step towards the realization of a project which had occupied the thoughts of many Frenchmen during the previous half-century. Its grant, however, produced a prolonged diplomatic struggle, in which the sultan sought to assert his prerogative against the viceroy; and the British government also steadily opposed, both in Cairo and Istanbul, a project which threatened their vested interest in the Overland Route and railway. This is not the place to enter into the details of the negotiations and intrigues which surrounded the cutting of the canal. They continued, as we shall see, beyond the death of Sa'īd Pasha, and well into the reign of Ismā'īl.

One consequence of the military and diplomatic defeat inflicted on Muḥammad 'Alī in 1840–1 had been, as we have seen, the requirement that he should comply with the Convention of Balta Liman, and dismantle his system of monopolies. By various means, he had succeeded in practice in largely evading this demand, as did 'Abbās after him. The real breakdown of the monopoly system came with the accession of Sa'īd, who abandoned the expedients used by his predecessors to control the market and to interpose between the cultivators and the European merchants. At the same time, governmental direction of agriculture also came to an end, and the peasant in this respect began to experience a new freedom. This coincided with changes in the land-law during Sa'īd's reign, which greatly increased the property rights of peasants in their land, and ended the collective responsibility of villages for the payment of taxes. The Egyptian peasantry thus entered a new and unprecedented phase of agrarian and social individualism.

In the Egyptian Sudan, the abolition of monopolies had consequences of particular importance. The small group of European merchants in Khartoum particularly resented their exclusion from the potentially highly profitable ivory trade of the upper White Nile. During the 1840s this had been handled by small annual expeditions sent out by the governors-general. In 1848, Muḥammad 'Alī, as a result of British pressure in Cairo and Istanbul, finally agreed to end the monopolies in the Sudan, but it was not until 1851 that a private European trading expedition at last managed to make its way up the White Nile. It was the first of many. The European merchants met with little success among the Shilluk, and their main contacts were at first with the Bari tribe, living much farther south, beyond the territories inhabited by the nomadic Nuer and Dinka. The Bari had access to considerable quantities of accumulated ivory, and there were fair prospects for the development of legitimate trade. In the middle 1850s also, the European traders and their servants entered the great river-system of the Bahr al-Ghazal, and penetrated the swampy plains inhabited by Dinka, to the higher lands on the fringe of the Azande territory in the south-west. This again was ivory country.

Within the course of a few years, both these regions, the upper White Nile and the Bahr al-Ghazal, had become notorious for the abuses committed by the traders and their retinues. From the published writings of European travellers and humanitarians, an oversimplified picture has been derived: namely, that the unhappy situation which developed in the southern Sudan was the result of predatory slave trading, carried out at first by European merchants, then by a variety of Sudanese, Egyptians and Levantines, who succeeded them in this unconscionable traffic. Recent research has demonstrated that slave trading was only one factor in a complex situation, in which a multi-racial frontier society, outside the limits of regular administration, confronted traditional tribal groupings.[1] The traders had a margin of superiority over the tribes, in organizational skill and in the possession of firearms. Hence, where trading became difficult, as it soon did, because the tribes of the upper White Nile and the Bahr al-Ghazal were unused to commerce, and had little desire for trade goods, the frustrated merchants were able to use force to obtain ivory.

Enslavement and the slave trade developed within the context of this wider confrontation. They were at first on a small scale, and slaves were not a commercial end in themselves. The determination of the traders to obtain ivory, by force if need be, led from 1854 onwards to raids into the interior, and to the establishment of fortified trading-stations, staffed with their agents and guarded by their private armies. Such a station was known in Arabic as *zarība* or *daym*, the former term meaning originally a cattle-enclosure, the latter a settlement. The traders used their troops to intervene in local tribal hostilities, which in turn provi-

[1] See Richard Gray, *A history of the southern Sudan 1839–1889* (Oxford, 1961), on which the following account is largely based.

ded booty in the form of cattle or slaves. The cattle were more acceptable than trade-goods for the purchase of ivory: the slaves were used in
partial lieu of wages for the servants and soldiers of the merchants.
Slave trading on the upper White Nile thus developed as ancillary
to the ivory trade: and although the acquisition of slaves for
sale in the north increased as time went on, they formed a very small
proportion of the total exported from the Sudan. The traditional
hunting-grounds (the southern fringe of Darfur, the Nuba Mountains, the upper Blue Nile and the Ethiopian marches) remained of
primary importance.

In the Bahr al-Ghazal, the course of events was slightly different,
since from the start trading-stations were established. These dominated
the weaker tribes in the central sector of the region, who were reduced
to vassalage. The Dinka of the swamps, however, although subject to
raids, remained unconquered and put up effective resistance to the
intruders. The Azande of the highlands on the Nile–Congo watershed
were also not easy to subjugate, and a kind of symbiosis developed
between their chiefs and the merchant-princes who penetrated their
country. Apart from the traders who entered the Bahr al-Ghazal by way
of the Nile (the *baḥḥāra*, as they were called), the region was also entered from the north (Kordofan and Darfur) by the *jallāba*, northern
Sudanese, who carried on an old-established petty trade across the
frontier of Islam and brought back slaves from the southern tribes. The
foundation of trading-stations for the *baḥḥāra* gave protection to the
jallāba, and facilitated their penetration deep into the Bahr al-Ghazal.
They entered the region by hundreds, either as independent traders or
as agents of large-scale slave traders in Kordofan and Darfur. The consequence was a considerable expansion of the slave trade by the overland route.

Although European merchants played the leading part in opening up
the commerce of the White Nile and Bahr al-Ghazal, their domination
of the trade of these regions was short-lived. Their numbers were
reduced by fighting and disease, and European export firms, trading
profitably in Cairo, had little incentive to hazard their capital in the
Sudan. By the end of 'Abbās's reign, the chief traders in the south and
south-west were men of local or at least of Levantine origin. These merchant-princes, notable amongst whom were the Egyptian, Muḥammad
Aḥmad al-ʿAqqād, on the White Nile, and the Sudanese, al-Zubayr
Raḥma Manṣūr, in the Bahr al-Ghazal, inherited their predecessors'
trading-stations, administrative staffs and military retinues of Danāqla

(i.e. tribesmen of the Dongola region) and Shāyqiyya, and, in the Bahr al-Ghazal, private armies of slaves, known as 'bazingers'.

There thus existed, beyond the pale of Turco-Egyptian administration, a very extensive area dominated by the frontier-society of the traders' establishments. The conscience of Europe, sensitive as ever in the nineteenth century to slavery and the slave trade, stirred up Sa'īd to an attempt to extend governmental control over the White Nile. At the beginning of his reign he forbade the introduction of slaves into Egypt proper. In 1855 he established a government post and garrison at the mouth of the Sobat, and appointed a governor for the new White Nile Province. The garrison, however, failed to establish itself, and was withdrawn in 1857. In 1861, a Dunqulāwī trader named Muḥammad Khayr, who had been driven out by the Shilluk in the previous year, gathered a private army, mounted an expedition, and established himself in the Shilluk country. Having done this, he sought recognition from the governor-general in return for the payment of tribute, and in 1863 nearly achieved this. He was however killed in the interior. The appointment of a powerful merchant-prince as the representative of the Turco-Egyptian government was an expedient that was employed later, as a means of establishing the nominal authority of the viceroy over areas he did not in fact control.

The break-through of the European merchants into the upper White Nile had been achieved partly by missionary pressure. The *Propaganda Fide* had quickly realized the significance of Salīm Qabūdān's expeditions, and the creation of the Vicariate Apostolic of Central Africa in 1846 was the first step in sending a mission to the newly accessible territories. A group of Catholic missionaries established their headquarters at Khartoum in 1848, and (like the European trading community) sought an opportunity to overcome the resistance of the administration, and to go up the White Nile. Success for both parties finally came in 1851, when Ignaz Knoblecher (Knoblehar), the Slovene head of the mission, obtained from the Emperor Franz Joseph the appointment of an Austrian consular agent in Khartoum, with whose support the restrictions on travel to the upper Nile were overcome.

The Catholic mission on the White Nile was even more short-lived than the commercial domination of the Europeans. A missionary arrived at Gondokoro, among the Bari, and in 1853 a station was set up there. From the outset its existence was precarious. Ignorance of tribal usage led to constant misunderstandings with the Bari, and the site was fatally unhealthy. In 1854 the one surviving missionary withdrew, to found the station of Holy Cross among the Dinka, farther north. Knoblecher, in 1855, revived the station at Gondokoro, but it remained an isolated and threatened enclave among the suspicious and hostile Bari. The high death rate of missionaries continued, so that Holy Cross was abandoned in 1859 and Gondokoro in 1860. A mission by the Franciscans, which re-established Holy Cross and established a station among the Shilluk at Kaka in 1862 proved equally unsuccessful.

THE REIGN OF ISMĀ'ĪL, 1863-79

With the accession of Ismā'īl, the son of Ibrāhīm Pasha, in January 1863, Egypt again passed under the control of a dynamic and ambitious ruler, who was to resume the political aims of his grandfather. He endeavoured to safeguard and strengthen his autonomy in Egypt, to maintain relations with the European powers (especially France), and to extend the Egyptian empire in Africa.

He had in the first respect a good deal of success. During most of his viceroyalty, his Ottoman suzerain was Sultan Abdülaziz (1861-76), with whom he usually had friendly relations. The two rulers exchanged visits, Ismā'īl going to Istanbul to be invested as viceroy, while Abdül-aziz visited Egypt in 1863 – the only Ottoman sultan apart from Selīm I to do so. In these favourable circumstances, Ismā'īl obtained two important concessions. In 1866 he was accorded a firman making the succession hereditary by primogeniture in his own line. Under the earlier firman, granted to Muḥammad 'Alī in 1841, the succession to the viceroyalty followed the Ottoman practice of passing to the eldest male. On the deaths of both Ibrāhīm and 'Abbās I attempts had been made to set this provision aside, in favour of their sons, but the plots had failed. By obtaining this change in the law of succession, Ismā'īl eliminated one cause of instability in the hereditary viceroyalty, although the restriction of the right of succession to his own descendants aroused the jealousy of other members of the viceregal family. A second concession which Ismā'īl obtained from the sultan was the grant of a special title, to denote the unique status of the viceroy of Egypt amongst Ottoman provincial governors. The title obtained was that of 'khedive' (through Turkish from the Persian *khidīv*, originally meaning 'king'), which had been unofficially used from the time of Muḥammad 'Alī. It was formally conferred by a firman in 1867. The privileges granted to Ismā'īl were finally consolidated in the sultan's firman of 8 June 1873.

Ismā'īl's relations with the European powers were more complex.

Although Muḥammad ʿAlī had made use of expatriate advisers and technicians, and had conducted diplomatic relations through the European consular representatives in Egypt (since, as a vassal of the Ottoman sultan, he had no independent international standing), he had always succeeded in preventing any infringement by them of his power in Egypt. His two clashes with the European powers, at Navarino in 1827 and in Syria during 1839–40, had deprived him of his external conquests, but had not affected his internal autocracy within Egypt. Ismāʿīl was to be less successful than his grandfather in managing the Europeans, and, as we shall see, European intervention was to bring about his deposition in 1879.

The causes of Ismāʿīl's lack of success in this respect were not wholly personal. He inherited from his predecessors a situation which already threatened to get out of hand. The finances of Egypt, precarious even in the time of Muḥammad ʿAlī, were undermined by the abolition of the state monopolies. ʿAbbās, in spite of his retrenchments, left the treasury in debt. The debts were considerably increased by Saʿīd, who obtained loans from European bankers. Saʿīd had also committed his successor to the Suez canal project by two concessions in 1854 and 1856 respectively. The latter granted to the Suez Canal Company a strip of land linking the line of the canal to the Nile, by means of which a freshwater canal could be constructed, and also included an undertaking by the viceroy to supply labour for the construction of the canal. A clash developed between Saʿīd and de Lesseps, who in 1859 began work on the canal, in spite of the opposition of both the viceroy and the sultan.

Ismāʿīl, who sought the retrocession of the strip of land between the Suez isthmus and the Nile, and wished to end the undertaking to supply labour (which was having a detrimental effect on agriculture), had to pay a heavy indemnity to the Canal Company. In addition he accepted and paid for the unsubscribed shares which de Lesseps had unsuccessfully attempted to unload on Saʿīd. The canal project was thus a factor in the growing indebtedness of Ismāʿīl, which was also partly due to the payments he had to make for the firmans concerning the right of succession and the khedivial title.

At the beginning of his reign, however, the financial prospects of Egypt seemed bright. Owing to the American Civil War (1861–5), cotton everywhere was at a premium. A fresh boost was given to the cultivation of Egyptian long-staple cotton, which had been allowed to decline in quantity and deteriorate in quality since its early exploitation in the time of Muḥammad ʿAlī Pasha. The price of Egyptian cotton increased fourfold during the war years, but with the end of the Civil War the boom suddenly collapsed, creating a problem of peasant indebtedness and ending one of the principal financial supports of Ismā'īl's policy. While his resources diminished, his ambitions increased, and by 1876 the khedive's debts amounted to nearly £100 million, two-thirds of which consisted of foreign loans.

The canal project and the cotton boom affected Egypt in other ways. They stimulated European immigration into Egypt, which had been at a standstill in the last years of Muḥammad 'Alī and during 'Abbās's reign. The average annual immigration between 1857 and 1861 was 30,000 persons; by 1865, it had risen to 80,000 persons, and even after the end of the cotton boom it remained at 50,000. While not all these immigrants by any means became permanently resident in Egypt, they constituted a serious administrative problem, since by treaties, known as Capitulations, with the Ottoman sultans (going back originally to the sixteenth century), the Europeans and Americans were largely immune from the jurisdiction of the Egyptian courts and police, and were exempt from Egyptian taxation. Even before his accession, Ismā'īl had attempted to modify the capitulatory regime, but had met with no success. A long series of negotiations with the capitulatory powers, begun in 1867 by Nubar Pasha, Ismā'īl's Armenian minister, resulted in 1875 in the setting up of Mixed Courts. These, staffed by Egyptian and foreign judges, administered codes based on French law, and had jurisdiction in civil and criminal cases where an Egyptian and a foreigner (or two foreigners of different nationalities) were parties. The reform thus resulted in some modification of the capitulatory regime: at the same time it marked an important step in the internationalization of control over Egypt.

This indeed was at the heart of Ismā'īl's problems. His difficulties with the foreign communities were aggravated by the fact that behind them lay the European powers, with whom he had to deal. A similar complication affected his relations with the foreign financiers, although the political consequences of this did not become apparent until late in his reign. A further turn was given to the screw since two of the powers chiefly concerned, namely Britain and France, were, as they had been since the beginning of the century, competitors for influence in Egypt. In Ismā'īl's reign, their rivalry came to a head over the Suez canal project. In March 1866 the sultan granted a firman authorizing the construction of the canal (which by then was far advanced), and in November 1869 the new waterway was opened to shipping.

As we have already seen, trade had preceded the flag in the opening up of the Equatorial Nile and the Bahr al-Ghazal, and Sa'īd's attempt to maintain a government garrison at the mouth of the Sobat had been a failure. In 1863, however, a new incentive was given to Egyptian expansion up the Nile by the arrival in Cairo of J. H. Speke and J. A. Grant, who had explored the route from East Africa to Lake Victoria, and had then descended the Nile to Gondokoro and so on to Cairo. This demonstration of the river as a practical highway to the lacustrine Bantu kingdoms, with the possibility they offered of legitimate trade, aroused Ismā'īl's interest. A garrison was established among the Shilluk late in 1863, and the White Nile Province returned to somewhat precarious existence. An attempt was made to police the White Nile.

More vigorous action was, however, needed to carry the khedive's authority up the river, and in 1869 Ismā'īl appointed the English explorer, Sir Samuel Baker, to command an expedition intended to crush the slave trade, to establish Egyptian administration throughout the Equatorial Nile, and to set up trading-stations. In spite of enormous initial outlay, Baker's expedition achieved remarkably little of permanent value. He succeeded in establishing his advanced base at Gondokoro, and in 1872 he reached Masindi, the capital of the interlacustrine kingdom of Bunyoro. But, although Baker had imposed recognition of the khedive's authority on the merchant-prince of the Upper Nile, Muḥammad Abu'l-Su'ūd, the representative of the firm of al-'Aqqād, he had by no means carried out an effective annexation or established Egyptian administration in the region. Moreover, to survive he had been forced to have recourse to the predatory methods of the ivory merchants, and had created among the Bari a deep animosity.

Baker was succeeded as Ismā'īl's agent in the south by another Englishman, Charles George Gordon, who in 1873 was appointed governor-general of Equatoria. Like Baker, he failed to achieve the grand design of bringing the interlacustrine kingdoms under the effective suzerainty of the khedive, and, lacking this natural commercial outlet, Equatoria was less a highway to the centre of Africa than a cul-de-sac. Within the limits set by inadequate finance, poor communications and insufficient personnel, Gordon strove to reconcile the Bari and other tribes to Egyptian rule, and to establish the framework of an administration based on a chain of garrison posts. One of the principal difficulties in creating an administrative system was its completely alien quality. Gordon himself and many of his chief subordinates were Europeans or Egyptians. At a rather lower level, he had to depend upon the diaspora of northern Sudanese, especially Danāqla, who had originally come to the region in the retinue of the ivory and slave merchants. Now, although nominally the soldiers or servants of the government, they had the local knowledge and influence to render themselves largely immune to Gordon's authority. When Gordon resigned in 1876, Equatoria, outside its provincial capital at Lado (near Gondokoro) and its riverain garrisons, was still largely unadministered.

Neither Baker nor Gordon was concerned with the Bahr al-Ghazal. Here Ismā'īl endeavoured to establish his overlordship through the agency of a private adventurer named Muḥammad al-Bulālāwī, who claimed Moroccan origin, and had established his personal rule in part of the region. With troops supplied by the governor-general and some backing from the khedive, al-Bulālāwī set to work in 1869 to reduce the *zarības* of the merchant-princes to submission. He soon clashed with the greatest of them all, al-Zubayr Raḥma Manṣūr,[1] by whom he was defeated and killed in 1872. Ismā'īl deferred to the accomplished fact by appointing al-Zubayr governor of the Bahr al-Ghazal in December 1873.

This appointment of a merchant-prince as khedivial governor had important consequences. Like other operators in the Bahr al-Ghazal, al-Zubayr sent his trading caravans north to Darfur and Kordofan. The route ran through the territory of the nomadic Rizayqāt, a tribe of Baqqāra, or cattle-Arabs, with whom al-Zubayr had an agreement. When the Rizayqāt broke this agreement in 1873, Zubayr launched a punitive campaign against them. This in its turn led to a clash with their nominal overlord, Sultan Ibrāhīm of Darfur, who failed to co-operate with al-Zubayr.

We have already seen how in 1821 the *Defterdār* conquered Kordofan, the outlying eastern province of Darfur, but had been unable to over-throw the sultanate in its heartland. Muḥammad 'Alī continued to have ambitions in that direction: he gave asylum to a pretender to the throne of Darfur named Muḥammad Abū Madyan, a son of Sultan 'Abd al-Raḥmān al-Rashīd. The death of Sultan Muḥammad Faḍl in 1838 or 1839, and the accession of his son, Muḥammad Ḥusayn, offered Muḥammad 'Alī an opportunity to intervene in Darfur on behalf of his protégé. An expeditionary force was assembled in Kordofan in 1843, but the invasion was suddenly cancelled, and Abū Madyan returned to Cairo. Sultan Muḥammad Ḥusayn ruled until 1873, although in his

[1] Al-Zubayr's name appears in the contemporary European writings under such forms as Zubair, Zubeir, Zibēr and even Sebehr.

later years his sight failed, and affairs were managed by his sister. His son, Ibrāhīm, had thus only newly come to the throne when the confrontation with al-Zubayr took place, and hostilities broke out.

Al-Zubayr's victory over a Fūrāwī army in January 1874 led to formal intervention by the khedivial forces. The governor-general, Ismāʿīl Pasha Ayyūb, brought an expeditionary force to the western boundary of Kordofan, while al-Zubayr, advancing from the south, defeated and killed Sultan Ibrāhīm at the battle of Manawāshī in October 1874. He entered the capital of the sultanate, El Fasher, five days before the governor-general. When, in the following year, al-Zubayr learnt that he was not to administer the province he had conquered, he went to Cairo to plead his cause with the khedive. He was too powerful and dangerous a person to be allowed to return, and he remained in Cairo, under easy conditions of house arrest, until 1899, when both the Turco-Egyptian regime and the Mahdia which succeeded it had passed into history.

Thus during the reign of Khedive Ismāʿīl an enormous area of territory in the south and west was added to the Egyptian Sudan. There were also attempts at expansion in the east, but these were less successful. Just as the khedive appreciated the potential importance of the Nile as a route to the Equatorial lakes, so he realized that the cutting of the Suez canal would increase the commercial and strategic importance of the Red Sea and its southern approaches. As early as 1865 he had obtained from the Ottoman sultan the grant of Suakin and Massawa, formerly held by his grandfather. Ismāʿīl claimed that this gave him rights on the Somali coast, and during the next four years Egyptian authority expanded from the ports of Berbera, Bulhar and Zeila. From the last town, in 1875, an Egyptian force occupied Harar and established a garrison there. Once again, as in the time of Muḥammad ʿAlī Pasha, Egyptian expansion threatened Ethiopia. In 1871 one of Ismāʿīl's expatriate officials, J. A. W. Munzinger Pasha, a Swiss, was appointed governor of Massawa, and subsequently of the whole littoral region. He was making preparations for war against the newly crowned Ethiopian ruler, Yohannes IV, when he was killed in a Somali ambush (1875). His aggressive policy survived him, but in 1875 an Egyptian force was defeated at Gundet in the Ethiopian highlands. A larger expeditionary force under the sirdar (commander-in-chief), Muḥammad Rātib Pasha, was then organized, but equally met with disaster at the battle of Gura (1876). The two defeats were a serious blow to Ismāʿīl's military prestige, and marked the end of his imperial expansion.

At this time of gathering crisis, Gordon returned for his first period of office as governor-general of the Sudan (1877-9), not merely of Equatoria as in 1873-6. He was faced with a difficult situation: a settlement was needed with Ethiopia; Darfur was in revolt against khedivial rule; in the Bahr al-Ghazal, al-Zubayr's son, Sulaymān, remained to watch over his father's interests and to stir up trouble for the Egyptians. In 1877, furthermore, the khedive concluded a Slave Trade Convention with Britain, by which the sale and purchase of slaves in the Sudan were to end by 1889. From July 1878 Gordon was solely responsible for the execution of this policy – an impossible task with the men and money available to him.

Gordon's governor-generalship was, in spite of his high purpose and daemonic energy, a failure. He was unable to reach a lasting settlement with Ethiopia. He sustained the Egyptian garrisons in Darfur, but was unable to heal the underlying causes of the revolt, which lay deep in Fūrāwī separatism. Although at first he conciliated Sulaymān, the son of al-Zubayr renewed his rebellion in 1878, and was hunted down and shot in the following year. The attempt to carry out the Slave Trade Convention – for which Gordon assumed the prime responsibility in 1878 – made him odious to many vested interests in the Sudan, and the task was impossible of fulfilment with the resources at his disposal. In June 1879, Khedive Ismā'īl was deposed; and Gordon resigned in the next year.

The last years of Ismā'īl's reign were a period of growing tension in both Egypt and the Sudan. In both countries, traditional society was breaking up under the pressure of modernization, although this process was by no means as far advanced in the Sudan as in Egypt, and hence the form of the reaction differed in the two territories. In Egypt, the tightly-knit village communities had since the time of Muḥammad 'Alī undergone dissolution. The more individualistic structure of rural society offered opportunities to the richer peasant families, from whom the government authorities appointed the village *'umdas*. The powers and status of these men increased in the later part of Muḥammad 'Alī's reign and in the time of 'Abbās: they received a set-back under Sa'īd. One of his measures had unforeseen consequences: he ended the exemption of their sons from military conscription, and thereby opened the way to the rise of a class of native Egyptian officers. Under Ismā'īl the *'umdas* regained their political and social position. He resumed Muḥammad 'Alī's policy of appointing them to governorships, and in 1866 he inaugurated a quasi-parliamentary body, the Assembly of

Delegates (*Majlis shūrā al-nuwwāb*), indirectly elected and heavily weighted in favour of the rural representatives, who were mostly village notables.

Another factor in the decline of Egyptian traditional society was the spread of western education. This had been neglected by the government under 'Abbās and Sa'īd, although schools set up by Christian missionary organizations and by the minority communities stimulated popular interest, especially in the towns. The reign of Ismā'īl witnessed new developments in the provision of European-style education by the state. The Assembly of Delegates served as a sounding-board for the khedive's ideas, and in 1867 a project for the founding of provincial primary schools was adopted by the Assembly. From this developed the Primary School Law of 1868. The recruitment of teachers for schools of the new type remained a problem. In 1871 'Alī Mubārak, one of the leading Egyptian reformers, opened a college known as *Dār al-'Ulūm* to provide higher education in both Islamic and western subjects. In the following year, fifty students from al-Azhar, who had received a traditional Islamic education, were selected for training in *Dār al-'Ulūm*. By 1879, there were about thirty modern state primary schools in Egypt (the great majority of them in Cairo), while the number of foreign and community schools rose from 59 to about 150.

The great influx of foreigners, especially Europeans, into Egypt has already been noted. The immigrants were agents of westernization. A leading part in the modernization of Egypt was played by the expatriate experts and technicians (and, in the Sudan, the expatriate administrators) employed by the khedive, such as, for instance, Edouard Dor, the Swiss inspector-general of schools from 1873 to 1880, or the numerous veterans of the American Civil War, who, like the Napoleonic officers of an earlier generation, resumed in Egypt their frustrated careers. Equally, the control of Egyptian commerce and finance passed increasingly into European hands. This became startlingly clear in 1875. The khedive was virtually bankrupt, although the sale of his Suez canal shares to the British government postponed the crisis for a year. In 1876, however, an institution, the *Caisse de la Dette Publique*, was set up to organize the service of the Egyptian debt. It had four members – British, French, Austrian and Italian. Shortly afterwards a British and a French controller were appointed to supervise Egyptian revenue and expenditure. The internationalization of the finances had political consequences. The British and French governments, not hitherto directly concerned, brought pressure to bear, and an international commission of inquiry was set up in 1878. As a result of its findings, the khedive accepted the principle of ministerial responsibility, and set up a cabinet under Nubar Pasha which included a British and a French minister.

The Egyptians reacted in various ways to the tensions of Ismā'īl's reign. Continuing rural discontent produced agrarian revolts, mainly in Upper Egypt, of the type that had become traditional. But although these threatened security locally, they could not endanger the khedivial regime, which had ample powers of control at its disposal. The peasant revolts were essentially primitive and backward-looking. A more serious development in these years was that of ramified subversive movements, which had their agents and supporters among the westernized governing and military élites and even in the viceregal family itself. These movements had at first little ideological content or elaborate organization. They were more or less ephemeral and secret associations of persons with grievances. Their origins and development are equally obscure, and their story is very much a matter of conjecture.[1] It has been surmised that their appearance was influenced and facilitated by the spread of Freemasonry in Egypt. It is also true that the Sufi orders and the artisan guilds offered prototypes of cellular organizations of élites.

Out of the tangle of aims and motives of the subversives, two or three main strands may be distinguished. By the mid-1870s, half a century had elapsed since the introduction of conscription, and twenty years since Sa'īd had extended it to the sons of the village headmen. In the interval, there had grown up a body of native Egyptian officers. They found themselves frustrated in their careers by the Turco-Circassians, who held the highest commands. The disasters of the Ethiopian campaign of 1876, when the Circassian sirdar had been ignominiously routed, destroyed once for all the prestige of the Turco-Circassian élite. Almost certainly in the same year, a group of Egyptian officers, amongst them the future leader Aḥmad 'Urābī, began to meet secretly and air their grievances – at that time grievances against the regime personified by Khedive Ismā'īl.

A second strand was composed by the intellectuals, who had been influenced by the ideas and institutions of Western Europe, and saw in liberalism and nationalism means to overthrow the autocracy of the

[1] The investigations of Dr Jacob M. Landau, 'Prolegomena to a study of secret societies in modern Egypt', *Middle Eastern Studies*, 1965, 1, 2, 1-52, are of seminal importance in this connection.

khedive and the domination of the Europeans. But by this time, there was also developing a reaction against European ideas: a desire to show the intellectual sufficiency of Islam, and to use the faith as a rallying-point against European political ascendancy – not only in Egypt but in the Islamic lands generally. The most able propagandist of this political pan-Islamic doctrine was the Persian, Jamāl al-Dīn al-Afghānī, who was in Cairo in 1869 and again from 1871 to 1879, and found many disciples among the younger politically conscious Egyptians. Although liberal, nationalist and pan-Islamic views were widespread among the malcontents, they were never synthesized into a systematic ideology. Subsequently (after Ismāʿīl's time) the nationalist element came to preponderate.

The ambiguity of these movements of dissidence in the early phase, the narrowly personal character of their grievances and objectives, is demonstrated by their links with members of the viceregal family. The alteration of the dynastic law of succession in 1866 had cheated the expectations of Ḥalīm Pasha, the last surviving son of Muḥammad ʿAlī and heir-presumptive under the old law. There are obscure but signifi-cant indications linking Ḥalīm with the subversives. He was prominent in Egyptian Freemasonry. Suspected of plots against the khedive, he was exiled from Egypt in 1868. From 1876 (again the critical year) there is more evidence of Halīm's activities, and James Sanua (Yaʿqūb Ṣanūʿ), a leading political journalist, was writing on his behalf. Tawfīq Pasha, Ismāʿīl's son and successor, had earlier been one of Sanua's patrons, and was also associated with Egyptian Freemasonry.

At the end of Ismāʿīl's reign, an understanding seems to have developed between the khedive and the subversives, on account of the growing European financial and political domination of Egypt. In February 1879 a gathering of Egyptian army officers, who had been put on half-pay as an economy measure, mobbed Nubar, the prime minis-ter, and his British minister of finance. They were rescued by the personal intervention of Ismāʿīl, who was strongly suspected of having instigated the incident. In April 1879, the secret army officers' society came into the open as the nucleus of a National Party, which included also religious leaders, intellectuals and politicians. The khedive, on 7 April, dismissed his French and British ministers, and appointed as prime minister Sharīf Pasha, who was connected with the National Party. The alliance between the khedive and the National Party was, however, of short duration. Under pressure from France and Britain, Sultan Abdülhamid deposed Ismāʿīl on 26 June. The accession of his son, Muḥammad Tawfīq, did nothing to resolve the tensions in Egyptian politics. A revolutionary situation developed, in which the leadership was assumed by the Egyptian army officers. This produced the so-called 'Urābī rebellion of 1881-2, which had as its consequence the British intervention and occupation of Egypt.

A dangerous situation developed also in the Egyptian Sudan during the last years of Ismā'īl's reign. Here the critically important element in the population was the diaspora of northerners, especially the Danāqla and Ja'aliyyūn, who had long established themselves and their trade in Kordofan and Darfur, and who since the middle of the century, as has been seen, had extended their operations to the Equatorial Nile and the Bahr al-Ghazal. On the whole they had gained enormously from the period of Turco-Egyptian rule. They had profited from greater public security and wider opportunities for commerce, and a few of them, notably al-Zubayr Raḥma, had become men of outstanding importance. Nevertheless, they had recently suffered a check, with the extension of the khedivial administration to Equatoria, the Bahr al-Ghazal and Darfur. The removal of al-Zubayr and the killing of his son had deprived them of two of their leaders. Gordon's measures against the slave traders, which included the harrying of the *jallāba* by the Baqqāra tribesmen in 1879, had placed their profits and careers in jeopardy.

Apart from the northerners, whose inter-relationships and communications formed a web, linking the main Nile with the new territories in the south and west, there were numerous sectional interests which had suffered from the Turco-Egyptian regime. The Fūr, who had only recently lost their independence, remained separatists at heart, and resistance continued around a series of shadow-sultans from the old dynasty. The nomads felt themselves increasingly under the pressure of khedivial administration – with Ismā'īl's acquisition of the Red Sea littoral and Darfur, the ring closed on the Beja and the Baqqāra respectively. The administrators found their prospects blighted by the recruitment of alien European and American officials to hold the chief positions. Moreover the expatriates were Christians, and the Sudanese (unlike the Egyptians) had rarely seen a Christian before the Turco-Egyptian conquest.

The revolutionary movement that declared itself under the Mahdi in 1881 was very different from the contemporary movement in Egypt, and (in spite of suspicions at the time) there is no evidence of their being organically connected. The Sudanese movement had much more in common with the earlier agrarian risings in Upper Egypt: its ideology was religious and millenarian, and totally lacking in those echoes of western liberalism and nationalism which characterized the 'Urābī movement. It began as a revolt of the *fakīs*, the indigenous Sudanese holy men. Its leader, the Mahdi, was a Dunqulāwī of the diaspora. It quickly attracted to itself the various elements of discontent, and within a few years had subverted khedivial rule in the Sudan.

CHAPTER 2

ETHIOPIA AND THE HORN [1]

The nineteenth-century history of the portion of Africa bordered by the Red Sea, the Gulf of Aden, the Indian Ocean, the Juba River, and approximately the 35th degree west and the 5th degree north is a story of the transformation of a conglomeration of tribes, principalities and kingdoms, some loosely connected with the Ethiopian state of those days, others independent, into a united Ethiopia and a series of European colonies along the coasts. Though the final stages of this process took place in the last quarter of the century, the forces which caused it appeared much earlier. The peoples of the area, who had not been part of any major international developments after the interests of the Portuguese and the Ottoman Turks had clashed there in the sixteenth century, were faced, within the span of a generation or two, with a completely new political and economic environment, caused by the rise of Muḥammad 'Ali's Egypt and the reawakening of European interest in the area. After two centuries of relative isolation and stagnation, the pace of events began to quicken; new challenges brought new responses, and a period of important developments was inaugurated.

ETHNIC, RELIGIOUS AND POLITICAL DIVISIONS, c. 1800

As far back as recorded history goes, the two main elements of the region's population were the peoples speaking Cushitic and Semitic languages. By the beginning of the nineteenth century large migrations and a continuous process of assimilation had created a very complex picture with a number of Cushitic tribes or population groups surrounding as well as interspersed among more or less semitized Cushites in the northern and central highlands. The high degree of assimilation, the long common history of much of the population and their adherence to Christianity or Islam, had wiped out or weakened tribal or ethnic dividing lines in large parts of the region. Linguistic and cultural affinity are therefore as important as ethnic origin in the grouping of the population.

[1] In this chapter a rigorous scientific transcription of Ethiopian names has been discarded in favour of a simple system which will be readily comprehensible to English readers. [General Eds.]

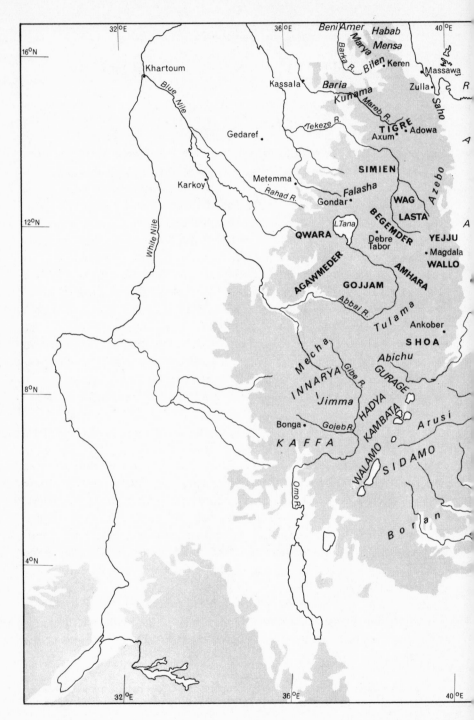

2 Ethiopia and the F

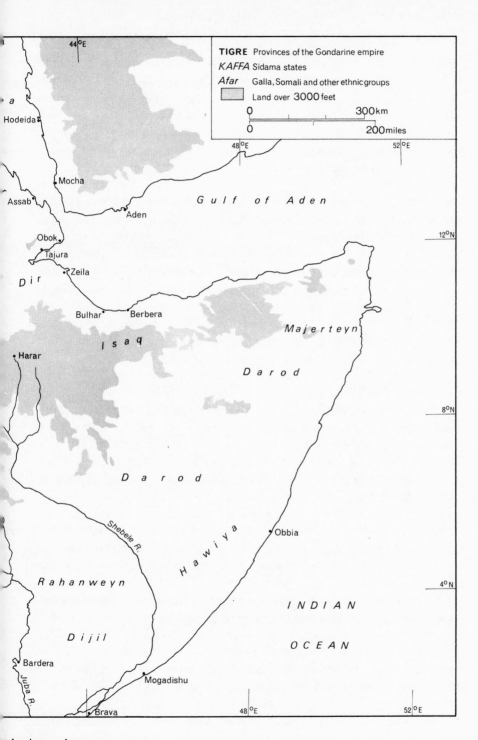

TIGRE Provinces of the Gondarine empire

KAFFA Sidama states

Afar Galla, Somali and other ethnic groups

Land over 3000 feet

0   300 km

0   200 miles

48°E   52°E

a

Hodeida

Mocha

Assab

Aden

Gulf of Aden

12°N

Obok

Tajura

Zeila

D i r

Bulhar   Berbera

Majerteyn

I s a q

Harar

D a r o d

8°N

D a r o d

Shebele R.

H a w i y a

Obbia

R a h a n w e y n

4°N

I N D I A N

D i j i l

O C E A N

Bardera

Juba R.

Mogadishu

Brava

48°E   52°E

arly nineteenth century

53

For many centuries the northern and central highlands had been dominated culturally and politically by the Semitic-speaking Christian Tigreans and Amhara. From the hinterland of Massawa in the north, they cultivated the plateau region as far south as the Abbay and a line drawn roughly south-east from the great bend of the river to the edge of he escarpment. This territory constituted the Ethiopian state of the early nineteenth century, nominally ruled by the emperors at Gondar. Its main political divisions were: Tigre in the north, Simien, Begemder, Amhara, Wag and Lasta, Yejju and Wallo in the centre, and Gojjam and Shoa in the south. In addition to the Tigrean and Amhara population, the region contained several pockets of Cushitic Agaw, most of whom had been christianized but not linguistically assimilated: the Bilen in the north, the Agaw of Wag and Lasta in the central highlands, the judaized Falasha and the largely pagan Kemant north and west of Lake Tana and the population of Agawmeder west of Gojjam. Along the western border some pagan Negroid tribes were also subject to the Gondarine empire; the best known of these were the Kunama and the Baria in the north-west. But after the Amhara, the most important ethnic group in the Gondarine empire were the Galla.

By 1800 the great northward migration of these mainly pastoral Cushitic tribes had come to an end, leaving the Barentu Galla in the highlands east of the Rift Valley, the Mecha Galla in the west, mainly between the Abbay and the Gojeb tributary of the Gibe (or Omo), and the Tulama, Abichu and others in between, where some lived within the Shoan vassal state of the Gondarine empire. Other groups had settled farther north in the foothills and mountains along the eastern escarpment. They became known, from south to north, as the Wallo, the Yejju, and the Raya (or Azebo). Of these, the Wallo and the Yejju not only lived within the boundaries of the Gondarine empire but played a central political role there. A Yejju family had, in fact, become the most powerful political factor in the empire towards the end of the eighteenth century.

Once a culturally homogeneous people, the Galla had by the nineteenth century lost many of their common characteristics through intermarriage and assimilation with the ethnic groups of the regions which they had overrun, through adaptation to new physical and socio-political environments, and through conversion to Christianity or Islam. The Wallo and Yejju in particular had been profoundly affected; they were agriculturists, with aristocratic ruling families little different from those of the Amhara; some of them were Amharic-speakers, either because they had changed their language or because they were, in fact, not of Galla origin at all. The common bond here was Islam, rather than ethnic or linguistic conformity. The Raya, on the other hand, were still largely pagan herdsmen.

Many of the central Galla had become cultivators, but remained largely pagan, and retained elements of the egalitarian, republican political system of their ancestors. In Shoa, however, the process of christianization had begun and the eastern Barentu had adopted Islam. Finally, the Arusi and the Borana Galla, south of the Awash and east of the lake region, still lived as nomadic herdsmen in their highly structured democratic age-group system known as the *gada* system, unaffected by either Christianity or Islam.

Although the Galla had overrun most of southern Ethiopia and absorbed many of the Sidama tribes, there still existed at the beginning of the nineteenth century some Sidama kingdoms or principalities in the south-western corner of the region. The most powerful and best known was Kaffa between the Omo and the Gojeb. During the first quarter of the century its king reportedly ruled or received tribute from thirty-eight kingdoms. Other Sidama kingdoms of importance were Hadya, Kambata and Walamo, between the Omo and the lake region. Though Christianity, and in the eastern parts Islam, had been introduced among the Sidama, pagan beliefs and practices had persisted, and the isolated Christian population in Kaffa, for example, was on the verge of reverting to paganism. The Gurage, south of the Awash and west of Lake Zway, had been most strongly influenced from the north. They spoke a Semitic language and some of their tribes were self-consciously Christian, others Muslim.

To the north and east of the Gondarine empire, along the Red Sea coast and in the Danakil depression, a number of tribal groups mainly of Cushitic language and Muslim faith had their homes. Those living north and west of Massawa were fairly small in size; some, for example the nomadic Beni Amer, were independent of the empire, others were linked by kinship and political ties with the population of the highlands, and the Habab, Mensa and Marya were still largely Christian at the beginning of the nineteenth century. The nomadic Afar or Danakil, and the related Saho south of Massawa, were Muslim and practically independent, although the political power of the Tigrean rulers was felt among the Saho and northern Afar, particularly in connection with salt production and trade. The only ruler to exercise authority over significant sections of the Afar population was the sultan of Awsa, who controlled the cultivable land around the lower course of the Awash.

From the Gulf of Tajura, the whole Horn to the east and south was occupied by the Somali, an ethnically, linguistically, and religiously (Muslim) homogeneous people. They had for centuries been expanding southwards, displacing in the process earlier Galla and Bantu popula-tions.[1] By 1800 they had reached but not crossed the Juba river. Starting from the Gulf of Tajura and following the coast of the Gulf of Aden and the Indian Ocean, the most important clan groups were the Dir (Isa and Gadabursi), Isaq, Darod, Hawiya and Dijil. In the hinter-land, the Darod had also occupied Ogaden north of the Shebele river, while the Rahanweyn had settled between the Shebele and the Juba. Except for some population in coastal settlements, all but the Hawiya and Rahanweyn were nomadic herdsmen, and centralized government was almost non-existent.

The most important points through which external influences reached the isolated region were the coastal centres, Massawa on the Red Sea, Tajura, Zeila and Berbera on the Gulf of Aden, and to a lesser extent Mogadishu and Brava on the Indian Ocean. It was through these places that the trade with the outside world flowed, pilgrims to Mecca and Jerusalem departed and returned, and occasional foreigners brought new ideas and new skills to the region. Because of the proximity of the Ethiopian escarpment to the coast opposite Massawa, this excellent harbour functioned as the main gateway to Ethiopia. The sixteenth century attempt to convert northern Ethiopia into a province of the Ottoman Empire had failed, but the Turks had held on to the small island of Massawa and claimed suzerainty over 'Habashistan'. Though they administered the port and levied duties, it was only occasionally that their presence obstructed Ethiopian trade; still less did it pose any threat to Ethiopia. The Turks had allied themselves with the Belew on the mainland and appointed as their *na'ib* the chief at Arkiko opposite the island. Before 1800 the pashas of Jedda had stopped sending gover-nors to Massawa, and the *na'ib* had become the *de facto* ruler also at Massawa. He occupied a rather strange position since he acknowledged the overlordship of both the sultan and the *ras* of Tigre and was re-warded by both. The first arrival in 1813 of representatives of Muḥam-mad 'Ali's Egypt did not alter the situation. The small garrison of sixty

[1] This, at least, is the picture to be derived from Somali oral traditions. However, it may be, as argued by Professor Herbert Lewis ('The origins of the Galla and Somali', *Journal of African History*, 1966, **7**, 27–46), that the southward expansion was really an expansion of Islam – of Muslim Somali at the expense of pagan Somali. [Ed.]

soldiers could easily be evicted by the *na'ib*, and this actually happened in 1826 because of a quarrel between him and the governor.

The second most important port in the area was Zeila, the main outlet for the trade of the small city state and region of Harar, as well as of Shoa and the Galla and Sidama territories of the south-west. It had a permanent population of Somali, Afar and Arabs, ruled by an emir who acknowledged the Sharif of Mecca as his overlord. Thus it was nominally incorporated in the Ottoman Empire, but the bond was tenuous. Though it had no permanent population, Berbera was the scene of a very important annual fair where caravans from the interior met Arab and Indian merchants. The surrounding Somali tribes controlled the place, and any Ottoman claim must be regarded as extremely shadowy. This was also true of the small Afar ports including Tajura.

The trade which had given rise to and maintained the Red Sea and Gulf of Aden ports was largely transit trade between the Ethiopian highlands on the one hand and Arabia and beyond on the other. Obviously this trade depended on political conditions not only in Ethiopia but in the whole of the Middle East. Conditions during the latter part of the eighteenth century had not been favourable to this trade, and the prosperity of the commercial communities was dwindling at the turn of the century.

The situation on the Somali coast south of Cape Guardafui was somewhat different. The hinterland was politically less organized and the long distance trade less extensive. During the seventeenth century Mogadishu, the most important of the coastal centres, had fallen under Omani authority, along with other East African ports. By the beginning of the nineteenth century, however, the Omani influence had weakened. With the exception of Mogadishu, the ports were in the hands of local Somali rulers, of whom the most important was the sultan of the Majerteyn to the north.

THE CLOSING DECADES OF THE *ZAMANA MESAFENT*

The closing period of the Gondarine empire is known in Ethiopia as the *Zamana Mesafent*, lit. 'the era of the princes'. It was characterized by a complete breakdown of imperial authority and by increasing regionalism. Kings were enthroned and dethroned at the whims of governors, who fought among themselves for the position of *ras* of the kingdom or *ras bitweded*, lit. 'the favourite duke'. From the beginning of the nineteenth century the Ethiopian monarchy existed only in name, only as the symbol of a polity which had once been powerful. In theory the king of kings still conferred ranks and governorships and withdrew them at will, but he had no real power. He had no army of his own and almost no revenue. In the 1830s Sahle Dengel's regular income is reported to have been 300 thalers annually from the Muslim merchants of Gondar.[1]

The rulers of the country were the *ras*es and the *dejazmach*es of the various provinces. They kept the revenues of their provinces and commanded their own armies. The most powerful had made their positions hereditary. Nevertheless, the awe in which the Solomonic dynasty had been held still lingered on and prevented any attempts to usurp the throne itself. The aspiration of the most powerful *ras*es was to become *ras* of the kingdom and thereby guardian of the king of kings. The struggle for this supreme position, and continuous attempts by all governors to increase their domains at the expense of their neighbours, caused a state of almost constant small-scale warfare.

The situation was further aggravated by developments in the Ethiopian Church, which had in the past, together with the monarchy, been the strongest unifying factor in the Ethiopian state and had traditionally acted as a mediator in political conflicts. Though the clergy in some cases still tried to play this important role, the unity of the Church was itself threatened by the growing intensity of the doctrinal disputes which had arisen from attempts to explain the genesis of the nature of Christ. Various factions fought each other by both spiritual and temporal means and sought the support of regional rulers or political factions. As a parallel development, the revival of Islam at the turn of the century increased the religious consciousness and commitment of the Muslim communities in Ethiopia. Muslim merchants carried their faith to new centres, and Islam was gaining ground at the expense of Christianity. The political influence of the Muslims increased, along with the power of the Gallas in the Gondarine state. On the other hand, the distinction between the Amhara-Tigre and the Galla nobility was to a certain extent disappearing. Leading members of the politically most important Galla families had accepted Christianity, at least nominally; they had married into the Amhara nobility, including the imperial family, and the shifting alignments in the political conflicts often ignored the question of religion. But there were large sections of the Christian population who resented this state of affairs. They would

[1] W. P. E. S. Rüppell, *Reise in Abyssinien* (Frankfurt am Main, 1838, 1840), II, 173-4.

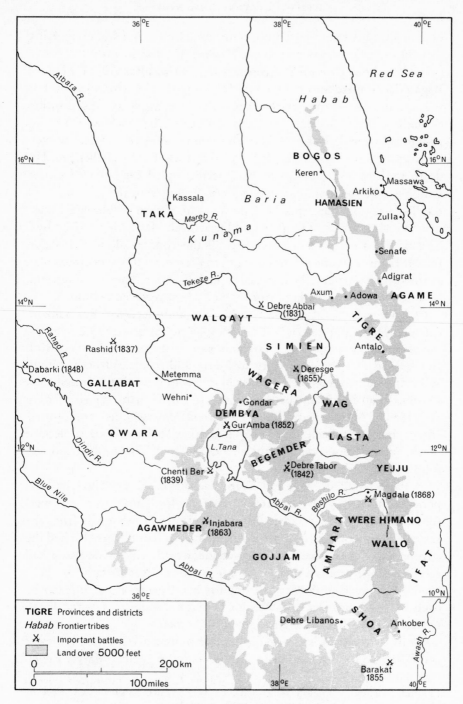

3 Ethiopia in the *Zamana Mesafent*

eventually find their most important spokesman and leader in King Tewodros, who put an end to the *Zamana Mesafent* in 1855.

In 1820 the *de facto* ruler of central Ethiopia was Ras Gugsa Mersa of Begemder, a member of the powerful Yejju dynasty, founded by Ras Ali Gwangwil in the 1770s. Gugsa had strengthened his position through successful campaigns and marriage alliances, and made his provincial capital, Debre Tabor, the main centre of political power. During the last years of his life his position was hardly challenged. His death in June 1825, however, became the signal for renewed power struggles. Those most immediately concerned were the governors of the Tana region: Dejazmach Haile Maryam Gebru of Simien, Dejazmach Goshu Zewde of Gojjam and Dejazmach Maru Aklu of Dembya. The domains of the latter included all the country along the Sudan border from Agawmeder in the south to Metemma in the north, as well as the districts around the imperial capital, Gondar. They were referred to as *Yemaru Qims*, the land from which Maru received tribute.

In the first battle Maru and Gugsa's son and successor, Ras Yimam, defeated Haile Maryam, who died soon after. In the struggle over the accession to Simien, Haile Maryam's son, Wibe, emerged successful. But he had lost some territory to Maru, and so the alliances shifted. Wibe and Yimam marched against Maru, who now allied himself with Goshu. In an important battle at Koso Ber in Gojjam, the latter were defeated and Maru killed. Yimam conferred Yemaru Qims on his brother Marye, but Dejazmach Kinfu and his mother Welette Tekla, a niece of Maru, successfully reclaimed their lands. In 1828 Yimam died and was followed as *ras* by Marye.

In these conflicts Shoa and Tigre had stayed aloof. Tigre had experienced its own period of turmoil after the death in 1816 of its powerful ruler, Ras Walde Sellassie. In 1822 Dejazmach Sebagadis from the eastern district of Agame emerged as the new ruler of Tigre. He had the advantage of easy access to the outside world. His predecessor had received some modern firearms as a gift from Great Britain, and Sebagadis continued to collect firearms for his Tigrean army. In 1827 he even made an unsuccessful attempt through a letter to George IV to recruit a small British cavalry force of 100 men.[1]

From 1828 onwards Sebagadis became more active in the politics of central Ethiopia, attempting to form a coalition against Marye. Rebel-

[1] Public Record Office, F.O. 1/2, fol. 6. William Coffin, who carried this letter to England, produced an English 'translation', fos. 1–2, containing an invitation to occupy Massawa, but there is no mention of this in the original.

lions and campaigns followed, but the co-ordination was poor and Marye defeated or outmanoeuvred his opponents one by one. At the beginning of 1831, the power struggle culminated in a major campaign. Marye collected a sizable army from Begemder, Yejju and Wallo, called on Goshu, Kinfu and Wibe to join him with their armies, and crossed the Tekeze into Tigre. In a fierce battle near Debre Abbai, Sebagadis, the last outstanding leader of the Tigreans during the *Zamana Mesafent*, was defeated and executed.

Marye, too, fell in the battle and was succeeded by his brother Dori. He returned to Debre Tabor, where he died in June. The chiefs and generals elected his thirteen-year-old nephew, Ali Alula, *ras* of the kingdom. A council led by his maternal uncle, Dejazmach Amede of Were Himano, was appointed to guide the young *ras* in state affairs. Ali's mother, Menen, became the most influential person at his court. Though born into the leading family of Muslim Wallo nobility, she had accepted Christianity when she became a member of Gugsa's family. Dejazmach Amede and her other Muslim relatives made several attempts to assert their influence and accelerate the pace of islamization in Begemder. Ali vacillated, but Menen was shrewd enough to realize that a balance had to be kept. Moreover, she was strong enough to carry out her policies, balancing Yejju-Wallo against Gojjam, Dembya and Simien. The French traveller Arnauld d'Abbadie, who met her in 1839, summed up his impressions of her: 'Cupide, avare, astucieuse, violente, ambitieuse, despote, vaniteuse et coquette, elle passait pour reculer devant aucun moyen.'[1]

The chief who benefited most from the outcome of the battle of Debre Abbai was Wibe. None of Sebagadis's many sons was strong enough to command the obedience of his brothers or the heads of the other leading families in Tigre. Although he was faced with much resistance, Wibe therefore made himself the ruler of all northern Ethiopia from the Red Sea to his home province of Simien. For about twenty years, he was in all but name the equal of Ras Ali. During the 1830s he did not, however, make any open attempt to challenge the *ras* or his guardians. In the Lake Tana region as well as between Lasta and Yejju-Wallo, the local feuds continued. The death of Dejazmach Kinfu in 1839 brought about significant changes. Ali offered Kinfu's lands to Birru, the ambitious son of Goshu of Gojjam. But no sooner had Kinfu's heirs been defeated by the Gojjamis at Chenti Ber and Birru installed himself at Gondar, than Ali reversed the appointment and conferred

[1] Arnauld d'Abbadie, *Douze ans dans la Haute-Éthiopie* (Paris, 1868), 183.

Yemaru Qims on his mother Menen. She installed her husband Yohannes, a son of Tekla Giyorgis, as emperor.

This increase in Ali's and Menen's power was as unwelcome to Wibe as to Goshu and Birru. A coalition was formed with the aim of overthrowing the Yejju dynasty. Wibe had prepared himself by bringing a new Coptic bishop, Abba Salama, to the country. Salama's predecessor Qerlos had failed to unite the Church, largely because he supported the strictest 'monophysite' faction, the *Karra Haymanot*. Ras Gugsa and his successors preferred to co-operate with the most prominent Ethiopian leader of the clergy, the *ichege*. The holders of this office in the 1820s and 1830s were adherents of the doctrine known as *Sega Lijoch* or *Sost Ledet*, which had followers both in Shoa and throughout the central provinces, particularly in the capital. When Qerlos died about 1829, the leaders at Debre Tabor and Gondar did nothing to bring a successor from Egypt. The arrival of Salama in 1841 gave Wibe the opportunity to pose as the leader and protector of the Christian community. This gave an additional dimension to the civil war of 1841–2 at a time when there were also signs of an approaching confrontation between Muslim Egypt and Christian Ethiopia.

As early as 1821 Egyptian forces in the Sudan had penetrated into the western borderlands of Ethiopia, primarily in search of gold. The following year the commander, Muḥammad 'Ali's son Ismā'īl, was killed by the chief of the Ja'ali, Mek Nimr, who then fled to the Ethiopian province Walqayt. Egyptian forces followed him into Taka and also appeared in Gallabat. They withdrew without having clashed with Ethiopian forces, but returned again in the late 1820s on slave-raiding expeditions. Many chiefs who had traditionally paid tribute to the Ethiopian governors in the highlands were subdued, but an attempt in 1832 to take and hold Gallabat was given up in the face of Ethiopian opposition. Taka was raided in 1832 and 1834, and from there the Egyptian forces pushed on towards the Red Sea coast. In 1834 the Habab accepted Egyptian overlordship. In the borderlands between the Tekeze and the Rahad, the Egyptians were less successful. A raid into Gedaref by some of Mek Nimr's men led to a counter-attack by Egyptian troops on Walqayt in 1835. They came in force and ransacked the province, but there was no question of holding it permanently. In an encounter with some of Wibe's forces, they were defeated and barely escaped to the lowlands. Farther south new attempts were made to gain permanent control over Gallabat because of its commercial importance. In 1837 an Egyptian force invaded the highlands through Metemma.

This time the threat was felt as far as Gondar. Dejazmach Kinfu collected his forces, followed the retreating Egyptians until he caught up with them near Rashid, and defeated them in a fierce battle. This increased the self-confidence of the Ethiopians in the area, but did not take the pressure off the frontier. The Egyptians continued their activity along the frontier into 1838, but there were no major clashes.

At first Ethiopian reactions to the Egyptian threat were local and momentary. It was only gradually that the rulers became aware of the Egyptian activities as an overall threat to Ethiopia. In this process the Europeans in Ethiopia, who for various reasons were concerned about Muhammad 'Ali's eventual plans to conquer the country, played an important role. The missionaries, explorers and adventurers, who had entered the country in unprecedented numbers, advised the rulers and offered to carry messages to Europe requesting assistance against Egypt. At Gondar the French brothers d'Abbadie offered to be the envoys of the emperor and Ras Ali, and in 1838 actually took charge of letters requesting assistance from France and England. But the front was far from united. In 1838 Dejazmach Amede was prepared to ally himself with Muhammad 'Ali in order to convert Ethiopia into a Muslim state. He died soon after, but as the intentions of Wibe and his allies to oust Ras Ali became more and more evident, the latter seems in his turn to have played with the idea of seeking an alliance with Muhammad 'Ali to save his own position. Envoys passed between the two, and there were reports of an understanding couched in the terms: 'Your friends shall be my friends and your enemies shall be my enemies.' An Egyptian army appeared once more at Wehni in 1841. Ali was openly accused by his enemies of having adopted the Muslim faith.[1]

When Abuna Salama arrived in 1841, he was persuaded to excommunicate Ali. Wibe could march on Gondar and Debre Tabor, quite confident that Ali's position with his Christian subjects had been considerably weakened. He was joined at Gondar by Birru Goshu with the army of Gojjam. Early in February 1842, Ali met them outside Debre Tabor with a large army consisting mainly of Galla warriors. The story of the battle and the events that followed is almost incredible. First Ali's army was soundly defeated and fled. Then one of his few Christian allies, Birru Aligaz from Yejju, returned in the evening to make his submission to Wibe, but found that he could capture him

---

[1] Mordechai Abir, *Ethiopia: the era of the princes* (London, 1968), 112–16. Abir's account of Ethiopian–Egyptian relations in this period is both detailed and convincing. He concludes: 'It is more than likely that they [i.e. Ali and his mother Menen] appealed to Ahmad Pasha [Egyptian governor of the Sudan] for help, using Islamic affinity as an incentive.'

instead, whereupon the other victor, Birru Goshu, decided to escape to Gojjam. Abba Salama lifted the excommunication of Ali and negotiated the release of Wibe. Ali then helped his former enemy to recapture Simien, though he had in the meantime given it to his ally, Wibe's brother Merso. Neither side gained much from this war. Wibe once more concentrated his attention on Tigre and the Red Sea coast. Relations between him and Ali remained tolerably good for about five years.

With Birru Goshu, on the other hand, no reconciliation was effected, and almost every year following the battle of Debre Tabor, Ali invaded Birru's lands in Gojjam without, however, being able to capture his enemy. At times Goshu agreed to participate in the campaigns against his son, but just as often the two were united against Ali. The latter also had rebellions to deal with in Lasta, Yejju, and Wallo, where Birru Aligaz and Amede's son Liben defied his authority. Though successful in many campaigns, Ali was totally incapable of bringing peace to central Ethiopia. In 1845 his relations with Salama deteriorated, because the latter quarrelled with the *ichege* on doctrinal and other grounds. Moreover, Salama had excommunicated King Sahle Sellassie of Shoa because of his support of *Sost Ledet* ecclesiastics in Shoa, and this had implications for Ali, who was himself a supporter of this faction. In 1846 the break became complete. Salama excommunicated Ali, Menen and other followers of the *ichege* and his doctrines, and left Gondar for Tigre. This may have caused tension between Ali and Wibe, and it was probably to test the obedience of his nominal vassal that Ali requested his participation in the 1846 campaign against Birru Goshu. Wibe refused, and this time Ali invaded Wibe's southernmost province, Wagera. Wibe remained on the defensive in Simien, and Ali decided not to penetrate into this mountainous area with his Galla cavalry.

Both Wibe and Ali had good reasons to avoid a major clash. Wibe's hold over Tigre depended very much on his presence there. Members of the Tigrean aristocracy defied his authority whenever possible. Balgada Araya Sellassie, for example, who controlled the essential salt imports into Tigre, took the opportunity to proclaim himself governor of all Tigre when Wibe was away at Debre Tabor. Wibe also had to deal with the *na'ib*, who in his absence had advanced inland. Here the issue at stake was really access to the coast, which meant, among other things, the opportunity to import firearms. In December 1843 Wibe's army raided the Semhar on the coast and forced the *na'ib* to pay compensation for his raids into the highlands. But the real threat in the north came from the Egyptians, who were slowly extending their rule from Kassala eastwards. Wibe counter-attacked in 1844 by campaigns into Habab and as far west as Baria and Kunama, but failed in his attempts to gain control over the coast. On the advice of French missionaries, he appealed to the French government to support his claims, but in vain. Instead, at the end of 1846 Massawa was once again placed under Egyptian rule. In March 1847 Egyptian troops landed at Massawa and soon after crossed to the mainland. The *na'ib*, who had managed until then to maintain a certain autonomy *vis-à-vis* both Wibe and the governor of Massawa, was stripped of all power and Egyptian garrisons were stationed at Arkiko and Monkullo. The chiefs of the small ports and coastal settlements south of Massawa were also called upon to accept Egyptian rule, and there were reports in 1847 of Egyptian plans to take control of the salt plains east of Tigre. This time the Egyptian take-over meant a real change. The nominal Turkish claims were replaced by a strong government opposed to Ethiopian interests.

All this happened while Wibe was guarding Simien against the expected invasion of Ali. In June 1847, however, Ali and Wibe came to terms with each other. Wibe could return to Tigre, and late in 1848 he once again sent his army into Semhar and threatened Massawa itself. The Egyptians gave up Monkullo and paid off the Ethiopians to save Arkiko and Massawa. In the following year the Egyptians withdrew again from Massawa, and a Turkish governor took over the administration. In the Habab, Bogos and Baria districts, however, raiding continued from both sides. For many of the northern tribes who had been almost independent a generation earlier, the struggle between Egyptians and Ethiopians for control meant payment of double tribute and sometimes enslavement.

Ali's reasons for calling off his campaign against Wibe in 1847 had nothing to do with the Egyptian activities. A new and dangerous rebel, his own son-in-law, Lij Kassa Haylu, had been added to his earlier enemies. Son of a chief from the border province of Qwara, and through his father the half-brother of Dejazmach Kinfu, Kassa had nevertheless been unable to prevent Menen's accession to Yemaru Qims in 1840. During the following years he alternated between the life of a *shifta*, a highwayman, on the western frontier, and service as a soldier of fortune to various chiefs, including Ras Ali. A popular commander, he was by 1845 important enough to be offered the governorship of Qwara and Ali's daughter Tewabech in marriage. But Kassa was far from satisfied with a minor province on the outskirts of Yemaru Qims. In October 1846 he rebelled against Menen, invaded Dembya and defeated the armies sent against him. Early the following year, when Ali and Menen were occupied with the campaign against Wibe, he captured Gondar, collected the tribute and appointed his own men to administer the capital. In June Menen returned and immediately marched against Kassa. In the battle which followed, Kassa won a complete victory and captured both Menen and her husband, the puppet emperor. In exchange for the release of Menen, Kassa demanded and received the governorship of Yemaru Qims. Next Kassa turned his attention to the western frontier, where Egyptian forces had invaded his territories. He occupied Metemma without difficulty and pushed on into the Sudan to gain a more decisive victory over the Egyptians than his brother Kinfu had at Rashid ten years earlier. Instead he was defeated in March 1848, when he tried to capture a small fortified Egyptian position at Dabarki, about 200 kilometres west of Metemma, and had to retreat to the Ethiopian highlands. The outcome of this battle had tremendous implications for Kassa's future outlook in military matters. Henceforth his military programme included drill and discipline, fortifications and, above all, the acquisition of artillery.

The defeat almost cost Kassa his governorship, but he managed to rebuild his army in time and come to terms with Ali. He loyally served the *ras* until 1852, when the relations between the two deteriorated once more. Kassa refused to appear before the *ras* when called. As in 1839, Ali chose Goshu of Gojjam to destroy his enemy, offering him Kassa's governorship. After a few months in Qwara to strengthen his army, Kassa invaded Dembya. In a fierce battle on 12 November, he defeated his enemy's numerically superior forces at Gur Amba north of Tana. Goshu died in the battle and the remains of his army hurried back to Gojjam. Kassa offered to negotiate, but Ali refused. Instead he called for reinforcements from several of his other vassals including Wibe. Kassa met these united forces in Taqusa north of Lake Tana, and again won a decisive victory, on 12 April 1853. After burning down Debre Tabor, he crossed into Gojjam and finally faced Ali at Ayshal. In a bloody battle on 29 June, Kassa was once more victorious. Ali fled to Yejju and made no serious attempt to collect a new army. The following year Kassa dealt successfully with Birru Goshu, who had defied Ali for more than ten years. At first Wibe agreed to accept Kassa as Ali's successor. But when Kassa took the title of *negus* (king) in 1854 and showed signs of aspiring to the position of king of kings (*negusa nagast*), Wibe collected all his forces for a final showdown. Kassa invaded Simien, and at Deresge on 9 February 1855, he won his crowning victory. He lost no time in putting the seal on it. Two days after the battle he was anointed and crowned king of kings by Abuna Salama in Deresge Maryam church. He chose as his throne name Tewodros. What remained to be settled was the question of Shoa's independence.[1]

Throughout the *Zamana Mesafent*, Shoa had enjoyed a *de facto* independent status. It had a well-established ruling dynasty and paid no tribute to Gondar. Sahle Sellassie (1813–47) accentuated this sovereign status by taking the title of *negus*, which was not used by vassals of the Gondarine emperors. Though Ali signed himself Negus Ali in a treaty with Great Britain in 1849, he did not claim kingship before his own people. Sahle Sellassie on the other hand, who claimed to belong to the Solomonic dynasty, might have aspired to occupy the imperial throne, but there are no indications that he seriously thought along such lines.

On the contrary, Sahle Sellassie seems to have been quite happy to stay out of the power struggles in the Gondarine state and to concentrate on the consolidation and expansion of Shoa as an independent political entity. This he did with great success, subduing the Galla tribes who made up the major portion of the population, partly by diplomatic intrigue and marriage alliances, partly by military campaigns in which the use of firearms tipped the scales in his favour. To Ifat in the north-east and Shoa proper in the centre, he added new territories inhabited by Galla in the south and west. In spite of several rebellions and other setbacks, a cholera epidemic and two years of drought in the 1830s, Sahle Sellassie managed to consolidate his power, to establish fairly regular taxation procedures and, generally speaking, to provide his subjects with more security and prosperity than the population enjoyed elsewhere in Ethiopia at the time. The new conquests of Galla territories in the south and west provided new opportunities for both local and transit trade. As a result, Sahle Sellassie could acquire firearms though still in very limited numbers. Political integration, assimilation and growth of trade were all facilitated by the Shoan ruler's tolerance in religious matters. On the one hand, he allowed church leaders an important role as his advisers and definitely supported a policy of christianization and amharization in his territories. On the other hand, there was no question of suppressing Islam or discriminating against Muslim traders.

In his internal ecclesiastical policies, Sahle Sellassie was less successful. Of the factions in the Church he was probably most inclined to support the *Sost Ledet* school. But when he attempted to demonstrate

[1] Abir, *Ethiopia*, 27–43, 95–143, and Sven Rubenson, *King of Kings Tewodros of Ethiopia* (Addis Ababa, 1966), 15–45.

his independence of Gondar also in ecclesiastical affairs by appointing high church officers on his own authority, they were accused of belonging to the opposite party, *Hulet Ledet*. The *ichege*, who at the time represented the central authority of the Church, protested, and Ali ordered Sahle Sellassie to obey the instructions of the Gondarine ecclesiastic. The Shoan king first refused, but then gave in under the threat of excommunication and a possible invasion by Ali's forces. He complied with the orders of the *ichege* and, at the risk of rebellion in some parts of his country, banished the opponents of *Sost Ledet*, only to find Abuna Salama in charge at Gondar and the ecclesiastical policies there reversed after the battle of Debre Tabor. Unwilling to make a complete turnabout again, Sahle Sellassie suffered excommunication by Salama in 1845. This time, however, Ali was on his side, and the unwillingness of the *abuna* to lift the excommunication of the Shoan ruler contributed to his own arrest and exile to Tigre in 1846.

The following year Sahle Sellassie died and was succeeded by his son Haile Malakot. A series of new Galla rebellions were successfully dealt with and, after some resistance, Ali agreed to recognize Haile Malakot's title as king. Nevertheless, the position of the new and young king was not as well-established as his father's when the political independence of Shoa was finally challenged by Tewodros in 1855.[1]

In several respects the last decades of the *Zamana Mesafent* foreshadowed coming developments. The country's long period of isolation came to an end. The religious resurgence of Islam made itself felt in some areas, and the revival of the Red Sea trade increased communication throughout the Gondarine state and with the Galla and Sidama territories beyond its boundaries. Christian missionaries, both Protestant and Catholic, entered the country and, though they did not win many converts, their very presence, often at the courts of the most important of the political leaders, had an unsettling effect in many ways. Their preaching and teaching introduced new ideas and new elements of tension, and their offers of political advice and of their services as emissaries to Europe opened alternative roads of action for the Ethiopian rulers. In addition, a number of other Europeans came to Ethiopia as explorers or to seek personal gain or influence for their home governments.

In the 1840s Britain and France opened competing consulates at Massawa, and during the same decade they negotiated their first treaties with Ethiopian rulers. Captain W. C. Harris led an official British

---

[1] Abir, *Ethiopia*, 144–82.

mission to Sahle Sellassie, which resulted in a treaty of friendship and commerce between Shoa and Great Britain, signed on 16 November 1841. For Sahle Sellassie, the contact was important as a means of acquiring firearms, including a few small cannon. For the British it was a question of opening up new markets for Indian trade and of fore-stalling the French. In 1839–40 a French emissary, Rochet d'Héri-court, also spent some six months at Sahle Sellassie's court. In 1843 he returned on a semi-official mission, handed over some gifts, and negotia-ted an agreement, which mentioned French military assistance against Muslims or other foreigners, protection of Ethiopian pilgrims to Jeru-salem and the privileges of French merchants in Shoa. The validity of Rochet d'Héricourt's document was, however, questioned by the French government itself soon after the envoy's return.[1] In 1849 a second treaty was negotiated between Ali and Walter Plowden, British consul to 'His Majesty of Abyssinia'. Plowden was instructed to sign the largely commercial treaty with the emperor at Gondar, but had to accept Ali's signature instead, albeit with the title 'King of Abyssinia'. According to Plowden, Ali showed no interest and, when he finally agreed to listen to the draft of the treaty,

... he kept talking to his favourite *shoomeree* about a horse that was tied in the tent ... I begged his attention to what was being read, to which he assented, and yawned exceedingly ... the Ras said that he saw no harm whatever in the document; on the contrary, that ... it was excellent, but appeared to him exceedingly useless, inasmuch as he did not suppose, as Abyssinia was then constituted, that one English merchant would or could enter it in ten years.[2]

Though Wibe and Sahle Sellassie were somewhat more active, the initiative in these relations normally came from the European side. The Ethiopian rulers accepted the gifts of firearms with pleasure, and showed some sporadic interest in technical innovations brought to their atten-tion. But there was no active, sustained response to the European interest such as manifested itself later in Ethiopia as elsewhere in Africa. There was also no indication that Ethiopia would unite to chart its own unique course as she did during the second half of the century.

For the population in general and the peasantry in particular, the closing decades of the Gondar era must have been a time of many sorrows. Although there was sufficient land, and although agricultural production was both diversified and adequate for their needs, the pea-

[1] Archives du Ministère des Affaires Etrangères (A. E.), Mémoires et Documents, Abyssinie 1, 306–7, Affaires Etrangères to the French consul, Jerusalem, 8 April 1846.
[2] Walter Chichele Plowden, *Travels in Abyssinia and the Galla country* (London, 1868), 420.

sants laboured under many disadvantages even in peaceful times. The land tenure system was very complicated. Some peasants owned the land they tilled, and paid taxes to the sovereign. Others were tenant farmers on crown lands. Others again were tenants on the lands of the nobility or of the Church, and paid taxes and other dues to these landlords. Church ownership of land was permanent and no taxes were paid to the state. Fiefs granted to other landholders were either permanent and inheritable, or temporary, burdened especially in the latter case by a variety of obligations, such as the collection of taxes and tribute, the raising of armies, etc. In the final resort the burdens were shifted to the tenants, who paid taxes usually in kind or in the form of *corvée* labour. In much of the country, taxation was based on the principle of tithes of everything produced, but there was much arbitrariness and exploitation. At the end of the period Plowden draws the following picture of the plight of the peasantry:

The prosperous or adverse condition of a village depends almost entirely upon the rapacity or moderation of its immediate chief . . . The imposts are numerous, but vary according to the traditional customs of each village. They pay a certain portion in kind to the Ras, or other great chief, and sometimes a regular tax in money; besides this they must furnish oxen to plough the King's lands: their immediate governor then takes his share in kind of every grain – say a fifth, and feeds besides a certain number of soldiers at the expense of each householder; he has rights to oxen, sheep, and goats, butter, honey, and every other requisite for subsistence; he must be received with joy and feasting by his subjects whenever he visits them, and can demand from them contributions on fifty pretexts – he is going on a campaign, or returning from one; he has lost a horse, or married a wife; his property has been consumed by fire, or he has lost his all in battle; or the sacred duty of a funeral banquet cannot be fulfilled without their aid.[1]

The unceasing campaigns of the *Zamana Mesafent* aggravated the situation. The soldiers lived by requisitioning if they were in friendly territory and by looting if they were in enemy territory. Sometimes the peasants found no other means of surviving than by joining the bands of pillaging soldiers. Most of the travellers of the period, except those who visited Shoa, commented on the insecurity and poverty, which even led to depopulation in some areas. In this situation the longings for a restoration of the monarchy, and of law and order, were expressed in Messianic terms, as a hope that the coming of the legendary Tewodros was imminent. According to the Ethiopian apocalyptic work

[1] Great Britain, Parliamentary Papers (P.P.), *Correspondence respecting Abyssinia 1846–1868* (London, 1868), 107, Plowden to Clarendon, 9 July 1854.

Fikkare Iyesus, Tewodros was God's promised king, who would come to rule the world in righteousness, peace and prosperity after a long period of war and famine, of corruption, perversity and lawlessness, and of the rule of imposters and women.[1] So great were the expectations of the coming of Tewodros during the *Zamana Mesafent*, that the missionary Samuel Gobat was referred to the prophecy about Tewodros when he asked a Falasha what he knew about Messiah. But some were losing hope. 'The time fixed by this prophecy is elapsed, and Theodore has not appeared', was the sad comment given to Gobat by his learned Orthodox friend Habte Sellassie.[2]

For the last and most successful of the *mesafent*, the role was cast. Kassa, the former *shifta*, proclaimed that he was the eagerly awaited Tewodros.

THE REIGN OF TEWODROS

In Tewodros II Ethiopia received a very different kind of ruler from any she had known for several generations. In terms of his background and his rise to power, he can be called the last of the *mesafent*; in terms of his aspirations and his policies, however, he belongs to the modern period in Ethiopian history. Tewodros is the father of modern Ethiopia in the sense that he conceived the idea of a united, strong and progressive Ethiopian state and was the first to attempt its realization.

Tewodros's first concern after his great military victories was to re-establish the prestige of the Ethiopian monarchy. In the choice between succeeding Ras Ali as the guardian of a puppet emperor and usurping the throne for himself, he did not hesitate to choose the latter alternative. The revolutionary element in this action was not so much the actual usurpation of the throne as the fact that Tewodros took this step without at the time of his coronation claiming Solomonic descent. Tewodros's claim to be the 'Elect of God' was not dynastic but personal. He undoubtedly regarded his rise to power as the result of divine intervention. In 1862 he wrote to Queen Victoria:

Because my fathers the emperors had sinned against our Creator, He took away their kingdom from them and gave it to the Gallas and the Turks. But now the Creator has given me life, lifted me out of the dust and endowed me with power, and He has placed me over the kingdom of my fathers. By the power of God I have removed the Gallas from power.[3]

---

[1] René Basset, ed., *Les apocryphes éthiopiens, XI, Fekkaré Iyasous* (Paris, 1909), 25–8.
[2] Samuel Gobat, *Journal of a three years' residence in Abyssinia* (London, 1834), 173.
[3] P.R.O., F.O. 95/721, fo. 126; P.P., *Correspondence 1846–1868*, 224, Tewodros to Victoria, 29 October 1862.

It was only later in his reign, when he began to suspect that foreigners despised him as an upstart, that 'the son of David and of Solomon' found its way into his official titles. During the first years of his reign he often stressed the difference between himself and his predecessors, for example to Plowden in March 1856:

Till now Ethiopia has been without a Sovereign, but now that by the grace of God I wear the Crown, I shall not depart from those usages that become all Sovereigns.[1]

Plowden was impressed and somewhat disturbed by the religious zeal and energy of this 'slave of Christ', as Tewodros often called himself. After his first interview with the king he reported:

He is persuaded that he is destined to restore the glories of Ethiopian Empire, and to achieve great conquests; of untiring energy, both mental and bodily, his personal and moral daring are boundless ... Indefatigable in business, he takes little repose night or day; his ideas and language are clear and precise; hesitation is not known to him; and he has neither councillors nor go-betweens.... His faith is signal; without Christ, he says, I am nothing; if he has destined me to purify and reform this distracted kingdom, with His aid who shall stay me: nay, sometimes he is on the point of not caring for human assistance at all, and this is one reason why he will not seek with much avidity for assistance from or alliance with Europe.[2]

Armed with the conviction that he was called to translate the Tewodros legend into reality, and strengthened by the sanction of the Church for his coronation, Tewodros turned to the tasks of completing the re-unification of the country, introducing reforms in State and Church, and preparing for a crusade against the 'Turks'.

Of the major provinces, only Shoa had remained unaffected by Tewodros's earlier victories. Soon after his coronation, the king marched south, overcame the resistance of the Wallo Galla and captured their stronghold Magdala, which was later to become his state prison, treasury and last refuge. In October he proceeded to Shoa. There resistance was poorly co-ordinated, probably because King Haile Malakot was ill and died ten days before the decisive battle at Barakat on 19 November. After the battle the defeated Shoan chiefs surrendered and handed over Haile Malakot's young son and heir, Menelik. Haile Malakot's brother, Haile Mika'el, was appointed governor of Shoa, and Tewodros returned to Gondar through Gojjam. If conquest had meant unification, the task would have been completed. But it did not.

[1] P. P., *Correspondence 1846–1868*, 165, Plowden to Clarendon, 5 March 1856.
[2] *Ibid.* p. 148, Plowden to Clarendon, 25 June 1855.

Rebellions had already broken out, and Tewodros was to spend most of his reign in the field against rebels and rivals.

In Gojjam, Tedla Gwalu of the old ruling family there had raised the standard of rebellion, and in Simien, Neguse and Tesemma Walde Mika'el, grandsons of Wibe through their mother and best known as Agaw Neguse and Agaw Tesemma, had done the same. Tedla Gwalu's troops were no match for the emperor's army as he passed through Gojjam, but the leader was not captured, nor was the province pacified. Neguse and Tesemma, who had invaded Dembya and captured Gondar, withdrew to the north before Tewodros arrived in the capital. The emperor was expected to follow, and the British consul expressed the hope that 'one more battle will decide between anarchy and order – between a vigorous monarchy, or a feudal oligarchy and consequent barbarism'.[1] Instead Tewodros turned once more to Wallo, where his governor, the Galla chief Dejazmach Liben, had rebelled. Magdala was recaptured and Liben replaced by one of the emperor's closest associates. But though Tewodros spent much of 1857 on campaigns there, the resistance was not broken. A swift campaign in Gojjam followed in November 1857. Again Tewodros was victorious in battle, but Tedla Gwalu escaped.

In the meantime Neguse and Tesemma were again attempting to extend their power southwards. Tewodros's governor in Wag and Lasta, Wagshum Gebre Medhin, went over to them. In March 1858 he was defeated, captured and hanged together with eight other rebel leaders. Tesemma was chased back from Wagera. Once again, however, the emperor did not follow up his victory by invading Tigre, but turned east to deal with a new large army of Galla horsemen under a Galla chief named Amede Beshir. In a campaign which lasted for more than one year, Wallo felt the full impact of the king's army. As Tewodros became more and more exasperated at the unceasing rebellions, he began to permit his troops to pillage and slaughter the cattle of the peasants, which had been strictly forbidden during his earlier campaigns. It was also from this campaign that Tewodros's secretary and chronicler, Debtera Zeneb, began to report the mutilation of hundreds of captured soldiers, albeit with the justification that they had already received amnesty several times.[2]

In Shoa, Haile Mika'el remained a loyal governor for three years, but when he was incapable or unwilling to deal decisively with a rebellion

---

[1] *Ibid.* p. 171, Plowden to Clarendon, 5 August 1856.
[2] [Zeneb], *Yetewodros Tarik* (The chronicle of King Theodore), ed. and publ. by Enno Littmann (Princeton, 1902), 35–45.

led by his brother Seyfu, he was replaced by his brother-in-law, Abboye, and another person from the court of Sahle Sellassie, named Bezabeh. In October 1859 Seyfu captured the Shoan capital Ankober. Tewodros hurried to Shoa to support his new governors. Seyfu was defeated and died soon after. After this expedition, Tewodros finally decided to deal with Neguse and Tesemma, who by now controlled most of northern Ethiopia, in spite of the fact that the king had appointed leading members of the Tigrean aristocracy as his governors. From one point of view Agaw Neguse was the most dangerous of all Tewodros's early enemies. Prompted or advised by the Catholic missionaries in Tigre, he had approached Napoleon III for recognition as the rightful ruler of Ethiopia. Late in 1859 a French mission under Count Stanislas Russel arrived at Massawa to see what could be done to promote French and Catholic interests by supporting Tewodros's rival. The emperor reached Adowa in January 1860, just in time to stop the eventual alliance. Neguse and Tesemma fled westwards. Later in the year Tewodros fought a new campaign in Wallo and also marched against his nephew Gared Kinfu who had joined the northern rebellion. Gared had attacked and fatally wounded Consul Plowden in February, just as the latter had left Gondar to go to Massawa. Now he was killed and hundreds of his followers massacred. However Tewodros's friend and adviser, John Bell, also lost his life in the battle. In January 1861 the forces of Neguse and Tesemma were decisively defeated and the leaders executed near Aksum.

This victory marked the peak of Tewodros's military control over the country. Except for minor outbreaks of insurrection among the Wallo Galla, the country was comparatively peaceful for about two years, and the king could devote more of his time to foreign affairs, in particular the Egyptian activities on the western frontier. The probability of a major campaign against the Egyptians, however, called for action against Tedla Gwalu, who had continued to defy the authority of the king. Early in 1863, Tewodros met the rebel at Injabara in one of the most bloody battles of his reign. The Gojjamis were defeated, but once again Tedla Gwalu escaped. In the same year a new and serious development took place in Shoa. After about five years of loyal service, Bezabeh declared the independence of Shoa and proclaimed himself king. The campaign which followed in Wallo and Shoa was a turning-point in Tewodros's career, in as much as he failed to lead his army to victory in the battlefield.

A new wave of rebellions followed in 1864. In the north-west a chief called Tiso Gobaze captured all the country between the Tekeze and Lake Tana, including Gondar. In Wag and Lasta, Gebre Medhin's son, Gobaze, raised the standard of rebellion and quickly became one of Tewodros's most powerful enemies. He threatened all Tigre, as did Tiso Gobaze from the west. Tewodros's governors were unable to put up much resistance, and the province fell to Wagshum Gobaze and his Tigrean lieutenant Kassa Mercha. During the first months of 1865 Tewodros made his last attempt to subdue Wallo and Shoa. He was heavily defeated, and after April 1865 there is no evidence that he ever passed south of Magdala. On 30 June 1865 Menelik succeeded in escaping from the mountain fortress where he had lived as a kind of state prisoner, albeit well treated, for almost ten years. The Shoans rallied to the young prince, who replaced Bezabeh and proclaimed himself king. He even began to use the title king of kings.

Thus the emperor was by 1865 encircled on all four sides by powerful rebels or rivals, Menelik, Tedla Gwalu, Tiso Gobaze and Wagshum Gobaze. His empire consisted mainly of Begemder east of Lake Tana and a few districts south of the lake, altogether about one-fifth of the Ethiopia he had once attempted to control. Within this area he continued to operate until his fall in 1868. But it was too small to bear the burden of his large army. By 1867 the army had begun to disintegrate, and by the end of the year it had fallen from the 70,000–80,000 that Tewodros had commanded at the peak of his career to some 10,000 men. Several of the rebel armies were far superior in numbers. Though a foreign intervention eventually became the immediate cause of Tewodros's fall, it was clear in 1867 that he had failed in his attempt to reunify Ethiopia and that his end was imminent.

The ultimate reasons for Tewodros's failure were as complex as his personality and the political situation which he wanted to master and change. His upbringing in a monastery and his early life as a *shifta* had endowed him with a strong sense of destiny and dedication to the task before him, but also with a despotic determination to overcome all opposition. His great will-power and the qualities of leadership which he demonstrated as a military commander were, however, not matched by prudence and the ability to solve political problems. He tended to resort to violence as a means of solving all problems, even those that clearly called for patience and compromise. Seen in the context of the regionalism and anarchy of the preceding period, Tewodros's programme for his country was almost unbelievably ambitious. It was by no means a simple question of supreme control over an otherwise intact feudal structure. Tewodros's reform policies amounted to nothing less than a call for national renewal and modernization. Although he failed, the historical significance of Tewodros's reign lies in that it initiated the unification and modernization processes by revealing the problems involved and making the first attempts to find solutions.

The feudal pattern of political life was challenged in several ways. The emperor resolved that governors and judges should be his personal, salaried appointees, and that a national army under his command should replace the feudal levies of the past. Early in his reign he reorganized the army and created new units in which he mixed soldiers from various provinces. He tried to introduce drill and discipline and to replace pillaging by regular wages or allowances. He made attempts to increase and control revenues, but the difficulties were overwhelming, not the least being the complete lack of a national bureaucracy to undertake the new tasks. For governors he relied heavily on the old ruling class, in most cases appointing members of the highest nobility as governors: Gebre Medhin in Wag and Lasta, Liben in Wallo, Haile Mika'el in Shoa and Araya Sellassie and Kassa Sebagadis in Tigre. Tewodros thus tried to limit the political and military power of the ruling class without significantly changing its composition. He seems to have believed that he would somehow be able to win the co-operation of the nobility for his programme. In this he turned out to be mistaken, but it may be doubted whether he had much choice.

Because Tewodros's concept of national renewal was basically religious, his most obvious ally was the Church. In 1854 he had called Abuna Salama to Gondar and the two had agreed on terms of mutual support. Both were eager to put an end to the doctrinal divisions which plagued the Church (see above, pp. 62–4). At the same time the king accepted the principle of separation between spiritual and secular powers, though it turned out to be a difficult distinction to make in the Ethiopian context. The king's hostility towards Islam, which did not, however, include a policy of forcible conversion, may have been politically motivated. But his manifest desire to initiate a spiritual and moral reformation in the Christian population can hardly be explained entirely from political motives. By condemning the clergy for their ignorance and immorality, he showed that he included them among those who needed reform. Though his attitude towards the Protestant missionaries was ambivalent, he allowed them, in the face of ecclesiastical opposition, to import and distribute Amharic Bibles and to teach and preach. He read the Bible in Amharic rather than the church language Ge'ez, and contemplated the introduction of Bible reading and exposition in Amharic into the church services. He tried to enforce monogamy and to curtail the slave trade. He stressed his responsibility as the 'Elect of God' to see to it that justice prevailed, that the poor received their right in the courts and that the needy were cared for, and he set an example himself in these respects. His justice was severe. Execution or mutilation was the normal punishment for murder, robbery and rebellion. But his sense of justice led him to discontinue the established practice that kinsmen of a missing homicide had to answer with their lives or a ransom even if they had nothing to do with the crime. In all this the king was probably inspired as much by the Tewodros legend as by his contacts with foreigners and, had there been no other issues involved, the clergy might have continued to support him.

It was on the question of the economic privileges of the Church that co-operation broke down. Tewodros needed finance on a completely different scale from any of his predecessors if he was to succeed in establishing a central administration and a national army. One possible source of additional revenue was taxation of church lands. In 1856 Tewodros proposed a reform by which each church should have sufficient tax-free land to support two priests and three deacons, the minimum number needed to celebrate mass. All other church lands would be confiscated and distributed to farmers who paid taxes. The surplus clergy would be given the choice of farming unprivileged land or joining the king's army as soldiers! Though Tewodros justified this reform by referring to the distribution of lands to the tribes of Israel in the Old Testament – when the Levites were awarded tithes but received no share in land at all – he was no doubt also influenced by knowledge about the land policies of the Reformation in northern Europe. The clergy won the first round by referring to the venerated ancient code, the *Fetha Nagast*, which upheld the right of the Church to keep whatever had become its property. In 1860, however, the king carried out a unilateral confiscation of church lands in areas under his control. But there was no popular basis for this policy. The conflict with the Church contributed in large measure to Tewodros's fall, and his immediate successors made no attempts to continue his policy.

In the field of foreign relations Tewodros's short reign was of particular importance. The opening-up of the country, distinguished by British–French rivalry and competition between Catholic and Protestant missions, continued and accelerated. The significant change was a change in attitude on the Ethiopian side. Tewodros understood as no Ethiopian ruler before him that he had to make the European interest in his country serve the national interests of his people. He also saw the Egyptian expansion as a long term threat which called for an active diplomacy.

When Plowden asked him in 1855 to ratify the 1849 treaty signed by Ras Ali (see above, p. 69), Tewodros objected to the clause which granted judicial rights to foreign consuls, on the ground that it would trespass upon his sovereignty. It was, in fact, the only clause in the treaty that was not reciprocal. He then informed the consul that he intended to send an embassy of his own not only to Britain but to other European powers as well. On the formal level his foreign policy was clear: he would enter into negotiations on equal terms only, and he would take the initiative himself whenever he believed it to be in his own interest. In spite of all the internal turmoil, he made several unsuccessful attempts in the following years to establish contacts with European governments, particularly the French and British. The French would not forgive him in that, at the request of Abuna Salama, he had banished the Catholic bishop, de Jacobis, from Gondar and limited the freedom of action of the Catholic mission. The British, though represented at his court by Plowden and, later, Cameron, failed to understand his personality and his intentions.

Tewodros's foreign policy had two main aims: the educational and technological advancement of his country, and the containment and reversal of Egyptian expansion. In the technical field, armament was the obvious priority, but in addition to gunsmiths, carpenters, masons, wagon- and boat-builders were welcome. When the king found that one of the Protestant lay missionaries knew the skill of rock-blasting, he commissioned him to lead road construction. His main supply of technical expertise was the group of missionaries from the St Chrischona Institute in Switzerland, where lay missionary artisans were trained. Only in 1866, when he held Consul Cameron and the special British envoy Rassam as hostages for craftsmen and equipment, did the British government respond, but by then it was too late. The few Ethiopians trained by the missionaries were not sufficient to reach even the first stage of a technical break-through, and Tewodros's plans to send promising candidates abroad never materialized.

The internal turmoil prevented Tewodros from embarking on any crusade against the 'Turks', as all Muslim neighbours were called by the Ethiopians. Until 1862 the western frontier remained quiet, but then a considerable Egyptian force appeared at Metemma and Tewodros prepared to act. He knew, however, that the European powers might not approve of hostilities against Egypt or the Ottoman Empire, and decided to sound the governments of Britain, France, Austria, Prussia and Russia on the impending war and solicit their moral, and possibly material, support. Only Paris sent a reply, and instead of referring to the threat of Islam, it implicitly rebuked Tewodros for his treatment of the Catholic mission. The king's disappointment knew no limits. But when the Egyptians withdrew again from Metemma, he turned once more to the internal problems of his country. The only significant change in the power balance between Ethiopia and Egypt during his reign was the new grant of Massawa to Egypt in 1865.

The negative response to Tewodros's diplomatic offensive of 1862, particularly the British failure to send any reply whatsoever, had unwelcome consequences for the Europeans in Ethiopia. Consul Cameron had been asked to go to England personally and to return with Queen Victoria's reply. Instead he mailed the emperor's letter and visited the Sudanese border provinces before returning. This aroused Tewodros's suspicion, and when a courier arrived from London in November 1863 without any message to the emperor, but with instructions to Cameron to leave Ethiopia and stay at Massawa, the storm broke loose. Cameron and his staff were arrested and chained in January 1864. Together with two missionaries, Stern and Rosenthal of the Falasha mission, who had been arrested some months earlier on other grounds, they were sent to captivity at Magdala. When the news reached London, the Foreign Office drafted a letter for the queen's signature and appointed Hormuzd Rassam of the British staff at Aden to carry it to Tewodros. When he finally reached the king's camp in January 1866, he was well received and the captives were temporarily released. The British had accepted an Ethiopian embassy to London, but an unfortunate mistranslation of the English text made Tewodros believe that Rassam was empowered to grant him more material proof of England's goodwill. In fact, he was advised to '... consult with him [Rassam] concerning what you require of us, and he will do it for you ...'.[1] Tewodros decided to detain Rassam and send the missionary Flad to England with requests for armament experts and equipment. The British government went as far as sending people and equipment to Massawa, but said that they would have to be exchanged for the captives on the frontier, and Flad was instructed to inform Tewodros that a British army would come to

[1] Hormuzd Rassam, *Narrative of the British Mission to Theodore* (London, 1869), II, 31–9.

rescue the prisoners if he did not let them go. In the meantime the final and rapid decline in the king's power had set in, and there was no route open by which to bring in the assistance. The Europeans in the king's service did their best to satisfy his increasing obsession with bigger and bigger mortars.

Diplomatic measures having failed, the British government decided to send a military force to release the captives. British and Indian troops numbering 32,000 under the command of Sir Robert Napier were landed at Zulla near Massawa and marched inland in January 1868. Tewodros made no attempt to block their way or harass their lines of communication. In October he had burned his capital Debre Tabor, and headed for Magdala taking his artillery with him. He arrived about two weeks before Napier. On a small plain just below the fortress, the only battle of the campaign took place on Good Friday, 10 April 1868. It was a violent but brief struggle. As soon as the Ethiopians came within the range of the British rifles, they were mown down. Of some 4,000 Ethiopians engaged, which was almost all that was left of Tewodros's once invincible army, 700–800 lay dead and twice the number were wounded. On the other side about 2,000 were engaged, twenty wounded, two fatally. The following day Tewodros released the prisoners, and on Sunday the other missionaries and artisans were also permitted to leave and reach the British camp in safety. Napier demanded that the king should surrender and, when he refused, Magdala was stormed on Easter Monday. Tewodros dismissed his last faithful followers, and just before the first British soldiers reached him, he shot himself.

Both in the most immediate and in a wider sense Tewodros destroyed himself. It was the internal political problems and Tewodros's method of tackling them that caused his fall, not the British army. Tewodros summarized them himself in a letter to Napier: 'My countrymen have turned their backs on me . . . because I imposed tribute on them, and sought to bring them under military discipline.'[1] In Ethiopian history, the British expedition to Magdala is but an incident. Napier had assured the population and their chiefs that Tewodros was his only enemy and that once he had liberated the Europeans, he would leave the country immediately. On this assurance, the rebel governor of Tigre, Dejaz-

[1] Trevenen J. Holland and Henry Hozier, *Record of the expedition to Abyssinia* (London, 1870), II, 42. The role of Tewodros, his complex personality, the aims of his policies and the causes of his failure are all more or less controversial issues. For the sources and further explanation of the interpretation presented here, see Rubenson, *Tewodros*, 46–92, and Donald Crummey, 'Tewodros as reformer and modernizer', *Journal of African History*, 1969, 10, 3, 457–69.

mach Kassa Mercha, and to a lesser extent Wagshum Gobaze, had not only granted the expedition the right to march through their territories, but assisted it with guides, provisions and pack-animals. Napier kept his promise and departed, rewarding Kasa with gifts of arms and ammunition. The expedition in itself was in no way part of a colonial venture. On the contrary, the British government decided to have nothing more to do with Ethiopia. The significance of Magdala lies in the distorted picture of Ethiopia to which it gave rise outside the country. The ease with which the 'invincible' Tewodros was overthrown and the country 'occupied' was remembered, but the conditions under which this took place were suppressed or forgotten. The opinion that the Ethiopians 'after Tewodros' would not offer serious or united resistance to any invasion gained ground and played its role in later attempts to conquer the country.

THE INTERREGNUM OF 1868–71

The Ethiopia left behind by Tewodros was as disunited as that of the *Zamana Mesafent*. But there were differences. No representative of the Yejju clan made any bid for supreme power. None of the three strongest contenders, Menelik of Shoa, Gobaze of Wag and Lasta and Kassa of Tigre, came from the Lake Tana region which had dominated the political life of the country for some 250 years, and none of them thought in terms of reinstating the practice of puppet emperors at Gondar. They all saw the need for consolidation of power and the importance of foreign contacts. On the other hand, they were all prepared, in varying degrees, to retreat on the question of a unitary state.

In many respects Menelik's position was the strongest. As the only son of the last king of Shoa, he had almost no opposition in his own province. The Galla of central Ethiopia, who had suffered most during the reign of Tewodros, also seemed prepared to accept his leadership. Haile Mika'el's and Bezabeh's co-operation with Tewodros had given Shoa longer periods of peace than other areas had enjoyed, and when Bezabeh finally rebelled he was strong enough to withstand the attack of the emperor's army. As a result the relative prosperity of the province continued and provided Menelik with a financial base for political action. He approached the British government, was recognized by Britain as king of Shoa in 1867 and opened a consulate at Aden in 1869. He stressed the importance of free access to the sea at Tajura and Zeila for Shoan caravans and asked for firearms from England. Whether his aspirations at this time went beyond the autonomy and prosperity of Shoa is difficult to know. In his foreign correspondence he styled himself 'King of Kings Menelik of Ethiopia'. On the other hand, he came to terms with Gobaze without too much difficulty, although the latter had publicly proclaimed himself king of kings at Gondar. The two princes agreed on Beshilo as the boundary between their territories, which left Wallo to Menelik. Temporarily at least, both seemed to prefer to acknowledge each other's claims to kingship rather than continue Tewodros's unification policy at the expense of further bloodshed.

Wagshum Gobaze's position was much more difficult than Menelik's. He had a bigger army and a greater reputation as a general than his two rivals. He was also the most immediate successor of Tewodros in the sense that he inherited the central parts of Ethiopia. He had just defeated Tiso Gobaze and taken possession of Gondar when Magdala fell. He was not slow to proclaim himself king of kings under the name of Tekla Giyorgis. By most foreign observers, he was regarded both as the most ambitious and the most suitable successor of Tewodros. But he did not have, as Menelik and Kassa did, a large province of his own to fall back on for support. In the eyes of Tedla Gwalu's son Desta, now a rebellious governor of Gojjam, he was only 'the son of that little piece of salt from Seqota [the capital of Wag and an important transit market for salt]'.[1]

The central provinces generally had become exhausted by the turmoil and destruction of Tewodros's last years. Political stability was non-existent; in three years Tekla Giyorgis was obliged to appoint or accept three successive governors in Gojjam. Finally, access to the sea depended on relations with the ruler of Tigre.

Though Dejazmach Kassa had for some time been in Gobaze's service and was his brother-in-law, he had in 1867 occupied most of Tigre on his own and no longer regarded himself as the vassal of the former *wagshum*. He came from the most important families of Tigre, and had met with very little resistance there. Members of the British expedition, however, reported that their ally was a weakling, who could hardly be expected to hold his own, and few doubted the outcome of the expected invasion from Gondar. Kassa chose another line of action from his rivals'. He refused to recognize Tekla Giyorgis as emperor in exchange for a *ras* title, but made no immediate claim to the throne. Instead he

---

[1] Bibliothèque Nationale, MS Collection Mondon-Vidailhet, no. 72, 9 r. In addition to the Ethiopian chronicles, e.g. those in the Mondon-Vidailhet collection, see G. Douin, *Histoire du règne du Khédive Ismaïl. L'Empire Africain* (Cairo, 1936–51), III: 2, 287–361, for the years between the reigns of Tewodros and Yohannes.

increased his prestige by bringing a new *abuna* to succeed Salama, who had died in captivity at Magdala, and calmly awaited the expected attack. On 10 July 1871, his small but well-equipped army met the numerically much stronger forces of Gondar on the banks of the Asem river outside Adowa. Tekla Giyorgis was defeated and captured and the way to the throne was open to Kassa. In January 1872, with due observance of all ancient ceremonies, the new king was crowned in Aksum as 'King of Kings Yohannes King of Sion of Ethiopia'.

The accession to the throne of Yohannes IV was of great significance. In the power struggle of 1868–71, Tekla Giyorgis represented the restoration of the Gondarine empire. He chose Gondar as his capital and rebuilt its many churches which Tewodros had burned down. He showed through his settlement with Menelik and his offer to Kassa, that he was prepared to share power along feudal lines. His very throne name pointed to the days before the decline of Gondar as the centre of political power. The battle of Asem thwarted this attempt, and thereby sealed the fate of Gondar and the central Amhara provinces as leaders of the political development in Ethiopia. Essentially, of course, it was Tewodros's doing. His reign, immediately following the civil wars of the *Zamana Mesafent*, had impoverished the area to such an extent that there was hardly any base for immediate reconstruction. The political centre of gravity moved first to the north, which was of great importance in the confrontation with Egypt and the first stages of Italian imperialism, then to Shoa as the heartland of modern Ethiopia.

GALLA STATES AND COASTAL SULTANATES 1820–75

In varying degrees, the same external factors as influenced developments in Ethiopia in the *Zamana Mesafent* and the reign of Tewodros, also affected the Sidama and Galla of the south and the coastal sultanates and their hinterland. For the south, the most important of these factors were the revival of the Red Sea trade and the reactivation of Islam as a missionary movement. The products in highest demand, slaves, gold, ivory and other luxury goods, originated in the Galla and Sidama areas. The caravan trade followed two main routes: from Massawa through Adowa, Gondar and Gojjam, and from Tajura and Zeila through Awsa or Harar and then Shoa. That Ethiopian merchants, mostly Muslims, profited from the trade as middlemen is obvious; so did the Ethiopian rulers by taxing the caravan trade wherever possible. For the emergence of Shoa under Sahle Sellassie, the increase in trade

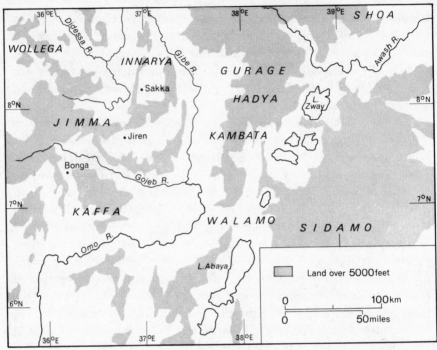

4 Galla kingdoms

undoubtedly played a significant role. But the regions most profoundly affected by it were those south of the Abbay and south-west of Shoa, particularly the area between the upper Gibe and Didessa. Caravans from the north and east converged on this area to exchange their salt (used in the shape of bars, *amole*, as regular currency), cloth, copper, beads, and metal products, for the ivory and musk of Kaffa and Walamo, the gold of Wollega, and above all for slaves from the whole region. In spite of the civil wars, enslavement on a large scale of Christian or Muslim Ethiopians, being illegal, was difficult and dangerous. Therefore the slave traders pushed farther south, and the 'Abyssinian' slaves in such high demand in Arabia were mostly Galla, Gurage, Walamo or Kaffa. Slave labour was common in Sidama societies and among the Galla who had become agriculturists. Slaves were mostly acquired through warfare. The increasing demand in the slave markets undoubtedly contributed to the continuous wars and raids which plagued the whole region, but the demand for children, young girls in particular, also resulted in kidnapping.

For the development of large-scale, organized trade, however, some security was essential, and this need was probably one of the factors behind the creation of the Galla kingdoms on the upper Gibe about 1820–30. There were other factors as well: the penetration of Islam into the area and the impulses received from the Ethiopian political structure in the north and probably from the Kaffa monarchy in the south as well. The impact of Islam seems obvious; other influences are less tangible.[1]

The best known of the Gibe kingdoms were Limmu-Innarya and Jimma-Kakka. The former was founded by a Limmu Galla called Bofo Abba Gomol, and reached its peak during the reign of his son Ibsa Abba Bagibo (1825–61). Its chief market town, Sakka, became the commercial centre, not only of Innarya, but of the whole region. After a war between Innarya's neighbours to the west had closed a rival route, the trade between Kaffa and Gojjam was for some time practically monopolized by Innarya. Many Muslim merchants from the north settled at Sakka, and before long a thriving Muslim community, including religious leaders, existed there. Bofo adopted the Muslim faith, and was followed in this respect by many of his subjects. The egalitarian structure of the Galla tribal society was transformed within decades into a despotic monarchy with a well-organized hierarchy of officials. But the hegemony of Innarya was soon to pass to an area still closer to the main sources of the coveted merchandise.

About 1830 Sanna Abba Jifar succeeded in uniting many of the Jimma Galla under his rule as king of Jimma-Kakka, known also as Jimma Abba Jifar. As Bofo before him, Abba Jifar adopted Islam and encouraged the spread of Islam among his subjects. Before long the ruling and merchant classes were all Muslim. Administration was centralized and controlled by the king through a gradually developed bureaucracy. Jimma derived its wealth partly from intensified cultivation, but above all from the handling of the transit trade which its markets, particularly the capital, Jiren, gradually captured from Sakka. While the irresistible expansion of Shoa thwarted all Innarya's attempts to expand towards the north and north-east, Jimma met less resistance in the south. Together Shoa and Jimma cut off Innarya from Walamo and, as Jimma expanded, Innarya also lost its common border with Kaffa. In a number of clashes in the late 1830s and 1840s, Jimma defeated its neighbours on all sides, including Innarya itself. When Abba Jifar died in 1855, Jimma was by far the most powerful state of the region. It suffered a temporary setback in 1859 when Innarya, Guma and Gera united against Abba Jifar's son Abba Rebu and killed him in battle.

[1] Abir, *Ethiopia*, pp. 44–94.

Under Abba Jifar's brother Abba Boka and his son Abba Gomol, Jimma was further consolidated and extended. It was as the ruler of a small but wealthy state, strongly committed to Islam, that Abba Jifar II, soon after his accession to the throne in 1878, confronted Menelik's Shoa.[1]

The chief suppliers of slaves and ivory, Kaffa and Walamo, though economically exploited, retained their independence throughout the period. Islam gained access through merchants, but its impact was much weaker than among the Galla. Because of its fame and possibly because of the remnants of Christian community life there, Kaffa became for a few years during the reign of Tewodros the main target of the Capuchin mission led by Cardinal Massaia. No major changes, however, took place in the Sidama kingdoms until the arrival of Menelik's armies in the 1880s and 1890s.

Among the tribes along the Red Sea coast as well as among the Somali and the eastern Galla, the revival of Islam also had lasting consequences. The Habab, Mensa and Marya tribes abandoned their Christian faith for Islam. The Afar, the Somali and many Galla who had been Muslims for centuries, renewed their religious commitment. Only the southern Galla, the Arusi and Borana, remained unaffected. For the coastal sultanates and later for Harar and the Afar of the salt plains, the revival of the trade also brought with it Egyptian and European attempts to gain control.

The first Egyptian attempt to obtain a foothold south of Massawa was a landing at Berbera in 1821. Local opposition forced the Egyptians to withdraw. In the 1830s Zeila came under Muḥammad ʿAlī together with the coast of Yemen, but there was no occupation or Egyptian administration of the port. The lease of Massawa by Egypt in 1846 led to a brief period of Egyptian activity along the Afar and Somali coasts, but it was not until the reign of Khedive Ismāʿīl that Egyptian plans were to materialize (see below, pp. 93–5). By then European powers had also entered the scene. The British East India Company signed a commercial treaty with the Somali controlling Berbera in 1827, and after the occupation of Aden in 1839 Britain kept an eye on the opposite coast from there. In 1840 a French company bought the Red Sea port of Edd from the local ruler, but the claim was allowed to lapse. In 1862 the French government acquired Obok through a treaty with the local sultan and three other Afar chiefs. In spite of some serious doubts about the right of the chiefs who ceded the place to do so, this claim was

---

[1] *Ibid.* and Herbert S. Lewis, *A Galla monarchy* (Madison, 1965).

maintained and eventually became the basis for French Somaliland. In 1869, finally, an Italian shipping company bought Assab from the local sultan for 6,000 Maria Theresa thalers, in order to establish an Italian colony there. But neither France nor Italy did much to consolidate their holdings or gain influence over the hinterland until about 1880. The only area in which the European presence had begun to take on colonial aspects was the hinterland of Massawa and Bogos.

Notwithstanding Ottoman, Egyptian and European claims, the local Afar and Somali administered the ports and controlled the trade routes with little outside interference. In some respects the contacts with the interior were as significant as the new pressures on the coast. The economic interdependence between the Afar tribes and the highland population was enhanced by the increase in the caravan trade. The growing volume and pace of the trade increased the demand for *amole*, the all-important salt currency, and with it the importance of the old ties and co-operation between the Taltal and the Tigreans. For the southern Afar, the rise of Shoa offered new opportunities. The shortest route from Shoa to the coast passed through Afar. Most of the transit trade, mainly in slaves, was in the hands of Harar and Afar merchants, and the latter managed to divert more and more of it to their main port Tajura at the expense of Harar and its traditional outlets, Zeila and Berbera. It was the nomadic Adoimara tribes and their sultan at Tajura who benefited most from the rise in trade. The sultanate of Awsa, ruled by an Asaimara family, saw a period of decline during the first half of the nineteenth century. In the 1840s, fighting and raiding caused serious disruptions of the trade. Conditions seem to have improved when the sultan of Awsa, Anfari (1800–62), reasserted his power about 1850. His son and successor, Muhammad Anfari, had close ties with Shoa, and acknowledged Menelik as his suzerain until the Italians managed to win him over in the late 1880s.

Although Harar lost much trade because of the growing importance of the route to Tajura, the old city state remained throughout the nineteenth century a leading commercial centre and the focus of Muslim worship and learning for the whole Horn. Its role in the diffusion of Islamic teaching among the Gurage and the southern Galla was crucial. Harar was ruled by a family of local emirs, who were also the leading merchants of the town. They claimed that the surrounding Galla and Somali were their subjects, but beyond the respect accorded to them for spiritual and historical reasons, they had little authority beyond the city walls and could at times barely protect the fields of the townspeople in the immediate neighbourhood. Through inter-marriage and payments to Galla chiefs, a precarious balance was kept. The security of the trade route to Shoa depended on the close co-operation between the emirs and the Shoan rulers and on the fact that Galla and Somali merchants stood to lose to the Afar if the route was closed. The situation in the direction of the coast was more complicated because of the rivalry of Zeila and Berbera. At Zeila a Somali merchant, Haji Shirmarke Ali Salih, became governor about 1840. A quarrel among the Haber Awal Somali, who controlled Berbera, gave him the opportunity to establish his authority also over this port. His attempts to monopolize the trade brought him into conflict first with the emir of Harar, who managed to unite the Haber Awal clan against him, and then with the British at Aden when he tried to blockade Berbera. Finally his rivals at Tajura caused his fall in 1855 by accusing him of being a British spy. His successor at Zeila, the Afar slave trader Abu Bakr, became a dominating figure on the coast and remained in power also when the Egyptians occupied the region.

In the interior of the Horn the general southward migration of the Somali continued throughout the nineteenth century, newcomers pushing earlier occupants in front of them. Only the sedentary Rahanweyn offered effective resistance, co-ordinated from about 1840 under the leadership of the Geledi clan. The migrating Darod groups were forced to turn west and began to cross the Juba, initially in small groups as clients of the Galla. About 1865 their numbers had increased sufficiently for them to force the Galla farther west. Along the Indian Ocean coast, the sultan of the Majerteyn retained his independence until the Italians arrived. Farther south on the Benadir coast, however, the sultan of Zanzibar claimed jurisdiction as successor of the Omani rulers. His claim was established, but he was forced to share actual power with the local Somali rulers. The governor of the Benadir coast resided at Brava, which was therefore more firmly under Zanzibar rule. Mogadishu, on the other hand, was really controlled by the sultan of the Geledi, and minor ports were in the hands of members of other clans. The only representatives of the sultan of Zanzibar were customs officers, who collected the income of a trade which had been much less influenced by new demands and forces than that of the Red Sea and Gulf of Aden.[1]

[1] See, in addition to Abir, *Ethiopia*, I. M. Lewis, *The modern history of Somaliland* (London, 1965), 27–39.

THE CONFLICT WITH EGYPT

In spite of border incidents, raids and counter-raids, it had often seemed during the half century following Muḥammad ʿAli's conquest of the Sudan as if Egypt and Ethiopia would avoid a full-scale war with each other. Ethiopia had no fixed boundaries in the modern sense of the word; peoples and tribes mattered more than territory. The vaguely tributary but autonomous and unprotected lowland tribes had formed an Ethiopian buffer zone in the west and north. But as Egyptian garrisons and administrative centres moved into the borderlands, Ethiopian governors counteracted by establishing more and more effective control over whatever remained. By about 1870, 'no man's land' had practically disappeared. The Ethiopians and Egyptians had come face to face along a frontier which, roughly speaking, left the Semhar, Habab, Beni Amer and northern Baria under Egyptian rule and the Marya, Mensa, Bogos, Kunama and southern Baria under Ethiopian rule. Massawa was again in Egyptian hands, granted to Khedive Ismāʿil by the sultan in 1865.

Before his coronation Yohannes could do very little about Egypt's consolidation of her territories on the Ethiopian frontiers. He had the expected attack of Tekla Giyorgis to think about and, moreover, needed good relations with Egypt in order to obtain a new bishop from Alexandria. But he was aware of the problem, and replaced the governor of Hamasien, suspected of secret contacts with Egyptians, by Ras Walda Mika'el, from whom he mistakenly expected more loyalty.

Matters were complicated by the European presence in the area. The missionary activities of Italian and French Lazarists had resulted in fairly large Catholic communities both in Akele Guzay and Bogos. These communities looked to the French consular representatives at Massawa for protection, and almost regarded themselves as French subjects. There were reports that the Catholics of Akele Guzay refused to pay taxes to the Tigrean ruler in 1869, referring to the French consul as their government. The predictable reaction to this was persecution of the Catholics, and complaints and questions directed both to the consul and to Napoleon III.[1] The crucial area, however, was Bogos. The Lazarist mission there had been established in the early 1850s, about the same time as the first Egyptian raid reached the area, and the missionaries, particularly Father Stella, had repeatedly assisted the

[1] France, Ministère des Affaires Etrangères (A. E.), Correspondance politique, Massouah 3, Munzinger to A. E., 1 June 1869; Mémoires et Documents, Abyssinie 3, Kassa to Napoleon III, 10 March 1870; Douin, *Ismaïl*, III: 2, 306.

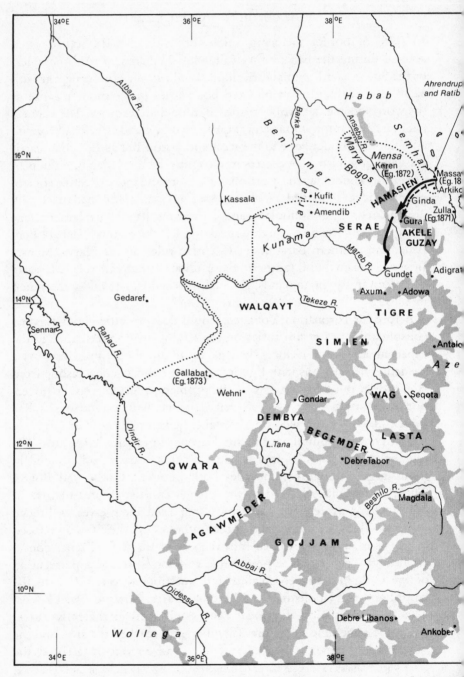

5 The Et[

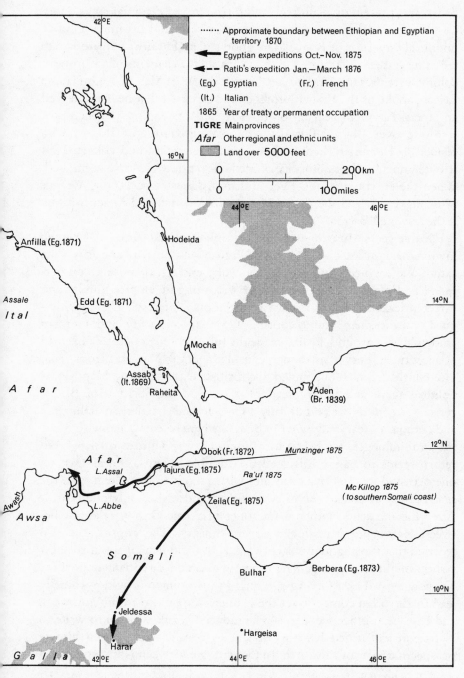

conflict

consular representatives in reclaiming people and cattle taken as booty to Kassala. Stella acquired land on a large scale and became a kind of unofficial governor of Bogos. The good soil and healthy climate attracted other settlers. By the end of the 1860s, all the elements of a European colony were present. The former French consul at Massawa, Guillaume Lejean, spoke of the French protégés and reported that he had received an official Egyptian declaration in 1864, acknowledging a French protectorate over Bogos. But the Ethiopian governor of Bogos, who resided in Hamasien, had made no such concession and collected his tribute, much to the annoyance of Stella. Egyptian raids also continued. When the Egyptians took over Massawa, Lejean's successor, Werner Munzinger, advised the French government to act, and to act quickly, if they wanted Bogos.[1]

For five years Munzinger would continue to plead for official French involvement, at least in the form of French support for 'une Abyssinie catholique', which alone would be strong enough to pose a counter-threat to Egypt. In fact, Munzinger was a private empire builder and cared little about either French or Ethiopian interests. Explorer, linguist, businessman and colonist, of Swiss nationality and German academic background, he had made the future colony of Eritrea his field of activity. He served as French consular agent at Massawa from 1864, vice-consul from 1866, joined the British expedition to Magdala as political agent and interpreter, and then held the position of British consular agent as well until July 1869. He had married an Ethiopian and became a great landowner in Bogos, where he competed with Stella for local influence. He held a low opinion of the Tigrean ruler, who in return seems to have mistrusted the 'double-consul', and at least on one occasion in 1868 bypassed him with a letter to Napoleon with the remark: 'Your consul serves two masters and he has only one heart.'[2] After the incidents with the Catholics in Akele-Guzay, relations between Kassa and Munzinger became uneasy. The consul was also worried that the negotiations between Kassa and Ismā'il about the new bishop might lead to a general *rapprochement* and Egyptian support for Kassa against Tekla Giyorgis, which in his opinion would eventually lead to Egyptian control over the country and an end to mission work and European influence. In 1869 he induced Walda Mika'el to write to Napoleon and urged his government to consider supporting him as prospective ruler of the north. In the struggle between Kassa and Tekla

[1] A. E., Corr. pol., Massouah 3, Lejean to A. E., 5 April 1865; Munzinger to A. E., 15 October 1865. See also Douin, *Ismaïl*, III: 1, 277–80.
[2] A. E., Mém. et Doc., Abyssinie 3, Girard to A. E., 22 December 1868.

Giyorgis, Munzinger's and the missionaries' sympathies were on Tekla Giyorgis's side.[1]

The outcome of the Franco-Prussian war put an end to all hopes of French intervention, and had immediate repercussions for Ethiopia. Munzinger decided to change sides. But before doing so he wrote a final letter as vice-consul to Kassa, threatening him with the fate of Tewodros, which he (Munzinger) would make him share if he did not improve his treatment of the Catholic missionaries.[2] Then, on 23 April 1871, he took up his new position – as Egyptian governor at Massawa. Instead of protecting European interests against Ethiopia and Egypt, and at times Ethiopian interests against Egypt, he became the tool of the Egyptian expansion. After one month he made his first proposal to Cairo to annex Bogos and Marya. Particularly if Tekla Giyorgis attacked Kassa, the opportunity should not be missed. As for Hamasien, Munzinger assured the Egyptian government that he only needed to say a word and the whole population would side with Egypt. Except for his own role the programme was not new. He had accused Isma'il of precisely these plans, including clandestine dealings with Ethiopian chiefs, two years earlier.[3]

Kassa's sudden and decisive victory over Tekla Giyorgis in July 1871 (see above, p. 83) caught Munzinger unawares. Among the emperor's captured papers, Kassa found evidence that the missionaries had offered to solicit French support for Tekla Giyorgis. The persecution which now followed drove many Catholics in Akele Guzay to ask for Egyptian protection, and Munzinger advocated immediate military action. But when he was called to Cairo in March 1872, it was to reach agreement about the occupation of Bogos and surrounding areas, where the population reportedly also wanted to become Egyptian subjects. The submission of the Marya chiefs was secured by negotiation, and Munzinger expressed the 'hope' that Bogos would follow their example. But he also asked for and received reinforcements. In June he occupied Bogos and fortified its capital, Keren. He reported that he would have liked to go on to Hamasien, 'the key of Abyssinia', at once, but having no orders to do so, he would wait for Yohannes's eventual counter-attack as a pretext for occupying Hamasien.[4]

[1] A. E., Corr. pol., Massouah 3, Munzinger to A. E., 18 November 1869; Walda Mika'el to Napoleon III, 22 August 1869; Munzinger to A. E., 31 August 1869; Douin, *Ismaïl*, III: 2, 298–307.

[2] J. de Coursac, *Le règne de Yohannès – depuis son avènement jusqu'à ses victoires sur l'armée égyptienne* (Romans, 1926), 86–7.

[3] Douin, *Ismaïl*, III: 2, 302–3 and 321–4.

[4] *Ibid.* 327–33, 337–44, 356–7.

Yohannes was hardly prepared to deal with the Egyptian aggression in 1872. He had not yet been to Gondar to receive recognition as emperor by Tekla Giyorgis's former vassals in central Ethiopia. When the occupation of Bogos took place, he was suppressing a revolt among the Azebo Galla. He immediately returned to Adowa with his army but made no counter-attack. Instead he charged J. C. Kirkham, a British soldier who had risen to the rank of general in his service, with a mission to the capitals of Britain, France, Germany, Austria and Russia. Yohannes asked for the moral support of the European powers in solving his territorial conflict with Ismā'īl. In London Kirkham proposed that the British government should nominate, alone or together with other governments, an arbitrator to decide on the boundary question. He also emphasized Ethiopia's need for a port on the Red Sea. He gave two reasons: the high customs duties levied by the Egyptian authorities at Massawa, allegedly 36 per cent on imports as well as exports, and the Egyptian embargo on arms. These complaints were not without foundation. Indian merchants operating from Aden also complained about rising duties, and in 1873 sporting guns were included in the arms embargo. With Zulla and Anfilla also occupied, Egypt completely controlled the foreign trade of northern Ethiopia. In 1872 Munzinger proposed an occupation of the Taltal salt mines which would give Egypt considerable control also over Ethiopian internal trade.[1]

The British government wanted no involvement in Ethiopian affairs, and neither Bogos nor the question of a port were mentioned in the Queen's and Lord Granville's replies to Yohannes. Nevertheless Kirkham's mission was not without effect. Ismā'īl was asked some embarrassing questions about his intentions, and decided to redirect his expansion to less sensitive areas. This made it possible for Yohannes to consolidate his position internally. In February 1873 he received recognition as emperor at Gondar. The following year he obtained the submission of Gojjam and Yejju. With Menelik, some kind of agreement about mutual recognition was reached, and Yohannes could return to Tigre before the rainy season of 1875 considerably stronger than he had left it two and a half years earlier.

In the meantime, however, the Egyptians had strengthened their overall position by occupying Gallabat and all the remaining ports south of Massawa: Edd, Assab, Raheita, Tajura, Zeila, Bulhar and

[1] P.R.O., F.O. 1, 27 B contains the important documents on the Kirkham mission. See also Douin, *Ismaïl*, III: 2, 373–87, 403–9.

Berbera. Munzinger had been promoted to pasha and governor-general of eastern Sudan and the Red Sea Coast and resided at Keren. His successor at Massawa, Arakil Bey, wanted more action and advised Cairo early in 1875: 'The necessary instruments to conquer Abyssinia are good maps, some intelligent officers and three or four thousand well-armed men.'[1]

In July and August Munzinger received instructions to occupy the hinterland of Tajura, to establish contact with Shoa, and if possible to incite Menelik to attack Yohannes. The emperor had moved his forces close to the northern boundary, and the possibility of an attack on Bogos could not be discarded. By early September over 4,000 additional Egyptian troops had arrived at Massawa, and by the middle of the month Ismā'īl was ready to give the final orders. Four expeditions were launched simultaneously: McKillop Pasha to the Somali ports on the Indian Ocean, Ra'uf Pasha from Zeila to Harar, Munzinger from Tajura to Awsa and Shoa, and Arakil and Ahrendrup Bey from Massawa towards Adowa. McKillop was turned back from Brava after British protests. Ra'uf occupied Harar without difficulty on 10 October, and ushered in ten years' of Egyptian rule there. Munzinger was less fortunate. On 14 November he was ambushed by the Afar and killed, together with about one third of his small force. The main force under Ahrendrup's command started their march inland on 2 October. The Ethiopian army in Hamasien retreated into Sera'e and on to the Mareb. Ahrendrup followed.

Yohannes delayed mobilization until 23 October and crossed the Mareb with his main force only during the night before 16 November. The battle which immediately followed near Gundet lasted only a few hours, but left 1,800 Egyptians dead on the battlefield. Ethiopian losses were less than half of this. Of great importance to Yohannes were the cannon and about 2,000 modern rifles captured. The Egyptians immediately withdrew to Massawa. Instead of following up his victory, Yohannes returned to Adowa and offered Ismā'īl peace, pleading: 'My brother, you are not greater than your forefathers and we are not less than ours. What is the purpose of dismantling the frontiers of this kingdom?'[2] The offer was not accepted. A new Egyptian army of some 15,000 men under the commander-in-chief of the Egyptian armed forces, Rātib Pasha, and an American chief-of-staff, General W. W. Loring, were already on their way. Attempts to win Ethiopian allies resulted in Walda Mika'el's desertion, but Menelik was unmoved

[1] Douin, *Ismaïl*, III: 3 B, 705.   [2] *Ibid.* III: 3 B, 850–1.

by Egyptian offers to recognize him as emperor if he joined hands with them. Yohannes mobilized again. The cause was presented as a choice between Christianity and Islam. Troops from as far off as Gojjam and Shoa helped to swell the numbers, probably to 100,000. This time Yohannes met the Egyptians in Hamasien and defeated them decisively at Gura in a three days' battle, 7–9 March 1876. The Egyptians evacuated the highlands except for Bogos, which was left in Walda Mika'el's hands. Yohannes appointed his most prominent general, Ras Alula, governor of Hamasien, and returned to Adowa.[1]

When Yohannes did not follow up his two victories by attacks on Keren and Massawa, he was probably influenced by the traditional Ethiopian concept of warfare as limited campaigns, to establish relative superiority of strength as a basis for redistribution of power and lands in situations of conflict rather than a persistent, all-out struggle to destroy the opponent. For him the war of 1875–6 was primarily a defensive operation, but, in addition, he also seems to have thought that his victories entitled him to certain rewards. The immediate reason for calling off the campaign was the Egyptian peace initiative which followed directly after the Gura battle. On instruction from Cairo, the Egyptian commander-in-chief started by requesting the restitution of all arms lost by the Egyptians in the two battles, and repatriation of all prisoners of war. Yohannes agreed to release the prisoners, but refused to return the captured arms, and added that if the Egyptians wanted peace they should hand back Bogos and pay an indemnity. Once the prisoners had been released, it was Egypt that asked for additional territory and an indemnity to cover the expenses of the war. When negotiations broke down, the British suggested that a European officer be appointed to find a peaceful solution. The choice fell on General Charles Gordon, about to return to the Sudan as Egyptian governor-general. His first proposals to Yohannes in February 1877 included the preservation of the frontiers existing before the war, free trade and free passage for envoys through Massawa, the import of arms and ammunition through Massawa within 'fixed limits', and an Egyptian undertaking to stop Walda Mika'el from raiding over the boundary. These terms appeared to meet several important Ethiopian needs, but also raised the problems of the undefined pre-war frontiers and the interpretation of 'free trade' and 'fixed limits'. No major concessions were intended. Bogos

[1] *Ibid.* III: 3 A, 602–27, 3 B, 629–1028 for the most detailed and best documented account of the whole war.

would obviously remain Egyptian, and 'limits' as narrow as 50 pounds of gunpowder, 10 muskets and 500 percussions caps annually were discussed in Cairo![1]

Yohannes all but ignored Gordon's proposals. He had moved his residence to Debre Tabor and was consolidating his power in central Ethiopia. In June 1876 Menelik had denounced the Egyptian attacks on Yohannes, the occupation of Harar and the blockade of the ports, in a very strong letter to Ismā'īl.[2] In a solemn agreement in March 1878, the internal relationship between Menelik and Yohannes was also settled in Yohannes's favour. Therefore the emperor was in a strong position when Gordon came to Debre Tabor to make a final attempt in September 1879. Gordon was determined to obtain the best terms possible for his master the khedive, but he also admitted privately: 'Now Johannis will not give me his help for nothing when I persist in keeping what we have stolen from him' and '. . . I have abused them [the Ethiopians]; for they (*like us*) want an eye for an eye, and twenty shillings for one pound.'[3] Yohannes asked for the retrocession of Metemma, Shanqella (the lowlands below the Blue Nile gorges) and Bogos, the ports of Zulla and Anfilla, a new bishop and either one or two million pounds or Massawa as well. He also brought up the question of international guarantees for any treaty signed. Gordon, who had been instructed to cede neither Bogos nor a port, could do nothing. During the following years, Yohannes made several unsuccessful attempts to gain British, French and German support for his plans to obtain a port, threatening otherwise to reopen hostilities with Egypt. But it was only when the victorious Mahdists threatened to wipe out the Egyptian garrisons on Ethiopia's boundaries that the British finally decided to meet Yohannes at least half-way. In June 1884 the so-called Hewett treaty (negotiated for Britain and Egypt by Sir William Hewett) brought the conflict with Egypt to an end. Yohannes was promised free transit through Massawa under British protection for all goods including arms and ammunition, and the restoration of Bogos, including all Egyptian property left behind at Kassala, Amedib and Keren by the evacuated garrisons. The Amharic version of the treaty clearly defined 'free transit' as 'duty-free'. For all practical purposes Ethiopia had therefore regained its ancient port. In return for this Yohannes

[1] Sven Rubenson, 'The Adwa Peace Treaty of 1884', *Proceedings of the Third International Conference of Ethiopian Studies*, I (Addis Ababa, 1969), 228–9.

[2] Abdin Archives, Soudan, Carton 5.2.7, Menelik to Ismā'īl, 16 June 1876.

[3] George Birkbeck Hill, ed., *Colonel Gordon in Central Africa 1874–1879* (London, 1881), 402–3, 408.

promised to facilitate the withdrawal of the Egyptian garrisons through Ethiopia to Massawa, and this he also did. The Egyptians evacuated Harar, which was left to a local emir, and most of the ports to the south of Massawa.[1]

The victories of Gundet and Gura and an unyielding, increasingly skilful diplomacy aided by favourable circumstances had restored to Ethiopia her north-western and northern borderlands and guaranteed her access to the sea. The Egyptian threat had been successfully averted. By 1884, however, European interest in the coasts of the Red Sea and Gulf of Aden had increased to the point of partition, and Ethiopia was destined to lose again within a few years all that she had gained.

[1] Rubenson, 'Adwa Peace Treaty', 230–6.

CHAPTER 3

THE MAGHRIB

POLITICAL, SOCIAL AND ECONOMIC CONDITIONS
BEFORE 1830

It is customary to link together the different states of north-west Africa, the Maghrib. But they were, in fact, very varied. They differed from each other and they did not constitute any form of political unity. Turkish suzerainty existed over Algiers and Tunis, but not over Morocco.

This suzerainty was, as it has often been described, largely fictive and mainly ceremonial, but it did have some real meaning. It was in Istanbul, in Smyrna and in Anatolia that the governments of Algiers and Tunis recruited their garrison troops (the *ojaq*). When the Porte was in peril in some way (as in 1795 against Tripoli, in 1810 against Crete, and most notably at the time of the Greek war of independence), then it received assistance from its vassals. Morocco, which was fully independent, was a country where political unrest and agitation were frequent. The sovereign was a hereditary monarch, but he had to be proclaimed sovereign by the different tribal and military units which covered most of the territory, as well as by the principal town organizations. In a sense therefore it could be said that the Moroccan monarchy was also elective. There had been many succession struggles; regional and local preoccupations could express themselves through the issue of a sovereign's proclamation; at times, revolt can almost be described as endemic, particularly during the rule of Mulay Sulaymān (1792–1822). In the regency of Algiers the dey was chosen by the Turkish garrison. He ruled with a council and he was directly responsible for the government of a large central area of the regency, including Algiers and the plain of the Mitidja, which was known as the Dar al-Sulṭān. The remainder of the territory was governed by semi-independent beys, appointed by the dey, usually in return for some advantageous fiscal retribution. But these beys were far from constituting dynasties. They could be dismissed and there were many examples of such dismissal, sometimes followed by execution. The political organization of Tunis differed considerably from that of Algiers, since a hereditary dynasty had established itself there since 1705, with Husayn b. 'Alī. It had succeeded in identifying itself more closely with

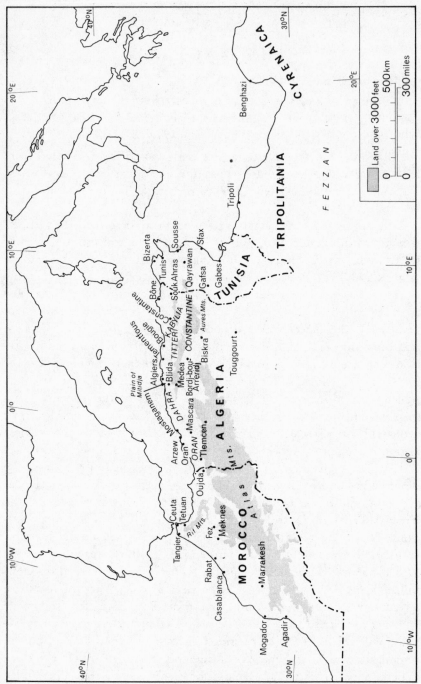

6 The Maghrib

the population than was the case in any other Maghribian state and appeared as the most stable of them all.

The population of these territories was also varied. In Algiers and in Tunis it was the Turks who were socially the most prominent and politically the most powerful, although non-Turkish Muslims were numerous in Algiers. They were usually soldiers and invariably town-dwellers. There was also a section of the population known as *kuloglus*, who were descendants of mixed Turco-Arab marriages, and there were Andalusians, descendants of the Moors driven from Spain. In Morocco there was a special armed force, used by the dynasty, which was recruited from Sudanic Africa. A Jewish population was scattered through the towns and villages of the region, and its largest grouping was in Tunisia (where there were some 20,000, including 15,000 in Tunis itself). The commerce of Algiers came to be largely dominated by Jewish merchants. Europeans were also scattered throughout the area, the largest group being in Tunisia where, in 1836, they numbered about 12,000, coming mainly from Malta and Sicily. This contrasts with the few hundred Europeans who lived in Morocco or in Algeria.

It is difficult to estimate the total populations of the territories, since contemporary estimates vary enormously and since such records as do exist are often taxation lists and are notoriously unreliable. The most careful calculation has been made for Algeria (within its present frontiers), and it has been estimated that there the population numbered about 3 millions in 1830. About the same time the population of Tunisia was probably over 1 million and that of Morocco in the region of 3 to 4 millions. Thus, while Turks, *kuloglus*, Jews, Andalusians, Sudanese and Europeans were to be counted in thousands or in hundreds, the bulk of the population was numbered in millions. It consisted of Arabs and Berbers. In Algeria the Berbers constituted about half of the total population, in Morocco probably more than half. In Tunisia, however, the Berber-speaking population was small (and it could have been for this reason that the regency of Tunis seemed the most united of the Maghrib territories). The Berbers were in many ways a contrast to the Arabs, with their particular language, their own customs, laws, forms of landholding and religious observances.

Thus, in terms of politics and of population, the region is one of diversity. But there were many similarities between the different countries. In each of the three territories the controlling military forces were primarily concerned with the raising of money by taxation and with the maintenance of order. Sometimes they were supplemented in these tasks by auxiliary forces (*makhzin*) which were given particular privileges; often purely local arrangements were made. Socially too there was a rough unity, in spite of such differences as those between Berber and Arab, or between those who were largely sedentary in their way of life and those who were largely nomadic. The basis of social organization was the family and the basis of tribal unity was family relationship. Among Berbers a dozen or more families formed a group, a number of such groups formed a *jemā'a* and several *jemā'a* formed the political unity of the tribe. Among Arabs the *douar* brought together different family units, and could sometimes unite people of very different origins. According to geographical and historical circumstances, Arab tribes varied in size, and the power of their leaders varied considerably, but some form of tribal unit was usually present. There were two other means whereby individuals and whole tribes could identify themselves with larger groupings. The one was the leagues or alliances (*çoffs*) which existed in some parts of the territories; the other was the religious organizations or brotherhoods or *ṭarīqa* (*confréries* as the French called them), which were often devoted to the cult of a particular saint or a particular form of religious emphasis. The latter, which spread across the Maghrib, were particularly active at the end of the eighteenth and beginning of the nineteenth centuries.

In terms of economic life there was an obvious and basic unity. The populations were dependent upon the land and were engaged in a subsistence economy. Within this generalization there was necessarily a wide variety of different activities, determined by the conditions of the soil and the amount of rainfall. But generally speaking the Berber populations in such regions as the Kabyle mountains practised an intense cultivation on small areas of land, producing grain, vegetables, oil and fruit; the Arab populations, cultivating larger areas of land, raised sheep (or camels to the south) and grew cereal crops. There were some big landowners who let their lands, or who had them farmed by a type of serf, but the usual pattern was of the peasant landowner with rudimentary equipment, striving to exist within a framework of poverty.

There was, however, a great deal of commercial activity. The variety of agricultural production gave rise to extensive exchanges, organized in a complicated manner. There was also an important artisanal activity, much of which was centred in the towns or in the more densely populated Berber villages. Particular regions had their specialities, and the production of certain textile goods was often the result of an extensive division of labour, which has sometimes been compared to a form of industrial capitalism. However the numbers engaged in these activities were relatively small. There were few large towns in Algeria; in the eastern region there was only the one town of any importance, Constantine, which had a population of some 25,000 at the time of the French conquest; Algiers itself had a population of about 50,000. Morocco had more towns, but less than one-fifth of the population could be described as urban, and the largest town, Fez, had less than 100,000 inhabitants. Tunis was the biggest town of the Maghrib (with about 120,000 people living there), while other towns, such as Bizerta, Sousse, Sfax, Gafsa, Kaizouan, were very active and made Tunisia the most urbanized of the three territories. Nevertheless it is unlikely that much more than a fifth of the total population lived in towns.

Some of the trading movements were purely local, others involved the provision of the whole territory with some particular textile, leather or metal-work. But in addition three main trading movements can be seen. There was the trade which followed the littoral, east–west and west–east, and which included the important organization of pilgrimages to Mecca. There were the trans-Saharan caravans which were often in the hands of specialized tribes. There was also Mediterranean trade, almost entirely in the hands of European and Jewish merchants. Woollen products, oil, wax, dates, Saharan products and sometimes cereals were exchanged for European goods. The Maghrib states were also famous for their piracy, and the existence of pirate ships outside the Mediterranean was occasionally recorded. But modern evidence shows that, like the Mediterranean trade, piracy was a small, entirely marginal activity. From time to time there was a flourish of activity, and at Tunis the enterprise was well organized. But it seems that the reports of this activity were highly exaggerated in Europe.

In general the Maghrib states resembled other parts of the Mediterranean, such as Corsica, Sardinia, Sicily and Calabria. They were poor countries. They suffered from periodic famines, notably that of 1815 and the following years; there were epidemics of plague, such as those of 1784, 1793 and 1817–18. It seems probable that the population as a whole was declining. But the Maghrib was also a closed world, conscious of its Islamic vocation and officially anxious to avoid contact with Europe. It was this world which was broken into by the French in 1830.

THE INITIAL FRENCH OCCUPATION OF ALGIERS, 1830-4

The French conquest of Algiers in 1830, and the colonization and settlement of Algeria which continued until 1962, would be notable if only because it was one of the first important European interventions on the African continent. Yet the decision to launch an expedition against the ruler of Algiers and the determination to make Algeria an area of French settlement, were arrived at in strange ways. They were neither the result of ideas which had been carefully elaborated, nor of interests which had been able to assert themselves. It would be true to say that French conquest and colonization were policies which emerged out of uncertainty and confusion.

Relations between the beys of Algiers and successive French governments had been bad for many years. One important reason for this was the financial imbroglio, which had developed during the days of the French Directory (1795-9), and which concerned two Jewish merchants living in Algiers, called Bacri and Busnach. They had supplied wheat grown in Algeria to the French armies; but they had indulged in a complicated series of credit manoeuvres and, with the connivance of certain French statesmen (who were probably corrupt), they had succeeded in associating the moneys owed to them with the moneys which they owed the bey. The situation became more difficult as Bacri and Busnach, with a number of associates, increased their own claims. The dey thus found himself at the centre of the imbroglio, and in a position to claim that the French government had been acting dishonourably towards him. From 1824 onwards, the French consul in Algiers, by name Deval, had the reputation of working with the Jewish financial houses. Thus it was that in 1827, the dey, believing that he had been shown little consideration and that he was being duped, is supposed to have allowed his irritation to get the better of him and to have struck Deval with a fly-swat. This alleged insult did not seem to have caused much excitement or indignation at first. Subsequently, however, the French government began a blockade of Algiers.

Since the final downfall of Napoleon in 1815, government in France had been based upon the Bourbon monarchy and on a limited parliamentary system, where the vote was given to a small, wealthy section of the population. Since the accession of Charles X in 1824 a conflict had been developing between him and a form of middle-class liberalism, primarily over the way in which this parliamentary government was to develop. It was this conflict, in its political, social and cultural aspects, which appeared important. The Algerian affair was never in the fore-front and was not a major preoccupation of any of the protagonists. But as the blockade proved ineffective, and as the various attempts at *pour-parlers* failed, more than one government became aware that their Algerian policy was open to criticism and that it could become an element affecting French internal politics. A number of officers, for technical reasons, suggested that the blockade ought to be abandoned and that armed forces should land on the Algerian coast. From this the idea grew that some resounding success in attacking Algiers could embarrass the opposition and would strengthen the government's domestic position. However, the discussion remained vague and a good many courses of action seemed open. At one time the possibility of entrusting the attack to the pasha of Egypt was considered. It was also thought that the conquest of the Regency by the French (or their agents) would form part of a general partition of the Ottoman Empire, and that this might even be accompanied by a general revision of Euro-pean frontiers. There were discussions about the economic possibilities of developing Algeria, but few people were well informed, and they were conducted mainly in terms of Algeria as a traditional sugar producing colony, or in terms of the French government's ability to control econo-mic affairs. There was little discussion about the intrinsic value of the territory, and the suggestion that the dey's treasure could be profitably seized by the French seems to have been put forward late in the day.

The French government announced in January 1830 that they inten-ded to send an expedition to Algiers. In May some 37,000 soldiers embarked in a fleet which crossed the Mediterranean. They started to land in the bay of Sidi-Ferruch on 14 June and were unsuccessfully engaged by the dey's troops, supported by reinforcements from the interior. The fort which protected Algiers was captured, and on 5 July the dey signed an agreement surrendering Algiers to the French in return for promises to respect the liberty and the property of all the inhabi-tants. A few days later Bone was captured and troops disembarked at Oran.

It is not clear what the French government intended to do with its victory. But whatever was in the minds of the officers who had ran-sacked their archives for maps and accounts of the area, the most important members of the government had no long-term plans for a French Algiers. With the exception of people in Marseilles who were interested in any activity in the Mediterranean, the French population showed little interest in the campaign. Although the elections were deliberately timed so as to coincide with the news of military success, the results were disappointing. The opposition was returned as powerful as before. Charles X attempted to remedy the situation by using emergency powers, but the result was the revolutionary days of 27, 28, 29 July 1830, when Paris and then the rest of France turned decisively against the king. The king abdicated, and he was replaced by his cousin, the Duke of Orleans, who became king as Louis-Philippe.

The new government was particularly embarrassed by the conquest of Algeria. It was determined to demonstrate that it was a pacific government in international relations, in spite of its revolutionary origins. An expansionist policy in the Mediterranean could compromise this conciliatory policy, especially with the British government. Yet it was clear that the rapid return of the expeditionary force (even had this been possible) would have been dangerous since many of the officers were reported loyal to Charles X. Thus it was in an atmosphere of particular confusion that the need to decide what to do about Algiers was admitted. The first commander-in-chief to be appointed by the Orleanist government was General Clauzel, a believer in the possibilities of French colonization; the second, General Berthezène, was an honest and straightforward soldier who thought that the difficulties of colonization were overwhelming; the third, Rovigo, believed that the French should behave as the complete masters of the population and owners of all the land. There was a lack of co-ordination between Paris and Algiers; the French found it difficult to establish an administration, and they were forced to rely upon individuals who belonged to the Jewish community or who were descended from the Andalusian Moriscos. These, by character as well as by ethnic appurtenance, were unrepresentative of the population as a whole; there was a conflict between the military and the civil administrations; there were uncertainties concerning the extension of French power into regions other than Algiers, notably within the beylicates of Oran and Constantine; there was a flurry of speculation over land which had been rapidly acquired, and a number of French settlers and investors found themselves cheated; many of the settlers came from amongst the Paris poor and were totally unsuited for the agricultural work to which they were directed.

While the opponents of colonization emphasized the difficulties of soil and climate, and while those who had particular interests in the French West Indies or elsewhere resented the prospect of developments which could only benefit Marseilles, the belief persisted that French greatness could be served by the possession of Algiers and its region, and that somehow Algeria could come to represent for France what India was for Britain. Perhaps this belief was all the more influential because it was vague and indefinite. The situation became all the more complicated when for a time certain French officers thought that one means of governing these territories was by coming to agreements with the Tunisian ruling dynasty and entrusting members of this family with the task of ruling.

A French commission was appointed to inquire into the situation in 1833. Its report condemned much of what had taken place since 1830. The army had committed atrocities; the civil authorities had respected neither the property nor the religion of the Algerians; agreements made had not been kept; those European settlers who had made their appearance had been rapidly disillusioned and discouraged; speculators were blamed for much that had gone wrong. Nevertheless, the commission recommended that the regency should continue to be occupied by France and by France alone. It was suggested that this was the will of the French population and the commission envisaged the possibility of Algeria being colonized by French and other European settlers who would be able to maintain just relations with the indigenous populations. Eventually, it was thought, the colony would be able to pay for itself. A further commission in 1834 confirmed these findings, but insisted on prudence in the establishment of the colony. It claimed that the French army should intervene only in the towns of Algiers, Bone, Oran and Bougie and in the regions surrounding them.

After some hesitation the French government accepted the principal part of these conclusions. Doubtless this was the first manifestation of something which was to be constantly present in the history of French Algeria. Few French governments felt strong enough to withdraw from Algeria and to face the accusations of weakness and of betraying French interests, which would have united the divided oppositions of the French political scene. Therefore they pursued their Algerian venture with the intention of limiting it to the coastal regions.

REACTION OF THE ALGERIAN POPULATION,
FRENCH CONQUEST TO 1848

The reaction of the population of Algeria to the French incursion was a complicated one. It would be wrong to suppose that there was a generalized and consistent hostility. The French army and administration found themselves in contact with a society which already had its own political issues and divisions. There were occasions when this society found in the French a factor which brought about unity, but this was rare and temporary. At first, the French presence could appear to be an additional factor in the complexities of Algerian politics rather than a dominating influence; there were very few occasions when a French officer was able to impose his authority without taking account of existing situations.

In Algiers itself resistance to the French was slight, in spite of the fact that the invasion had been expected and that the dey had had more men under arms than the French had landed. But the Turkish military contingent had declined in numbers; the dey had little contact with the population of the town; the bourgeoisie, whether Jewish or Moor, had been in favour of capitulation; the representatives of the *makhzin* tribes were only interested in maintaining their fiscal and territorial privileges and they had no attachment to any particular government. The first French administration in Algiers, therefore, found no organized resistance and was able to collaborate with the bourgeoisie.

But outside Algiers the situation was different. At Tementfous, about 30 kilometres to the east of Algiers, a number of tribal and religious leaders met towards the end of July 1830 in order to discuss their reaction to the French invasion. Whether the resistance of areas outside Algiers was in any way linked to this meeting is not clear. Nevertheless the first French attempt to occupy Bougie was repulsed; although the French succeeded in establishing relations with the bourgeoisie in Bone, the population from the surrounding hills intervened and fought fiercely before they were driven back. Although the Bey of Titteri had sent his submission after the fall of Algiers, he resisted the French in Medea both in 1830 and in 1831. The Bey of Constantine, al-Ḥājj Aḥmad, who was a *kuloglu*, had taken part in the defence of Algiers, but he had refused to surrender. His resistance necessarily gave the signal to the whole region since most of the population held land directly from him. The *makhzin* here was not a group of privileged tribes but rather a collection of tenant farmers, so that they were ready to respond to the bey's call. He maintained his resistance until he was defeated in 1837. Even then he personally continued to fight in the Aures mountains. His resistance however did not affect the great feudal families of the region, such as the Ben Gana and the Mokrani. Nor could it extend to the western beylicate where conditions were different.

In the west, and in the centre, there was a great social variety. There were important differences between town and country and between mountain and plain. There was a contrast between the privileged tribes, the *makhzin*, and the remainder, as there was between those tribal units which were under the control of great hereditary chiefs and those which maintained a looser organization. There were Arabs and Berbers. There were tribal leaders and units which had interests in the towns and contacts with the *kuloglus*, the *ojaq* or the bourgeoisie. There is reason to believe that before 1830 relations between all these different groups were becoming increasingly difficult and that there was already a search for some acceptable and agreed authority. There had been an emphasis on the importance of Islam, and there were various religious brotherhoods which were particularly strong in this area. These were the Tijāniyya, the Ṭayyibiyya, the Darqāwiyya and the Qādiriyya. The founder of the Tijāniyya order had fled to Morocco in 1789 when he had been persecuted by the Turks in Algeria; its main centre was in southern Titteri. The Ṭayyibiyya had played an important role in Morocco and their power in Algeria was extensive. The Darqāwiyya had opposed the Turks, and the Qādiriyya was said to be the most powerful order in the whole of Algeria, being very strong in the plains of Oran. The Qādiriyya had a record of conflict with the other orders.

The French invasion added a further complication to an already complex situation. In 1830 there was a movement of the population away from Oran, and there was an unsuccessful attempt on the part of Clauzel to introduce a Tunisian bey. The *kuloglus* of Tlemcen turned to their traditional source of help, the Sultan of Morocco. At that time he was Mulay 'Abd al-Raḥmān, who was reluctant to find himself in conflict with the French, but found himself obliged to collaborate with some of the religious orders and to establish a deputy in Tlemcen and a base in Mascara. The French eventually came to an agreement with him in 1832 to withdraw from Algeria. This left the Algerian tribes dependent upon the Qādiriyya organization, which was all the more incensed against the French because the French had reached agreement with some of the former *makhzin* unities, their traditional enemies. In other words the old hostility against the Turks and the *makhzin* took on a new aspect, that of a tribal jihad, since it was the French who were now the allies of the *makhzin*.

The religious leader of the Qādiriyya at this time was Mahieddin, whose headquarters were at Guerna, near to Mascara. He had for many years been hostile to the *makhzin* and during 1832 he led various attacks against the *makhzin* of Oran, proclaiming these attacks as a holy war.

But he was not successful and, deciding that it was necessary to have a younger and more warlike leader, it was one of his sons, 'Abd al-Qādir, who was chosen. This choice was also a religious choice. 'Abd al-Qādir had been to Mecca and was renowned for his piety as well as for his military prowess. But although the twenty-four-year-old leader was proclaimed in November 1832 as the leader of several tribal groupings, it should not be thought that his authority was recognized everywhere. There was no unity of the indigenous populations against the French. There were many rivals, both individual and tribal, who refused to accept that 'Abd al-Qādir had any form of superiority, and he found himself in conflict with the Darqāwiyya and with the Ṭayyibiyya. It was, as it happened, a French general, Desmichels, who first calculated that by making an agreement with 'Abd al-Qādir French influence would be most easily established. It was this treaty which, in 1834, stated that 'Abd al-Qādir enjoyed sovereignty over western Algeria apart from Oran, Arzew and Mostaganem, and suggested that he was the commander of the faithful. But 'Abd al-Qādir was forced to overcome many Arab and Berber enemies before he was able to affirm himself; at times he benefited from French supplies and arms; at times part of the process of affirmation was to show his hostility to the French. His position was strengthened still further when in 1837 he signed an agreement with a French general who had already defeated him, General Bugeaud. This, the treaty of the Tafna, redefined and extended the area of 'Abd al-Qādir's sovereignty. The French held Oran, Arzew, Mostaganem and Mazagran in the Oran beylicate; in the central beylicate they held Algiers, the coastal region and part of the plain of the Mitidja.

These treaties between the French and 'Abd al-Qādir reveal a certain confusion in the minds of the French generals. Both gave rise to strong criticism, since many of the French could not see why they should build up the strength of their chief enemy. There was also confusion because the Arab and French texts of the treaties did not agree. Desmichels had concealed some of the concessions to 'Abd al-Qādir in the French text, whilst some secret clauses in the Tafna treaty suggested that Bugeaud was expecting some personal financial gain from his negotiations. Nevertheless 'Abd al-Qādir was able to extend his power into the eastern region and to consolidate his position in the west and centre. He realized that he could not be a permanent ally of the French, and he realized the dangerous implications of French settlement on the land. He was forced to organize his territories increasingly on a religious basis. He came into conflict with the Tijāniyya order, which refused to recognize his rule and entered into agreements with the French.

In the east, the French general Clauzel had failed to capture Constantine in 1836, but his successors were successful the following year. They attempted to persuade Aḥmad Bey to sign a treaty with them, but he refused, and the French were obliged to establish some sort of indirect rule in the province. This meant an increase in French commitment and the need to keep a land route open between Algiers and Constantine, going across territory which 'Abd al-Qādir claimed by the treaty of the Tafna. Towards the end of 1839 a violation of this territory caused 'Abd al-Qādir to declare a state of war and to invade the plain of the Mitidja, the main area of French settlement. The renewal of conflict meant the end of any French hope that they could rule Algeria through 'Abd al-Qādir. It also meant the end of the policy of limited occupation.

By 1840 the European settlers in Algeria numbered about 25,000, of whom slightly less than half were French (the remainder being Italian, Spanish and Maltese, together with a sprinkling of other nationalities). There was always a movement of Europeans away from Algeria, and many of the settlers were totally unfitted to be pioneers. The army was spread over a wide area and, in 1840, many of the French soldiers were suffering from illness. There was therefore little effective resistance to 'Abd al-Qādir. The Mitidja was devastated; some of the tribal units which had allied themselves to France became uncertain in their loyalty. Many, including the Berbers from Kabylia, began to harass the French even in the outskirts of Algiers. The whole French position seemed threatened.

The period which followed was one of continual and cruel war. It was clear that no French government in Paris could consider abandoning Algeria. It was therefore necessary to drop the idea of limited occupation and to proceed to a position where France was militarily superior. It was Bugeaud who was appointed governor-general and commander-in-chief and who, with forces which often exceeded 100,000, pursued a rigorous attack on real and potential enemies. He sent his men on raids throughout the territory, destroying the crops, cattle and food reserves, and sought to control the means of communication and internal trade. He tried to build up a network of tribes favourable to the French and one by one he attacked 'Abd al-Qādir's supporters. After 1843, when 'Abd al-Qādir was forced to take refuge in Morocco, resistance to the French was organized by the Ṭayyibiyya, and a young marabout who took the name of Bou Maza became the leader of both Arabs and Berbers in the Dahra and Ouarsenis regions, and his insurrection had wide repercussions. In 1845 and 1846 'Abd al-Qādir attempted to organize one last movement against the French. By 1847 both Bou Maza and 'Abd al-Qādir were forced to surrender. The 1850s saw the conquest of the Kabyle mountains and a further suppression of revolts. By the 1860s, when Napoleon III was mid-way through his reign, it could be said that Algeria was conquered.

From the French point of view this war was accompanied by a great deal of confusion. There was disagreement between Paris and Algiers, a constant conflict between military and civilian authorities, uncertainty about the principles of administration and colonization. The *bureaux arabes*, a form of which had been instituted in 1833 and which were reformed and extended in 1841 and 1844, set out to provide specialist information about Arab and Berber society and tried to serve as an intermediary between the French command and the indigenous chiefs. These officers, however, often found themselves acting as if they were the sole administration. Having tried unsuccessfully to govern by means of the Turks and the *makhzin*, Bugeaud chose to rely on the native aristocracy. In many cases he preserved the administrative structure of 'Abd al-Qādir, entrusting considerable powers to these chiefs, but always hoping that with increased security he would be able to reduce the size of their administrative units and to limit their power. Thus the French administration governed both directly and through native institutions which it shaped and manipulated. In certain sectors, such as justice, the French chose to act as if they were in France, and they decreed that French law should apply, thereby reducing (at least theoretically) the judicial powers of the chiefs.

It is possible to measure some of the effects of this period on the French in Algeria. Attempts, favoured by Bugeaud, to promote military colonization, so that the soldier would both settle and farm in the country which he was conquering, were accompanied by other attempts at both official and private colonization. By 1846 the European population numbered nearly 110,000 (with the army being almost the same size), the French still being very clearly in a minority. But only 15,000 of these were rural settlers, the remainder living in the towns. However this did not reduce the European desire to acquire land, even if it had to be cultivated by Muslim farmers, and during the 1840s and 1850s, the lands which were consecrated to religious purposes, *hubūs* lands, and the tribal lands were made available to settlers. In some cases the

French administration decided that certain areas of land were not needed by a tribe, and by this policy, known as *cantonnement*, tribal groups were forced to make do with less, and often with inferior, grazing land.

The effect of this period of war and colonization on the indigenous populations is harder to measure. It was clearly a period of destruction. It was a particularly cruel war, but it is impossible to make any overall estimate of the demographic and economic effects. It has been suggested that in the forty years from 1830 to 1870 several hundred thousands were killed. Certainly there was an important emigration of the Algerian population into Morocco, and most of the existing urban centres saw a considerable decline in their indigenous populations. Both Bugeaud and 'Abd al-Qādir practised the *razzia*, the raid into territory and the capture or destruction of its cattle and food. Some peoples must have been raided by both sides. The result of this was a considerable reduction in the number of cattle kept and in the amount of land cultivated. The persistence of famine and cholera can be partly explained by this destruction.

These demographic and agrarian catastrophes would in themselves explain the economic depression into which many areas of the country decayed. But other factors were important. The increase in the numbers of European traders and the sale of European products, the scarcity of money, the dislocation of urban organizations, the increase in the amount of taxation demanded both by the French and their nominees, the rise in the cost of food and raw materials, meant that there was a crisis affecting all forms of economic activity. The political crisis was also widespread. Such organization as existed under the Turks had been destroyed both by 'Abd al-Qādir and by Bugeaud. In its place there was a mixture of military, administrative and feudal authorities. Algerian society was being pulverized and there did not seem to be any way whereby it could recover.

FRENCH ADMINISTRATION, 1848–70

The constitution of the Second Republic of 1848 proclaimed Algeria to be an integral part of French territory; the doctrine of 'assimilation' was stated, which was eventually to culminate in the belief that Algeria was an extension of metropolitan France. From March 1848 the French population of Algeria was given the right to elect deputies to the Assembly in Paris; from August 1848 a number of administrative matters in Algeria were to be dealt with by the relevant ministry in Paris; from December 1848 Algerian territory was divided into civil and military regions, and in the former, Oran, Algiers and Constantine became three departments, administered by prefects, sub-prefects and mayors (the majority of whom were appointed by the prefects). The prefects were only obliged to correspond with the governor-general on matters directly concerning 'colonization'; otherwise they dealt directly with the Algerian department of the Ministry of War in Paris and with other appropriate ministries. The military territories were governed by the governor-general, the generals, officers in charge of the sub-divisions, the *bureaux arabes*, and the native chiefs who formed part of the administrative system.

The politicians of the Second Republic were determined that Algeria should be useful to them. After a Parisian workers' insurrection in June 1848, and with a persistent economic crisis making employment difficult, it was suggested that a solution might be found in the organized emigration of Parisians to Algeria. Between October and December 1848, more than 13,000 settlers were transported across the Mediterranean and were supposed to find specially created villages awaiting them (particularly in the Oran region). In reality the preparation had been quite inadequate, and although still more settlers were drafted towards Algeria, the whole operation was a failure. Many died; more returned to France; most protested against deplorable conditions and against the military control to which they were subjected.

The failure of this attempt at official colonization was a sign of the failure of the Second Republic's attempt at governing Algeria as a whole. Civilian power proved ineffective. Soon the generals were in command and the right of the settlers to elect representatives to the Chamber of Deputies was suppressed. Nevertheless the settlers continued to dominate the economic life of the territory. By 1851 there were some 131,000 European settlers, of whom more than 30,000 were engaged in agriculture, the growing of cereal crops, tobacco and the raising of cattle. It was possible to import Algerian products into France without paying duty. The risings and protests of the Muslim population were ineffective and disorganized, and certain tribal lands were severely reduced in area so as to make way for European settlement. But the years from 1848 to 1851 were also difficult years. There was a plague of locusts; there was drought; cholera and smallpox were severe. The whole future of French Algeria appeared to be doubtful. Economically speaking, Algeria still had a considerable commercial deficit, and there was no sign of any crop which would transform this situation. The difficulties appeared infinitely greater than the prospects.

On 2 December 1851 Napoleon III was brought to power in France by a coup d'état. He was regarded by the French settlers in Algeria with mixed feelings. They voted against him in the referendum, and they resented his action in liberating 'Abd al-Qādir (who had been held prisoner in France since 1847). But he spoke of developing and assimilating 'the vast kingdom which lay opposite to Marseilles'. However, it seems likely that the extension of French power, during the 1850s, towards the Sahara, and the conquest of the Kabyle regions, were not so much deliberate acts of policy on the emperor's part, as initiatives taken by the soldier commanding in Algeria, Maréchal Randon, and actions which were somewhat forced by continued flurries of resistance to French rule. Over Algeria, as in other matters, the emperor was hesitant. Although he was usually more preoccupied with different aspects of foreign and domestic policy, he was prepared to experiment with an assimilation policy and with a civil administration controlled by a Ministry for Algeria and for the Colonies. Under this form of government more territory was made available for settlers, and the loss of land, combined with fears and rumours of further losses, caused a certain effervescence to start up amongst many tribal units. The conflicts between the settlers and the army, and between the civil administration and the army, became more bitter, and Napoleon III became very aware of them during a visit to Algiers. It was in these circumstances, and because of his desire always to take the initiative, that in December 1860 the system whereby power was concentrated in the hands of a governor-general was re-established. The principle of association was affirmed rather than the principle of assimilation. A number of individuals came to the fore who proclaimed that the role of the Europeans in Algeria should be essentially an urban and commercial one, whilst the indigenous population should be protected and their rights to their lands should be guaranteed. Thus it was suggested that the policies followed in the past had been mistaken, and that in the future colonization was a matter for bankers and industrialists rather than the settlers. The new policy seemed to reach its climax when, in 1863, Napoleon declared that Algeria was not, properly speaking, a colony, but an Arab kingdom, and that he was as much the emperor of the Arabs as he was emperor of the French. This statement was modified in 1865 when, after another visit, Napoleon III defined Algeria as an Arab kingdom, a European colony and a French military camp. Nevertheless the emperor's policies were new, and as such they were deeply resented by the settlers and were opposed by much of the administration.

It should be emphasized that Napoleon III was in no sense someone who sought to preserve the traditional Arab society. His admiration for Arabs and his conviction that the persistent extension of European settlers into Algeria would be disastrous were linked with the belief that reforms should be applied to the indigenous populations. Thus it was intended that a survey should be carried out of all land, whether individually or collectively owned, with the hope that ownership would eventually become concentrated in individuals or in villages. It was thought that in this way the population could more easily transact affairs amongst themselves and with Europeans. Similarly a municipal reform sought to create communes, sometimes, if there was an appreciable number of Europeans in the neighbourhood, *communes mixtes*, which would replace the tribe, supposedly an anachronism. By a law of 1865 it was ordered that both the Algerian Jews and Muslims could be considered as French subjects, entitled to enter the French army and civil service. They could also be classified as French citizens provided that they renounced Muslim or Jewish religious laws (an act which only a few individuals from either community chose to do). A number of schools were created, some of which were Franco-Arab, others being especially designed for Arabs. The papacy was allowed to create two new dioceses and the Bishop of Algiers became an archbishop. Above all, a vast programme of public works was envisaged, to be undertaken by private companies, closely surveyed by the state, in return for large concessions. From 1867 there was a complete customs union with France.

It was largely because of these efforts that Algeria hardly settled down during the Second Empire. The administration was opposed to many of the emperor's ideas and sought to sabotage his efforts in various ways. The army, having extended its hold over the Kabyle regions by allying with a small number of important families, turned against these families and sought to destroy their influence. The settlers were fearful of being absorbed into Muslim society and they were anxious about their economic privileges. When Monseigneur Lavigerie arrived as the Archbishop of Algiers in 1867, he attacked the policies of the emperor, maintaining that Muslims should be converted and criticizing the actions of the military. The settlers, often assisted by officers and by civilian administrators, and sometimes by politicians in Paris, pressed the government to change its policy and to modify, if not to abandon, the idea of the Arab kingdom. From 1868 there were several commissions studying various projects of reform, and in March 1870 it was agreed that a civil administration should be set up. The hostility of the settlers to Napoleon III was shown dramatically in Algeria's reply to the referendum of 8 May 1870. Whereas in metropolitan France a majority of five to one approved the emperor's recent liberalization of the constitution, in Algeria a small majority (of the French citizens) voted against him, whilst about one third of the electorate abstained altogether.

Relevant to the failure of the Second Empire in Algeria was the series of natural disasters which marked its closing years. A plague of locusts, cholera and an earthquake in the region of Blida combined to make the period from 1866 calamitous. The European settlers suffered, and a crisis of confidence led to a falling off of investment funds. But it was the indigenous population which suffered most as their slender resources disappeared. They had been encouraged to sell food for exportation, and in order to pay taxes they had been forced to sell immediately after the harvests. Therefore they had to face a succession of bad harvests without stocks. For 1868 one contemporary source quotes a figure of 300,000 deaths, and it was generally believed that the intensity of the catastrophe was to be explained by the inadequacies of Napoleon's ideas and policies.

THE REVOLT OF 1871

The news of the Franco-Prussian war (France declared war on 15 July 1870) was not greeted with any enthusiasm by the European settlers. They foresaw a French victory and a further reinforcement of military authority in Algeria. But the news of French defeats, the capture of the emperor and the proclamation of the Republic (4 September 1870) transformed the situation. In Algiers and in other towns a series of popular committees were set up which organized the dismissal of many of the existing civil officials and sought to humiliate the military. The interventions of the French government (meeting in Bordeaux since Paris was besieged by the Germans) met with violent opposition. Attempts to satisfy the settlers, such as the decrees which were issued at the end of 1870 and at the beginning of 1871, drastically reducing the power of the army and the *bureaux arabes* and extending the power of the civil administration, were still judged insufficient. One of the decrees, which naturalized the Jewish community, led to much protestation, since it was alleged that it was unpopular amongst the Muslims and it was feared that it would lead to an increase in the political power of Jewish consistories. But all these activities became much less important when the European settlers realized that they were facing a considerable movement of rebellion amongst the Muslim populations.

It is striking to note that the Europeans were reluctant to believe that there was any serious possibility of revolt. The last rebellion had been in 1864, supposedly the work of the religious brotherhoods, encouraged by the news of war in Europe and by the reductions in the French army so that troops could be sent to Mexico. It was claimed that the same situation could not recur in 1870 or in 1871, and it was suggested that news of revolt was a fabrication by the army and the *bureaux arabes*, seeking to demonstrate how they were needed in Algeria. But, in fact, many authorities and experts had been expecting revolt and had commented on the tenseness of the situation. There were regions where this tension had been increased by the news of the Franco-Prussian war and of the emperor's fall from power. By September 1870 there were those who claimed that insurrection was imminent.

The first signs of revolt came in January 1871, when there were mutinies amongst Muslim soldiers who were in the French service. These were usually small and isolated affairs, associated with the soldiers' reluctance to be posted to France. But one mutiny did develop and led to a fierce attack being made on the town of Souk-Ahras. In February there were serious disturbances eighty kilometres north-west of Constantine. In mid-March one of the most powerful chiefs of the eastern region, Muḥammad al-Muqrānī, launched a large force against the strategic position of Bordj-bou-Arreridj. This attack was initially successful, but it was not followed, as had been hoped, by any general rising of the great feudal leaders. In April, the leader of the Raḥmāniyya brotherhood, al-Ḥasan, after some hesitation, decided to support Muqrānī's movement and proclaimed a holy war against the French. This led to the rising of the Berber tribes in the Kabyles, a very different sort of revolt to al-Muqrānī's. It was the failure of the rebels to organize any effective unity which was the principal cause of their defeat. The French were able to deal with them separately. There were large areas where there was little or no revolt, such as the south of Oran and many parts of the Algiers region. In fact two-thirds of the Muslim population abstained from any association with the rebellion. There was a shortage of arms, and the ending of the war with Prussia meant that the French army could be reinforced. Al-Muqrānī himself had seen the revolt as a means of negotiating with the French from a position of strength, and it does not seem as if he ever seriously considered ending the French presence. He unsuccessfully tried to submit to the governor in Algiers, but he was killed fighting in May 1871. Although his brother continued resistance until January 1872, the majority of the rebels had surrendered or had been overcome by the autumn of 1871.

The French had lost about 2,600 dead (many of whom had died from disease and not from fighting). It has never been possible to estimate the number of Muslims killed in the insurrection, although all observers thought that their losses were heavy. Many of those who had taken part in the rebellion fled into Tunisia (some 16,000 according to one estimate), and the repression which followed the ending of the revolt must have contributed to that movement. A massive fine was imposed on all those tribal groupings which had supposedly been involved, and for twenty years many of them were engaged in paying this off. Vast areas of tribal land were confiscated. By 1875 it was said that this amounted to 574,000 hectares.

In considering the causes of this rebellion, it is necessary to avoid over-simplification. Al-Muqrānī had reasons of his own to be dissatisfied with the French, and it could be that he was preoccupied with his own debts, whilst al-Ḥasan was influenced by his son's political ambitions. The political activities of a number of French officers, effecting reconciliations amongst the çoffs and leagues, had led to confusion, and some Muslims seem to have thought that they were being encouraged to revolt against the settlers. News from France and the agitation amongst the urban Europeans had led to the belief that French power was vacillating. The decree naturalizing the Jewish population had been deeply resented. But amongst all these considerations there was one which was overwhelming. From the last months of the Second Empire onwards it had been realized that a civil regime was going to replace the existing military regime. This was greatly feared and bitterly opposed. For the Muslim populations such a regime meant the intensification of colonization, and that meant the loss of land to Europeans. This apprehension, the essential cause of the revolt, was well justified. It was the terrible irony of Algerian history that the insurrection of 1871 actually facilitated what it sought to prevent, the installation of civil government and the beginning of a new era of colonization. The period of revolts had ended; the tribes were ruined and crushed; the political and economic domination of Algeria by Europeans had been firmly established.

TUNISIA 1830–70

The French presence in Algeria necessarily had its effect on Algeria's neighbours. In Tunisia the French conquest had coincided with a crisis in relations both with the European powers and with the Ottoman Empire. With the first, the Tunisian government had had to sign instruments agreeing to abandon the slave trade and to give European consuls the right to deal with all legal issues which involved Europeans. With the second, there was considerable apprehension that the Ottoman government, reacting against loss of power in Algiers, would assert its authority in Tunisia. In 1836 a Turkish fleet was sent to Tripoli and its commander requested that Tunisian troops should assist it. The Tunisian bey, Muṣṭafā, accepted this, but was fearful that, once the dissident tribes in Tripolitania had been subdued, then the Turks would turn on Tunis. In these circumstances the bey expected the French to protect him against the Turks, whilst believing that the Turks were a protection against French encroachments.

Aḥmad Bey (1837–55) continued to try and steer Tunisia through this middle course. He maintained friendly relations with the European powers, especially France, and he insisted upon the religious ties between Tunis and Istanbul, whilst rejecting all Ottoman claims to establish any form of sovereignty over Tunis. Part of the policy of rejecting Ottoman control was to place some tribal leaders in positions of authority, thus underlining their link with the bey. The reputation and grandeur of the beylical office was made visible in great palaces and effective in a large army (trained by French officers). The disadvantage of these policies was their expense. The Tunisian exchequer was suffering from the loss of income which followed from the abolition of the slave trade. There was doubtless too a great deal of inefficiency and corruption. But the result was that the Tunisian authorities had to borrow money from foreign banks (mainly French) and had to try various expedients for raising money by national loans. Foreign merchants tended to secure the government's bills at advantageous terms and thereby increased their influence. This in turn led to greater importance being given to the role of European consuls in Tunis, who were traditionally concerned with protecting their nationals against Muslim laws and customs. Under Aḥmad Bey's successor, Muḥammad Bey (1855–9), foreigners were granted the right to own property in Tunisia, thus opening the country to further economic penetration, and beginning an era in which the British, French and Italian consuls were to seek greater influence, and a reform movement was to attempt to modify the absolutism of the bey's rule. This coincided with the reign of a new bey, Muḥammad al-Ṣādiq.

A constitution was introduced in 1860 which made Tunisia into a form of constitutional monarchy. Ministers were to be responsible to a council, most members of which were chosen by the bey, although others were co-opted, and a system of compulsory retirement was established. This council was charged with the most important matters of government. It was not long however before this system collapsed. The bey's ministers found it too easy to ignore the council; the tribal leaders objected to the council challenging their rights; the consuls, especially that of France, saw the council as a check on their influence. But most important was the increasing indebtedness of the bey, who accepted some loans on remarkably disadvantageous terms. He was forced to increase taxation and to extend it to categories of the population who had hitherto enjoyed exemption. There was a widespread rising against the government in 1864, and Britain, France and Italy sent naval detachments to Tunisian ports in order to protect their subjects and to bring pressure on the bey. The French consul was particularly active in mediating between the rebels and the government and in persuading the bey to abolish the 1860 constitution and to abandon reforms.

Once the bey had returned to arbitrary government, there seemed to be nothing to prevent the country from moving to economic ruin. By the late 1860s it seemed that there would have to be a declaration of bankruptcy, and there were well-grounded British fears that this would lead to French military intervention. The upshot was the loss of Tunisian economic independence. An international commission was set up which controlled all state expenditure and which drew up the budget. Attempts were made to reinvigorate the economy, but often they came to very little because of the obstructive tactics pursued by the prime minister and other officials. Rivalry amongst the European consuls was intensified after the French defeat in 1870, when the Italians (who had more than 7,000 nationals in the country) attempted to become dominant. The British consul endeavoured to resolve the situation by a formal declaration that Tunisia was a Turkish possession, which therefore came under the provisions of the 1856 Treaty of Paris and had an international guarantee, whilst at the same time gaining concessions for British business men. The French responded by revealing evidence of the corrupt practices of the chief minister. This led to the appointment of Khair al-Din, a leading reformer who attempted to modernize the administrative system and stimulate agriculture and artisanal production. International rivalry remained a dominant factor.

MOROCCO 1830–73

Morocco had been directly affected by the French invasion and colonization of Algeria. The presence of the French drew Morocco out of her isolation and made it impossible for the sultan, Mulay 'Abd al-Raḥmān, to maintain the fiction that Europeans were of no interest to his government or peoples. In 1830 Moroccan troops intervened in Tlemcen and Oran, and in the 1840s 'Abd al-Qādir derived support from the west. When he took refuge in Moroccan territory, a French army invaded Morocco and the French navy bombarded the Moroccan coast. The result was that there was a generalized movement of rebellion against the sultan and an increase in European activities in Moroccan ports and towns. The British government brought pressure to bear on the sultan and encouraged him to defy the French. The French increased their consular representatives and gained shipping and mining concessions. The Spaniards, who possessed territory on the Moroccan mainland, were determined not to be ousted by the other European powers, and in 1848 they seized some small islands off Zaffarin and attempted to extend their influence in the Rif mountains. During the Crimean War, both the British and French sought to buy additional supplies of wheat and wool in Morocco in order to supply their armies.

Britain persuaded the sultan to sign a treaty in 1856, to which other European powers could adhere, whereby Moroccan trade was freed from almost all its monopolies, the import duties were fixed and British subjects could own property in Morocco. The French refused to sign and endeavoured to attract Moroccan trade through Algeria. The Spanish government also refused to sign, and took advantage of certain incidents to land an army in Ceuta and to occupy Tetuan in 1860. The death of the sultan was invariably the occasion for revolt in various parts of the kingdom. When Mulay 'Abd-al-Raḥmān died in 1859, increasing European influence and the victories of the Spaniards encouraged two major revolts against his son, Sīdī Muḥammad (1859–73). The one was in the south, where Raḥāmna tribesmen besieged Marrakesh. The other was in the mountains of the north, in the region of Kurt, and was led by a pretender who claimed special religious and miraculous powers. It was not until 1862 that both rebellions were overthrown, and it was in the same year that the Spanish government accepted to withdraw from Tetuan on receipt of a heavy indemnity.

From this time onwards the sultan's position was particularly difficult. His advisers were divided amongst those who saw all that was happening as the result of European penetration and who urged adherence to a rigid, traditional, anti-European attitude, and those who believed that it was necessary to modernize and to improve the administration. Sīdī Muḥammad oscillated between these policies. He was not helped by antagonisms amongst the European consuls, nor by the European residents' determination to maintain their privileges. His authority was diminished in many parts of the country and he suffered from the reputation of being an unlucky ruler. Rumours about his health in 1866 helped to create an effervescence amongst tribal units. The closing years of the 1860s were marked by bad harvests, plague and a falling off of European trade and investment. The coincidence of these crises had a catastrophic effect on most parts of Moroccan society. The movement of population to the towns was increased; internal trade diminished; the government's revenue fell dramatically. It was in response to this crisis that when Mulay Ḥasan succeeded his father in 1873, he inaugurated an era of reforms.

TRIPOLI 1830–70

In Tripoli, the Qarāmānlī dynasty was failing in strength by the time of the French attack on Algiers. The pasha had lost prestige as the European consuls had increased their influence, and in August 1830 a French admiral forced him to sign a treaty with France, whereby he agreed to abstain from any activity hostile to the French in Algeria and to suppress piracy. The loss of the pirate trade led to a financial crisis, and the pasha was forced to seize property and to debase the currency. His debts mounted and when, in 1832, a British squadron came to Tripoli and tried to compel him to settle his accounts with British traders, he was obliged to try and levy taxes on those tribes which had enjoyed exemption. The result was widespread rebellions, both in the Fezzan district in the south (which had been conquered in 1811), and in the coastal region, which led to Yūsuf Qarāmānlī's abdication in 1832. But two rival pashas were proclaimed, the one the son and the other the nephew of Yūsuf, the one recognized by the French consul, the other by the British. The issue was only resolved in 1835, when the Turks intervened and established direct rule, via various administrative centres, in Tripolitania and Cyrenaica. Their interest in the trans-Saharan trade caused them to come into rivalry with the French as they expanded southwards (the French reached Touggourt from Algeria in 1854), whilst in Cyrenaica political and social life came to be dominated by the order of the Sanusiyya. The governor of Tripolitania from 1867 to 1870 was 'Alī Riḍā Pasha, who was active in trying to develop the resources of the area. However his decision to attract French settlers aroused British distrust, and the period from 1870 onwards opens in the shadow of European rivalry.

CHAPTER 4

THE NINETEENTH-CENTURY JIHADS IN WEST AFRICA

The history of West Africa in the nineteenth century is chequered with jihads – Islamic holy wars. While differing in place, timing and execution, all show religious and political similarities, and all brought about important changes in the societies in which they occurred. It is the purpose of this chapter to describe these jihads. But first it is necessary to describe the situation in the Islamic world at large at this time. For the West African jihads, while in some respects local movements, were, in other respects, associated with events and movements taking place across that wider world.

THE ISLAMIC WORLD IN THE EIGHTEENTH AND EARLY NINETEENTH CENTURIES

Islam is a religion and a way of life. It was also once a great world power. From the seventh century AD, Muslims embarked on a course of imperial expansion which extended over Persia, much of the Byzantine empire, reached eastward to the river Indus and westward into North Africa and southern Spain. Thus secured, Islam remained, throughout the Middle Ages, powerful and self-sufficient. It is true that by the end of the fifteenth century, the Muslims had lost Spain to the *Reconquista*. But they contained the main assault of Christendom – the Crusades – with ease and, confident within the circle of their vast territorial dominion, they were well content with the majesty of their intellectual and spiritual achievements. By the sixteenth century Islamic dynasties were ruling much of India, while in the west the Ottoman Turks were masters not only of the Middle East and North Africa, but also part of the Balkans. In 1529 they threatened Vienna. But this was the apogee of Islam's worldly greatness. For reasons which cannot be explained here, the power of the Turks then receded, and the lands of Islam passed more and more under European tutelage or direct control. Egypt fell to the Napoleonic conquest. In India the long reach of British imperial government constantly extended until, by 1897, it was possible for a British missionary to observe, complacently but truthfully, 'Our

Queen has, in fact, more Mohammedan subjects that has the Sultan of Turkey.'[1] Not only did non-Muslims dominate Muslims in the temporal sphere. In many parts of the Islamic world Christian missionaries were free to attack the Faith – though they made few inroads into it – with an impunity which owed something, at least, to the strength of Christian arms. At the same time, Islamic intellectual life, burdened with centuries of theological conservatism and the literary accretions amassed by the habit of derivative scholarship, lost much of its vigour and become imitative and formal.

This was a traumatic situation for Muslims of ardent spirit and active mind. Inevitably it produced a reaction. By 1872 W. G. Palgrave, in his notable *Essays on Eastern Questions* was describing 'The Mahometan Revival', the beginnings of which he discerned some hundred years earlier.

Among the dramatic manifestations of this revival was the well-known Wahhābī movement, an angry surge of Islamic fundamentalism that swept the slothful Turk out of Arabia and established its first, puritanical regime there from *c.* 1747 to 1812. It quickly spread to India, where its flames burned fiercely in the climate of Muslim resentment against British occupation, and caused the imperial government much anxiety, as Palgrave shows.

The Wahhābī movement had an electrifying effect on the Islamic world. Not all of that world accepted its rigorously fundamentalist doctrines. But few Muslim societies escaped the sting of the Wahhābīs' revolt against Islam's lethargy and its otiose way of life. In particular the Sufis – that is, the members of the Islamic mystic orders – reacted strongly. For the Wahhābīs bitterly attacked mysticism, with its tumid thaumaturgy, tomb-worship and ecstatic ritual, as being unsanctioned by the authority of the Koran and the precedents of the Prophet Muḥammad. This challenge provoked the Sufis into a defence of their cherished beliefs and practices. The result was a Sufi revival – part of the total upsurge of the times – which reached a climax during the second half of the eighteenth century in the mosque of al-Azhar in Cairo. It was the Khalwatiyya order of Sufis that initiated the movement and largely organized it. But it embraced many others, including the ancient Qādiriyya, which it spurred into renewed and militant activity. In the end, the revival led to the founding of a new, most vigorous order, the Tijāniyya, which spread rapidly across the western Islamic world, including the western Sudan.

[1] C. H. Robinson, *Mohammedanism: has it any future?* (London, 1897), 50.

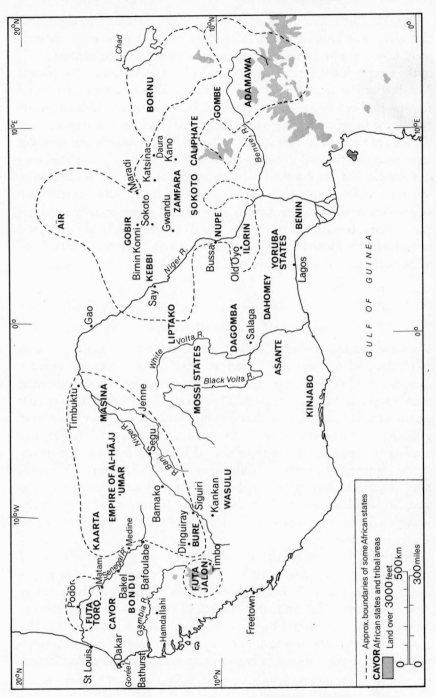

7 West Africa c. 1865. (Based on map 4 in J. D. Hargreaves, *Prelude to the partition of West Africa* (London, 1963))

But, like Christians in medieval times, many Muslims in the eighteenth and early nineteenth centuries looked beyond the powers of ordinary men, however pious or divinely inspired, 'to unravel the confusion . . . in the tangle of the times'[1] and awaited a God-sent messiah, the Islamic Mahdi. For the catastrophic events which had overturned their world seemed to them to portend the End of Time – a reasonable conclusion within the belief-system by which they lived – before which must come the Mahdi to preside over the millennium. Their actions and attitudes were thus conditioned not only by immediate political and social considerations, but also by their conviction that the divine consummation was nigh and that they had a duty to prepare for it. This belief, which was widespread throughout the Islamic world, was especially strong in West Africa. It is against this background of intellectual and ideological excitement, sharpened by millenarian expectancy, that the events about to be narrated should be understood.

EARLY ENDEAVOURS TOWARDS ISLAMIC REFORM IN THE WESTERN SUDAN

The first attempt to bring about Islamic reform, or more precisely revolution, in the western Sudan was that of the eleventh-century Almoravids (Arabic al-Murābiṭūn), whose movement is fully discussed in volumes 2 and 3 of this history. The subsequent course of Islam in the ancient empires of Ghana, Mali and Songhay can be followed in volume 3. Some scholars are inclined to trace an active and continuing tradition of Islamic reform from the Almoravids down to the jihads of the nineteenth century. Others regard the Almoravid movement as a single, dramatic event that had important repercussions at the time, but did little to influence the subsequent history of Islam in the Sudanic countries, except perhaps to leave behind a folk memory of reforming militancy.

More obviously influential as a determinant in shaping attitudes of mind among western Sudanese Muslims was the career of the fifteenth-century 'ālim, that is Muslim scholar, Abū 'Abdallāh Muḥammad b. 'Abd al-Karīm b. Muḥammad al-Maghīlī al-Tilimsānī (d. 1504). He was endowed with a powerful but orthodox mind and a ferocious conviction of his own righteousness. After a turbulent career in the Maghrib he removed to the Sudan. On the way he visited Aïr, Takedda, Katsina

---

[1] From an unpublished Hausa poem by Shehu Usuman dan Fodio. See M. Hiskett, 'Hausa Islamic verse: its sources and development prior to 1920', Ph.D. thesis (London, 1969), 453.

and Kano. In the last two cities he gave courses of instruction in Koranic studies and Islamic law. He then moved on to Gao, the capital of the Songhay sultan, al-Ḥājj Muḥammad Askīya. To the latter's questionnaire on matters of law al-Maghīlī replied with a series of *fatāwī* (*responsa*), some of which are preserved. These *fatāwī* offered a theoretical basis for Muḥammad Askīya's attempts to establish Islam as the state religion in Songhay. They remained available to legitimize the reforms of later generations of Muslims. Al-Maghīlī's presence farther south, in Hausaland, already faintly islamized by this time, led to the setting up of coteries of local Muslim scholars (Arabic *'ulamā'*, plural of *'ālim*). In the course of generations they multiplied and their literary endeavours gave rise to an indigenous Islamic literature in classical Arabic that kept the ideals of orthodox Islam alive in the hearts and minds of their fellow Muslims. Al-Maghīlī was also a member of the Qādiriyya order of Sufi mystics. His example inspired the devotion of succeeding generations of western Sudanese Muslims to the order, as their writings make clear.

Especially significant was al-Maghīlī's contribution to Islamic messianism. He believed himself to be the *mujaddid* of his time, the centurial 'Renewer of the Faith' and precursor of the Mahdi. He thereby established, or greatly helped to establish, those chiliastic expectations that later proved to be powerful adjuncts to Islamic reform and revolution in West Africa. His name will be mentioned again, on more than one occasion, as this chapter proceeds.

The Fulani are a people of Negro origin, who stem from the Halpular of the middle Senegal valley. At an early date, probably before the eleventh century AD, they came into contact with Berber pastoralists drifting southwards from the Sahara whose culture and occupation was similar to their own. Through inter-marriage they acquired a lighter skin colour than other more sedentary peoples living in the same area. Their language, which belongs to the West Atlantic group, is related to Wolof. They originally followed an African religion, which still survives among many of them. But at an unknown date before the fourteenth century, a number of them converted to Islam, as a result of North African influences, probably reaching them through the empire of Mali. Some of these converts, among them the Torodbe, often known by the Hausa form of their patronym, Toronkawa, abandoned their ancestral nomadism and became sedentary and clerical as a result of adopting Islam's literate culture.

According to their own traditions the Toronkawa began a long, slow migration out of Senegambia in the fifteenth century, which took them east towards Hausaland. Here groups settled, including the family of the Shehu Usuman dan Fodio (Arabic: Shaykh 'Uthmān b. Fūdī), an account of whose career will figure largely in this chapter. But other clerical Fulani remained behind in Senegambia, where they continued to live as small Muslim minorities among their pagan fellows. It was in Senegambia, among these Fulani, that jihad began in West Africa. The first occasion was *c.* 1680, when a certain *'ālim*, Mālik Si, came to Bondu, to the south of the pagan kingdom of Futa Toro. There he fought a holy war that resulted in the setting up of an Islamic state. He was followed in 1725 by Alfa Ba, who declared jihad against the pagan Fulani in Futa Jalon and founded the Muslim dynasty of the Almamys. This survived until the French occupation of Futa Jalon in the nineteenth century.

In 1776 'Abd al-Qādir, another Fulani Muslim, and his Tukolor followers, overthrew the Denianke dynasty in Futa Toro and set up an Islamic theocracy, based on the election of the *'ulamā'* to local councils. He then undertook further jihads against the population in the areas between the Senegal and Gambia rivers.

These early jihads clustered in the far north-west corner of the Sudan, more than a thousand miles away from the Hausa kingdom of Gobir, where the first major jihad of the nineteenth century in West Africa broke out. This jihad in Hausaland was, in certain obvious respects, the precursor of subsequent jihads described in this chapter. It occurred in social and political circumstances that were not necessarily duplicated in earlier and ethnically somewhat different societies. It would therefore be rash to assume a direct link between the early jihads in the Senegambia area and the major eruptions of the nineteenth century farther to the south-east. For instance, the writings of the nineteenth-century jihadists hardly support the notion that they were in any direct fashion inspired by events in seventeenth- and eighteenth-century Senegambia. Their attention focused with much greater interest on the fifteenth-century world of al-Maghīlī, on the distant ideal of Mecca and Medina, the holy places of Islam, and on literary rather than practical paradigms. All the same, these early adventures no doubt played a part in encouraging later movements of Islamic reform in the western Sudan, including that of the Shehu Usuman dan Fodio in Hausaland.

More profound, though cumulative over many generations, was the influence of some saintly Saharan clans, especially the Kunta of Timbuktu. This clan had been, at least since the fifteenth century, instrumental in the spread of Islamic literacy and Sufi mysticism in the Sahara. Shaykhs of the Kunta were luminaries of the Qādiriyya order. They were widely acclaimed as *walīs*, holy men possessed of miraculous powers. Their tombs were to be seen in the oases and along the caravan routes of the Sahara and the northern edge of the Sudan, places of pilgrimage for Saharan and Sudanese Muslims. The charismatic example of this clan must have done much, over generations, to formulate the attitudes and condition the minds of the Sudanese peoples who later became involved in the jihads. In particular, the pattern of religious exercises and visionary experience of the Kuntī shaykhs is reflected in that of the jihad leaders of the nineteenth century.

THE JIHAD IN HAUSALAND

Islam probably first appeared in Hausaland – one cannot be wholly certain because the sources are inconclusive – in the fourteenth century. It was brought from the kingdom of Mali by 'Wangarawa' traders, probably members of the Dyula community. But it did not become firmly established until the end of the fifteenth century, after al-Maghīlī had done his work. Even then, it was by no means generally accepted. It became the religion and way of life of small literate élites. It influenced the court circles only superficially. The mass of the people continued in their traditional polytheistic beliefs and were at first barely touched by this exotic monotheistic faith. Gradually Islamic mores and attitudes, if not full Islamic confession, became more pervasive however. This created a situation described, after an Arabic term, as 'mixed' Islam – that is, Islamic and indigenous African religious customs and practices existing eclectically together, sometimes with integration, at other times merely in parallel. This mixed Islam was characteristic of much of the western Sudan, including Hausaland, over the four centuries that preceded the jihads.

On the twenty-ninth of the Islamic month of Ṣafar, in AH 1168/15 December 1754, the Shehu Usuman dan Fodio, who was referred to above (his full Arabic name was 'Uthmān b. Muḥammad b. Muḥammad b. Ṣāliḥ), was born in Maratta, in the Hausa kingdom of Gobir, near present Sokoto. He came of a scholarly family, one of a larger community of Muslim Fulani, of which his father was the *imām* – that is, the religious and temporal leader. The community, in turn, belonged to the great Fulani clan of the Toronkawa which, as was explained in the preceding section, had begun to emigrate out of Senegambia towards

Hausaland in the fifteenth century. In the course of this migration some members of the clan, the *shehu*'s family among them, settled in Gobir. Here they lived as literate Muslim groups, in the midst of, but holding largely aloof from, the surrounding preliterate culture. They maintained close links with their nomadic, cattle-rearing kinfolk, the Alibawa, the Sullebawa and others, who also moved to and fro across Hausaland, but they no longer kept cattle, except a few favourite animals, which they retained for sentimental reasons. They devoted themselves mainly to the profession of Islamic education and scholarship. How they earned their living is not entirely clear, since they claimed to eschew the patronage of the Hausa courts, by which other Muslim literates in Hausaland lived. But their skill as scribes and teachers must have contributed something to their livelihood.

These scholarly Muslim Fulani were an intellectual élite, as, too, were similar groups of literate Berber Muslims with whom they were closely allied by marriage and common interests. By the end of the eighteenth century the situation in which they pursued their calling was particularly conducive to intellectual endeavour. For the locally composed writings in classical Arabic that are our sources for this period reveal a lively controversy in Hausaland, in which various groups of Muslims took up positions, from extreme rigorism to total quietism, towards the mixed Islam by which they were surrounded. Most rigorous of all were men like the early eighteenth-century Muḥammad al-Barnāwī, who roundly condemned all un-Islamic survivals and deviations from strict orthodoxy, and the Berber Shaykh Jibrīl b. 'Umar, who espoused the harsh doctrine that any sin – in which, of course, he included all non-Islamic practices – was equivalent to apostasy. It is said that he tried to start a jihad in Agades, but had no success, apparently because his doctrines were too extreme even for his own supporters.

At the other end of the scale were pacific Muslim literates who lived by the patronage of the Hausa courts – as scribes, counsellors, horoscopers, rain-makers and the like – and were thus prepared to countenance a broader compromise with African religion as the price of their comfortable, privileged status. As the 'Hausa Chronicle' succinctly puts it, 'At this time all the Hausa kings gave judgement arbitrarily, without laws; learned Mallams [Hausa *malam*, the equivalent of Arabic *'ālim*, a learned man] were attached to them, but they did what the kings ordered them.'[1] These quietists, some of whom probably combined

[1] In J. A. Burdon, *Northern Nigeria: historical notes on certain tribes and emirates* (London, 1909), 94.

trading interests with their literate functions, were opposed to any disturbance of the *status quo*, whether by peaceful means, or by jihad. Most were Hausa. But it seems that some, at least, were clerical Fulani, seduced away from the austere independence of their ethnic fellows. They were certainly not unlearned, however, and some of them appear to have been sincere Muslims who genuinely eschewed violence and believed in the possibility of *tajdīd*, peaceful reform.

The debate between these two groups, and others in between, was conducted through classical Arabic prose and verse – for Arabic was the legal and liturgical language of these scholars – and sometimes by verbal confrontation. It was constantly nourished by returned pilgrims, who intervened on the authority of famous shaykhs whom they had consulted in Mecca, Medina, Cairo and Fez, all centres of learning and of the contemporary ferment of ideas.

The young Shehu Usuman received a conventional Islamic education. He proved to be highly intelligent, pious and of scholarly bent. In the course of it he came under the influence of teachers who had become imbued with the spirit of Islamic reform described above. Such a one was an uncle, 'Uthmān Bindūrī. Another was Jibrīl b. 'Umar, whose iconoclastic teachings certainly impressed him, although he by no means accepted them, at least not during his early life. Later, when certain broken ideals of the jihad caused him bitterness and disappointment, he moved closer to Jibrīl's views. By 1774, when he began to take an active part in the theological argument, he and his associates emerged as moderates, rejecting the extremism of Shaykh Jibrīl but also condemning the total complacency of the quietists. The *shehu's* theology is discussed in some detail below. But it may be summed up at this point by stating that he and his party took their stand on the letter of the Mālikī rite, as interpreted by *ijmā'* – the consensus of the Muslim scholars. He has sometimes been portrayed by European commentators on his life and times as a fanatic, a Muslim zealot and so on, but this is a judgement that fails to take account of contemporary Islam. Measured within the cincture of his day, the true moderation of the *shehu's* views at this time – that is, before the jihad of 1804 – is apparent from a passage in an early work, *Ihyā al-sunna* (*Revivification of orthodoxy*), in which he stresses that the common people should not be subjected to excessive fault-finding, nor be expected to conform to standards of Islamic observance beyond their capacity to attain.

But his moderation in no way diminished his enthusiasm for reform. In early manhood he began to experience a sense of divine election which convinced him, as it had convinced al-Maghīlī three centuries earlier, that he was the *mujaddid* of his time and people – that is, the centurial 'Renewer of the Faith' whom God sends once in every hundred years, to reform Islam and prepare the way for the Mahdi. Moreover, the *shehu* and his followers believed that he was the last of the *mujaddids* and that the coming of the Mahdi was therefore very near indeed. In this he reflected, in the peculiar circumstances of late eighteenth-century Hausaland, and in an intensely personal manner, the widespread messianic expectations in the outside Islamic world referred to above, and he was certainly indebted to the example of al-Maghīlī.

About 1774, when he was twenty years old, he set out on his chosen career as an itinerant Muslim missionary, preaching up and down the Hausa kingdom of Gobir, and then the neighbouring kingdoms of Zamfara and Kebbi. His main purpose was to reform imperfect Muslims – that is, to combat the mixing of Islam with polytheism – but it seems he also made some efforts to bring about the conversion of outright pagans. He did not confine his activities to preaching, however. Probably anticipating an eventual confrontation with the king of Gobir, he set up certain alliances that had strategic and political as well as religious objectives, against a time when he might have to resort to physical instead of intellectual persuasion. There is no doubt that the clan organization, which linked the Toronkawa not only with their nomadic Fulani kinsfolk, but also with certain Berber Muslim clans, greatly assisted him in forging these alliances. It continued to aid him when he came to fight the jihad.

About 1780, fortified by the extent and depth of his support in Gobir, Kebbi and Zamfara, he approached Bawa Jangwarzo, the powerful but ageing king of Gobir. He demanded from him somewhat uncompromisingly that he conform more strictly to Islam. Bawa Jangwarzo was nominally a Muslim. But the society over which he ruled was typical of mixed Islam, and it is clear that his authority still depended largely upon his role as protector of the ancestral polytheistic cult. Thus he could not, even had he wished to do so, convert to full Islamic confession and constitutional orthodoxy with the completeness which the reforming *shehu* demanded. So he temporized and plotted to assassinate the *shehu*; then lost his nerve and conceded certain of his demands.

In 1789–90 Bawa Jangwarzo died. He was succeeded, briefly, by Yakubu and then, in 1794–5, by Nafata, who reigned until *c.* 1801. This was a period of ambiguous relations between the *shehu* and the Gobir establishment. Nafata was openly hostile, but the *shehu* seems, none-theless, to have been able to dabble in court affairs, particularly in a succession struggle, in a way that suggests the court was faction ridden and that he had the support of at least one of the factions. At any rate, he secured the appointment of Yunfa, a son of Nafata, to the throne of Gobir (1801–8). At first he was able to dominate him. But it became clear, even to Yunfa, that no permanent accommodation with the Muslim reformers was possible, except by an unacceptable sacrifice of traditional authority. The *shehu*, for his part, seems to have become increasingly persuaded of the futility of compromise with the tradi-tional rulers and more apt to consider the alternative of a forceful solution. A series of crises ensued, including, so Fulani sources allege, another unsuccessful attempt, this time by Yunfa, to assassinate the *shehu*. The final incident – the capture of a party of the *shehu*'s supporters by Yunfa's soldiers and their release in a counter-attack by their Muslim fellows – which precipitated armed conflict, was probably not intended by either side. But it was of a kind inevitable in the tense atmosphere then prevailing.

The *shehu*, adopting an established method of signalling withdrawal of allegiance from a Hausa ruler, emigrated to the farthest boundary of Yunfa's kingdom, and out of his jurisdiction. Here, in Gudu, he set up an embryonic Islamic state with himself as *imām*, or temporal and religious head. This was seen by Yunfa as rebellion. He at once dis-patched a punitive force against the Muslim rebels. The armed clash that resulted sparked off what now became the Fulani jihad in Hausa-land. This culminated in the setting-up of a Muslim empire ruled by the jihadists from their walled city of Sokoto.

THE IDEOLOGICAL, SOCIAL AND POLITICAL
BACKGROUND TO THE JIHAD

Before describing the campaigns of this jihad, it is appropriate to consider in more detail the motives and inspirations that persuaded the *shehu* to act as he did, as well as the circumstances that contributed to his success.

It has been seen that the millenarian excitements abroad in the Islamic world from the fifteenth century onward were reflected in the role of *mujaddid* which the *shehu* felt called upon to assume. But his inspiration was wider than these messianic expectations alone. From about 1789, when he was thirty-six years old, the *shehu* began to experience visions. There is no doubt that he believed sincerely in their divine origin. They clearly exerted an important influence on his behaviour. The visions, which were usually introduced by periods of fasting, lonely vigils and other ascetic exercises, form a sequence in which the full nature and implications of his divine election were made clear to him. Thus in a vision of 1789 he believed he was given the power to work miracles. In another, he was given a special *wird*, a Sufi litany, which enabled him to intercede with God on behalf of his followers. Later, he experienced visions in which the twelfth-century founder of the Qādiriyya, 'Abd al-Qādir al-Jīlānī, appeared and directed him as to his future course of action. In a climacteric vision, which occurred in 1794 and which vividly recalls the *mi'rāj* – the Prophet Muḥammad's ascension through the Seven Heavens until he finally arrived before the throne of God – he was presented before the heavenly company of Islamic luminaries who constitute the *silsila* or mystical genealogy of the Qādiriyya, including the Prophet Muḥammad himself. On this occasion 'Abd al-Qādir al-Jīlānī, commanded by Muḥammad, enturbaned him as '*imām* of the *walīs* [Muslim holy men]' and presented him with 'the Sword of Truth, to unsheath it against the enemies of God.'[1] After this profoundly exciting experience, the sources record that he composed the militant 'Qādirī Ode', which presaged jihad, and that he also 'began to incite [his followers] to arms, saying to them, "Verily to make ready weapons is *Sunna* [the orthodox way of Islam, based on the precedent of the Prophet]"'.[2] This took place in 1797, that is, some seven years before the outbreak of the jihad. Finally, in 1804, 'Abd al-Qādir al-Jīlānī again appeared and instructed him to proceed on the momentous *hijra* or emigration to Gudu mentioned above.

However one chooses to explain the psychological and emotional origins of such supernatural experiences, their symbolism, in the *shehu*'s case, seems clear. They reflect his strong sense of personal identification with the Qādiriyya, which he saw as the vehicle for reform in the Sudan, and an increasingly militant determination to promote this reform, if need be, by arms. The vision of 'the Sword of Truth' was a turning-point at which this determination received the sanction both of the Prophet himself and 'Abd al-Qādir al-Jīlānī.

This interpretation of the visions becomes more persuasive when one

[1] M. Hiskett, *The sword of truth* (New York, 1973), 66.

[2] *Tazyīn al-waraqāt* of '*Abdullāh b. Muḥammad*, translated with an introductory study of the author's life by M. Hiskett (Ibadan, 1963), 105.

learns that the *shehu*, his family and his followers were deeply involved in a Sufi network extending from Hausaland into the Sahara, North Africa, Egypt and, ultimately, Mecca and Medina. Their involvement included not only membership of the Qādiriyya but also links with other powerful orders such as the Shādhiliyya and the Khalwatiyya, mentioned above as the focus of the eighteenth-century Sufi revival at al-Azhar. From the list of Sufi personalities with whom the *shehu* and his associates are known to have had contacts, among them Shaykh al-Mukhtār of Timbuktu, a member of the Kunta clan, it is obvious that they must have been exposed to the ideological excitements that this revival aroused. Living in Hausaland, they were not, of course, directly affected either by European imperialism – although eddies of resentment at the Napoleonic occupation of Cairo may well have reached the western Sudan – or by the decline in Ottoman power, which were adduced above as being in part responsible for the general Islamic revival of the day. But this in no way precluded them from sharing enthusiasms which suffused the whole Islamic world, nor from reacting to them in ways which heightened their sense of involvement in the peculiar problems of the Sudan.

But the inspiration that the *shehu* and his small band of disciples drew from the Qādiriyya cannot explain the amount of popular support that they enjoyed, sufficient in the end to bring about the military conquest of Hausaland. For there is no reason to suppose that Qādirī enthusiasm also inspired the predial serfs and pastoral nomads who made up the jihad armies (for despite the tensions between opposing groups of agriculturalists and pastoralists described below, contingents from both fought side by side in the *shehu*'s forces). To explain their role in the victorious holy war one must seek local and more mundane causes.

Even though they were not influenced by specifically Qādirī fervour, these illiterate supporters of the *shehu* may well have shared in a more general kind of Islamic excitement. For the preaching of Islam was established in the western Sudan well before 1800, and an oral Islamic verse literature in the vernacular languages, Fulfulde and Hausa, existed before the jihad, although it had probably not, at that time, attained the status of a written literature. Its message of divine punishment and reward may have been persuasive for certain individuals who listened to the verse sermons of Muslim preachers. But more easily documented are certain social and political factors, the first a long-standing tension between peasants and nomads.

Right across the area that later became the empire of Sokoto, the pattern recurred of the nomadic Fulani clan leader and his followers enjoying the hospitality of a Hausa ruler in whose domains the clan had grazing concessions. Then the clan leader became resentful at restrictions which the Hausa king imposed upon the clansmen to protect his own indigenous subjects – limitations on the use of water sources, penalties for grazing across crops and the like. When the jihad broke out, the clan leader rose in sympathy with the *shehu* and fought his own 'holy war' against his Hausa host, ousted him and emerged as the local emir within what, in due course, became the Fulani empire. One documented example is that of Zabarma, in northern Kebbi. Here the emergence of a certain Abubakar Luduje as a victorious jihadist was preceded by much tension and bloodshed between his nomads and the Zabarma peasants over grazing rights. In Hadejia, which before the jihad was part of Bornu, a similar situation developed. After a history of squabbling between the dour Hadejia peasantry and the Hadejia Fulani, Sambo, a younger brother of the *ardo* (Fulfulde, clan leader), led a 'jihad' in the chiefdom and ousted the chief 'so that he might establish the whole *Sunna* and set up the truth'.[1]

Slavery, or more precisely the violent process of enslavement, was something else that caused discontent in Hausaland. It, too, was a factor giving rise to support for the jihadists, as the sources clearly show. The reformers were themselves slave owners and probably took part in slave raids. But they were scrupulous. They enslaved neither fellow Muslim nor their nomadic kin. Not so the Hausa. There is sufficient evidence that slave-raiding was an essential part of the Hausa economy and that Muslims as well as non-Muslims fell victims to it. Certainly the nomadic cattle Fulani frequently did. Since the enslaving of Muslims not of servile parentage is forbidden by the *Sharī'a*, Muslims may have turned to the reformers to uphold their rights under Islamic law. Non-Muslims may have been tempted to convert and join the reformers so as to gain protection.

There are good, but not conclusive, reasons for believing that slave-raiding in Hausaland became more prevalent during the eighteenth and early nineteenth centuries, because muskets became available in the area during that period. First, the possession of these weapons would have conferred superior fire-power on the privileged *sarakuna*, the courtiers and royals of the Hausa courts who possessed them, thus increasing the yield from raiding. Second, the possession of muskets by one Hausa ruler would be apt to set off an escalating rivalry in which all rulers

[1] An unpublished 'Chronicle of Hadejia', in M. Hiskett, Ph.D. thesis, 527.

would require more and more of the weapons. Since slaves were the main currency through which they were obtained, this, too, is likely to have intensified the whole enslaving process. This hypothesis serves to account for the fact that enslavement contributed to a 'peasants' revolt' in 1804, whereas, as far as is known, it had not done so over several preceding centuries.

Another factor which could have contributed towards disturbing the stability of Hausa society would be cowrie inflation caused by an influx of European-borne shells from the coastal trade area. But the evidence for this is far too slight to do more than draw attention to the possibility.

Also, the reformers accused the Hausa rulers of tyranny and corruption. This was to be expected. It is prudent, therefore, to bear in mind that what seemed corrupt and tyrannical to Muslim reformers, dedicated to the exotic *Shari'a*, may have been acceptable to those who understood the system and how to operate within it. Nevertheless, there is a ring of truth about many of the reformers' accusations. No doubt tyranny and corruption of a kind intolerable in any society did weigh in the scales that tipped in their favour.

Some have thought to see in the jihadists' success the consequence of a general decline in the power and authority of the Hausa states. The chronic factionalism of the courts has been predicated in support of this, for instance in Kebbi and Gobir. Such an interpretation is unconvincing however. For there is evidence that the free play of factional rivalry was an accepted method of establishing the succession in many Hausa kingdoms.[1] Thus it is risky to postulate decline on this ground alone, and there is but slender evidence elsewhere to uphold the theory that the Hausa dynasties were near to decrepitude at the end of the eighteenth century. On the contrary, Gobir, for one, seems to have been full of vigour, having swallowed most of Zamfara and part of Katsina on the eve of the jihad. The 'nationalism' which surged up in Kebbi after this chiefdom's partial defeat by the jihadists, belies the notion that it was moving towards dissolution. In Kano, perhaps, the Hausa dynasty was somewhat discredited. But overall there is little to support the view that the jihadists merely toppled worm-eaten structures. The better opinion is that they succeeded despite the strength of their opponents.

[1] Michael Crowder, *Revolt in Bussa* (London, 1973), gives a detailed account of the succession procedures in pre-colonial Borgu, which, although not a Hausa state, may provide a valid analogy.

THE CAMPAIGNS OF THE JIHAD

A detailed account of the campaigns which made up the jihad in Hausaland is not possible here. What follows is but a broad survey of strategy and tactics.

The Gobir forces were powerful, their commanders tenacious. The war which now ensued was protracted, the outcome often uncertain. All the same, it seems that the Muslim commanders, especially the *shehu*'s younger brother, 'Abdallāh b. Muḥammad, known in Hausa as Abdullahi dan Muhammadu, his second son Muhammadu Bello and Aliyu Jedo, a Fulani clan leader, understood the art of war better than their Hausa opponents – perhaps due to the fact that the first two at any rate were literates fully familiar with the extensive Islamic military literature in classical Arabic. Moreover, all three, especially Aliyu Jedo, may have taken part in slave-raiding and cattle razzias with their nomadic Fulani kin and Tuareg allies, and gained practical experience of warfare in the kind of country across which they now led the jihad. Abdullahi dan Muhammadu proved to be a master of surprise. And he understood the sensible military doctrine that to surmount a seemingly impassable natural obstacle is frequently less costly than to make a frontal attack against a prepared opponent. Muhammadu Bello emerged as an expert cavalry commander, especially skilled in co-ordinating the cavalry arm with the formidable Fulani archers. Of particular tactical elegance was the battle before Gwandu (1805), during which he used his cavalry to draw the Gobir cavalry into the volleys of his archers.

The *shehu* in person took little part in the fighting, but he directed the overall strategy. This consisted of securing the left flank by seizing Matankari and Birnin Konni; striking south-east from Gudu, in Gobir, to gain control of the neighbouring chiefdom of Kebbi; then establishing a base line along the valley of the Zamfara river and pivoting on Birnin Kebbi in the west and Kanoma in the east. Thus poised, the Muslims were assured of ample grazing and cereal crops, as essential to their armies as is petrol to a modern army, and went on to besiege and capture the walled towns of Kebbi, Gobir and Zamfara. This was not easy. They were at first poorly equipped, their councils sometimes uncertain and divided. They suffered several sharp reverses, particularly at the battle of Tsuntsua in 1804 and the battle of Alwassa in 1805. But in September 1808 Alkalawa, the capital city of Gobir, fell to a three-pronged attack. The way for this had been opened up by their success at Fafara (1806), a key battle which knocked both the Tuareg and the

Katsina allies of Gobir out of the war, and so secured the Muslims' eastern flank.

The fall of Alkalawa brought about the final collapse of Gobir. But it did not end the war. The jihad, at first a series of limited and largely defensive actions within Gobir, Kebbi and Zamfara, had by now burgeoned into an open war of conquest against the surrounding kingdoms of Kano, Zaria, Nupe and others, including the ancient Islamic kingdom of Bornu. These outlying campaigns, though inspired by the *shehu*, were conducted by clan leaders within the Fulani genealogical network. When successful, they became emirs, that is, military governors of the territories they had conquered, and thenceforth stood in feudatory relationship to the *shehu*. By 1812 a Fulani Muslim empire was in being, deliberately constructed, as far as possible, according to the received Islamic constitutional pattern. It was even styled a 'caliphate' (Arabic *khilāfa*), in conscious imitation of the classical Islamic polity. This caliphate consisted of a western half, ruled from Gwandu by Abdullahi dan Muhammadu, and an eastern half, ruled by Muhammadu Bello, of which the newly founded walled city of Sokoto became in due course the capital. In theory, the *shehu* presided over both halves, but in fact he devoted himself more and more to scholarship, and left the administration of the empire to his two lieutenants.

The empire's most northerly point of direct control was Birnin Konni. Beyond this it enjoyed an alliance with the friendly Tuareg Muslim kingdom of Aïr. It was still threatened, though never mortally, by the Hausa rump kingdoms of Maradi and Daura Zango and later Tsibiri, where representatives of the old dynasties still held out. Border warfare continued between Sokoto and these Hausa rump kingdoms for several generations. The south-eastern boundary remained open and was constantly pushed forward until finally stabilized by the British occupation early in the present century. By 1812 it had reached, approximately, the Benue river. The western edge of permanent control settled along the Niger river, although a tenuous authority may have extended to the west bank of the river. In 1817 a jihad was launched in Ilorin that led to the setting-up of a Fulani emirate in what had been a dependency of the old Yoruba kingdom of Oyo. The eastern border of the empire remained in dispute for many years and in 1812 it still ebbed and flowed just east of the emirate of Gombe.

In 1817 the *shehu* died. The Fulani caliphate passed to Muhammadu Bello. He became the consolidator and administrative architect of an empire won by his father's charismatic leadership.

RELATIONS BETWEEN THE JIHADISTS AND
AL-KANAMĪ OF BORNU

The kingdom of Bornu lies to the east of Hausaland. About 1812, when the shape of the new Fulani empire was established, the western boundary of Bornu marched with the eastern borders of the Fulani emirates of Hadejia, Katagum and Gombe. Its eastern boundary passed approximately through the centre of Lake Chad. It therefore belongs more to the central than to the western Sudan. Yet it was so closely associated with the jihad in Hausaland that some account of that association is appropriate, as part of the whole story of the jihad.

Before the jihad in Hausaland, southern Bornu comprised the kingdoms of Hadejia, Jama'are, Katagum and Misau and was governed by the Galadima, a senior Bornu official. Around 1805, the leaders of certain Fulani clans that had long been settled in these states revolted against their Bornu overlord. In this they were following the example of the jihadists in Hausaland. Mai Aḥmad, the ruler of Bornu at the time, believing the rebels to be acting in collusion with the jihadists in the Hausa kingdoms, protested to Shehu Usuman dan Fodio and demanded that he use his influence to restrain them. This produced no result and the Fulani in Bornu continued their successful rebellion. Although they suffered some initial defeats, by 1808 they had driven the *mai* out of his capital, Birnin Ngasargamu. Mai Aḥmad died shortly after this and his successor, Mai Dunama, called to his aid a certain Shaykh Muḥammad b. Amīn b. Muḥammad al-Kānamī, a Kanembu *'ālim* settled in Ngala, south of Lake Chad. Al-Kānamī took up arms on the *mai*'s behalf and in a series of campaigns scotched what had now become a thorough-going attempt by the Fulani to conquer Bornu, although he was unable to recapture the western provinces, which became emirates of the Sokoto empire. As a result of his campaigns al-Kānamī gained such material power and moral influence that he first rendered the *mai* subservient and later ousted his dynasty, that of the Saifawa, which had ruled Bornu for almost a thousand years. He then became the sole ruler of the empire, thus founding his own dynastic line.

Al-Kānamī was a devout Muslim. He was not a jihadist. He fought his campaigns to protect the territorial integrity of the Bornu empire and to preserve the Islamic *status quo* within it. There is no substantial evidence that, in imposing his own authority over Bornu, he was preoccupied with notions of reform. It is true that, sporadically, he tried to enforce conformity to orthodox Islam, sometimes with considerable severity. But this may have been simply a reaction to the criticisms levelled at him by the Sokoto jihadists. On the other hand, in the correspondence that he conducted with the jihadists in Sokoto, protesting, like Mai Aḥmad before him, at the Fulani aggression in Bornu, he demonstrated an easy-going attitude towards mixed Islam that contrasts strongly with the fierce iconoclasm of the Fulani reformers. He emerges from this correspondence as an Islamic empiricist, not an idealist. Nonetheless, he shared certain important attitudes and spiritual techniques with the reforming jihadists. First, he was rooted in Islamic literacy. In Ngala he was the centre of a group of '*ulamā*'. By his teaching and his reputation he set up a religious network among the Kanembu and the Shuwa Arabs of the Chad area. It was because he was known as a *walī*, a holy man with miraculous power, that Mai Dunama had turned to him in the first place. It was his standing as an intellectual and spiritual leader that enabled him to muster the force necessary to contain the Fulani rebels. Not only did the people of Bornu respond to his call: he also had the support of powerful Muslim groups from beyond the borders of the Bornu empire, especially from Murzuk. He had performed the great pilgrimage *c.* 1790 and this, too, contributed to his religious leadership. It seems that, in the course of his journey to and from Arabia, he took the opportunity to establish good relations with Muslim literates in Tripoli, Wadai and Bagirmi. These proved useful in due course. Finally, like Shehu Usuman dan Fodio and later West African jihadists, al-Kānamī was a visionary who claimed that his actions were directed by the Prophet Muḥammad during miraculous visitations. And, like Shehu Usuman, he was a member of the Qādiriyya, who from time to time invoked the aid of the founder, 'Abd al-Qādir al-Jīlānī.

The significance of Muḥammad b. Amīn b. Muḥammad al-Kānamī in the history of the nineteenth-century jihads in West Africa is this: his career demonstrates the importance of ideas as weapons in the struggle between Islamic revolutionaries and the defenders of the Islamic *status quo*, that is mixed Islam. The Hausa rulers were well-armed, tenacious opponents who fought hard and resourcefully against the jihadists. But they lacked political and ideological unity and their weapons were man's, not God's. Al-Kānamī led a united people and his panoply included many of the same ideas that fired the spirit of jihad. The Hausa kingdoms fell. Bornu survived. In part this was due to its political and territorial cohesion, which was not shaken even by a change of dynasty. But equally important was al-Kānamī's genius in turning potent ideas to his own ends.

THE THEOLOGY AND LAW OF THE FULANI REFORMERS

The reformers' theology is of more concern to specialists in Islamic studies than to the general reader. Nevertheless, some account of it is fitting in this chapter, if only to show how theology and politics were inseparable in the minds of the Muslim reformers of eighteenth- and nineteenth-century Hausaland, as for most Muslims at that time.

The *shehu* wrote many books in classical Arabic on theological matters, a few before but most after the successful conclusion of the jihad in Gobir, which took place in 1808, often in apology and justification for having resorted to that drastic measure. Their numerous and complex themes and arguments were drawn from the whole wide range of Islamic classical and post-classical theological literature. But he was particularly indebted to the fifteenth-century theologians Muḥammad b. 'Abd al-Karīm al-Maghīlī, already mentioned above as a forerunner of the nineteenth-century reform movement, and to Jalāl al-Dīn al-Suyūṭī, an Egyptian. Neither of these two scholars was an especially original thinker. Both recensed the orthodox theology of the Mālikī rite and discussed mysticism and Islamic messianism. It was by their emphases rather than by any intellectual innovations that the *shehu* and his fellow reformers were influenced.

Four main heads of argument stand out from the mass of theological detail with which the reformers', particularly the *shehu*'s, writings are concerned. The first relates to the *mujaddid* and the Mahdi, and how to recognize the signs of their coming. It is a complicated matter, involving an understanding of prophecies, genealogies and portents, as well as the close study of *ḥadīth* – that is, the traditions recording the sayings and acts of the Prophet Muḥammad. All of this was of more than just intellectual interest in the context of the reform movement because, as was explained above, messianic expectations and the *shehu*'s role as a *mujaddid* supplied much of the rationale for reform and jihad.

The second head concerns the nature of sin. To rigorists like Shaykh Jibrīl b. 'Umar, all sin was equivalent to apostasy. But more moderate minds, such as the *shehu*'s, shrank from this stark absolutism. They preferred to regard sin as a continuum ranging from mere venial disobedience to, in the last resort, apostasy. The problem which this argument posed was particularly acute in an environment of mixed

Islam, and yet more so in the context of jihad. For, while the question of whether a particular act of disobedience constitutes sin or not, is a matter for God to decide and, if necessary, requite in the hereafter, apostasy from Islam merits instant death. Thus it was vital to establish apostasy, as opposed to mere disobedience, in order to justify jihad against those who themselves claimed to be Muslims, as the Hausa frequently did. Conversely, as the *shehu* well understood, to shed Muslim blood unjustly imperilled a man's own salvation. It was also possible to argue that, under certain circumstances, the Hausa were Muslims, but rebels against the Islamic state. Thus war against them was just, but did not entail the ultimate penalty attaching to apostasy. This, of course, had to do with how captives were treated. So the argument went round and round, in search of legal justifications for what were, in the end, subjective decisions.

Associated with this problem of jihad was that of *hijra* or emigration out of 'the territory of unbelief'. The Prophet Muḥammad's *hijra* from Mecca to Medina, before he launched his jihad against the unbelievers of Mecca, was a precedent which Muslim activists were inclined to follow. The quietists, on the other hand, argued that the obligation had lapsed after the Prophet's *hijra* and that to remain within the territory of unbelief was in order, provided that the Muslim could practise his religion without hindrance. Understandably, this controversy took on more than a theoretical significance in a society where many Muslim literates enjoyed good livings from the patronage of the Hausa courts. The *shehu* composed an exhaustive work on the subject entitled *Bayān wujūb al-hijra 'alā al-'ibād* (*Explanation of the necessity of 'hijra' to the worshippers*), in which he examined all aspects of the problem and, as his title indicates, concluded that *hijra* was obligatory under the circumstances obtaining in Gobir in 1804. He appealed to many authorities for his arguments, but seems to have been especially indebted to the fifteenth-century North African jurist, al-Wansharīsī.

The third head concerns the role of the *'ulamā'*, particularly their prescriptive role and their responsibility for the cure of souls in the Muslim society of the western Sudan. In the environment of mixed Islam, semi-literates, who had a smattering of Arabic but no depth of understanding of the Islamic scriptures, enjoyed a heyday. Their contribution was not to strengthen orthodoxy, however, but to abet the process of mixing Islam and animism, against which the reformers had set their faces. Not only that. The true *'ulamā'* are a pillar of any orthodox Muslim society and an estate of the Islamic realm. No Islamic leadership can tolerate a rival to them and still hope to establish a power based on Islamic constitutionalism. Al-Maghīlī had protested against the activities of these fraudulent *'ulamā'* in fifteenth-century Songhay. The nineteenth-century reformers of Hausaland were equally concerned to expose similar impostors in their own day.

The fourth head concerns the conflict between personal interpretation and authoritative precedent. It involves such complex matters as the use and abuse of *'aql* (reason, intellect), the weight to be attached to *ijmā'* (the consensus of the learned), the place of *taqlīd* (passive acceptance in matters of faith), the limitations on *ta'wīl* (interpretation, especially of the Koran) and the like. Once again, the arguments raised by such considerations were far from simply academic. In mixed Islam there was a constant temptation to attempt to justify pre-Islamic survivals by stretching a point or appealing to a far-fetched interpretation or shaky authority. Indeed, it seems clear that this was the practice of the quietists among the *'ulamā'* of Hausaland, who were referred to earlier in this chapter, and perhaps too of the fraudulent scholars just mentioned. The reformers' position may be described as 'Ash'arite' (approximately equivalent, perhaps, to Thomist in Christian theology), after the tenth-century Islamic theologian, al-Ash'arī, whose authority they constantly invoked. They did not entirely reject *'aql* and *ijtihād* (personal interpretation), but they regarded both as strictly subordinate to *ijmā'* and were concerned lest excessive argumentation should prove divisive in the Muslim community. At the root of their concern is apparent a desire to knit together and stabilize that community in a form consonant with their own theological assumptions.

In Islam the law – comprising *fiqh*, the corpus of legal theory and the *Sharī'a*, the canon law – is inseparable from faith and religious observance. Thus the Shehu was a jurist as well as a theologian. He and his younger brother, Abdullahi dan Muhammadu, expounded in their writings the theoretical basis upon which the law and constitution of the Fulani state rested. The *shehu*'s second son, Muhammadu Bello, also contributed to this literature. But his main achievement was to give the constitution practical shape.

The Fulani jihadists have sometimes been described as fundamentalists. A cognate argument, which has recently been advanced, is that, whereas the Middle Eastern reformers of the nineteenth century were truly 'reformers' in that they sought 'to restore the basic principles of Islam in the light of the contemporary situation', the West African jihadists, including the Shehu Usuman, were revivalists rather than reformers in that they sought 'not to accommodate or adjust, but rather to rediscover and revive . . .'.[1] The distinction is helpful in drawing attention to certain characteristics of the West African jihads which differentiate them from modernist movements elsewhere in the Islamic world during the nineteenth century. It is also justified at a semantic level by reference to the term *mujaddid*, 'renewer', which the *shehu* adopted as a title. But the dichotomy it proposes is perhaps too simple to be wholly acceptable. For it seems to ignore both the reality of the situation with which the *shehu* was trying to grapple, and also where the roots of his thinking really lay. In the first place, Islam in the Sudan had always been mixed. Thus in the local context there could be no question of rediscovering or reviving a state of lapsed perfection (the suggestion, which has sometimes been made, that he, like other West African jihadists, was harking back to a 'Golden Age' of Songhay Islam is not convincing; Askīya Muḥammad, although he occasionally receives commendation in the Fulani Arabic sources, does not emerge as one of the *shehu*'s heroes). To what extent, then, was the *shehu* a fundamentalist and a revivalist, attempting to recreate in the Sudan the Islamic ideal of a distant Arabian past?

It is true that he constantly appealed to a patriarchal model and that his constitutional terminology reflects this. But the appeal had more to do with sentiment than reality. For when one traces his ideas back to their sources, it becomes clear that they sprang from the exuberant thought-world of al-Maghīlī and al-Suyūṭī, representatives, respectively, of fifteenth-century Maghribian and Cairene civilization, not from the stark simplicity of barely literate patriarchs in the utterly different intellectual and physical milieu of seventh-century Arabia. It was a thought-world swollen with legalism of a complexity of which the early fathers can have had no concept. At the same time it was vibrant with messianic longings and gnostic techniques for mystic understanding that left their simple, bare-bones theology far behind. But the intricate pattern of the *shehu*'s mind was not only indebted to the teeming abundance of fifteenth-century thought. It was also nourished from the equally prolific harvest of the eighteenth-century al-Azhar, the focus of a new, intense phase of Islamic fervency.

The truth is, the Shehu Usuman dan Fodio was an idealist, essentially the product of the era in which he lived, not of a remote past. He strove through all means open to him – by the persuasions of an ardent

[1] John Ralph Willis, '*Jihād Fī Sabīl Allāh* – its doctrinal basis in Islam and some aspects of its evolution in nineteenth-century West Africa', *Journal of African History*, 1967, **8**, 3, 44.

preacher, by the symmetry of legal argument and by the ruses and stratagems of war – to make real the projections of his visionary mind. When it suited his purpose he appealed to the past. Otherwise, he made use of the proximate ideas and sentiments of his day. None of the terms 'fundamentalist', 'revivalist' or 'reformer', although, for convenience, the last has been used throughout this chapter, is wholly adequate to sum up a man of so many parts and the works he wrought.

Much interesting discussion has revolved round the question, Was the Shehu Usuman a social reformer? Of course many of the objectives of his movement can be accepted as what moderns would call 'social' reform – judicial and administrative honesty, the rule of law, female education and so on. In particular, he often preached against the un-canonical taxation imposed by the Hausa rulers, and demanded the imposition of only those forms of taxation allowed by the *Sharī'a*. Much has been made of this by those who see him as a social reformer. But to argue thus may be to misunderstand his motives. In the first place, it is by no means certain that Hausa 'uncanonical' taxation bore more harshly on the people than the canonical taxation of the *Sharī'a*. Indeed, to judge from the reports of Heinrich Barth and the other West African travellers who visited areas where traditional forms of taxation survived even after the jihad, these were often surprisingly mild. Canonical taxation may sometimes have been more severe. But what is more important is the reasoning that lay behind the *shehu*'s preaching. It seems clear that his objection to such taxes as *jangali*, the cattle tax on nomads, *kurdin gari*, a tax levied on townspeople, *kurdin salla*, a tax levied at the time of the Salla festivals and so on, was that they were uncanonical and thus contrary to the will of Allāh, not that they were socially unjust. In general, it needs to be remembered that the *shehu* lived in a society very different from those modern ones in which the notion of social reform arises out of a particular course of social and political development not duplicated in other societies and cultures. For instance, his cosmology was still the beautiful, symmetrical archi-tecture of the medieval imagination, and with it was associated a particu-lar view of man's life on earth, and of human society, which saw little point in striving for material improvements. For him and his fellows the world of time was but a painted harlot and the end of all human endeavour was to attain the eternal perfections of Paradise. If one accepts the view of J. Huizinga,[1] then to speak of 'social' reform in the

[1] *The waning of the Middle Ages* (Harmondsworth, 1968), 36 and *passim*.

context of such a belief system seems far-fetched. But if one wishes to argue that the social nature of reform is always basic and that it is merely the way it is presented that varies according to the age and society, then, no doubt, it is possible to think of the *shehu* as a social reformer.

THE RESULTS OF THE FULANI REFORM MOVEMENT IN HAUSALAND

Another of the interesting problems which the reform movement in Hausaland bequeathed to present-day scholarship is to decide to what extent the reformers succeeded in their aims. Did they, as they intended, establish the basic Islamic institutions and change Hausa society significantly to conform to them? Or did they leave that society much as they found it, as some scholars have argued?[1] The answer to this question is somewhat subjective and is also a matter of emphasis as much as fact. The present author's view is that they did succeed, not wholly, of course – what human endeavour ever does? – but in several important respects.

Polytheism was not entirely extinguished by the jihad. For military conquest can seldom, of itself, force men to abandon their beliefs and customs. But what it can do is set up the institutions that, given time, will persuade them or coerce them into doing so. This the jihad did. It set up a unified Islamic feudality where previously there had been a mere collection of particularist and warring chiefdoms. It introduced the full *Sharī'a* where there had been, as far as is known, only unwritten customary law decked out with whatever Islamic decorations the Hausa chiefs found it convenient to adopt from the rag-bags of their subservient *'ulamā'*. Neither the constitution nor the law were perfect replicas of the Islamic ideal envisaged by the *shehu*. But in time both moulded the society into a more orthodox Islamic way of life than existed under the Hausa chiefs. Especially is this true of the cities and larger villages. But in the countryside the old pre-Islamic, African ways survived – and still do – although it would be rash to under-estimate the strength of sentiments of Islamic identity even among the Hausa peasantry.

Also important in influencing Hausa attitudes was the vernacular written literature which the reform movement may have created and

[1] See for instance M. G. Smith, 'Historical and cultural conditions of political corruption among the Hausa', *Comparative Studies in Society and History*, 1964, **6**, 2.

which it certainly established as a permanent institution. The reformers employed the device of circulating written manuscripts of religious verse in both Arabic and the vernaculars, Fulfulde and Hausa, as part of the propaganda of their movement. The practice of committing this vernacular religious verse to writing, in *ajami*, a modified form of the Arabic script, then became implanted in the society in the post-jihad period. Thus there quickly grew up a theological, legal, devotional and astrological literature, as well as a form of verse-chronicling, in the two main vernaculars, especially Hausa. This was accessible, through public recitation, to the vernacular-speaking population, even if non-literate, in a way that the earlier, esoteric Arabic literature of Islam had never been. The impact of this literature is to be recognized in the widespread acceptance among the Hausa of Islamic notions of life, death and the hereafter, of Islamic time-keeping and the Islamic calendar; also their addiction to Islamic horoscopy, geomancy and the way in which Islamic djinns have largely taken over the roles of the ancestral spirits of the indigenous *bori* cult.

One crucial test of a Muslim society is how its members think politically. There can be little doubt that the Islamic caliphate, with its centre at Sokoto and its surrounding feudatory states, became the accepted polity of Hausaland. It survived in the Native Authorities of colonial northern Nigeria and was still reflected in northern Nigerian political attitudes from 1950 onward, during the era of the rise of modern political parties in Nigeria, as Hausa political verse of that period clearly shows. This polity was the creation of the reformers.

Sufism certainly existed in Hausaland before the reform movement. But there is no reason to think it was more than the confession of a Muslim minority. After the jihad it became, in the form of the Qādiriyya and the Tijāniyya orders, a feature of Hausa life. Some Tijānī votaries claim that their order made its first appearance in Hausaland during the *shehu*'s lifetime, and that he approved of its teachings. This is not impossible although it remains unproven. But it was certainly well established there by *c.* 1850, and there is evidence that its doctrines were being preached in Zaria during the reign of Abdul Karimi (1834–46).[1] Both orders play very important roles at the present day, religiously and politically. Both claim the *shehu* as one of their immediate founders in Hausaland and owe their expansion largely to the climate of Islamic fervency engendered by the reform movement.

[1] See M. Hiskett, Ph.D. thesis, 292.

For all these reasons it is the present writer's conclusion that the *shehu*'s reform movement resulted in a decisive change of direction that swung Hausa society, firmly and explicitly, into the orbit of the Islamic world, where previously it had hovered uncertainly on the fringe.

The jihads about to be described have been less thoroughly studied than that of the Shehu Usuman dan Fodio, partly, at any rate, because they gave rise to less literature which can be used as source material. In some cases even such basic matters as chronology are uncertain, and the small core of definitive knowledge which scholars possess has to be filled out by recourse to information which is still the subject of research. The task of this section is to state what is known with reasonable certainty and to describe the more important opinions and theories which scholars have advanced, without engaging in controversy, except marginally.

THE JIHAD OF AḤMAD B. MUḤAMMAD B. ABI BAKR B. SAʿĪD IN MASINA

The study of this man's career is complicated by the multiplicity of names under which he appears. Among the more common are Ahmadu Lobbo, Shehu or Seku Ahmadu, Hamad Bari and Ahmadu Hammadi Bubu. Frequently, Amadu does service for Aḥmad or Ahmadu. The confusion is further confounded by the fact that his son, Aḥmad b. Aḥmad, is also often referred to as Seku or Shehu Ahmadu, and so too is the well-known Sultan Aḥmad b. ʿUmar of Segu, the son of al-Ḥājj ʿUmar b. Saʿīd, whose jihad is described below. These variants of the Masina jihadist's name are basically naturalized African versions of the classical Arabic Aḥmad or Shaykh Aḥmad, to which clan patronyms have been added. The full classical Arabic form of the name is almost certainly that given in the heading of this section. He will, therefore, be referred to throughout this chapter as Aḥmad b. Muḥammad.

Aḥmad b. Muḥammad was a Fulani *ʿālim* who was associated with the Shehu Usuman dan Fodio. He is reputed to have studied under him. Whether he actually fought in the *shehu*'s jihad, as is sometimes claimed, is uncertain. But it is clear that the Fulani reform movement was in part seminal to the jihad upon which he embarked.

In 1810 – or some say as late as 1818,[1] the chronology is uncertain –

[1] W. A. Brown, 'The caliphate of Hamdullahi ca 1818–1864: a study in African history and tradition', Ph.D. thesis (Wisconsin, 1969), considers that the military phase of Aḥmad b. Muḥammad's movement commenced in this year.

he raised a jihad against the Fulani *ardo'en*, the traditional and faintly Muslim chiefs in Masina, whom he accused of idolatry. Certainly they were tributary to the pagan Bambara of Segu, and the society over which they presided was typically one of mixed Islam. The jihad quickly extended to include the Bambara among its targets, also the Bozo and other pagan or partially islamized groups in the area. It eventuated in the establishment of a large empire ruled from Hamdallahi, which Ahmad b. Muhammad founded as his capital city. He died in 1844 and was succeeded by his son and grandson (both also called Ahmad), who ruled until the empire was overthrown by al-Hājj 'Umar b. Sa'īd in 1862.

A number of factors contributed to the ideological excitement and political and ethnic discontent which Ahmad b. Muhammad was able to exploit in order to get his jihad under way. As in Hausaland, so in the area of the Niger bend, formerly nomadic Fulani had become settled, forming literate Muslim enclaves in the midst of surrounding paganism. Unlike the Fulani *ardo'en* of Masina and the rather supine *'ulamā'* of Jenne, both of whom had come to terms with the pagan Bambara, many of these literate Muslim Fulani were enthusiasts for Islamic re-form and intolerant of the compromise in the midst of which they lived. It seems certain that their attitude had some of its roots in the same ideological debate that was described as taking place in Hausaland during the late eighteenth and early nineteenth centuries, although this is less well documented than in the Hausa case. But it is supported by the fact that Ahmad b. Muhammad, himself a Qādirī, at first enjoyed the support of the Qādirī Kuntī shaykhs of Timbuktu whose leader, Ahmad Bakkā'ī, was a prominent spokesman for Islamic reform, and also of course by the fact that he was a pupil of the Shehu Usuman dan Fodio. He must, therefore, have been exposed to many of the ideolo-gical pressures that influenced his master.

One authority sees Ahmad b. Muhammad's jihad as arising out of the tension between, on the one hand, the established *'ulamā'* of Timbuktu and Jenne, who tolerated the mixed situation, and, on the other hand, Sufi activists, who did not.[1] If this is so, it is certainly likely that their inspiration sprang from the same general Sufi revival, stemming from al-Azhar, that made such an important impact on the reformers of Hausaland.

Another factor that may have helped Ahmad b. Muhammad to gain support was the decline of the *arma* – the mulatto descendants of the

[1] John R. Willis, Review of Jamil M. Abun-Nasr, *The Tijaniyya, a Sufi order in the modern world*, in *Research Bulletin of the Centre of Arabic Documentation*, 1965, **2**, 1, 45.

Moroccan alcaids of Timbuktu. This encouraged both the Muslim *'ulamā'* and certain Fulani clan leaders to hope to reassert their own power, lost at the time of the Moroccan conquest. The jihad offered a way to achieve this. In Masina itself some of his support came from Tukolor and Fulani, who saw in the jihad a means of achieving independence from Bambara overlordship, exercised from Segu; from escaped slaves of the Bambara; and from other persons and groups of inferior status in Bambara society.

Not all the support which Aḥmad b. Muḥammad at first enjoyed was constant however. Both the Qādirī Kuntī establishment of Timbuktu and the Sokoto establishment, also Qādirī, who had at first been well disposed toward him, later turned against him. This was in part due to the extreme rigour of his theology. But it was also because, having set up his theocracy in Masina, he treated both with contumely, criticizing their theology, questioning their legal rulings and withholding the deference which their seniority in the Qādiriyya led them to expect. Indeed, he is reputed to have claimed the rank of *amīr al-mu'minīn*, Commander of the Faithful, in the Sudan, thus challenging the Sokoto right to this title. Another factor which probably antagonized the Kuntī shaykhs of Timbuktu and also the *'ulamā'* of Jenne, who had at first supported him, was that his jihad had a disastrous effect on the trade of that essentially commercial city. For both these parties, despite their religious profession, were active and prosperous traders. Finally, there was by Aḥmad b. Muḥammad's day a considerable Tijānī presence in Masina. This gave rise to a faction which was opposed to his militant Qadirism.

But despite this opposition, Aḥmad b. Muḥammad succeeded in building an Islamic theocracy based on Hamdallahi, which extended over Masina, and claimed some authority over Segu, Timbuktu and its surrounding Tuareg and Songhay principalities, and Kaarta. This theocracy, which eschewed the more elaborate Islamic constitutional titles and was styled simply *dina*, from Arabic *dīn*, 'religion', was characterized by constitutional simplicity and strict adherence to the letter of the *Sharī'a*, as interpreted by the Mālikī school of law. Aḥmad b. Muḥammad ruled through a grand council of forty elders, over provincial governors who were related to him by kin and clientship. This suggests that, like the Fulani reformers in Hausaland, much of his support was drawn from among fellow members of the Fulani genealogical tree and perhaps also from the Qādirī hierarchy. These governors, in their turn, supervised a network of *'ulamā'* and notables who exercised local authority. A particularly important part was played by provincial *qāḍīs*, the Muslim administrators of the *Sharī'a*. Thus, as in the Sokoto empire, but in a more direct fashion, the company of Muslim literates was elevated to the status of an estate of the realm. A number of Western scholars have remarked on the strict legal construction of the Masina constitution. One authority regards it 'as near the ideal nomocratic state as is likely to be achieved'.[1] It has been contrasted with the catholicity and intricacy of the Sokoto caliphate. There is no doubt that Aḥmad b. Muḥammad's constitutional rigorism reflected his religious preferences. Nevertheless, it also owed something to circumstances. In Hausaland the jihadists took over a number of ancient Hausa kingdoms that must have been politically advanced long before Islamic constitutional ideas became assertive in the area. It was not practical for the reformers to sweep these structures entirely away and replace them with the perfect Islamic constitutional model, although they tried their best to do so. Aḥmad b. Muḥammad, on the other hand, inherited in Masina a well defined territorial entity, the government of which seems to have been much less convoluted than those of the Hausa kingdoms. Thus his task was easier and he perhaps made a virtue of necessity.

Attention was drawn above to the Sufi ideology which informed both the reformers of Hausaland and Aḥmad b. Muḥammad. There is another religious similarity between them which strengthens the presumption that both drew their inspiration from common and wider Islamic sources. Like Usuman dan Fodio, Aḥmad b. Muḥammad claimed to be the *mujaddid*, the centurial precursor of the Mahdi. It is generally accepted that he did not lay claim to being the Mahdi, but at least one authority believes he proclaimed himself the prophet's successor and the twelfth *imām* after him and sent letters to the sultan of Morocco, to the Shehu Usuman dan Fodio and to 'the four corners of the earth', demanding that every Muslim swear *bay'a*, allegiance, to him in recognition of this claim.[2] If this is true, it is almost as pretentious as a claim to the mahdiship. It certainly indicates that Aḥmad b. Muḥammad, in common with other West African jihadists before and after him, was affected by the climate of messianic expectancy prevalent in the Islamic world of the eighteenth and nineteenth centuries, and

[1] J. Spencer Trimingham, *The influence of Islam upon Africa* (Beirut, 1968), 16.

[2] John R. Willis, 'The nineteenth-century revivalist movement in the western Sudan: literary themes, sources, and influences'. Unpublished paper presented at the School of Oriental and African Studies Seminar on 'Islamic influences on the literary cultures of Africa' (March, 1968), p. 22.

was apt to exploit it. So, while his movement owed its immediate origin to a confluence of local causes, a number of important aspects of it fit into the broader pattern which encompasses the jihad of Shehu Usuman dan Fodio before him, and that of al-Ḥājj ʿUmar b. Saʿīd, who followed him.

THE JIHAD OF AL-ḤĀJJ ʿUMAR B. SAʿĪD B. ʿUTHMĀN AL-FŪTĪ AL-TIJĀNĪ

The jihad of al-Ḥājj ʿUmar b. Saʿīd, sometimes known as al-Ḥājj ʿUmar Tal, differs from those of the Shehu Usuman dan Fodio and Aḥmad b. Muḥammad in one important respect. It took place during the full tide of French colonial penetration into West Africa. In consequence, it has often been presented as a movement of African resistance against European colonialism. Such an interpretation, although not entirely invalid, is too simple, as this section will seek to show.

Al-Ḥājj ʿUmar b. Saʿīd was born in Futa Toro about 1794. He spent many years in Mecca and Medina, where he was appointed *khalīfa*, vicar, of the Tijāniyya order in the Sudan by a certain Muḥammad al-Ghālī. He then returned to the Sudan via Egypt and in or about 1848 founded an Islamic theocracy in Dinguiray. From here, with Tukolor support, he launched a jihad against the pagan Bambara in 1852 or 1853. By 1862 he had destroyed Masina, taken Hamdallahi and set up a substantial empire, at the same time clashing with the French who were advancing into the Sudanese interior from Senegal.

THE PILGRIMAGE OF AL-ḤĀJJ ʿUMAR

Pilgrimage was important for several West African jihadists. The Shehu Usuman dan Fodio was never able, for family reasons, to perform the great pilgrimage to the Hejaz, in Arabia, although he is said to have performed a lesser pilgrimage to Agades, in the Sahara, to visit the tombs of certain *walīs*, or holy men, enshrined there. But his inability to perform the great pilgrimage seems only to have intensified its significance for him. He composed a number of poems, some in classical Arabic and some in Fulfulde, in which he describes it in passionate and imaginative language that shows how it had become for him a visionary ideal equivalent to an actual, physical meeting with the Prophet Muḥammad. This poetry makes it clear that he contrasted an ideal of Islam, as he fervently pictured it unfolding before the pilgrim to the holy places, with the reality in the Hausa kingdoms. Also important for him in forming this ideal picture were the accounts that he received from returned pilgrims such as, for instance, his teacher Jibrīl b. 'Umar. Another jihadist, al-Ḥājj Maḥmūd, who led a minor jihad in the area of the bend of the upper Volta *c.* 1850, is also believed by his countrymen to have performed the great pilgrimage and to have vowed to fight for Islam in the course of it.

Al-Ḥājj 'Umar did perform the pilgrimage to the Hejaz and this was a formative event in his life. He, too, contrasted an Islamic ideal, which for him was amply confirmed by what he saw and heard around him in Mecca and Medina, with the disenchanting reality of mixed Islam in the western Sudan. The experience was seminal in arousing his reforming zeal. All the same, his attachment to the recently founded Tijāniyya order, into which he was initiated in the Sudan by his teacher 'Abd al-Karīm b. Aḥmad al-Naqīl, was strong even before he left for the Hejaz. It was in the company of this teacher that he first decided to go on pilgrimage and it is clear from his own account of this period of his life in his well-known work *Rimāḥ ḥizb al-raḥīm 'alā nuḥūr ḥizb al-rajīm* (*The lance of the party of the Compassionate [God] at the throats of the satanic party*) that he was filled with religious excitement long before his departure.

When he reached the Hejaz, he tells how

I heard that my lord Muḥammad al-Ghālī was in Mecca the Honoured, devoting himself to the service of God, and I was overjoyed at that. I asked God Most High to give me the benefit of meeting him. In the purity of His grace God answered my prayer and brought us together in Mecca the Honoured, after afternoon prayer, in the Place of Abraham. We discussed together for a while and he was greatly pleased with me and honoured me when he perceived my sincerity.[1]

He then entered Muḥammad al-Ghālī's household and studied under him for three years. At the end of this period Muḥammad al-Ghālī, acting on instructions allegedly given him by the founder of the Tijāniyya, Aḥmad al-Tijānī, who appeared to him in a vision, gave to al-Ḥājj 'Umar an *ijāza* – a licence – appointing him vicar of the Tijāniyya in the Sudan. This occurred in September 1822. Al-Ḥājj 'Umar then left the Hejaz and travelled to Egypt, possibly via Syria. In Egypt he spent some time in the al-Azhar, where he formed important connections with a number of Sufi shaykhs active at that time. From

[1] *Rimāḥ* (Cairo, n.d.), 181. There is some doubt concerning the chronology of this early period of al-Ḥājj 'Umar's life. I have followed the dating given in B. G. Martin, 'Notes sur l'origine de la Ṭarīqa des Tiğāniyya', *Revue des études islamiques*, 1969, **37**, 2, 281f, but according to a different tradition he did not leave Senegal till 1825.

Egypt he returned to the Sudan, probably by way of North Africa, and then travelled to Bornu. There he quarrelled with Shaykh al-Kanamī over his attempt to introduce the Tijāniyya into this strongly Qādirī area. From Bornu he moved on to Sokoto, where he was present during the year 1826. He left Sokoto in 1837, having married a daughter of Sultan Muhammadu Bello. In 1838 he passed through Masina and Segu, but received a hostile reception and moved on to Futa Toro. Here he met with opposition from the local *ʿulamāʾ*, and went off to Dinguiray, close to the borders of Futa Jalon. By 1848 he had set up his theocracy in Dinguiray and compelled the submission of neighbouring chiefs. The next stage in his turbulent career was full-scale jihad.

Unlike his two predecessors, Shehu Usuman dan Fodio and Aḥmad b. Muḥammad, al-Ḥājj ʿUmar b. Saʿīd travelled extensively in the outside Islamic world before he became a jihadist. He also travelled widely within West Africa, visiting all the main centres of religious education along his way. These experiences were not only educative: his travels outside West Africa must have impressed him with the strength and solidarity of Muslim society in such metropolitan centres of Islam as Mecca and Cairo, and underlined for him the inadequacy of mixed Islam in his homeland. At the same time, he was exposed to all the ideological and intellectual currents which were sweeping across Islam in his day. Their impact is clearly reflected in the pattern of his subsequent career, for he showed himself to be receptive to several new and radical ideas and introduced them into the Sudan, as will be explained when his theology is discussed below. As for his West African journeys, they must surely have served to drive home the lesson that reform and jihad had already succeeded here and there in the Sudan. Why then should they not succeed for him? But perhaps the most significant fact about his travels is this. They made of him a Muslim ideologue, through and through. It is to this that one should look to understand what happened next.

THE JIHAD OF AL-ḤĀJJ ʿUMAR

Al-Ḥājj ʿUmar b. Saʿīd fought his jihad on two fronts: against his African enemies, both pagan and Muslim, and against the French. The campaigns have been described in detail elsewhere.[1] Only the broad outlines will be given here.

[1] For instance in A. S. Kanya-Forstner, 'Mali-Tukulor', in Michael Crowder, ed., *West African resistance* (London, 1971). I am largely indebted to Dr Kanya-Forstner's study for the summary of the campaigns which follows.

Following an established pattern for jihad, the jihadist first performed his *hijra*, emigration, out of the territory of unbelief, in this case Futa Toro, to Dinguiray, where he set up an armed camp. He now demonstrated that he possessed not only religious charisma but also powers of leadership of a more worldly kind. For he created an army that, within the limits of his resources, was well trained, well officered and well organized. Clearly, too, he possessed some skill in the business of soldiering.

The army consisted of the *talibes* (Arabic *ṭālib*, student, disciple), his original followers who had emigrated with him out of Futa Toro. They made up an élite corps of mounted shock troops. Converted polytheists, *sofas*, and conscripted levies formed the infantry *corps de bataille*, while Fulani irregulars were used as auxiliary cavalry. The permanent force probably consisted of about 12,000 men. But in certain battles al-Ḥājj 'Umar was able to field as many as 15,000 and even 30,000. The regular troops were armed with a variety of weapons: muskets, rifles purchased from coastal traders or captured from the French, and traditional arms. They are said to have been supported by a corps of gunsmiths who maintained the firearms and manufactured ammunition. No doubt this corps could service flintlock muskets and supply locally made ball and powder. One wonders, however, how well they were able to cope with the miscellany of European rifles which the army also apparently possessed. It is difficult to believe that al-Ḥājj 'Umar's gunsmiths, without access to the proper workshop facilities required to repair precision weapons and to manufacture cartridge ammunition, can really have kept such weapons in service for any length of time.

In 1853 al-Ḥājj 'Umar declared holy war against all infidels in the Sudan. By 1854 he was in control of many of the Bambara and Malinke states in the upper Niger and Senegal basins. He then went on to conquer Kaarta. By 1862 he had destroyed the empire of Masina and occupied Hamdallahi. His conquests now formed a great wedge of territory, stretching from the lower Senegal in the west to Timbuktu in the east; from Guémou in the north to Dinguiray in the south. But in 1863 a substantial body of his non-Tukolor subjects rose in revolt against him and besieged him in Hamdallahi. Early in 1864 he was killed while trying to break this siege.

During the period of his jihad against his African opponents, al-Ḥājj 'Umar b. Sa'īd also fought several major actions against the French. The first was at Bakel, in 1855, when his forces raided the French post and kidnapped the commander. In 1857 he attacked the French fort at Medine, but was repulsed with severe losses. In 1859 he attacked a French post at Matam. In the same year the French attacked and took his fort at Guémou.

By all accounts al-Ḥājj ʿUmar's troops fought valiantly in these actions. The *sofa* battalions and their supporting cavalry appear to have had some knowledge of elementary battle drill. But in the pitched battles their formations quickly broke up into formless frontal assaults, carried out with great impetus, but helter-skelter and, more often than not, across open ground. They offered rewarding targets to the French-officered African regulars, in their tight squares and with their measured fire control. The drenching volleys usually saturated the attack before the jihadists with their inadequate weapons could get within killing range. But those who did acquitted themselves well. They cost the French sixteen dead and sixty-three wounded at Médine, thirty-nine dead and ninety-seven wounded at Guémou. These are higher casualties than were usually sustained by European-led troops in battle against indigenous forces in West Africa. And they were enough to harass the French. For by 1863 General Faidherbe thought it worthwhile to seek al-Ḥājj ʿUmar's co-operation and sent Lieutenant Mage to Segu to treat with him. By this time however the revolt against him was in full swing, and after his death it fell to his son, Aḥmad b. ʿUmar, to negotiate with the French envoy.

Although al-Ḥājj ʿUmar died before his empire was finally consolidated, it did not pass with him. It continued, in an uneasy relationship with the French, until his son, Aḥmad b. ʿUmar, was finally defeated by them in 1893. It then passed completely into French control. What were the forces that enabled al-Ḥājj ʿUmar to gain such success as he enjoyed?

Part of his jihad took place outside his own homeland, Futa Toro. Also, he was supported by many Tukolor emigrating out of Futa Toro. Indeed, he actively, and sometimes forcibly, encouraged this emigration, and profited from the disturbed conditions created by the French intrusion into that area in building up his Tukolor contingents. All of this has caused his movement to be interpreted as one of Tukolor imperialism manned by Tukolor Muslim émigrés. Such a view is plausible. First, the Tukolor were already heirs to an imperial tradition. In 1776 ʿAbd al-Qādir and his Tukolor supporters had launched a successful jihad in Futa Toro, ousted the Denianke dynasty and set up their own Islamic state. Second, al-Ḥājj ʿUmar's movement was seen as

Tukolor imperialism by certain non-Tukolor groups within his empire who, as was said above, reacted to his jihad by revolting against him.[1] On the other hand, the direction of his jihad, after the subjugation of Kaarta, was down the Senegal, toward his homeland in Futa Toro, where he had been spurned by the local 'ulamā'. This shows him as a Muslim reformer, concerned to mend the ways of his own community, rather than as an imperialist, intent on territorial expansion. Moreover, although many of his supporters were Tukolor, a substantial number were not. This strengthens the view that it was Islamic fervour, not ethnic solidarity, that bound them to him. Finally, the revolts against his empire bear more than one interpretation. No doubt there was an ethnic element in them. But equally important may have been such factors as the resentment of the Qādiriyya at Tijanist domination, as well as the hostility of the 'ulamā' of Jenne and the Kuntī shaykhs, each of whom had reason to feel threatened by his radical Islamic attitudes.

It was not only the French intrusion that created disturbed conditions from which al-Ḥājj 'Umar was able to profit. His was the third in a line of major jihads. The two earlier ones had created their own oppositions, made up of the disappointed and the dispossessed. For instance, there was certainly a Tijanist opposition to Aḥmad b. Muḥammad in Masina. And, if there is no hard evidence, there is at least a strong hint of Tijanist opposition to the Qādirī establishment in Sokoto *c.* 1850. Al-Ḥājj 'Umar's radical Tijanism must have been attractive in these various pockets of discontent, which then became recruiting grounds for his jihad.

There are also indications that al-Ḥājj 'Umar's movement, like that of Aḥmad b. Muḥammad, appealed to the slave population. He seems to have invited the defection of slaves to his own community, particularly from the pagan Bambara. Indeed the overt reason for declaring jihad was a quarrel over a slave who had escaped from 'the territory of unbelief' into 'the territory of Islam' – that is, al-Ḥājj 'Umar's community – and whom he refused to return.

Finally, some have thought to recognize in his movement a self-consciously black African form of Islam reacting against the ascendancy of Muslim Berbers and Fulani. Such an interpretation risks foisting colour attitudes on to a society that may not have thought in such terms.

[1] See also H. J. Fisher, 'The early life and Pilgrimage of al-Ḥājj Muḥammad al-Amīn the Soninke (d. 1887)', *Journal of African History*, 1970, **11**, 1, where it is argued that the jihad of Muḥammad al-Amīn was, to a large extent, a Soninke movement of resistance against Tukolor imperialism.

It is indeed possible that black Muslim literates like al-Ḥājj ʿUmar, who had covered the pilgrims' circuit – North Africa, Arabia, Cairo, perhaps Syria, maybe Istanbul – were stung to resentment by the colour prejudice that certainly existed in the Ottoman Empire and adjacent areas of the Islamic world during the nineteenth century. But a doubt attaches to the notion that his followers, illiterates for the most part, for whom blackness was a normal, not exceptional human characteristic, can have thought of colour as a sensitive issue. Resentment at enslavement and dissatisfaction with the exclusiveness of Qādirī aristocracies are more convincing reasons to explain the measure of al-Ḥājj ʿUmar's popular support.

THE THEOLOGY OF AL-ḤĀJJ ʿUMAR

The central fact of al-Ḥājj ʿUmar's theology is his ardent attachment to the Tijāniyya, and his career was probably the most important factor in establishing this new order in West Africa. Nevertheless, although he differed in this respect from the Shehu Usuman dan Fodio and Aḥmad b. Muḥammad, both of whom were faithful Qādirīs – although tendentious tradition does claim that the *shehu* converted to the Tijāniyya late in life and Tijānīs claim him as a *quṭb*[1] – it was a difference of direction rather than of kind. For there is no doubt that al-Ḥājj ʿUmar was inspired by the same spirit of Sufi revivalism that informed his predecessors. Not only was he a Tijānī. He also exhibits clear evidence of having come under the influence of the Khalwatiyya, the order which stood at the head of the Sufi revival, in an even more direct fashion than did the Shehu Usuman. During his four years in Cairo he was in constant intercourse with certain Khalwatī shaykhs. As B. G. Martin perceptively remarks, 'Fondamentalement, la nouvelle Ḥalwatiyya égyptienne et son rejeton, la Tiğāniyya, participent d'une vague commune de prosélytisme et d'expansion musulmannes. À l'origine de tout ce mouvement se trouvent la force spirituelle et l'impulsion organisatrice données par Muṣṭafā al-Bakrī et par son groupe.'[2] It was with the successors of Shaykh Muṣṭafā al-Bakrī (d. 1742) that al-Ḥājj ʿUmar consorted in Cairo. His indebtedness to the Khalwatiyya is apparent from his *Rimāḥ*, where he advocated *khalwāt*, retreats (it is from this Arabic word that the order takes its name) characteristic of

---

[1] See the quotation from a Hausa poem in Hiskett, *The sword*, 162.
[2] 'Notes sur l'origine de la Ṭarīqa des Tiğāniyya', 278. I am greatly indebted to Dr B. G. Martin's discoveries for my understanding of al-Ḥājj ʿUmar's association with the Tijāniyya and with mahdism.

the Khalwatiyya. Thus, whereas Shehu Usuman and Aḥmad b. Muḥammad represent the impact of Sufi revivalism on the ideology of the Qādiriyya, al-Ḥājj ʿUmar was a direct participant in that stream of Sufi endeavour that had created the Tijāniyya by way of the Khalwatiyya. Part of his particular contribution to West African Islam was to establish the new Tijāniyya firmly in the area and infuse it with a strong colouring of Khalwatī mysticism.

In a number of other respects, al-Ḥājj ʿUmar demonstrates that he was essentially a product of the intellectual and ideological climate of his time. Like the Shehu Usuman he experienced visions. The visionary background to his appointment as Tijānī *khalīfa* has already been described. It was a divine voice that first summoned him to jihad on 5 September 1852. Like Shehu Usuman he experienced a visionary visitation from the Prophet Muḥammad. There is no reason to think that all this was in conscious imitation of the *shehu* – although there may have been some unconscious influence. Rather, both men were filled with mystic fervour which caused them to expect visions as part of their divine election.

In one particular, however, al-Ḥājj ʿUmar may have gone further than Shehu Usuman in exploiting mystic techniques. For he made especial claim to the gift of *istikhāra*, that is, a special esoteric formula that assured him of direct divine guidance in time of difficulty. The *shehu* too laid claim to divine guidance. But it seems less prominent in his total theology than in that of al-Ḥājj ʿUmar. Indeed, the latter's success in resorting to *istikhāra* probably accounts for his extraordinary hold over his followers.

Messianism also featured prominently in al-Ḥājj ʿUmar's mystic programme. Like the West African jihadists before him, he did not claim to be the Mahdi. But his followers certainly did make messianic claims on his behalf. An interesting document dating from the late 1850s and composed by one of al-Ḥājj ʿUmar's more ardent followers, has recently been published.[1] In it the claim is made that al-Ḥājj ʿUmar is the vizier – that is, the lieutenant or right-hand man – of the Mahdi. The tone of the document, its appeal to fantasy and the barely literate Arabic in which it is written, clearly demonstrate the hectic and popular impact of the Segu jihadist's messianic pretensions. For instance, he was widely referred to as *mujaddid al-dīn al-muḥammadiyya*, 'the renewer of the Muslim faith', and his enemies claimed that he sacrilegiously

[1] B. G. Martin, 'A Mahdist document from Futa Jallon', *Bulletin de l'I.F.A.N.*, 1963, 25, B, 1–2.

identified himself with ʿĪsā (Jesus) who, in Islamic millenarianism, will return with the Mahdi.[1]

One interesting development in al-Ḥājj ʿUmar's theological thinking is the way in which he adapted and enlarged the notion of jihad. He taught that jihad was a continuum, beginning with *jihād al-qalb*, 'jihad of the heart', that is, a personal battle with carnal lusts, required to purify the soul; then *jihād al-qawl*, 'jihad of words', in discharge of the Koranic injuction to 'command the right and forbid what is disapproved of', that is, a jihad of preaching and intellectual persuasion, and finally *jihād al-sayf*, 'jihad of the sword'. These degrees of jihad were certainly known to the reformers of Hausaland. But they did not give the first two such prominence as did al-Ḥājj ʿUmar, who erected them into doctrinal pillars of his movement. In doing so, he clearly revealed his Tijanist persuasions, for 'jihad of the heart' is basic to the order's teaching.

Closely associated with his teachings on jihad were those concerning *hijra*. Like the Shehu Usuman dan Fodio, he regarded *hijra* out of the territory of unbelief as obligatory, and like him he relied largely on al-Wansharīsī as his authority for this. In his case, as in the case of the *shehu*, *hijra*, which he performed to Dinguiray, was a deliberate part of the process of legitimizing jihad by resort to Prophetic precedent.

The sixteenth-century Muslim theologian, ʿAbd al-Wahhāb al-Shaʿrānī, also exerted a formative influence over al-Ḥājj ʿUmar's theology. It was from him that he derived his doctrine, revolutionary in the Sudan, that there is no need for a Muslim to adhere to any one of the four orthodox rites. This is certainly in marked contrast to the teaching of the Shehu Usuman dan Fodio, for whom adherence to the Mālikī *madhhab* was most important. Equally original in the context of his place and time was al-Ḥājj ʿUmar's rejection of *taqlīd*, passive acceptance of authority and precedent in matters of faith, and his elevation of *ijtihād*, personal interpretation. Indeed, he warned of the dangers of too great reliance on the *Mukhtaṣar* of al-Khalīl and the *Risālah* of Ibn Abī Zayd, both standard texts for legal education among the reformers of Hausaland. Pursuing his distrust of legalism even further, he opposed the virtues of the *awliyāʾ*, Muslim holy men, marabouts, to the formalism of the *fuqahāʾ*, the canon lawyers. He thereby seems to have elevated the *awliyāʾ* to the status occupied by the *ʿulamāʾ* in Shehu Usuman dan Fodio's scheme of things, and he certainly differed radically

---

[1] Willis, *'Jihād Fī Sabīl Allāh*, 403, n. 31. Dr Willis has undertaken a number of studies in depth of al-Ḥājj ʿUmar's theology, to which I am much indebted.

from the strongly nomothetic preferences of Aḥmad b. Muḥammad. He also raised *ḥaqīqa*, gnosis, above *'ilm*, intellectual knowledge of the Islamic religious sciences. Here, too, he was more innovative than both the Shehu Usuman and Aḥmad b. Muḥammad.

One other aspect of al-Ḥajj 'Umar's theology distinguishes him from his predecessors in reform. He was deeply concerned with 'reconciliation' and with the unity of the Muslim community, which he regarded as disastrously divided by *fitna*, civil and ideological discord. This view was not of itself original. Shehu Usuman dan Fodio was also concerned to create and preserve the unity of the *umma*, the Muslim community. What was new was al-Ḥajj 'Umar's diagnosis of the cause of *fitna* and the remedy he proposed. The *shehu* saw the cause as being the discordant wrangling of self-styled mallams, who would do better to rely obediently on *ijmā'*, the hallowed consensus of the Mālikī *'ulamā'*; and he was especially severe in his condemnation of *'aql*, the impertinent presumptions of human reason in conflict with the benign and unifying authority of revelation. Al-Ḥajj 'Umar took a different view. He saw the *'ulamā'* as the cause of *fitna*, not the instruments for healing it. For him the remedy lay in abandoning divisive loyalties to the four orthodox rites, sanctified by *ijmā'*, and he believed that the best hope for unity lay in adherence to the Tijāniyya. This, too, was an original contribution to Sudanese Islam.

'UMAR'S RELATIONS WITH THE FRENCH

Tukolor tradition insists that al-Ḥajj 'Umar had no wish to fight Europeans, only black infidels. It certainly seems that his clash with the French was due more to circumstances than to deliberate intent. He began his jihad at the same time that the French began their penetration into the interior. At some point the two were bound to collide. Certain French activities, especially the alliances into which they entered with indigenous rulers to whom al-Ḥajj 'Umar was opposed, precipitated the collision and forced his hand. But that to fight the French was not his intention is supported by the fact that he twice proposed collaboration to the French government of Senegal and was rebuffed on each occasion.

In fact, there is no reason why al-Ḥajj 'Umar should have felt compelled to wage jihad against the French. In Islamic law Christians are not infidels but 'People of the Book', that is, scripturaries, who have received revelation, but of a lesser order than that vouchsafed to Muslims. The received attitude towards them in al-Ḥajj 'Umar's day was, therefore, that when peacefully domiciled within Islamic territory, they had the status of *dhimmis*, that is, non-Muslim subjects of the Islamic state who, on payment of tribute, the canonical *jizya*, were entitled to practise their religion and pursue their livelihoods without hindrance. There is evidence that this is how al-Ḥājj 'Umar initially regarded the French. He is reported in a French source to have said 'Les blancs ne sont que des marchands . . .'[1] and demanded dues from them for the privilege of trading in his territory. These dues he seems to have regarded as *jizya*. Had the French been willing to pay them and had they confined themselves solely to trading, it is unlikely that al-Ḥājj 'Umar would have included them among those against whom jihad was obligatory. But in regarding them as *dhimmis* he certainly failed to understand both the nature of their imperial ambitions and also the quality of their unwillingness to accept client status.

All the same, there may have been some element of resentment at colonial intrusion, if not in al-Ḥājj 'Umar's personal attitude, at least in the attitudes of his followers. Many of the *talibes* came from areas which were under direct French domination, or had suffered from French punitive action. It is they, rather than al-Ḥājj 'Umar himself, who may have been eager for a confrontation. Once committed to fighting the French, al-Ḥājj 'Umar naturally exploited the prevailing sentiment of Islamic militancy and declared jihad against them as well as against his African enemies.

Despite the violence which accompanied his career – and in his place and time he had no monopoly of violence – and the sensational aura that surrounded his messianic claims, al-Ḥājj 'Umar b. Sa'īd was a Muslim intellectual who made a serious and original contribution to the development of Islam in West Africa. The true appreciation of his importance depends as much upon the dignity of his intellectual and spiritual achievement as upon his notoriety as an opponent of French imperialism.

CONCLUSIONS

It was suggested at the beginning of this chapter that the nineteenth-century jihads in West Africa, despite differences in local circumstances, show broad religious and political similarities. It is now the moment to draw together these threads of motive and causation and sum up the consequences of the jihads.

[1] Reported by Willis, 'The nineteenth-century revivalist movement', p. 24 as part of a statement by al-Ḥājj 'Umar in the course of a meeting with Governor Grammont in 1847.

The first common factor was the presence of mixed Islam. It seems certain that this system of accommodation and compromise, evolved over several centuries, did end by grating against an Islamic idealism, that grew up alongside it, in such a way as to cause frustration to the idealists and provoke them first to protest and then to militancy. Thus intellectual argument followed by military conquest is a general characteristic of the reform movements – al-Ḥājj 'Umar's 'jihad of words' and 'jihad of the sword'.

But what lay behind this militancy? Why was the system of mixed Islam not acceptable to all, as it was to some? The answer lies in a multiplicity of factors. First, the growth of Islamic literacy in certain minority groups, especially the sedentary Fulani, captured imaginations and created a mood of Islamic perfectionism that made mixed Islam more and more offensive. Second, the general climate of religious excitement, particularly the Sufi revival at al-Azhar, animated the whole Islamic world in the eighteenth and nineteenth centuries and certainly extended into the Islamic Sudan. Sometimes this was expressed through militant Qadirism, at other times through militant Tijanism. Third, Islamic messianism, also part of the general Islamic revival, was particularly strong in the Sudan and gave to events in that area a sharp edge of urgency which precipitated militancy. Also part of the pattern of Islamic religious excitement, but playing its own key role, was pilgrimage. This seems to have been a trigger which activated the reform process. Sometimes, as in the case of al-Ḥājj 'Umar, it was a direct experience for the personalities concerned. In other cases, typically that of the Shehu Usuman dan Fodio, it worked at second hand, through literary influences and contacts with returned pilgrims.

The secular motives and causations – in so far as they can be separated from the religious and ideological – are more difficult to define, largely because the sources, almost exclusively religious in content and purpose, are uncommunicative about political and social matters. So, many of one's conclusions rest on inference.

In the Hausa case, tension between nomads and peasants was important. The present author knows of no documentary evidence to demonstrate that this was also a factor in the later jihads. Nevertheless, since the whole Western Sudan shared a common economy of peasant agriculture and nomadic cattle-rearing, it is probable that it was.

Slavery is another factor which operated in the Hausa case. Aḥmad b. Muḥammad was indebted, in some measure, to the support of servile orders. There is evidence, too, that al-Ḥājj 'Umar's movement attracted escaped slaves. And it also appears that his Tijanism drew in a number of the common people – the underprivileged and the dispossessed? – as against established Qadirism, which had become identified with aristocratic interests.

Some have thought to recognize not only a conflict between nomads and peasants, slaves and enslavers, commoners and aristocrats, but also between urban and non-urban intellectuals in all these jihads. Thus the clerical Fulani of Hausaland, who self-consciously avoided the Hausa courts, which were of course situated in the walled towns, were at odds with the urban mallams, who were clients of Hausa patronage. Aḥmad b. Muḥammad and his followers ended by crossing swords with the Kuntī *shaykhs* of Timbuktu and the *'ulamā'* of Jenne – and here trading interests certainly seem to have had a cooling influence on the ardour of these urban Muslims that their non-urban co-religionists escaped. Likewise, al-Ḥājj 'Umar fought against an established, city-centred Islamic dynasty that the urban realities – the need to govern, to trade and to balance conflicting interests within the political community – may have rendered flexible and thus vulnerable to reformist propaganda. This evidence is impressive. Nonetheless, in the present author's view, an attempt to see the 'urban' and 'non-urban' conditions as the determining factors in these situations leads to over-simplification. More probably, many occasions of self-interest, of which those associated with the urban condition were only some, contributed to drawing the teeth of Islamic ideology and promoting compromise.

Some of the consequences of the nineteenth-century jihads in West Africa will already be apparent. First, they gave power to a new governing class, sometimes though not always of a different ethnic group from that displaced. Most tried to substitute an entirely new political and constitutional system for what existed before. Their success was often substantial but seldom complete.

Second, the jihads greatly accelerated the dissemination of Islamic literacy, particularly in Hausa and Fulfulde-speaking areas, and they also led to the wider dispersal of Muslim literates and to the setting-up of additional centres of Islamic education, especially in the southern areas of the western Sudan. While this certainly strengthened orthodoxy where Islam was already well established, it also, paradoxically, extended the area of mixed Islam. For the Muslim pietists who described the state of Islam in these newly 'converted' areas make it clear that they were still confronted with the ancient problem of mixing.

Third, the jihads led to the setting-up of characteristically Muslim city centres such as Sokoto and Hamdallahi. In consequence, whereas much Islamic intellectual activity during the pre-jihad era had taken place among nomadic Berbers and in the small settlements of the clerical Fulani, it now became increasingly concentrated in large, permanent walled cities. Thus a strong push was given to the process of urbanizing West African Islam.

Fourth, the success of the jihads strengthened the hold of Islamic political and social institutions over the populations subject to them. Thus there grew up, in due course, a sentiment of Islamic solidarity in these areas that still differentiates them from other areas of West Africa where Islam is faint or sporadic. One manifestation of this is that in the course of the political prelude to West African independence, the 'jihad areas', especially northern Nigeria, tended to be pan-Islamic in their aspirations, in contrast to the pan-Africanism of non-Islamic areas. Sometimes, too, the heritage of the jihads accustomed Islamic populations to assume superiority over non-Muslims, which made it difficult for them to adjust to a situation in which political power passed, either wholly or partially, to non-Muslims at independence.

Not only in politics but also in education, the heritage of the jihads has been far-reaching in its effects. Broadly speaking, the non-Islamic areas of West Africa, which had no significant indigenous tradition of literacy before the Europeans arrived in their societies, have seized upon Western education avidly and have quickly made it their own. Not so in the Islamic areas, where the jihads have created a strong sentiment of Islamic identity. Here, the new secular education of the colonial administrations had to compete with an entrenched system of Islamic literacy and education. The progress of Western education, and thus of twentieth-century technology, was therefore slow and was resisted all along the line by the *'ulamā'*, at any rate until recently. This has meant that when, during and just after the Second World War, such Islamic areas did begin to awake to the need for secular, Western education, they had much leeway to make up to avoid being dominated by technically and educationally more advanced non-Muslims.

But not only did Islamic areas have to make good lost ground. Even when convinced of the necessity for Western education, they still retain a strong attachment to their inherited Islamic system of education and way of life. Thus one of the problems facing present-day educationists in these areas is how to integrate the two systems – the Islamic and the Western – in such a way as to preserve the inherited Islamic culture and at the same time prepare the people to take their place in the modern world.

Finally, the jihads greatly strengthened the hold of the Sufi orders, especially the Qādiriyya and the Tijāniyya, in West Africa. These two orders are now widespread and deeply rooted where the jihads took place. Their influence is not negligible in areas of faint Islam. Wherever they are found, their importance is not only religious. They also play a crucial political, social and educational role. They are, perhaps, the most important of all Islamic institutions in West Africa sustaining Islam, both as a religion and a way of life, at the present day.

CHAPTER 5

FREED SLAVE COLONIES IN WEST AFRICA

Strictly speaking, the only European colony on the Western side of Africa before the end of the eighteenth century was Portuguese Angola. Elsewhere Europeans who settled to trade paid rent for their settlements to African rulers. Sovereignty was not surrendered. African rulers followed the precedent set in 1482, when the Portuguese were grudgingly permitted to build a fort at Elmina in return for a regularly paid rent. There were a few exceptions to this rule, but normally European traders were only allowed to settle in West Africa if they made regular payments in return. There was no transfer of sovereignty in these settlements.

All along the coast African rulers and European traders were united by the reciprocal obligations of 'landlord' and 'stranger'.[1] The landlords protected their strangers and undertook to provide them with trade. Hence, in the period of the slave trade, Europeans did not appear in West Africa north of the equator as invaders or masters, but as equal trading partners.

Whatever misery they brought to those they purchased and shipped across the Atlantic, European slave traders were welcomed by their African customers. They offered, in return for slaves, a wide range of manufactured goods otherwise unobtainable in West Africa. Both trading partners, African and European, received the commodity they wanted, and made the best bargain they could. Yet, though individual Africans might often outwit their European customers, the overall economic advantage lay with the Europeans. In return for slaves, wealth-creating human machinery, they gave expendable consumer goods, turned out in growing volume by the expanding economy of industrializing Europe.

As the technological gap between Africa and Europe, not strikingly great at the first period of contact in the fifteenth century, steadily widened, Europeans became obsessed with it. They tended increasingly

[1] See Vernon R. Dorjahn and Christopher Fyfe, 'Landlord and stranger', *Journal of African History*, 1962, 3, 3, 391–7; also H. W. Ord and others, *Markets and marketing in West Africa* (Edinburgh, Centre of African Studies, University of Edinburgh, 1966), 1–25.

to equate European society with 'civilization' and contrast it with the 'barbarism' of African societies. This implied a moral as well as a technological difference. The assumption that Europe was morally superior to Africa was reinforced by the Christians' belief that theirs was the only valid religion. Protestant Christians, from the late eighteenth century, were inspired to preach their gospel to the whole world; Catholics too revived their missionary tradition. Protestant or Catholic, they interpreted the Christian religion in a Eurocentric way which tended to overlook its origins in Asia and its long continuance in Egypt and Ethiopia. The moral values associated with European missionary Christianity were the moral values of Europe.

The trans-Atlantic slave trade made nonsense of these claims. So long as Europeans were buying and selling human beings in West Africa, it was not possible to maintain, in good conscience, that they were morally superior to Africans. If they were really more moral, they would have to give up such obvious immorality. Hence the voices of protest against the trans-Atlantic slave trade, which had been raised almost from the period it began, roused a widening sense of shame as the eighteenth century advanced.

Moral arguments were reinforced by economic arguments. In a period when free trade principles were an exciting new technique for advanced intellectuals, the slave trade was denounced as an outmoded waste of economic resources. Those who were unmoved by humanitarian appeals could be stirred by arguments which declared that it would be better business to treat the mass of Africans as customers, and sell them factory-produced goods, than to look upon them merely as bodies for sale as labour overseas. Thus, it became possible for small but well organized protest groups to mount an ultimately successful campaign against a deeply entrenched organization which had for centuries provided wealth and employment for shipowners, manufacturers, planters and a host of associated interests.

THE FOUNDING OF THE SIERRA LEONE COLONY

The British anti-slave trade movement is customarily associated with Thomas Clarkson, who organized the campaign, and William Wilberforce, its spokesman in Parliament. Behind the scenes, modest and unobtrusive, was Granville Sharp, who in 1772 brought James Somerset[1]

---

[1] The report in T. B. Howell, *A complete collection of state trials 1771-1777* (London, 1814), spells 'Sommersett'. Sharp (who knew him) spelt 'Somerset' which I have preferred.

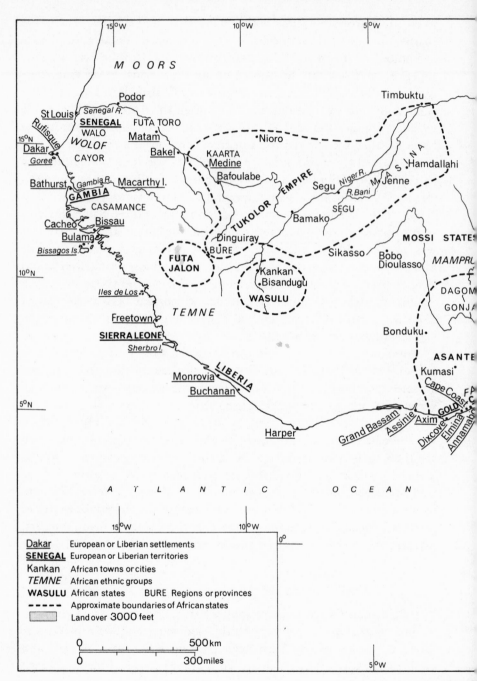

8 West Africa i[...]

AÏR

Agades

5°E   10°E   15°E

15°N

SOKOTO

Sokoto
Gwandu

·Katsina   Ngasargamu

·Kano

CALIPHATE

Birnin Gwari   Zaria

BORNU

N U P E

Bauchi
Gombe

10°N

Old Oyo

Bida

Yola

ILORIN

Ilorin

Benue R.

·Ibi

ADAMAWA

Oyo· **YORUBA**
Ibadan **STATES**

Lokoja

M T S.

·Abeokuta

C A M E R O U N

I B O

Ijebu-Ode· **LAGOS**

BENIN

DAHOMEY

Benin City

omey

IBIBIO

Lagos

IBIBIO

·Calabar

Porto Novo

Cotonou

Whydah

Badagry

Palma

·Benin City

5°N

NIGER

ITSEKIRI

Keta

Brass

E F I K

Bonny Opobo

·Duala

Fernándo Po

Principe

São Tomé

Libreville

0°

Annabon

5°E   10°E   15°E

teenth century

173

before the courts, and extracted from Lord Mansfield, the lord chief justice, the declaration that there was no law under which a former slave could be claimed in England by his former master and sent back to slavery across the Atlantic.

Somerset's Case is often misrepresented. It did not declare unequivocally that slavery could not exist in England. Nor did it impel black servants in England to leave their masters *en masse* (as some historians have supposed). Not until a dozen or more years had elapsed was there any substantial unemployed group of Africans in England. These were not runaway servants, but refugees who had made their way to London at the end of the War of American Independence, chiefly ex-sailors from naval ships, or escaped plantation slaves. Sharp organized a committee to relieve them. As well as giving temporary relief, the committee proposed that they should be sent to Africa to a new permanent home of their own. The government, anxious to be rid of an unwanted vagrant black community, agreed to ship them to Sierra Leone.[1]

The selected site, the Sierra Leone estuary, had been an important trading centre since the first period of African contact with Europeans. The wide river-mouth, with deep water along the southern shore, gave passing ships one of the few safe anchorages on the long surf-bound coast. A fresh stream supplied drinking water, and there was plenty of accessible timber for firewood. The ruler who controlled the watering-place had regular opportunities for trade, and received a steady revenue from watering and customs duties. At this period it was part of the Temne kingdom of Koya.[2]

Sharp devised the settlement in terms of the current Eurocentric vision which dreamed of spreading higher moral values over a barbarous world. He drew up a constitution (slightly ante-dating that of the United States) to establish an egalitarian, self-governing community, which he named the 'Province of Freedom', as an exemplar of Christian liberty set down in a country long given over to the slave trade.[3] In May 1787 about 400 settlers reached Sierra Leone. The British naval captain in charge of transporting them negotiated a treaty with King Tom, the Temne ruler at the watering-place, who allowed them to establish a settlement. They then elected one of themselves, Richard Weaver, governor, according to Sharp's directions. For, once

[1] For a full account see Christopher Fyfe, *A history of Sierra Leone* (London, 1962).

[2] See E. Ade Ijagbemi, 'A history of the Temne in the nineteenth century', unpublished Ph.D. thesis (Edinburgh, 1968).

[3] See John Peterson, 'The Enlightenment and the founding of Freetown', in Christopher Fyfe and Eldred Jones, *Freetown: a symposium* (London, 1968).

they were settled, the naval ships sailed away, leaving them a self-governing community for which the British government had no further responsibility.

King Tom was subordinate to Naimbana, the regent of the Koya Temne. When he died in the following year, Naimbana notified the settlers that a new treaty must be negotiated. Here he was following established precedent in the relations of 'landlord' and 'stranger'. Europeans made their tenancy agreements with an individual landlord: when he died a new agreement had to be negotiated with his successor. Naimbana assumed that the newcomers were settling in the ordinary way as tenants. Nevertheless the treaty he and his chiefs put their marks to (but could not read) in August 1788, declared that he was surrendering all claim to the land he was granting, for himself and his successors, in return for a consignment of trade goods. Thus inadvertently he renounced sovereignty over land, and admitted into West Africa a completely new principle which transferred sovereign rights to aliens.

From the first, the history of the province of Freedom was unfortunate. The heavy annual rains began as the settlers landed, before they had time to build adequate houses. Many fell sick and died. The country was unsuited to the kind of farming they were used to; gradually they began drifting away. About 200 struggled bravely on until 1789 when they unwisely took sides with some neighbouring European slave traders in a dispute with King Tom's successor, King Jimmy. In retaliation he burnt their town and they dispersed over the surrounding country.

Sharp could not afford to re-found the province himself, but persuaded richer supporters of the anti-slave trade movement to help. In 1791 the Sierra Leone Company was established in London to take over the land Naimbana had granted. Financed by shareholders' money, administered by a board of directors, it could no longer allow responsibility to a community of self-governing settlers. The 'Province of Freedom' never revived. The Company's settlement was to be governed on a colonial pattern. Henceforth policy was decided in England by the directors, particularly by the chairman, Henry Thornton, a London banker, and was carried out in Sierra Leone by the Company's employees.

Otherwise the Company's underlying intentions were close to Sharp's. Like him they wanted to plant on this slave-trading coast a settlement from which Christianity and European morality would radiate over a benighted continent. For, having renounced the slave trade, the directors and their employees could appear in West Africa not only as benefactors, but also (a new guise for Europeans) as moral superiors.

The Sierra Leone Company had commercial as well as ideological aims. Its sponsors hoped to combine profit with philanthropy, substituting trade in vegetable produce for trade in slaves. But their 'true principles of Commerce' (as they put it[1]) were like those of the slave trade – exchanging European manufactures for African produce. Thus the economy remained tied to Europe.

The Company recruited settlers across the Atlantic in Nova Scotia and New Brunswick, among communities of former slaves who had escaped from their masters during the War of American Independence. Evacuated at the end of the war by the British armies, they had been promised grants of land. Many never received them. Fearful that without land they might be pushed back into slavery, they sent a delegate, Thomas Peters, to London to obtain redress. He made contact with the directors, who promised his people a home.

About a thousand 'Nova Scotians' (as they were called in Sierra Leone) crossed the Atlantic in 1792. Like the first settlers they arrived at the beginning of the rains; like them, they and the Company's European officials suffered heavy initial mortality. Their early misfortunes, many of them inseparable from the foundation of almost any pioneer settlement, were later much publicized by opponents of the abolitionists, and helped to give Sierra Leone its much exaggerated title of 'White Man's Grave'.[2] But after these initial difficulties the Nova Scotians settled down easily. They were industrious and enterprising – having already displayed enterprise and initiative in running away from their masters, and then venturing across the Atlantic. Many were literate; most had practical skills. They were already organized into religious congregations under their own pastors, Methodist, Baptist, and the Countess of Huntingdon's Connexion (an offshoot of Methodism). The Company recognized their self-reliance by allowing them to elect representatives responsible for their own local affairs.

The Company's sponsors assumed, as Granville Sharp had done, that the settlers would live by farming. But they had neither capital nor suitable land for growing export crops. Those who farmed did so chiefly for subsistence. To prosper they had to trade. They put their trading profits into building houses to live in, or to let to Europeans, investing in house property as the only way of securing a regular income from their accumulated savings.

[1] See *Sierra Leone Studies* (old series), 1932, 18, 26–77.
[2] Particularly in Anna Maria Falconbridge, *Two voyages to Sierra Leone* (London, 1794).

Freetown, laid out by the Company's officials, and built by the Nova Scotians, was planned on the North American pattern, with wide intersecting streets and houses spaced out on large building-lots, an urban setting wholly different from the layouts of neighbouring African towns. The settlers put up frame houses, mounted on a foundation of laterite stone, reminiscent in style of the colonial architecture familiar to them in North America, which in elaborated forms were to provide a model for Freetown buildings for the next hundred years or so.

With their sense of moral authority the Sierra Leone Company's directors coupled a sense of racial authority. A systematic, fully-fledged theory of race was not formulated in Europe until the middle of the nineteenth century in the writings of Robert Knox and Arthur de Gobineau.[1] Nevertheless the basic social assumption of the American colonies, that white must rule and black obey, was already widespread in Europe – though not yet in West Africa, where white slave traders still acknowledged the authority of black rulers. Hence, though the directors were ready to allow the settlers some measure of local self-government, they retained ultimate power themselves. Important policy decisions were made in London and executed in Sierra Leone by white officials. To some Nova Scotians this seemed a perpetuation in Africa of the racial domination they had suffered under in America.[2]

Before leaving Nova Scotia they had been promised land in their new home, free of rent. This promise, made them by John Clarkson, the abolitionist's brother who organized the emigration and was appointed the Company's first governor, totally misrepresented the directors' policy. The Company's prospectus stated explicitly that a small annual quit-rent must be paid for all land granted.[3] When, therefore, after Clarkson had left Sierra Leone, they were asked to pay, they felt they had again been cheated, as in Nova Scotia, by white men's promises. The directors, far away in London, could not understand how deeply this grievance rankled. They could not perceive that the settlers regarded landownership as a badge of newly won freedom, so that any threat

[1] For the development of racial theories see Philip D. Curtin, *The image of Africa* (Madison, 1964).

[2] See P. E. H. Hair, 'Africanism: the Freetown contribution', *Journal of Modern African Studies*, 1967, 5, 4, 521–39, for the settlers' 'Africanism'. Dr Hair overlooks, however, the 'Europeanism' of the Company and its officials.

[3] See N. A. Cox-George, *Finance and development in West Africa: the Sierra Leone experience* (London, 1961).

to it seemed like a threat to reduce them to slavery again. Instead, the Company insisted that the quit-rent must be paid, seeing refusal to pay simply as ingratitude.

Under the strong governor, Zachary Macaulay, open conflict was averted. After he left, the government lost control. Extremists among the settlers drew up their own laws,[1] to be enforced without reference to the Company. In September 1800 armed rebellion broke out. The officials and the few settlers who stood by them were outnumbered, until unexpectedly a British transport arrived with a garrison of soldiers and 550 new settlers on board. With this reinforcement the government quickly put the rebellion down.

The newly arrived settlers were Jamaican Maroons. Descended from a community of runaway slaves, predominantly of Asante origin, they had lived as free men in the mountains of Jamaica until deported to Halifax, Nova Scotia, for making war against the Jamaican government. Eventually they were shipped to a new home in Sierra Leone. After a period of initial antagonism the two settler groups, Nova Scotians and Maroons, integrated gradually into one community with its own distinctive Eurafrican culture.

In the Sierra Leone Company's settlement, Naimbana's treaty of 1788 was taken at its face value. Neither government nor settlers supposed that they were under Temne sovereignty. When King Jimmy's successor, another King Tom, and Farama, who became King of the Koya Temne after Naimbana died, tried to insist on making new treaties, as required by customary usage, their demands were refused. Ignoring the rules which bound landlord and stranger, the Company's officials maintained that full perpetual sovereignty had been ceded, as stated in the written treaty.

So long as the Temne rulers had believed that the settlers were 'strangers' of the familiar type, they were ready to welcome them. Once they realized they were invaders, come to dispossess them, they grew increasingly hostile. When they saw British troops arriving with the Maroons, they realized they must act at once if they were ever to regain their land. In November 1801 King Tom's army attacked Freetown. The settlers were taken by surprise, but rallied and drove the invaders away, then counter-attacked and drove the Temne from all the neighbouring towns. A second Temne attack, a few months later, was equally unsuccessful. It was henceforth clear that no African force could dislodge the invaders. In 1807 the Temne rulers accepted what they

---

[1] Printed in Christopher Fyfe, *Sierra Leone inheritance* (London, 1964), 124–6.

could not remedy, and signed a peace treaty which gave the colony full possession of virtually the whole peninsula. Thus, the planting of a colony ostensibly dedicated to principles of humanity and justice deprived the Temne of land they had held unquestioned all through the long period of the slave trade.

The Sierra Leone Company's hopes of making profits were frustrated by the long Anglo-French wars which began in 1793. Their ships were regularly captured; Freetown was sacked by a French naval squadron in 1794. By the beginning of the nineteenth century the Company was virtually bankrupt, and kept going only by subsidies from the British government. In 1808 the government took over completely. The Company was wound up, and Sierra Leone became a British colony. The existing pattern of government remained. The absentee powers exercised by the board of directors were henceforth exercised by the secretary of state and his staff. Governors and officials ruled in the name of the Crown instead of the Company. The settlers' own elected representation, which had disappeared after the rebellion, was not revived.

THE SUPPRESSION OF THE SLAVE TRADE

The Act for the Abolition of the Slave Trade passed by Parliament in 1807 enabled the British government to introduce measures for the active suppression of the trade.

Sierra Leone became an important base in the British anti-slave trade campaign. From 1808 ships of the British navy were stationed off the West African coast to intercept ships carrying slaves illegally. Intercepted ships were brought to Freetown, where a court of vice-admiralty was constituted. Captain and crew were prosecuted, and if the prosecution was successful the slaves were freed. So long as the Napoleonic Wars lasted any ship could be intercepted. With peace, in 1815, the naval squadron was restricted to British ships. Severe penalties already deterred British subjects from trading directly in slaves (though they could still participate indirectly, by selling to foreigners the trade goods used in exchange), so international co-operation was needed if the naval squadron was to take any effective action.

A series of bilateral treaties, the first signed in 1817, between the British and other governments, obliged either party to allow its ships to be searched for slaves by the navy of the other. In practice this meant leaving enforcement to the British navy with its large, full-time West African squadron. Only the governments of the recently belligerent

France and the United States objected (conceding a right of search over their shipping had been the immediate ground for American hostilities against Britain in the war of 1812), and employed their own naval enforcement procedures.

International courts, called courts of mixed commission, were constituted under these treaties in ports on both sides of the Atlantic.[1] The West African court was in Freetown. When a slave ship was brought in there, two judges heard the case, one British, one representing the country of the ship's origin. If they disagreed, the decision was referred to an arbitrator chosen by lot from two commissioners representing the two nations concerned. If it was established that the ship was trading illegally, the human cargo was freed and the ship and remaining cargo were impounded; the captain and crew were sent home to be tried by their country's laws.

Despite this enforcement apparatus, the slave trade still went on. Brazil and Cuba developed intensive sugar production during the early nineteenth century, opening a large market for slaves. As Edmund Burke once prophesied, 'So long as the slavery continues, some means for its supply will be found.'[2] A naval squadron cruising along hundreds of miles of coast could not hope to intercept more than a few slave ships. Hundreds of slaves might be captured and freed, but thousands were disembarked into slavery across the Atlantic. Shippers were not discouraged by captures: losses were amply offset by the profits on the ships that eluded the ineffective blockade. By the late 1830s the numbers of slaves shipped from West Africa were still comparable with those of the 1800s.

Sir Thomas Fowell Buxton, a Member of Parliament who had devoted himself to the anti-slavery cause, suggested a remedy.[3] He proposed that British naval officers make treaties all along the coast with African rulers, who would renounce the slave trade and cede land for British settlements. Here planters and produce traders would settle and provide alternative commodities for export to Europe. Like the sponsors of the Sierra Leone Company, Buxton saw his colonization scheme as a means of raising the moral level of Africa, as well as tying it more firmly to the European economy, and extending British political influence.

The British government, anxious for domestic reasons to please

[1] See Leslie Bethell, 'The Mixed Commissions for the suppression of the transatlantic slave trade', *Journal of African History*, 1966, 7, 1, 79–93.
[2] Edmund Burke, 'A sketch of the Negro code', *Works* (London, 1829), IX, 281.
[3] Thomas Fowell Buxton, *The African slave trade and its remedy* (London, 1840).

Buxton, approved his proposal and sanctioned a grandiose steamship expedition up the Niger to plant one of Buxton's colonies at its confluence with the Benue. The expedition (of 1841) was a disastrous failure; most of the members died of malaria.[1] Interest in West African colonies faded away.

But the navy followed Buxton's suggestions. Navy officers took to landing at suitable places along the coast, where they would cajole or force the rulers to make anti-slave trade treaties. Then they destroyed any slave-trading establishments, burning the slave 'barracoons' and warehouses, and freeing the slaves within the rulers' territories. These measures were hamstrung for several years by legal actions brought in the English courts by slave traders who claimed damages for the destruction of their property. Not until 1848 was it laid down that officers could not be held personally responsible. Yet even this policy was only slowly effective: driven from one part of the coast, the slave traders would reappear in another. What finally ended the trade was the ending of slave imports across the Atlantic by the governments of the recipient countries.

In 1864 the last slave ship was adjudicated in Freetown; in 1865 the last cargo of slaves was freed in Havana. For over fifty years the governments of Europe and America had mouthed disapproval of the slave trade and tried half-heartedly to suppress it. But while slaves were in demand it still went on. Only in an era of fast-growing machine technology, when the transatlantic slave plantation system and the human trade that fed it were no longer economically necessary, was it brought to an end.

SIERRA LEONE AND THE LIBERATED AFRICANS

The anti-slave trade campaign caused a demographic revolution in Sierra Leone. In 1808 the Colony had about 2,000 inhabitants. By 1811 the influx of people freed from the slave ships had more than doubled the population. The number freed in the year 1816 alone exceeded the total number of Nova Scotian and Maroon settlers combined.

The 'Liberated Africans', as they were officially styled, or 're-captives', as they may more conveniently be called, had to be maintained in the colony. Brought in by naval ships from all parts of the coast, from homelands extending from the Senegal to the Congo (a few even came

[1] For the Niger expedition of 1841 see C. C. Ifemesia, 'The "civilizing" mission of 1841', *Journal of the Historical Society of Nigeria*, 1962, **2**, 3, 291–310.

from East Africa, even as far away as Lake Malawi), they could not possibly be repatriated. Even had repatriation been possible, the re-patriated would have risked being immediately re-enslaved. Some were taken into European or settler households in Freetown as servants. Some were enlisted as soldiers. The rest were settled in villages in the country round Freetown.

Most officials saw the recaptives as a problem: Sir Charles MacCarthy, who governed Sierra Leone from 1814 to 1824, saw them as an oppor-tunity. Fired by the kind of vision that had once inspired Granville Sharp and the sponsors of the Sierra Leone Company – the creation in Sierra Leone of a centre from which Christianity and civilization would be diffused over Africa – he took the recaptives as the means to fulfil his vision. He proposed to transform them into a Christian population who would spread new ways to the unenlightened.

MacCarthy planned to settle recaptives in tidy villages, laid out in English style round a nucleus of parish church, parsonage and school-house. There they would learn from missionaries a new religion and a new way of life. Missionaries were already available for the task. The Church Missionary Society, from 1804, and the Wesleyan Missionary Society, from 1811, had agents in Sierra Leone. The CMS was ready to collaborate officially with the government. The obstacle most gover-nors would have found insuperable was finance, for the end of the Napoleonic Wars brought a period of sudden retrenchment. British colonial policy was entering the era which grudged every penny spent on the colonies. But MacCarthy, a persuasive enthusiast, won over the authorities in London, who authorized the outlay of large sums of British tax-payers' money to carry out his grandiose, expensive schemes.[1]

Missionaries were put in charge of the recaptive villages as govern-ment officers: hence they could use secular as well as religious authority to impart their message. But little authority was needed. The recaptives were immediately responsive. Lacking a common language, they were ready to learn English to communicate with one another. Cut off from the community-based religions of their homelands, they listened with interest to Christian preaching which invited them into a new life of salvation to match their new life of freedom. They began adopting European names (usually the name of a missionary, official or promi-nent settler). They took to wearing European-style clothes, and learning

[1] For the development of the recaptive community see John Peterson, *Province of Free-dom: a history of Sierra Leone 1787–1870* (London, 1969).

the skills imparted in the schools – or at least seeing that their children learnt them.

It proved impossible to recruit enough missionaries to staff all the villages, where the population swelled yearly with fresh importations from the slave ships. Missionaries fell ill and died or had to be invalided home. Lay officials were substituted, sometimes Afro-Americans or Afro-West Indians who had emigrated to Sierra Leone to seek their fortune. Nova Scotian and Maroon settlers too were employed in charge of villages. Indeed the settlers played a large part in the transformation of the recaptives. A black Christian community, living in European style, they formed a reference group for the recaptives to copy, particularly those who worked in their households. Some preferred to attend the settler churches rather than the missionaries' churches. Similarly the already established recaptives influenced those who were newly arrived, particularly their own countrymen, taking them into their homes and initiating them into a new kind of life.

Soldiers disbanded from the Royal African Corps and the West India Regiments after the Napoleonic Wars were also settled in the colony. Some stayed in Freetown, forming their own suburbs; the rest MacCarthy sent to found villages in outlying parts of the peninsula. They, too, with skills learnt from Europeans and small pensions, were a reference group for the recaptives. A few prospered as traders or petty officials, but despite their advantages most merged before long into the recaptive population.

Not all went quite as MacCarthy had planned. Much of the lavish expenditure was diverted into useless channels – vast Gothic churches with massive towers that collapsed, enormous bales of clothing and other equipment that rotted unissued in the stores. Some of it was appropriated by ill-supervised European officials. Nevertheless, within a decade or two of MacCarthy's death his dream had come true. The recaptive population had been transformed in the way he intended. Though perhaps 5 per cent remained Muslims, and others still clung to the religions of their distant homelands, most became church-going Christians. Yet they were ready to interpret their religion in their own way. Despite missionary disapproval, some indigenous practices (like communicating with the family dead) were unobtrusively incorporated into Christian worship.

Government supervision of the recaptive villages was often lax and ineffective: some of the smaller villages had no official in charge. But the people created their own local government institutions. They elected their own headmen, and formed benefit societies, which also served as a means of settling disputes among the members and preserving law and order. The majority of the recaptives were Yoruba, captured during the civil wars that devastated Yorubaland during the 1820s. They introduced their own *egungun* society, and even established their own hierarchy of government, with a 'king' to whom all Yoruba in the colony gave allegiance. The government normally refused to give any recognition to any of these recaptive institutions. Nevertheless it was they rather than the government that kept order in the villages, and enabled the recaptives to evolve as a law-abiding, peaceable, self-respecting community.

THE GAMBIA

British traders had long been established in the Gambia River.[1] From 1661 the Royal African Company occupied a post on James Island, until it was destroyed by the French in 1779. During the Napoleonic Wars all the French West African possessions passed into British hands: at the peace it was agreed that Gorée and Senegal be restored to the French. But to allow British traders to retain a foothold on that part of the coast, and in particular to let them participate in the export trade in gum (then used for glazing textiles), a new British settlement was established in 1816 on Banjul Island, re-named St Mary's Island, in the Gambia.

In the usual way a treaty was made with the king of Kombo, who was promised an annual payment of the customary kind. Like Naimbana in Sierra Leone, he put his mark to a document he could not read, and thereby renounced all further claims to the island. In his own eyes he remained the owner: in British eyes he had transferred sovereignty.

The Gambia settlement was also intended for use in the naval campaign against the slave trade. Recaptives were sent there as settlers, and a small town, named Bathurst after the secretary of state for the colonies, was laid out on the island on the Freetown gridiron plan. Disbanded soldiers were also settled there. Thus the Gambia colony, like the Sierra Leone colony, had as its permanent population a nucleus of non-indigenous Africans, in addition to the transient population of European traders, officials and missionaries, and indigenous (chiefly Wolof) traders and labourers who moved in from the surrounding countryside.

As in Sierra Leone, enterprising Afro-Americans came back across

[1] See J. M. Gray, *A history of the Gambia* (Cambridge, 1940).

the Atlantic to seek their fortune. Among them was Thomas Joiner, a Mande in origin, who had been enslaved and taken to America, where he had managed to save money and buy his freedom.[1] Then he returned to Africa, took up trade, prospered and settled in Bathurst as a merchant and government contractor. He also owned ships which he sent trading along the coast. He died in 1842, as one of the most prominent men in the town.

Christian missionary efforts tended to be concentrated on Sierra Leone. In the Gambia there was only a small station of the Wesleyan Missionary Society to educate and preach to the recaptives. Hence their transformation was slower than it was in Sierra Leone. Nevertheless they, too, accepted the new ways they were offered, became Christians and adopted a European style of life. As in Sierra Leone, they formed their own benefit societies and elected their own unofficial local government, forming a distinctive self-reliant society in their new homeland.

TRADE IN VEGETABLE PRODUCE

Where the slave trade was suppressed, alternative sources of export produce had to be found, to give the inhabitants something to exchange for the imported manufactures they had come to rely on. Coastal Sierra Leone was covered with fine forest trees. An Irish trader, John McCormack, began felling timber in 1816 and exporting it to Britain. A flourishing timber trade grew up, chiefly to supply the British dockyards. The Temne, Bulom and Susu rulers in the timber-producing areas welcomed the timber traders, who restored them the rents and customs they had lost when they had to give up the slave trade. As the suitable trees were felled along one river bank the traders moved on to the next. Gradually the country was deforested; the secondary bush that grew up was useless for export. By the 1860s, when in any case iron ships were replacing wooden, most of the available timber had been cut. Thus the timber trade, like the slave trade, consumed natural resources and gave expendable consumer goods in return.

Vegetable oils were in growing demand in Europe for lubricants, cleansers and food. So groundnuts, palm oil, palm kernels and benniseed provided alternative export commodities. Charles Heddle was the pioneer in the groundnut trade. The son of a Scottish army doctor and a

[1] For Joiner and the Bathurst community in the nineteenth century see Florence K. Mahoney, 'Government and opinion in the Gambia 1816–1901', unpublished Ph.D. thesis (London, 1963); also Florence K. Mahoney, 'African leadership in Bathurst in the nineteenth century', *Tarikh*, 1968, **2**, 2, 25–38.

Senegalese mother, he traded in the Gambia, then in Freetown, building up a large fortune from import–export trading and property investment. Eventually he retired to an opulent château in France. Heddle was the first to realize that the fine colourless oil inside palm kernels was a saleable commodity, as well as the thick red oil from the pulp in which the kernels were embedded.

In this way Freetown and Bathurst became the centres of a flourishing export trade. Trade in vegetable produce replaced trade in human beings – as the abolitionists had long envisioned. But an internal slave trade was still needed to supply labour to harvest the vegetable produce. No longer exported across the Atlantic to work directly for Europeans, slaves were now sold within coastal West Africa to work indirectly for the European market.[1]

Nor was there any change in 'the true principles of Commerce' – the exchange of African raw materials against European manufactures. Vegetable produce was exported unprocessed: factories to express groundnut oil, opened in Freetown in the 1840s, soon closed. Indeed as the import–export trade in vegetable produce expanded, the West African economy was tied more and more closely to that of Europe.

SOCIAL CHANGE AND THE CREOLE DIASPORA

The economic opportunities represented by this growing import–export trade underlay the transformation of the recaptives. Instructed in the capitalist ethic of early nineteenth-century Protestantism, with its emphasis on hard work, thrift and individual initiative, the enterprising soon abandoned subsistence farming in the villages for petty retail trade in Freetown, or produce-buying in the surrounding country. Street traders would save their penny profits, put up a stall, and eventually build a shop. Produce-buyers, working at first as agents for a European or a Freetown settler, would branch out on their own. In 1842, John Ezzidio, a recaptive from Nupe country and a dedicated Methodist, was taken to England by a Methodist missionary and introduced to English exporters. On his return to Freetown he set up as an import–export trader. Within a few years he was importing £3,000–4,000 worth of goods a year.

The emergent capitalist recaptives traded almost on an equal footing

---

[1] See Christopher Fyfe, 'Opposition to the slave trade as a preliminary to the European partition of Africa', in *The theory of imperialism and the European partition of Africa* (Edinburgh, Centre of African Studies, University of Edinburgh, 1967), 129–43.

with the few European traders in the colony, who did business on the same sort of scale as they did. Though the settler population still resisted accepting recaptives as social equals, they were forced to accept them as economic superiors, and to sell them land in the exclusive central part of Freetown.[1] For the recaptives, like the settlers, put their profits into land and houses to obtain an income from invested capital. Thus a *rentier* class could emerge. By mid-century those who had entered the colony not long before naked and penniless were turning themselves into a prosperous bourgeoisie, building substantial houses, furnished with imported luxuries, to advertise their new-found status, like their equivalents in Europe and America.

Ambitious for themselves, they were even more ambitious for their children. Here the missionary societies were ready to help. In 1845 the CMS opened a grammar school in Freetown, and in 1849 a secondary school for girls, catering not only for the colony but for children from the Gambia and other parts of the coast. The other missions followed their example. Nor was higher education ignored. As early as 1814 the CMS had opened an institution to train recaptives as teachers and missionaries. After various vicissitudes it was refounded in 1827 at Fourah Bay, east of Freetown. As the century advanced it became less exclusively a missionary institution; students were also accepted for general higher education. In 1876 Fourah Bay College, as it had by then become, was affiliated to the University of Durham, to enable students to receive a degree from a British university.

Children born to recaptives were known in Sierra Leone as 'Creoles', a name which then became attached to all their descendants – even to those who adopted their way of life. Young Creoles, educated by the CMS or sent abroad by wealthy parents for higher education, began entering the professions. Two qualified as doctors in Britain in 1859, James Africanus Horton and William Broughton Davies; they were commissioned as army officers and served twenty years in West Africa, both retiring with the rank of lieutenant-colonel. Horton published several books on medical and political subjects.[2] Others qualified as lawyers; the most famous was eventually knighted as Sir Samuel Lewis.[3] Others entered the ministry as pastors or missionaries, or went into government service and rose to senior posts.

Yet the government was slow to recognize the demands for repre-

[1] See Arthur T. Porter, *Creoledom* (London, 1963).
[2] Horton's most interesting book is *West African countries and peoples* (London, 1868).
[3] For whom see John D. Hargreaves, *A life of Sir Samuel Lewis* (London, 1958).

sentative government voiced in the Freetown newspapers which began appearing in the 1840s and 1850s. Autocratic rule by governor and council was given up in the Gambia, more dominated by European business than Sierra Leone, in 1843. Executive and legislative councils were constituted – the former composed entirely of officials, the latter with one or two unofficials added. Not until 1863 was a similar change made in Sierra Leone. Ezzidio was one of the first unofficial members. But no further representative institutions were conceded, and policy remained firmly in official hands.

The Sierra Leone colony peninsula and its environs could not satisfy the ambitions of this enterprising population. Many still longed for their far-off homelands. In 1839 a group of Yoruba recaptives bought a convicted slave ship and sailed down the coast to Badagry, the port from which many thousands of Yoruba had been shipped. On their return they petitioned the government to found a British colony there.[1] Official help was refused, but nevertheless they streamed back unsponsored, returning to their astonished families like Joseph returning from Egypt to his brethren.

At the invitation of these 'Saro' (as they were called in their Yoruba homeland – a corruption of 'Sierra Leone'), the Church Missionary Society and Wesleyan Missionary Society established missions among them. Recaptives and Creoles played a large part, working as teachers and missionaries. In 1864 the most prominent recaptive missionary, a Yoruba, the Reverend Ajayi Crowther, was made a bishop of the Church of England. He became head of a CMS mission to the Niger peoples, leading a wholly African mission church, run entirely by recaptive or Creole agents.

All along the coast there were openings in government and mission service, as trading agents or private traders, as craftsmen or professional men, for those educated in Sierra Leone. Many went to swell the recaptive community in the Gambia, as officials, pastors and teachers, or to trade in groundnuts. Creole traders were established on MacCarthy's Island, 150 miles up the Gambia river. Creole women dominated the trade in kola nuts between Bathurst and Freetown. Others, men and women, traded along the river banks north and south of Sierra Leone.

Though the Gold Coast colony had its own European-educated élite, Creoles found plenty of openings there too. They also settled in Lagos before it became a British colony.[2] Freetown Christians opened

---

[1] Petition printed in Fyfe, *Sierra Leone inheritance*, 147–9.

[2] See Jean H. Kopytoff, *A preface to modern Nigeria: the 'Sierra Leonians' in Yoruba 1830–1890* (Madison, 1965).

the first church in Lagos; Freetown Muslims opened the first mosque. Others traded up the Niger and in the Niger delta.

During the 1820s it had been proposed in London to abandon Sierra Leone (which was supposed to be particularly unhealthy for Europeans), and move the naval base and the courts of mixed commission to the Spanish island of Fernando Po. A naval officer, Captain W. F. Owen, who conducted the first scientific surveys of the coasts of tropical Africa, was sent with a party of recaptive artisans and labourers from Freetown to lay out a site.[1] The plan came to nothing, but the recaptives remained. Emigrants from Freetown joined them, settling as traders and planters, forming a British Creole population in a Spanish colony.

Thus the recaptives, gathered in from the coast, scattered over it again, a far-ranging diaspora, bringing with them the new religion, skills and way of life they had learnt in Sierra Leone.

LIBERIA[2]

There are many similarities between the founding of the Sierra Leone colony and the founding of Liberia. Both were founded by sponsors who were seeking a distant receptacle for undesirables of a different skin colour. Both were seen as weapons against the slave trade. Both served, and were meant to serve, as a means to implant an alien religion, morality and way of life in Africa. Both purported to be grounded on principles of peace and philanthropy, but maintained themselves by war and conquest.

By the beginning of the nineteenth century nearly a quarter of a million Afro-Americans in the United States were free. Yet they were not full citizens. In the slave-owning states they appeared as a menace – a threat to the cherished white faith that slavery and colour must go together. In the north they were an anomaly. 'The laws, it is true, proclaim them free,' wrote Henry Clay, 'but prejudices more powerful than laws deny them the privileges of freemen.'[3] Americans in name, they were excluded from the aspirations the new republic claimed to offer its citizens – a living reproach to American idealism.

Thomas Jefferson spelt out the situation as he saw it in his *Notes on*

---

[1] Owen's reports are in the Public Record Office, series C.O. 82.

[2] For the early history of Liberia see C. H. Huberich, *The political and legislative history of Liberia* (New York, 1947).

[3] Quoted in Early Lee Fox, *The American Colonization Society* (Baltimore, 1919), 33.

the state of Virginia published in 1794, in which he anticipated un-systematically the theories of race enunciated systematically some seventy years later. He declared it impossible for black and white to live together in the same society in America. Instead he turned to a pro-posal, already current for a couple of generations,[1] that the black population be sent away to some distant home of their own. This proposal interested the missionary-minded: the Reverend Samuel Hopkins of Baltimore, a friend of Granville Sharp's, was planning to use Afro-Americans to preach Christianity in Africa. Thus the 'colon-ization' movement in the United States united two dreams – the 'purification' of white America from its 'black taint', and the Chris-tianization of Africa.

When therefore the American Colonization Society was founded in Washington in 1816, it had many influential sponsors.[2] Some supported it to be rid of an embarrassing social incubus; some hoped that by drawing off the free black population slavery could be entrenched more firmly; some dreamed missionary dreams. All apparently saw Africa (as their ancestors had seen America) as *tabula rasa*, where colonists could fulfil their potentialities undisturbed.[3] Disapproval of the slave trade enabled them (as it had once enabled the sponsors of the Sierra Leone Company) to take up a position of moral superiority, and assume un-questioningly that their efforts would bring benefits to Africa.

When their aims were so divided, it is no wonder that most of the proposed beneficiaries were suspicious. Despite all the Society's efforts, throughout the whole period of colonization from 1816 to the 1840s, less than 17,000 ever emigrated. The rest no more wanted to settle in Africa than their white compatriots wanted to settle in Europe.

To fulfil its aim adequately, the American Colonization Society needed official backing. The government of a country so recently liberated from colonial status could not directly participate in overseas 'colonization'. Indirectly, however, money was made available under the Slave Trade Act of 1819. The Society's settlement was designated a home for slaves captured in transit across the Atlantic by the United States navy, where recaptives could be settled at public expense, as British-liberated recaptives were in Sierra Leone. Thus the Society received official countenance; government agents accompanied the

---

[1] See D. B. Davis, *The problem of slavery in Western culture* (Ithaca, 1966), 310.

[2] For the American Colonization Society see P. J. Staudenraus, *The African colonization movement 1816–1865* (New York, 1961).

[3] For Africa as a *tabula rasa* see also George A. Shepperson, 'Africa, the Victorians and imperialism', in *The theory of imperialism*, 175–85.

prospectors for a suitable site. The colony was a private venture, not a colony of the United States.

Afro-Americans had already on their own initiative been making contact with Africa. Paul Cuffee, a Massachusetts ship-captain of part African, part Amerindian descent, had visited Sierra Leone, made friends with the settlers, and in 1816 took over a party of Afro-American immigrants to Freetown. Thus American colonization in West Africa antedated the foundation of the American Colonization Society, and was begun by a man of African origin. The Society's first agents, inspired by Cuffee's example, went to Sierra Leone in 1818 to look for a suitable site in the neighbourhood.

The sponsors of the American Colonization Society, like the sponsors of the Sierra Leone Company, knew nothing of West Africa and its long tradition of friendly, institutionalized relationships between Africans and Europeans. Obsessed with the sense of their own superiority, contemptuous and ignorant of African usages, they assumed the African peoples would receive their agents as god-like benefactors, and be glad to cede them land. The coastal Temne could tell a different story of the dangers of letting aliens settle in their country. Hence it proved impossible to negotiate a permanent site near Sierra Leone. A temporary site on Sherbro Island, south of the Sierra Leone peninsula, was provided by a Nova Scotian settler, John Kizzell, who traded there. But when the first group of immigrants arrived, it turned out to be ill-adapted for settlement, and they had to abandon it.

Unable to find any other nearby site, dissuaded also by the Sierra Leone government from planting American settlers so close to a British colony, prospecting agents went down the coast to Grand Bassam. Here a site was offered, but on the usual terms, in return for an annual rent; sovereignty was refused. This was not acceptable. Finally in December 1821 the Society's agent, Dr Eli Ayres, and a United States naval officer, Lieutenant R. F. Stockton, landed at Cape Mesurado, in the lee of which there was a better anchorage than could generally be found elsewhere on a coast which European sailors had shunned for three centuries. Here they began protracted negotiations with King Peter, the ruler of the indigenous De people.

Farther south, towards Cape Palmas, lived the Kru and Grebo peoples, known collectively to Europeans as Krumen, a seafaring community with a distinctive and unusual way of life. Leaving home young, a Kru would serve on board European ships, particularly British naval ships, or on shore at a European trading establishment. There had been a Kru community in Freetown since 1793. Every few years he would return home for a while with his earnings, then go out and work again. Eventually he would retire and settle back permanently in his own country.

Accustomed to working for foreigners, the Kru sometimes tended to identify with foreign interests. Ayres and Stockton found Kru allies in their negotiations with King Peter. Indeed later Kru tradition declared that it was they who were chiefly responsible for getting the settlement founded – a responsibility many of them would one day lament.[1]

King Peter, like any ruler along the coast, was ready to welcome 'strangers' who came to trade in the familiar way and who undertook the recognized obligations towards their landlord. But he hesitated to renounce sovereignty; the decision was put off from day to day. At last Stockton cut his hesitations short by pointing a pistol at his head. The king then agreed – and at that moment (so Stockton related) rays of sunshine burst symbolically through the clouds. Like Naimbana and the Temne chiefs, King Peter and the De chiefs put their marks to a treaty ceding land in perpetuity in return for an assortment of trade goods. The Americans congratulated themselves on their bargain, Ayres reporting to the Society that they had acquired a million dollars worth of land for goods worth 300 dollars.

The settlers, who had been waiting in Freetown, arrived in January 1822 to found their new home, Liberia – the land of the free. Their capital was called Monrovia, after James Monroe, president of the United States. Like the early Sierra Leone settlers they suffered from initial hardships, disease and mortality. The Society's agents went home ill. But the survivors struggled on, led by two settlers, Elijah Johnson and the Reverend Lott Cary, a Baptist preacher, who assumed charge. The Board of the Society, however, despite its claims to be providing its protégés with opportunities and a chance to rise in the world, would not recognize Johnson and Cary as agents. Rather than trust a non-white settler with responsibility, they sent out white agents to die or be invalided home.

Defrauded of their land, the neighbouring peoples remained unreconciled. The settlers, sensing their hostility, built stockades in the North American frontier tradition, with cannon mounted. Faced with these evidences of military occupation, the De, like the Temne against Freetown, attempted a surprise attack in November 1822. Like the Temne, they were defeated. A second attack was similarly unsuccessful.

[1] See P.R.O., F.O. 367/138, petition enclosed in Admiralty to Foreign Office, 11 March 1909.

A passing British naval ship then landed some officers and sailors who helped negotiate a truce and stayed on for a few weeks. Some have suggested that British intervention saved Liberia. But the settlers had already entrenched themselves permanently. Better armed and better organized than their opponents, they had proved that whatever local rebuffs they might occasionally suffer, they, like the Sierra Leone settlers, were not to be dislodged from their new home by an African enemy. Hence the anniversary of the second battle has been rightly celebrated in Liberia as a public holiday. To the Americo-Liberians the victory had moral overtones. It was taken to represent the triumph of civilization over barbarism. Inspired, like their white contemporaries in the American West, with the pioneer's sense of the ethical rightness of his advance, they saw their success in the teleological terms which for another century and a half were to give Europeans and Americans (of whatever colour) the belief that their aggressions represented the spread of enlightenment.

The Americo-Liberian immigrants were busy pioneers. They laid out Monrovia like a North American pioneer town and extended their 'frontier' round it, with farmsteads hacked out of the bush. Like the first Sierra Leone settlers, they hoped to make a living by farming: like them they were to find eventually that only trade could bring them profit. Some had capital and traded in export produce, even sending their own sailing ships back and forth across the Atlantic. Many were articulate and well educated. In 1830 James Russwurm, one of the first black Americans to have graduated from an American university, founded a newspaper to voice their views, the *Liberia Herald*. Missionary societies opened schools for their children in addition to the publicly supported schools, which tended to be hampered for lack of funds.

Though Liberia was intended as a home for recaptives, the United States navy seldom appeared off the West African coast. Over a period of forty years only 5,722 recaptives were brought in. Called 'Congoes', because the first shipload came from the Congo, they tended to be segregated in communities of their own, forming a small uninfluential group in the population. Thus the demographic patterns of the Sierra Leone and Liberia colonies differed. In Liberia, American immigrants predominated; in Sierra Leone, recaptives soon outnumbered the original settlers.[1]

[1] For comparisons of Sierra Leone and Liberia see Edward W. Blyden, *Christianity, Islam and the Negro race* (London, 1887); and John D. Hargreaves, 'African colonization in the nineteenth century: Liberia and Sierra Leone', *Sierra Leone Studies* (new series), 1962, **16**, 189–203.

Americo-Liberian culture tended therefore to be far less African than Sierra Leone Creole culture. In Sierra Leone Krio developed as the vehicle of everyday speech, an Africanized Creole language. In Liberia the English language persisted in a recognizably American form, nurtured by missionary contacts from across the Atlantic.

Other settlements were established along the coast on land ceded by the inhabitants. Some were started by settlers from Monrovia, some were sponsored by the American Colonization Society, or by other colonization societies in the United States who sent out immigrants. Wherever they settled the slave traders were expelled, if need be by war. By mid-century the coastline stretching from the Sherbro country of Sierra Leone as far south as the country beyond Cape Palmas had been included in the Liberian sphere.

Despite occasional small wars, relations between the immigrants and the indigenous population were on the whole amicable at this period. The Americo-Liberians brought the opportunities of trade formerly brought by slave traders. Hence, even though they had expropriated the land they settled on, they were still welcomed for the economic advantages they brought. Some settlers felt strong missionary obligations towards their new neighbours: Lott Cary opened a school in the interior to spread the Christian religion and new skills.

Private colonization societies in far-off America were not really competent to govern settlements on the West African coast. In 1839 most of the settlements united into the Commonwealth of Liberia, virtually self-governing, but still with a governor appointed by the American Colonization Society. In 1841 for the first time a governor of part-African descent, John J. Roberts, was appointed (though even he was nearly white). In 1847 the Commonwealth was transformed into the independent Republic of Liberia, in order to give the state a recognized international status. (The settlement of the Maryland Colonization Society at Cape Palmas, constituted as a separate republic in 1853, joined Liberia in 1857.)[1]

The new republic was launched by a declaration of independence, with a constitution on the American model, drawn up by a white Harvard law professor, with a president, two houses of congress and a supreme court. Like the constitution of the United States it made no provision for political parties. But the Liberians, unlike the Americans, remained true to the principles of the Founding Fathers and avoided a

[1] For Maryland see documents in P.R.O., F.O. 47/12–13; also J. H. Latrobe, *Maryland in Africa* (Baltimore, 1885).

rigid two-party system. Despite some awkwardness in the constitution (until 1907, for instance, the presidential term lasted only two years, which meant incessant electioneering), it supplied a workable instrument of government by which power was transferred peaceably from president to president, save for one coup d'état in 1871. In this respect Liberian politics made a striking contrast with the bloodstained politics of the republics of Latin America.

Revenue was raised chiefly through customs duties, the regular expedient for tax-gathering in an impoverished colonial economy where it is difficult to raise direct taxes. Though the long Liberian coastline had never been an important centre for European trade, a few British traders were settled in isolated places. They resented having to pay customs duties and complained to their government in London. Lord Palmerston, the foreign secretary, refused to listen to their complaints. He approved of Liberia as a weapon against the slave trade. When President Roberts visited England, he received him cordially. The British government recognized Liberia officially in 1848 (the United States government, fearful of having to receive a black ambassador in Washington, delayed recognition until 1862), and presented the republic with an armed schooner.

Nevertheless the British traders remained resentful, evaded payment of duties, and incited their Kru neighbours to do the same. Hence a tradition of hostility grew up between the Kru round Cape Palmas and the government in distant Monrovia. Over the following generations, and into the 1930s, a series of wars was fought between the Kru and the government, the Kru often supported covertly by Europeans.

Similarly in the Gallinas country adjoining Sierra Leone a British trader refused to pay customs to Monrovia and incited his Vai neighbours to repudiate Liberian rule. After two decades of dispute and armed hostilities the British government ended the altercation summarily. The governor of Sierra Leone appeared in Monrovia in 1882 with a large naval escort, forced the Liberian government to surrender all claims to the Gallinas country, and annexed it.

These disputes and wars soured relations between the Americo-Liberians and the indigenous peoples. The hopes expressed in earlier days of integrating into one united Christian nation gradually lost their appeal. Liberians also grew increasingly suspicious of Europeans, feeling that 'some Europeans have always been at the bottom of every war which has been fought between the colonists and the natives'.[1]

---

[1] Abayomi Karnga, *History of Liberia* (Liverpool, 1926), 23.

They were also divided by a bitter legacy brought across the Atlantic – the strife between those with part-European ancestry and those without. President Roberts was almost white, and though his successor Stephen Benson was black, mulattoes tended to hold the highest offices and to look down on those darker skinned than themselves. The champion of the blacks was Edward Blyden. Born in the West Indies of unmixed African ancestry, partly educated in the United States, Blyden came to Liberia in 1851 and worked there as a teacher and in government service. Adopting the racial theories current in Europe, he sought to preserve the purity of the 'Negro race' in Africa and America from the contaminations of white interbreeding and European culture. In his writings may be found the first expression of the cult of 'African personality'.[1]

The import–export economies of the British and French West African colonies expanded steadily, linked to easily accessible mother countries. Liberia faced growing economic competition. British colonial mail steamers, the lifeline of trade, stopped calling at Monrovia in 1858. Sailings across the Atlantic were irregular. Hence, the customs-based revenue was meagre. In 1870 President Roye went to England to raise a £100,000 government loan on the London stock exchange. The only terms he could obtain were so unfavourable that he was greeted with fury on his return. Already hated by the mulatto élite because he was black, he was accused of trying to establish a dictatorship, was imprisoned and charged with high treason. He escaped, but was drowned trying to leave the country.

In the confusion much of the loan money disappeared; a large slice had already stayed in England in the promoters' pockets as commission. Altogether it was reckoned that only about a quarter of it reached the Liberian treasury. Instead of benefiting from an injection of capital, the impoverished republic was henceforth burdened with heavy interest payments to foreign shareholders, whose claims had to be satisfied every year out of the exiguous revenue.

As the period of the European scramble for Africa approached, Liberia showed up clearly as a potential victim. The high hopes of its early years had faded. Crippled financially by foreign debt, divided among themselves and against their neighbours, unable to resist European aggression, the Liberians seemed to be sustained by little more than 'the Love of Liberty' which, as their motto proclaimed, 'brought us here'.

[1] For Blyden see (in addition to his own published works) Hollis R. Lynch, *Edward Wilmot Blyden: Pan-Negro patriot 1832–1912* (London, 1967), and Edith Holden, *Blyden of Liberia* (New York, 1966).

LIBREVILLE

During the period of the July Monarchy in France (1830–48) the British and French were often in colonial rivalry. From the late 1830s Frenchmen were propounding plans to extend French influence in West Africa. In 1839 a French naval officer, Edouard Bouët-Willaumez, cruising down the coast, persuaded rulers at Cape Palmas and at the mouth of the Gabon estuary to make treaties ceding land to France – acting on his own initiative without orders from the government, in a style often followed by French officers in nineteenth-century Africa.[1]

Renewed British interest in West Africa manifested in Buxton's proposals, in the Niger expedition of 1841, and by revived official concern for the Gold Coast, spurred the French into a Buxton-type policy of their own – the so-called 'foothold policy' (*politique des points d'appui*).[2] Fortified French posts were to be planted at suitable places on the coast to encourage French commerce, to help suppress the slave trade, and above all to help check British expansion. In 1842 treaties were made at Grand Bassam and Assinie (in the modern Ivory Coast), and at Gabon, to enable posts of this kind to be built. As in Sierra Leone and Liberia, the Africans who affixed their marks to the treaties specifically renounced sovereignty.[3]

At Gabon land was ceded on the north shore of the estuary, and Fort d'Aumale was built. The Gabon estuary was an old trading centre, where the coastal Mpongwe had for centuries exchanged slaves and ivory with Europeans for manufactured goods. Like Freetown, and to a lesser extent Monrovia, it formed a fine natural harbour. For a short period the French began fortifying it as a naval base, but the project was abandoned early in 1848.

The main trading centre was a couple of miles up river at King Glass's town, where white traders, chiefly British and American, gathered. In 1842 the Reverend J. Leighton Wilson, an energetic American missionary, established a Congregationalist mission there. King Glass and other neighbouring rulers also made treaties with the French, renouncing sovereignty and accepting French protection. As

---

[1] For the early years of French colonization in Gabon see Hubert Deschamps, 'Quinze ans de Gabon: les débuts de l'établissement français, 1839–1853', *Revue française d'histoire d'outre-mer*, 1963, **50**, 283–345 and 1965, **52**, 92–126.

I am grateful to Professor John Hargreaves of the University of Aberdeen for advice on this section.

[2] For which see Bernard Schnapper, *La politique et le commerce français dans le Golfe de Guinée de 1838 à 1871* (Paris, 1961).

[3] Schnapper, *La politique*, 98.

in Sierra Leone, the full implications of the treaties were only understood after they had been made. When King Glass hoisted a British
flag, a French gunboat forced him to remove it. When King Denis, a
treaty chief on the south shore, went on trading in slaves, the French
navy intervened. As elsewhere, the European suppression of the slave
trade undermined African sovereignty.

French entrepreneurs dreamed of making Gabon a plantation colony.
But the Mpongwe, like the other peoples of coastal West Africa, had no
tradition of working for Europeans as agricultural labourers: their
relations with them were normally those of equal trading partners.
Hence it was impossible to recruit plantation labour locally. In 1846 the
government agreed to supply recaptive labour. A captured slave ship,
the *Elizia*, was brought into Gorée with about 250 slaves on board,
shipped from Loango, north of the Congo mouth. Most were sick or
dying, but thirty were sent to Gabon where they were put to work –
not however on plantations, but on the naval works, not yet abandoned.
Three years later Bouët-Willaumez, now in charge of the naval squadron, sent off another fifty-two of the *Elizia* survivors to Gabon –
twenty-seven men, twenty-three women and two children.

Bouët-Willaumez, like MacCarthy in Sierra Leone, saw in his policy
something that transcended mere administrative or economic convenience. In the tradition inaugurated by the Sierra Leone Company
and followed by some of the sponsors of Liberia, he dreamed of 'a new
creation, from which African civilization and French occupation will, I
hope, derive some fruits'.[1] In Gabon, as in Sierra Leone, recaptives
were to be settled in a village specially laid out for them, named
'Libreville'. A suitable site was found on the plateau above the fort –
so suitable that a year later (1850) the French authorities abandoned the
fort by the swampy waterside and moved up themselves. Thus Libreville became an official capital as well as a recaptive village, laid out like
Freetown and Monrovia as a planned city, in contrast to the surrounding African towns.[2]

In Libreville as in Sierra Leone the recaptives settled down to a new
way of life. They elected their own mayor. Catholic missionaries of the
Holy Ghost Mission, established near the fort in 1844, ministered to
their religious needs. But they disappointed those who were looking for
plantation labour. Like the Sierra Leone recaptives, they farmed, if at
all, only for subsistence or for the local market. Most took jobs with

[1] Schnapper, *La politique*, 98.
[2] For the development of Libreville see Guy Lasserre, *Libreville: la ville et sa région*
(Paris, 1958).

the government. Gabon no more became a plantation colony than Sierra Leone.

Libreville fits only marginally into the category of 'freed slave colonies'. The tiny recaptive settlement was eventually absorbed by the adjoining French official town, and by the Mpongwe and other villages that came clustering round as suburbs. The recaptive descendants merged into the growing population, some of whom were immigrants from their own Loango homelands. Little more than the name 'Libreville' has survived to recall the original purpose of the plateau settlement.

CONCLUSION

Though the European scramble for Africa only began in the last quarter of the nineteenth century, already in the first three-quarters the European powers were encroaching. The planting of freed slave colonies in West Africa belongs to this 'proto-partition' period in which the coming partition was foreshadowed.

The sponsors of the colonies, dedicated as they were to opposing the slave trade, saw no need to question the rightness of what they were doing. Their colonies were intended as centres from which European ways were to radiate to enlighten a benighted continent and open it up to European trade and influence. They voiced the sense of collective moral authority that was later to be embodied in the justificatory international documents of the 'scramble' period – the published Acts of the Berlin Conference of 1884–5 and the Brussels Conference of 1890.

In the early history of these colonies, then, one can see how, in Basil Davidson's words, 'British and French abolition of the slave trade went hand in hand with the rise of a new imperialism.'[1] Intended to help the peoples they were planted among, the colonies deprived them of land and sovereignty. They introduced an alien way of life, including a novel pattern of race relations which assumed that whites should rule and blacks obey. Thus the planting of these colonies provided a model for the future extension of European sovereignty, and softened West Africa for the coming European partition.

[1] Basil Davidson, *Black Mother* (London, 1961), 243.

CHAPTER 6

WEST AFRICA IN THE ANTI-SLAVE TRADE ERA

European relationships with West Africa in the first three-quarters of the nineteenth century were to a large extent dominated by the European effort to end the trans-Atlantic slave trade and to replace it by trade in the agricultural produce of West Africa. This led in part to the foundation of Sierra Leone and Liberia, the strengthening of British and French trading depots in other parts of the coast, a new European curiosity about the interior of Africa, and a renewed interest in effecting social and cultural change in Africa through Christian missions. This range of activities became an integrated programme of the abolitionists – stopping the slave trade, maintaining an anti-slavery naval squadron to enforce the prohibition, expanding 'legitimate trade', supporting missionary activities and exploration of the interior. These activities encouraged the involvement of Europeans in Africa, and several European and American nations came to participate in them to a greater or lesser extent. Abolition of the slave trade became the most common ideology to justify to the European public the expense and the fact of this involvement. This ideology was particularly strong in Britain, and from Britain it affected other countries. For example, owing to the tradition of Anglo-French rivalry in West Africa, the British example ensured the wholesale adoption of the abolitionist programme in France. Consequently, in the written European sources on Africa in this period, whether from missionaries, explorers, 'legitimate' traders, naval officers or government officials, the theme of abolition looms large, often disproportionately large, and the period 1807 to about 1870 in West African history has often been called the anti-slave trade or abolitionist era. The aim of this chapter is to assess the significance of European activities in West Africa in this period and thus to examine the validity of this title.

The essentially Eurocentric description of West African history in the pre-colonial nineteenth century implied by this title involves distortion in a number of ways. It seems to project onto the West African peoples the European preoccupation with the slave trade and its abolition. The protagonists of this view suggest or imply that the slave trade dominated the West African economy; that raiding for slaves was the basic cause and purpose of West African wars; that such slave wars or

the economic effects of the slave trade were the main factors in the rise and fall of West African states.[1] Accordingly, the issues for or against abolition are treated as the dominant themes of West African history in the nineteenth century, and the impact on West African states and peoples by Europeans preoccupied with the slave trade and its abolition is exaggerated. It is often overlooked that for all the effort of the abolitionists, European influence by 1870 remained limited virtually to the coast. For most West African peoples and states, the Christian abolitionist factor, if it existed at all, was very marginal in this period.

This tendency to exaggerate the role of Europeans as a factor of change in West African history before 1870 has led to another kind of distortion. Not only are the main events of West African history explained largely in terms of the single factor of the slave trade or its abolition; often the colonial period is allowed anachronistically to cast its shadow backwards to an undue extent. Because the abolitionist movement in many respects prepared the way for the colonial period, some historians go further and treat West African history between 1800 and 1870 only as a prelude to, if not an integral part of, the colonial period. They write with an underlying assumption that European rule was inevitable or imminent throughout the abolitionist era. They regard European officials who pursued policies advancing the areas of European control generally as the bold and far-sighted ones, and those who did not as hesitant, obstructionist and retrogressive.[2] They obscure or ignore the difference between the spread of European influence in the so-called informal empire and the formal exercise of sovereignty in the establishment of colonial rule, and they attribute to European officials in the former areas initiatives which they did not possess before the 1880s.[3] Consequently, they see European activities before 1870 as

[1] For a recent statement of this view, see A. G. Hopkins, 'Economic imperialism in West Africa: Lagos 1882–92', *Economic History Review*, 1968, **21**. For a critique, see J. F. A. Ajayi and R. S. Smith, *Yoruba warfare in the nineteenth century* (Cambridge, 1964), 123–5.

[2] See, for example, the relative treatment of General Louis C. Faidherbe and John Pope-Hennessy, e.g. on pp. 100 and 168 of J. D. Hargreaves, *Prelude to the partition of West Africa* (London, 1963). In popular textbooks, only the expansionist governors like Bouët-Williaumez, Faidherbe, MacCarthy, MacLean and Glover are mentioned by name. J. D. Fage, *A history of West Africa: an introductory survey* (Cambridge, 1969), while careful about the limits of British power, tends on pp. 162–3 to exaggerate the extent of French expansion.

[3] Even a careful historian like J. D. Hargreaves, discussing the development of groundnuts in Senegal in the 1850s, says: 'Thus began the exploitation of Senegal's major cash crop, which did not require government colonization schemes or the alienation of African land to settlers. But the cultivation and marketing of groundnuts on any really extensive scale would require stable political conditions in the Senegal region and France still possessed neither the power nor the political skill to provide them.' (*West Africa: the former French states* (Englewood Cliffs, New Jersey, 1967), 82.)

having caused revolutionary changes in West African social and economic systems, as well as decadence in the political systems, and other consequences of European dominance, which did not come about until the colonial period, and even then not precipitately in most places.

THE ISLAMIC ADVANCE

It should be emphasized, therefore, that for the vast majority of West Africans in the first three-quarters of the nineteenth century, Islam, not the Christian abolitionist movement, was the revolutionary factor creating larger political systems with new economic opportunities, and establishing new religious obligations and social values. By 1800, Islam was of course already a dominant religion in the Sudan, where for centuries it had competed with traditional African religions, not only as a set of personal beliefs but also as communal law, a source of social and cultural values and a complete way of life. Several Muslim rulers of Mali and Songhay had turned to Islam in their efforts to build supra-ethnic states and empires in the western Sudan. They used Muslim scribes and judges and legal precepts, much to the chagrin of traditionalists, especially in the rural areas. With the decline of Songhay, even though Islam continued to spread as a personal religion, there was a resurgence of traditional political systems and ethos and more accommodation of pre-Islamic religious ideas, as the Denianke Fulani and Mande came to power in Senegambia, the Rari took over in Masina, and the Bambara of Segu and Kaarta came to dominate a good deal of the western Sudan.[1] This in turn provoked a whole series of Islamic reform movements in the eighteenth and early nineteenth century aimed at establishing Muslim political control and the Islamic way of life throughout the western Sudan.[2]

This new advance in Islam began when Fulani religious leaders established theocracies in Futa Jalon and Futa Toro in the Senegambia region. From there it spread to northern Nigeria, where between 1804 and 1810 Usuman dan Fodio led a movement that conquered the old Hausa states and established over them a series of theocratic emirates owing allegiance to a single caliph whose capital was located at Sokoto. The older 'Habe'[3] rulers had represented Hausa ethnic rule and an

[1] See B. O. Ọlọruntimẹhin, *The Segu Tukulor empire* (London, 1972), 8, 21–2, 34, 36 and 317.

[2] These movements are examined in detail in chapter 4 of this volume.

[3] 'Habe', a Fulani word meaning 'strangers', is here and elsewhere used to designate the Hausa rulers of the pre-jihad period.

accommodation between Islam and traditional Hausa culture. The confrontation between them and the new theocratic emirates was the dominant historical factor throughout Hausaland for most of the nineteenth century. Pockets of Habe resistance remained unconquered. The new Fulani rulers spoke Hausa. They adopted and adapted Hausa political, social and military institutions, but Islam became established as the dominant way of life, regulating public and private law and personal morality. For the first time, the Hausa states were brought together within a single religious and political system. What is more, this movement thrust itself beyond Hausaland into Nupe, Ilorin, Gwari, Bauchi, Gombe, and Adamawa, establishing Fulani dominance and the frontiers of Islam as an aggressive force among peoples hitherto little touched by Islamic influences. The efforts of the Fulani to supplant the Kanuri in control of the Bornu empire provided an opportunity for the reforms of Muḥammad al-Amīn al-Kānamī, with the consequent collapse of the ancient Saifawa dynasty and the rise of a new Kanembu dynasty and Shuwa Arab bureaucracy. Like its bitter enemies in the Sokoto caliphate, the Kanembu dynasty combined religious and political leadership in the hands of the ruler, and placed the basis of the political order no longer in traditional custom but in Islamic law.[1]

Following this example, the Cisse of Masina led a revolution in 1818 to topple the Rari dynasty and the Arma, the descendants of the Moroccan conquerors of Songhay. They established a theocratic state where a council of Muslim scholars, led by the caliph with his capital at Hamdallahi, regulated public law and private morality according to Islamic tenets. One result of this successful revolution was that the new rulers sought to establish the independence of Masina and to end its subordination to the Bambara of Segu, whose regime remained based in traditional religion. This provoked war between the caliphate and the Bambara until the 1860s, when the Tukolor became a threat to both and encouraged them belatedly to make common cause.[2]

The Tukolor revolution which was launched around 1848 was perhaps the most militant attempt to use Islam as an instrument of large scale state-formation in the Western Sudan. Led by al-Ḥājj 'Umar b. Sa'īd Tal, the *khalīfa* of the Tijāniyya in West Africa, Tukolor aristocratic and military castes sought to establish a new theocratic regime

[1] M. Last, *The Sokoto caliphate* (London, 1967); L. Brenner, *The Shehus of Kukawa* (London, 1973); R. A. Adeleye, *Power and diplomacy in northern Nigeria* (London, 1971).
[2] A. Hampaté Ba and J. Daget, *L'empire peul du Macina* (Paris, 1962); W. A. Brown, 'Towards a chronology for the caliphate of Hamdullahi (Masina)', *Cahiers d'études africaines*, 1968, **8**, 3, 428–34.

over Segu, Kaarta, and some parts of Senegambia. The result was a confrontation between Tukolor social and political institutions as expressed in the ethos of Tijānī ways of Islam on the one side and Bambara institutions and culture on the other. The attempt to expand down the Senegal threatened to shut off the French from the waterway vital for the gum trade with the Moors of southern Mauritania, and the French resisted this. The expansion into Masina provoked not merely theological disputations with the caliphate at Hamdallahi, but also a series of wars in one of which al-Ḥājj 'Umar himself lost his life. Thereafter, the dominant theme of the history of the area, until the French conquest began in the 1880s, was the effort of Ahmadu, al-Ḥājj 'Umar's son and successor, to maintain Tijānī rule over the vast empire with the help and sometimes in the face of the rivalry of competing relatives and powerful Tukolor *talibes* (lieutenants).[1]

From the 1860s onwards, Islamic influence moved southwards to the edge of the forest zone. First, there was the attempt of Samory Toure to reconstruct various Mande peoples and states into a vast political system. He was himself not learned, but as an enlightened long-distance trader brought up in the tradition of the Dyula, he chose to use Islamic education, legal precepts and ideology in his endeavours at state formation.[2] This further encouraged colonies of Dyula traders, settled all along trade routes connecting the trading centres of the Sudan to the capitals of the forest and coastal states, to convert their mercantile and religious dominance into political hegemonies in places like Sikasso, Bobo Dioulasso and Bonduku.[3] Farther west in Senegambia in the same period, Islamic religious leaders or marabouts were establishing Koranic schools, and acting as political and commercial advisers among the Wolof, Temne, Lebou, and others. They made charms for the aristocratic castes and, tried to win influence over them. In these and other ways, they expanded religious and commercial opportunities for Muslims and, as the opportunity arose, they built up Islamic communities that exercised a good deal of political influence if not power. While no major Islamic states emerged, the political, social and religious consequences of the spread of Islam from the 1860s to the 1880s were far more significant than those of the advancing frontiers of European influence.[4]

[1] Ọlọruntimẹhin, *The Segu Tukulor empire*.
[2] J. Suret-Canale, 'La Guinée dans le système colonial', *Présence africaine*, 1960, **29**, 9–44.
[3] R. R. Griffeth, 'Dyula recruitment techniques in the West Volta region' (African History Colloquium on West African State Formation, UCLA, 1970).
[4] M. A. Klein, 'The Moslem revolution in nineteenth century Senegambia', in D. F. McCall, N. R. Bennett and J. Butler, eds., *Western African history* (London, 1969).

Farther east, in the forest states, this Islamic resurgence had important repercussions though it did not become the major factor of change. In the Volta region, the use of Muslim scribes and mounted mercenaries encouraged a new efficiency in state administration as far south as Asante, but the Islamic factor remained marginal in the expansion of the Asante empire and its conflict with the coastal peoples.[1] The establishment of Fulani rule in Ilorin was a result, not a cause, of the collapse of the Old Oyo kingdom. Fulani expansion and the mass movement of people helped the rapid spread of Islam in major Yoruba towns in the nineteenth century. However, it was the traditional Yoruba institutions, political systems and religious ideas that dominated and shaped the reconstruction and reorganization that followed the foundation of new political centres.[2] Similarly, while Ilorin and Nupe expansion into the northern parts of the Benin empire helped to spread Islam and to reduce the influence of the Benin monarch, the monarchy itself and the traditional religious and political systems survived.

EUROPEAN COASTAL ENCLAVES

European trading posts existed all along the coast, and it was here that the European impact was most evident. At some of these trading posts, forts had been built to protect the trade from European rivals and hostile African neighbours. At others, barracoons were erected to store slaves pending the trans-Atlantic journey. Some of the best known forts and barracoons were built in St Louis, Gorée, Rufisque, and St Mary's Island in Senegambia; Bissau in former Portuguese Guinea; Elmina, Anomabu, Cape Coast and Christiansborg (Accra) in modern Ghana; and Whydah in Dahomey. Around these trading posts, a mixed population had grown up, even by 1800, owing more allegiance to the European traders than to the neighbouring African states. Apart from the handful of European traders at each station, there were mulattoes – usually products of the union of European fathers and West African women, educated around the forts, on trading vessels or in Europe – holding administrative, commercial and military positions at the forts and helping to extend European commercial interests among neighbouring African peoples, or along the waterways and other trading

[1] N. Levtzion, *Muslims and chiefs in West Africa* (Oxford, 1968); I. Wilks, 'Ashanti government', in C. D. Forde and P. M. Kaberry, eds., *West African kingdoms in the nineteenth century* (London, 1967).

[2] J. F. A. Ajayi, 'The aftermath of the fall of Old Oyo', in J. F. A. Ajayi and M. Crowder, eds., *A history of West Africa*, II (London, 1974).

routes into the interior. A few African neighbours came to attach themselves to these stations as traders, labourers or deck hands on the trading vessels. The largest group, however, were slaves and emancipated slaves who did the menial work, head-loading goods, looking after the slaves in the barracoons, and providing labour at the ports. The resulting communities of strangers were developing into municipalities under European control and with varying degrees of independence *vis-à-vis* the neighbouring African states, depending on the size of the community itself or the power and cohesiveness of the neighbouring state. The size of St Louis (12,000 by 1837), its recognition with Gorée, and later Rufisque and Dakar, as municipalities by revolutionary governments in France, with defined governmental institutions, helped to consolidate their position as independent communes.[1] On the Gold Coast, the neighbouring Africans recognized European control in the forts but not beyond them. Some states claimed to be overlords with the right to collect tax for the land on which the forts were built. Other states depended to some extent on the forts for protection against hostile neighbours, and the governors of the forts therefore wielded influence beyond the forts.

These European-controlled municipalities and enclaves provided the bases for European activities in the anti-slave trade era. New enclaves were established, notably the settlements of Europeans and freed slaves in Freetown and surrounding villages of Sierra Leone, and of Afro-Americans and freed slaves in various colonies on the Liberian Coast, as well as French trading posts at Grand Bassam, Assinie and Libreville (Gabon).[2] The population, power and influence of these centres grew in the course of the nineteenth century and they became important markets on the coast and gateways to the interior. They expanded their influence either through agreements with neighbouring Africans, as on the Gold Coast, or through naval and military force, as on the lower Senegal, in Cayor and Lagos. But it is important not to antedate or exaggerate this influence. European power was based on a superiority of naval power, which was effective on the sea coast even though African canoes had the advantage in the lagoons and creeks. Military power on land, as Governor MacCarthy discovered on the Gold Coast in 1824, was more uncertain, because there was no such predominance in the armament available to either side. While Europeans had the advantage of discipline and superior techniques, Africans had the advantage of

[1] Hargreaves, *West Africa*, 62–77; G. W. Johnson, *The emergence of black politics in Senegal* (Stanford, 1971), chapter 1.　　　[2] See chapter 5 of this volume.

numbers and better knowledge of the forested terrain. Even where Europeans could use African allies and auxiliaries, they found military expeditions which would be adequate to ensure victory very expensive and they resorted to them rather sparingly. Thus until 1880, African political and religious systems, though increasingly under pressure, remained dominant even on the coast.

ATTACK ON THE SLAVE TRADE

As mentioned earlier, the attack on the slave trade was the initial justification for the expansion of European and American interests in West Africa. Opposition to the trade developed gradually in Europe towards the end of the eighteenth century, when a significant and growing number of people began to point at the cruelty and inhumanity of the traffic in human beings as well as at the wastefulness of cheap enforced labour. The campaign against the trade gained support partly from the liberalism associated with the age of the French Revolution, with its attack on privilege and oppression, partly also from the new economic ideas of the era of industrialization, in which a labour-intensive economy was being undermined by the introduction of mechanical devices. It was by no means easy to persuade those with vested interests in the trade to give it up, but a number of factors combined to persuade the British government to outlaw the trade in 1807. These factors include the depression in the British maritime trade following the American War of Independence, the decline of several of the West Indian islands which had passed their optimum stage of exploitation, the growing fear in the West Indies of the large number of rebellious slaves, the rise of an East Indian lobby and, above all, the religious revival associated with John Wesley, who made abolition a cardinal principle of the Evangelical faith and a popular cause. Denmark, whose participation in the trade was not substantial, had given up the trade in 1802. Sweden and the Netherlands followed in 1813 and 1814 respectively. A combination of those opposed to the trade and those who wished to enhance the value of their slaves got a bill through the United States senate to prohibit the trade from 1808, but few people expected the law to be seriously enforced, especially when the expansion of cotton production in the southern states called for additional labour. However, once the British, who had handled the largest share of the trade in the eighteenth century, decided to give it up, it was in their economic interest to persuade others to give it up as well.

The British thus took the lead from 1807 onwards in discouraging the export of slaves from West Africa to the New World. They had to persuade other European traders not merely to co-operate in outlawing the trade but also to permit or to assist the British navy in enforcing the ban on the transport of slaves by sea. In France, where the abolitionist movement had gone out of favour with the rise of Napoleon, it required diplomatic pressure to persuade the restored monarchy to prohibit the trade in stages between 1818 and 1823. Similar pressure brought Spain into line, and Portugal agreed to abolition north of the Equator, though these agreements had little effect in Brazil and Cuba, where labour-intensive cultivation of coffee and sugar respectively was being rapidly expanded. The British navy operated from Freetown and Fernando Po. When the French navy joined in after 1820 they operated from Gorée. Courts of mixed commission were set up in West Africa, the Caribbean and South America to try captured ships suspected of dealing in slaves. The United States government resisted the naval initiative from Britain, and instead offered half-hearted action by the United States navy operating from the Liberian and United States coasts.

Up to 1840, this campaign on the seas made little impact on the West African coast[1] The naval patrols stimulated interest in the European enclaves on the coast, and the slaves set free by the courts were swelling their population. But the export of slaves hardly diminished.[2] American, Brazilian and other traders based in the New World replaced Europeans as the main exporters. The anti-slavery laws, international treaties, and the rules under which the naval patrols operated were tightened up, so that a ship could be judged a slaver from its equipment and not from the actual presence of slaves who, if a ship was about to be apprehended, could be thrown overboard, with costs recoverable from insurance companies. Even then, no significant decline was noticeable till the 1840s, when both Britain and France changed tactics from action on the high seas to attempt closer economic blockade and inshore activities in West African ports. It was only at this stage that the abolitionist movement began to impinge on the lives of the coastal peoples. Such close blockade required the co-operation of the coastal rulers, the negotiation of a whole series of slave trade treaties, and the constant threat of naval attacks.

The attitude of the coastal rulers was dictated by three basic considerations. The first was political. Many of the rulers, whether they were

[1] C. Lloyd, *The navy and the slave trade* (London, 1949), 89, 115.
[2] P. D. Curtin, *The Atlantic slave trade: a census* (Madison, 1969), Tables 67, 68.

economically dependent on the slave trade or not, resented foreign powers coming to dictate to them what or what not to trade in. They viewed such dictation as an attack on their sovereignty. This was why the abolitionists often resorted to treaties including promises of some compensation to the chiefs and the encouragement of alternative trade. But the Europeans insisted on the right to enforce the prohibition unilaterally. It was soon clear that both the British and the French were using the slave trade treaties to improve their economic influence in West Africa *vis-à-vis* other traders such as the Brazilians and Portuguese, and to make inroads into the right of independent action by the coastal states. Many of the smaller states, especially those whose capitals were close enough to the coast to be bombarded, yielded to the pressure. Some, like Lagos and Bonny, had their unco-operative rulers deposed and were thus forced into agreement. Others like Dahomey, while willing to trade in palm oil with the British and the French, refused to compromise their sovereignty and were distant enough from the coast to ignore the naval threat.

The second consideration was economic. Many of the coastal towns were formerly fishing villages which had become organized for the slave trade. The trade had become central to their life. They could not retain their population or level of prosperity if they gave it up, unless they found an equally prosperous alternative 'legitimate' trade. In some areas there was gold, gum, indigo, ivory or other produce which had formed part of the trade of the eighteenth century, but the most important new trade was in palm oil. Where, as in the Niger delta, the palm oil trade developed quickly, there was a smooth transition, and economic fears were not as important a consideration as political fears. In other places, such as Badagry, where the palm oil trade was either non-existent or slow to develop, the economic factor was predominant. Other crops such as coffee, cotton or groundnuts were slower to become established. It was not until the 1860s that the groundnut trade can be said to have effectively replaced the slave trade in the Sine-Saloum and Casamance regions of Senegambia. Cotton had to wait till the colonial period.

A third consideration, concerning the nature of slavery generally in West African society,[1] went beyond the question of finding substitute staples for the European trade. The coastal rulers who sold slaves thought in terms of domestic slavery in Africa, where there was deprivation of liberty and of the comfort and support of one's own relatives,

[1] J. F. A. Ajayi, *Christian missions in Nigeria 1841-91* (London, 1965), 53-6.

but not of the basic rights and attributes of human beings as in slavery in the New World. Much of the argument about the cruelty and inhumanity of the slave trade was therefore lost on them. Domestic slavery seemed to them an essential aspect of social and economic relationships. While free men could share their labour through mutual aid or age grade organizations, or through customary service to elders, in-laws and rulers, slavery was the most usual method of recruiting labour to work on the farms of the wealthy or in iron or gold mines. In long distance trade, slaves were used not merely to transport goods, but sometimes also in business transactions as a form of large-scale, self-exporting currency. Slavery provided a means of recruiting needed skilled labour, such as blacksmiths, veterinarians to look after horses and cattle, weavers, etc., from one community to another. Similarly, skilled slaves were used in war, or in administrative positions in which loyalty to the ruler was more important than the local political influence of the official. Some of these officials like the *kachella* of Bornu or the *wombai* of Kano were important notables. Some individual lieutenants of the jihadists, who were of slave origin, such as Mustapha who became emir of Nioro in the Tukolor empire, rose to very high office.

It is not surprising therefore that while some West African rulers did not hesitate to support the end of the external slave trade, most were reluctant to give up the trade, and none considered giving up domestic slavery or the internal trade that nourished it. As long as European, particularly British, capital investments were financing cotton plantations in the southern United States, sugar in Cuba, and coffee in Brazil, and were giving insurance cover to slave ships and encouraging the South American governments to act independently of Spain and Portugal, the demand for slaves remained strong, and the coastal states found ways of evading naval patrols so as to supply the demand. After Brazil's final effective abolition of the trade in 1850, its volume was more than halved. Following the US emancipation proclamation of 1863, Cuba was left as the only significant importer. The naval effort against the trade could now be concentrated, and by 1866 the Atlantic slave trade was virtually extinguished.[1]

LEGITIMATE TRADE AND DOMESTIC SLAVERY

One constant aim of the abolitionists, as we have seen, was that the end of the trans-Atlantic slave trade should not mean a reduction in the volume and value of the European trade in West Africa. Until about

[1] D. P. Mannix and M. Cowley, *Black congress* (New York, 1962), 263–87; Curtin, *Atlantic slave trade*.

1850, there was little reduction in the trade between West Africa and America, though it came to be concentrated on Brazil, Cuba and the southern states. Gradually, trade with America declined as the United States itself drifted into isolation after the Civil War. By 1888, traffic between Lagos and Bahia had to be specially revived for the benefit of returning emancipated slaves. On the other hand, trade with Europe was expanding all the time, thus bringing to an end the old triangular pattern of trade linking Europe with West Africa and the New World.

In order to expand 'legitimate' trade so as to sustain and increase the trade with Europe, the abolitionists were initially anxious to develop agricultural plantations in West Africa. The various European enclaves along the coast were viewed not merely as trading posts, but also as centres from which the settlers and freed slaves could engage in large-scale cultivation of produce, the export of which would replace the doomed trade in slaves. Sierra Leone and Liberia were the most important centres of these agricultural experiments, but not the only ones. On the Gold Coast, in Nigeria, Bathurst, Fernando Po and other places, missionaries tried to establish coffee and cotton plantations. The French made elaborate plans for plantations on the Lower Senegal to be worked by indentured labour recruited from among former slaves around St Louis or from neighbouring African states, and to be protected by armed forts at Podor, Bakel and Medina. In 1818, Julien Schmaltz was sent there with troop reinforcements, agricultural experts and machinery. He and his successor, Baron Jacques François Roger, failed to get the plantations going. The traders of St Louis did not like the scheme since it was likely to endanger their gum trade. As the African neighbours were hostile, the labour was not forthcoming, and the notion of large-scale French colonization proved unrealistic.[1] A similar British attempt at establishing a model farm at the confluence of the Niger and the Benue in 1841–2 was dismally unsuccessful.[2]

The failure of these efforts at agricultural plantations was another reason why the abolitionist movement could not make the sort of impact on the West African scene that had been expected. Liberian coffee achieved some success, but was soon driven off the market by Brazilian coffee. Some cotton was exported from Senegal, but by 1840 it was clear that West Africa was not suitable for large-scale plantations or colonies of settlement under European leadership. The high mortality rate of European residents was a factor. There was also ignorance of tropical

[1] G. Hardy, *La mise en valeur du Sénégal de 1817 à 1854* (Paris, 1921).
[2] C. C. Ifemesia, 'The "civilising" mission of 1841', *Journal of the Historical Society of Nigeria*, 1962, **2**, 3, 291–310.

8-2

agriculture, except among a few Liberian settlers, who were not anxious to recreate in Africa the farm life from which they had escaped in America. One significant effect of these failures was to convince the rising Western-educated élite in West Africa that there was little money to be made from new methods in farming. They turned to the more prosperous import/export and distributive trade, and directed their educational endeavours towards literary and commercial goals to the neglect of technical and agricultural possibilities.[1] The expansion of 'legitimate' trade in West Africa therefore was to take place, not in the European enclaves, but within the existing African agricultural systems, and without unduly disturbing existing patterns either of production or of political authorities.

The increased demand for cash crops was met largely through the local initiative of coastal entrepreneurs in stimulating expansion of the production of palm produce, ivory, gum arabic, shea butter and indigo in the interior. Sometimes the vital necessity for certain European goods, in particular guns and gunpowder, encouraged the rulers and war chiefs in the interior to take a hand in organizing the production, transportation to the coast, and sale of these products.[2] More often, these activities were handled by local and long distance traders within the existing market system. The result was that the expansion of 'legitimate' trade did not lead to changes in the social structure which the abolitionists had expected in terms of undermining the basis of domestic slavery.

The commercial success of some of the freed slaves who returned from Sierra Leone or the New World, and of others who attached themselves to the missionaries, did represent the rise of a new class who owed their origin to the abolitionists. But outside the European enclaves, their influence lay in the future. True, there was an increased emphasis on entrepreneurial skills rather than descent in appointing heads of Houses, as the family units were called in the coastal towns of the Niger delta. But this was a process that had been going on during the slave trade era. Neither the isolated examples of people of slave origin, such as Jaja who achieved high office in the nineteenth century, nor the occasional slave riots in Calabar, where social mobility was restricted and oppression heightened by the competition of the élite as to the number of slaves they killed at funerals, implied that the abolitionists had achieved a social revolution in the delta city states or elsewhere

---

[1] J. F. A. Ajayi, 'The development of secondary grammar school education in Nigeria', *Journal of the Historical Society of Nigeria*, 1963, **2**, 4, 522.

[2] For the Ibadan example, see B. A. Awẹ, 'The Ajele system', *Journal of the Historical Society of Nigeria*, 1964, **3**, 1, 47–60.

outside the European enclaves.[1] The development of cash crops through 'legitimate' trade did not lead to a general emancipation of domestic slaves or the growth of a sturdy, free peasant class. On the contrary, the demand for more agricultural produce was met largely by increasing the domestic slave labour force.

The abolitionists were at pains to explain why the expansion of 'legitimate' trade failed to effect changes in West African social structure in this period. They argued that this was because palm fruits, ivory, shea butter, indigo and gum were not really produced, not specially cultivated; that they were collected, and in this they were not unlike slaves; and that the socio-economic system that had sustained the slave trade[2] could absorb the expanded collection of the new staples without any fundamental changes. The weakness of this argument is that the cultivation of groundnuts in Senegambia in this period produced no significant change. Although it has been suggested that the income from groundnuts was more widely distributed than the income from slaves – the same may be said of palm oil[3] – any effect of this could only have been in the long run. There was little change as long as the pattern of production, transportation and marketing remained the same. Change was more rapid in the colonial period because, although cotton, cacao, and other cash crops were developed within the same system, the Europeans had first destroyed African sovereignty, taken the initiative, and were no longer confined to the coast. The cultivation of groundnuts, of itself, marked no departures from the system that had produced slaves, ivory, palm oil, or gum. The increased production of palm oil was no easy, effortless exercise. The collection of palm fruits, the manufacture of palm oil, transportation to the coast, and organization for export, raised the same problems of scale of production, land tenure, and marketing organization that groundnuts raised and other cultivated crops were to raise later. In the abolitionist era, these problems were tackled within the existing pattern of markets, with domestic

[1] R. Horton, 'From fishing village to city state: a social history of New Calabar', in M. Douglas and P. M. Kaberry, eds., *Man in Africa* (London, 1969); K. K. Nair, *Politics and society in old Calabar* (London, 1972).

[2] Polanyi and other economic anthropologists have described this as an example of the 'archaic economy' in which there is an absence of a money economy, and a predominance of the middleman role of state monopolies or coastal entrepreneurs linked with overseas interests and exclusive practices such as the restrictive trust system (K. Polanyi, 'The economy as instituted process', in K. Polanyi, C. M. Arensberg and H. W. Pearson, eds., *Trade and markets in early empires* (Glencoe, Ill., 1957) and *Dahomey and the slave trade* (Seattle, 1966)).

[3] For arguments about the distribution of income from groundnuts, see M. A. Klein, *Islam and imperialism in Senegal* (Stanford, 1968), 45–7; from palm oil, see U. I. Ukwu, 'The development of trade and marketing in Iboland', *Journal of the Historical Society of Nigeria*, 1967, 3, 4, 647–62.

slave labour for the collection, manufacture and transportation, and the trust system for the export. Thus the increased production of palm oil and groundnuts in this period created no social revolution because, in spite of the pressures of abolitionists, the West African political, social, and economic systems proved able to meet the changing demands of the coastal trade through adaptation rather than revolution.

The abolitionists themselves came to recognize this. Most traders adjusted themselves to operate within the existing African political and socio-economic systems. They were usually linked with the coastal middlemen through the trust system, and they often joined in resisting attempts of other Europeans seeking to bypass the middlemen and penetrate into the interior. Domestic slavery came to be accepted as an essential part of the existing social system necessary for economic development. Even missionaries, who had at first opposed domestic slavery and would not accept owners of domestic slaves as members of their church, began to modify their views. From the 1840s until the late 1870s, there was to be heard little criticism of the system of domestic slavery. The Church Missionary Society formally pronounced that, while polygamy was an absolute sin capable of no amelioration, domestic slavery was a social evil that would be gradually ameliorated by the expansion of Christianity.[1] The missionary practice of buying slaves to be emancipated and used as servants, or the apprenticeship system practised in Sierra Leone and Liberia, or the indentured labour system (*régime des engagés à temps*) operated by the French in Senegal, were little different from domestic slavery.[2] Thus even the legal emancipation of slaves in the European enclaves was slow to produce significant changes. Accusations of slave-holding after emancipation, or of the recruitment of labour under conditions hardly distinguishable from slavery, were widespread in Lagos, Freetown and St Louis till the 1870s.[3]

[1] Ajayi, *Christian missions*, 105–8.

[2] R. Pasquier, 'À propos de l'émancipation des esclaves au Sénégal en 1848', *Revue française d'histoire d'outre-mer*, 1967, **54**; F. Zuccarelli, 'Le régime des engagés à temps au Sénégal 1817–48', *Cahiers d'études africaines*, 1962, **2**, 3. One important side effect of the emancipation of slaves at Saint Louis and Gorée was that it favoured the incoming French business houses at the expense of the Creole community.

[3] See J. U. J. Asiegbu, *Slavery and the politics of liberation, 1787–1861* (New York, 1969), in particular 38–47. He compares on p. 53 the British schemes for the emigration of freed slaves from Sierra Leone to the West Indies with the Victor Régis scheme for recruiting indentured labour from Dahomey for the French West Indian islands.

THE MISSIONARY IMPACT

The nineteenth century saw not only a great expansion of European trade in West Africa but also a spectacular growth of European and North American missionary activities. This urge to convert West Africans to Christianity was an important factor in the abolitionist movement. Evangelical Christianity operated partly as cause, partly as an effect of the movement. Some abolitionists in the early nineteenth century argued that the expansion of European trade and the spread of European customs and ideas must precede and induce in the African a frame of mind ready to accept Christianity. Others believed that Christianity should precede, pioneer and, through religious change, induce the Africans to desire European trade goods and European social and cultural values. All were agreed that in whatever order, Christianity, European commerce and 'civilization' were aspects of the same revolution that was about to sweep through Africa.[1] They expected a much more rapid and more far-reaching change than was ever to take place in West Africa in the nineteenth century. Nevertheless, the missionary movement was important in stimulating new interest in the European trading centres and in pushing European influence into the hinterland.

In Senegal, St Louis and Gorée had long been centres of unsuccessful attempts by Catholic religious orders to establish Christianity in West Africa. From about 1846 onwards, these missions were revived by the Holy Ghost Fathers. The area around the trading port of Bathurst in the Gambia became a centre of Methodist activities. However, Sierra Leone was the most important missionary centre of West Africa. The Nova Scotians, settlers from Canada, brought their own churches with them, and set the example for a significant later development of independent African churches. The Church Missionary Society began work in Sierra Leone in 1804 and the Methodists in 1811. Their work among the freed slave villages was of crucial importance. They helped to create out of the different linguistic groups from all over West Africa a new society dominated largely by English-speaking Christians, but with a distinctive social and religious life rooted in traditional African cultures.[2] In turn, their success in the villages created an opportunity for using Sierra Leone as a laboratory for the study of West African languages, from where interpreters, teachers and missionary agents

[1] T. F. Buxton, *The African slave trade and its remedy,* reprint (London, 1967).
[2] J. Peterson, *Province of Freedom: a history of Sierra Leone, 1787–1870* (London, 1969).

could be recruited for work in other parts of West Africa. In Liberia, the Methodist Episcopal and Protestant Episcopal Christians and the Southern Baptist Convention worked from the 1830s onwards, mostly among the Afro-American settlers and freed slaves, and later began to penetrate into the interior along the main rivers and trade routes.

On the Gold Coast, the Basel Mission (1828) and the Bremen (or North German) Mission (1847) were important in the areas around Accra and Aburi, and Keta. The most important centre, however, was Cape Coast, where the Methodists became well established in the 1830s and 1840s under the dynamic leadership of Thomas Birch Freeman. From there the Methodist Mission began to expand into Badagry and Whydah, and made tentative approaches to Asante. In Togo and Dahomey, the Basel and Bremen missions extended their activities to the Ewe, among whom they achieved some of their most significant successes in terms of conversion, education, and impact on the life and culture of the people. The Catholics from the Society of African Missions, having failed to establish themselves in Sierra Leone, reopened an old mission in Whydah in 1861.[1]

In Nigeria, the missionaries concentrated their activities in three main areas. The CMS and Methodists came in through Badagry to Abeokuta in the 1840s. In 1851, having joined in inducing the British to intervene militarily in the disputed succession in Lagos, they moved in with Akintoye, the restored monarch. The Baptists arrived in 1853 and joined the movement into the Yoruba hinterland. The second area was the south-eastern corner of the country, Calabar and the Cross river basin, where Scottish Presbyterian missionaries concentrated their attention. The third area was the Niger valley, where the CMS established the Niger Mission in 1857, which was extended to the delta in 1861.

As far as conversion was concerned, there was no mass movement to join the Christian churches. The most significant successes were in the coastal European enclaves among freed slaves and trading communities, who saw in Christianity and close identification with European culture, an avenue to a new life with good commercial possibilities; St Louis, Freetown, Monrovia and Lagos thus became the leading centres of Christianity in West Africa. Yet, even in and around Freetown, in spite of the magisterial powers given to Christian pastors in the 1820s to compel attendance at church and to persecute anti-

[1] C. P. Groves, *The planting of Christianity in Africa*, ii (London, 1957).

Christian behaviour, African cults and Islam survived, and traditional religious values retained an important influence over everyday behaviour even among the converts. Outside the European enclaves, missionaries were welcomed to settle in some places and rejected in others. In a few places, as at Abeokuta, depending on the political situation or the ability of the man himself, the missionary could become very influential. But while there were some few conversions, usually of domestic slaves, or of people uprooted by war or in other ways disadvantaged in society, there were no conversions of whole communities or of influential members of society. Some people took the attitude that the missionary approach to religion only represented yet another insight into the nature of the supernatural and tried to add the white man's deity to the pantheon of the gods. Children were sent to school or to live with the missionaries to become devotees of this new God or to learn new skills, such as the art of reading and writing. Thus by 1880, although the Christian missions had made useful contacts, and through their linguistic and educational work among the freed slaves sowed many potentially fruitful seeds, the Christian revolution had so far failed to get under way.

The missionaries became increasingly anxious to encourage European political control as a necessary step to securing social and religious change. As they moved beyond the European-controlled enclaves, either along the coast or into the interior, they were following the traders or encouraging the traders to follow them. The alliance of missionaries and traders, often using abolitionist arguments to secure the support and protection of their metropolitan governments, was the most important factor in the expansion of European influence in West Africa in this period.

IMPERIAL EXPANSION AND ABOLITION

European expansion followed two different paths: the expansion of areas under direct European control and power on the one hand and, on the other, the expansion, not of power but of influence among independent African states. The first method was initially favoured by the abolitionists. The aim was to multiply the number of forts and trading enclaves ruled and policed by Europeans; to cultivate areas around these colonies, where Europeans, Afro-Americans, freed slaves under European or American control, and others would trade, develop plantations, and establish a new type of society that would grow and, as the European colonies in America had come to dominate the continent, would eventually replace or absorb the various African states. Sierra Leone and Liberia were only the beginning of this movement. Both expanded along the coast, thanks to the naval patrols, but expansion inland was limited. It was the difficulties encountered by these settlements and the disastrous failure of other attempts, like that of the French on the Lower Senegal and of the British at the confluence of the Niger and Benue, that discouraged this idea. Economic growth was slow, and the high rate of mortality, the administrative difficulties and the hostility of neighbouring African states were all deterrents. The idea of direct control was therefore abandoned. The only other example was the annexation of Lagos, which was in a sense an extension of the colonization of Sierra Leone, dictated by the large number of Yoruba among the freed slaves in Sierra Leone, itself a result of the Yoruba wars of the early nineteenth century. But the Lagos example merely confirmed that, as far as the expansion of legitimate trade was concerned, nothing was to be gained from undermining existing African political and economic systems by extension of the areas under European control. It was better to co-operate with independent African states which were capable of expanding export trade through the use of domestic slaves. By 1865, a special committee of the British Parliament reported against further extension of direct control. Expansionist ardour roused by Captain Faidherbe was also at a low ebb in France until the late 1870s owing to internal divisions and the 1870 war with Germany.

Along the coast, co-operation with African states was secured in a number of ways. Usually the slave trade treaties included clauses guaranteeing freedom of movement for European traders and sometimes for missionaries as well. Some even included clauses for the abolition of such customs as human sacrifice, the killing of twins, panyarring (kidnapping for debt), trial by ordeal, and others judged repugnant to European susceptibilities and therefore bad for the expansion of 'legitimate' trade. The ability of naval patrols to enforce these clauses gave the naval officers and consular agents a basis for interfering in the internal affairs of the African states. They used the treaties to intervene in disputed successions, to enforce their own settlement of trade disputes, or to insist on particular trade policies or procedures for the regulation of trade and the resolution of trade conflicts. The best known example of this was in the Niger delta, where the exercise of European influence became institutionalized in the courts of equity. In theory, these courts, consisting of the consul, European traders and local rulers, did not diminish the autonomy of the delta states, since they were constituted by treaty agreements and regulated only the external trade. However, the presence of the naval patrols meant that the consuls could enforce decisions of the courts even if the local rulers did not like them.[1]

Farther inland, European influence depended on the good will of the rulers secured through missionaries, traders or the visits of envoys. Only in Senegal, because of the navigability of the river, was influence bolstered up not merely by the building of forts, but also by the use of troops recruited largely from freed slaves – the *tirailleurs Sénégalais* – officered by Europeans or *métis*. Through military action, the Moors were kept to the right bank of the river, al-Ḥājj 'Umar barred from access to the river, treaties of protection signed with Walo, and Cayor put constantly under pressure. These military activities notwithstanding, Captain Faidherbe, the active governor of the French enclaves in Senegal from 1854 to 1861, did not extend the area of direct French control beyond the coastal communes. The political and economic systems of even the neighbouring states of Walo and Cayor, though changing internally from the impact of Muslim reformers, remained largely immune to abolitionist and French colonialist pressure. The French were not in a position to rule these states, or to interfere with the institution of domestic slavery on which their economy depended. Both states had to be reconquered when French political expansion began in earnest in the late 1870s.

The British on the Niger faced the hostility of the delta states, and this with the high rate of mortality in the rainy season proved effective in minimizing British naval action till the 1870s.[2] Naval power extended British influence along the lagoon east and west of Lagos, but rivalries with the French prevented further annexation. Expansion inland was discouraged by the expense and uncertainties of military action on land. The British relied on alliances and playing one state against another. Only on the Gold Coast, where the coastal states were weak and divided and there was a threat of their being engulfed by the more powerful Asante, did the British feel a challenge to face the difficulties of military expeditions. In 1824, Governor MacCarthy lost his life trying to check Asante expansion. His death was avenged in 1826. Thereafter, George Maclean acted as arbiter for the Fante states and

[1] Dike, *Trade and politics*.
[2] C. C. Ifemesia, 'British enterprise on the Niger', Ph.D. thesis (University of London, 1969).

built up a judicial system for resolving their differences. This was later extended and consolidated by treaties in which the chiefs allowed the British jurisdiction over offences which British traders and missionaries regarded as repugnant. As the British took over Danish and Dutch forts, the Fante increasingly challenged British jurisdiction. Hemmed in between rising British power and Asante threats, they tried to end their divisions and form a confederacy. It then appeared as if the British might be pushed out of the Gold Coast. In 1874, the British therefore mounted an expensive war, and defeated the Asante, but withdrew as the expense of military control was still beyond available local resources. Instead, the informal jurisdiction in Fanteland was converted into formal annexation.[1] This was one of the clearest signs that a new determination to expand political control in Africa was rising.

As the determination to move inland grew, the attitude to domestic slavery seemed also to change. African political and economic systems had proved able to supply an increasing volume of legitimate trade, but had, as we have seen, insisted on confining European power to the coastal enclaves. Arising largely out of intra-European rivalries, European ambitions in Africa now went beyond the increase of 'legitimate' trade. It became necessary to stake out claims for the future, to prospect for minerals, to build railways, and to participate directly in the trade and agricultural development of the interior. African states began to be criticized for being small, for restricting trade with too many toll posts, for frequent closures of roads, and exclusion of foreigners from particular markets. Domestic slavery began to be attacked, and encouragement given to slaves of hostile African neighbours to escape and seek emancipation. In this way, constabularies and armed police, as well as porters of European goods and cannon for the inland advance, began to be built up on the coast. The abolitionist slogans proliferated. Middlemen traders and coastal rulers like Jaja, Nana, and others who opposed these moves were denounced as slave traders and removed in the 1880s, even though it was known they had never taken part in the trans-Atlantic slave trade. As the Europeans penetrated into the Sudan belt, the Islamic states were also portrayed as oppressive and decadent, having departed from the ideals of their founders and having no other function but to raid for slaves. Slaves were encouraged to riot and desert, and were turned into soldiers to be used against their former masters.[2]

---

[1] Fage, *A history of West Africa*, 142–6.
[2] See for example F. N'Diaye, 'La colonie du Sénégal au temps de Brière de l'Isle (1876–1881)', *Bulletin de l'Institut Fondamental d'Afrique Noire*, series B, 1968, 30, 2.

Yet as British and French rule began to take shape, the predominant attitude was to be cautious in the emancipation of domestic slaves, so as not to injure the economy of the newly acquired territories. Emancipation was phased. Slaves were encouraged to buy their own freedom; their children were declared free, but only on reaching manhood after a period of apprenticeship. Fear of brigandry and indiscipline through sudden emancipation led to the establishment of 'Freed slaves' homes' or 'Villages de liberté' which were in fact sources for recruiting labour for the colonial masters.[1] In some cases, as in the delta, much to the chagrin of missionaries, the initial move was not towards emancipation but towards strengthening the hands of the masters over the slaves. In fact, emancipation of domestic slaves was a gradual process that took place, not in the nineteenth, but in the twentieth century.

CONCLUSION

The intention of the abolitionists to change the face of West Africa had not made much progress by 1870. The European presence on the coast had become significant. The trans-Atlantic slave trade, at least, had come to an end and the whole trans-Saharan trade was declining. West Africa, from being essentially northward looking, began to turn more attention to European trade, missionary activities and other influences from the coast. Sierra Leone, Liberia, the four communes of Senegal, Bathurst, the Gold Coast forts, Lagos, and other European enclaves were expanding, but not yet to the extent of threatening the political and economic systems of the surrounding African states. The basis of European power was not military but naval. This restricted European power to the coastal enclaves, discouraged much expansion and encouraged co-operation with independent African states. As a result, the area of direct European power was severely limited and the theme of abolition was marginal except along the coast. For most of West Africa, the Islamic advance in the Sudan belt and the internal politics of the states of the forest zone were far more significant.

[1] F. de Kersaint-Gilly, 'Essai sur l'évolution de l'esclavage en Afrique Occidentale Française', *Bulletin du Comité d'Études Historiques et Scientifiques de l'Afrique Occidentale Française*, 1924, 7; D. Bouche, 'Les villages de liberté en A.O.F.', *Bulletin de l'Institut Français d'Afrique Noire*, series B, 1949, 11. G. O. Olusanya, 'The freed slaves' homes', *Journal of the Historical Society of Nigeria*, 1966, 3, 3.

CHAPTER 7

THE FOREST AND THE
SAVANNA OF CENTRAL AFRICA

REGIONAL DIVISIONS

The history of Central Africa in the nineteenth century covers two broad geographical zones. The equatorial zone comprises Africa's largest surviving area of tropical rain forest, together with the adjacent woodland on the fringe of the central Sudan. The savanna zone, in the south, stretches from the Atlantic in the west to the middle Zambezi in the east, and is mainly light woodland, rather than true savanna grassland. The whole region was, and is, one of the most sparsely populated of the habitable areas of Africa, currently averaging about six people to the square kilometre, or about one sixth of the density found in the wooded areas of West Africa. Central Africa has no great concentrations of rural population, such as are found in the Niger delta to the west, or in the interlacustrine highlands to the east, and the only urban growth has been in recent commercial, administrative and mining centres such as Duala, Bangui, Kinshasa, Luanda and Ndola.

Late in the nineteenth century Central Africa was divided into four political zones which are reflected in the subsequent history of the area. The central and north-eastern zone consists of the republic of Zaïre, an area of about 1 million square miles and twenty million people, who were ruled during the first half of the twentieth century by Belgium. The south-west consists of Portuguese-speaking Angola, an area of half a million square miles and five million people. In the quarters adjacent to these two huge territories there developed the spheres of British influence in the south-east, and of French influence in the north-west. The Cameroun section of the French sphere was under German rule from 1884 to 1914, and a small pocket of the northern Gabon forest is Spanish-speaking. Three of the four main colonial influences had their roots in the pre-1875 period. The Portuguese and French had traded extensively along the coasts north and south of the Congo river from the fifteenth and seventeenth centuries respectively, and the Portuguese had created settlements in Angola and Benguela. The northward expansion of Dutch and English-speaking settlers in southern Africa was creating reverberations across the Zambezi into southern Central Africa by the mid-nineteenth century. In the fourth quarter, that of

Zaïre, the roots of external influence also lay in the pre-1875 era, but in this case a dramatic change of leadership occurred. The economic system pioneered from the east coast by Swahili and Arab initiative, was captured and transformed into a European colony by Belgian-led initiative from the Atlantic coast.

The study of nineteenth-century Central Africa involves much more than seeking the roots of twentieth-century colonialism. With adequate research it will one day be possible to reconstruct a detailed account of the pre-colonial societies of the area. The oral traditions are fresher than for earlier periods, the eye-witness accounts more plentiful, the institutions more closely related to the present, and the ethnic rivalries and partnerships more alive. From this wealth of evidence the complex structure of government institutions and trading systems could be recreated. This pattern of sometimes very localized societies, rather than the four quadrants of the modern map, should form the primary focus for the nineteenth-century historian. From there, he must seek to understand the tensions and alliances, the loyalties and fears, the unity and conflict which were central to the lives of people in many hundreds of societies and communities. The peoples of these communities spoke 200 or more different languages, Bantu languages in the forest and the south, Central Sudanic and eastern Niger-Congo languages in the north. They occupied a wide range of different ecological environments, the most favoured being the medium rainfall belts immediately north and south of the forest. Their everyday economic activities ranged from forest gathering, through grain and tuber cultivation, to nomadic pastoralism, with a significant minority graduating out of primary food production to become handicraft specialists, caravan traders or political and religious leaders. So far, however, research is in its infancy, and a survey based on the work undertaken in the 1960s is liable to dwell on economic factors, and more particularly on factors of trade, to the detriment of politics and religion, demography and nutrition, law and social organization.

THE LUNDA EMPIRE

The history of the savanna half of Central Africa, although but dimly illuminated by the standards of West African historiography, is already considerably better known than the history of the northern forest and beyond. By the end of the eighteenth century it had evolved several large-scale political institutions and far-reaching economic systems. The most important of these was the Lunda empire. This empire had

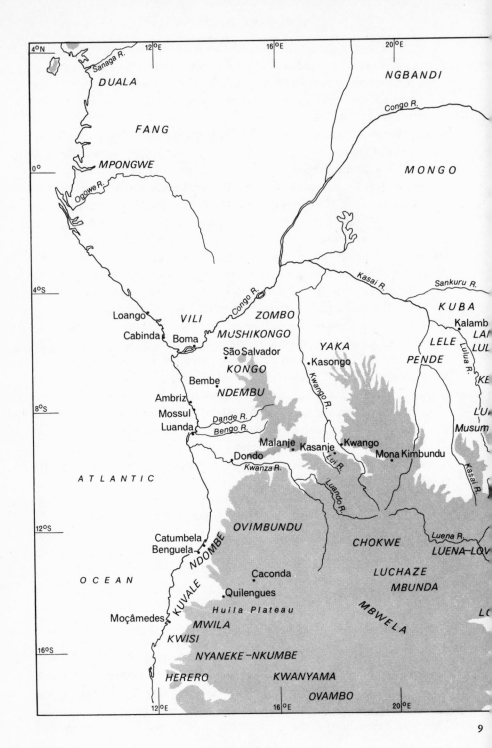

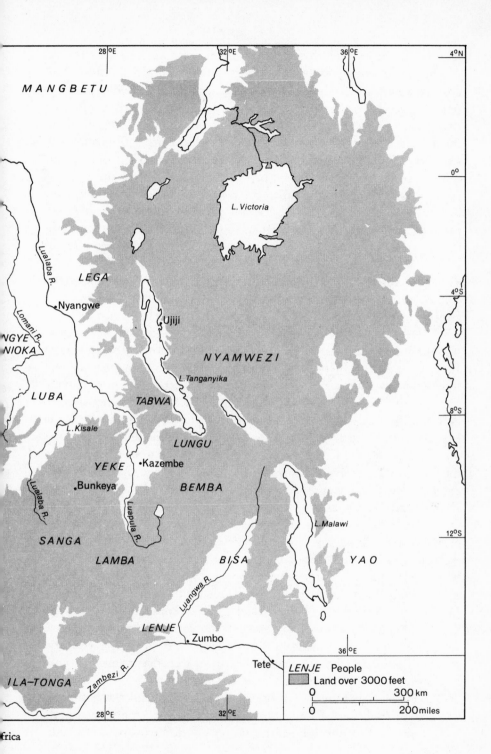

MANGBETU

L. Victoria

LEGA

•Nyangwe

•Ujiji

Lualaba R.

Lomani R.

NGYE
NIOKA

NYAMWEZI

L.Tanganyika

LUBA

TABWA

L.Kisale

LUNGU

YEKE

•Kazembe

•Bunkeya

BEMBA

Luapula R.

Lualaba R.

SANGA

L.Malawi

LAMBA

BISA

YAO

Luangwa R.

LENJE

•Zumbo

ILA-TONGA

Zambezi R.

Tete•

LENJE People

Land over 3000 feet

0   300 km

0   200 miles

frica

225

its roots in the eighteenth century. From about 1700, or a little before, the fusing of new commercial opportunities with old political skills enabled a Lunda dynasty to emerge which rapidly came to dominate the upper Kasai basin. As the empire developed, Lunda peoples colonized the central provinces, while their agents spread Lunda political influence among numerous surrounding peoples. During the first three-quarters of the nineteenth century the central part of this Lunda domain continued to thrive and prosper. The hub of the empire was a royal capital or compound called the *musumba* which was rebuilt anew by each successive king. A successful and long-lived ruler attracted courtiers and retainers who built satellite compounds at the *musumba*, until it came to resemble a town, with well-fenced courtyards, broad streets, and a great piazza for public functions. The *mwata yamvo* (or *mwant yav*) ruled this metropolitan complex with two sets of supporters. The traditional elders, descendants of early Lunda clan leaders, were custodians of continuity, rooted in the soil. Some held hereditary posts associated with leading figures of the Lunda 'creation'. One such figure was the influential *lukonkeshia*, 'mother of the nation', who governed an independent sub-court where she entertained state visitors and received tributary taxes of her own. The second set of supporters were bureaucratic office-holders, appointed by the king, and responsible to him for the day-to-day administration of the over-kingdom. These functionaries operated both as senior court dignitaries and as travelling government agents. Until at least the middle of the nineteenth century the forces of unity remained effective in Lunda. Village chiefs paid their tribute even when they lived as much as two months' journey away from the capital. Official *tukuata* travelled the length and breadth of the empire checking caravans, escorting foreign travellers, and warning chiefs whose tribute was late, or inadequate. This continued political well-being was reflected in great stability at court. During the period between 1790 and 1873 the empire appears to have been ruled by three great rulers, Yavo ya Mbanyi (early nineteenth century), Naweji ya Ditende (*c.* 1821–*c.* 1853) and Muteba ya Chikombe (*c.* 1857–1873). Even allowing for disputed successions and short intermediate reigns, this continuity was remarkable in so large and diverse a country, especially at a time when fundamental changes were occurring all around in eastern, western and southern Central Africa.

One factor governing the success of the Lunda empire was the old and strong tradition of unity which related both to the early Lunda migrations, and to the eighteenth-century political expansion. In addition to these quasi-nationalist sentiments of unity, the country was held together by its government. The administrative structure, evolved over many generations, stabilized by many checks and balances, tested by many succession crises, had acquired a certain political permanence. An equally important factor of stability was the economic basis of Lunda power. This basis began with agriculture. The capital was situated in open country with perennial streams and good rainfall. Even at the height of his power, a *mwata yamvo* continued to take personal care of his plantations and regularly visited his large cassava fields manned by serf labour. A safe agricultural base was necessary to sustain the small towns which developed around the court. A second source of Lunda wealth was derived from the copper mines in the south-eastern part of the empire. Copper crosses called *muambo*, weighing two or three kilograms each, were widely disseminated across the savanna. Lunda craftsmen were skilled at converting these copper ingots into an alloy which made fine trade wire. This wire was wrapped round elephant hairs to form bangles, both for personal ornamentation and as a ready form of currency. Both the province of the Lualaba and the eastern, Kazembe province of the Luapula included copper in the tribute payments which they remitted to the *mwata yamvo*. Another important item of trade, and of tribute, was salt, which was scarce and valuable in all the Lunda territories, and had to be imported from both the eastern and the western marches of the empire.

In addition to its internal prosperity, Lunda enjoyed a considerable level of wealth derived from its external trade. One feature of this was the slave trade. In the early nineteenth century, as in the two preceding centuries, the Atlantic slave trade remained the most pervasive factor of foreign influence in Central Africa, even in the savanna heartland 1,000 kilometres from the coast. As yet no detailed, quantitative analysis of the nineteenth-century slave trade from Central Africa has been attempted, but in about 1850 Magyar estimated that one-third of all the slaves leaving Luanda and Benguela in the previous hundred years had come from the Lunda territories. This would suggest that at least two or three thousand slaves a year were being sent out from the Lunda sphere of influence. Even if the true figure were to be considerably less, it raises serious questions as to why Lunda should have become involved in the trade and how the victims acquired their slave status.

Some of the slaves exported from Lunda were undoubtedly prisoners of war. The empire had constant difficulty in defending its northern border, which never lay very far from the *mwata yamvo*'s capital. The king himself frequently led wars against Kete and Luba border groups who threatened his capital. A second share of the export slaves appears to have been collected within the empire as part of the tax system. In 1847 Rodrigues Graça made an estimate of the tribute revenue which the *mwata yamvo* received at approximately annual intervals. The estimate listed thirty-six chiefs who contributed slaves and ivory to the royal exchequer, as well as locally produced iron, copper, hoes, bows, spears, food, palm oil, skins, raffia, cloth and earthenware. Small chiefs paid as little as 600 milreis (£130), but more important chiefs such as Kasongo and Kanioka, when not in revolt, paid the equivalent of 12,000 and even 16,000 milreis. The total revenue, according to Graça, came to about 260,000 milreis (£60,000), substantially more than the colonial revenue of Angola for the same year.[1] The manner in which the *mwata yamvo* prevailed upon his subject chiefs to pay tribute was apparently threefold. Some military force was used, and chiefs reported that government officials 'seized' their children and ivory, if tribute had not been adequately paid. Secondly the veneration in which the *mwata yamvo* was held must have been a powerful deterrent to those contemplating tax evasion. Thirdly, the tribute system was a two-way exchange, and loyal chiefs were rewarded with foreign cloth, ornaments, beads and rum in which the *mwata yamvo* virtually held a trade monopoly. The integrity of the empire was thus maintained by armed strength, by religious sanctions, and by the judicious use of material rewards.

The internal slave trade, on which the wealth of both chiefly and royal courts was partly based, still needs much clarification. One important factor was probably judicial action in sentencing criminals, or alleged criminals, to slavery. When Rodrigues Graça explained to provincial Lunda chiefs that Portugal had outlawed the slave trade, they protested. Portugal, they said, continued to transport convicts to Angola, and so why should not the Lunda be allowed to transport convicts to Portugal? A second means whereby people fell into slavery was in numerous small-scale feuds, either between chiefs, or over disputed succession within a state. Explanations of enslavement in Lunda are closely tied to the relationship between ruler and ruled, and the concept of 'slavery' may often have been not very different from that of 'subject'. Thus a chief, under extreme pressure, might have been able to use considerable discretion in selecting 'slaves' among his entourage of serfs.

[1] Joaquim Rodrigues Graça, 'Viagem', in *Annães do Conselho Ultramarino* (Lisbon, 1855), 145–6.

A controlled trade in slaves was capable of assisting in the growth of political authority. Chiefs were intimately involved in the administration of justice and in the conduct of both local and national wars, the two important means of obtaining slaves. They also controlled the redistribution of foreign goods, thus gaining further power. One factor in the trade which, surprisingly, does not seem to have been significant, was the sale of guns and powder. As late as 1875, Pogge reported that guns were worth very little in Lunda compared to the high prices offered by peoples nearer the coast. Some guns were in use, but were exceedingly ineffective in Lunda hands, even at a range of twenty paces. In 1874, when a chief who controlled the western route to the Lunda capital planned to take over the government by a military coup, he recruited Chokwe musketeers as mercenaries to assist him. In 1876, when Pogge gave the new *mwata yamvo* a single breech-loader, this was an event sufficiently important to be recorded in Lunda tradition as having increased the power of the ruler. In general it would seem, therefore, that although foreign trade played an important role in the power-structure of the empire, this role did not involve the significant supply of firearms.[1]

Although the century before 1875 was marked by conspicuous stability in the heart of Central Africa, and by long uninterrupted reigns at the courts of the Lunda kings, changes of great importance were taking place in all the peripheral areas of southern and western Central Africa. In the west these changes involved the opening of southern Angola to long distance trade and to foreign settlement, the expansion of the Ovimbundu trade network into the upper Zambezi basin, the undermining of the Kimbundu–Kasanje trading axis of Angola by Chokwe expansion into western Lunda, and the development of the proto-colonial Luso-African society of the Luanda hinterland. In the east the main developments were the growth of trade from the lower Zambezi into eastern Central Africa, and the establishment of Nyamwezi, Swahili and Arab trade routes between eastern Zaïre and the Indian Ocean. Each of these developments had effects which, as will be seen, undermined the old political and commercial systems, so that in the 1870s Lunda suddenly disintegrated, and the central rump of the empire was overrun by invaders and torn by factionalism.

[1] Paul Pogge, *Im Reiche des Muata Jamvo* (Berlin, 1880); A. Petermann, 'Ladislaus Magyar's Erforschung von Inner Afrika', in *Petermanns Geographische Mitteilungen* (Gotha, 1880); Joaquim Rodrigues Graça, in *Annães do Conselho Ultramarino*.

SOUTH-WESTERN ANGOLA

The late eighteenth century marks the beginning of several important changes in the western part of Central Africa. For over a century the region had been dominated by the Atlantic slave-trading system. In the second half of the seventeenth century the forces of Portuguese conquest had spent themselves, and the trading system had become dependent on a working relationship between Portuguese traders and a series of frontier states such as Matamba, Kasanje and later Bihe. Portuguese enterprise was restricted to two spheres of influence, in the hinterland of Luanda and Benguela; beyond that the effects of overseas trade were transmitted by African enterprise. From the 1780s the Portuguese began to make fresh attempts to gain information about the remoter parts of Central Africa and to establish new areas of activity and more direct trading links with the interior. The Luso-African sphere acquired a new dynamism and began to push its frontier outwards.[1] In the south this process began when several expeditions were sent from Luanda to explore the lands in the far south-west of Angola.

South-western Angola had not been greatly influenced by external events in the first three-quarters of the eighteenth century. Along the coastlands a few small groups of Herero-speaking pastoralists, such as the Kuvale and Ndombe, remained largely isolated and self-sufficient. What external contacts they had were either with client groups of Kwisi hunter-gatherers, or with the larger Bantu nations of the highlands who occasionally raided cattle below the Chela escarpment. On top of the south-western plateau the Mwila peoples were organized into kingdoms such as Huila and later Njau. It was these kingdoms which first established regular trading contacts with the Atlantic markets. In the late eighteenth century ivory began to flow northwards through Quilengues to Benguela, and a few Portuguese tried to settle in and around Huila, but their settlements did not survive. Slavery was still the staple of the Benguela trade, and southern slaves were unpopular, as well as being hard to obtain in such a sparsely peopled area. Neither the Huila market, nor a coastal expedition organized in 1785 by the Baron of Moçâmedes, was of any immediate consequence. Farther east, indirect trading influences were beginning to percolate inwards at about the same time. The Nkumbe sold ivory to Ovimbundu intermediaries

[1] For a clear analysis of the Luso-African sphere of influence in the eighteenth century see two articles by Jean-Luc Vellut: 'Relations internationales du Moyen-Kwango et de l'Angola dans la deuxième moitié du XVIIIe s.', in *Études d'histoire africaine*, I, 75–135; 'Notes sur le Lunda et la frontière Luso-Africaine (1700–1900)', in *ibid.* III, 61–161.

at Caconda, but rigorously excluded the Portuguese and their agents clad in European dress. The Ovambo made their first outside contacts with ivory merchants in Damaraland in the south. Not until the mid-nineteenth century did these indirect trading links give way to more direct foreign contact between the peoples of the south-west and the traders.

In 1840 merchants from Luanda founded the trading port of Moçâmedes on the south coast and began to seek direct access to the highland ivory markets. Within a few years they had opened the route as far as the Nkumbe, and even the Ovambo, and trade increased to include cattle, slaves, gum, orchilla and wax. A major new trading axis had thus been created to parallel the older systems of Luanda and Benguela. In 1849 the new colony was strengthened by the admission of Portuguese refugees from Brazil who introduced sugar and cotton planting in watered pockets of the coastal desert. The cane was used for rum to increase the inland trade, and the cotton became reasonably profitable when prices rose during the American civil war. The Moçâmedes colony was further strengthened in the 1860s by the arrival of Portuguese fishermen who successfully established a coastal fishing industry. The fishing port also developed market gardens from which to supply foreign whaling fleets. All of these new industries were in part based on the local absorption of slave labour which could no longer be legally exported. But they also represented a real attempt at white colonization, as opposed to white trading, in Central Africa. As such the Moçâmedes colony formed an important stage in the Portuguese transition from an exclusively mercantile economy to one including agricultural settlers.

Attempts to use the toe-hold gained in Moçâmedes to extend the new southern colony into the highlands met initially with sharp resistance. The coast was sparsely occupied and defended, but the plateau was organized into militant kingdoms. In the late 1850s Portuguese military expeditions reached Humbe, despite Ngambwe resistance and long-range Ovimbundu and Kwanyama opposition, but they were soon forced to withdraw to Huila. Meanwhile long distance Ovimbundu raids for cattle and slaves became increasingly severe in the south. On one occasion the raiders even descended into the desert and threatened Moçâmedes. They were bought off with European goods as protection money. Military opposition was not the only barrier to the extension of the southern colony. Settlers who had reached the foot-hills found the plateau unsuitable for tropical agriculture. Various colonizing ventures failed before Boer trekkers from South Africa arrived in the early 1880s, and effectively began to clear the highlands of both trees and people in order to facilitate white settlement. The early trading communities had in the meantime become increasingly Africanized and subject to Nkumbe political control.

Two sets of commercial rivals challenged the growth of southern Portuguese trade. From south-west Africa traders penetrated the Ovambo and Okavango regions to capture much of the ivory market and develop a trade in ostrich feathers. The southern traders were accompanied by influential Christian missions. The Ovimbundu traders from the north found that the best way to buy southern ivory was with cattle. They obtained their cattle with European trade-goods in the far east of Angola, in the Zambezi region. By the 1870s the extensive networks of inter-regional trading were causing a decline in the supply of ivory, and all three major buyers were competing for the Ovambo trade by the 1880s.[1]

SOUTH-CENTRAL ANGOLA

The commercial network of south-central Angola also began to expand towards the east in the late eighteenth century. The Portuguese and the Ovimbundu had long been anxious to gain access to the upper Zambezi basin, both in order to open up new spheres of trade and to seek a possible land route to Mozambique. Two major barriers lay in their way. In the north the Chokwe were hostile to foreign penetration and had developed very little trade which might afford an opening. In the south the Mbundu chiefs prevented the passage of caravans in order to protect their own slave and ivory trade. When a route to the east was finally pioneered from Bihe, it crossed a stretch of uninhabited land between these two blocks and reached the Luena–Lovale lands along the Luena and upper Zambezi rivers. This route to Lovale was first described by a trader who had reached the Zambezi from the west in 1794. The new opening probably had considerable effects on the trade of the southern Zaïre region. Lunda copper went to Lovale, for instance, and the Lovale had become skilled in the making of copper wire. Eventually copper crosses from Katanga were being traded right through to Benguela. By 1800 the governor of Angola was speculating that the upper Zambezi might be an extension of the Lualaba which,

[1] Carlos Estermann, *Ethnografia do Sudoest de Angola*, 3 vols. (Lisbon, 1956, 1960, 1961). Alfredo de Albuquerque Felner, *Angola: apontamentos sôbre a colonizaão dos planaltos e litoral do sul de Angola*, 3 vols. (Lisbon, 1940). J. J. Monteiro, *Angola and the River Congo*, 2 vols. (London, 1875). This section owes much to the advice of W. G. Clarence-Smith, who has since written a history of south-western Angola, 'Mossamedes and its hinterland 1875–1915', Ph.D. thesis (London University, 1975).

amazingly but correctly, he thought might be the upper Congo. He was also aware that the upper Lualaba was one source of Lunda copper. Thus by opening a route to Lovale, a new communication had been established with Katanga which bypassed both Kasanje and the metropolitan areas of the Lunda empire in the north. Chiefs along this new high-road into the interior soon began to benefit from their position. Angarussa, who controlled the upper Kwanza crossing, charged up to 200 fathoms of cloth for each caravan that passed eastward, and a further two or three slaves on the return journey. He also accepted commissions from traders to waylay their rivals. In view of the profitability of the new opening to the east, other nations began to offer alternative routes, so that they too might draw profit from trade tolls. The Mbundu, in particular, opened up access to the remote Mbwela lands of the south, where slaves were particularly cheap.

THE LOZI

The western traders who reached the Zambezi hoped to go on to the rich lands of the Lozi along the river between Lovale territory and the southern bend of the Zambezi. They were not welcomed by the Lozi, who showed little enthusiasm for trade. Only much later did the Lozi become linked to the trans-African trade routes. The Lozi were essentially a pastoral people, who kept fine cattle both on the banks of the river and on islands in the flood plain. They used large canoes to ferry their cattle to the richest or safest pastures. The Lozi probably had an organized political and economic system, even in the early nineteenth century. The rulers operated a system of tributary exchanges whereby production of many goods was stimulated: the king received canoes, weapons, iron tools, meat, fish, fruit, salt, honey and a range of agricultural foods including maize and cassava. In return he lent to his subjects cattle, all of which belonged to him. Silva Porto, visiting Lozi in 1853, listed twenty-eight 'tribes' who came under the jurisdiction of the king and supplied the central authority with their specialized products.

From about 1840 to 1864 Bulozi (or Barotseland) was ruled by Sotho conquerors from the south called the Kololo.[1] They arrived on the Zambezi after several years of marauding in Botswana, with occasional forays as far afield as Namibia and Rhodesia. Their main base was in the southern part of Bulozi, between the Chobe and Zambezi rivers. Their economy continued to depend to a significant extent on cattle raiding,

[1] See also below, pp. 341–3.

but two new sources of wealth became important when they reached the Zambezi. One was the old Lozi flood-plain economy, which the Kololo effectively took over. They became as skilled as the Lozi in the management of canoes, and in the collecting of tributary payments from the many sectors of the plain. The second new dimension was external trade. Before the Kololo invasion the Lozi had rebuffed the traders who came from the west via the court of the Lovale king, Kinyama. The reason, in all probability, was that this rich agricultural area was not a potential source of labour exports. On the contrary it imported labour, and Mulambwa, the Lozi king in the 1830s, had nothing to offer to slavers. The advent of long distance trade occurred at a later date along the more southerly Mbunda–Mbwela route. About 1850, 'Mambari' traders from Angola began to frequent the southern Kololo area, below the flood-plain, where they found people more willing to sell slaves. These slaves, obtained as a byproduct of cattle raiding, were of no immediate economic benefit to the pastoral, pre-dominantly non-agricultural Kololo society. Soon after its opening, this southern route was enhanced by the development of ivory trade. A combination of rising prices, soaring demand and the abolition of the Portuguese royal monopoly on the Angola coast made it profitable to carry ivory 1,400 kilometres to the Atlantic. This trade proved attractive to the people of the flood-plain, as well as to the southern Kololo, and in 1854 Livingstone pioneered a northern trade route to Angola, which was later used by at least one Kololo-led caravan. This northern trade may have intensified conflict between the northern and southern poles of the Kololo kingdom. The traders may have become indepen-dent of both Lozi and Kololo traditionalists, and so helped to cause the breakdown of political stability. This breakdown occurred in the 1860s, after the death of Sekeletu, the second Kololo king. When a strong king re-emerged in the 1870s, it was no longer a Kololo leader, but Lewanika, king of the Lozi. Although the rise of the western ivory trade may have facilitated the Lozi 'restoration', ivory also helped to cause its downfall. After a few years of independence, Lewanika came under the influence of ivory hunters from southern Africa who even-tually brought colonial conquest in their wake.[1]

[1] Eric Flint, 'Trade and Politics in Barotseland during the Kololo period', *Journal of African History*, 1970, 11, 1. António Francisco da Silva Pôrto, *A travessia do continente africano* (Lisbon, 1936) and *Viagens e apontamentos de um Portuense em África* (Lisbon, 1942). David Livingstone, *Missionary travels and researches in South Africa* (London, 1857).

THE OVIMBUNDU KINGDOMS

One of the most important developments in the south-west of Central Africa between the late eighteenth and late nineteenth centuries was the growth in power and prosperity of the Ovimbundu kingdoms. This growth was linked to both southern and eastern trade developments. The Ovimbundu states may have been founded by seventeenth-century immigrant groups. By the eighteenth century they had crystallized into half a dozen major kingdoms with several lesser satellites on the periphery. Their early history was noted for the long distance raids organized to obtain cattle for themselves and slaves for Benguela. Gradually some states developed into regular trading centres to find a surer and more permanent means of prosperity than plundering. Other states profited from the routes which crossed their territory by charging tolls or supplying services and food.

The most important of the trading kingdoms was Bihe. It was the easternmost of the Ovimbundu states and therefore had the most ready access to the interior. It seems that Bihe also had an established prosperity, which may have formed the basis for its entry into long distance commerce. Bihe had a particularly good supply of iron, and so became a centre of iron working, supplying hoes and other implements to neighbouring peoples. Immediately east of Bihe was a pottery industry, which supplied a wide area where sandy soils made good-quality potting clay scarce. The profits from local trades, together with the experience in communications, may have stimulated the growth of Bihe entrepreneurship in organizing slave, ivory, wax and, later, rubber caravans. Initially, in the first half of the nineteenth century, the main route out of Bihe ran north-west towards the Kwanza. An important fair flourished at Dondo, the main crossing point into Portuguese Angola. Two other Ovimbundu states also lay along the north-western routes, at Ndulu and Bailundu. They became important as trading kingdoms, either in their own right or as agents of the transit traffic. The more direct exit for Bihe trade was to the Benguela coast, but this involved crossing the whole Ovimbundu territory and paying protection money or other dues to several intermediate states. A variety of routes was used, passing either through Bailundu or through Huambo depending on political conditions. The growth of this direct trade to the coast led to the founding of a new Portuguese trading settlement at Catumbela. This was more accessible from the plateau than Benguela, which had been geared to the southern trade through Caconda. The number of traders grew steadily; in 1879 Silva Porto travelled from Catumbela to Bihe in a month and met about forty caravans. The growth of entrepreneurship gradually affected all the Ovimbundu states, as increasing numbers of long distance caravans were sponsored. The development of these wealthy, experienced, commercial kingdoms gradually came to be felt as far afield as Luba and Kuba.

THE CHOKWE

A fourth topic in the history of south-western Central Africa was the creation of an entirely new trading 'empire' by the Chokwe. These pioneers struck northwards from the uplands of eastern Angola to capture part of the trading system of the Congo basin. The Chokwe had played a very slight role in Central African trade in the eighteenth century. Their country was remote and underpopulated, and they took little part in the supply of slaves. Their main exports were ivory and wax, but in the heyday of the slave trade, they were difficult to transport and less profitable than slaves. The Chokwe did, however, manage to sell some of their commodities, and in return specialized in the purchase of flintlock muskets. In the 1840s a great change occurred among the Chokwe. The trade in wax from Benguela and Luanda rose some thirty-fold, as trading houses tried to remain solvent despite the decline of the slave trade. Chokwe wax went both to Kasanje and nearby markets on the route to Luanda, and to Bihe, for transmission to the Benguela coast. Chokwe wax was highly esteemed and was collected from carefully prepared log hives. Production occurred throughout the upper Kasai woodland and even beyond into Luchaze territory, though transport costs reduced the profits farther east to a marginal figure.

Another important change occurred among the Chokwe, when a rapid rise in the ivory trade came to overshadow wax production. The Chokwe played a large part in the revival of ivory which followed the abolition of the Portuguese royal monopoly in 1834 and the consequent rise in prices. The Chokwe had the advantage of being skilled hunters. They were also expert gunsmiths and had been able, through their wax trade, to build up and maintain a substantial armoury of guns. Thirdly, the Chokwe woodland was the nearest region to the coast in which elephants were still plentiful by the late 1840s. Under these conditions, the Chokwe were able to take up intensive ivory hunting. The volume of the exploitation, however, soon depleted the elephants. New hunting grounds had to be sought and the Chokwe sent out hunting parties to the north and east. They offered their skills to the Lunda, in whose territory elephants were still available. One half of the ivory shot in Lunda was kept by the Chokwe hunter and the other half went to the Lunda chief. Both the chief and the hunter usually sold their ivory to Kasanje and Bihe traders, who had travelled in the hunters' wake, and switched part of their interest from slaves to ivory. By this adaptation to new circumstances the traditional large-scale trader continued to prosper for a few years longer. At the same time the Chokwe emerged as a new entrepreneurial group in the Kasai basin.

The increase of Chokwe prosperity had the primary effect of increasing Chokwe population. The ivory which they hunted was primarily converted into women. These women were bought from Kasanje and Bihe caravans at increasingly favourable rates as the demand for slaves, and especially women slaves, slackened on the coast. In Chokwe society, investment in women was the soundest means of economic development. Agriculture prospered, families increased and by the 1850s the upper Kasai was beginning to experience a shortage of cultivable farmland. As a result a slow process of migratory expansion began towards the north. Chokwe villages moved a few miles at a time beyond the national frontier, occupying forested river banks and other familiar terrain. The migrants avoided conflict with the Lunda by occupying the more wooded areas and by contributing, through trade and hunting, to the economic well-being of their neighbours.

Having successfully exploited first wax and then ivory until each was exhausted, the Chokwe economy underwent a third change in the late 1860s and began to embark on the production of rubber, tapped from forest vines. In the Chokwe home territory this activity was very short-lived, because of the wasteful methods used for tapping latex. The rubber collectors had to move north, thus swelling Chokwe migrations, and spreading the rubber trade along the forest galleries of the Kasai basin.

The exhaustion of ivory and rubber along the upper Kasai caused important changes in the Chokwe economy. From being mainly producers, who sold to the established caravaneers from Kasanje and Bihe, the Chokwe became traders who fetched their ivory from the middle Kasai and eventually from among the Luba. To do this they established their own long distance caravan system, with their own routes, carriers and leaders. Once they had launched into the business of carrying, the Chokwe began to rival the old entrepreneurs. Furthermore, when they reached the Lulua and Luba areas, they found themselves among people who hunted their own ivory and tapped their own rubber, so that the traditional skills of the Chokwe as producers became super-fluous. They gradually adapted to the single role of trading inter-mediaries.

In the short space of fifty years the Chokwe had risen from being a small, remote, forest people to being one of the most dynamic economic forces in Central Africa. They had also become one of the most power-ful military forces, and their early, inconspicuous migrations were in-creasingly replaced by violent raiding. By the 1870s they were a match for any rival including the large, organized empire of their Lunda neighbours, which they succeeded in subverting and almost destroying.[1]

NORTHERN ANGOLA AND LUANDA

The history of northern Angola in the nineteenth century involved changes of a rather different kind from those at work in southern Angola during the same period. In the south new trading axes were being pioneered to tap a wide variety of new resources and commodi-ties and to stimulate new economic growth and diversification. In the north the nineteenth century was associated with decline and retrench-ment. It was, however a decline in slave trading which should have released new forces of positive growth. For a long time this growth was not greatly in evidence, and Luanda stagnated. When the history of this period comes to be written, one will of course have to treat with caution the perennial traders' cry that business had been ruined. It is, neverthe-less, true that such trade as there was on the old slave route through north-central Angola continued to decline after its hinterland had been partially captured during the eighteenth century by Loango in the north and Benguela in the south. Despite the decline of this route, the western coast of Central Africa remained the most lucrative slaving area on the Atlantic during the nineteenth century. A British Foreign Office estimate of the total slave exports from 1817 till 1843 gave the figures shown opposite.[2]

The striking thing about this table is that only 4,400 slaves were listed as shipped from Luanda, barely 7 per cent of the total listed from Benguela and less than 3 per cent of the Cabinda figure. Although some of the unclassified 'Angolan' slaves may also have come from Luanda, one can nevertheless assume a serious decline in the city's trade.

---

[1] Joseph Miller, 'Cokwe expansion 1850–1900' (mimeographed, Madison, 1969), and 'Cokwe Trade and conquest', in Richard Gray and David Birmingham, *Pre-colonial African trade* (London, 1970); Gladwyn M. Childs, *Umbundu kinship and character* (London, 1949).

[2] Philip Curtin, *The Atlantic slave trade* (Madison, 1969), 261.

Loango	1,100
Malembo	26,800
Cabinda	102,500
Congo river	16,400
'Angola'	144,100
Ambriz	30,600
Luanda	4,400
Benguela	58,400
Total	384,300
Annual average	14,800

The decline was also felt at other points along the route into the interior. In 1790, before the Napoleonic wars had reduced the overall quantity of shipping available to slaving interests, Kasanje was still the focal point of the Luanda trading system. For over a hundred years it had effectively controlled a large share of the trade between the Lunda empire and the west coast. The Portuguese, however, driven by falling profits, were no longer satisfied with the old broker kingdoms and sought direct contact with their suppliers. In 1806 Anastacio and Baptista, two Luso-African *pombeiros*, reached the Lunda capital of the *mwata yamvo*, and were able to reveal to the Lunda details of the European trading system so long concealed by Kasanje middlemen. Two years later an embassy from the *mwata yamvo*, and another from his mother, the *lukonkeshia*, arrived in Luanda to present royal letters to the Portuguese governor. This breach of the Kasanje barrier by diplomatic envoys led to the creation of new commercial routes which by-passed the Imbangala territory altogether. The resulting decline of Kasanje led to increasing disputes between the Portuguese and the Kasanje kings. These disputes finally led to a major war in 1850 in which the kingdom was disrupted and the Portuguese *feira*, or staple market, was moved back to Malanje in Portuguese-held territory. Although Kasanje was subsequently re-established, and although in 1852 David Livingstone was able to receive copies of *The Times* there, it no longer flourished. Malanje became the departure point for caravans to the interior, and its trading houses became fully capable of equipping long distance traders. By the 1870s all that remained of the long association between the Kasanje plain and Angola were a few Portuguese cattle ranchers and sugar planters. Most caravans used other routes, leaving Kasanje independent, but largely deprived of its life-blood.

A second major change in the Luanda system came in mid-century with the penetration of Ovimbundu and later Chokwe enterprise into the Kwango–Kasai region. The effect of this was to cut across the old east–west trade routes and replace them with new north–south routes. This was not done without a struggle, and battles between Kasanje and Ovimbundu caravans occurred even before the Chokwe captured a share of the trade. In the south, as seen, this growing north–south trade triggered off a major northward expansion of Chokwe peoples. In the north, as will be shown later, it began to affect peoples on the forest fringe who had little previous contact with market-oriented trade. On the central routes, however, the effect was to depress trade yet further and cause the Portuguese to think once again about developing the local economic potential of their coastal provinces in Angola.

There had been attempts in the eighteenth century to diversify the economy of Angola by investing in the salt and hide industries, and by introducing Iberian technology into the iron-working industry. These endeavours had come to nothing, however, and in the early nineteenth century the colony was as dependent as ever on the slave trade. Even food and building timbers were brought in from Brazil. A large proportion of the 2,000 white inhabitants of Luanda city were deported criminals, and much of the military garrison consisted of local African convicts. The rest of the population consisted of a few hundred mulattoes and free Africans, and some 3,000 slaves, many of them charwomen and laundresses. The 'colony' was divided into about a dozen districts ruled by ill-paid and ill-trained government agents. Their main function, and incidentally their main source of income, was the forced recruitment of conscript carriers to be hired to passing traders. This conscription led to severe forms of extortion, and the contract was between the agent and the trader only, not between the carrier and the trader. As the slave trade declined, efforts were made to seek new trade goods and a new hinterland. As early as 1790 the Portuguese had tried to expand northward along the coast. They had been severely defeated by the ruler of Mossul, who continued to dominate the coast north of Luanda for many years. In 1855 the Portuguese tried to overcome this barrier by establishing a garrison at the English settlement of Ambriz. They had little success in attracting more trade, however, and their high tariffs drove the traders to the neighbouring bay of Kinsembo. Despite the difficulties, some agricultural produce began to flow into Luanda by the 1860s. Cotton, coffee, beeswax, and palm oil were all produced by small-scale African farmers and collectors in the Kwanza, Bengo and Dande valleys. Farther inland, cattle-keeping revived in importance, and when a steamer service was introduced on the lower Kwanza, attempts were made to establish sugar plantations there. In Cazengo and Golungo Alto a few Portuguese traders branched into coffee planting, but the colonial economy remained weak even in the last quarter of the nineteenth century.[1]

SOUTHERN CENTRAL AFRICA

When one moves eastward, beyond the immediate sphere of Luso-African influence in western Central Africa, one eventually enters a region in which the earliest international trade came across eastern and south-eastern Africa from the Indian Ocean. This commercial penetration of southern Central Africa, like the Atlantic penetration of western Central Africa, was marked by several distinct phases, each pioneered by separate groups interested in exploiting different resources. In the north of the southern savanna the two spheres of economic influence were linked by the growing political and commercial empire of the Lunda. In the south an economic watershed divided west from east, and parts of southern Zambia remained a no-man's land unvisited by foreign caravans until the nineteenth century. The fact that this region was untapped by direct long distance trade did not mean that its population was inactive. On the contrary, many interesting developments were taking place, particularly on the fertile Tonga plateau. The Tonga were mixed farmers and pastoralists who remained isolated from the outside world until colonial times, although after the 1830s they experienced periodic cattle raids from the Kololo and Ndebele. They did not, however, constitute exclusively self-sufficient subsistence communities. Within a middle Zambezi framework they operated a system of exchanges and specialisms which supplemented their subsistence activities. The Tonga had valuable supplies of salt with which they could purchase goods of external origin. On the other hand they lacked good quality iron ores, and so had to rely on imported hoes and other metalwares. Other items of exchange, such as shells, beads and cloth, filtered through from farther afield and reached the Tonga after multiple exchanges had taken place among neighbours who were trading in fish, grain, game, ochre, building materials and specialized items of food. These exchanges enabled Tonga communities to build up a small quantity of material wealth which could be converted either into

[1] J. Lopes de Lima, 'Ensaio sôbre a statistica d'Angola ê Benguella', in *Ensaios sôbre a statistica das possessões portuguezas*, III (Lisbon, 1846). J. J. Monteiro, *Angola and the River Congo*, 2 vols. (London, 1875). E. Alexandre da Silva Corrêa, *História de Angola*, 2 vols. (Lisbon, 1937).

personal ornaments or exchanged for food in times of famine and hardship. They did not become specialists in trading, or in any form of market-oriented production, as did the Chokwe or the Lozi, but they nonetheless took steps to increase their economic well-being, and to cushion themselves against economic disaster.[1]

Eastward from this central region where the penetration of nineteenth-century trade was only slightly felt, were the lands of the Luangwa and Luapula basins, where direct and strong contacts with the outside world developed during the nineteenth century. The earliest of these contacts was with the lower Zambezi. Already in the eighteenth century the people of the middle Zambezi bend, especially the Lenje, had been conducting some trade with the Portuguese at Zumbo. A more important trading state in the area, however, was the eastern Lunda kingdom of Kazembe.[2] This important state had been established in the mid-eighteenth century by groups of Lunda explorers, colonizers and fortune hunters. In an otherwise sparsely inhabited region, they found that the Luapula valley contained a flourishing community centred on the fishing industry. The diversity of the Luapula economy somewhat resembled that of the upper Zambezi. The migrants from Lunda were able to contribute in several ways to its growth. They were probably able to introduce cassava as a new and hardy staple crop, with a higher yield than the traditional grain crops. The Lunda immigrants were also able to establish a pattern of administration which encouraged economic co-operation. The early *kazembes* built a state structure, and imposed a produce tribute on the various peoples of the region. The Lunda tribute system of two-way exchanges between the king and his chiefs was probably used to redistribute the surplus. The Lunda colonization of the Luapula also increased external trade. In particular salt was sent west to the court of the *mwata yamvo*. It is likely, though not yet adequately proven, that the eastern Lunda of Kazembe also supplied slaves to central Lunda, both for internal reabsorption, in agriculture, and for relaying to the Atlantic. In the early years Kazembe received its exotic imports from the Atlantic. Metal wares, ornaments, shells, and even crockery, were carried from the west coast over enormously long lines of communication. Much shorter, however, and potentially more important, was the trading axis between Kazembe and the lower Zambezi.

[1] Marvin Miracle, 'Plateau Tonga entrepreneurs in historical inter-regional trade', *Rhodes-Livingstone Journal*, 1959, **26**.

[2] Kazembe was the hereditary title of the ruler of this Lunda state. Kazembe is here used to denote the state ruled by the *kazembe*s.

By the 1790s Kazembe and the Zambezi Portuguese were each anxious to establish direct trading links. Indirect trade between them had been in the hands of the Bisa, who conveyed slaves, ivory, and copper to the Portuguese and carried cloth back to Kazembe. At first Bisa trade was only a small branch of Portuguese business, along with ranching, gold panning and local slave trading in the Zambezi valley. Gradually, however, they became aware of Kazembe's potential value as a gateway to the interior. In 1798 an expedition led by Francisco de Lacerda e Almeida was instructed to sign a treaty with the third *kazembe* and open a road to the west. The *kazembe*, although anxious enough to attract traders, naturally had no intention of allowing foreigners to open his much cherished route *à contra costa*. The Lunda knew all about the economic advantages of the strategic middleman. Lacerda e Almeida's great expedition therefore failed in its economic aims, if not in its scientific ones.

The second Portuguese attempt to establish links with Kazembe started from the west. The two Portuguese-speaking *pombeiros*, agents of a European trader at Kasanje, who visited the *mwata yamvo*, also had instructions to travel to Tete on the Zambezi. They reached Kazembe safely in 1806 and, after being delayed for four years, were eventually allowed to complete their journey. On their return they were again waylaid in Kazembe and relieved of the presents they carried. These presents had been sent by the Portuguese to induce chiefs of the interior to direct their trade to the Zambezi rather than the Atlantic. This journey of the *pombeiros* was undoubtedly one of the most dramatic and famous episodes in the annals of African exploration, but it did little to increase the eastern trade of Kazembe or to further Portuguese trading ambitions in Central Africa. By 1831, when the Portuguese made their third attempt to open trade with Kazembe, the situation had altered and the king had established contact with the expanding trade systems of East Africa. Monteiro and Gamitto found him disdainful of their goods. He was unwilling to accept plain cloth at any price, and he would not pay ivory or copper for even the better quality coloured and woollen materials, but only rather inferior slaves. The Portuguese penetration from the south-east was thus halted, and the way opened for a new enterprise to move onto the Central African scene from the Zanzibar coast.[1]

[1] Ian Cunnison, 'Kazembe and the Portuguese', *Journal of African History*, 1961, **2**. A. Verbeken and M. Walraet, *La première traversée du Katanga en 1806* (Brussels, 1953). Nicola Sutherland-Harris, 'Zambian trade with Zumbo in the Eighteenth Century', in

Swahili-Arab penetration of north-eastern Zambia and south-eastern Zaïre was more like the Chokwe penetration of western Lunda than the Portuguese activity which it superseded. The Swahili-Arabs probably began to arrive in the early nineteenth century, although it has been suggested that by the time of Lacerda's visit to Kazembe a few traders had already reached the Luapula.[1] They came as peaceful traders, and settled in small compounds near established local chiefs while they built up their trade in slaves and ivory. Caravans were periodically sent back to the coast, and returned not only with new trade-goods but also with more guns and powder. As the Swahili-Arab trading-posts increased their military establishment, the factories became stockades or even forts. Eventually the traders became sufficiently well-established to overthrow the local chiefs and gain independent political power for themselves. Thus they slowly undermined the communities on the eastern fringe of the Lunda empire, just as the Chokwe were undermining those on the west. In both cases ivory was the fundamental stimulus to advance; but in both cases a trade in slaves, including women slaves, was an important secondary activity.

The development of Swahili-Arab ruled communities in Kazembe's sphere of influence was especially significant in the 1850s and 1860s. Kazembe itself was not initially subject to outright challenge, but many of the eastern chiefs, who had previously been under its influence, were now more directly under Swahili-Arab influence. Kazembe seems to have retained considerable control over the supply of ivory from beyond the Luapula, but in the 1860s this supply was either becoming exhausted or being tapped by rival west-coast traders. The kingdom was probably also losing its grip on the important copper trade. As a result Kazembe's power and prestige was definitely on the wane by the time Livingstone visited the capital in the 1860s. By 1872, the influence of the traders had become so strong that they became involved in serious political disturbances in which the seventh *kazembe* was replaced first by the eighth *kazembe* and soon after by the ninth *kazembe*. This disruption was part of a pattern which was to become familiar in other

Gray and Birmingham, *Pre-colonial African trade*. F. J. de Lacerda e Almeida, *Travessia da Africa* (Lisbon, 1936). A. C. P. Gamitto, *King Kazembe*, tr. Ian Cunnison, 2 vols. (Lisbon, 1960). Andrew Roberts, 'Pre-Colonial trade in Zambia', *African Social Research*, 10, 1970. Andrew Roberts, 'Tippu Tip, Livingstone, and the chronology of Kazembe', *Azania*, 2, 1967.

[1] The term 'Arab' has often been applied to coastal Muslims more properly called Swahili. Tippu Tip, the greatest 'Arab' trader of all, was probably more African than Arab by culture, race, and language, and would be described today as a Swahili. The term Swahili-Arab is used throughout in referring to East Coast traders since the contemporary nomenclature is so unclear.

parts of Central Africa. Failure to satisfy rising expectations created by the opening, or increase, of external trade, led to situations of internal conflict which could easily be exploited by outside agents. The situation was made more volatile by the rapid increase in the supply of guns. In the first half of the nineteenth century guns were rare in southern Central Africa. A few were brought in by traders, but they were inefficient and short-lived weapons, which few people learnt to use with any skill. They became a symbol of power, a badge of office, but not a real military asset. The development of the ivory trade in the period after 1850 brought in new entrepreneurs, such as the Chokwe and the Swahili-Arabs, who had a much larger supply of guns and, above all, were much more skilled in their use than the population which they met in the remote interior. The new traders rapidly gained considerable power and prestige, and were often only too willing to accept invitations to support one faction or another in the internal disputes of states such as Kazembe, thus weakening the old order and increasing their own power.

The third major people to penetrate Central Africa from the east, along with the Portuguese and the Swahili-Arabs, were the Nyamwezi. The Nyamwezi acquired their commercial skills, and accumulated their capital, in the internal trade of western Tanzania. They became important traders of iron, salt, hoes, cloth, food and other local staples or specialties. At about the same time that the Swahili-Arabs were beginning to seek access to the interior of East Africa to buy ivory, the Nyamwezi were beginning to seek access to the coast to buy foreign cloths, beads and copper. By the 1850s the Nyamwezi, like the Swahili-Arabs, had become large-scale caravan operators in East Africa. Their major trading partner was Kazembe, from which they bought ivory and Katanga copper. In the 1850s the Nyamwezi began to circumvent Kazembe, in order to trade more directly with the copper-producing areas. In this the Sumbwa Nyamwezi were particularly successful, and became known in Katanga as the Yeke.

The Yeke penetration of Kazembe's western domains, and of the frontier-lands of *mwata yamvo*'s Lunda, began, like the Chokwe penetration in the west and the Swahili-Arab penetration in the east, as an essentially peaceful commercial operation. The Yeke were welcomed because they brought foreign goods, increased the scope for local exchanges, and put a new value on commodities which were previously hard to export because of transport difficulties. In particular, the Yeke traded with chief Katanga of the Lamba. They bought large copper ingots, moulded in the traditional cross form, but weighing as much as a man could carry.

Although the Yeke had penetrated the Lamba country in the capacity of traders, they soon began to aspire to political power under the leadership of Msiri, the son of an early Sumbwa trader. Msiri made use of his superiority in firearms to dominate his neighbours and spread fearsome rumours of his military prowess. His first conquests were made on behalf of local chiefs who welcomed his help in suppressing insubordination. In return they gave him captives, whom he could use as porters to carry ivory and copper to Unyamwezi. Msiri rapidly followed up this success by challenging the power of chiefs Katanga and Mpande, whom he overthrew, to make himself master of the Lamba and Sanga peoples. He then directed new campaigns against the Luba, in the north, until by about 1870 he had sufficiently gained in power to challenge the overlordship of Kazembe. Thus at the same time that the Swahili-Arabs were weakening the power of Kazembe in the east, the Yeke were breaking his authority in the west, to declare themselves an independent nation. Yeke independence not only reduced the size and power of Kazembe, but also threatened its route to the *mwata yamvo*'s capital.

The success of Msiri led many peoples from all parts of Katanga to join him. He called his new heterogeneous kingdom Garenganze, and by the 1880s his capital, at Bunkeya, had grown to over forty villages of followers who had migrated to safety under his suzerainty. By intervening in the disputes of his neighbours, Msiri was able to spread his influence to cover most of the area between the upper Lualaba and the Luapula, a vast territory carved out of the two main branches of the Lunda empire. Garenganze became one of the most important and most successful conquest states of nineteenth-century Central Africa. Its initial success may have been associated with the advent of plentiful and effective guns, but in his administration Msiri adopted traditional and well-tried methods of government. A Lunda-type system of provincial governors administered his more remote subjects, and levied the ivory tax which lay at the base of Msiri's wealth. A hierarchy of war chiefs organized expeditions against Msiri's Luba and Lunda enemies. The Yeke military élite, numbering perhaps some 2,000 men, was armed with guns, while the bulk of the state's armed force consisted of locally recruited soldiers with lances, bows, and other traditional weapons.

Although Msiri's empire was apparently a more aggressive, military kingdom than the old Lunda states, it remained, like them, dependent on trade for prosperity and long-term success. Ivory remained Msiri's foremost source of state revenue, and he held a monopoly of tusks from elephants killed on his land. Garenganze was so remote from the major trade arteries that elephants were still plentiful after the 1870s, and could provide an important revenue to the state, when most regions nearer to the coasts had been almost hunted out. In a second revenue-earning field, the copper industry, Msiri began by imposing a percentage levy on production, but soon moved towards a state monopoly, recruiting Yeke smiths to smelt copper and produce wire, bracelets and ingots for the surrounding markets. The supply of slaves to Garenganze was mainly satisfied by warfare, but Msiri also instituted orders of merit with treasured emblems of office which could be purchased by donating slaves to the royal court. Slaves were also a current means of paying fines for judicial infringements. Finally, Msiri gained control of the salt springs of Mwashya, and the marsh salt supplies of the Lualaba, which gave him an important stake in the internal trade of Katanga.

The original outlet for the Yeke trade was eastward via Kazembe, or other Luapula crossings, to Unyamwezi and Zanzibar. With the decline of Kazembe, Msiri began to seek new caravan routes. He established direct links with the Lovale by about 1870, and thereby became linked to the expanding Ovimbundu trade system of southern Angola. Caravans from Bunkeya began to travel fifteen hundred kilometres right through Bihe to Benguela on the Atlantic. From the west Silva Porto, an established Portuguese trader, began sending caravans from Angola to Bunkeya. Msiri was able, by means of this new link, not only to export additional quantities of ivory and slaves, but also a certain amount of rubber and wax. In 1875 Vernon Cameron followed much of this route in his journey across Africa from east to west, and met a 'Nyamwezi' caravan in Angola. In the next decade Frederic Arnot came up the route from the Atlantic to establish the first Christian mission in Katanga.[1]

Although the Lunda state of Kazembe was perhaps the major kingdom to attract Swahili-Arab and Nyamwezi traders into the south-eastern quarter of Central Africa, two other kingdoms of rather different character were also important. These were Bemba and Luba.

The Bemba state developed during the nineteenth century to cover much of the plateau country east of Kazembe, between the Luapula and Luangwa valleys. The origins of the kingdom probably reached back into the seventeenth century, and may have been vaguely related to early Luba or Lunda states, but the emergence of an important terri-

---

[1] Auguste Verbeken, *Msiri: roi du Garenganze* (Brussels, 1956).

torial claim by the *chitimukulu*, or king, only took place from the late eighteenth century. The reasons for the rise and expansion of the Bemba state are not at all clear. It has been suggested by Roberts[1] that the initial stages of Bemba expansion were related to raiding. The Bemba homeland was poor in many respects, and the Bemba took to raiding their neighbours for cattle, for salt and probably for many other regional products which they themselves did not produce. By the end of the eighteenth century the *chitimukulu* began to found Bemba chiefdoms in the raided lands and to appoint to them relatives who would tie the new lands to a central dynasty. Among the earliest 'colonies' was the western chiefdom of Ituna, the ruler of which was given the title *mwamba*. This expansion was rather different in character from the expansion of Lozi or Kazembe, which started with a comparatively wealthy nucleus, based on rich fishing, cattle-keeping, or farming, and gradually expanded to bring neighbours into an increasingly diversified sphere of economic exchanges. The Bemba, in contrast, started out as a poor group of military raiders and expanded into the better endowed country around them.

The Bemba kingdom received a new stimulus to expansion when, about 1850, it began to establish contact with the Swahili-Arab traders moving into the territories around the south of Lake Tanganyika. The Bemba country still had supplies of prime-quality ivory which it could offer to such traders. Furthermore, the Bemba pattern of raiding was eminently suited to the capture of slaves. Since Bembaland was too poor for large-scale, slave-using agriculture, as in Lozi or even Chokwe regions, a slave surplus was available for export. In about 1860 Chileshye, the *chitimukulu* who had pioneered the first phase of Bemba expansion, died and was succeeded, after an interval, by Chitapankwa. He began to make use of the country's new-found trading potential to acquire guns, which had not been used in the establishment of the kingdom, but which became a major factor in its later expansion. Guns increased the scope of Bemba slave raiding and elephant hunting, and from about 1870 consolidated their relations with the East Coast traders, including Tippu Tip. Guns also helped in the successful Bemba repulsion of their Ngoni neighbours in the east.

Although the Bemba state can be described as a 'brigand' kingdom, like those of the Yeke and Chokwe, the Bemba showed considerable skill in creating political cohesion within their domains. The first link

[1] A. D. Roberts, *A history of the Bemba: political growth and change in north-eastern Zambia before 1900* (London, 1973), 125-7.

was in family ties between the central rulers and the appointed governors of the conquest territories. To enhance the loyalty of these governors, appointments were not made for life, but were subject to promotion and advancement. The second unifying factor in Bemba was a ritual one. Local chiefs came to pay their tribute to royal chiefs in order to obtain religious sanction for their office. It may be that, as in Kazembe, material exchanges were also a part of the tribute system, thus making loyalty profitable as well as spiritually comforting.

By the 1870s the Bemba economy had successfully integrated the needs of local commerce with the opportunities of external trade. Trade did not consist simply in the exchange of guns for slaves, but in the circulation of a wide range of commodities. Spears and hoes could be exchanged for cloth, either bark cloth for immediate use, or imported cloth, which was commonly preserved as a current means of exchange. Cloth in turn could be sold to buy salt, and salt was a recognized means of buying slaves. Thus a wide range of forms of production and of trading prosperity was fostered before the final sale of slaves for guns. To conclude: as Roberts has demonstrated, the power of Bemba chiefs was due to their ability both to sustain local interchange of goods and labour, and to attract long distance trade.[1]

THE LUBA EMPIRE

The history of the Luba is one of the most interesting and important stories in Central Africa. The traditions refer to 'empires' as far back as the fifteenth century, and archaeological excavations have shown that as early as the eighth century some areas which were, or later became, Luba, had achieved a high degree of technical ability in the field of metallurgy and may even have been part of an early trading system. Until the end of the eighteenth century, however, the Luba apparently remained divided into small or medium sized states; Kikonja controlled the Lualaba lakes, and their dried fish industry, while other states specialized in salt production or oil palm cultivation. Among the Songye to the north, raffia cloth was produced both as a commodity and as a currency, which circulated widely among the Luba. Related peoples in the south worked copper which they sold to the Luba principalities.

Among the Luba, trade, or more precisely the exchange of produce,

[1] A. D. Roberts, *History of the Bemba*, 182–214. See also Marcia Wright and Peter Lary's useful and well-documented article on the history of this region, 'Swahili settlements in northern Zambia and Malawi', *African Historical Studies*, 1971, 4, 3, 547–73.

was mainly conducted through the system of tribute and reward. It was a vertical exchange, with producers paying a part of their produce in kind to the chief and receiving in return material rewards derived from the tributes of others. Such a system did not encourage horizontal trade directly between producers, and did not lead to the emergence of full-time professional traders, or even part-time, dry-season, traders. The incentives which enabled a 'class' of traders to emerge among the decentralized Nyamwezi and Bisa did not operate among the centralized Luba kingdoms. On the other hand, when outside traders established links with Luba leaders, these rulers were immediately in a position to go into business as monopolist entrepreneurs, and thus greatly to strengthen their economic and political standing.

The growth of Luba under the impact of long distance trade came last in a series of political developments which spread across the southern savanna from both east and west. Maravi in the east and Kasanje in the west had been seventeenth-century trading empires. In the eighteenth century the twin empires of Lunda and Kazembe had grown to dominate the western and eastern trades. Finally in the late eighteenth and early nineteenth century the effects of long distance trade began to be felt among the Luba. The state which most rapidly and successfully responded to these new opportunities was Luba Lomami. It was probably the largest and most centralized Luba state, with an effective mechanism for collecting tribute from producers in a rich and varied economy.

The first traders to reach Luba Lomami were Bisa ivory traders. They had been trading in the Kazembe region since about the 1760s, but by the 1800s ivory was becoming scarce, so they began to push northwards. The market for ivory which they created had a stimulating effect on many aspects of the internal trade of Luba. Durable goods such as cloth, mats, bracelets, rings, hoes, axes and hides were exchanged and hoarded until sufficient capital had been accumulated to buy tusks. The tusks could then be sold, subject to royal or chiefly supervision and taxation, to the Bisa. The main items acquired in return were cotton cloth, beads, and in some areas cattle. The Bisa used no guns in their penetration of Luba, either as trade-goods, or as a means of hunting elephants. They did not even have guns for their own protection, and relied instead on their stable relationship with the Luba rulers. Any attack on them would have been damaging to the new centralized commercial economy from which the Luba aristocracy was so greatly benefiting, and would therefore have been internally suppressed without use of Bisa arms. The advance of the Bisa trading front through the Lualaba–Lomami basin was preceded by the advance of a Luba political front. Pioneering chiefs moved into the virgin lands and arranged the purchase of ivory which they then transferred to central depots. They simultaneously created a more or less permanent Luba political superstructure. The Bisa followed behind, selling their cloth and beads in the new outposts of Luba frontier society.

The expansion of Luba was concentrated in the reigns of three great rulers. Ilunga Sunga (c. 1780–c. 1810) began the process with an unsuccessful attack on the Kalundwe in the west. Meeting strong resistance in that direction, he turned eastward and rapidly spread Luba influence over the region between the Lualaba and Lake Tanganyika. One of his sons, Kumwimba (c. 1810–c. 1840), carried Luba expansion still farther. He first of all conquered the Lualaba lakes and took over the rich fishing and palm oil industries. He then moved southwards to control the copper workings of the Samba. At the same time, in response to the continuing ivory trade, he consolidated Luba domination over the conquered eastern territories and created a new, north-eastern province in Manyema. By the time the Luba empire was at its height, under Ilunga Kalala (c. 1840–c. 1870), it was at the centre of a wide-ranging and varied international trade. In the east, oil and salt were brought across Lake Tanganyika from Ujiji in return for arrow poisons, drums and slaves. In the south-east the empire was linked to its main long distance customers via the Bisa. In the south-west a new link was developing with the Bihe–Lovale route, along which the Ovimbundu were carrying copper and slaves to the Atlantic. In the west Luba was in contact with Lunda through the Luba Kaniok kingdom. In the northwest an important trade including palm cloth, baskets, iron, zebra skins, and fish was carried on with the Songye and, through them, with peoples as far away as the Kuba.

About 1870 the economic and political growth of Luba began to weaken. In his study of the savanna kingdoms, Vansina attributed this decline of Luba to institutional instability, especially in the succession system. An open succession system, far from being a safeguard against the advent of incompetent rulers, appeared to be a major cause of weakness, leading to constant feuding between royal factions, and laying the country wide open to foreign interference through ready-made fifth columns. He saw a further weakness in the overwhelming importance of the king. The fortunes of empire appeared to fluctuate with the personality of the ruler, and no government seemed capable of compensating for the personal inadequacies of the king. This interpretation of Luba history in structural and personal terms may have been largely inspired by the nature of the historical evidence. Even in the nineteenth century this consists, for the most part, of oral chronicles, which inevitably lay emphasis on the exploits of great men, and blame national calamities on the deficiencies of weak ones. Such emphasis, however, may obscure some of the less visible changes, particularly in the economic sphere. During the period 1800 to 1870, there had, in fact, been only one great ruler in each generation and, although disputes and short reigns had intervened between these three great reigns, the overall pattern was one of growth and stability. What caused this pattern to change radically after 1870 was a fundamental change in the country's external relations. This had the effect of increasing internal dissension, but the structural defects which then became apparent were the consequences, and not the causes, of Luba decline.

A crucial factor in the decline of Luba was probably the exhaustion of its ivory supplies. So long as ivory was available, Luba maintained a stable working relationship with the foreign trading groups. By 1870 the most important of these were the Yeke-Nyamwezi in the south and the Swahili-Arabs from Ujiji in the north. When ivory became scarce, the Yeke-Nyamwezi concentrated increasingly on copper, and in the 1860s began to conquer the copper producing areas of chiefs Mpande and Katanga. Their success was increased by the first large-scale use of guns in the region. The creation of Msiri's state based on military power and direct exploitation, rather than trade, presented one major threat to Luba. A second and even more serious threat arose on the northern frontier among the Swahili-Arabs. These Swahili-Arabs had overtaken the Luba frontier of expansion, and were driving north into the forest in search of ivory by more direct means than state trading. Luba was then cut out from both the northern and the southern trading circuits. This situation of declining opportunity occurred just when Luba most urgently needed outside trade contacts to buy guns. These new weapons had suddenly become crucial for military survival. In the absence of any ivory to sell, the Luba attempted to buy guns with slaves. The traders, however, accepted slaves only at very low prices, and when nothing more profitable was available. Thus to get guns in the 1870s, Luba had rapidly to expand its slave trade, thereby causing a new set of problems. The empire was now enclosed, north and south, by strong, gun-using, trader-states, which prevented slave-seeking expansionist wars by the Luba. In fact, the roles were reversed, and Luba was in danger of becoming the raiding ground of others. In order to obtain slaves for sale, Luba rulers had to find them internally, thus causing new conflicts and tensions, and further damaging their declining authority. The result, during the 1870s and 1880s, was that Luba began to break up into warring factions, each faction trying to capture the kingship and re-establish authority where a previous ruler had failed. The more the country declined, however, the more it became prey to Yeke-Nyamwezi and Swahili-Arab slave raids. Eventually the Yeke kingdom of Garenganze in the south, and the Swahili-Arab kingdom of Nyangwe in the north, imposed foreign 'pacification' over the area they had so effectively disrupted. This domination by the new trader-states did not last long, however, and within a decade they were challenged, in their turn, by yet stronger and more determined traders, who took over their political and economic systems, and harnessed them to Leopold's Congo Independent State.[1]

The demise of the Luba-Lomami empire was closely matched by the decline and fall of the older and more influential empire of the *mwata yamvo* of Lunda. Until the 1870s Lunda had survived in strength and stability. But the forces of change crept closer during the century, and eventually removed both the western and the eastern spheres of influence. It was the Yeke who reduced the power of the *kazembe* in the east. The Chokwe did the same to the *mwata yamvo* in the west. With the final decline of the overseas slave trade, the kings of Lunda had sought alternative items of state trade such as wax, ivory and rubber, but each had proved a very temporary solution to the fundamental decline of export revenues. For a time the flow of slaves was reversed, as Lunda sold slaves eastward to the Luba in return for ivory, but this too was a short-lived phenomenon. The Chokwe continued to expand and increase their power at the great western market of Mona Kimbundu. As the *mwata yamvo* became unable to meet the expectations of even his closest supporters, factions arose to replace him and stem the catastrophic decline of the empire. One of these factions called in Chokwe mercenaries to support its cause. The result was but a temporary restoration of central power. Soon the Chokwe began to settle in central Lunda in increasing numbers. They overran the kingdom which, having lost its provinces to new gun-using trader-armies from east and west, now lost its capital as well.[2]

[1] Jan Vansina, *Kingdoms of the savanna* (Madison, 1966), 227–44; Anne Wilson, 'Long distance trade and the Luba Lomami empire', *Journal of African History*, 1972, **13**, 575–89.
[2] L. Duysters, 'Histoire des Aluunda', *Problèmes d'Afrique centrale*, 1958, **12**.

NORTHERN CENTRAL AFRICA

The history of the equatorial north is rather different from the history of the Central African savanna. Changes from the outside were slower to penetrate into the forest. By the nineteenth century, however, an increased tempo of change was being felt among all the peripheral peoples of the forest. In the west the forested segment of the Atlantic coast belatedly became a maritime trading sphere. In the south a whole complex of agricultural, commercial, and political changes began to percolate northward from the societies of the savanna. In the east an almost revolutionary set of explosions occurred, as Swahili-Arab traders broke into the forest in a desperate last effort to maintain their ivory trade. And finally in the north the centuries-old interaction between forest and woodland peoples was deeply affected by the military expansion of several savanna states.

In the huge central forests, where people were often scattered as thinly as three or four to five square kilometres, change remained slow. A shifting balance was maintained between three groups, the farmers, the fishermen and the nomadic hunters. There was, of course, some overlap in their activities, as farmers often hunted and fishermen sometimes farmed. There was also some interdependence, as when hunters bought grain or farmers bought fish. These occasional contacts, or even a more permanent, symbiotic, relationship between agriculturalists, and client hunters, did not, however, lead to the development of markets, trade routes, kingdoms, and to the regular, institutionalized communications which became so important to some peoples of the more favoured savanna. This lack of large states and absence of contacts with the outside world did not imply, as has sometimes been supposed, a complete stagnation or a lack of historical evolution. It did, however, mean that the galaxy of minute polities showed considerable diversity, as each village or group of villages evolved its own method of meeting the challenge of its environment. The rich variety of cultures was expressed not only in improved material possessions, but also in the sophisticated social structures developed to meet the needs of small-scale communities.

The most specialized of the forest peoples were the various Twa or Pygmy groups. In the nineteenth century they were probably declining as a proportion of the population, if not in absolute numbers, by gradual absorption into neighbouring societies. The first facet of their distinctive culture to be lost was apparently language, and by the twentieth century at least all surviving Pygmy groups spoke the Bantu or Central Sudanic languages of their agricultural neighbours. Evidence for a more wholesale shift from hunting and gathering to iron-age farming is difficult to obtain, but the process undoubtedly went on, and many forest farmers owed part of their cultural and demographic heritage to the Pygmies.

The second distinctive group to occupy part of the forest were the river-line fishermen. Small, stretched-out communities of fishing folk developed their specialized way of life along the Lualaba, the Ubangi, the Kasai and many other waterways of the Congo basin. Many of these communities remained inward-looking, but a few developed outward contacts on a growing scale. The Bobangi, in particular, mounted long distance expeditions by canoe. During these ventures they came into contact with other river peoples and acted as long distance commercial carriers. By this means contact was established between the Teke, and other savanna peoples of the lower Congo and Kasai, and the riverain peoples of the forest. By the late nineteenth century some waterways were carrying a heavy traffic in food and ivory.

By the nineteenth century the farmers probably outnumbered the hunters and fishermen in all but the densest forest, like that of the Ituri, or the most waterlogged river basins such as the Ngiri. Even at the heart of the forest region, the farmers were receptive to changes in crops and technology, as well as to new ideas about the management of small societies. The large and diverse Mongo nation, which occupied much of the low central land of the Congo basin, has clear folk memories of immigrants joining the society from the north over many generations. The Mongo pattern of succession and inheritance, which distinguishes them from their neighbours, may be a social trait introduced by immigrants. Although the peoples of this remotest forest heartland welcomed change, their remoteness militated against them. In addition their sparsity of population was probably not conducive to fostering such agricultural change as occurred, for instance, in the more populous Kasai region of the southern forest.

The best documented of the changes which influenced the periphery of nineteenth-century equatorial Africa occurred in the west. The forested segment of the Atlantic coast had had an altogether different history from that of West Africa or Angola during the slave trade era. In the far north, along the southern shore of the Bight of Biafra, lay an area which had been little favoured by seventeenth- and eighteenth-century traders. Dutch, English, and French vessels made occasional

visits to the coast, but no trading posts or ports were regularly established. As a result of this neglect by foreign traders, Cameroun was one
of the few parts of Africa with plentiful supplies of good quality ivory
near the coast. About 1800 ivory was fetching £240 a thousand kilograms in this area, the value being made up of fifteen thousand kilograms of salt, seventeen kegs of powder, fifty 'Tower' proof guns, ten
pieces of Indian 'baft', ten pieces of Indian 'romal', forty cheap
Manchester prints, twenty good-quality prints, two kegs of brandy,
thirty copper pots-and-pans, and a residual sum in beads, ironmongery,
crockery and cutlery. The superior quality of the ivory attracted increasing numbers of traders, but they found negotiating a delicate
business. The tastes and demands of the Duala merchants, and of their
inland suppliers, fluctuated disconcertingly with changing fashions. To
transact any business, gifts had to be given to the local trade prince, and
goods of the right variety and quality had to be offered for sale. Excessive importations of any particular kind of cloth rapidly depressed its
price. Spirits formed a major part of the trade, but their sale involved
acrimonious bargaining, because of the common European practice of
adulterating the liquor.

The development of the ivory trade in Cameroun also brought
traders to the coast who were willing to deal in slaves. Although
Cameroun slaves had a reputation for being weak and sickly, the numbers exported in the early nineteenth century were rising, and the area
became important in the last stages of the trans-Atlantic traffic. Business
was further enhanced by the sale of palm oil, beeswax, ebony and red-
wood, so that as many as twenty-five ships at a time were sometimes
reported in the Cameroun estuary. The growth of trade had a markedly
divisive effect on the political structure of the Duala peoples who controlled it. The practice of paying 'comey' to the chief off whose shore a
ship anchored created strong incentives for each village, or even each
section of a village, to claim independence and the right to levy
'comey'. One major division occurred in Duala society in 1814, when
chief Mbele, known to the traders as King Bell, lost his dominant position and was faced with the rival kingdom of King Akwa. The two
kings dominated the estuary for a time, but the process of political
fission continued, and by 1861 there were at least three trade kings on
the estuary. It may be that 'secret' societies, such as Mikuka and
Bangolo, had become more important than the trade princes in controlling the Duala communities.

The survival and growth of the Cameroun slave trade had the effect of attracting official British interest to the Bight of Biafra from the 1820s, when efforts were being made to suppress the traffic. In 1827 a British naval base was established on the island of Fernando Po. A small settlement of freed slaves, similar to that of Freetown in Sierra Leone, grew up at Port Clarence, and in 1843 the Baptist Missionary Society arrived to care for the spiritual life of the recaptives. The mission also began to establish settlements on the Cameroun mainland and, under the guidance of Alfred Saker, Jackson Fuller and George Grenfell, the Baptists became the most important mission in the area until the German colonial occupation of 1884. While missionary influence grew, the British government also began appointing consuls for the Bight of Biafra to encourage mainland chiefs to outlaw the slave trade, and to promote a more 'honest' conduct of the 'legitimate' trade. The suppression efforts of Beecroft, Hutchinson and Burton were arduous, but slow-yielding. As late as 1861 a ship from Montevideo was caught buying 400 slaves in exchange for rum. Gradually, however, the export of palm oil rose to become the major commodity of Cameroun trade.

The trade of Cameroun used two forms of money as well as credit transactions. In transactions with inland suppliers and producers, the Duala calculated their prices with the copper manilla, a heavy open anklet. About twenty manillas were called a bar, a money of account worth about one quarter of a pound sterling. In transactions with Europeans, a different unit of account was used called the 'crew'. This consisted of a variable assortment of trade-goods, some of them large items, such as guns and powder kegs, and some measurable goods such as alcohol, cloth and metal. Although the crew was apparently linked to the price of a measure of palm oil, it could be used in any financial transaction; pilot dues, for instance, were measured in crews at the rate of one crew per metre of draught.

In addition to calculating 'prices', and to bargaining over quantities in an assortment of goods, traders also faced the difficult matter of negotiating credit. Credit was supplied by the ships, not by the Duala. Goods were unloaded, valued, and then despatched to the inland markets, while captains awaited their payment. If they were lucky, and got quick and full payment, they could hope for profits of 100 per cent and more. For those less lucky, the risks of this 'trust' system were high, and many ships suffered long hold-ups, or even lost the entrusted cargo altogether. The oil traders welcomed the appointment of British consuls, and the establishment of courts of equity, not only because they would reduce the competing slave trade, but also in the hope that they would assist in the recuperation of bad debts.[1]

Southward from Cameroun lay another area with a similar history. The coast of Gabon had been comparatively unimportant in the early centuries of European trade. It was of fairly difficult sailing access, and had only attracted the occasional vessel seeking ivory, wood or slaves. The Gabon hinterland was even more densely forested and thinly populated than that of Cameroun. Here too, however, the growing demand for ivory brought increased trade. The main trading people were the Mpongwe, living on the Gabon estuary. They were merchants, middlemen and commercial entrepreneurs, similar in many ways to the Duala. Each chief tried to control a slice of the trade. Here, too, the slave trade increased in the early nineteenth century, with the rise in general trading activity, and traders dealing with the Spanish-speaking Americans were especially prominent. One difference between Cameroun and Gabon was that in Gabon the French, rather than the English, took the official initiative in trying to suppress the slave trade and to increase the production of 'legitimate' commodities with which the Gabon peoples could earn their foreign exchange requirements. Despite the official contacts initiated by France, and the establishment in 1848 of Libreville, the French Freetown, trade was very much dominated by British interests before 1875; French industrial manufacturers were unable to compete with the cheap and plentiful cottons and metalwares brought in by the British, and also by the Americans. The growth of trade in ivory and wood was very slow in causing a decline in the slave trade. From the 1840s the slave trade shifted from the relatively well-patrolled Gabon estuary to the many creeks farther south, where vessels could hide and be supplied by small canoes carrying slaves through numerous waterways. Not until the 1860s did the real end of the slave trade set in.

In the early part of the century, the Gabon trade was conducted by a complex system of credit. This credit seems to have operated in two directions at once, thus giving maximum profit to the middlemen. The European traders landed their goods at the settlements of the Mpongwe trade princes such as King Denis and King Glass and then waited, sometimes a year or even eighteen months, while the goods were relayed by a system of multiple exchanges to sources of production in the interior. When the supply of ivory began to decline, the firms tried to stimulate it by increasing credit, but this tended to aggravate the delays. At the

[1] J. Bouchand, *La côte du Cameroun* (Paris, 1952).

same time that Europeans were supplying credit from the coast, ivory producers in the interior were apparently sending tusks to the coast also on credit. They too had to wait a long time for their profits and lost a percentage every time their tusk changed hands. This multiple exchange through a wide range of middlemen seems to have been temporarily reduced as the Mpongwe gained a monopolist grip on the trade routes. When they did so, however, their position as middlemen was rapidly challenged from both ends. From the interior it was challenged by the Fang expansion, and from the coast by the European penetration.

One of the most dramatic features in the nineteenth-century history of Cameroun and Gabon was the enormous and rapid expansion of the Fang peoples. In the eighteenth century the Fang, Bulu and Beti had lived in the Sanaga region of eastern Cameroun near the northern border of Bantu speech. They seem to have come under pressure from raiders in the north such as the Bamum, the Chamba and, by the mid-nineteenth century, the Fulani of Adamawa. This pressure set in motion a series of leap-frogging migrations towards the south, into the Cameroun and Gabon forests. These migrations, in which each village moved a few miles at a time, in a manner similar to the contemporaneous Chokwe migrations in the south, eventually led to the colonization of a large section of the western equatorial forest by twenty or so culturally and linguistically related groups. The area they occupied seems previously to have been scantily populated. This may have been due to a reduction of population, caused perhaps by the slow drain of the slave trade, or by the introduction of such diseases as smallpox and sleeping sickness. Alternatively the dense forest may have not previously been attractive to agriculturalists and hunters, who preferred the forest margin when this was not threatened by savanna raiders. The advance parties of the Fang dispersion seem to have been capable hunters, and by the 1840s they were trading ivory for guns with the Gabon estuary. The acquisition of guns, and the new profitability of ivory-hunting, speeded the Fang advance towards the Gabon estuary and Ogowe river, thus severely restricting the Mpongwe sphere of influence.

The second major change in Gabon came in the 1860s and 1870s when three new developments occurred. Firstly, the credit system on which the old trade was based broke down. Secondly, Europeans, notably Paul du Chaillu, began to explore the interior of Gabon for themselves, and discovered direct access to the commercial hinterland.

Thirdly, ivory became exhausted and rubber became the major export. These three developments were closely related to one another. The Ogowe basin had several advantages as a source of rubber. Slaves, no longer in much demand for export, could be used to collect the rubber, which then reached the coast by the well-established river transport system. Canoe carriage made rubber and timber profitable export commodities, even though they were only worth about one-twentieth of the value of ivory. European firms therefore began setting up trading posts along the rivers and used the Mpongwe as hired agents. Trade was further increased by experiments in ground-nut and palm oil trading. The French, however, remained minor participants in the new commercial growth, and by the early 1870s were on the point of abandoning their settlements altogether. They never took such an active step, however, and within a decade Gabon was becoming a prized colony in France's Equatorial African empire.

One of the notable features of Gabon was the absence of any large political systems. None of the peoples, least of all the Fang, had administrative structures covering more than a single village or a group of adjacent villages. South of the Gabon the situation was different, and some of the people of the upper Ogowe and of the coastlands conducted trade with the Teke and Loango kingdoms north of the Congo river.[1]

The lower Congo area, athwart the southern boundary of the forest, was a much older area of external trade than Gabon. In the three centuries before 1790, slaving had gradually expanded from the Congo estuary, not only southward into Angola and eastward into the Kwango and Kasai basins, but also northward along the Loango coast. In the Loango kingdom which had come to dominate that coast in the seventeenth century, a growing dependence on the slave trade had had a number of effects. Firstly, it had led to the development of a large local population of slaves, who formed the basis of wealth in the kingdom. The more slaves a chief owned, the more land it was possible to cultivate and the higher his economic and social standing became. Secondly, the development of trade had meant that officers such as the Mafouk, who were responsible for trade negotiations, had become enormously powerful, usually at the expense of the monarchy. Thus the traditional structure of a great political and religious king supported by a large royal family was subverted. The power of the king was reduced,

[1] H. Deschamps, *Quinze ans de Gabon* (Paris, 1965). P. Alexandre, 'Proto-histoire Beti-Bulu-Fang', *Cahiers d'études africaines*, 1965, 5. H. Brunschwig, *Brazza explorateur* (Paris, 1966).

the pattern of succession was disrupted, and power shifted in fact, if not in theory, to the commercial officials and the slave-owning agricultural aristocrats. This pattern, with a weak nominal king and a range of powerful notables, apparently survived until the colonial period. From the 1860s the slave trade from the interior no longer supplied overseas markets but met the Loango demand for 'domestic' slaves.[1]

The south side of the Congo river, once the centre of the Kongo kingdom, had, by the nineteenth century, long since ceased to be a single empire. The royal dynasty still reigned in São Salvador, and was still revered in a spiritual way by many Bakongo peoples. It held no political authority, however, beyond the confines of the village-capital, and the Kongo people were no longer even recognized as a single 'tribe', but were seen as three separate peoples, the Mussorongo in the north-west, the Mushikongo in the centre and the Zongo in the east. Among these peoples a certain amount of European cultural influence survived; the 'kings' had to be crowned by a Christian missionary, and often went to considerable pains to obtain one from neighbouring Angola. Literacy and a knowledge of Portuguese were also significant among the various Kongo peoples, and in 1856 Alfredo de Sarmento was allowed to inspect the important royal archives, which were still being maintained. From the documents, he compiled a list of the twenty-eight kings who had reigned in the 200 years since the battle of Ambuila. These archives were unfortunately destroyed by fire towards the end of the century.

Although the Kongo region no longer represented a recognizable political entity, it remained an area of important trading activity. In the north, the Congo river was a favoured slaving area until the 1870s. The many creeks and islands made clandestine traffic easier than on the open coast, and the rapid current helped sailing vessels to get away quickly beyond the range of the coastal squadron. Boma was an important centre for receiving the slave caravans, which arrived loaded with cassava and beans to feed the waiting slaves in the barracoons. Monteiro, who studied the working of the slave trade in the 1860s, attributed its survival to three causes. The first was drought and famine, which caused subsistence communities to reduce the pressure of population by the short-term, but short-sighted, expedient of selling members of the community. The second factor was a judicial system which had come to make enslavement the punishment for even minor offences; this punishment was sometimes meted out not only to the

[1] Phyllis M. Martin, *The external trade of the Loango coast* (London, 1972).

offender but also to his family. A twisting of the judicial system to benefit chiefs in their capacity as judges, was a widespread effect of the slave trade. The third cause of the survival of extensive slavery was thought by Monteiro to be the widespread belief in witchcraft. Disease, death and other misfortunes were commonly thought to be caused by witches who had to be condemned. This belief may have been heightened by outbreaks of smallpox, and by the nineteenth-century spread of sleeping sickness from the Gabon coast.[1] These secondary factors, which facilitated slave trading, were of course all subordinate to the fact that the price of labour in the Atlantic basin remained higher than the price of any commodity which the lower Congo could produce. By the 1870s, however, the price of labour had fallen, and the operation of a free market had been broken by the European political decision to stop the slave trade. Both African and European traders had to seek new avenues.

The British and Dutch seem to have been most successful in diversifying their trade, and by the 1870s were sending half a million pounds' worth of European goods to the lower Congo each year for legitimate purchases. This trade was believed to be rapidly increasing, so that by the early 1880s British trade with the Congo was of comparable significance to that with the Niger. The main exports were palm oil and palm kernels, but a number of other trade items were encouraged. Ground-nuts were exported both from the river and from the coast. Coffee was grown in the Ndembu region north-east of Luanda and exported via the Congo coast to avoid Portuguese duty. Ivory was brought to the coast by Zombo traders from the Kwango regions, and some vine rubber was being produced by 1875. Red gum and white gum were produced and exported. Attempts were made to found mining companies to take over the Bembe copper mines, but both a Brazilian and a British company failed to compete successfully with traditional small-scale methods of extracting the malachite. The caravans reaching the coast were paid in local produce, notably salt and dried fish, as well as in imported cloth, manillas and other manufactures. Several thousand heavy flintlock muskets were imported each year and were very popular; although used with minimal skill, the noise of a large, overloaded musket was a major factor in deciding the outcome of village warfare. The Sorongo, who carried out a profitable piracy at the Congo mouth, were also able to mount small cannons on canoes to very good effect.

[1] J. J. Monteiro, *Angola and the river Congo*, 2 vols. (London, 1875).

Eastward from the lower Congo was the lower Kasai basin, a populous area of grass-covered hills and forested valleys, which much impressed the European explorers and colonizers of the 1870s and 1880s. The area was ethnically very fragmented, as shown in the previous volume of this history. Some peoples, such as the Yaka and the Pende, had been brought under a form of unitary government by immigrant Lunda chiefs. Others, notably the Kuba, were governed by their own system of kingship. Others again were divided into independent chiefdoms and villages. These mainly lived at a self-sufficient subsistence level, with little regional or external trade. Typical, perhaps, were the Lulua at the heart of the Kasai basin.

The Lulua included substantial numbers of Luba immigrants among their number and some of their chiefs may have been of Lunda origin, although they did not recognize the supremacy of the *mwata yamvo*. These chiefs constantly disputed seniority among themselves. Their wealth was based on the tribute of their subjects who brought gifts of food, game-meat and craftsmanship in filial duty. In return they gave presents or held a feast with music and dancing. The rich agriculture was already based on the American crops, cassava and maize, supplemented with more nutritious crops such as ground-nuts and palm oil. The Lulua also grew and smoked tobacco and hemp. They were efficient artisans, ironworkers, weavers, potters and builders. Until about 1870 the Lulua peoples apparently produced nothing which was directly aimed at the export market. They were too far removed from the savanna markets to organize a transport system which could realize new economic potentials. A certain amount of indirect filtration of foreign goods may have reached them, as they reached their Kuba neighbours, from the trading areas of the lower Congo, or from Lunda, but only after about 1870 were they brought into the Central African caravan trading network. One opening was created by the arrival of Chokwe caravans, who established an important market at Kalamba.

The first item of trade to be exported from the Kasai was of course ivory. It was sold not only to the Chokwe, but also to Portuguese traders from Malanje. The Portuguese obtained contract porters from the Nzinga chiefs inside Angola. These carriers were bound to the expedition for its duration, which might be several years. Lopes de Carvalho and Saturnino de Souza Machado, for instance, travelled widely, storing goods in well-guarded camps, and only returned occasionally to Angola to sell their accumulated ivory. They carried with them salt, cloth and beads, which they traded for local valuables includ-

ing copper crosses and young women, until they had acquired a sufficiently attractive range of goods to buy ivory. In one transaction
Carvalho paid two children, five copper crosses, 5,000 cowries and 200
Venetian beads for a slightly damaged tusk. The Kasai ivory trade did
not flourish long, however, and within a few years the local supply was
exhausted. The Lulua began fetching it from their neighbours the
Songye, but very soon they ran up against the Swahili-Arab ivory-
hunting frontier. They thus became trapped in the same way that the
Luba had. The rapidly rising expectations of the people, and more
especially of the chiefs, had been met entirely by capitalizing on wasting
assets. When ivory was exhausted they were driven to seek desperate
alternatives. One of these was slaves.

At Kalamba, in the 1870s, a slave sold for sixteen metres of calico,
or six kilograms of gunpowder, or a musket. The majority of slaves
were women and children bought for resale within Africa. Many communities could afford to buy slave-women once the high-priced competition from the Atlantic coast had been removed. Only at this late
date did the trade introduce muskets on a large scale. This led to a
demand for powder, and a charge of gunpowder – measuring about
three thimbles – became a unit of currency. It could be used for the
purchase of food and household goods and for the valuation of export
commodities. The third export to develop from the Kasai was rubber,
sold in piles of 100 balls. The rubber was of good quality, and relatively
unadulterated, but inflation rapidly set in and the weight of the balls
shrank to only twenty-five grams in a few years. This rubber trade
eventually caused great hardship in the Congo basin. Just when the
supply was becoming scarce, and chiefs were desperate to extract
additional export revenue, a new political factor was introduced into
the situation: the Congo Independent State took over the government
of the Lulua. It used force on a wide and systematic scale to impose
compulsory rubber collecting by its subjects.[1]

Beyond the Kasai, in the far eastern part of the Congo forest, people
remained untouched by the growing turbulence of long distance trade
until very late in the pre-colonial period. When external influences did
penetrate, however, they had even more violent consequences than in
the west. Trade was introduced by Swahili-Arabs whose ivory supply
in the upper Lualaba basin had become exhausted. This, as has been
shown, led to severe disruption among the southern Luba, as traders
and chiefs resorted to slave trading and gun running to maintain their

---

[1] C. S. L. Bateman, *The first ascent of the Kasai* (London, 1889).

economic status. In the north, the Swahili-Arabs decided to move on to new ground and brave the dangers of the forest, in the hope that the rewards would more than compensate for their losses. They recruited local armies and began attacking forest communities, taking prisoners either for sale elsewhere or to be locally ransomed for ivory. On his great trans-African journey, Stanley hired Tippu Tip and his mercenaries to accompany him down the Lualaba towards the Congo river proper. Within five years Tippu's men had blazed a trail of destruction almost as far as Stanley Falls. When the Swahili-Arab progress down-river was stopped by the return of Stanley as Leopold's colonizing agent, they turned eastward and penetrated the forests of the Aruwimi basin, wreaking further havoc, but finding new riches of ivory.

To complete this survey one must look finally at the far north of Central Africa. During the nineteenth century, this area was affected by three different sets of external influences. The first, from the west, was the invasion of Fulani pastoralists from Nigeria, who set up the emirate of Adamawa in central Cameroun. The history of this great equestrian dynasty belongs more properly to the history of West Africa, but the consequences of its slave raids and conquests were felt deep into the south and east. Refugees fell back into the Cameroun forest, and victims were rounded up by raiding horsemen on the eastern plains of the Central African Republic. The second external influence in the northern woodland was the 'Arab' slave-raiding from the states on the southern side of the Sahara. By the end of the nineteenth century the raiders had reached the Ubangi river, and slaves from the Congo forest were being brought up by canoe to the departure points for the Sahara crossing. Finally the third external influence was the ivory trade from Khartoum. The Khartoumers employed a system of raids and ransoms which was not dissimilar to Tippu Tip's exploitation on the other side of the forest. Unlike him, however, they had not penetrated very far into the forest before the whole ivory-raiding system was brought to an end by the colonial partition. The southward advance of the Khartoumers was, moreover, delayed by the organized resistance of the Mangbetu kingdom on the Uele river.

The upper Uele basin, in the north-eastern corner of Central Africa, was rich agricultural farmland comparable to the banana groves of the East African lake region. The closely-settled Mangbetu practised agriculture of a quality not seen in the millet-growing plains of the northern savanna. Their plantains throve with a minimal investment of labour, and were supplemented by crops of American origin, including excellent maize and cassava. They practised almost no animal husbandry, but received game-meat from client groups of Pygmies. Mangbetu smiths produced a sophisticated range of spears, swords, scimitars, adzes, knives and cutlasses, which they sold to their less skilled neighbours. They also manufactured jewelry out of copper brought in rough rings from Hofrat en Nahas in Darfur. The Mangbetu had a more extensive and centralized form of government than any of their neighbours either in the southern forest or in the northern Sudan belt. The king received regular tribute from his people, and held court in a royal complex occupied by his wives, courtiers and retainers, which reminded a European visitor of the great Lunda capital. In the late 1860s King Munza, after demonstrating his military power, was able to receive the first Khartoum ivory traders peacefully and on his own terms. This advent of foreign traders, however, rapidly turned sour on him, and the Mangbetu, like the Luba on the opposite side of the forest, were undermined by increasing numbers of gun-using traders. The garden-land of the upper Uele became a scene of violence and destruction, and the Mangbetu were unable to preserve their prosperity and independence.[1]

To the north and west of the Mangbetu and of their Central Sudanic neighbours, stretched a huge belt of eastern Niger–Congo peoples of rather different cultural origins. Among these were the Baya, Banda, Ngbandi and Azande. The bulk of these peoples lived in the open woodland, but some had colonized the forest margins, and a few had even migrated farther south and been absorbed into Bantu societies. In the late eighteenth century some of these eastern Niger–Congo peoples began to be conquered by Azande dynasties, of the Avungara clan, who spread eastward towards the headwaters of the north Congo basin and the Nile watershed. The conquerors sought new land, new rivers, new hunting grounds, and new subject peoples to be adopted and acculturated. The Avungara political system, although it grew rapidly during the nineteenth century, did not retain any cohesion, but fragmented into rival factions at each generation. By the 1870s there were numerous Azande kingdoms, each ruled by proud Avungara chiefs. These chiefs, however, were quite unable to resist the challenge of the Khartoum ivory traders, who rapidly spread into their territories. The traders developed an almost permanent state of war with the Azande, whom they greatly feared for their alleged cannibalism, and whom they consequently called the Niam-Niams.

[1] Georg Schweinfurth, *The heart of Africa*, 2 vols. (London, 1873).

In the region west of the Azande, another powerful clan, the Bandia, launched itself on an expansive career of conquest and state-building. The Bandia were of Ngbandi origin, and for some centuries had been spreading eastward up the Ubangi valley. Late in the eighteenth century they founded three or four kingdoms in areas they had colonized, and whose culture they had partially absorbed. The most powerful of these seems to have been the kingdom of Bangassou, founded among the riverain Nzakara whose old ruling clan was replaced by a new Bandia dynasty. Bangassou soon came into contact with the traders of the central Sudan. Whereas the fragmented, acephalous peoples of the Ubangi were unable to organize either resistance or co-operation, Bangassou was able to negotiate with slave dealers from a position of strength. The Bandia became prosperous middlemen, but only male slaves were sold to the trans-Saharan traders, since women and children could not survive the long overland journey to the north. Women captives were retained by the Bandia rulers, and played an important role in building the prosperity and population of their kingdoms. Sparseness of population was a major economic and political weakness among all Ubangi peoples, and the success of the Bandia, like that of the Chokwe in the south, was in large measure due to their absorption of additional people, and particularly of women who could enhance the demographic growth rate. Thus the Bangassou 'sultanate' flourished in the nineteenth century, while all around it the northern woodland was sparsely occupied by small, isolated, frightened villages of eastern Niger–Congo peoples, cowed under the shadow of the slave trade.[1]

CONCLUSIONS

The long-term significance of nineteenth-century development in Central Africa remains hard to judge. The real achievements in the economic and political management of small or medium societies were obscured, firstly by the destruction associated with the scramble for ivory and slaves, and secondly by the imposition of European rule. The destructiveness of the ivory trade, especially in its terminal stages, has been emphasized in the foregoing pages. The rising tide of violence, which began with the old Atlantic slave trade, increased rather than abated with the development of the ivory trade, and embroiled many more of the peoples of Central Africa, even into the heart of the forest. All peoples became accustomed to treating strangers as hostile. The

[1] Éric de Dampierre, *Un ancien royaume Bandia du Haut-Oubangui* (Paris, 1967).

violence was compounded by the gun trade as manufacturers and dealers sought outlets for their weapons in a period of rapidly advancing technology. The advent of colonial rule did not always bring an alleviation of the widespread suffering. The early colonial period in Central Africa was harsh and exploitative to a degree unmatched in the rest of Africa. It did, admittedly, see a suppression of the gun traffic. But French, Belgians and Portuguese all used extensive forced labour, and all surrendered part of their colonial sovereignty to concessionary companies, which were subject to few of the constraints imposed on democratically elected metropolitan governments. In the south-east corner of Central Africa, the peoples of modern Zambia, although also under chartered company rule, may have fared a little better and been subjected to less extreme forms of physical brutality and degradation. In all four regions, nevertheless, much individual hardship was suffered through labour-recruiting methods. The sparsity of population meant that labourers were taken to remote regions for long periods of time. To the victim, this contract labour often appeared very similar to the old nineteenth-century slavery. This was especially so in the case of labourers sent to the island plantations of São Tomé, whence they rarely returned.

The positive legacies of the nineteenth century became deeply hidden in the early decades of the colonial period. The economic achievements of Central Africans had represented real advances in the exploitation of their natural resources. Local economic networks throughout the southern savanna, and in the more accessible parts of the forest, were linked to the major commercial highways, so that produce from even remote parts of Africa began to reach world markets. Local economies were enhanced by increased consumption of traded commodities like salt, copper ornaments and textiles. In some areas, an expanding economic activity was matched by a growing political structure, which brought new forms of political integration to a formerly fragmented area. In the last quarter of the nineteenth century, however, these economic and political systems suddenly seemed inadequate to meet the challenge of outside economic enterprise and outside political ambition. The weaknesses which underlay the sudden loss of African initiative and the assumption of control by Europeans were many. Foremost, perhaps, was the inability of unaided African enterprise to evolve more efficient methods of bulk transport than caravan porterage. Railways and river steamers gave Europeans the economic means to compete profitably with traditional caravanning. Their military technology gave them the political means to compete with African kings and, more significantly perhaps, with the Arab and Swahili trade-princes whose power had been growing so rapidly in the last pre-colonial decades. As the Belgians advanced into Zaïre, as the Portuguese turned their trading posts into a colony, and as French and British companies staked out their claims, it seemed that the achievements of the past would count for nothing. All that went before was deemed irrelevant by the colonizers, and, all too often, by the colonized as well. But the legacy of business acumen and political ability was not totally submerged. Central Africans slowly found out that the small man could adapt, and could challenge the colonial monolith, the private lorry driver could compete with the international railway company, and the small retailer could thrive in conjunction with the foreign wholesaler. Although this African re-awakening was slower in Central Africa than in West Africa, or even East Africa, it did occur. Gradually the dismissal of the past was reversed and the old skills were adapted to the new circumstances in resistance, in co-operation and finally in re-emergence.

CHAPTER 8

EAST AFRICA: THE EXPANSION
OF COMMERCE[1]

MUSLIM SETTLEMENTS ON THE COAST

Until the end of the eighteenth century the inhabitants of the islands and ports of East Africa had very little to do with those of the interior. The East African coastal belt belonged to the rest of the continent only in a geographical sense. Events at the coast passed almost unnoticed in the interior, while people living along the coast were rarely touched by what happened up country. The East African littoral was more a part of the Indian Ocean world than of the African continent. From the second century at least, Arabs from the south of Arabia and the Persian Gulf had been trading to East Africa, following the monsoon winds. They transacted their business in the ports and went back with the trade winds to India or beyond. During Muslim times, some of these Arabs and Persians, especially the Shirazi, began to build fortified urban settlements on the coast and the offshore islands. The earliest of these known so far was at Manda in the Lamu archipelago, and dates to the ninth century. Zanzibar and Pemba were probably occupied soon after this. The Islamic settlements at Mafia and Kilwa were built mainly in the twelfth and thirteenth centuries, and a score of other stone-built towns were added during the next two hundred years. Thus by the fifteenth century a considerable population of immigrants had settled in the islands and ports of East Africa.

The immigrants settled among the Africans or attracted a population of the local inhabitants into the new towns. This mingling of different races and cultural backgrounds resulted in the evolution of a coastal society deriving its characteristics from both cultures. It was largely Islamic: the immigrants dominated the economic life of the coastal states and were in the main Muslim; and the settlements were in regular contact with other Islamic states around the Indian Ocean. Through intermarriage between the immigrants and the Africans a mixed population known as Swahili came into being. Leadership in the coastal city states was shared by both Muslims and non-Muslims, with the Muslims wielding predominant influence in most. A coastal language, Kiswahili, evolved with a Bantu grammatical structure, taking its

[1] Professor Webster wrote the sections of this chapter relating to the interlacustrine region, while the rest is the work of Dr Unomah.

vocabulary from African languages and Arabic. Each of the coastal settlements developed as an independent state, with little attempt to dominate the others politically, although some like Mogadishu and Kilwa became commercially more important than the others. The economy of the states was greatly dependent on commerce across the Indian Ocean with Arabia, India and the Far East. With the aid of the monsoon winds, the Arab traders of the Persian Gulf carried products such as ivory, gold, gum copal, mangrove poles and slaves to the markets of Asia and brought back cowries, porcelain, cloth and other commodities. Increasingly, it was the gold trade from 'Zimbabwe' and Sofala that was at the core of this commercial system. This trade brought such wealth to the traders that the coastal states enjoyed great prosperity. Some of the states like Kilwa and Mafia had domed mosques and houses and minted their own coins.

It was this prosperity, and especially the gold trade, that partly ex-plains the determination of the first Portuguese voyagers in the area to wrest control of the Indian Ocean trade from the Arabs by bringing the East African coast under their sway after 1500. In a series of military expeditions, the Portuguese succeeded in conquering all the coastal states and establishing a nebulous political control along the whole East African coast. For two centuries they drained the resources of the area, especially the gold of Sofala. Their weak and avaricious bureau-cracy and monopolistic economic policies slowly strangled the vitality of the trade, causing a marked decline all along the coast. Some of the more prosperous states were utterly ruined by the persistent military operations organized by the Portuguese against resistant coastal com-munities. Undeterred by the high-handed manner with which the Portuguese officials suppressed these risings, the Swahili did not relent in their effort to throw off the Portuguese yoke. Mombasa set in motion the resistance movement, which culminated by 1699 in the expulsion of the Portuguese from the coastal belt north of Cape Delgado. Mombasa appealed for aid to the ruler of Oman who had by 1652 driven the Portuguese from Arabia and regained Muscat. Omani intervention in East Africa from about 1669 resulted finally in the capture of Fort Jesus at Mombasa and the expulsion of the Portuguese.

In eight centuries of settlement the coastal Muslims do not appear to have ventured far inland. Neither their flourishing international trade nor the intrusion of the Portuguese provided any incentive for the Arabs and Swahili to attempt to explore the East African hinterland for economic resources or political allies. Many commodities exported from the East African ports before the nineteenth century came from the interior, but it remains unclear how these reached the coastal markets. The goods probably passed from hand to hand through a series of regional trading networks until they finally reached the coast. The East African peoples who constituted the final link between the interior and the Swahili-Arabs probably included the Yao of south-eastern Tanzania, the Nyika who live behind Mombasa, and the Zaramo. There is no evidence that the coastmen travelled into these countries. The initiative for transporting the products of their areas or those purchased from peoples immediately surrounding them would seem to have rested entirely with the peoples of the interior.[1]

The fact that the interior Africans did not open relations with the coast until the end of the eighteenth century can be partially explained by the situation in the interior. The years from 1500 to 1800 were marked by considerable population movements throughout this region. Sparsely populated areas were settled, larger societies were created and new states were founded. Until this had occurred it is probable that no large-scale trade could develop.

In north-eastern Tanzania the migration of a large group of people from the steppe of the Nguru mountains into the Usambara region led to state re-organizations and the rise of the Kilindi state of Usambara. A similar process led to the formation of the kingdom of Ugweno in northern Pare and several other fragmented societies to the south of it. Farther inland the Kimbu and Nyamwezi peoples settled in their respective areas between the middle of the seventeenth and the end of the eighteenth centuries and evolved a social and political system common among the peoples of what has been described as the '*ntemi* region' of Tanzania.[2] This was also the period of the Nilotic and Paranilotic intrusion into the interlacustrine region. In fact one gets the impression that the new arrivals moved into very sparsely settled areas among peoples with a low level of political organization. Except for Bunyoro, states of considerable size controlling large populations were a development of the post-1750 period, even in Buganda and Rwanda. By 1750 density of population and political organization favoured the expansion of, and greater interaction among, the regional trading networks, including that of the coast.

[1] This seems to be the consensus of historians of the early history of the coast. See for example G. S. P. Freeman-Grenville, 'The Coast, 1498–1840', in R. Oliver and G. Mathew (eds.), *History of East Africa*, vol. 1 (Oxford, 1963), and F. J. Berg, 'The coast from the Portuguese invasion to the rise of Zanzibar Sultanate', in B. A. Ogot and J. A. Kieran (eds.), *Zamani: a survey of East African history* (Nairobi, 1968).

[2] A. Shorter, *Chieftainship in western Tanzania* (Oxford, 1972), chs. 1–3.

By the middle of the eighteenth century a number of well-organized states had emerged in the interior, the rulers of which were able to provide protection for caravans to travel to distant markets. It is likely that it was about this time that the Nyamwezi began to engage in trade over long distances. By the beginning of the nineteenth century, they were trading as far as the copper belt of Katanga and modern Zambia. The opening by the Nyamwezi of the caravan routes to the coast about the beginning of the nineteenth century was merely an eastward expansion of their flourishing trading network. Pioneer traders, like princes Mpalangombe and Ngogomi, are said to have carried iron from their kingdom of Usaguzi to be sold in Ugogo. They are believed to have heard of the existence of the Indian Ocean when they reached Uzaramo and to have decided to see it for themselves. At the coast they found beads and cloth and discovered that ivory was in high demand. According to Nyamwezi tradition, this opened the Nyamwezi country to external trading, for the adventurers returned home and began to gather ivory to be carried to the coastal markets for sale. Kafuku, the son of Imaliza, chief of one of the Sumbwa states to the north-west of Unyamwezi, imitated the Usaguzi pioneers and so became the first of the Sumbwa traders to travel to the coast. By about 1840 Swahili-Arab traders had begun to travel to Unyamwezi and other parts of the East African interior in search of ivory and slaves.

SAYYID SAʿĪD

Although the coming of Nyamwezi traders provided the impetus for Swahili-Arab penetration inland, there was another vital force that made this penetration more systematic. This was the personality of the *imam*, Sayyid Saʿīd b. Sulṭān, who came to power in Oman about 1806. From the beginning of the eighteenth century, Omani rulers had regarded the East African coastal towns as part of their political domain. Their claim derived from Omani military assistance to the inhabitants of the East African coast against the Portuguese. With the expulsion of the Portuguese, the Omani rulers had tried to establish their overlordship over East African peoples by setting up their governors in some of the important towns like Mombasa, Zanzibar, Lamu, Pate and Kilwa. But Omani overlordship remained nebulous for more than a century. The rulers were too preoccupied with local problems in Arabia and the Persian Gulf to be able to enforce their authority over the East African coastal settlements. The Omani governors therefore pursued independent policies. The governor in Mombasa, particularly, who had been chosen from one of the oldest and best-established Omani families there – the Mazrui – ceased to pay allegiance to Oman, especially after the change of dynasty which brought the Busaʻidi to power in 1741. The Mazrui instead began to extend Mombasa's influence to the other towns along the coast.

When Sayyid Saʻid b. Sulṭān became the ruler of Oman in 1806, he spent the first few years of his reign trying to consolidate his position. By 1814 he had become secure enough on the throne to attempt to bring his East African dominions under firmer control. He needed to exploit the resources of East Africa to enable him to carry through his project of building up a strong navy for Oman. The first opportunity to pursue his plan occurred during the conflict between Mombasa and Lamu from 1810 to 1812. Mombasa had attacked Lamu in a bid to set up a Mombasan governor there. Although Lamu defeated the combined forces of Mombasa and Pate, she continued to fear further aggression from Mombasa. The people of Lamu thus appealed to Sayyid Saʻid to send them a governor and garrison as protection. The Omani ruler readily complied with their request in 1813, and so secured a base off the Benadir coast from where he was to embark upon the Omani reconquest of the coast.

In 1814, on the death of the governor of Mombasa, Aḥmad b. Saʻid al-Mazrui, Sayyid Saʻid tried to re-establish his authority over the new Mazrui ruler of Mombasa, Abdullah, by demanding that he send the customary present by which all new governors recognized Omani overlordship. In response, Abdullah b. Ahmad sent only trifles to demonstate his defiance of the Omani ruler. Sayyid Saʻid at first ignored this, because he faced fresh troubles in Oman which turned his attention from East Africa. By 1822, however, he was again strong enough to send a fleet to Pate to intervene in a dynastic dispute in which Mombasa was seeking to establish its own candidate, Fumoloti. With Omani intervention, Fumoloti was driven from Pate, and Saʻid b. Sulṭān's candidate was installed in office. However Saʻid had to maintain this governor in office by sheer military might, and between 1823 and 1845, he had to send five expeditions to Pate to restore political control.

Following its victory in Pate, the Omani fleet attacked Pemba and captured it, thus depriving Mombasa of its major source of grain. Both Brava and Lamu acknowledged the sovereignty of Oman. The inevitable confrontation between Oman and Mombasa was postponed for a time by the establishment of a British Protectorate over Mombasa by

Owen in 1824, upon the request of the ruler of Mombasa. Owen had taken the action before seeking approval from the British government, and after a series of negotiations, the protectorate was repudiated in 1826. Almost immediately, Saʿīd b. Sulṭān invaded Mombasa. Several truces were concluded, but Mombasa violated the terms of each almost as soon as Saʿīd b. Sulṭān's men had left. Finally, in 1837, the Omani ruler took advantage of a dynastic dispute among the Mazrui to seize the most prominent members of the ruling family and exile them to the Persian Gulf, where they died in captivity. After the elimination of the troublesome Mazrui, Sayyid Saʿīd steadily gained supreme control all along the East African coast from Mogadishu to Cape Delgado.

During his visits to East Africa between 1822 and 1839, the Omani ruler gained a better appreciation of the importance of this part of his domain for his economic prosperity and political security. He had a strong inclination towards commerce, and easily perceived the enormous economic potentialities that East Africa held out to him and his Omani subjects. In 1840 therefore he moved his capital from Oman to Zanzibar and set about trying to reorganize the economy of the East African city-states.

One of the measures which he undertook to achieve his purpose was to provide Zanzibar with a major export crop. After experimenting with a number of crops, he discovered that cloves proved most suitable to the geographical conditions of the islands of Zanzibar and Pemba. He therefore embarked upon their cultivation with great enthusiasm; he was said to have maintained about forty plantations personally. He encouraged the Arab residents of both islands to cultivate the crop, and persuaded other Arabs in Oman to come to Zanzibar and avail themselves of the new opportunity. In the course of a few years the revenue yielded by cloves became the economic mainstay of the two islands. By the 1860s Zanzibar and Pemba had become the world's major producers of the crop, exporting about 11,000,000 kilograms annually.

Sayyid Saʿīd would seem to have appreciated from the outset that a ready supply of capital and expert organization of finance were vital for the realization of his objective. Aware that neither would be readily forthcoming from Oman, he sought to attract Indian financiers, the so-called Banians, whose ability in these matters he had experienced in Arabia. A few Indians had been active in East Africa before the coming of Sayyid Saʿīd. The sultan encouraged more to settle in the coastal ports through generous concessions. The number of Indians grew rapidly from a handful to about 2,000 in 1840 and to over 5,000 by the

1850s. It was these men who provided the finance to revive the trade of the coastal towns. Sayyid Saʿīd and most of the great Arab merchants became highly indebted to them financially; the Indians controlled the customs houses, and a great proportion of the export–import trade of the East African coast was in their hands.

European traders were also encouraged. Although some of them, like the French, had been trading for slaves before Saʿīd's time, this trade had declined markedly after the signing of the Moresby Treaty in 1822. By its terms Saʿīd made the sale of slaves to the subjects of Christian powers illegal throughout Zanzibar's dominions. But the development of clove production had revived Zanzibari trade with European nations, and the sultan further encouraged this by regularizing the import duties, imposing a flat rate of 5 per cent in all the ports of his domain. He also signed treaties with the USA, France and Britain between 1833 and 1844, which enabled these countries to set up consulates in Zanzibar to look after the interests of their respective countrymen. Moreover, to sustain the interest of the foreign traders, Sayyid Saʿīd sought to diversify the commodities that Zanzibar offered for export. His desire to achieve this made him turn to the East African interior, to tap its resources.[1]

SWAHILI-ARAB TRADE ROUTES: INLAND PENETRATION AND ITS EFFECTS

One of the products of the interior which had for long attracted a great deal of foreign interest was ivory. This commodity was no longer available in any significant quantity near the coastal ports. By the end of the eighteenth century, interior peoples, particularly the Nyamwezi, had begun to bring down elephant tusks to the coast in locally organized caravans. It became clear that enormous elephant herds existed in the far interior. Sayyid Saʿīd developed an interest in the trade, and from the 1830s was reported to have begun to send annual caravans numbering about a hundred men to various parts of the interior to explore their ivory potentialities. This began the systematic penetration by the Swahili-Arabs of the hitherto unknown hinterland. Other merchants followed his example. With capital borrowed from the Indian com-

[1] On the coastal situation see R. Coupland, *East Africa and its invaders* (Oxford, 1938), particularly ch. 10; Sir J. Gray, *History of Zanzibar to 1856* (London, 1962), 133–54; the same author's 'Zanzibar and the coastal belt, 1840–1884' in Oliver and Mathew (eds.), *History of East Africa*, I, 212–51; N. R. Bennett, *Mirambo of Tanzania* (New York, 1971), 13–23.

mercial houses in Zanzibar, coastal traders led caravans of porters laden with a variety of goods, including cloth of various sizes and qualities, beads, copper wire, hats, guns and gunpowder, into the interior in search of ivory. Other caravans also brought down slaves, who were needed not only for export to Arabia and Asia, but also to work the great plantations in Zanzibar and Pemba.

The traders travelled by diverse routes and traversed the countries of nearly all the peoples of the interior. Three main sets of routes can however be distinguished. There was a southern set which diverged inland from Kilwa and passed through territories inhabited by such peoples as the Yao, Hehe, and Bena, in the direction of Lake Malawi, and beyond to the Bemba country in present-day Zambia. There was a northern set of routes based on Tanga which passed up the Pangani valley through the plains of Upare into the Kilimanjaro area inhabited by the Chaga. There was also another route used largely by the Kamba of Kenya that went far into the heart of modern Kenya. In between the northern and southern routes were a number of central routes that went directly westward from the Mrima coastal ports of Bagamoyo and Sadani. One of these bypassed the dry Gogo country and traversed the Sangu country to the shores of Lake Tanganyika. Another passed the country of the Gogo into Unyamwezi and thence through the Uha territory to Ujiji. A branch turned northwards from Tabora in Unyamwezi and, passing via Usukuma and Karagwe, continued to the interlacustrine kingdoms of Buganda and Bunyoro. There were numerous other routes which were less commonly used or which acted as feeders to the main ones. They tapped the resources of peoples like the Nyiha, Fipa, Tongwe and the Ha of the extreme south-west and north-west of modern Tanzania. While slaving dominated the southern routes, the central and northern routes were at first dominated by ivory; slaves became more important during the 1860s.

The central routes went farthest into the interior and were the principal arteries by which the ivory of the mainland reached the coastal markets. Along these routes the Swahili-Arabs used trading centres like those of Zungomero, Tabora, Kwihara, Msene, Ujiji and Karagwe. By the 1850s Tabora had become the major trading centre for the Arab and Nyamwezi traders in the interior, and had become the inland entrepôt for the merchants. As early as the 1850s, the Indian financiers found it necessary to send an agent to Tabora to represent their interests. And when the trade began to be disturbed in Unyamwezi around 1860, the sultan appointed a political representative among the

Arabs of Tabora. A commercial link was thus forged between the coastal communities and those of the mainland. This interaction was to have a serious impact on the economic, social and political life of all the peoples of the interior.

While hardly any part of the interior was unaffected by the commercial invasion of the coastmen between 1800 and 1870, yet the degree, nature and duration of such contact varied greatly from region to region. A great part of modern Kenya received no direct coastal contact until the 1860s, for Masai and Kwavi raiding rendered most of Kenya unsafe for peaceful trading. Moreover the Masai became involved in a serious civil crisis from about 1850, which further discouraged Swahili-Arab penetration. As we shall see later, most of the trade in this region was transacted by Kamba middlemen.

Similar circumstances prevented the coastmen from trading extensively for ivory in the south-eastern region of Tanzania. Here the migrant Ngoni, offshoots of the great South African outburst, were a cause of trouble from the 1840s on.[1] Two main Ngoni contingents reached East Africa between about 1840 and 1845. One, the Maseko, travelled up the eastern bank of the Shire and the eastern shore of Lake Malawi, passing through the territory of Yao and Nyasa peoples before settling to the north of the upper Rovuma, in the territory of the Nindi and Ndendeule around modern Songea. The other contingent, the Jere, crossing the Zambezi higher up than the Maseko, moved up the watershed to the west of Lake Malawi to the highlands of Ufipa, which overhang the south-eastern corner of Lake Tanganyika. Here its leader, Zwangendaba, died sometime between 1845 and 1848. The Jere thereupon broke up, two large sections moving southwards into northern Malawi, two others dispersing northwards up both sides of Lake Tanganyika, while two more sections moved round the north-eastern corner of Lake Malawi, and settled among the Pangwa, immediately to the north of the area settled by the Maseko. At first these placed themselves under the suzerainty of the Maseko king. Later, around 1862, they fomented a rebellion among the subject peoples of the Maseko and drove them from the eastern side of the lake. Thenceforward there were two Ngoni states to the north-east of Lake Malawi, that of the Njelu in the region of Songea and that of the Mshope to the north of it. It has been calculated in a recent study that the combined population of the Njelu and Mshope kingdoms in the early 1880s may have been of the

[1] P. M. Redmond, 'A Political history of the Songea Ngoni', Ph.D. thesis (University of London, 1972). See also chapter 9.

order of 20,000. Of these only some 2,000 would have been the migrants from Ufipa or their descendants. The remainder would have been Pangwa, Nindi, Ndendeule, Nyasa and other indigenes of the area who had been incorporated by the Ngoni into their settlements and into their regimental system.

The expulsion of the Maseko was, however, no simple transfer of power from one Ngoni group to two others. Many former subjects of the Maseko, mostly Nindi and Ndendeule who had undergone some twenty years of forcible assimilation to Ngoni methods of warfare and government, and who had then joined in overthrowing the Maseko yoke, moved off upon campaigns of conquest and plunder independently of the Njelu Ngoni. Nindi raiding parties, known to their victims as Mafiti, devastated the region between Songea and Lindi, occupied till then by Mwera and Makonde. Ndendeule raiders, often known as Magwangwara, went north-eastwards towards Kilwa and the Rufiji, scattering the Ngindo and Matengo, and here and there establishing petty conquest states like that of the Mbunga in the upper Rufiji valley. Other Magwangwara raided westwards into the Lake Malawi basin, terrifying the Nyasa and Manda fishermen of the lakeshore. Thus, although the Njelu Ngoni occupied the core of the Maseko territory, establishing there a stable and highly centralized monarchical state, the indirect effect of their conquest was to spread a ripple of violence, raiding and destruction through virtually all the peoples living between the northern half of Lake Malawi and the Indian Ocean coast. As Livingstone noted when setting out on his last African journey in 1865, large areas in the hinterland of Kilwa and Lindi, which had formerly been dotted with prosperous villages of Makonde and Matambwe, were now all but uninhabited, and were to remain so for decades to come.

In remarkable contrast to the largely passive reaction to Ngoni and Ngoni-ized raiders which was shown by the stateless and mainly matrilineal and agricultural peoples of southern Tanzania, was that of the patrilineal, cattle-owning tribes of the highland region stretching to the north and north-east of Lake Malawi. Here the Sangu, the Bena and the Hehe all responded positively to the Ngoni menace, adopting Ngoni weapons and military tactics, and amalgamating the many small statelets in which they had earlier been organized into a few large ones, well capable of resisting the Ngoni and, later, of keeping the Swahili-Arab traders under good control. The Sangu, who had lived closest to the Ufipa Ngoni settlement of Zwangendaba, emerged as a formidable military power in the 1840s and 1850s.

The turmoil in the south and the emergence of strong groups such as the Ngoni, Sangu and Hehe increased the number of people who ultimately ended up in the slave caravans to Kilwa, even though the Ngoni assimilated rather than sold their war captives. During this period the peoples of southern Tanzania were more closely linked to the commerce of the Lake Malawi region than they were to the Tabora trading network. Furthermore, because of the insecurity of the area, the Arab and Nyamwezi ivory traders tended to avoid the south.

Local disturbances were not uncommon in the other regions of East Africa. The Sangu people terrorized the south-western parts of Tanzania from the 1830s; the Wanyamwezi experienced severe internal crises within their states, and wars between them were common from the 1860s to the end of the 1880s; the Gogo before the 1840s, by their extortionate *hongo* (toll) demands, forced the Swahili-Arabs to avoid their territory on their way to and from the interior; and the Zaramo are said to have resisted any large Arab penetration of their country. In general, however, the penetration of coastal traders was encouraged by the societies living along the central route. The Nyamwezi rulers in particular were keen to trade with them and often gave them protection, and the commoners offered their labour and piloted the caravans. With Nyamwezi co-operation, coastmen were able to travel to other parts of the interior and collect ivory. The general atmosphere in the western interior was never as unsettled as in the Masai and the Ngoni areas.

The result was that most of the peoples of the central sector – the Nyamwezi, Shambaa, Gogo, Sukuma, Jiji, Haya and Ganda of the interior – came under greater Arab commercial influence than other East African peoples. Furthermore, the impact of the coastmen was more severely felt in these regions than elsewhere.

Since outside contact with the interior was largely commercial, the aspect of African life most immediately affected by the contact was economic. The sudden boom in the ivory trade stimulated a remarkable increase in economic production and commerce. Until the coming of the coastmen, Africans of the interior had valued ivory as an item for ritual or ornament; it did not constitute a notable trade item. Little time was therefore devoted to its procurement. The collection of tusks was merely incidental to the killing of elephants for food or the protection of crops and people. Among many East African peoples, elephants and other large game were traditionally hunted by teams of about twenty or more hunters of proven ability, who set out during the dry season with spears, bows and poisoned arrows, clubs and axes, as

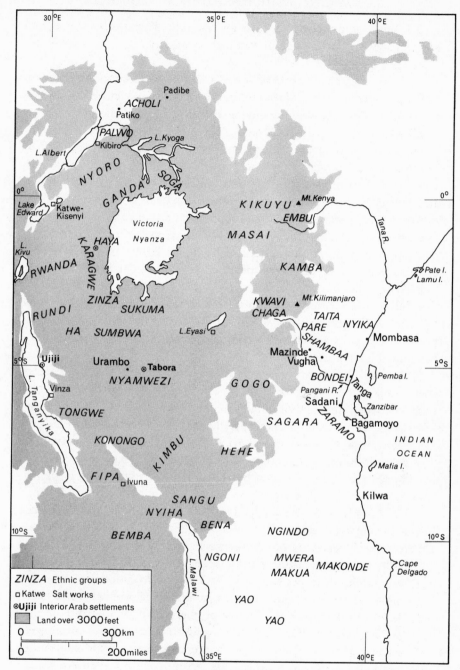

30°E   35°E   40°E

Padibe
ACHOLI
Patiko
PALWO
L.Albert   Kibiro   L.Kyoga
NYORO
GANDA   *SOGA*
0°
Lake Edward   Katwe-Kisenyi
Victoria Nyanza
KIKUYU   Mt.Kenya
EMBU
MASAI
0°
L.Kivu
HAYA
KARAGWE
RWANDA
KAMBA
Pate I.
Lamu I.
RUNDI
ZINZA   *SUKUMA*
KWAVI
CHAGA   Mt.Kilimanjaro
TAITA
PARE   *NYIKA*
Tana R.
HA   *SUMBWA*   L.Eyasi
SHAMBAA
Mombasa
5°S
Ujiji
Urambo   ⊙ Tabora
NYAMWEZI
GOGO
Mazinde
Vugha
BONDEI
Tanga
Pemba I.
5°S
Vinza
TONGWE
L. Tanganyika
Pangani R.
Sadani
ZARAMO
Zanzibar
SAGARA
Bagamoyo
KONONGO
KIMBU
HEHE
INDIAN
OCEAN
Mafia I.
FIPA   Ivuna
Kilwa
10°S
SANGU
NYIHA
BENA
NGINDO
10°S
BEMBA
L.Malawi
NGONI
MWERA   *MAKONDE*
MAKUA
Cape Delgado

ZINZA   Ethnic groups
□ Katwe   Salt works
⊙ **Ujiji**   Interior Arab settlements
▨   Land over 3000 feet
0   300 km
0   200 miles

35°E   40°E

10   East Africa

well as protective charms, to chase away or kill elephants menacing the life or crops of the society. Individual hunters hardly ever set out to kill elephants.

As ivory became a source of added wealth, a corresponding change in the purpose and organization of elephant hunting occurred. Hunters went out, not merely with the objective of driving away the animals, but to kill as many as possible and collect the tusks. The number of expeditions increased in each season, and people without the traditional hunting skills adopted new methods of ensnaring the animals. In Ugogo and Unyamwezi, parties went out into the forests searching for and collecting the tusks of elephants that had died of thirst during drought. The desire to collect and sell ivory privately, without sharing the revenue with any other members of the community, hastened the decline of the community system of hunting, particularly when more firearms began to be imported into the interior from about 1860. With guns, men could hunt in small groups. Young men no longer had to go through a long period of apprenticeship before they could join the 'guilds' of hunters in their attack on the herds. Inevitably, what had been a community activity increasingly became a specialist's occupation for skilled adventurers.

Professional elephant hunters thus emerged. Among the Nyamwezi, such hunters spent most of their time following the herds, and eventually extended their activities far beyond the limits of their localities or kingdoms. One such renowned ivory hunter in the Nyamwezi kingdom of Unyanyembe was nicknamed *Kapiga-miti* ('He even shot down trees'). The son of a Konongo immigrant, he moved away from the centre of the kingdom to a place which he called Igoo to exploit the elephant resources of the south-eastern portion of Unyanyembe. In a folksong composed in his praise, he was said to have 'exterminated the elephants in the swamps and ravaged the east with his [gun]fire'. He travelled widely to such places as Mambulozi and Milumo to hunt elephants.[1] There were many other renowned hunters of his status in Unyanyembe during his time, men like Kapanda, Mlivbe and Mkuvba.

In the northern interlacustrine area, similar developments have been recorded by Adefuye in his study of the Palwo, who lived in the northern province of Bunyoro. According to Adefuye, the coming of the coastmen inspired the elephant hunters to form a guild called the *aligo*, whose 'major occupation was to secure ivory for alien Arab and

[1] This theme is dealt with more fully in A. C. Unomah, 'Economic expansion and political change in Unyanyembe, *c.* 1840–1900', Ph.D. thesis (University of Ibadan, 1973), 86–7.

Nyamwezi traders. The *aligo* regulated prices, controlled recruitment into the occupation and organized large-scale hunting expeditions'. When firearms became common in the area and hunters began to use them to kill elephants, it became unnecessary for new hunters to undergo long apprenticeships before killing their first animals, and becoming full-fledged *aligo*. Individuals began to organize their own private expeditions, without the assistance of other members of the *aligo*. Thus the importance of the *aligo* declined, the guild collapsed and individuals sold their tusks at uncontrolled prices.[1]

Among the Chaga and Pare of the highland region of north-eastern Tanzania, it is known that the communities living in the more forested parts where elephants were found, organized hunting expeditions to supply ivory to the coastal merchants. At Ngofi in northern Ugweno (northern Pare) for example, the Pare were stimulated by the trader Msukuma to intensify the hunting of elephants in the area. By 1862 some Pare had begun to use the opportunity of the Arab commercial impetus to organize hunting expeditions to Nbaga in the far south of Pare.

Outlining the main ivory producing areas of the interior in 1857, the European traveller R. F. Burton remarked that the Doe hunted elephants in the vicinity of Shakini, not very far from the coast. The Zaramo, he said, as well as the people of Khutu, had killed off the animals in their respective areas. One of the great interior ivory markets had been established at Zungomero in Khutu country by the early 1850s. According to Burton, the Sagara contented themselves with keeping a look-out for the bodies of animals that had died of thirst or of wounds received elsewhere. It is very likely that, with the increase in the ivory trade and the introduction of guns around 1860, the Sagara changed their system of gathering tusks. The Gogo in central Tanzania trapped animals in pits. Their country being dry, elephants frequently died during the long droughts, and the Gogo got much of their ivory from the remains of dead elephants. In Buganda, the ruler, Mutesa (1856–84), secured ivory not only by organizing raids on weaker neighbours, but also by maintaining a body of professional hunters who supplied him with ivory. Even in the less accessible parts of East Africa such as Kenya, much ivory was acquired by the Bantu and Nilotic peoples, particularly those living between the Nyandarua range and river Tana in the south-east.

[1] A. Adefuye, 'Political history of the Paluo, 1400–1911', Ph.D. thesis (University of Ibadan, 1973), 129–31.

EXPANSION OF AFRICAN TRADING ACTIVITY

Along with the intensification of ivory hunting came an expansion both of the areas within which Africans traded and of the scale of their commercial organization. This was particularly the case among the Nyamwezi, the Kamba and the Shambaa. The Nyamwezi, as we have noted above, played a part in initiating the contact between the coast and interior. The fact that the Swahili-Arabs began to tap the ivory of the interior at its sources did not result in the decline of Nyamwezi commercial activity. Rather, the coming of the coastmen greatly stimulated the expansion of Nyamwezi long distance trading, for these people were not content, like many other African groups, to sell their products locally to the coastal middlemen. They took an ever increasing part in the various aspects of the trade. The youths, whether they were of commoner or noble families, sought employment in the trade as porters, caravan guides, and recruiters of labour. Many acted as allies of the slave traders in their plundering of weaker communities, particularly in the Manyema country of the eastern Congo basin. They did so with such enthusiasm that they became some of the best known professional carriers in East Africa. By the 1860s the trade had become such an integral part of their life that porterage had even become one of the main tests of manliness. This is suggested in some of the traditions recorded among one of the Nyamwezi groups, in which it was stated that those men who had travelled to the coast were highly regarded in Nyanyembe society. They had entered great houses at Unguja (Zanzibar) and returned to relate their experience to their people.[1] According to one European observer, 'not one of them was allowed to marry before he had carried a load of ivory to the coast, and brought back one of calico or brass wire'.[2]

The number of Nyamwezi adults who travelled to the coast each year is by no means easy to estimate. In 1890, the German, F. Stuhlmann, estimated that up to a third of the male population of Unyamwezi went there each year as traders and porters. If this is an accurate assessment of the numbers involved in what was by 1890 already a declining trade, an even higher proportion of the male population may have been involved around 1860, when the trade was at its height. For

[1] Unomah, 'Economic expansion in Unyanyembe', 100. The information is based on traditions collected in Unyanyembe in 1968.

[2] A. J. Swann, *Fighting the slave-hunters in Central Africa* (London, 1910), 78–9. Burton also remarked that 'porterage on the long and toilsome journey is now considered by the Wanyamwezi as a test of manliness . . .' (R. F. Burton, *The lake regions of Central Africa* (New York, 1960), II, 13–23).

since the menfolk travelled out during the dry seasons, some of them staying for some time on the coast waiting to be enlisted in returning caravans, there must have been a great shortage of labour in Unyamwezi to attend to dry-season tasks such as hut building, honey collecting and the preparation of the soil for the women to plant. This probably explains why, as we shall see later, the Nyamwezi became buyers rather than sellers of slaves.

Besides providing the bulk of the carriers for Arab and Swahili caravans, the Nyamwezi also fitted out their own. Nyamwezi rulers, who received great supplies of ivory by gift, tribute and confiscation, were able to take part in the international ivory commerce as entrepreneurs. The same was true of subordinate chiefs, great hunters, medicine men and even ordinary citizens. By the end of the 1850s the Nyamwezi had more caravans trading to the coast from Unyamwezi than the coastmen. These Nyamwezi caravans consisted of individuals carrying their own goods, and petty proprietors, hiring only a few porters each, travelling together for protection. Often one of the proprietors was recognized as the leader of the caravan and played the role of spokesman for the party in their negotiations with the peoples whose territories they traversed. Thus, for the Nyamwezi who had been trading over long distances before the coming of the Swahili-Arabs, commerce from the coast enlarged the scale of their own trading activities.

Another area where the coastal commercial intrusion led to a remarkable upsurge in African commerce was the Kamba country. The Kamba people lived mainly in the Machakos and Kitui districts of present-day Kenya, an area infested with tsetse, and subject to drought and famine. In such times of stress, Kamba families often emigrated in great numbers seeking refuge among neighbouring Bantu peoples like the Kikuyu and Embu. It would appear that this harsh environment forced the Kamba to establish various kinds of trading arrangements with their surrounding peoples long before the coastal trade began. They were experts in the production of poisoned arrows, which they exchanged for food. Also, in the course of searching for water holes and new sites for settlement, they became familiar with the surrounding neighbourhoods and this prepared them for the kind of role they were to play in the era of the caravan trade.

After a disastrous famine in 1836, which forced a great proportion of the Kamba to seek refuge among the Rabai near the coast, the Kamba were exposed to new influences and opportunities which enabled them to play a major role in the commerce of the Kenyan interior. They came in contact with coastal merchants who wanted ivory in exchange for foreign manufactured goods. These coastal traders were reluctant to trade into Kenya for fear of the Masai. The Kamba therefore seized the opportunity offered by this situation. From about 1840 the Kamba began to play the role of middlemen between the Africans of the Kenyan interior and the Swahili Arabs. They organized caravans that tapped the resources of most parts of Kenya and, until the 1860s, virtually monopolized the trade of this area. They traded as far into the interior as Ndia, Chuka and Embu, and along the more northerly routes leading to Mathira and Laikipia. These latter passed through the Metumi and Gaki regions, where ivory was said to have been plentiful. The European traveller, J. L. Krapf, noted in 1848 that Kamba caravans reached the coast every week bringing down some three to four hundred *frasilahs* of ivory. Krapf estimated that such caravans consisted of from three to four hundred persons.[1]

Kamba traders monopolized the middleman trade for about a decade by employing a variety of stratagems. While they encouraged the Embu and Kikuyu to produce ivory for sale, they discouraged them from by-passing the Kamba traders and carrying their goods straight to the coastal markets. This they did by spreading false reports about the situation on the coast, and by raiding Embu and Mbere caravans whenever they tried to reach the coast. The Kamba also used similar tactics to dissuade the Swahili and Arab traders from going into the interior. They spread stories of the fierce Masai, of Kikuyu and Embu hostility to traders, and of the difficulties of trading along the route controlled by them. In the 1860s the Kamba lost their monopoly of this route when Arab traders began using it, but they were not forced out of the trade. Instead they changed their role. They began to act as ivory collectors, travelling into the less accessible parts of Kenya, where they bought the tusks and carried them to the major routes to sell to the Arabs. They also sold foodstuffs to the passing caravans.

The third area where the coming of the Swahili-Arabs stimulated and increased African commerce was in Usambara. Here the chief of the province of Mazinde on the caravan route, Semboja, established control over the road leading on into the interior. He had moved his capital from Nguwa to Mazinde as a vital step towards the achievement of this

---

[1] J. L. Krapf, *Travels, researches and missionary labours . . . in eastern Africa* (London, 1869), 248. The above interpretation of Kamba motivation follows I. N. Kimambo, 'The economic history of the Kamba, 1850–1950', in B. A. Ogot (ed.), *Hadith*, 2 (Nairobi, 1970), 81; but see also Lamphear's chapter 'The Kamba and the northern Mrima coast' in R. Gray and D. Birmingham (eds.), *Pre-colonial African trade: essays on trade in central and eastern Africa before 1900* (London, 1970).

objective. He also sponsored the movement of Shambaa traders and hunters into the southern Pare plains in order to exploit the commercial opportunities of that region. For example, Semboja sent his son-in-law, Kihungwi Mgalu, to Mamba where, after asking the permission of the Mamba ruler Kihungwe, he established a town and began to collect ivory. Kihungwi attracted a number of Shambaa followers and built the fortified town of Kihurie. From here the Shambaa not only hunted but tried to gain control of the trade from the adjacent Pare kingdoms, as well as to collect tolls from caravans coming from the interior. The goods collected were sent to Mazinde, whence Semboja transported them to the coast. Other Shambaa trading settlements were founded at Mariranga, close to an important caravan camping station in Gonja, and also at Buiko to ensure the supervision of the western route.[1]

Large-scale African involvement in commerce occurred in almost all parts of East Africa in this period. But, unlike the Nyamwezi and the Kamba, most of the interior peoples did not carry their goods to the coast, but bartered them locally to the visiting coastal or Nyamwezi merchants. Often the rulers, such as Kimweri ya Nyumbai of Usambara, Mutesa of Buganda, and the rulers of the Ufipa and Nyiha peoples, tried to monopolize the trade. Markets were established near the royal palaces, and each ruler devised various means of collecting local trade-goods which he exchanged for the exotic articles brought in by the alien merchants.

The ivory and slave trade led to a significant increase in the production of and trade in other products of the East African interior, particularly iron, salt, tobacco and foodstuffs. Inter-state trading had been in existence long before the arrival of the Arabs, but these commodities were traded only within a short distance from their points of production. With the influx of more people into the interior from the coastal region and the great intermingling of people from different regions of East Africa, the demand for the various products increased. Iron was in great demand, but the areas where it was produced were few and the technical knowledge of smelting was limited to particular families. With the coming of the coastal traders, it became possible for the iron produced in the far interior to reach people nearer the coast. The Gogo, Sagara and Zaramo all demanded iron implements in exchange for ivory and foodstuffs. Therefore, all caravans travelling from the interior to the coast carried new and old iron implements, especially hoes, with which they purchased food, settled road tolls or procured coastal pro-

[1] I. N. Kimambo, *A political history of the Pare of Tanzania* (Nairobi, 1969), ch. 10.

ducts. Most of these iron hoes were produced in the Sumbwa, Zinza and Konongo areas. Nyamwezi traders are known to have been in the habit of travelling to the iron producing regions to secure their supplies. Even the coastal traders and some of the European travellers had to send their servants to these regions to buy hoes. Consequent on this expansion of the hoe market, production was considerably increased, so that one family of ironsmiths composed a working song in which they boasted that only the charcoal of the *mubanga* tree brought the cloth of the coast.[1]

Among the Pare, the Swahili-Arab trade indirectly stimulated an increased production of iron. The Pare had been the chief suppliers of iron to the inhabitants of the mountain regions of north-eastern Tanzania. The demand for Pare iron, according to I. N. Kimambo, increased from the beginning of the nineteenth century. The cause of the increased demand was the military rivalry among the rulers of the Chaga who inhabited the slopes of the Kilimanjaro mountain. Kimambo believes that 'it is likely that there was a connection between this rivalry and the development of long distance trade from the coast to the interior of the Pangani river basin'. Suggesting that the Chaga trade contacts with the coast may have dated to about the end of the eighteenth century, he feels that the rivalry among the Chaga rulers was probably the result of competition among them for the control of the trade. Raids and counter-raids characterized the Chaga rivalry. There was consequently an increased demand for Pare iron to forge military weapons with which to equip the armies of the Chaga rulers. Similar increases in iron production have been reported for Uhehe and Ufipa, and also among the Palwo of northern Bunyoro, where the intensification of hunting created an expanding demand for spears.[2]

The production of salt was similarly affected. Although most communities knew how to produce salt in their various localities by various methods, the trade in ivory had the effect of expanding the area over which white salt from the great salt pans of places like Uvinza in western Tanzania, Lake Eyasi in central Tanzania and Ivuna in the extreme south-west of the same country was distributed. Salt was in high demand, and, as the explorer Burton remarked in 1857, there were areas

[1] A. D. Roberts, 'Precolonial trade among the Nyamwezi of Tanzania' (University of Zambia, history seminar paper, June 1962), 8.

[2] I. N. Kimambo, 'The Pare', in *Tanzania before 1900*, 26–7; it is important to note that iron production was increasing in the nineteenth century in areas outside the range of Arab commercial influence, thus the degree of direct Arab inspiration may have been exaggerated in those areas that felt direct Arab influence. See R. Herring, 'Iron production and trade in Labwor' (Dalhousie University, African Studies seminar papers, 1973).

where nothing else but salt would be accepted in exchange for other trade items. The result was that the salt works, particularly those of Uvinza, were considerably intensified.

THE INTERLACUSTRINE AREA

By 1750 at least, an extensive trading network and commercial system had developed around the salt works of Katwe and Kisenyi in the Lake Edward–Lake George region of what is today south-western Uganda.[1] According to tradition, Katwe salt was discovered in ancient times by a hunter called Murogo, his descendants becoming the ritual heads of the salt works until the colonial period. Three types of salt were mined; one a rare variety, fine and white from Kisenyi, which was supplied exclusively to the chiefs; the second, ordinary cooking salt; and a third, a rock salt for animals. The Katwe–Kisenyi works possessed three advantages over other salt areas such as Kibiro in Bunyoro and Uvinza in Tanzania. They could be worked all the year round, rather than only in the dry season; the extraction process involved less labour than at Kibiro; and a number of specialized iron working centres – Kayangwe Buhweju, Kayonza and Bugangaizi – were located in close proximity.

While salt and iron were the staples of the commercial system, a variety of other products was exchanged in a string of markets around the shores of the lakes and at inland market centres such as Ishaka in Igara, Rukinda in Rujumbura and Ibanda in Buzimba. Sorghum, peas and honey were traded from Kigezi and Rwanda, millet from Nkore and Toro, dried bananas from Buganda, Bwamba and eastern Zaïre, coffee from Karagwe and Buganda, skins and hides from Rwanda, Mpororo, Nkore, Mwenge, special soft skins worn by chiefs from Bugangaizi, barkcloth from Buganda, and copper wire from the Konjo. So much had the society moved out of a subsistence economy that numbers of people had migrated into the area to engage full-time in specialist occupations, becoming entirely dependent upon the market economy for their daily necessities. Besides the salt and iron workers, these migrants included the canoe builders and transporters on the lakes, and traders such as the people of Butumbi who formed the major trading link in the salt–iron exchange between Kayangwe and Katwe.

From early in the eighteenth century the Bito chiefs of Kisaka had regulated the trade on behalf of the *omukama* of Bunyoro, until 1830,

[1] The material which follows on south-west Uganda is based on E. R. Kamuhangire, 'The pre-colonial economic and social history of East Africa with special reference to the south-west Uganda salt lakes region' (Historical Association of Kenya Conference, 1972).

when Toro gained control, until ousted by Kabarega, who in turn was displaced by the British. The chiefs of Kisaka appointed agents to collect taxes from both miners and traders and to maintain law and order. Commerce was almost entirely in the hands of the agricultural peoples and had been created to meet their needs. Clearly commerce was stimulated by the population increase through the northward migration of the agricultural Kiga of Kigezi during the nineteenth century as well as by the influx of Ganda refugees.

It was the Ziba and Haya, who for long had traded in the Katwe–Kisenyi commercial network, who introduced first the Nyamwezi and then the Arabs to the trading network. Prior to this neither ivory nor slaves had been trade-goods. By the usual interlacustrine practice, one tusk of any elephant killed belonged to the king. The Nyamwezi, whose traders reached as far north as Bunyoro and Alur, began to organize elephant hunting expeditions with a consequent abuse of ancient practices. As a result the ivory trade was confined to the palaces of the chiefs, and many Nyamwezi took service as royal hunters. The slave trade did not become an important economic factor, but some few recorded instances indicate the potential in that trade for disruption of the indigenous commercial system.

While the ivory trade brought new products into the market and increased the number of traders, it does not seem to have been the cause of any notable acceleration or change of emphasis within the economy. Partly this was because the ivory trade was a separate trade, conducted in the palace, firearms thereby being controlled and monopolized by the political leaders, unlike other products, which moved into general commercial circulation. Barkcloth and the skins of Bugangaizi, for example, continued to possess greater prestige than coastal cloth. The outsiders were far from their trading-posts; they were few and totally dependent upon local goodwill. They never approached the stage of displacing local traders or turning them into commercial clients, as along the Kamba routes discussed above, or of influencing politics, as among the Nyamwezi. The Nyamwezi and Arab traders formed merely another element within a flourishing indigenous market economy.

During the eighteenth century a change in the power relations among the states of the interlacustrine region occurred. Olimi Isansa, *omukama* of Bunyoro, had decided to strengthen his kingdom's southern frontier by permitting the establishment of local and tributary sub-dynasties in Kooki, Kitakwenda and Kisaka. In the course of his southern campaigns, Isansa clashed with the high priest of the Chwezi cult in Bwera.

Henceforth, at least in the regions south of Bunyoro, the cult no longer supported either the political or military objectives of the Bito dynasty. This marked the beginning of the decline of Bunyoro and the rise of Buganda and, to a lesser extent, Nkore.[1]

Since at least the reign of Mawanda in the early eighteenth century, the political organization of the kingdom of Buganda had been such that the geographic expansion of the state contributed to the strengthening of royal power. Consequently strong and ambitious kings sought to expand the state. During the reigns of Kabakas Junju and Semakokiro in the later eighteenth century, the expansion of the kingdom was spurred and its direction determined by the desire to reach, and possibly control, the commercial systems radiating from Kiziba and Karagwe to the south and the salt lakes region to the west. Junju began with the conquest of the Nyoro province of Buddu and then proceeded through a combination of force and diplomacy to bring the Nyoro sub-chiefdom of Kooki into tributary relationship. Ganda settlers moved into Kooki, rose to prominence at court and gradually transformed that chiefdom from pastoralism to a Ganda-like agricultural economy. The steady Ganda penetration of Kooki throughout the nineteenth century, including the acceptance of Ganda officers as 'advisers' and 'trainers' in the army, resulted in the complete absorption of Kooki into Buganda by the end of the century.

For centuries Kiziba had been a sub-chiefdom and tributary state of Bunyoro. By the late eighteenth century, Kiziba had secured its independence, but it was a small Bito state in a Hinda world. Neighbouring states such as Karagwe and Kyamutwara had ambitions to bring Kiziba into clientage. First under Junju, and increasingly in the nineteenth century, Kiziba turned to the Ganda as a counter-force to its Hinda neighbours. In spite of two attempts to limit the Ganda presence, as the century advanced Kiziba became more and more a satellite of Buganda, which used it as a base from which to control commerce and spread its influence over Kyamutwara and Karagwe.[2] Kyamutwara was fragmented after a Ziba–Ganda invasion, and Speke in 1861 recorded that King Rumanyika I of Karagwe recognized the superiority of Kabaka Mutesa. In 1876 Stanley described Karagwe as tributary to Buganda.

[1] Here and in what follows the authors are indebted to E. R. Kamuhangire's paper 'Bunyoro and Rwanda, the changing balance of power and its effects upon the marcher region c. 1650–1900: a case study of the Bachwezi and Nyabingi cults' (Dalhousie University African Studies Conference, 1974).

[2] F. X. Lwamgira, Amakuru ga Kiziba, 2nd ed. (Tabora, 1949), translated by E. R. Kamuhangire as 'The history of Kiziba'. A. G. M. Ishumi, 'The kingdom of Kiziba', Journal of World History, 1971, 13, 4, 714–34.

Even if these travellers' reports were exaggerated, it would seem that Buganda held a paramount presence in the south by the 1870s. Presumably the Ganda were primarily preoccupied with controlling the trade routes and the supply of firearms. The increase in Ganda activities along the western shores of the Victoria Nyanza was paralleled by a growing control and domination of the lake trade in ivory. After 1870, the Nyanza was well on its way to becoming a Ganda lake, a supremacy which Arab and Swahili traders found it expedient to recognize.

Buganda's expansion to the south had been induced by commercial considerations and facilitated by her ability to replace Bunyoro as the protecting power to small client chiefdoms threatened by the Hinda. It was in essence the same combination which drew the Ganda towards the salt lakes, even if the results – from the viewpoint of Buganda – were not as impressive. The political situation around the salt lakes was complicated by three other factors, the fragmentation of Mpororo, the ambitions of Nkore and the foundation of the state of Toro.

Around 1750 Mpororo had been the largest state in the west. By 1800, partly as a result of internal instability and partly from Rwandan pressure, Mpororo had collapsed and fragmented into a number of small and mostly ineffective petty states. Nkore and Rwanda were the chief beneficiaries, Nkore gaining as a result a large territory, an influx of new settlers and the Mpororo royal drum. In the eighteenth century, the former tributary state of Buhweju had declared its independence from Bunyoro, and in the nineteenth century came under the growing influence of Nkore. Even the sub-chiefdom of Kitakwenda, which remained loyal to Bunyoro until the onset of the colonial period, had to reckon with the growing influence of Nkore, and upon occasion probably paid tribute both to Bunyoro and Nkore.

To some extent, Buganda was frustrated around the salt lakes by the ambition of Nkore to become the paramount successor-state to Bunyoro. While Nkore's expansion towards the lakes may be interpreted as an effort to control the trading routes between them and Kiziba and Karagwe, yet it seems clear that pastoralist-dominated states such as Nkore were slower to react to the economic stimulus of commercial networks than were more agriculturally orientated kingdoms such as Buganda or even Toro. To the rulers of Nkore in the nineteenth century, the fertile grazing lands of the salt lakes region – among the best in the entire interlacustrine area – probably held a greater attraction than its flourishing commercial centre and trading network.

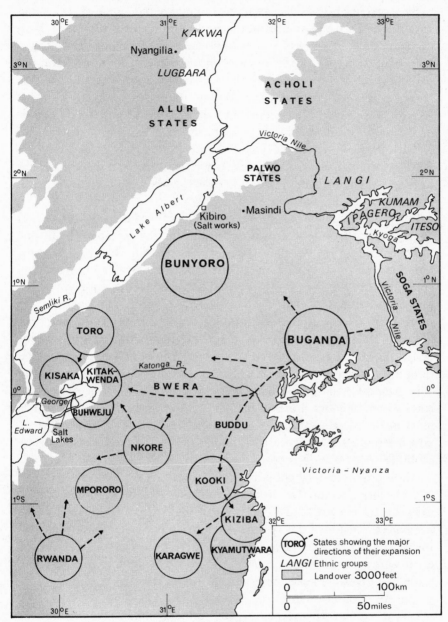

Map labels

KAKWA

Nyangilia.

LUGBARA

ACHOLI
STATES

ALUR
STATES

Victoria Nile

PALWO
STATES

LANGI

Lake Albert

Kibiro
(Salt works)

•Masindi

KUMAM

PAGERO

ITESO

L. Kyoga

BUNYORO

SOGA
STATES

Victoria Nile

Semliki R.

TORO

BUGANDA

KISAKA

KITAK-
WENDA

Katonga R.

L. George

BWERA

BUHWEJU

BUDDU

L.
Edward

Salt
Lakes

NKORE

KOOKI

Victoria – Nyanza

MPORORO

RWANDA

KIZIBA

KARAGWE

KYAMUTWARA

TORO States showing the major
directions of their expansion
LANGI Ethnic groups
Land over 3000 feet
0   100 km
0   50 miles

11   Bunyoro and her neighbours: late eighteenth to mid-nineteenth centuries

Bunyoro reached its nadir with the simultaneous break-away around 1830 of the Palwo provinces in the north and of the province of Toro in the west. Toro's secession was organized by Kaboyo, a prince of the Nyoro royal house. Realizing the significance of the commerce and grazing lands of the salt lakes, Kaboyo made their acquisition a priority. In time he was successful in bringing the Nyoro sub-chiefdom of Kisaka, which held direct control of the salt works and grazing lands of Busongora, into tributary relationship to Toro. From the time of Kabaka Suna (c. 1824–54), Ganda forces periodically raided into the salt lakes area. These Ganda raids, as well as those into the Soga states to the east, gave the impression that the Ganda were more inclined to raid than to trade for ivory.

Buganda's major problem around the lakes was her inability to find an ally and collaborator. It was not until Kabarega came to the throne of Bunyoro (c. 1868) with the ambition of restoring the prestige of his kingdom, beginning with re-conquest of the Palwo and Toro, and conscious of how important to his ambitions was the control of commerce and firearms, that Toro increasingly turned to Buganda for protection. This was the opportunity for which Buganda had been looking. Kabarega succeeded in defeating Toro and taking over control of the salt lakes' commerce. Late in the century economic considerations also led the British to fix upon the salt lakes as a major objective.[1] The Anglo-Ganda-Toro alliance to drive the Nyoro out of the salt lakes was merely one more stage in the history of economic imperialism to control this flourishing industry and market economy, a history which stretches back at least to the foundation of the Chwezi dynasty around the fourteenth century.

Another commercial network spread out from the Kibiro salt works and Masindi iron industry in northern Bunyoro. The Parombo trading network among the Alur to the west of the Albert Nile seems to have been one extension of this system, which stretched northward to include the Nyangilia iron industry among the Kakwa and Lugbara. In the eighteenth and nineteenth centuries, Nyoro immigrants and Parombo trade had probably been important factors in the significant expansion of the Alur state system.

In the eighteenth century Nyoro influence had spread along the southern littoral of Lake Kyoga, and a severe famine in the north around 1785–92 had greatly accelerated the south-westward migration

---

[1] J. F. M. Wilson, 'The pre-colonial history of Toro', M.A. thesis (Makerere University, 1973); H. Basaliza, 'Toro in transition', undergraduate research essay (Makerere University, 1971).

of the Paranilotic Teso and Lwo-speaking Lango out of Karamoja and into areas north of Lake Kyoga. During the nineteenth century Lake Kyoga developed into an important trading artery connecting Bunyoro, Busoga, Palwo, Lango and Teso with markets and traders operating both north and south of the lake. Iron hoes made in Bunyoro were the major staple of the trade, exchanged initially for goats and later for ivory.[1]

Following their secession from Bunyoro around 1830, the Palwo welcomed first Nyamwezi and then coastal traders into their markets.[2] The Palwo were particularly interested in securing firearms, their first priority being to sustain their newly won independence, their second to re-establish the Palwo wing of the Bito to the throne of Bunyoro. It seems logical that the first people around Kyoga to grasp the significance of firearms would have been the numerically weak but singularly ambitious Palwo, living on the borders of the potentially powerful and hostile state of Bunyoro, and also, that it would have been the bilingual Palwo who first introduced the Lwo-speaking Lango, Ipagero and Kumam to the hoe and ivory trade. Finally, the bilingual Ipagero and Kumam (Lwo and Teso) in turn attracted the Iteso to the markets of northern Busoga.

As a consequence of the Kyoga commercial system, the kings of Bunyoro and the Palwo recruited Lango mercenary soldiers, while some Soga states recruited Iteso as a counter-force to the growing influence of Buganda. The first mention of Lango mercenaries occurs in the reign of Rwakabale, king of Bunyoro, in the 1840s and 1850s. Kabarega of Bunyoro, after 1868, paid particular attention to the Kyoga trade and the recruitment of mercenaries. It was his success both around Kyoga and the salt lakes which drew these commercial systems with their important gun trade under Bunyoro's control and into the service of Kabarega's ambitions. Despite their efforts to ally with the Egyptians to the north, the Palwo were unable to compete with the Nyoro in the recruitment of mercenaries or in the attractions they could offer traders. Ultimately Kabarega defeated the Palwo and, as with the Toro, brought them back within the kingdom.

The evidence neither proves nor disproves that it was the alien traders who linked the regional trading networks. The unusual physical

[1] No one source covers the Lake Kyoga trading network; sources used for the above reconstruction include Peter Odyomo, 'Consensus and leadership in the Alido confederacy in nineteenth century Lango', in *A history of Uganda*, vol. II (Nairobi, forthcoming). See also J. B. Webster *et al.*, *The Iteso during the Asonya* (Nairobi, 1974).
[2] Adefuye, 'Political history of the Palwo'.

appearance of the aliens and the presence of guns in the markets stand out both in travellers' reports and oral tradition, but whether this proves that it was they who linked the regional networks is indeed debatable. The following groups have been reported in the mid-nineteenth century as traders in Karagwe: Rwanda, Suwi, Nyamwezi, Ziba, Haya, Nyankore and Nyoro. It seems difficult to believe that they had all been drawn into trade as a result of the Swahili-Arab penetration.

Outside Karagwe, the influence of coastal or Nyamwezi traders as a political factor in the northern interlacustrine states was negligible. The Arab presence in Karagwe resembled the situation to the south rather than to the north. The coastmen were numerous enough to be 'asked by a ruler to help in maintaining his rule, or by one of the contenders for the throne . . .'. They lived in 'secluded communities which they established as trading centres and appointed one of their number as a governor . . .'. Some intermarried with local Africans, but Islam did not spread outside their kinship circles. Despite the numerous alien traders, and perhaps reflecting the pastoralist nature of the society, a historian of Karagwe has concluded that here the strength of the Swahili-Arab traders was such as to prevent the emergence of any class of successful entrepreneurs among the Banyambo people.[1]

AGRICULTURAL CHANGES

The impact of coastal commerce on agriculture was equally impressive. Commerce created landless people who were either resident in the main trading centres or in transit on the caravan routes. The traders often needed provisions, not only for immediate consumption, but also to carry away for use in areas where grain could not be easily procured. On the central Nyamwezi route, for example, it was difficult to purchase food either in the large arid region occupied by the Gogo or in the uninhabited forest expanse between the last villages of Unyamwezi and those in the Gogo area, generally described as the *mgunda mkali* (harsh wilderness). Caravans travelling to the coast often tried to take as many provisions for the march across this arid zone as they could carry. The demand for provisions resulted, at times, in an inordinate rise in the price of foodstuffs, and thus African farmers were induced to produce more. Nyamwezi territory was also affected, and there was a conscious effort to increase the food supply, but many Nyamwezi youths went

[1] I. K. Katoke, 'Karagwe: a pre-colonial state', *Journal of World History*, 1971, **13**, 3, 536–7.

away from home to trade, or from the 1860s were recruited into the standing armies of warriors like Mirambo and Mkasiwa, and this had a major impact on Nyamwezi agriculture. Many families made good this labour shortage by buying slaves to cultivate their fields. The great merchants themselves, including the resident coastal traders, maintained farms of considerable size which were worked for them by numerous slaves and free servants. Speke remarked in 1861 that the Arabs appeared to be great farmers, because they had cattle stalls attached to their houses. The coastmen introduced new foods such as rice, cassava, pawpaw and citrus. Tutsi with large herds of cattle also came in great numbers and settled in various parts of Unyamwezi. The hitherto swampy wastelands (*mbuga*) began to be utilized for the cultivation of rice. Thus Unyamwezi was described by Burton as the garden of inter-tropical Africa with the people as the proprietors of the soil.

Wherever large numbers of people are engaged exclusively in specialized occupations such as mining, smithing, irrigation works, trading and transporting (and in the Katwe–Kisenyi commercial system trading caravans contained between eighty and a hundred traders), farmers have an opportunity to secure a part of the new wealth by increasing production beyond subsistence levels. The descriptions by Stanley (1889) and Lugard (1891) of Kitakwenda, a tributary state to Bunyoro east of Lake George, indicate that farmers were also sharing in the commercial prosperity of the area.

The entire distance thence [from the lake-shore] to Kitari in Ankori is an almost unbroken line of banana plantations skirting the shore of the Lake and fields of Indian corn, sugar cane, eleusine and holcus which lie behind them inland, which are the properties of the owners of the half-dozen salt markets dotting the coast.

There is a very great deal of cultivation all along the line we came today, and here at our camp there are forests of bananas, and acres of potatoes in every direction.[1]

One significant impact of the coastmen on the peoples of the interior was therefore the transformation of economic production and commerce from formerly localized standards. This was what Richard Gray and David Birmingham have described as a change to a 'market-oriented economy' which 'generated new forms of wealth...'. 'A whole range of goods (e.g. ivory, cattle, wax) acquired new economic values

[1] The first quotation is from H. M. Stanley, *In darkest Africa*, II (London, 1890), 326, and the second from F. D. Lugard, *The rise of our East African empire*, II (London, 1893), 262.

which they had not possessed in the subsistence economy. Organized markets handling a multiple exchange of goods were often developed.' This transformation seems always to have involved the invention, or introduction, and growing acceptance of an indigenous or imported currency, enabling traders to bring an increasing number of commodities within a common frame of values. New means of capital accumulation were found, a new field of consumer demand for imports was created and, above all, new forms of economic specialization were stimulated. The production of export goods, whether by miners, hunters or craftsmen, assumed an unprecedented importance, while individuals, and in some cases whole communities, began to adopt the role of professional merchants.[1]

SOCIAL CHANGES AND THE SLAVE TRADE

Directly or indirectly, the penetration of the Swahili-Arabs left a significant imprint on the social life of East African peoples. As was the case with economic changes, these changes differed in their nature and extent according to the intensity of the trade and the nature of the commodities exchanged. The trade in slaves brought great disruption to the areas from which they were obtained. The port of Kilwa grew important from the 1750s as a slave exporting town, because of the increased demand for labourers to work in the plantations on the French islands of Ile de France and Bourbon. With the introduction of the plantation economy in Zanzibar by Sayyid Sa'id at the beginning of the nineteenth century, the African inhabitants of the fertile regions were pushed away into the less fertile southern and eastern parts of the island. The labour needed to cultivate the cloves could not be fully supplied by the island population, so Sayyid Sa'id and the other Arab plantation owners had to look to the mainland for the needed labour supply. This further increased the demand for African slaves and the importance of Kilwa as the main slave port.

The Yao living behind the port of Kilwa, who had long been involved in its commerce, seized the opportunity of the increasing slave demand to play a dominant role in its supply. Armed with trade guns, they raided the Makua and Makonde on either side of the Ruvuma; while to the north of them the Mafiti (Nindi) and Magwangwara (Ndendeule) raiders from the former Maseko-Ngoni kingdom created additional havoc from the 1860s on. The Ngoni themselves did not usually sell

---

[1] Gray and Birmingham (eds.), *Pre-colonial African trade*, 3-4.

their captives, since they were always in need of agricultural labour to feed their standing armies and the large concentrations of people at their capital and provincial centres. But, as described earlier (p. 279), Nindi and Ndendeule who had undergone military training in the Maseko regiments during the 1850s became the scourge of surrounding areas during the next two decades.

The trade in slaves in other parts of the interior would not appear to have assumed any major significance until after the 1850s. This was particularly true along the central and northern routes. The slavers arrived in the wake of the ivory traders. They seem to have succeeded in capturing men in places like Usagara, Uzaramo and Usambara. At Khutu, for example, there was a class of people known to European travellers as 'touters', who oppressed the people with their terrorist activities. Farther inland, the Nyamwezi did not respond enthusiastically to the opportunities offered by the coastal slavers. They had taken to the ivory trade and needed men to conduct it gainfully. Moreover they were strong enough in their respective communities to deter Swahili-Arab parties from attacking them. The Nyamwezi people therefore did not sell their own people. However, individuals or small groups of people did engage in slave hunting. They hid along unfrequented paths and captured women and children who passed by. These slave hunters were known as the *vbungi-vbungi* in Unyanyembe. They were a social nuisance and the community frowned on their practices. Offenders were severely punished when captured.[1]

The Nyamwezi nonetheless participated in the traffic in men. Some of their great rulers, like Mirambo of Urambo or Nsimba Kavbung'ando of Uluila, sold war captives, especially if they were too old to be easily integrated into their armies. Nyamwezi traders, even porters, travelled to Ujiji and to Buganda to buy slaves. Some of them co-operated with the coastal slavers to raid the fragmented Manyema communities in eastern Congo. It would appear however that the greater proportion of the slaves purchased by the Nyamwezi in the Congo or from the Ganda were not exported outside East Africa. Some were kept by the Nyamwezi themselves as domestic servants, others were given in exchange for ivory and foodstuffs in Ugogo. Swahili-Arabs, on the other hand, found great difficulty in transporting their slaves to the coast, and thence to Zanzibar or Arabia, because by the 1850s the British had stepped up their attempts to bring the slave trade to an end on the East African coast. Therefore, those who led slaves from the interlacustrine

---

[1] Traditions collected by A. C. Unomah in Unyanyembe, 1968.

regions and the Congo basin kept them in Tabora until they could be sent to the coast in small groups. Many of the slaves could not be transported from Tabora, and were therefore retained as domestic servants of the coastmen. Thus in Unyamwezi the slave trade did not produce the same kind of disruptive effects seen in other areas. It was instead a factor of population growth, and there are many families, both in Tabora and in the rural areas of Unyamwezi, who trace their origins to the period of the slave trade.

We may then say that the slave trade affected African society in two widely different ways according to the kind of role that each society played. For those communities that were the victims of the slavers, the trade was a factor of great social dislocation and even anarchy. This was the experience of the Makonde and Makua in south-eastern Tanzania, the Fipa and Nyiha in south-western Tanzania, the states to the north and south-west of Buganda and to some extent of the Pare and Chaga. Among these peoples raids, wars and the overpowering of the weak by the strong in society became a feature of social relations. Farms, villages and houses were devastated and there was a great deal of violence done to the social, economic and political system of the people.

Among other peoples like the Nyamwezi and the Gogo, the slave trade was a factor of population redistribution and economic advancement. During the nineteenth century, the dry and thinly populated Gogo country was traversed by large ivory and slave-trading caravans, and the Gogo demanded slaves in exchange for the little ivory that they were able to produce. A considerable proportion of the slaves leaving Unyamwezi were sold to the Gogo, who employed them in the cultivation of the soil.

In response to the menace of the slave-raiders many peoples had to devise means of self-protection. Both the Nyiha and the Fipa people, for example, built 'heavily fortified villages'. The reports of European travellers in East Africa at this time contain references to the fact that most East African peoples surrounded their villages and residences with walls and trenches, which probably date from the period of the slave trade.

Changes in the structure of societies also occurred in areas not seriously affected by the slave trade. In Unyamwezi, for example, the former straggling villages became more compact. This was partly because of the great numbers of people brought in by the trade in ivory, but the internecine wars among Nyamwezi states to win control of the trade were also an important factor. Large towns like Isiunula, Uramba,

Inala, Mfuto and Ivbelamafipa, which contained thousands of people, sprang up in Unyanyembe. The great merchants of the states, the *vbandevba*, built these *miji* (or large walled homesteads) in which were concentrated hundreds of their clients and dependants. Some of the Nyanyembe villages were strongly fortified and garrisoned by regiments of soldiers. The market town of Tabora became a sort of urban centre, where the cultures of the Swahili-Arabs and various East African peoples were mingled. Its population was estimated at about 20,000 people in the 1890s.[1] Mirambo's fort in Ulyankhulu contained about 10,000 people, with about 5,000 more living outside its walls. In the 1870s an LMS Missionary considered a 'village' of 4,000 souls in Mirambo's sphere of influence to be a comparatively small one. Considering that villages in Unyamwezi tended to be small and dispersed, this suggests the kind of change that had taken place in the settlement patterns in Unyamwezi since the 1840s. Greater 'urbanization' also occurred among the Chaga, Pare and to a lesser extent among the Palwo.

Contact with the Swahili-Arabs had a considerable impact on traditional African cultures and values. In the first place, Africans developed an increasing taste for foreign commodities. All sorts of cloth, including American calico, the *kaniki*, *joho* and *debwani*,[2] began to be in demand. There was also a market for beads, copper wire, hats, umbrellas, tents, guns and gunpowder. As many of these commodities were items of dress, the traditional fashions gradually underwent great changes. Skins and locally made cotton and bark cloths gave way to imported materials. This is clearly reflected in the reports, photographs and drawings of European travellers who passed through East African communities at the time. R. F. Burton, for instance, in his description of the dress of the people whose countries he visited between 1857 and 1859, shows that imported cloth was fast displacing the indigenous cotton, bark cloth or skins as the most important item of dress in most of the Tanzanian interior. He referred to the Zaramo as 'wealthy enough to dress well'. Almost every man, he said, could afford a *shukkah* (or loin cloth) of unbleached cotton. There was hardly any place visited by the great traveller where the people had not begun to dress in imported cloth, especially on important occasions. The wealthy classes wore superior stuff. Adefuye notes that, in northern Bunyoro, 'wealth and

---

[1] P. Maze, 'Vicariate de Tabora', tyepscript, Archives of White Fathers, Via Aurelia, Rome.

[2] These are local names for various kinds of imported cloth. *Kaniki* was a dark blue calico. *Joho* was the commonest woollen cloth in the interior. *Debwani* was a cheap cotton cloth imported from Oman. For notes on cloth imports see Burton, *Lake regions*, II, 395-9.

status began to be reflected in the manner of dressing. The *jaghi* and *batongole* (important political functionaries) wore imported cloths even on ordinary days. Their wives wore gold bangles.' Even the common people appeared in imported cloth, and those who dressed in the traditional bark cloth were often not allowed to come near the centre of activities. In Buganda cotton cloth from the coast was preferred to the high quality bark cloth produced locally. The *kabaka* and the great chiefs of Buganda always dressed in foreign materials. As in Unyamwezi and most other parts of East Africa, the adoption of the colourful imported fabrics went hand in hand with the borrowing of Arab fashions. The rulers and commoners who could afford cloth made them into robes similar to those worn by the coastal traders. Mutesa of Buganda was described by the missionary, R. P. Ashe, as clothed 'from head to foot in a snowy white robe'. His *katikiro* (chief minister) wore 'Arab costume, a snowy gown of fine cotton, over which he wore a long mantle or robe of rich black cloth heavily embroidered with gold'. Even the royal pages were said to dress in Arab fashion.[1]

Even those peoples who took little active part in the ivory trade were affected by this cultural change. Among the Gogo, Burton reported that a skin garment was as rare as a cotton garment in the interior. The men wore Arab check or dyed Indian cotton. Even among the nomadic Masai, who have on the whole been notorious for their resistance to foreign influences, there were reported to be some who had 'exchanged their hide tents for the hut and the skin for cotton cloth' in Ugogo.[2]

Like imported cotton cloth, copper wire, made into coiled bracelets known as the *kitindi*, also became popular among many East African peoples as an item of ornament. In Ugogo men and women wore it, as well as anklets and necklaces of beads. The Masai women wore *kitindi* of full and half sizes, above and below the elbow. The *kitindi* was also popular among the Nyamwezi and Ha people of western Tanzania.

Another way in which the coastmen affected the culture of the East African peoples was in the art of building. The rectangular houses which are now common in the whole of the area would appear to have spread to the interior during this period. Most peoples had built circular huts before the nineteenth century, but from the beginning of that century, Africans adopted the rectangular buildings common among the coastal Swahili. In Pare, for example, the rectangular building style was spread through the agency of the Shambaa traders. In

[1] The sources of the quotations in this paragraph are Burton, *Lake regions*, I, 109–10; Adefuye, 'Political history', 134–5; and R. P. Ashe, *Two kings of Buganda* (London, 1889), 59 and 55.   [2] Burton, *Lake regions*, I, 305.

Unyamwezi the coastmen built flat-roofed *tembes* which were copied by the Nyamwezi people.

Trade with the coast stimulated movements and intermingling of people of different ethnic or racial origins. The result was that new social relations were forged between the coastmen and those of the interior, as also among the different peoples of the interior themselves. The security of the coastmen in the interior depended largely on the co-operation of their hosts. They had therefore to reach some form of understanding with the rulers of the African communities considered powerful enough to offer them protection. Sayyid Sa'īd of Zanzibar is known to have entered into agreements with a number of interior rulers and to have exchanged gifts with them in the attempt to ensure the safety of coastal caravans. The traders themselves often stayed in or around the houses of the African rulers, where goods were brought to them for sale or from where they sent out their factors to collect merchandise. These traders tried to sustain the favour of the rulers by making gifts, paying transit fees or assisting the rulers in local political struggles. In a few cases the coastal traders married into the royal houses, consolidating their common interests through kinship.

However, relations between the coastmen and the peoples of the interior were not always cordial. There were cases where the former were unable to sustain the friendship of the African rulers, as in Urambo, Puge, Uvinza and some parts of Uha. Some of the powerful coastal traders, like Hamed b. Mohammed (known more commonly as Tippu Tip), were a terror to many African communities. Tippu Tip and his followers raided African societies and used their military might to get what they wanted. In Unyanyembe one of the rulers, Mnywasele (1859–61), had reasons to disagree with the coastmen and tried to expel them from his country. In the long disturbances in Unyamwezi between 1861 and about 1875, the Swahili-Arabs assumed the role of overmighty subjects in the small Nyamwezi states by raiding for ivory, cattle and foodstuffs. This is not to say, however, that they usurped the political position of the local rulers.

Among the Africans of the interior, new social relationships were formed. The Nyamwezi, for example, because they began to travel extensively between their country and the coast and to other parts of East and Central Africa, ensured safe passage by entering into joking relations, known as *utani*, with nearly all the peoples through whose territory the trade routes passed. The *utani* relationship ensured for them the friendship of all the societies with whom the link was maintained. Through the caravan trade, ideas and beliefs were spread from their regions of origin to other parts of East Africa. According to Kimambo, the idea of spirit possession was unknown among the Pare until it was introduced by the visiting Shambaa traders.[1] In Unyamwezi, the rituals of the society of medical experts, known as the *uyege*, were carried to other communities at this period. Such medicine men (*waganga*) were found along the routes in the company of caravans as guides or porters, who rendered their services whenever called upon. This was also the time when the Tutsi introduced the Chwezi cult into Unyamwezi. It attracted so many adherents that the ruler of Unyanyembe in 1860 tried to expel the Tutsi herdsmen from his territory.

Muslim religious ideas made little impact on the Africans at this period. The only area where Islam secured a foothold for a time was in Buganda. Here Kabaka Mutesa, who reigned for most of the period under review, sympathized with the religion of the Arabs for nearly ten years. He observed the Ramadan fast, and tried to force his subordinate chiefs and pages to adopt Islam. About 1875, however, he suddenly changed in the face of severe outside pressures, particularly the Egyptian attempts to gain control of the headwaters of the Nile, and gave up the religion. Those of his pages who would not abandon the faith and insulted his royal person by what the *kabaka* regarded as their religious fanaticism, were now persecuted. Islam thus suffered a severe set-back, and from then until his death in 1884 the *kabaka* began to dally with Christianity in both Roman Catholic and Anglican forms.

In Unyanyembe also, some of the ruling aristocracy were said to have adopted Islam. Isike, for example, was reported to be observing the Ramadan fast by the 1880s. In 1883 he compelled the White Fathers resident in his state to send him the Ramadan presents. A number of other princes and chiefs as well as the local concubines of the Arabs of Tabora were believed to have been converted to the Muslim faith. In Unyamwezi Islam secured no significant following; in Buganda a minority of people remained loyal Muslims. Among the interior peoples only the Yao became strongly attached to the Muslim faith through contacts with the east coast.

Outside these three areas, Islam made no headway in the East African interior. Nor did the Arabs themselves appear keen to spread the faith. They and their Muslim followers regarded themselves and were seen as special people. They were known as *waungwana* or 'civilized persons', as against the African infidels, and they did not show any desire to

[1] Kimambo, *Political history*, 189–90.

raise the Africans to the status of 'civilized' by converting them in large numbers.

Another significant impact of the caravan trade on the social life of the Africans was the modification of the traditional determinants of social status. Formerly it was the possessors of grain, the great ritual experts, and the hunters of game who wielded influence in East African society. These were the people who provided for the community the necessary protection against hunger, disease and enemies. With the advent of the coastmen and the introduction of imported commodities and new opportunities, the old order began to yield place to a new. The possession of the traditional status determinants was no longer enough to command high social influence. Those who were in trade were often able not only to amass more grain, but also to own quantities of imported commodities, which enabled them to offer their people security against hunger and the danger of hostile enemies. Hence the trading community, including the resident coastmen, became people of outstanding social influence. They had multitudes of followers, they lived in larger houses, they maintained extensive farms and consequently had considerable stores of grain and livestock. Most important, they often had firearms and gunpowder in their possession, so that they became useful allies to their host societies in cases of invasion. Moreover, having travelled outside their own community, they possessed a broader general experience. They thus formed a kind of agricultural and commercial élite.

Among the Nyanyembe of Unyamwezi, to be an average hunter was not enough to win high social respect. It was necessary to hunt elephants that earned the coveted coastal beads, wire and cloth. Elephant hunters became so important in the social life of the people that they were an indispensable group in the election and coronation of the Nyanyembe rulers. They formed themselves into a guild known as the *uyege*, and it became the practice that the closing ceremony, before the Nyanyembe ruler was recognized as a full-fledged *ntemi*, was the ritual shaving of his hair while he was sitting on the carcass of an elephant killed by the *Wayege* for the purpose. By this practice the *ntemi* was in essence initiated into the guild of hunters. In other words, membership of the *uyege* was regarded as a necessary status which the *ntemi* must attain before he could be acceptable.

A similar development has been reported among the Palwo during the same period. Elephant hunters became very important socially. They held lengthy and elaborate social functions, they married many wives and purchased new slaves. Even slaves who became successful hunters moved up the social ladder. This change was reflected in the politics of the people, because the fishermen, who had previously had more wealth and so higher social influence in the traditional society, were gradually displaced by the elephant hunters and traders.

THE POLITICAL IMPACT OF THE COASTMEN

The Arab impact on the politics of the East African peoples was profound. One of the immediate results of the increasing interaction between the coast and the interior was the extension of Zanzibari influence. As we have noted earlier, Sayyid Sa'īd, when he embarked upon his commercial invasion of the interior, attempted to ensure the safety of the coastal traders by entering into trade treaties with some of the rulers of the interior states. His successor, Sayyid Bargash, maintained this relationship by corresponding with African rulers and through exchanges of gifts, as with Mutesa of Buganda, Mkasiwa of Unyanyembe and Mirambo of Urambo. In these ways the influence of the Zanzibari sultan spread into the interior; his letters of introduction given to Europeans and others travelling into the East African hinterland were treated with respect, and the Zanzibari flag borne by the coastal caravans was recognized and honoured.

Zanzibari influence was established in the interior through the medium of the coastal traders themselves. They founded trading colonies in various places where they lived 'comfortably or even splendidly'. Commenting on one of the Arab settlements in Unyanyembe in 1857, Richard Burton remarked that the 'gardens are extensive and well-planted, they receive regular supplies of merchandize, comforts and luxuries from the coast, they are surrounded by troops of concubines and slaves . . . rich men have riding-asses from Zanzibar and even the poorest keep flocks and herds'.[1] They also derived a great deal of political power and influence from their possession of large quantities of guns and gunpowder, and private armies numbering in some cases up to 300 men. For the East African peoples, therefore, the relative affluence displayed by the Arabs of the interior was a reflection of the wealth of the coastal communities and the power of the Zanzibari sultan. The Arabs, because of their control of the commerce of the interior and the attendant social prestige which they enjoyed, easily gained the confidence of the rulers of the societies in which they settled.

[1] Burton, *Lake regions*, I, 328.

They sent gifts to the rulers, gave various forms of assistance to factions of the ruling aristocracies, and in some cases made their presence felt by raiding weak communities.

A typical example of an area where the Swahili-Arab commercial community exercised this kind of political influence was Unyanyembe. Here two main colonies of coastmen were to be found, at Tabora and Kwihara. One missionary described Tabora as 'a second Zanzibar without the sea . . .'. From the time of Ntemi Ifundikila of Unyanyembe (c. 1840–58), the coastmen maintained congenial relations with the rulers of the state. One of the prominent Unyanyembe Arabs, Mohammed b. Juma, married the eldest daughter of Ntemi Ifundikila. On the death of Ifundikila, his successor, Mnywasele, gained the assistance of the powerful Arab community of Tabora and was able to expel his greatest political rival, Mkasiwa, from the kingdom. However, a year or two later, Mnywasele grew apprehensive of the power of the trading community of his state and tried to establish greater control over it. Being affected adversely by the *ntemi*'s new policy, the Nyanyembe turned against him and gave their support to the exiled political rival then living in the Nyamwezi kingdom of Ulyankhulu. Thus they became intimately involved in a political rising in Unyanyembe in 1860, which led to the overthrow of Mnywasele and the accession of Mkasiwa. From 1860 onwards the Arabs played an ever increasing role in the politics of Unyanyembe. They took an active part in prosecuting the war against the expelled *ntemi*, Mnywasele, who persisted in his attempts to defeat Unyanyembe and regain his power from 1861 until 1865. They also provoked hostilities with Mirambo of Urambo and dragged Unyanyembe into a prolonged war with Urambo, which lasted from 1871 until the death of Mirambo in 1884. During the war, they not only fought on the side of Unyanyembe, but they appealed to the sultan of Zanzibar for military assistance. Sayyid Bargash obliged them by sending about 3,000 troops to fight with the Nyanyembe people against Mirambo. Just prior to the Unyanyembe–Urambo wars, the sultan had appointed an Arab to act as his representative in Tabora and with the coastal community there.

The extent of this Swahili-Arab impact led the Europeans who passed through Unyanyembe at this time to conclude that Unyanyembe was under Arab control, and their conclusions have continued to be echoed by modern historians. It is the writer's belief that this conclusion is, to say the least, an overstatement of the extent of Arab influence. There is no doubting the fact that the coastmen wielded great political influence in Tabora and Kwihara. Because of the military resources at their disposal, and because they had been partly instrumental in the accession of the Nyanyembe *ntemi*, they were in a position to exercise some influence over the rulers of Unyanyembe. Nevertheless, they did not have the final say in the politics of that state. Rather the evidence suggests that power remained undisputedly in the hands of the traditional rulers of the state. Even between 1860 and about 1876, when Unyanyembe was in a precarious position politically, because of severe pressures from rival Nyamwezi states anxious to take over control of the ivory trade and political supremacy from Unyanyembe, Ntemi Mkasiwa of Unyanyembe nonetheless remained in control. This was true, despite the fact that he had to seek the assistance of the resident Arabs and other great men to fight his wars. Arabs were not the only foreigners to enjoy this privilege in Unyanyembe; other non-Nyanyembe African residents who had the means to wield such an influence did so. Tutsi herdsmen, and hunters and traders who had migrated into the state, were mobilized to increase the strength of the Nyanyembe army. The Arab role was therefore that of co-operating with the indigenous authority in resisting external aggression, which threatened their common security and commercial interests.

In fact, from the 1870s on, the security of the coastmen in the interior was wholly dependent upon the protection offered by the Nyanyembe warriors, like Magohe, Swetu, Kasuvbi and Inwele mwana Katwe, through whose efforts Mirambo was prevented from over-running Unyanyembe and driving them away.

In Ujiji, as in Unyanyembe, the coastmen had founded their own settlement away from the area occupied by the indigenous Jiji and Ha. Through the efforts of a Swahili-Arab called Mwinyi Kheri, the coastmen had entered into a relationship with the *mwami* (king) of the Ha, which allowed them to live in Ujiji with little interference from the Jiji ruler. To consolidate his position, Mwinyi Kheri married the daughter of the chief of Ugoyi, in whose district the trade town of Ujiji was founded. Thus the Arabs were able to control the trade passing through their colony and to hinder missionary activity on the shores of the lake. In Ujiji therefore they did not control the *mwami*. Their relationship was such that it was mutually beneficial to both sides.

The political relations of the coastmen with the interior states were determined essentially by their need to be on good terms with African rulers for political and economic security. The coastmen were generally respected for their wealth and were regarded as the bringers of prosperity. Moreover, they were often in possession of much-needed firearms, which made the African rulers court their support in wars against one another. This was their major source of influence. It is doubtful whether the coastal traders were any more the agents of Zanzibari imperialism than they were the propagators of Islam. Wherever they became involved in local wars on the side of one of the belligerent states or factions, or whenever they had to engage in wars against African rulers on their own, it was usually in defence of their commercial interests. They never fought to rule the people. The presence of the representatives of the Zanzibari sultan in Tabora and Ujiji was not a demonstration of Zanzibari political control over the African rulers and peoples; such officials were expected to take care of the commercial interests of the sultan and the great commercial houses of Zanzibar. They had very limited political power even over the Arabs themselves, and some of them were ejected from office by the Arabs of the interior without the prior approval of the sultan of Zanzibar.

The behaviour of the coastal traders in Buganda was not significantly different from those of Unyanyembe and Ujiji. In the reign of Suna of Buganda, Swahili-Arabs had reached the country and assisted the *kabaka* in a military campaign against the people of Busoga. About 1844 Suna's successor, Mutesa, came under the influence of Ahmad b. Ibrahim, who not only acted as the *kabaka*'s Muslim teacher, but also was believed to have at times been co-opted 'as a supernumerary member of Mutesa's state council'. His advice was sought on questions arising out of Buganda's contact with the outside world. Ahmad b. Ibrahim was, for example, a major figure in the negotiations between Kabaka Mutesa and the agents of the khedive of Egypt, who had come to Buganda with the objective of annexing it. Ahmad and other Zanzibari traders influenced Mutesa against the Egyptian envoy, because they feared that the Egyptian move would jeopardize their commercial interests in Buganda. He also assisted Emin Pasha's withdrawal of the Egyptian garrison at Mruli. More coastmen were concentrated in Unyanyembe, Ujiji and Buganda than in any other areas of the interior. Consequently the coastmen elsewhere exercised less political influence over interior rulers. Here and there, traders were known to have assisted one local ruler against another for various commercial reasons. Sometimes the coastmen fought directly against African communities, as in Uvinza, where Tippu Tip fought the Uvinza ruler over road tolls, or in Urambo and Kilila, where Mirambo engaged the Arabs in combat. However, these wars did not bring the Arabs political control.

Despite this extensive Swahili-Arab penetration of the interior, there was hardly any area where their influence resulted in outright political authority. Where the coastmen founded colonies, as in Tabora and Ujiji, one of the resident Arabs was appointed as the head of the expatriate community. But the powers of these men were often limited and, as has been shown above, they had very little to do with local African governments. The only known exceptions were Sayyid Sa'īd's conquest of Kaole to open the roads through Uzaramo, and the fact that the Doe were said to be paying tribute to Zanzibar in the 1850s.

While it may be true that the Swahili-Arab commercial invasion of the interior did not lead to their control of East African peoples, it nevertheless had a tremendous impact on the character of political authority and patterns of relationships both within individual states and between one state and its neighbours. One significant change that would appear to have swept through the whole of East Africa was an increasing dependence of political power on military rather than religious authority. Formerly, the major foundation of political power had been religious. The power of Pare leaders had been founded on their ability to make rain. Cult priests had wielded enormous influence among the peoples of south-eastern Tanzania. Rulers in Unyamwezi owed their positions to their descent from the founders of their societies, who were felt to have had immense ritual power. Such rulers had as their main socio-political functions the organization of prayers for rain during droughts, the performance of rituals to open the planting seasons, sacrifice to the state ancestors for the welfare of the community, and the proper administration of the food resources of the state. They were hedged round with religious taboos and hardly appeared in public during the day. Commoners seldom planned the overthrow of rulers, for the public would be apprehensive of the evils that would follow the accession of persons not related to the royal houses. Except within the interlacustrine region, inter-state hostilities generally took the form of minor raids, and able-bodied youths, recruited *ad hoc*, were able to take care of state defence. There were therefore no standing armies, and the question of war and peace was generally not one of the major problems with which rulers had to grapple. What the people demanded of the rulers, on the contrary, was security against both the uncertainties of the harsh East African environment and the displeasure of their state's ancestors. Rulers were therefore expected to possess the supernatural mediatory qualities that would enable them to provide these necessities.

With the coming of the coastmen, the religious basis of political power weakened in importance and rapidly gave way to more secular, military power. The reason was that changes had occurred in the economic, social and political conditions of East Africa. Arab trade had opened up new avenues of economic prosperity, and individuals and states vied with each other to gain the profits of the trade. Guns and gunpowder had been introduced by the coastal traders and, from the 1860s on enormous quantities of these foreign weapons found their way into various parts of the interior. The manner in which wealth and firearms were distributed among the people was to determine the nature of political relations both within individual states and between one state and the others. Those who succeeded in gaining wealth and weapons within a state often succeeded in taking over political power from the original ruling houses; those states with the easiest access to these new sources of power began to wield more influence over their less fortunate neighbours.

Taking first the changes in political activity within states, there was a marked intensification of the struggle for political power. Princes of the ruling lineages, who were able to gain sufficient wealth and accumulate the new weapons, often found no difficulty in attracting followers to themselves. Some of them readily found foreign allies. Such princes tended to defy the authority of ruling relatives and pose a threat to the stability of the state. They were very influential in society and with their wealth could lobby for the support of the king-makers. Furthermore, with the commercial upsurge of the period, political office began to offer more valuable rewards: the rulers received gifts from various sources; they exchanged their traditional tribute for new commodities from international markets; and they exacted a tribute in tusks. As in West Africa, some of the rulers even perverted the traditional judicial system in such a way as to enable them to supply their slave-trading clients with criminals convicted at their courts. The increased prestige and material rewards accruing to the ruler as a result of his office made the office more attractive to the princes than had previously been the case. Succession to the throne began to be more keenly contested. In some areas, bloody succession struggles became more common. In many areas, the traditional criteria for electing new rulers were thrown aside. Increasingly, the princes who had demonstrated their military superiority over their rivals were installed, whether they were qualified under the customary requirements or not. Often those princes who did not succeed in winning power indulged in acts of sabotage, aimed at the downfall of their successful rival. Some organized conspiracies, others boldly antagonized the ruler and created local political crises. There were also cases where disappointed princes moved away from the kingdom with their followers and imposed their rule over less powerful communities.

The significance of all this is that rulers of East Africa ceased to rely on their traditional religious authority for the retention of political power. They devised means either of weakening their opponents or of strengthening their positions through possession of secular sources of power. Some rulers tried to control the trade in firearms by establishing a royal monopoly over importation. This device was most successful in the kingdom of Buganda. It did not succeed in Usambara and Ufipa, where it was also attempted. Some rulers established a royal body-guard, occasionally enlarged into a standing army, thus making themselves more independent of the provincial chiefs. In some parts rulers tried to solve the problem of their recalcitrant relatives by appointing their sons, relatives, dependants, and even commoners upon whom they could rely, to chiefships in the outlying districts and provinces.

The shift in the basis of political power opened up opportunities for Arab traders to play a role in African politics, but also indicated that African societies were adapting themselves to the new circumstances in a manner which would make an Arab take-over more and more difficult to achieve. The situation might be contrasted briefly with the Egyptian presence in the northern interlacustrine region, where the aliens were primarily an army of occupation protecting their traders. With very little dependence upon Acholi rulers for their security, the traders were not inclined to involve the Acholi in trade except as menials, porters and interpreters. Since the military dictated policy, there was a strong reluctance to supply firearms to the Acholi. Thus, without the development of entrepreneurship, the accumulation of wealth or the possession of firearms, few of the factors which led to a change in the basis of leadership among the Nyamwezi were present in Acholi. The alien presence was almost entirely destructive. In response, some Acholi states migrated away from areas of alien concentration, others, such as Patiko, fragmented into insignificant political units. Only one Acholi state, Padibe, responded in the manner of the Nyamwezi states. Under Rwot (king) Ogwok, Padibe expanded its borders, developed a new bureaucratic structure, set up new industries such as weaving, began the adoption of Arab dress styles, and organized a standing army. Of all the Acholi states, only Padibe seems to have turned the alien presence to advantage.[1]

The turbulence that characterized the internal politics of the East African states in the era of the coastal trade derived not only from the competition among the princes; powerful commoners were also involved. We have seen above that in some parts of East Africa, as in Unyamwezi, trade with the coast was not successfully controlled by the states. Some commoners were able to amass enough wealth and military power to gain social and political recognition in their societies. Such successful merchants were able to bribe or buy their way into political offices. They formed the major support behind the contesting princes and often aligned with political factions in competition with one another. They constituted a new form of political élite, whose views could not be overlooked and who wielded notable influence on the rulers of their states. The basis of their influence was not their ritual knowledge, but their material wealth and military power.

This development was discernible in a number of East African communities. A typical example was the Shambaa country of Usambara from the time of the ruler Kimweri ya Nyumbai (that is, from the early nineteenth century to the 1860s). The shrines which constituted the strength of the Kilindi rulers of Usambara were in Vugha, the ritual capital of the region. Until the time of Kimweri, the kings' authority had depended largely upon their rain-making abilities and their right to arbitrate local disputes. The relative inaccessibility of Vugha further strengthened the kings' position, because it was easily defended. Multitudes of people thus fled to Vugha for protection, while witches and other social outcasts were often sent to the capital. As a result, its population was estimated to be 3,000 by the 1850s.

With the advent of the coastmen and the development of the caravan trade, the authority of Vugha was undermined and there was an increasing split in the centres of ritual and war. In the new situation, the commercial and military position of the district of Mazinde on the caravan route became much more important, and the power of the chiefs of Mazinde much more pervasive. This change in the relationship between Vugha and Mazinde was only fully felt after the death of Kimweri and the succession of one of his grandsons, Shikulwavu.

Although Kimweri had attempted to monopolize the trade with the coastal merchants, he had not been able to prevent his brother Semboja

[1] P. Owot, 'Padibe during the Aconya', in J. Onyangoku-Odongo and J. B. Webster (eds.), *The Central Lwo during the Aconya* (forthcoming).

from trading with the foreign merchants and accumulating wealth. Semboja also purchased huge quantities of firearms. Through trading, he came into contact with the Taita, with whom he later formed a political alliance. Young Shikulwavu was at an even greater disadvantage than Kimweri since, by social convention, he was supposed to be respectful to his uncles. The political realities forced him to try to control those who were his subordinate chiefs. This naturally led to disagreements with many of them and brought him into open conflict with Semboja. Ostensibly, this quarrel was over one of Semboja's slave women who fled to Vugha and was given sanctuary by Shikulwavu. Thereupon, Semboja called for the resistance of his Taita allies, and used his greater military power to storm Vugha successfully and kill Shikulwavu. His wealth, guns, and foreign support had thus given Semboja the means to challenge the ritual authority that had been the traditional basis of Shambaa political life.

After his victory, Semboja did not become king, but rather installed his son, another Kimweri, at Vugha, while he remained at his trading town of Mazinde from where he controlled Vugha. His success introduced a new era in the politics of Usambara. He had neither inherited the rituals of the Kilindi rulers, nor moved to the traditional capital, nor did he depend upon the local population for power. His authority depended on his superior military resources and an alliance with non-Shambaa peoples. In other words his authority was based on secular wealth and military power. His kind of politics was emulated by Shikulwavu's rightful successor, Chanyenghea. The latter joined the Bondei in effecting what has since been known as the Kiva rebellion. The Bondei had been brought under the power of the Kilindi rulers. They rebelled and killed all the members of the Kilindi dynasty whom they found to be in sympathy with Semboja. As a result of the Kiva rebellion the Bondei regained their independence, and with their support Chanyenghea gained control over much of eastern Usambara, while Semboja and his son held the west including Vugha. Thereafter each ruler sought foreign allies to buttress his position.[1]

Similar changes also occurred among the other peoples of eastern and north-eastern Tanzania. The Zigua, said to be originally peaceful, were 'rendered terrible by the possession of firearms ...'.[2] They ceased to follow hereditary chiefs, blood feuds became common and a number of petty chiefs sprang up whose powers depended entirely on

[1] The section on the Shambaa is based largely on S. Feiermann, 'The Shambaa', in *Tanzania before 1900*.   [2] Burton, *Lake regions*, I, 125–6.

their wealth, their weapons and their slaves. This was probably how individuals like Bwana Heri of Uzigua rose to prominence among his peoples.

Among the Pare, the caravan trade aroused rivalry among the chiefs. Geographically, the Pare were separated into two main groups, the northern and southern Pare. By the eighteenth century the Pare of the north had been brought together as a unit called Ugweno, and a single clan had become predominant. The rulers of Ugweno had been able to win and maintain their position because of their control of the society's initiation ceremonies and through the diffusion of a common legend of migration. However, in the late eighteenth century a section of the Ugweno known as Usangi broke away from the Ugweno community. Early in the nineteenth century, the authority of the Ugweno ruler over the remaining districts also began to weaken. This was as a result of the influx of coastal traders, who equipped the subordinate chiefs in charge of districts athwart the caravan routes with guns and gunpowder. Since the capital of Ugweno was remote from the caravan routes, the ruler was not as quickly affected by these foreign influences as were some of his subordinate chiefs. The latter were able to assert their effective independence, thus multiplying the states in Pare. The district of Hedaru, for example, is said to have broken into fourteen independent units.

Realizing his weakness *vis-à-vis* his subordinate chiefs, the Ugweno ruler of the time, Gbendewa, tried to arrest the break-up of the kingdom. He built a new and strongly fortified capital, raised a standing army for the state and a strong bodyguard for himself. Gbendewa succeeded in recovering some control in the northern districts of Ugweno, but, being militarily inferior to some of the southern chiefs, Gbendewa was unable to re-establish his authority over them. He therefore sought outside assistance. He allied with Rindi, ruler of the Chaga kingdom of Moshi. Moshi troops were brought in, and, with their help, Gbendewa organized a number of military expeditions into the southern districts. Although he succeeded in bringing some of the chiefs under his control, his alliance with Rindi turned into a double-edged sword. Rindi was as anxious as Gbendewa to control the caravan trade in the area. Upon discovering the weaknesses of Gbendewa during the joint expeditions in Ugweno, Rindi turned against Gbendewa and invaded the Ugweno capital to capture the cattle and other goods which Gbendewa had amassed. Southern Ugweno split into several tiny states in competition with one another for the control of the trade.

The political significance of the coastal trade with the interior peoples was more pronounced in Unyamwezi than in most other parts of East Africa for a number of reasons. Chief among these was the presence of a considerable population of coastmen who were resident in various parts of Unyamwezi, particularly in Tabora and Kwihara. These traders had at their disposal large quantities of guns and gunpowder and hundreds of slaves and servants. In Unyanyembe, the Arab community became an essential part of the new political élite of the kingdom, and after 1860 it played a vital role in the struggle for political authority. Another reason was that trade in Unyamwezi was not regulated as it was, for example, in Buganda. Consequently, more people, whether they were commoners or princes, were able to acquire the new sources of political power. The size of the trading élite with which the Nyamwezi rulers had to deal was therefore larger than those of Usambara, Pare or Buganda. Although the great merchant-princes of the caravan trade in Unyamwezi did not try to usurp the thrones of Unyamwezi and form new dynasties, they nevertheless wielded great influence in their respective societies, and often constituted a political élite upon whom princes depended in order to secure power.

Hence in many Nyamwezi states the matrilineal system of royal succession was undermined, because princes began to rise to political power more for their ability to defeat other rivals than because they were qualified under the traditional succession rules. Thus Mtyela Kasanda, otherwise known as Mirambo, came to power in Uyowa and Ulyankhulu after overthrowing better qualified princely rivals. He united both kingdoms into the larger state of Urambo. Similarly, Isale Swetu, who was popularly known as Ifundikila, of Unyanyembe, succeeded his father after eliminating rivals such as Mtanduki, Mkosi and the sons of Mpasi. At Uyui one of the princes struggling to come to power had to appeal to Ifundikila of Unyanyembe for assistance against rivals in the 1850s. This development has led some historians to conclude that succession in most of Unyamwezi at this time changed from matriliny to patriliny. This is an oversimplification of the nature of the change. Succession did not become patrilineal as such. It became competitive, and the strongest princes, some of whom were at times sons of the former rulers, succeeded to the throne. Unyanyembe is a typical example of such a case. The successors of Ifundikila, Mnywasele and Mkasiwa, were not his sons. They were relatives who had to compete with other princes before coming to power.

Princes who did not succeed in gaining political power in their states often indulged in subversion. In Unyanyembe they allied with the powerful Arab residents and influential indigenous merchants against the rulers. Thus Karunde joined forces with the coastmen and Mkasiwa to overthrow Mnywasele in 1860. When Mkasiwa came to power after the Unyanyembe crisis, many of his relatives continued to plot against him in a bid to seize the Nyanyembe throne. Some of these princes, like Nyungu ya Mawe, left the kingdom with their supporters and, after conquering less powerful peoples, imposed their rule on them. Nyungu went to Ukimbu, where he established the empire of Kiwele. Nsimba Kavbung'ando left Unyanyembe and founded the Uluila state, with his main base at Ngesela in Ukonongo. In other words, from about 1860 the increasing dynamism of politics in the states of Unyamwezi began to affect inter-state relationships. Large-scale wars became common, as rulers such as Mirambo of Urambo began to expand their kingdoms. Mirambo himself brought states under his power that were in no way related to his own, thus neglecting the traditional belief among the Nyamwezi people that only the descendants of the traditional rulers of a people, who had links with the state ancestors, could rule and make sacrifices to the state gods.

Rulers in Unyamwezi responded to the challenge of their age by attempting to secure possession of the secular sources of power as well as the ritual ones. They maintained bodyguards of young and dependable warriors. Some like Mirambo, Mkasiwa of Unyanyembe, Mtinginya of Usongo, Nyungu ya Mawe of Kiwele, maintained large standing armies, known generally as *ruga ruga*, which were armed with guns and spears. Some of the Nyamwezi rulers led the armies to battle. In such cases the rulers secured the loyalty of their soldiers and people through their personal charisma and sheer military genius. Those rulers who did not become warriors had to work out new political relationships with the powerful forces in their states to remain in power. Mkasiwa of Unyanyembe was an example of such: he avoided the battlefield after he became the *ntemi* of Unyanyembe in 1861, even though he ruled Unyanyembe during the most turbulent period of Nyamwezi history. He kept the throne by employing various skilful diplomatic and political devices to maintain the loyalty of his subjects and the Unyanyembe Arabs. For example, he sponsored the development of a standing army for Unyanyembe and paid experts from Buloha to train them in the Ngoni techniques of warfare. He then ensured that he had full control of the leadership of this army by establishing close ties with the four principal military leaders. He adopted one of them as his son, he married his daughter to another, and the overall head of the army was his loyal slave. Thus, although he allowed the military leaders to use their discretion in many matters, he nevertheless controlled policy-making in the state.

It is particularly difficult to sum up the Swahili–Arab impact in East Africa, because it was an interrupted historical process, the coastmen being overtaken by the intrusion of the Europeans. However, even without the Europeans, the relations between coast and interior would have changed drastically within a few decades, because ivory was a rapidly wasting natural resource. The disappearance of the elephant and appearance of the European invaders were almost contemporary phenomena. As ivory became scarce, would the coastal presence have faded, changed its economic objectives, or would it have caused a more intensive struggle between the two regions for control of a declining resource? Some will see in the relations between East Africans and Swahili-Arabs in the nineteenth century the classical pattern of economic penetration leading almost inevitably to political control. Others will argue that the Swahili-Arabs drew inland peoples into economic dependency, developing foreign tastes which contributed little if anything to their overall well-being or standard of living, and failing to provide them with the means or skills to establish a locally generated and self-sustaining improvement in the quality of life. Yet others will be impressed with the degree to which inland Africans participated in commerce in the nineteenth century, and will contrast this unfavourably with the limited commercial role which they played or were assigned in the later colonial period. For yet others, less interested in economic theory, nineteenth-century East Africa will remain a fascinating study of cultural and social interaction between two distinct and yet in some ways compatible peoples. In truth the complex events of East Africa in the nineteenth century can be made to lend some support to each of these views.

CHAPTER 9

THE NGUNI OUTBURST

By the mid-eighteenth century the greater part of South Africa had been settled by Bantu-speaking peoples through a prolonged process which may have begun as early as the third century AD. The Bantu replaced or absorbed earlier populations of San hunters and gatherers, and in some areas Khoi pastoralists also, though some survived in rugged or poorly watered country, or in dependence on Bantu groups. From these peoples the South African Bantu speakers had acquired a number of distinctive click consonants and incorporated them in their languages.

Bantu settlement was densest in the south-east, along the eastern coastal corridor between the Drakensberg mountains and the sea where the relatively high rainfall and fertile soils provided the most congenial conditions for human settlement. By 1800 the Bantu had reached the Great Fish river and had begun to spread into the lands to the south-west, between the Fish and Sunday rivers, named Zuurveld by the Cape Dutch settlers.

On the high veld, west of the Drakensberg and east of the Kalahari, the Bantu occupied much of the area of the modern Transvaal, Botswana, Orange Free State and the less mountainous parts of Lesotho, but had not in general advanced as far south as the Orange river.

Two main linguistic and cultural groups had differentiated themselves among the South African Bantu. The Nguni-speaking peoples lived along the eastern coastal belt between the Drakensberg and the sea, while the Sotho- and Tswana-speaking peoples occupied the interior plateau. West of the Kalahari, the Ambo and Herero in South-West Africa (Namibia) belonged to a third linguistic grouping.

In spite of linguistic and cultural differences the Nguni and the Sotho–Tswana peoples were in many respects very similar. Both groups were made up of communities of cattle keepers who also practised hoe agriculture. Both had patrilineal family systems. Both were organized in political units structured along basically similar lines. Though the two groups for the most part occupied distinct geographic areas, separation was by no means complete. Numerous communities of Nguni origin were scattered among the Sotho–Tswana peoples of

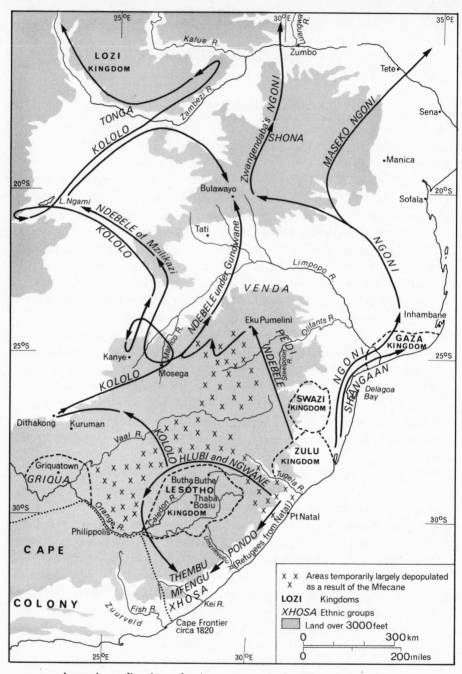

12 Approximate directions of main movements in the *Mfecane* in southern Africa

the Transvaal high veld. Sotho peoples lived alongside Nguni communities in the north-western corner of the eastern coastal belt, notably in the neighbourhood of modern Swaziland and north-western Zululand.

THE BEGINNING OF STATE BUILDING

Towards the end of the eighteenth century the political institutions of the southern Bantu were under increasing strain. Over much of South Africa settled farming was long established. In the healthy climate of South Africa, free for the most part from malaria or tsetse fly, the population had probably expanded fairly rapidly and was continuing to do so. The absence of written records makes any accurate quantitative analysis impossible, but the frequency of chiefdom fission revealed in traditional accounts suggests a very rapid growth indeed.

For peoples living near the periphery of settlement, the traditional process of chiefdom division and the removal of one section of the community to as yet unoccupied land could still go on. Even within the area long occupied by Bantu-speaking peoples, there were undoubtedly still pockets of uncleared land here and there. In areas well behind the frontiers of settlement, however, it became increasingly difficult for new chiefdoms founded by secession to find suitable grazing lands without coming into conflict with established occupiers. Continuing expansion to the south was coming to an end as a consequence of the establishment and expansion of the white colony at the Cape, where individual white families expanded rapidly into the Zuurveld to occupy large acreages for ranching. In 1811–12 the line of Bantu settlement was driven back when British troops drove the Xhosa from the Zuurveld back across the Fish river.[1]

On the interior plateau the effects of white expansion made themselves felt more indirectly. Groups of Khoi, known as the Korana, driven northward by the expansion of the Cape Colony, moved across the Orange and adopted a life of brigandage, preying on the most southerly Tswana and Sotho communities. They were followed by groups of mixed Khoi–White descent, who left the colony in response to increased racial discrimination. Under missionary influence this mixed community took the name Griqua, settled around the junction of the Orange and Vaal rivers and established a polity with its capital at Griquatown. Subsequent divisions over leadership led to a series of

[1] The first attempt by the whites to drive the Xhosa from the Zuurveld took place in 1779 but it had only very temporary success.

breakaways. Two further Griqua republics were founded, the most significant being that of Adam Kok with its capital at Philippolis in the modern Orange Free State. A fringe group known as the Bergenaars adopted a life of brigandage like the Korana.

Trade, as well as land shortage, may have intensified the movement to form larger political systems. Ivory was exported to the Portuguese at Delagoa Bay in return for cloth, beads and brass bangles. This trade extended into what became Zululand, and onto the interior plateau.[1]

On the interior plateau, the Pedi[2] established a substantial kingdom in the eighteenth century in the area around the Steelpoort river on a natural route to Delagoa Bay. Not very much is known about the early stages of the formation of the Pedi kingdom, but it seems that their forces were organized in age-regiments formed after the initiation of young males.[3] Among the Sotho peoples of modern Lesotho and neighbouring areas of the Orange Free State a somewhat similar tendency can be seen in the career of Motlomi, who built up a sphere of influence covering a number of chiefdoms by a policy of dynastic marriages and by exploiting his reputation as a rainmaker, a visionary and a man of wisdom and justice who could be relied upon as a fair arbiter of disputes. His hegemony fell short of real political control and dissolved on his death about 1815. By the early years of the nineteenth century the tendency towards the formation of larger states was so widespread that Alberti, a government official during the period of the Batavian Republic's administration at the Cape (1803–6), writing no doubt with reference mainly to the area near the eastern frontier of the Cape Colony, remarked that the most frequent cause of wars was the ambition of strong chiefs to establish paramountcy over others.[4]

THE NGUNI KINGDOMS

It was in the area now known as Zululand at the northern end of the eastern coastal corridor that expansive state building developed most fully and culminated in a dramatic revolution in the scale and nature of political organization which had far-reaching consequences. The region was long settled by Bantu peoples and a substantial population had

[1] See A. Smith, 'The trade of Delagoa Bay as a factor in Nguni politics 1750–1835', in L. Thompson, ed., *African societies in southern Africa* (London, 1969), 171–89.

[2] Attention has been drawn to the significance of the rise of the Pedi by M. Legassick, 'The Sotho-Tswana peoples before 1800', in Thompson, ed., *African societies in southern Africa*, 86–125.

[3] See D. R. Hunt, 'An account of the Bapedi', *Bantu Studies*, 1937, 5, 275–326.

[4] L. Alberti, *Description physique et historique des Cafres* (Amsterdam, 1811), 186.

grown up,[1] which could only find an outlet to suitable unoccupied land either by migration down the coastal belt or by crossing the Drakensberg onto the interior plateau. The way to the south was impeded by the large numbers of chiefdoms already established in Natal and farther south. Migration across the Drakensberg had taken place repeatedly in the past, leading to the establishment of numerous groups of Nguni origin amongst the Sotho–Tswana peoples of the Transvaal high veld,[2] but the increasing occupation of the high veld by the Sotho–Tswana peoples made movement across the escarpment a hazardous process. The northern part of this densely populated coastal strip was within easy reach of Delagoa Bay and was increasingly participating in the ivory trade. It was an area of contact between Sotho- and Nguni-speakers, whose closely related but slightly differing cultures and institutions could provide a natural stimulus to borrowing and innovation.

About 1790 there arose a number of powerful leaders of Nguni chiefdoms in this area, all of whom attempted by very similar means to build up kingdoms by forcing the chiefs of surrounding communities to accept their paramountcy. Of these leaders the three most powerful were Zwide of the Ndwandwe people, Sobhuza of the Ngwane (later to be known as the Swazi) and Dingiswayo of the Mthethwa group.

The increased tempo and scale of warfare which accompanied the rise of these enlarged states stimulated the development of military organization. One of the most vital institutions of the southern Bantu peoples was the system of manhood initiation, involving circumcision, followed by a period of ritual seclusion during which the initiates were instructed in the *mores* of the group and the behaviour expected of an adult man. Not only was the system of initiation of immense educational, cultural and psychological significance, but it was utilized by some groups in a military and political sense. The shared experience of initiation naturally created a sense of enduring fellowship amongst the initiates. Among many Sotho-speaking groups initiation schools were held on the prompting of chiefs, whenever they had a son of an age to be initiated. After the ending of such an initiation school, all the initiates who had participated in it constituted a group who would fight together in times of war under the leadership of their chiefly

[1] See e.g. the account of the journey through this area of the survivors of the wrecked Portuguese ship *São João Baptista* in 1622. C. R. Boxer, ed., *The tragic history of the sea* (Cambridge, 1959), 190–271.

[2] An analysis of the evidence concerning these groups is given by M. Legassick, 'The Sotho-Tswana peoples before 1800'.

age-mate. They might also be called upon for other forms of corporate activity, such as building a new cattle enclosure for the chief.

The traditional initiation rites could expose a community to considerable danger in times of hostility, particularly in a situation where traditional restraints on military activity were no longer fully operative. An enemy could gain an easy advantage by launching an attack when a high proportion of the young fighting men had been newly circumcised and were not in a position to take part in the fighting or even to defend themselves. In the circumstances of frequent and severe fighting which prevailed in Zululand at the end of the eighteenth century, the traditional circumcision and initiation rites were abandoned by a number of peoples.[1] In their place service in the age-regiments and participation in actual warfare served as the *rite de passage*, marking the transition from adolescence to adulthood.[2] This change, by divorcing age-regiment membership from previous participation in an initiation school, allowed the age-regiment system to be used in a much more effective manner, both as a system of military organization and as a means of integrating members of subordinate communities in an enlarged political system. Age-regiments could now be constituted on the sole basis of apparent age, and young men of conquered tribes could be enrolled in the regiments of their conquerors, where, by fighting alongside members of other groups, they would develop a sense of loyalty and common identity cutting across the boundaries of their original communities. The freeing of the age-regiment system from its original basis in circumcision school membership also destroyed any necessary connection between a particular regiment and a particular prince. Though age-regiments continued to be associated with particular royal households, the 'heads' (*makhanda*) of which served as their headquarters and rallying points, the age-regiments no longer necessarily constituted the personal following of the individual younger members of the royal family, but could become sections of a state army owing ultimate loyalty only to the king. Through this change the regiments could act as a centralizing rather than a centrifugal force.

[1] This argument is necessarily hypothetical. Its probability is strengthened by the fact that the Pondo are known to have abandoned initiation ceremonies when faced with circumstances of acute military danger resulting from the disturbances set in motion by the rise of the Zulu. M. Hunter, *Reaction to conquest* (London, 1961), 165.

[2] Thus among the Zulu young men were only permitted to wear the headring, the insignia of adulthood, and to marry after their regiment had been dissolved. Among the Ndebele young men were given the right to marry and the title *ndoda* (adult man) after a period of active service. Among the Ngoni young men were regarded as adult and were no longer permitted to drink fresh milk after they had served on their first campaign.

The ending of traditional initiation ceremonies and the introduction of the age-regiment system of military organization is sometimes associated with Dingiswayo, who is said to have forbidden the performance of the traditional rites until his conquests should be complete.[1] Though it is not impossible that such a development might have been the result of a single inventive mind, the virtually simultaneous appearance of this pattern amongst a number of different peoples makes it more probable that it arose naturally out of the stress of circumstances.

The growth of a series of large-scale kingdoms in the Zululand area inevitably led to conflicts between them, and thus to an increase in warfare, which in turn accelerated the process of institutional change. The first such conflict between the emerging blocs took place between Zwide and Sobhuza, who came to blows over disputed ownership of farming land along the Pongola river. Sobhuza was defeated and retired with his following into the heart of modern Swaziland. That area then had a mixed population of many small chiefdoms, some being Nguni speakers but the majority Sotho speakers. Using the age-regiment system in its then state of development, Sobhuza gradually brought the different chiefdoms of the area under his paramountcy. A large-scale state thus came into existence which over time developed into the modern Swazi kingdom. Its institutions were based on organizational principles of the Dingiswayo period, but these were subsequently modified as a result of contact with the more highly developed military system of the Zulu. It also adopted some of the political principles of the subjected Sotho population. Through the combination of these different organizational principles, together with the development of the peculiarly Swazi system of a division of authority between the king and the official queen mother, and by the growth of a system of personal clientage, a highly flexible system emerged which focused loyalty on the centre, while allowing considerable autonomy at the periphery to combine strong leadership with a relatively wide measure of participation in political decision taking.[2]

During the early years of the growth of his new kingdom Sobhuza was in a delicate position, and sought to avoid any further conflict with his powerful neighbour by making one of Zwide's daughters his

[1] H. F. Fynn, 'History of Godongwana (Dingizwayo) and (in part) of Chaka' in J. Bird, *The annals of Natal* (Pietermaritzburg, 1888), 1, 60–71.

[2] This account of the military and political organization of the Swazi kingdom is based on H. Kuper, *An African aristocracy* (London, 1947), and H. Beemer, 'The development of the military organization in Swaziland', *Africa*, 10, 1, 1937. See also J. D. Omer-Cooper, *The Zulu aftermath* (London, 1966), 49–56.

great wife. The same determination to avoid conflict governed Swazi relations with Shaka and his successor Dingane. The principle of relying on diplomatic methods and avoiding conflict with potentially more powerful enemies became an established Swazi tradition, which was scrupulously followed in later years in their relations with Europeans.

The elimination of Sobhuza from the Zululand arena left the two most powerful rulers, Dingiswayo and Zwide, face to face. After a series of engagements in which Dingiswayo generally had the advantage, a full-scale collision took place, probably in 1817. Dingiswayo marched with all his forces to meet his enemy, but as the two hosts prepared for battle he went with a small number of his followers to climb a hill from which he could look down on the battlefield. In so doing he fell into an ambush set by his enemy, was captured and subsequently put to death. Deprived of their leader, the Mthethwa forces broke up in confusion and Zwide was left apparently undisputed master of the situation.

SHAKA AND THE ZULU NATION

By this time however a new power was rising in the person of Shaka. He was born to a junior wife of Senzangakona, chief of the Zulu, then a relatively small Nguni chiefdom. While he was still a child, his mother, Nandi, made herself unwelcome at her husband's court on account of her ferocious temper. She was driven out with her son to take refuge amongst her mother's people. Shaka thus grew up among strangers without a father to protect him and suffered much from the taunts and humiliation of his playmates, made worse by his own proud nature and insistence on his chiefly descent. He grew up with a fierce determination to prove himself, a reckless courage and a thirst for power which was his dominant characteristic.

As a young man Shaka served in the age-regiments of Dingiswayo, where his acts of daring won him the title of 'Dingiswayo's hero'. When Senzangakona died Dingiswayo saw a chance to establish his influence over the Zulu by placing his protégé on the throne, and lent Shaka military assistance, with which he succeeded in killing the legitimate heir and establishing himself in his place.

Once established as chief of his own people, Shaka began to put the ideas he had developed while serving in Dingiswayo's army into practice, and in so doing carried the evolution of military and political institutions to a new stage. In the battles in which he had been involved, he had had plenty of opportunity to observe the military inadequacy of the traditional methods of fighting based on the use of long-handled javelins (assegais) which were hurled from a distance. These weapons and tactics, which had served well enough in the small-scale skirmishes of earlier times, were unsuitable for the large, set battles between thousands of men, which were now taking place as a result of the increase in scale of political and military organization. Shaka saw that the tactics of hurling javelins at a distance made close formation fighting impossible, and virtually ruled out the possibility of a really decisive encounter. If his men retained their spears and advanced right up to their enemies behind the defensive wall of linked body-sized shields, they would have their foes at their mercy, and be able to achieve really conclusive victory. Shaka thus armed his regiments with short-handled stabbing spears to be retained throughout battle on pain of death, and drilled them in close formation fighting.[1] The formation generally employed in set battles was known as the 'cow's horns'. The bulk of the army would be drawn up in a solid mass, several ranks deep, known as the 'chest'. In front of the chest, one regiment on the right and one on the left would be thrown out in more extended formation and with a gentle inward curve. The horns would move round the enemy and gradually close in. Their meeting would be the signal for the chest to move forward and destroy the entire hostile force trapped within the encircling horns.

The introduction of these new tactics necessitated prolonged drilling and was related to a further development, the introduction of continuous military service and the barracking of the age-regiments in special military settlements at the royal households, where they remained until formally dissolved and given permission to marry. As a result of this change the value of the age-regiment system as a method of integrating tribal aliens into the community was greatly increased. What was more, the whole balance of power within the political system was radically altered. With the introduction of continuous military service, the bulk of the young men of fighting age were concentrated at the royal households, constituting a permanent standing army at the ruler's immediate command. The rulers of territorial segments not only lost much of the fighting strength which would traditionally

[1] Fynn gives an account of a mock battle which Shaka arranged to convince his followers of the superiority of the new weapons and tactics. As in the case of the use of age-regiments for military purposes, the very rapid adoption of the new weapons by a number of peoples leads one to wonder whether this change may also have been a spontaneous development under stress of military circumstances rather than the invention of a single person. J. Stuart and M. D. Malcolm (eds.), *The diary of Henry Francis Fynn* (Pietermaritzberg, 1950), 16.

have been theirs, but such forces as they retained, made up of older married men, could not compare with those at the king's command. The possibility of a territorial segment head challenging the authority of the ruler or seceding with his local following was greatly reduced.[1] Thus the forces which had obliged chiefs to act with close regard to the advice of powerful segment heads and public opinion at large were considerably weakened.

The power which had been taken from the territorial chiefs now passed to the class of appointed officials known as *indunas*, especially the military commanders appointed to lead regiments and act as commanding officers at the royal homesteads. It is noteworthy that, while there is no evidence of Shaka summoning councils of heads of territorial segments, he was careful to consult closely with his *indunas*, and also to prevent the *indunas* from meeting in his absence.[2] The *indunas* were however in a much weaker position to challenge or restrain the will of the ruler than territorial segment heads under the traditional system. They owed their position to the ruler's appointment and could be removed by him. Above all they lacked the aura of royal descent, and so could neither seek to replace him nor secede to establish themselves as heads of separate communities. Thus, through a change in military organization necessitated by the employment of new tactics and the general development of the military situation, the traditional political system had been subtly transformed. From a decentralized, segmentary system within which power was shared between the ruler and other 'royals', and where the ruler's authority was severely limited, a much more highly centralized, militarist state had emerged with a ruler capable of exercising very wide powers indeed, through control over a large standing army exercised through a bureaucracy of appointed officials.

These changes had taken place without any breach of continuity or the introduction of radically new institutions. Existing institutions were developed and exploited in new ways to face the increasing scale of warfare. The concept of kingship played a particularly vital role, for it was inconceivable for chieftaincy to be exercised by anyone not of royal descent. The chief embodied the unity of his subjects, and this endowed him with theoretically absolute authority.

The circumstances in which the new politico-military system of the Zulu was born and began to grow were perilous indeed, for, soon after Shaka had established himself at the head of the Zulu, his patron

[1] See e.g. N. Isaacs, *Travels and adventures in eastern Africa*, ed. L. Hermann (Van Riebeeck Society, Cape Town, 1936), I, 149.
[2] Fynn, *Diary*, 283–4. Isaacs, *Travels and adventures*, I, 284.

Dingiswayo became involved in the conflict with Zwide which resulted in his death and the dissolution of the Mthethwa hegemony. Shaka had been summoned by his overlord to participate in the campaign, but took no part in the fighting, and on the news of the débâcle returned with his following intact. According to some sources he deliberately betrayed Dingiswayo's intended movements to the enemy, in order to open a way for his own ambitions.[1] In the immediate aftermath of the Mthethwa defeat, however, Shaka's small following was completely at the mercy of the vastly superior forces of the Ndwandwe. It was probably only the relative insignificance of the Zulu which spared them from immediate attack, and gave Shaka a vitally needed breathing space.

He used the time thus gained to bring surrounding communities under his paramountcy, incorporating their young men into his age-regiments. As Shaka continued the process of reconstituting the shattered Mthethwa bloc around himself, Zwide determined to intervene and despatched a number of his regiments to crush the newly rising power. A fierce battle took place at Gqokoli hill. Zulu fighting methods and superior discipline made up for inferiority of numbers, and the Ndwandwe withdrew, leaving a number of Zwide's sons on the field. The battle was narrowly won, however, and the Zulu regiments had been badly mauled. There was a pressing need for Shaka to increase the size of his forces if he were to face the full strength of the Ndwandwe. For this purpose he turned against a neighbouring chiefdom, the Qwabe, on the pretext that they had failed to come to his aid against Zwide. With the aid of a dissident section of the Ndwandwe, the Qwabe were defeated and their young men went to swell the Zulu forces.

Alarmed and infuriated at the repulse of his first expedition, Zwide sent his whole army against the Zulu (probably towards the end of 1818). Faced with this massive invasion, Shaka withdrew before his foes, destroying the food supplies along the way and harassing them with night attacks. Led on by their elusive enemy, the Ndwandwe advanced almost to the Tugela river, but by this time starvation was beginning to tell. As they retreated towards their own country, the Zulu hung around their rear. Then, as they were about to cross the Mhlatuse river, Shaka launched an all-out attack. Worn out by hunger and long marches the Ndwandwe broke and fled. To prevent them regrouping Shaka despatched some of his regiments to pass behind the

[1] Fynn, *Diary*, 15; P. R. Kirby, ed., *Andrew Smith and Natal* (Van Riebeeck Society, Cape Town, 1955), 87.

fleeing enemy and fall upon their civilian population, thus destroying their home base. These tactics were largely successful. Zwide himself narrowly escaped and with a remnant of his following established himself on the upper Nkomati river, where he gradually recruited his forces and prepared for a war of revenge. Other sections of his one-time following, and other peoples who had been associated with the Ndwandwe and found themselves involved in the disaster, fled northwards into the south of modern Mozambique. They included a strong section of the Ndwandwe forces led by Shoshangane.

As this confused mass of straggling groups fled northwards out of the immediate range of his regiments, Shaka was left without a serious rival. Thenceforth his army went out annually on campaign, defeating tribe after tribe, incorporating them in his growing kingdom or driving them out as homeless refugees, and seizing their cattle to swell the vast royal herds.

As his conquests expanded, Shaka employed his new system of military organization as a means of incorporating conquered peoples and building up a kingdom transcending the traditional political groupings. When a chiefdom was conquered it became an additional territorial segment of the kingdom. The bulk of its population continued to live together as a community on their existing lands or, in some cases, on new lands allocated to them by the king. They continued to be administered as far as local matters were concerned by their own chiefs. These however now held their positions at the pleasure of the king, and exercised their authority subject to his overriding authority. In some cases the ruling chief was put to death and a member of the royal line nominated by Shaka established in his place. The young men of fighting age, however, were taken away and incorporated in the royal age-regiments in accordance with their apparent ages. They drilled, danced and fought alongside their age-mates drawn from many different communities within the kingdom, thus acquiring loyalties and a sense of corporate identity transcending that of their own original community.

To accommodate the age-regiments, Shaka established a series of military towns in a central military area of his kingdom. Each of these towns was a royal household, containing a royal section with quarters for the king himself and the royal women, together with the huts of the soldiers. Each of the royal households was headed by a senior female relative of the king, and by a military *induna*, who acted as commanding officer. The system indeed was essentially the traditional system of royal households practised by all Nguni chiefs, adapted to a system of militarist organization.

There was a difference in Shaka's case, however, because he never officially married, and his households were headed, not by his wives, but by other senior female relatives. Shaka appears to have had an obsessive horror of producing an heir, and any woman found pregnant by him was put to death. At his royal households Shaka assembled large numbers of young women who were officially his wards. They were organized into age-regiments on the same principles as the men and took part in ceremonial dances and display.[1] When an age-regiment was deemed to have completed its period of active service and was dissolved, the corresponding female regiment would also be dissolved, and its members given as wives to the soldiers. During the period of active service, the young men were expected to remain strictly celibate. Breaches of this rule, which were understandably not un-common in view of the prolonged periods of service necessitated by continuing warfare, were punished by death when detected.

The sustenance of the regiments, so far as milk and meat were concerned, was supplied from the royal herds.[2] Each regiment had a herd of the king's cattle attached to it, and each herd was made up of beasts with a particular skin colouring. As the shields with which the warriors were equipped were made from the hides of these cattle, each regiment was distinguished by shields of a colour corresponding to that of the herd assigned to it. The logic of the whole pattern of military organization not only fostered the rapid development of common loyalties, and a sense of common identity amongst an originally heterogeneous population, but also focused loyalty and attention on the king. The soldiers lived at royal households under officers personally chosen by Shaka. The meat they ate and the milk they drank were supplied from the king's cattle, and the regiments had a direct interest in the success of the king's wars, by which the herds were maintained and expanded. It was the king who supplied them with their weapons. The king's participation was necessary also in the strengthening

[1] Some Sotho groups formed female age-regiments on the basis of female initiation ceremonies on the same lines as the male regiments. This practice was preserved in the Swazi kingdom until very recently. This may be the origin of what appears such an extra-ordinary feature of Shaka's kingdom. I have not been able to discover any reference to it among Nguni speakers in the pre-Shaka period.

[2] I have not been able to discover any account of how the regiments were supplied with their grain requirements. It is possible that some of the large numbers of young women assembled at Shaka's military towns engaged in agricultural work. The solution of this problem is of great importance for a fuller understanding of the working of Shaka's system.

ceremonies without which the regiments could not go to war with hope of success. Finally, it was the king who dissolved the regiments at the completion of their period of active service, authorized the wearing of the head ring, the insignia of adulthood, and provided the demobilized soldiers with their brides.

The logical simplicity and intense centralization of the military system, however, should not obscure other aspects of the political organization of the kingdom which tended to operate in a different way. Outside the military area, the subjected chiefdoms remained for the most part coherent communities under their own chiefs. Their sense of identity was thus preserved in spite of the centripetal pull of the age-regiment system. As the members of the age-regiments could look forward to demobilization, marriage and retirement within the area of their community of origin, the persistence of pre-Shakan loyalties would be bound to affect loyalties within the military system, just as experiences within the age-regiments would affect attitudes of ex-soldiers when they returned to their homes.[1] The danger to the kingdom was greatest when a chief with a powerful traditional follow-ing also became a leader within the military system. Just such a coinci-dence produced the only major split to occur during the lifetime of Shaka. Mzilikazi, the young chief of the Khumalo, an Nguni chiefdom which seceded from Zwide's kingdom to join Shaka, distinguished himself by his military abilities and became one of Shaka's most trusted generals. Sometime between 1821 and 1823, however, he rejected the authority of his overlord by refusing to send him the booty seized in a successful raid. Shaka sent his regiments to crush the upstart, but after bitter fighting, Mzilikazi made his escape onto the high veld of the modern Transvaal, where he began the process of building up a kingdom of his own on the Zulu model. His people came to be known as Nbebele.

As the Zulu kingdom expanded, its pattern of internal structure and external relationships was bound to become increasingly complex. The economic inefficiency implied by the concentration of such a large part of the available man-power in the military towns, and the high meat consumption of the young warriors, meant that the system could only be supported by the exploitation of surrounding peoples. Every year the regiments must go out and seize more cattle, but the process of raiding and violent seizure of livestock and other commodities was self-destructive. As communities were violently smashed and driven

[1] See the argument in J. D. Omer-Cooper, 'Aspects of political change in the nineteenth-century Mfecane', in Thompson, ed., *African societies in southern Africa*, 207–29.

from their homelands, expeditions had to go farther and farther to find worthwhile loot.

By 1824, Natal had been so fearfully devastated and denuded of its livestock that the Zulu regiments passed right through it to fall upon the Pondo. It became necessary, therefore, to establish more stable relationships with external groups, which could yield a steady supply of food and other requirements in the form of tribute. At the same time, with the expansion of Shaka's conquests and the fame of his power, surrounding peoples became increasingly interested in gaining his protection and thus immunity from attack. Sobhuza of the Ngwane (later Swazi) and, among the Sotho-speaking chiefdoms of the high veld, Moshoeshoe of the Sotho, and Sikonyela of the Tlokwa, all paid tribute to Shaka. The Thonga chiefdoms lying to the north of the Nguni, between Zululand and Delagoa Bay, accepted his paramountcy but were not completely incorporated in the kingdom. Thus, as it expanded, the Zulu kingdom came to be surrounded by vassal communities and client states in varying degrees of subordination, and the boundaries of the kingdom shaded off into a sphere of influence.

Shaka, like Dingiswayo, was careful to preserve trading contacts with the Portuguese at Lourenço Marques, and in 1825 a Portuguese visitor was present at his court. The Portuguese were not to be Shaka's only external trading contacts however. An English ex-naval captain, Farewell, became convinced of the profits to be gained from trade with the Zulu, as the result of a trading expedition he had made to Lourenço Marques. He succeeded in gaining support in the Cape for the idea of a trading expedition to the coast of Natal. After an abortive attempt at landing at St Lucia Bay in 1823 an advance party headed by Henry Fynn landed at Port Natal (modern Durban) in 1824 and succeeded in establishing friendly relations with the Zulu king. Thereafter, in spite of many vicissitudes, the small group of traders remained in Natal and was joined by a number of other white and coloured adventurers.

At the time of the arrival of the English traders, the population of Natal had been drastically reduced by Zulu armies and the devastation produced by other groups fleeing from them and one another. The miserable remnant of the population, which had lost all its cattle and was living on the borders of starvation, was in some sense part of Shaka's kingdom, in so far as its members refrained from partaking of new crops until the Zulu king had performed his first fruits ceremonies. On the other hand they were not fully incorporated in the Zulu state. Shaka gave his new friends permission to make use of a large part of

Natal, authorizing them to act as chiefs over the population there. The English traders thus became quasi-independent chiefs, each with his own following. Shaka expected them to support him with their guns when called upon for particularly difficult campaigns, but otherwise left them a good deal of autonomy.

In spite of the crushing Zulu victory on the Mhlatuse river, the Ndwandwe remained a political danger. In 1824 Ndwandwe agents infiltrated the Zulu court and stabbed Shaka quite severely. This took place when Fynn was visiting Shaka and gave him an opportunity to win the king's favour by dressing his wound. In 1826, a dispute broke out over the succession to Zwide. Sikhunyana was successful, but a disappointed rival, Somapunga, fled to Shaka and supplied information about Ndwandwe plans. Towards the end of 1826 Sikhunyana launched a full-scale invasion of the Zulu kingdom in the hope of avenging the defeat of 1818. By this time, the Ndwandwe had adopted Zulu fighting tactics and a sanguinary battle took place. Large numbers of cattle were seized by the victorious Zulu. After this defeat the Ndwandwe were unable to rally again. Some of them submitted to the Zulu, others fled to form part of the followings of Shoshangane or Mzilikazi.

For the last two years of his reign Shaka was faced with no serious external rival. The structure of the state he had built freed him from the restraints normally operative on rulers and allowed him to indulge to the full the despotic tendencies in his personality. The death of his grandmother, and then of his mother Nandi, early in 1828, provoked him into excesses of harshness, partly the outcome of his own morbid fears of mortality and partly perhaps as a deliberate attempt to strengthen his position against assassination by impressing on the people the horrors of a royal funeral.[1] By this time his people were growing weary of the rigours of the military system and the never-ending wars no longer justified by any direct military threat.

The mourning ceremonies for Nandi concluded in 1828 with a massive expedition through Natal to the lands of the tribes lying between the Umzimvubu and the frontiers of the Cape. To prepare the way Shaka had sent an embassy to the Cape under the care of Lieutenant King, but it met with a poor reception and failed to see the governor. Having no news of his embassy, Shaka listened to the advice of Fynn,

[1] It should be noted however that one of the apparently extraordinary aspects of the mourning for Nandi, the prohibition of sexual intercourse between married couples, was in fact a long-established tradition at the death of chiefs. See the account of the survivors of the wrecked ship *Stavenisse*. Bird, *The annals of Natal*, 1, 30–2. Alberti, *Description physique et historique des Cafres*, 171.

who warned him that the British regarded the tribes of the Cape frontier as being under their protection, and drew back. He left a message that he would return the next year and not rest until he had reached the Cape frontier and spoken with his English friends. Cheated of any major victory on his expedition to the south of his kingdom, Shaka immediately despatched his weary forces against the people of Shoshangane, who had by then established himself as the paramount power in southern Mozambique. The Zulu forces won an initial victory and forced Soshangane to move farther out of range, but they failed to capture any large herds of cattle and were decimated by starvation and disease.

While the army was away on this expedition, two brothers of Shaka, Dingane and Mhlangane, conspired with his trusted *induna*, Mbopha, and, finding a suitable opportunity, stabbed the Zulu king to death. Thereafter Dingane rid himself of his fellow conspirators and succeeded to the Zulu throne. In the immediate aftermath of the assassination the conspirators had pacified the surrounding people by proclaiming that they had killed the king on account of the atrocities committed for the sake of mourning for Nandi, and to put an end to the ceaseless wars. On his accession Dingane would seem to have intended to discontinue the system of full-time military service and allow the people to live peacefully in their homes. The relaxations, however, created the opportunity for secession and the powerful Qwabe, under Nqetho, broke away from the kingdom, beat off the army sent against it, and made its way through Natal to Pondoland. To preserve his kingdom Dingane was forced to keep the army occupied. On three occasions his forces were despatched as far as the Transvaal to attack the Ndebele of Mzilikazi. The system built up by Shaka thus proved to have a momentum which enabled it to survive the death of its founder, and the succession of a ruler very different in character, who did not share the preoccupation with war and glory which had inspired his great predecessor.

CONSEQUENCES IN NATAL

Though the rise of the Zulu kingdom was to have consequences for vast areas, some at an enormous distance, its heaviest impact outside Zululand was naturally felt in neighbouring Natal. At the beginning of the nineteenth century Natal was relatively densely settled by numerous Nguni chiefdoms. As Shaka established and expanded his kingdom in Zululand, the peoples of Natal were thrown into confusion by two

successive invasions of refugees fleeing southward across the Tugela
river. The passage of these groups through Natal drove a number of
Natal communities to flight and a life of plunder. Finally, behind the
mass of straggling refugees and wandering plunderers, came the Zulu
regiments themselves, as Shaka steadily extended his raiding farther to
the south-west. As a result the population of Natal was drastically
reduced for a time. About 3,000 people lived in the vicinity of modern
Durban in a pathetic state of poverty. They were found there by the
English traders who visited Shaka and they came to accept the traders
as their protectors and chiefs. Outside this area travellers passing
through Natal gained the impression that the country was almost completely uninhabited, though there were no doubt pockets of population
persisting in relatively inaccessible areas of mountain and forest.
Though loss of life must have been considerable the extensive depopulation which occurred was for the most part of a temporary nature.
The peoples of Natal had not been destroyed, but had taken temporary
refuge elsewhere and awaited the return of settled times to reoccupy
their homelands.

As refugees fled southward from Natal, many settled in the coastal
lands immediately to the south, in the neighbourhood of the Pondo
chiefdom then led by Faku. Others entered the area of mountain valleys
lying between Lesotho and the more densely settled lands of the coastal
corridor.[1] This area became known to the colonial authorities at the
Cape as Nomansland.

In these areas bitter and complex struggles ensued between rival
groups among the overcrowded refugees, and between refugee groups
and the previously established communities.

Amongst the refugee groups, Ncapayi of the Bhaca emerged as the
sole surviving major leader. His following came to consist of a highly
heterogeneous agglomeration drawn from many original Nguni chiefdoms. Faku, the Pondo chief, was even more successful than Ncapayi.
He managed to avoid any major conflict and maintained the fighting
strength of his people virtually unimpaired. Though most of his cattle
were carried off by the Zulu during their expeditions into his area in
1823–4 and 1828, he remained the most powerful leader immediately
to the south of Natal.

In 1829 the Pondo and Bhaca were faced with a new and formidable
menace. The Qwabe, one of the earliest communities to be incorporated

[1] The analysis given here is mainly based on A. T. Bryant, *Olden times in Zululand and
Natal* (London, 1929).

in Shaka's kingdom, rebelled against his successor, Dingane. Under the leadership of Nqetho, they fled through Natal and invaded Pondoland. The Qwabe were in effect a breakaway section of the Zulu. Masters of Zulu fighting methods and military organization, they might well have carried all before them.

Faku, however, made up in generalship for the Qwabes' superior discipline. He fell upon his enemy as they were moving in broken formation along the edge of cliffs overlooking the Umzimvubu river. In this situation the sheer mass of the Pondos' superior numbers was decisive. Many of the Qwabe were driven over the cliffs. Those who escaped were attacked once more by a Pondo ambush, which Faku had concealed near the ford over the river. Nqetho escaped with a small following but was subsequently attacked and killed by Ncapayi. The statesmanship and military skill of Faku thus prevented the tide of confusion and devastation sweeping down from Natal along the coastal corridor to the Cape colonial frontiers, and ensured that the Bantu population of this area would remain as a bloc preventing any rapid expansion of white settlement farther up the east coast.

Many of the refugees from Natal percolated down the east coast corridor, and settled as destitute refugees with the Thembu and Xhosa chiefdoms of the modern Transkei. They came to be known as Mfengu, a name derived from a verb meaning to beg for food. The Cape authorities referred to them as Fingos. Their coming added considerably to the problems of overcrowding in the lands beyond the Cape's eastern frontier. The tension which subsequently developed between the Mfengu and their hosts contributed a further element to the political complexities of the eastern frontier situation.

Two of the most powerful chiefdoms in the Natal area early in the nineteenth century were the Ngwane of Matiwane, who were settled on the edge of the escarpment near modern Wakkerstroom, and their close neighbours the Hlubi. As the process of building up enlarged political units developed in Zululand, and the rising powers began to compete with one another for the allegiance of the remaining independent chiefdoms, the Ngwane were attacked first by Dingiswayo and then by Zwide. To save their herds, they entrusted them to the safe keeping of their Hlubi neighbours, but these, seeing the Ngwane defeated, refused to return the cattle. Thus provoked, in 1821 the Ngwane launched a surprise attack on the Hlubi, killed their chief Mtimkulu, and caused most of them to flee over the Drakensberg under the leadership of Mpangazita. In 1822 the Ngwane were in turn attacked by

Shaka, and then fled across the Drakensberg in the wake of their old enemies.

CONSEQUENCES ON THE HIGH VELD

The sudden intrusion of Mpangazita and the Hlubi into the Trans-orangian high veld brought to an end the period of relative peace and prosperity among the southern Sotho peoples, and produced a violent upheaval and a new pattern of population distribution and political organization. The first major group with whom the Hlubi came in conflict were the Tlokwa, then living under the rule of an energetic queen, Mma Nthatisi, who was exercising the regency for her son, Sekonyela. The Tlokwa were driven from their homes and launched on a long career of wandering and rapine, which led them as far south as the Orange river and ultimately back to settle round the mountain of Jwalaboholo and Morabeng in the Free State near the north-east corner of modern Lesotho. In their long wanderings they drove many other groups from their homelands, forcing them in turn to fall upon others.

To add to the distress of the southern Sotho peoples, Mpangazita and the Hlubi wandered over much of the eastern part of the modern Orange Free State, fighting from time to time with the Tlokwa and like them raiding and devastating a wide area. The Ngwane, following in the track of the Hlubi, likewise fell upon any community who retained enough cattle to be worth raiding. They and the Hlubi fought a struggle to the death on the Orange Free State high veld, which ended with the defeat and break-up of the Hlubi, most of whom joined the ranks of their Ngwane conqueror, Matiwane. Thereafter Matiwane was attacked by a Zulu expedition[1] and an Ndebele raiding party. Food and cattle in the Orange Free State were virtually exhausted; Matiwane accordingly sought new sources of cattle amongst the Thembu people in the eastern coastal lands. In 1828 he led his people across the Drakensberg.

His arrival in the Thembu country, however, coincided with the alarm caused by Shaka's invasion of Pondoland, with the apparent intention of marching through the Transkei to the border of the colony. Matiwane was encountered by colonial forces sent to ward off the expected Zulu invasion. Being mistaken for the Zulu, his people were attacked and dispersed at Mbholompo. He himself eventually went back and placed himself at the mercy of Dingane. Fearful of retaining such

---

[1] N. J. van Warmelo, ed., *History of Matiwane and the Amangwane tribe* as told by Msebenzi to his kinsman Albert Hlongwane, Union of South Africa Department of Native Affairs Ethnological Publications, VII (Pretoria, 1938), 28–9. Bryant, *Olden times*, maintains that there is no Zulu tradition of this expedition.

a renowned warrior and leader in his kingdom, the Zulu king had him executed at Matiwane's Kop (later to be the scene of the killing of Piet Retief and his Boer comrades).

MOSHOESHOE AND THE SOTHO

The desperate and confused situation in the area of the modern Orange Free State and Lesotho provided the opportunity for an exceptionally able leader known as Moshoeshoe. Son of a relatively insignificant sub-chief of the Mokotedi, a small tribe belonging to the Kwena group, Moshoeshoe early displayed qualities of foresight and leadership which were to prove invaluable in the troubled times ahead. At an early age he saw the potential advantage of the defensive positions offered by flat-topped mountains, and established himself with his family and a small band of age-mates in a strong position on Butha-Buthe mountain in north-eastern Lesotho. The narrow access routes to his mountain stronghold were then fortified with dry stone walling. From this point Moshoeshoe led his followers on daring raids. His exploits and increasing wealth soon attracted a growing following. Soon after Mpangazita made his appearance on the high veld, the Tlokwa whom he had thrown in motion made an attack on Butha-Buthe. They failed to storm the heights, and in a counter-attack Moshoeshoe's men penetrated to the heart of the enemy camp. The Tlokwa then moved on, but about 1824–5 they returned again and this time made a determined attempt to besiege Moshoeshoe on his mountain. Moshoeshoe held on till his people were almost exhausted by starvation, when he was fortunate to win the support of the Ngwane, who drove the Tlokwa away from the mountain.[1]

The siege had revealed the weakness of his position at Butha-Buthe, and Moshoeshoe led his people on a dangerous march through country infested by cannibals and wandering bands of masterless men to the larger and more fully defensible hill of Thaba Bosiu. Secure in this virtually impregnable position, he was able to commence the task of gathering the remnants of many communities together in a single kingdom. In this task Moshoeshoe did not make use of the age-regiment system, but relied on more traditional means. He established his brothers and later his sons at key points in his kingdom, attaching to their followings the numerous small groups of refugees who came to

[1] Van Warmelo, ed., *History of Matiwane and the Amangwane tribe*, 24. T. Arbousset and F. Daumas, *Narrative of an exploratory tour of the north east of the Colony of the Cape of Good Hope* (Cape Town, 1846), 291–2, ascribes this intervention to the 'Matabele of Sepeka'.

him. Larger, more coherent groups, such as the Phuthi of Morosi, the Taung of Moletsane, and eventually the Tlokwa, were allowed to remain under their own chiefs subject to Moshoeshoe's paramountcy. Unity was consolidated by wide consultations and the pressure of common enemies.

When first established at Thaba Bosiu, Moshoeshoe acknowledged the paramountcy of Matiwane of the Ngwane and paid him a regular tribute. But, as Matiwane's depredations endangered the task of state building, Moshoeshoe paid homage to Shaka and called for the aid of Zulu regiments to rid him of this incubus. A Zulu expedition fell upon Matiwane and his following was severely mauled, but the expedition departed without overthrowing the Ngwane completely.

Moshoeshoe had earned the hatred of the Ngwane, and in 1827 they attacked Thaba Bosiu. The mountain stronghold proved too strong for them and shortly afterwards they moved off into the Thembu country, to meet their fate at Mbholompo. In 1831 Moshoeshoe was attacked by an even more dangerous enemy. An Ndebele force penetrated Lesotho and attempted to storm Moshoeshoe's mountain home. Once again the attackers failed in face of the natural defences of Thaba Bosiu, and were driven back by the hail of stones and missiles which the defenders hurled on them from above. Moshoeshoe bought peace from further such attacks by sending an embassy after the retreating Ndebele with a gift of fat cattle.

Hardly had this enemy drawn off, however, before Moshoeshoe's people began to be attacked by new foes. Griqua and Korana banditti turned their attentions to his kingdom which had almost the only substantial reserve of cattle remaining in Transorangia. For defence against these enemies, who specialized in lightning raids, Moshoeshoe's people relied on ambushes and night attacks. Appreciating the tactical superiority afforded by guns and horses, Moshoeshoe encouraged his people to acquire these valuable commodities by every means in their power. Within a short time the Sotho had developed their own breed of horse, the 'Basuto pony', and had converted themselves into a nation of mounted gunmen.

The depredations of the half-caste banditti also led Moshoeshoe to seek contact with the missionaries at Philippolis, and to invite them to settle with him. His message arrived just as a party belonging to the Paris Evangelical Missionary Society was waiting at Philippolis in the hope of proceeding to the Hurutshe country. Disappointed of hopes of their original field by the news of Mzilikazi's invasion of the area, they turned to Lesotho, and in 1833 established themselves there. Moshoeshoe had thus acquired valuable helpers and councillors when shortly afterwards he came in contact with the Boers of the Great Trek.

The disturbed conditions in Transorangia, provoked by the invasions of Mpangazita and Matiwane, led to great devastation and the temporary virtual depopulation of wide areas. While much of the population gravitated to the mountain area of Lesotho and the protection of Moshoeshoe, substantial numbers poured into the Cape Colony, where they were widely employed by white farmers.[1] After remaining in white service for some time and acquiring cattle, most of these refugees made their way back across the Orange and placed themselves under Moshoeshoe, who established many of them under the guidance of the French missionaries in the lands forming the angle between the Orange and Caledon rivers.

THE KOLOLO

In addition to those who were incorporated in the kingdom of Moshoeshoe or took refuge temporarily in the Cape Colony, a number of Sotho communities, driven from their homes in the course of the disturbances initiated by the Hlubi and Ngwane, fled northwards across the Vaal river. Amongst these were the Fokeng led by Sebetwane. In mid-1823 they and two other wandering Sotho groups converged by different routes on the Tlhaping chiefdom in which the London Missionary Society missionary, Robert Moffat, had established a station at Kuruman. Hearing news of the advance of the invaders, Moffat sought aid from the Griqua, and a force of about 100 mounted Griqua gunmen rode from Griquatown to the aid of the Tlhaping. In a battle on 26 June 1823 the invaders were driven back, and the Fokeng, subsequently known as the Kololo, turned northwards. Fighting and plundering as they went, they made their way through much of modern Botswana, then turned westward into the Kalahari and settled for a time near Lake Ngami. From there, after an abortive attempt to make their way to the west coast, they moved north again up to and across the Zambezi, settling on the lands near the junction of the Kafue and Zambezi rivers. Here they encountered an Ndebele force and, after an inconclusive struggle, the Kololo moved up the Zambezi and entered the territory of the Lozi. The Lozi kingdom was divided at the time by a succession dispute, and the Kololo succeeded in over-running it and

[1] For the scale of the migration of refugees to the Cape Colony and subsequent return see W. Lye, 'The distribution of the Sotho peoples after the Difaqane', in Thompson, ed., *African societies in southern Africa*.

establishing their own rule. In their new home they were attacked twice by the Ndebele and once by Nqaba, whose wanderings eventually brought him to the Barotse flood plain. The Kololo, however, had swiftly acquired a mastery of the use of canoes and, by making use of the advantages of their terrain, they were able to defeat all these attacks. Nqaba and his men were trapped on an island until exhausted by starvation. Nqaba himself was drowned in the Zambezi.

Under the wise rule of Sebetwane, the Kololo prospered and their rule seemed firmly established. Sebetwane adopted a deliberate policy aimed at attracting the loyalty of his new subjects. He married Lozi wives, consulted Lozi councillors and insisted that all his subjects were equally 'children of the chief'. Under his rule the conquered peoples were rapidly beginning to identify themselves as Kololo. Under Sebetwane also, the boundaries of the Lozi kingdom were considerably extended. Kololo rule was established over the valley Tonga, as far as the Victoria Falls.

On the death of Sebetwane in 1851, however, the trend towards the stabilization of the Kololo kingdom was reversed. His successor, Sekeletu, suffered from leprosy and developed a morbid fear of witchcraft. He was deeply suspicious of the Lozi and of potential rivals amongst the Kololo also. He surrounded himself with Kololo councillors and married only Kololo wives. His suspicious nature, and his withdrawal to a great extent from public affairs, allowed matters to slip from his control. The Kololo now began to act as an arrogant ruling class, demanding to be supported and served by the conquered peoples. Lozi loyalties began to shift to survivors of their royal dynasty, who had fled up the Leambye river and had managed to maintain their independence there. The numbers of the Kololo were declining fast as they succumbed to the malaria of the flood plain. While Sekeletu was yet alive, fears were openly being expressed that the kingdom would break up.

On his death in 1864 a succession dispute broke out. This was the signal for Sipopa, a descendant of the Lozi royal line, to launch an uprising aimed at the overthrow of the Kololo and the re-establishment of the Lozi dynasty. Divided amongst themselves, the Kololo were driven out and the Lozi dynasty was restored. During their period of rule, however, the Kololo had made a lasting impression. Their language has remained the basis of modern Silozi.

Livingstone visited the Kololo for the first time in 1851, the year of Sebetwane's death. The reception he received, and the impression he gained of the stability of the kingdom, encouraged him to make it the base for his journeys to Angola and down the Zambezi. On these expeditions he was accompanied by porters from the Kololo kingdom, some of whom settled in the Shire valley, married local wives and decided to stay on there when Livingstone took most of them back to their homes in 1860. The small group of sixteen who remained on the Shire river had a few guns that they had been given by the missionary. Above all they had experience of large state organization and a tremendous pride and self-confidence derived from their association with the warlike reputation of the Kololo (the majority of them were not in fact true Kololo). In the disturbed conditions of the Shire valley area at the time, where the local Manganja populace was a prey to raids by Ngoni, as well as by Yao and Portuguese slave raiders, the Kololo succeeded in establishing themselves as a ruling group and building up two Kololo kingdoms which effectively excluded the Portuguese and Yao raiders from the area, and even deterred the Ngoni from any major attack. They thus helped to preserve the population of the Shire valley from further devastations, and at the same time kept open the route through which the Scottish missionaries were able to penetrate into and establish themselves in modern Malawi.

THE NDEBELE KINGDOM

About 1821 the only major split within the Zulu kingdom took place when Mzilikazi, who combined military command in Shaka's kingdom with the chieftaincy of the Khumalo, defied the Zulu king and was driven with his followers onto the Transvaal high veld. The Sotho and Tswana communities living there did not possess the military organization and training to offer effective resistance, and Mzilikazi was able to embark on a career of widespread conquest, incorporating captives in his regiments and building up a powerful Ndebele kingdom organized on lines similar to that of the Zulu.

During his period in the Transvaal, Mzilikazi moved from a first base near the Olifants river in the eastern Transvaal to a position near the Magaliesberg range, not far from modern Pretoria, and finally to the Marico district in the western Transvaal. These moves were undertaken with a view to removing himself further from the danger of Zulu attack. Expeditions sent by Dingane did in fact attack him twice when he was settled in the area near Pretoria. In addition he was repeatedly attacked by groups of Griqua and Korana in alliance with Tswana chiefs. The guns and horses of the Griqua gave them an advantage which enabled them to seize large herds from the Ndebele and threaten the survival of the kingdom, though on each occasion Mzilikazi succeeded in counter-attacking his enemy while they were retiring with the loot, taking them by surprise and recapturing his stock. In response to this threat, Mzilikazi attempted to establish relations with the whites and invited a visit from the missionary Robert Moffat. This was to be the beginning of a life-long friendship of the Ndebele king for the stern missionary.

In 1835 Mzilikazi agreed to enter into a treaty with the Cape, in the hope that the colonial government would restrain the Griqua from further attacks. At the same time Ndebele regiments were kept on constant patrol to the south-east to fall on any attacking party. In spite of these precautions Mzilikazi still felt unsafe and had begun to spy out land to the north, with a view to a further move when he became involved in a conflict with the Boers of the Great Trek.

Early in 1836 Mzilikazi's regiments came across the wagons of a number of Boer trekking parties who had crossed the Vaal without giving prior notice to the Ndebele king. The Ndebele attacked the trekkers and, taking them by surprise, massacred a number of them. Those who survived, united under the leadership of Potgieter, recrossed the Vaal and beat off a mass Ndebele attack on a hill subsequently known as Vegkop.

In December 1836 the trekkers, aided by Griqua and African allies, launched a retaliatory expedition, captured one of Mzilikazi's military settlements and retired with large numbers of cattle. News of this campaign prompted the Zulu king, Dingane, to send another expedition against his old foe. The Zulu regiments did not achieve complete victory but inflicted heavy losses and drove off still more of Mzilikazi's cattle. In October 1837 the trekkers launched a further attack. In seven days of fighting, Mzilikazi's military settlements fell one after another and his people fled out of the Marico valley to the north.

During his period in the Transvaal Mzilikazi's activities resulted in widespread devastation and a substantial, if essentially temporary, redistribution of population. Wide areas around his successive encampments were left apparently deserted and the population tended to concentrate around the periphery of the Transvaal, in the vicinity of the Steelpoort river where the Pedi, after being defeated and temporarily scattered by the Ndebele, re-established and expanded their kingdom, in the Zoutpansberg area of the northern Transvaal and in Botswana to the west.

After the abandonment of the Marico district, Mzilikazi's following divided into two sections and made its way northwards.[1] One party, including the royal women and children, passed through the northern Transvaal, crossed the Limpopo and halted near the Matopos range in Rhodesia. With the other division Mzilikazi moved by a more westerly route through Botswana up to the Zambezi near its junction with the Kafue. There the Ndebele encountered the Kololo. After a brush with them, Mzilikazi turned south and made contact with the other section of his people. In the meantime the *indunas* of this party had given up their king for lost. They were about to establish his heir, Nkulumane, in his place, when he returned. Five of the *indunas* who were held responsible for this, together with the chief *induna* Gundwane, were put to death on the hill subsequently known as the 'hill of the *indunas*'. Nkulumane was almost certainly killed at this time, and Lobengula, later to become the second Ndebele king, only just escaped. The Ndebele then settled down in what was to become their permanent home.

In Matabeleland the Ndebele kingdom reached its full development. As the Ndebele were in origin a breakaway section of the Zulu, the principles on which the kingdom was organized were essentially those of the Zulu, using the age-regiments, which absorbed the conquered peoples. The Ndebele community thus came to include members derived from a large number of different peoples and three distinct language and culture groups. Some belonged originally to Nguni-speaking tribes, others were from the Sotho–Tswana group of peoples, who had been absorbed during the period in the Transvaal, while various Shona were absorbed after the final settlement in Matabeleland. These three groups came to form distinct prestige classes, the Nguni-speakers or *Zansi* ranking highest, the *Enhla* or Sotho–Tswana peoples second and the *Hola* (Shona peoples) lowest. Inter-marriage between these classes was restricted.[2] In this way the culture and language of the *Zansi* group were preserved. The high prestige of the *Zansi* group encouraged the other classes to seek to imitate them as closely as possible, and so fostered the eventual adoption of their Nguni language and culture by the entire community. In the Ndebele kingdom as in the Zulu, the structure of the politico-military system focused loyalty directly and intensely on the king, who was able to wield virtually absolute power.

[1] An account of the division of the Ndebele into two sections and their separate journeys is given by N. Jones (Mhlagazanhlansi), *My friend Kumalo* (Salisbury, 1945).

[2] This system has persisted until recent times. See A. J. B. Hughes, *Kin, caste and nation among the Rhodesian Ndebele*, Rhodes-Livingstone papers no. xxv (Manchester, 1956).

Whereas in the Zulu kingdom the army was only a part of the community, and the majority of the population lived in traditional fashion under territorial chiefs who were often the descendants of previously independent rulers, the Ndebele were initially a section of the Zulu army. Therefore the organization of the army was the organization of the state. The regimental towns were the administrative headquarters of the whole populace as well as the military centres.

The regimental towns thus became permanent territorial divisions of the community. Members of a particular regiment remained associated with their regimental town after they had been permitted to marry, and remained liable for military service, constituting a reserve force which could be called upon in time of emergency. Their sons became members of the regiment stationed at their fathers' regimental town, and in this way membership of particular regiments became hereditary. Only when growth of population warranted it did the king gather youths from various regimental towns and constitute a new regiment, establishing at the same time a new regimental town which in due course would become hereditary in the same way. Through this process the regimental system evolved away from its original age basis into something more like traditional territorial chieftaincies. This evolution was far from complete, however. The regimental towns were still military centres, which constituted the headquarters of regiments of youths who underwent a period of active service between certain ages marking the transition from adolescence to manhood. Above all they were under the authority of *indunas* rather than traditional chiefs.[1]

On their establishment in Matabeleland the Ndebele engaged in numerous expeditions against the Shona peoples, whose political system had already been thrown into confusion by preceding invasions led by Zwangendaba and Nqaba, leaders of two of the groups of refugees who had fled into Mozambique after the defeat of the Ndwandwe on the Mhlatuse river in 1818. A section of Zwangendaba's people under a woman leader, Nyamazana, had remained behind when the rest of his following crossed the Zambesi. They joined Mzilikazi, and Nyamazana became one of his queens. The Ndebele were thus able to establish their dominance over a substantial area. The area of their direct rule, however, probably extended very little if at all beyond the area occupied by their military settlements. In Mashonaland the Shona peoples regrouped themselves in a number of paramountcies and,

[1] See J. D. Omer-Cooper, 'Aspects of political change in the nineteenth-century Mfecane', in Thompson, ed., *African societies in southern Africa*.

though subjected from time to time to Ndebele raids, effectively preserved their independence.

Even within the area where Ndebele paramountcy could be said to have been accepted, moreover, the situation was highly complex. The primary method by which the Ndebele absorbed conquered peoples into their political system was by incorporating the young men in the regimental system. This continued in Matabeleland but, even while Mzilikazi was still in the Transvaal, it had ceased to be the only method by which alien groups were brought under his control. Moffat noted that at Mosega there were numerous villages of Hurutshe living under Mzilikazi, but in their traditional way.[1] In Matabeleland this occurred on a much larger scale. Though many Shona were incorporated in the age-regiments, there were many living in traditional style in their own villages right in the heart of the Ndebele country. Farther from the centre of the kingdom, Shona chiefs lived in various degrees of subordination to the Ndebele.[2] Ndebele prestige was so great, however, that even some of the loosely associated Shona groups came in time to adopt the Ndebele language and to regard themselves as Ndebele.

Influence was by no means all one way. In the Mutapa kingdom, and in that of the Rozvi empire which succeeded it in ruling over the Shona communities of the greater part of Rhodesia, a cult had grown up involving belief in a deity sometimes known as Mwari and sometimes as Mlimo. The deity was believed to communicate with man through the agency of spirit mediums. This cult was closely linked with the Rozvi political system. Mzilikazi in his later years began to consult the oracular utterances of the surviving cult priests, and under Lobengula their influence established itself more firmly. The Ndebele rulers thus became to some extent heirs to the religious heritage of the Rozvi kings, and the Ndebele kingdom was united with the still independent Shona paramountcies in a common framework of belief.[3]

After his brush with the Kololo, which led to his turning back from the Zambezi, Mzilikazi nursed a determination to avenge his defeat by destroying their kingdom on the Barotse flood plain. The Ndebele regiments were at a disadvantage in this watery terrain, however, and the expeditions sent against the Kololo ended in failure. The move to Rhodesia had, moreover, failed to place the Ndebele out of reach of

[1] R. Moffatt, *Matabele journals*, ed. J. P. R. Wallis (London, 1945), 1, 70.

[2] R. Brown, 'The external relations of the Ndebele kingdom in the pre-partition era', in Thompson, ed., *African societies in southern Africa*.

[3] For the significance of this development in later years see T. O. Ranger, *Revolt in Southern Rhodesia* (London, 1967).

Boer attacks. In 1847 a Boer commando, organized by Hendrik Pot-gieter and accompanied by Pedi auxiliaries, penetrated to the heart of Mzilikazi's kingdom and seized large herds of cattle. Once again, however, the Ndebele employed the same tactics they had used in the past against Griqua and Korana. In a night attack the Pedi were massacred and the cattle recaptured.

In spite of this attack, Mzilikazi remained anxious to establish good relations with the whites. In 1852 he agreed to a treaty with the Boers, which opened the way for Boer hunters to enter his territory. In particular he longed to see his old friend Moffat again, and was delighted when in 1854 the missionary visited him in his new home. Thereafter Moffat came again in 1857, and for the last time in 1860. Moffat did much to win concessions for white hunters and other visitors, and he also persuaded Mzilikazi to allow missionaries to settle in his kingdom. In Mzilikazi's last years white hunters and traders frequented his court in increasing numbers, and after the discovery in 1867 of gold at Tati, on the borders of his kingdom, the number of whites rose considerably. By this time, however, Mzilikazi had lost control of events. In his later years he suffered a great deal of pain from swellings in his feet and ankles which made him completely lame. The pain made him restless, and in his last years he was almost always on the move, carried about in a wagon Moffat had brought for him. He died in 1868.

His death left the people divided, for the fate of the legitimate heir, Nkulumane, was obscure. He was generally believed to have been killed at the time of the execution of the *indunas* who had contemplated placing him on his father's throne. There were rumours, however, that he had been spirited away and was living somewhere in South Africa. He was thought by some to have been identified in the person of a groom work-ing for Sir Theophilus Shepstone, who did his best to keep the rumours alive as a means of winning influence over the Ndebele kingdom.[1] An Ndebele embassy visited Natal to search for the prince, but it returned with a negative report, and the majority of the *indunas* placed Lobengula on the throne. One regiment, however, refused to recognize the new king, and it was only at the cost of a civil war that Lobengula con-solidated his position.

[1] R. Brown, 'The Ndebele succession crisis', in *Historians in Tropical Africa*, Proceedings of the Leverhulme History Conference 1960 (Salisbury, cyclostyled, 1962).

SHOSHANGANE AND THE GAZA KINGDOM

After the battle on the Mhlatuse river in 1818, in which Shaka's forces shattered the Ndwandwe, a number of groups who had formed part of or been associated with the Ndwandwe fled into southern Mozambique. They included the following of Shoshangane, the Jere under Zwangendaba, the Maseko under Ngwane and the Msene under Nqaba. All these groups made use of fighting methods similar to those of the Zulu, and built up their strength by incorporating captives in their forces. As they expanded they came into conflict and, after a complex struggle, Shoshangane emerged victorious. He was then able to build a powerful kingdom dominating the greater part of southern Mozambique and organized basically along Zulu lines. In his kingdom, as in Shaka's, a series of royal households provided the centres of military and political organization and the headquarters of regiments, which included young men captured from conquered communities, but, as in the Ndebele kingdom, members recruited from conquered peoples held a lower status than those who belonged to or were descended from the original nuclear group.

Outside the central area of the kingdom, numerous chiefdoms came under Shoshangane's paramountcy, but retained their separate identity and internal autonomy. Within this peripheral zone were the Portuguese settlements. At the time when the various Nguni-speaking groups of refugees invaded southern Mozambique, the Portuguese settlements were too weak to offer effective resistance. In 1833 the Zulu regiments of Dingane overran the fort at Lourenço Marques. In 1834 the Portuguese captain of Inhambane and all but ten of his men were killed in a clash with one set of Nguni invaders.[1] In October 1836 almost the entire garrison of Sofala was wiped out. The long established Portuguese market in Manica was closed, and the towns of Sena and Tete on the Zambezi were reduced to buying peace with an annual tribute. Divisions within the kingdom following Shoshangane's death allowed the Portuguese to improve their position to some extent. A dispute culminating in civil war took place between rival heirs, Mawewe and Mzila. With Portuguese help, Mzila finally succeeded in defeating Mawewe who had gained help and protection from the Swazi kingdom. Desultory warfare between Mzila and the Swazi continued until 1862,

[1] Portuguese sources generally do not distinguish at all clearly between the different invading Nguni groups. A recent attempt to disentangle the threads in this confusing period in southern Mozambique has been made by G. J. Liesegang, *Beiträge zur Geschichte des Reiches der Gaza Nguni im südlichen Mocambique 1820–1895* (Bromberg, 1967).

when he was succeeded by Gungunyane, who was finally overthrown, captured and exiled by the Portuguese in 1895.

NGUNI STATES IN THE FAR NORTH

After their defeat by Shoshangane, the three other migrating Nguni groups moved out of reach of his regiments. Zwangendaba and his followers (subsequently known as Ngoni) moved into the area of the Rozvi kingdom in modern Rhodesia. They halted for a time near modern Bulawayo and from there their forces attacked and killed the last Rozvi *mambo* at Thabazika Mambo. Thereafter Zwangendaba turned northward and on 19 November 1835, a day marked by an eclipse of the sun, crossed the Zambezi not far from Zumbo.

The Maseko remained for a time in southern Mozambique, then crossed the Zambezi between Sena and Tete about 1839. Thereafter this group (also known as Ngoni) moved through southern Malawi, passing round the southern end of the lake and crossing the Shire river from west to east. They then moved northwards into south-eastern Tanzania and under Ngwane's successor, Mputa, built up a substantial kingdom in the Songea district. Like Zwangendaba, Nqaba moved into Rhodesia and plundered parts of the Rozvi kingdom. Thereafter he moved farther west up the Zambezi where he was killed and his following dispersed by the Kololo.

After crossing the Zambezi, Zwangendaba moved northward in a series of stages interrupted by halts of several years' duration. Keeping between Lake Malawi on the east and the Luangwa river to the west, he eventually passed the northern end of the lake and reached a place in the Fipa country of south-western Tanzania called Mapupo. He died there about 1848. After his death disputes over the succession led to a series of splits, in which each group continued expanding and absorbing conquered peoples, with the result that Ngoni states made their appearance over a large area between lakes Malawi and Tanganyika, and even to the south of Lake Victoria.

CONCLUSIONS

At the heart of the whole vast chain of disturbances which spread itself over much of South, Central and East Africa, was the revolutionary process of political change in Zululand, which resulted in the emergence of a new type of state, militarist, highly centralized, and administered under the king by commoner *indunas* rather than royal relatives. The new political system not only produced a formidable military machine, but also provided a means of welding originally disparate peoples into a common identity within a greatly expanded political framework. This transformation took place, not by the borrowing of ideas from other societies, but by the adaptation of existing institutions of the southern Bantu-speaking peoples to the new purposes in a situation of crisis produced by intensified military conflict arising from land shortage and possibly also the expansion of trade.

The migrations to which this political upheaval gave rise led to the establishment of a whole series of powerful communities in South, East and Central Africa. On their migrations those wandering groups who had been in contact with the Zulu kingdom carried with them some of the basic principles of its organization, modifying them in various ways to meet the circumstances in which they were placed and planting them in the new areas in which they settled. Other peoples who were affected by the upheaval were also stimulated to organize themselves in larger units with stronger central leadership. Sometimes they borrowed methods derived from the Zulu system, sometimes they found different ways of achieving larger scale organization of their own.

In South Africa the upheaval resulted in the emergence of the Zulu kingdom itself. It also led to the creation of the Swazi kingdom, and of the Sotho kingdom of Moshoeshoe, both of which have retained their identity to the present time and evolved into independent nations. Though almost destroyed in the course of conflict with the Ndebele, the Pedi kingdom in the eastern Transvaal was also strengthened by the consequences of the disturbance and thus prepared to play an important role in the subsequent history of the Transvaal. It is now the basis of one of South Africa's 'Bantustans'. The flight of peoples out of Natal southward down the eastern coastal corridor and westward across the Drakensberg had as one of its results the intrusion of the Mfengu into the Transkei, resulting in further complications of the eastern frontier problems.

One of the most significant consequences of the upheaval for South African history is the substantial, if temporary, redistribution of population which it produced. The Bantu peoples, who had previously been fairly evenly distributed over their area of occupation, became temporarily much more concentrated, leaving large areas at least to all appearances virtually vacant in Natal, the Orange Free State and the Transvaal. Information about this situation reached the Cape through the English traders in Natal, and missionaries and travellers in the other areas. It came just at the time when sections of the white population in the colony, short of land and hostile to the policies of the colonial government, were contemplating a movement of secession. The news of vacant lands in the interior was followed up by the despatch of parties to Natal and the Transvaal. When the strength of Xhosa resistance, combined with the efforts of philanthropists in England, led to the frustration of hopes for further rapid advance up the east coast, trekkers poured out of the colony to the north, skirting Moshoeshoe's kingdom and moving into the relatively empty and desirable areas of Natal, the northern Orange Free State and the Transvaal. Even though the picture has subsequently been substantially altered by further white expansion, the pattern of white and African landownership in South Africa today still reflects the consequences of the wars and migrations which accompanied the rise of the Zulu.

CHAPTER 10

COLONIAL SOUTH AFRICA
AND ITS FRONTIERS

WHITE EXPANSION AND THE BRITISH OCCUPATIONS

When the British took possession of the Cape in 1795 they inherited from the Dutch East India Company a situation which already exhibited many of the most significant features which were to characterize the history of South Africa until well into the nineteenth century. Outside the wheat and wine-growing areas of the Cape, the settlers had developed a system of stock ranching, requiring the exploitation by individual white farming families of large farms worked with the assistance of non-European labour. This resulted in a continuous territorial expansion of the white settlement, which by 1795 had already resulted in the extension of the original tiny settlement around Cape Town to the Fish river, the Sneeuwbergen and the Khamies Bergen. This vast expansion, by scattering the white population so thinly that the growth of urban areas was severely restricted, inhibited the development of alternative economic opportunities for whites and encouraged further expansion.[1]

At first there was little resistance from San[2] and Khoi,[3] but white expansion at length resulted in a situation of endemic frontier conflict. In the north-eastern districts of Tarka, Sneeuwberg and Agter Bruintjies Hoogte, the San hunters mounted a ferocious resistance against further encroachment on their hunting grounds. In the Zuurveld, where white and African farmers were settled alongside each other, two frontier wars had left the issues between them unresolved.

In the course of their conflicts, the settlers developed the highly flexible and mobile commando system whereby settlers were called together to make war. This relieved the Company's government of substantial defence burdens, but at the same time made the settlers much more difficult to control. Military action against non-European peoples could be undertaken on local settler initiative, and the frontier farmers had a military system which they could turn against the government.

---

[1] See S. D. Neumark, *Economic influences on the South African frontier 1652–1836* (Stanford, 1967). H. B. van Ryneveld, ed., *Willem Stephanus van Ryneveld se Aanmerkingen over de Verbetring van het vee aan de Kaap de Goede Hoop 1804*, Van Riebeeck Society (Cape Town, 1942).

[2] The people commonly known by the derogatory term 'Bushmen'.

[3] The people often referred to by the derogatory name 'Hottentots'.

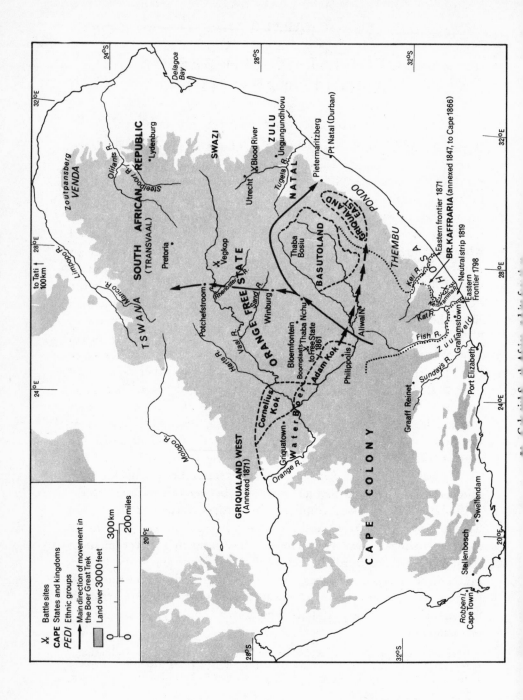

Map of South Africa in the nineteenth century

Battle sites
CAPE States and kingdoms
PEDI Ethnic groups
Main direction of movement in
the Boer Great Trek
Land over 3000 feet

300 km
200 miles

to Tati
100 km

Zoutpansberg
VENDA
Olifants R.
Steelpoort R.
•Lydenburg
SOUTH AFRICAN REPUBLIC
(TRANSVAAL)
Pretoria •
SWAZI
Utrecht •
×Blood River
ZULU
Tugela R.
Ungungundhlovu
× Vegkop
Rhenoster R.
ORANGE FREE STATE
Sand R.
Winburg
Bloemfontein •
Boomplaats ×
Thaba Nchu
× —1861
Adam Kok
Philippolis •
Vet R.
Vaal R.
Hart R.
Potchefstroom •
TSWANA
Limpopo R.
Molopo R.
Mariico R.
GRIQUALAND WEST
(Annexed 1871)
Cornelius Kok
Griquatown •
Water Boer
Orange R.
Thaba Bosiu
BASUTOLAND
Aliwal N •
GRIQUALAND EAST
PONDO
Pt Natal (Durban)
Pietermaritzberg
NATAL
THEMBU
Kei R.
X H O S A
Eastern frontier 1871
BR. KAFFRARIA (annexed 1847, to Cape 1866)
Natal strip 1819
Keiskamma R.
Kat R.
×
Neutral strip 1798
Eastern
Frontier 1798
Fish R.
Grahamstown •
Z u u r v e l d
Sundays R.
Graaff Reinet •
Port Elizabeth
C A P E   C O L O N Y
Swellendam •
Stellenbosch •
Robben I.
Cape Town

Delagoa Bay

24°S
28°S
32°S
28°S
32°S

32°E
28°E
24°E
20°E
32°E
28°E
24°E
20°E

Hand in hand with the territorial expansion of the white settler colony went the development and consolidation of a rigid system of class stratification based on race. The failure of early ideas of developing a white working class had been ensured by the importation of slaves. Thereafter the role of manual labour was to be almost exclusively confined to persons of non-European descent. While not averse to manual work where it was necessary for demonstrative purposes, or where non-white labourers were absent or insufficient for the fulfilment of the task, whites expected to occupy roles of authority and command. With the expansion of the colony a large proportion of the indigenous Khoi, whose lands were taken by the settlers, were incorporated in the white farmers' labour force. A process was established whereby the white dominated agricultural system expanded territorially at the expense of traditional systems, converting part of the indigenous population into labourers within the new economic order.

As this continued, the outlying members of the white group were increasingly isolated in the vastness of the interior, in physical danger from their non-European workers, as well as from independent African peoples on whose lands they were intruding. They were in danger also of cultural absorption by the non-European majority amongst whom they lived. In response they developed a powerful sense of racial community and exclusiveness and beliefs in inherent racial superiority, to justify and strengthen their dominant position. Anything which tended to weaken belief in intrinsic white superiority, or to hint at equality between persons of different race, came to seem a threat to their very survival.[1] These attitudes were further strengthened by the long struggle with the San, which took the form of a war of extermination. Hunting down the San like wild animals had a brutalizing effect on the settlers and cheapened the price they set on non-European lives.[2]

As these attitudes grew, they inevitably affected the status of persons of mixed descent. Originally freely accepted as members of the white community, the offspring of white amours with Khoi or slave women found themselves confined to the ranks of non-white labourers. Numbers of them began drifting out of the colony in the wake of the Khoi group known as the Korana, retreating before the advancing frontiers. They began settling in the relatively underpopulated lands around the Orange river, which still remained a no-man's land between the African peasant communities expanding from the north and the

[1] See I. D. MacCrone, *Race attitudes in South Africa* (London, 1937).
[2] See O. F. Mentzel, *A geographical and topographical description of the Cape of Good Hope*, III, ed. H. T. Mandelbrote, Van Riebeeck Society (Cape Town, 1944), 334–5.

colony expanding from the south. At the same time Khoi in the service of white frontier farmers, deprived of their lands by the settler advance and reduced to servile dependence on their white masters, nursed bitter grievances which could only too easily explode into violence and coalesce with frontier conflicts to produce a really severe upheaval.

Faced with the problem of tension between white and non-white, both along the frontiers of white settlement and between masters and servants within the settled area, the Dutch East India Company's government, through Maynier its magistrate at Graaff Reinet, had attempted to impose respect for the normal procedures of orderly government. Maynier made it clear that military action against the Xhosa of the Zuurveld was a matter of government policy and was not to be undertaken on local settler initiative. He also showed himself ready to listen to complaints of ill-treatment on the part of the Khoi servants. In response the settlers rose against the Company's rule.[1] In February 1795 Maynier was expelled and an independent republic of Graaff Reinet proclaimed. The movement spread to the adjoining magistracy of Swellendam, where a settler republic was similarly proclaimed a few weeks later. The underlying conflict between white and non-white on the frontiers and within the colony had produced the first serious uprising by the settlers against the metropolitan government, a conflict which the Company had failed to suppress by the time the British seized possession of the colony.

The first period of British rule, which lasted from 1795 until 1803, was a temporary occupation. The basic structure of the situation and the pattern of conflict to which it gave rise remained unchanged. Though the initial defiance of the frontier farmers towards the new ruling power was speedily and effectively crushed by means of an economic blockade of the frontier districts, which deprived the rebellious settlers of essential supplies of ammunition, the new administration adopted essentially the same policies to the frontier areas as its predecessor. Maynier was even sent back for a time as resident commissioner. Two further rebellions by frontier settlers took place in 1799 and 1801.

In the process of crushing the first and most dangerous of these, the British authorities unwittingly brought about the coalescence of class and frontier tensions, which posed the greatest danger to white settler frontier society. The British force sent to repress the rebellion of the eastern frontier farmers contained a corps of Khoi soldiery. Seeing

[1] See J. S. Marais, *Maynier and the first Boer republics* (Cape Town, 1944).

these in the company of British troops, Khoi farm servants thought that the British had come as their allies in a struggle with their white masters. They deserted their employers in large numbers, formed armed bands and began widespread pillaging of white farms. At the same time the Xhosa, misinformed by the rebellious settlers of the purpose of the British expedition and believing that plans were afoot to drive them from their homeland on the Zuurveld, joined with the Khoi bands in looting white farms. The combination of Xhosa numbers with Khoi fire-power and inside knowledge of settler property and affairs, resulted in widespread devastation. Farms were burnt and stock looted as far west as the Langekloof. Some farmers were reduced to living permanently in their wagons, clothing themselves and their families in animal skins. Only general exhaustion, the absence of further rich booty and quarrels between the Khoi and Xhosa enabled the British to patch up peace of a kind on the eve of their handing over of the Cape to the representatives of the Dutch Batavian Republic in 1803.

For the future history of South Africa the most significant development during the first British occupation was the introduction to the Cape of the new missionary-philanthropic movement, which was finding increasing favour with the rising middle classes in Britain and Europe generally. Dedicated to the christianization and 'civilization' of Africa, processes which they generally believed to be inseparable, the missionaries were agents of cultural change. Their programmes, initially at least, envisaged the creation of an African clergy taking the lead in developing self-sustaining African churches. It was also hoped to create an African middle class, which would adopt European technology and patterns of economic life, and transform African society on the model of western Europe.[1] By thus regenerating Africa with the Bible and the plough, by transforming African societies into modern communities of producers and consumers, the missionaries would encourage Africans to produce the raw materials needed by European factories and provide a market for European manufactured goods. In this way their endeavours directly served the interests of the commercial classes who so generously financed them. The aims of the missionary movement did not directly imply the extension of European political authority. They were not, however, necessarily opposed to it. Very often the missionary in his attempt to transform traditional

[1] See e.g. Dr J. Philip to J. B. Purney, Cape Town, May 1833, in D. J. Kotze, ed., *Letters of the American missionaries 1835–1838*, Van Riebeeck Society (Cape Town, 1950), 28–45; also the argument in Dr J. Philip, *Researches in South Africa*, 2 vols. (London, 1828).

African society would come to see the establishment of European rule as an essential or at least valuable aid to the attainment of his primary object.

These aims conflicted with the attitudes and interests of the Cape settlers, who needed to preserve their position as an exclusive dominant élite, reducing the indigenous peoples to a labouring class within an economic system controlled by whites.

On his arrival as agent of the London Missionary Society in 1799, Dr Jan van der Kemp identified himself closely with the Khoi, seeing himself as the protector of an oppressed people as well as their spiritual guide. The British authorities allowed him to gather Khoi around him, and promised him land on which his flock would be able to live without being forced to accept employment from the frontier farmers. Van der Kemp was still temporarily established on a vacant farm pending a final decision on the location of his proposed mission station when the Batavian authorities took possession of the Cape.

The brief period of rule by the Batavian Republic (1803–6) saw no vital change in the situation at the Cape. So far as the frontier was concerned, the new administration carried on much the same policies as the British. The idea of establishing mission stations for the Khoi was supported, and van der Kemp was given land at Bethelsdorp. The attempt to regulate the conditions of service of Khoi on white farms was also pursued, and the majority of them returned to work or settled down on the mission stations. Unsuccessful attempts were made to persuade the Xhosa to leave the Zuurveld. The period was one of unusual peace and apparent harmony. So far as the eastern frontier was concerned, however, it was essentially a peace of exhaustion. The underlying problems were far from being resolved and with the growth of population they soon reasserted themselves.

As the Treaty of Amiens, under which the Cape had been handed over to the Batavian Republic, proved no more than a truce in the long-drawn out struggle between Britain and Napoleonic France, the British took possession of the Cape once more in 1806. The second British occupation, like the first, initially had the character of a temporary occupation, until the colony was formally ceded to Britain under the terms of the general peace settlement of 1814.

Immediately after 1806 the British authorities at the Cape represented a high Tory government at home and tended to sympathize more with employers than employees. Like the colonists themselves, the authorities looked with a somewhat jaundiced eye on the mission stations for the Khoi within the colony, which were regarded as havens of idleness holding back much needed labour from useful employment on white farms. They were also suspicious of extra-colonial mission activity, but they could not ignore the growing political influence of the missionaries' supporters in Britain, and were determined to govern effectively and impose the rule of law on the frontier areas.

A major step in this direction was Governor Caledon's Ordinance of 1809 codifying regulations concerning the colonial Khoi. These regulations strongly favoured the white farmers as employers. Khoi were forbidden to move from one district to another without a pass from the local magistrate. Every Khoi had to establish a fixed address (i.e., on a white farm or recognized mission station). If he left that address, he must establish another fixed address within fourteen days on pain of arrest for vagrancy. These regulations gave the farmers a firm hold over their Khoi labour, and prevented them not only from withdrawing their labour altogether, but even from selling at the highest possible price, by making it very difficult for them to move around the country in search of higher wages. The farmers' hold over their Khoi servants was still further increased in 1812 by an ordinance under which a farmer who had maintained a Khoi child on his farm to the age of eight was entitled to apprentice him to a further ten years' service. Finally in 1819 Lord Somerset decreed that Khoi children left unprotected as a result of the death of their parents or any other cause should be apprenticed to Europeans until their eighteenth year.

Though favouring white farmers, the 1809 regulations also regulated the conduct of employers towards their servants in considerable detail. Relations between masters and servants were thus definitely brought within the sphere of the law and the unlimited patriarchal authority of the farmer on his *plaas* was undermined. In 1811–12 this change in relations between farmers and their non-white servants, which had begun with the magistracy of Maynier, made itself forcibly felt in the frontier districts. Stung by allegations that the administration had allowed atrocities against Khoi in the frontier districts, the governor, Sir John Cradock, ordered the circuit court to inquire closely into all complaints of mistreatment by employers of their non-white servants.

The so-called Black Circuit faithfully carried out its instructions. Many of the complaints brought forward turned out to be trivial or fabricated, but a good deal of cruelty was uncovered and two farmers were convicted of murder. The Black Circuit aroused a great deal of resentment among the frontier settlers.[1] Not only did it give rise to bitter feelings on the grounds that many farmers had been dragged away from their farms, leaving their families and property undefended, to answer charges which turned out to be insubstantial, but the principle that whites could be summoned to court to answer charges brought by their non-white servants struck at white racial pride, and weakened the farmers' authority over their servants by interposing the authority of the courts between them.

In 1815 the antagonism roused by the proceedings of the Black Circuit erupted into violence. A farmer named Bezuidenhout refused to answer a summons on a charge of maltreating a Khoi servant and was shot while resisting arrest. Members of his family vowed revenge and tried to raise a rebellion. The authorities took prompt action. The incipient revolt was quickly crushed and the ringleaders publicly hanged at Slachters Nek. This abortive uprising was the last of the series of frontier rebellions which had begun with the rising against Maynier in 1795. The stern action of the authorities effectively deterred any further repetitions, and ensured that hostility to the policies of the colonial government would in future express itself in withdrawal beyond the colonial frontiers rather than in armed rebellion within them.

In the same year that the Black Circuit was infuriating the frontier farmers, the British authorities intervened decisively on the settlers' behalf in the affairs of the Zuurveld. The Fish river had long been accepted by the colonial authorities as the legal frontier of the colony. The decision was now taken to make it an effective boundary between the colonists and the Bantu peoples. In 1811–12 British troops drove 20,000 Xhosa across the river, thus freeing the whole of the Zuurveld for settlement by whites whose growing families were hard-pressed for farms.[2] To safeguard the frontier, a series of military posts (the most important of which was Grahamstown) were established. By driving the Zuurveld Xhosa back upon their fellows beyond the Fish river, the colonial authorities produced serious conditions of overcrowding and tension beyond the river. In spite of the military patrols the situation in the Zuurveld remained too insecure to encourage white settlement.

Beyond the frontier the Qunukwebe and Ndlambe sections of the

[1] G. M. Theal, *History of South Africa 1795–1828* (London, 1903), 202–3, gives the settler point of view.
[2] 'Extract from Report of the Commission of Circuit to Lieutenant-General Sir J. F. Cradock, 28 February 1812', *Papers relative to the condition and treatment of the native inhabitants of Southern Africa*. Parliamentary Papers, 1835, part I, 111–14.

Xhosa were bitter at the loss of their homeland. In their frustration, they sought supernatural means to redress the balance of armaments and to provide them with the ideology for organization on the scale necessary for a war against the colony. Makanna, a subject of Ndlambe, taught that if the Xhosa would practise the strictest moral discipline the heroes of the past would return aided by a mighty wind to help them drive the white settlers from their ancestral homes. Inspired by this message, Makanna's following grew rapidly and the followers of other chiefs flocked to join Ndlambe. Resentment at this development, and conflict over grazing lands at a time of drought, led to a head-on clash between Ndlambe's people and the followers of Ngqika who had always lived beyond the Fish and bore no animosity against the whites. At the battle of Amalinde, Ngqika was heavily defeated and the unification of his followers with those of Ndlambe into a formidable block inspired by Makanna appeared imminent.

The colonial authorities acted quickly and prevented the merger from taking place. A colonial force went to the aid of Ngqika and recaptured numbers of the cattle he had lost to Ndlambe. The Ndlambes led by Makanna then invaded the colony. Grahamstown was besieged and its garrison hard pressed before reinforcements came up and the tide of battle turned. Colonial forces struck back across the Fish, and Makanna voluntarily gave himself up to save his people from further suffering. He was imprisoned on Robben Island and eventually drowned in an attempt to escape. In the settlement which followed the Xhosa resistance war of 1818–19, the British treated Ngqika as the paramount ruler of all the Xhosa living in the vicinity of the Fish river. In this capacity he was forced to agree to the cession of the land between the Fish and Keiskamma rivers. This area was to form a neutral strip kept empty of inhabitants of both areas.

The idea of an empty buffer zone between the races was a natural extension of the long established policy of attempting to resolve the problems of frontier tension by keeping the races apart. It was based on a failure to appreciate the fact that overcrowding among the Africans beyond the Fish was a main cause of frontier tension and that depriving them of still more land could only make the situation worse. It also ignored the fact that trade between the two groups had already made them mutually dependent to a considerable extent. Pressure from both sides ultimately resulted in the strip filling up with a mixed population of settlers and Africans, thus largely duplicating the problems that had existed on the Zuurveld before 1812.

In the meantime the reluctance of white settlers in the continuing conditions of insecurity to take up farms on the Zuurveld provided the occasion and the opportunity for the most ambitious attempt to grapple with the problems of the colony yet undertaken. The idea was to settle the Zuurveld with English settlers, each of whom would be given a farm of 40 hectares with an allowance of an extra 20 hectares to anyone who brought a farm labourer with him. The settlers were to work their land with their own labour and that of their families, together with any white farm workers they brought with them. By introducing a new farming pattern of intensive cultivation on small farms, a relatively dense white population would be established which would be capable of providing for its own defence. At the same time the Cape would relieve the mother country of some of its population, at a time when unemployment was giving grave cause for concern. A solid block of loyal British citizens would be established at the Cape to offset the somewhat dubious loyalties of the Dutch-speaking majority.

During 1820 about 10,000 British people were brought to the Cape, and the majority settled on small farms on the Zuurveld. The success of the experiment depended on the assumption that small-scale farming at the Cape was economically viable, an assumption contradicted by the whole past history of white farming in the colony. The scheme was misconceived and its collapse was hastened rather than caused by the particularly adverse climatic conditions of the first two years. The majority of the settlers remained dependent on rations supplied by the government until these were cut off. Most of them then left the land for the towns, while those who remained pressed for large farms of the type held by their Dutch-speaking neighbours.

Other measures taken by the authorities to encourage a more intensive use of land were equally unsuccessful. Provision was made for the traditional loan farm system of tenure to be converted into permanent ownership in return for an annual quit rent, thus allowing farms to be subdivided among heirs on the death of the owner. It was decided that crown lands still available in the colony would no longer be given out virtually free but sold by public auction. These measures together with the 1820 settlement merely increased the problem of land hunger and the tendency of the whites to go beyond the frontier in search of farms. At the same time they generated hostility against a government which seemed to be intent on making land hard to get and raising its price.

The resistance of the Xhosa on the eastern coastal corridor virtually brought further settler expansion in that direction to a halt, so the tide turned northwards. Though the north-eastern frontier of the colony was not substantially altered between 1798 and 1824 and farmers were sternly forbidden to go beyond it, the economic facts of life ensured that the border would be ignored. In 1820 farmers were already settled as far as the Orange river. Thus between 1800 and 1824 about 130,000 square kilometres of country previously occupied by San hunting bands was taken over by white farmers, and by 1825 no single independent band remained within this entire area.[1] The revision of the border, to bring it into line with the facts of settlement, took place between 1820 and 1824. The frontier was then extended as far as the Orange river in the north-east corner of the colony. By the time this revision was made, however, the land behind the new frontier was already fully settled and farmers were beginning to look across the Orange river, where the devastations of the wars associated with the rise of the Zulu had resulted in land lying apparently unoccupied and available for white settlement. Movement of settlers across the Orange began on a large scale in 1825. At first it took the form of temporary migrations under the impulse of drought and locust plagues, but by 1830 settlement north of the river was already assuming a permanent character and requests began to come from settlers for legal recognition of farms beyond the Orange. As early as 1829 some settlers had trekked as far as the Harts river and set up beacons there with their names on them.[2]

The beginnings of the extension of white settlement into the area of the modern Orange Free State coincided with the immigration into and settlement in part of the same area by a section of the Griqua. Consisting partly of pure Khoi and partly of persons of mixed European–Khoi descent driven out of the colony by the rising barriers of colour discrimination, the Griqua had settled along the north bank of the Orange, just to the west of its junction with the Vaal, in the closing years of the eighteenth century.

In 1800 the London Missionary Society missionaries, Anderson and Kramer, set up a station with the Griqua at Klaarwater (later known as Griquatown). They persuaded the heterogeneous community to adopt the name Griqua and establish a regular polity with a republican form of government. About 1820, however, conflicts within the Griqua community, and between the Griqua chief Adam Kok II and the missionaries, led to the deposition of the chief and the installation of the mission catechist Andries Waterboer in his place. Adam Kok and his

---

[1] P. J. van der Merwe, *Die noordwaartse beweging van die Boere voor die Groot Trek* (The Hague, 1937), 153–4.   [2] Van der Merwe, *Die noordwaartse beweging*, 233.

followers then seceded from the main settlement, and this was followed by further secessions of disgruntled Griqua, who under the name of Bergenaars took to a life of plunder raiding the Tswana tribes. In 1825 the missionary John Philip, anxious to persuade Adam Kok to settle down and to prevent him joining the Bergenaars, gave him permission to settle at the London Missionary Society's station for the San at Philippolis.

While Adam Kok and his followers were in the process of settling on the lands around Philippolis and establishing a second Griqua state there, they began to come under pressure from white settlers infiltrating into the same area. Protests backed by the missionaries proved of no avail. The Griqua lacked the social and political coherence to prevent their members succumbing to the temptation to rent farms to whites on long leases in return for immediate cash, nor did they have the military strength to risk a direct confrontation with the settlers. In 1835 Adam Kok journeyed to Cape Town to urge the governor to annex the land of his people as the only way of saving them from Boer encroachments. His efforts were in vain and he died on the return journey, leaving his successor Adam Kok III to face a problem which was to grow steadily worse in the future.

The northward expansion of white settlers to the Orange river and beyond provided only limited relief from the problems of land hunger in the colony. This expansion was largely undertaken by the sons of farmers already established in the north-eastern districts of the Cape. Much larger numbers remained dammed up against the eastern frontier, where rising population on both sides, and the economic interdependence of colonists and African peasants, had led to the breakdown of the policy of a neutral buffer zone. In times of drought farmers would lead their cattle deep into the neutral strip and beyond, and some began settling among the Xhosa far in advance of the colonial frontier.

Pressure of rising population was equally great in the other direction and much of the neutral strip had filled up with an African population. The permission of the colonial authorities for settlement in this area was given on the basis of good behaviour. The chiefs and their people lacked security of tenure and might find themselves driven from their homes at short notice. The point was emphasized in 1830, when Macoma was driven from the lands he had been allowed to occupy along the Kat river and they were used for an experimental settlement of Khoi (intended to provide the colonists with a defensive buffer). Resentment at the loss of land already taken by the whites was compounded by fear that they would soon take over the rest of the neutral strip, as they had previously done with the Zuurveld. Tension remained high and was exacerbated by measures taken to recover cattle stolen from the colony, which only too often resulted in the innocent suffering for the guilty.

In the meantime the philanthropic movement had been steadily gathering strength in Britain. From attacking the slave trade it had moved to seeking the abolition of the institution itself throughout British possessions, and to a general concern for the fate of aboriginal peoples in British colonies. In the Cape, slave owners were subjected to ever-increasing restrictions on their right to deal with their slaves as they pleased, and the eventual abolition of slavery could be seen to be only a matter of time. At the same time attention was focused on the lot of the settlers' free non-white employees. In his *Researches in South Africa* the missionary John Philip bitterly attacked the discriminatory regulations governing the right of the Khoi in the Cape Colony to move about the country in search of better wages or, to withdraw their labour from the whites altogether. These regulations, he argued, placed the Khoi in a situation of economic subjection to the whites even worse in some respects than slavery. They prevented the Khoi from bettering themselves economically and so providing a greatly increased market for British goods. In the atmosphere generated by this combined appeal to philanthropy and economic interest, the acting governor, Bourke, in consultation with the philanthropically minded frontier magistrate Andries Stockenstroom, framed Ordinance no. 50 of 1828. This abolished all discriminatory restrictions on the Khoi and placed them on a basis of legal equality with the settlers. On receiving it the British Parliament decreed that its provisions might not be altered without reference to the king-in-council.

The 50th Ordinance amounted to a revolution in the legal status of non-whites at the Cape. It constituted an attempt to reverse the trend towards increasingly rigid colour stratification which had characterized the history of the Cape settlement since the latter years of the seventeenth century. From the point of view of the settlers, the 50th Ordinance worsened the labour problems and added to the problems of security by permitting Khoi to wander about the country at will. It also struck at the heart of the deep-seated prejudices and beliefs about the proper relationships between the races which had grown up to rationalize and support the system of race–class stratification on which settler society was based.

When the decision to abolish slavery altogether was finally taken, the dissatisfaction of whites at the Cape reached a new peak. The abolition had long been anticipated, but the provision that ex-slaves after a period of apprenticeship to their former masters would come under the terms of Ordinance 50 and enjoy legal equality with whites was deeply resented.[1]

It seemed to the frontier farmers in particular that the alien government had no sympathy for their lot. It had failed to advance the frontier with the Xhosa. Under missionary pressure it tended to blame the whites for frontier tensions, and looked with disfavour on measures taken to preserve their security and recover their stolen cattle. It appeared determined to revolutionize the social structure on which their economic position, social status and physical security were based.

Just at this time the news was spreading that there were wide areas in the interior virtually uninhabited and suitable for white settlement. The idea of a mass secession, and the establishment of an independent polity beyond the frontiers of the colony, began to take form. In 1834 three small reconnaissance parties set out for the interior to examine the possibilities.

Before they returned, however, the situation was dramatically changed by the outbreak of another war on the eastern frontier. Governor D'Urban, who came out to the Cape to carry through the emancipation of slaves, brought with him instructions to look into the frontier situation and devise some other method of preserving security than periodical commandos sent to recover stolen cattle. On his arrival he consulted with the missionaries, and asked Philip to visit the frontier chiefs and inform them that he would soon be visiting them himself and intended to introduce a frontier system that would be more in their interest. Philip's tour had an immediately calming effect on the tense frontier situation but D'Urban, weighed down by paper work, postponed his visit to the frontier. At last the chiefs and their people became convinced that the message was a trap and that the colonial government was preparing to drive them still further back. In December 1834, the long accumulated tensions burst into violence and the Xhosa poured into the colony.

Wide areas in the frontier districts were devastated before the troops gained the upper hand and struck back far into Xhosa territory. D'Urban, who had at last reached the frontier area, was appalled at the

[1] Anna Steenkamp, 'Record or journal of our migration from our mother country to Port Natal', *Die Dagboek van Anna Steenkamp* (Pietermaritzburg, 1939). J. Bird, *The annals of Natal* (Pietermaritzburg, 1888), 459.

destruction. The Xhosa were stigmatized as irredeemable savages. The annexation of the area between the Fish and the Kei rivers as Queen Adelaide Province was proclaimed. The Xhosa were to be driven out of this whole area for ever.

D'Urban's annexation, and the prospect of abundant new farms in the Queen Adelaide Province, delighted the frontier farmers, who felt that they had at last a governor who understood and sympathized with their predicament. The 'extermination' policy, however, roused howls of missionary protest, which fell on sympathetic ears in England, where a Parliamentary Select Committee on Aborigines was meeting. The policy also proved beyond the military capacities of the authorities at the Cape. The Xhosa fought on desperately, and not only refused to be driven out of Queen Adelaide Province but even raided the settled districts of the colony. D'Urban substantially revised his original policy in favour of allowing the Xhosa to retain most of their lands in Queen Adelaide under direct British rule, while allowing a limited number of settlers to be established on farms in the area. His extreme dilatoriness, however, prevented his new policy from being understood in London. The secretary of state, Lord Glenelg, instructed him to prepare the public mind for the abandonment of the province, and informed him of the appointment of the philanthropically inclined Stockenstroom as lieutenant-governor of the eastern districts. The retrocession of Queen Adelaide Province,[1] which dashed all hopes of settler advance along the well-watered eastern coastal corridor and confirmed their worst fears about the British government's attitude to relations between the races, precipitated secession. In the last months of 1836 Dutch-speaking frontier farmers began streaming out of the colony heading northwards across the Orange for the wide empty lands their spying parties had visited.

THE GREAT TREK

The Great Trek was in one sense merely an accelerated phase in the long process of white expansion which had already brought the white farmers from the Cape to the Fish river, and at that very time was resulting in increasing settlement of the lands between the Orange and the Vaal. The white advance, long dammed up by the resistance of the Xhosa on the Eastern Frontier, dramatically changed direction and burst out to the north. Yet the Great Trek was different in its scale, its

[1] The evacuation of the province was finally ordered by D'Urban in October 1836. E. A. Walker, *A history of southern Africa*, rev. ed. (London, 1965), 190–3.

organization and its motivation from the previous and concurrently continuing movements of white expansion. Whereas settlers who went beyond the frontiers in the past had no intention of cutting themselves off from the colony, but rather hoped to draw the frontier after them, the Boers who took part in the Great Trek went with the determination to shake off the authority of the British government for ever and to establish an independent state based on their own principles. In this sense the Great Trek was a form of political protest, another in the series of revolts of frontier settlers against the agents of the metropolitan power which had begun with the expulsion of Maynier from his magistracy in 1795. It was a protest against the attempts by the British authorities, under pressure from the missionary-philanthropic movement, to modify the pattern of race relations within the colony and along its borders. The trekkers left the colony in protest against the ungodly equality implied in the 50th Ordinance and the general attitude of the British authorities, and determined to establish a society in which 'proper relations' between master and servant would be preserved.[1]

The nature and form of this movement of protest was not exclusively determined by developments within the colony. It was the wars and migrations started by the rise of the Zulu kingdoms which temporarily cleared the modern Orange Free State, Natal and the Transvaal of a large proportion of their population, created the possibility of mass emigration into the interior and determined the directions taken by the trekkers. Turning back from the densely populated eastern coastal corridor, the trekkers moved through Transorangia, skirting the heavily populated kingdom of Moshoeshoe, to pour into Natal and the Transvaal, where the African population had been drastically reduced by the regiments of the Zulu and Ndebele.[2] In its most fundamental significance the Great Trek was a phase in the long drawn out struggle between white settlers and Africans for the farming lands of South Africa.

The Great Trek was not just the movement of whites into the interior, it was the migration of an economic system, involving the exploitation of large areas of land by individual white farmers with the aid of non-white labour, and of principles of political and social organization related to that economic system. The nature of the white system of land exploitation implied continuous and rapid territorial expansion with growth of the white population. Each new area of white settle-

[1] See accounts given by participants in Bird, *The annals of Natal*, I, and by G. S. Preller, *Voortrekkermense* (Cape Town, 1920). See also E. A. Walker, *The Great Trek* (London, 1960).
[2] See ch. 9, 'The Nguni outburst', p. 352.

ment was bound to become a growth point for further territorial expansion, involving the take-over of lands occupied by African peasants, the expulsion of part of the population and the absorption of the rest as a strongly subordinated class of farm workers within the new socio-economic system.

This process naturally evoked bitter resistance from African peoples struggling to maintain possession of their lands and to maintain their political, social and cultural identity and independence. Superiority of armaments ensured that African resistance would generally be overborne. The process was complex. White society itself was based on, and derived its potential for expansion from, the employment of African labour. African leaders were active agents in the drama. African chiefs often understood clearly the nature of the threats which menaced their people and their traditional way of life. They attempted to meet them by a variety of means. The aid of missionaries was sought, both with a view to acquiring European knowledge, skills and weapons, and for the sake of the diplomatic support they could give to the chiefs who favoured them. Divisions between different European groups were consciously exploited and determined military resistance was offered when essential interests were threatened. Though these measures could not reverse the general tendency towards the expansion of white dominated society at the expense of independent African groups, the outcome in particular areas was often largely determined by the strength of African resistance, qualities of leadership and politico-military organization.

Moving out of the colony in a whole series of separate trekking parties, the emigrant white farmers converged on the neighbourhood of the Wesleyan Mission with the Rolong at Thaba Nchu. Some of them moved across the Vaal river where, arriving unannounced, they were mistaken by the Ndebele regiments of Mzilikazi for another Griqua invasion of the type that on two occasions had almost succeeded in overthrowing the Ndebele kingdom.[1] The Ndebele took the scattered trekkers by surprise, and two parties were virtually wiped out. The rest, however, were warned in time and beat off the first assault. Under the leadership of Potgieter, the trekkers retreated across the Vaal to a hill subsequently known as Vegkop, where they built a laager by linking their wagons in a defensive circle. Firing from behind this barricade, they drove off the attacking Ndebele, who retreated taking the trekkers' cattle with them. Potgieter and his

---

[1] See ch. 9, 'The Nguni outburst', p. 344.

party were helped by the Rolong chief Moroka to fall back on Thaba Nchu.

Conflicts over political leadership and disagreements over the direction to be taken by the Trek led to a division in the trekker community on the highveld. Potgieter and his supporters determined to revenge themselves on the Ndebele and to settle the lands beyond the Vaal, from where they hoped to make contact with the Portuguese in Mozambique. In January 1837, with the support of a number of Griqua and Rolong, they launched a reprisal raid against Mzilikazi and captured large herds of cattle. In celebration of their victory they established the village of Winburg, near the Sand river, as the base from which to pursue the struggle with the Ndebele king. In November 1837, a second attack was launched on Mzilikazi, and in nine days of fighting the Ndebele were driven from all their principal towns. Mzilikazi, who in the interval had been badly mauled by an attack from the Zulu regiments of Dingane and who was already contemplating movement to the north, abandoned the Transvaal, and his people set out on their migration to Matabeleland. Potgieter claimed the area previously occupied by the Ndebele by right of conquest, and permanent settlement by trekkers in the Transvaal was established at Potchefstroom on the Mooi river.

THE BOERS IN NATAL

The majority of the trekkers did not follow Potgieter, but accepted the leadership of Piet Retief, whose opinion was that the fertile lands of Natal, where the port already developed by the English traders offered an opening to the sea, should be the home of their new polity. Retief rode off to see Dingane and obtain his permission for the trekkers to settle in Natal. The Zulu king was deeply alarmed. Anxious to avoid an immediate conflict, he promised Retief that he would make him a grant of Natal if he would recover some cattle said to have been stolen by the Tlokwa chief Sekonyela.

The events which followed did little to calm Dingane's fears. Retief tricked Sekonyela into trying on a pair of handcuffs and held him prisoner until the cattle were surrendered. News came in of the Boers' victory over Mzilikazi and his flight from the Transvaal, and Retief wrote in hectoring terms pointing the moral and advising Dingane to consult the missionaries about the fate of wicked kings.[1] Finally the trekkers began pouring over the passes of the Drakensberg and settling

[1] Bird, *The annals of Natal*, i, 362–4.

in the Natal area, even before Retief had returned to claim his reward. Dingane massed his regiments and prepared for a desperate blow to destroy the immigrants and save his kingdom before it should be too late. Retief was given his piece of paper ceding possession of Natal. He and his companions were tricked into attending an assembly unarmed. They were seized and put to death. The Zulu regiments then set out at once to attack the scattered wagons of the trekkers unprepared. Caught unawares, some of the Boers were massacred, but others were roused by the sound of firing and the regiments were driven off with heavy losses.

Dingane had failed, but the position of the trekkers remained very precarious. As a result of divided leadership a Boer counter-attack ended in fiasco and flight, which gave it the name *Vlug Kommando*. Many abandoned hope and thought of returning to the high veld. However trekkers attracted by reports of the rich lands of Natal came up from the Cape. Others followed, inspired by the desire to aid their fellows in their hour of need. Andries Pretorius from Graaff Reinet, who had visited the trekkers soon after their arrival in Natal, came in with a strong following and assumed the military leadership. Strengthened by these reinforcements, the trekkers once more took the initiative. A powerful commando set out for Dingane's capital, Ungungundhlovu. They halted and built a laager on the banks of the Blood river. On 16 December 1838 they were attacked by the full strength of Dingane's forces. The close-packed regiments offered a perfect target for the trekkers' guns, and the Zulu were defeated with very heavy losses. The *Win Kommando* then marched on to the smouldering ruins of Ungungundhlovu, where the bodies of Retief and his companions were found, together with the deed of cession granting them possession of Natal.

By this time a small British force had arrived at Port Natal to watch the trekkers' proceedings. It was too small to do much, and its commander contented himself with arranging peace negotiations between the trekkers and Dingane before sailing away again. The trekkers had now clearly established themselves in Natal. Pietermaritzburg was founded as a capital, and the foundations of a republic laid. But their position remained a dangerous one while the Zulu kingdom, defeated but far from destroyed, was still ruled by Dingane.

At this point political division within the Zulu kingdom played into the trekkers' hands. Mpande, a brother of Dingane, broke away and sought the protection of the Boers. Then, with the support of a Boer commando marching in parallel with his own forces, he advanced to challenge Dingane for the Zulu throne. The two Zulu armies met at

Umgongo. Dingane was defeated and fled into Swaziland, where he was killed by a local headman. The Boer commando did not fire a shot, but reaped the fruits of Mpande's victory. The new Zulu ruler accepted the status of vassal of the republic and handed over huge herds of cattle, thus giving the expedition the title of the Cattle Commando.

The trekkers in Natal were then able to organize their polity around their capital of Pietermaritzburg. Though the disagreement on the high veld had led to the establishment of two distinct trekker groups, one in Natal and the other settled around Winburg and Potchefstroom in the northern Orange Free State and the south-western Transvaal, the sense of common identity and the feeling that they all formed a single *maatschapij* (company) remained strong. In October 1840 agreement was reached that they should form one republic based on Natal. The local governing committee on the high veld was to be a sub-committee (*adjunkraad*) of the Natal Volksraad, which was the supreme legislative authority for the whole emigrant Boer community. Geographical separation ensured, however, that this unification was no more than nominal. The Volksraad's authority was effectively limited to Natal. Even there, however, conflict between the elective principle embodied in the Volksraad, the principle of executive leadership as represented by Pretorius as *hoof commandant*, and the idea of direct democracy expressed in spontaneous assemblies of the *volk*, prevented the republic from following clearly thought out and consistent policies. Faced with the demands for land which it could not meet in spite of the vast areas it had acquired, demands for cattle which were far from being assuaged by the distribution of the vast herds acquired from Mpande, and by massive immigration into the areas under its authority of Africans returning to their homes now that the Zulu menace had been allayed, the republic adopted ill-considered policies towards its African neighbours which precipitated British intervention.

The Great Trek placed the British authorities in a difficult position. The emigrants were British subjects, and Britain could hardly deny responsibility for their conduct towards the indigenous peoples in the interior. This responsibility had indeed been specifically recognized in the Cape of Good Hope Punishment Act of 1835, passed in response to missionary and philanthropic concern about the fate of aboriginal peoples at the hands of colonists who were moving into the area of the Orange Free State before the Trek. Under this act British subjects could be tried at the Cape for crimes committed beyond its borders as far as the 25th degree of south latitude. To carry out this responsibility effectively, however, would mean extending British authority over the areas occupied by the settlers, once efforts to persuade them to return had proved abortive. Such a massive extension of British authority promised to be very expensive, and it was difficult to see where the process would end if the British government were to consider itself bound to follow its subjects wherever they might wander into the interior. The alternative would be to leave the trekkers to their own devices but, apart from moral concern about the fate of the aborigines, this line of policy promised formidable complications. The Boers in Natal might establish contact with a foreign power, thus undermining the security of the route to India, the ultimate purpose for which the Cape was held. The Boers, moreover, were settled to the north-east and west of a great mass of African peoples who bordered on the Cape. Conflicts between the trekkers and these peoples could only too easily have repercussions on the frontiers of the Cape, generating the very expenditure which it was desired to avoid. Caught on the horns of this dilemma, British policy vacillated between the extremes of annexation and abandonment in reaction to the developing situation in South Africa and political changes at home.

BRITISH NATAL

The initial British response to the situation created by the Trek was a refusal to accept that the trekkers could shake off their allegiance, yet the British drew back from the expense of enforcing that allegiance. Developments in Natal, however, led to the first step towards the assumption of authority over the emigrant farmers. Not only did news of foreign vessels calling at Port Natal raise fears of a foreign establishment on the coast, but philanthropic opinion, alarmed at the news of the Cattle Commando, was further incensed by a Boer raid on the Baca chief Ncapayi. Then, as it became known that the Natal Republic was contemplating seizing an area of land from the Pondo chief Faku, into which to settle its growing unwanted African population, action was precipitated by the danger that a chain reaction along the eastern coastal corridor might be set up with serious consequences for the eastern frontier of the Cape. Sir George Napier, who replaced D'Urban as governor in 1838, sent a British force to Natal. It was attacked and besieged by the republicans. Reinforcements were despatched and the Boers brought to terms. Then, as political institutions disintegrated, Britain took over the administration, and in 1845 Natal was formally annexed. Many of the emigrants, faced with the authority they had sought to escape and distressed by Britain's refusal to segregate the African population *en masse*, left the colony for the high veld. Their place was eventually taken by British settlers, which made Natal the most pronouncedly English-speaking area in South Africa.

Though immigration from Britain, which assumed substantial proportions in 1849–52, filled the gaps created by the exodus of the Boers, the white population in Natal long remained a tiny minority. The most important problems were relations with the Zulu kingdom and the policy to be adopted towards the large internal African population. The handling of these problems was entrusted to Theophilus Shepstone. The son of a missionary to the Xhosa, Shepstone had grown up amongst the peoples of the eastern frontier of the Cape. He served for a time as an agent of the Cape government among the Mfengu and the people of Ndlambe and Congo, and before being appointed in 1845 as diplomatic agent to the native tribes in Natal. His knowledge of African traditions and customs and his flair for diplomacy enabled him to exercise a profound influence over the Zulu king, Mpande. He was equally successful in establishing his influence over the Africans in Natal, with the result that the colony enjoyed a long period of peace. His success in winning the confidence of African chiefs and people led him to an insatiable ambition to bring more and more African peoples under his influence.

Shepstone's policy towards the African peoples was in principle little, if at all, different from that of the Voortrekkers. It involved the segregation of Africans in reserves where they would be ruled by their own chiefs under his ultimate supervision. The idea of removing the entire African population of Natal and settling them in lands to the south having been ruled out, a commission appointed in 1846 demarcated a series of fairly substantial reserves within the boundaries of the colony. Shepstone succeeded in persuading the Natal African population of between 80,000 and 100,000 to move into them without any bloodshed. The large reserves were subsequently the object of settler criticism, on the grounds that they constituted a military danger to the white community and inhibited the maximum exploitation of African labour. Shepstone himself continued to hanker after the policy of the Boer Republic of Natal, and in 1854 formally proposed a scheme to draw off a large proportion of the African population of Natal and settle them in Nomansland with himself as chief.[1] He hoped to be recognized

[1] E. H. Brookes and C. de B. Webb, *A history of Natal* (Pietermaritzburg, 1965), p. 58.

by the British government as an independent though financially subsidized ruler. This project was vetoed by the British high commissioner at the Cape, and the reserves remained.[1]

When Natal was annexed in 1845, it constituted an autonomous district of the Cape ruled by a lieutenant-governor with a wholly official executive council. The legislative authority for the district was the Cape legislative council. In 1856 Natal became a separate colony and gained a limited measure of representative government. A legislative council was set up with twelve elected and four official members. The franchise theoretically followed the colour-blind principle of the Cape franchise, but the conditions under which Africans could qualify for the vote were subsequently hedged about with such difficulties as to make it impossible for any significant number to do so.

In spite of the hut tax imposed on Africans living in Natal, the number of Africans seeking employment with whites failed to meet the demand. With the development of sugar plantations, which began in the coastal lands in the 1850s, the labour shortage became acute. The hut tax was raised sharply from seven to eleven shillings, but this device, while increasing revenue, failed to resolve the labour shortage, and in 1859 provision was made for the importation of Indian workers. The Indian labourers were bound to serve the master to whom they were allocated for five years. Thereafter they were free to enter into further labour contracts or not to work at all, and could change their residence. After ten years they were entitled to free passages back to India, but with the lieutenant-governor's permission they could exchange this for a grant of land. After the ten-year period they were entitled to a permanent right of residence in Natal. The first group of Indian immigrants arrived in November 1860 and thereafter their numbers rose rapidly. By 1885 the Indian population nearly matched the European.[2]

BRITISH FORWARD MOVES: KAFFRARIA AND TRANSORANGIA

The problem of relations between the emigrant Boers and the indigenous peoples, which had led to the annexation of Natal, were equally pressing in the area between the Orange and the Vaal. In that area two

[1] A commission set up in 1852 urged radical changes in the direction of decreasing the size of the reserves (*Proceedings of the Natal Kafir Commission 1852* (Pietermaritzburg, 1852)), but the recommendations were not carried out.

[2] Brookes and Webb, *A history of Natal*, 85.

Boer groups, pre-trek emigrants who still regarded themselves as British subjects, and trekkers who rejected British authority, were settled alongside the Griqua of Adam Kok and the Sotho of Moshoe-shoe. The two white groups were deeply suspicious of each other, but were united in rejecting the authority of the chiefs onto whose lands they had infiltrated. Attempts by Governor Napier to regulate the situation, by defining the frontiers of the chiefs and making treaties requiring them to return Boer offenders to the Cape for trial under the Cape of Good Hope Punishment Act, in return for annual subsidies, broke down on this point. In 1845 his successor, Sir Peregrine Maitland, attempted a new arrangement which would take account of the chiefs' incapacity to exercise authority over the whites. Each chief was to divide his land into an alienable and an inalienable area. No white would be entitled to rent land in the inalienable area. The chief's authority in the alienable area would be delegated to a British resident, who would exercise it over the whites there. This quasi-annexation proved highly unsatisfactory, as the resident lacked an adequate force to assert himself effectively over a white community, one section of which remained deeply hostile to British rule.[1] Tension between the whites and the African peoples persisted, and Transorangia remained in a chaotic condition dangerous to the security of the Cape.

In the aftermath of the 1834–5 frontier war, a treaty system associated with the name of Stockenstroom was never put into effect in the way which that official had intended. Considerations of expense led to its being whittled down to a form which promised little prospect of long term success. Its greatest weakness, as applied to the peoples of the eastern frontier and Transorangia, was that it laid great burdens on the chiefs without giving them adequate support and incentives. Chiefs along the eastern frontier found themselves placed in the increasingly intolerable position of acting as agents for the colonial authorities in recovering cattle said, often on the flimsiest evidence, to have been stolen by their people. In 1846 a relative of Chief Sandile was arrested in the colony for the theft of an axe. He was rescued by comrades who killed the Khoi policeman to whom he was handcuffed. The chief refused to surrender the culprits. The colonial forces crossed the frontier, and the War of the Axe began.

When Sir Harry Smith arrived as the new governor of the Cape and

[1] J. F. Midgley, 'The Orange River Sovereignty', *Archives Year Book for South African History*, II (Cape Town, 1949), 28–48.

high commissioner for the affairs of the interior in December 1847,[1] Xhosa resistance had been broken but a political settlement to replace the discredited treaty system had still to be devised. Harry Smith, who had had previous experience as a military commander in the war of 1834–5, then adopted the policy, towards which D'Urban had been groping in his revised plans, of extending British authority over the frontier peoples and guaranteeing them the possession of their lands under British administration.

He annexed the whole area between the Fish and Kei rivers, promising the Xhosa the continued enjoyment of their lands on condition of their becoming British subjects. The newly annexed area became the separate colony of British Kaffraria. Harry Smith's policy offered perhaps the best hope of bringing to an end the process of settler nibbling at African lands, and the accompanying endemic frontier tension. Unfortunately, it was carried through with more haste than foresight, and with a lack of adequate administrative resources, for which Harry Smith's bombastic theatricality provided no adequate substitute. Having as he believed impressed the Xhosa chiefs with British might by blowing up a wagon filled with gunpowder in their presence,[2] Harry Smith rode off hastily to Natal, to deal with the problem posed by trekkers abandoning that colony.

On his way he passed through Transorangia and speedily came to the conclusion that only the extension of British authority to the area could put an end to the chaotic situation, make orderly economic progress possible, protect the African peoples from being expropriated by the whites and prevent an explosion of violence which would inevitably spread to the Cape. At a hastily summoned conference at Bloemfontein, attended by Moshoeshoe as well as by a number of Boer leaders, he gained the impression that all parties would welcome the establishment of British rule, and soon after his arrival in Natal he proclaimed the whole area between the Orange and the Vaal annexed as the Orange River Sovereignty. Major Warden, who had acted as resident under the terms of the Maitland agreement, was appointed to head the administration.

Like his attempted solution of the eastern frontier problem, Harry Smith's annexation of the Orange River Sovereignty had much to

---

[1] High commissioner 'for the settling and adjustment of the affairs of the territories . . . adjacent or contiguous to the . . . frontier'. The title was first conferred on Sir Henry Pottinger who held office at the Cape from January to December 1847.

[2] According to one account the wagon failed to explode at all. J. M. Orpen, *Reminiscences of life in South Africa* (Cape Town, 1946), I, 331.

recommend it, but, as with the annexation of British Kaffraria, it was carried out too hastily and with inadequate consideration of the practical implications. In Britain the Free Trade movement, with its hostility to colonial expenditure, was growing stronger, and the news of Harry Smith's annexation received a very critical reception from officials in the colonial office.[1] The colonial secretary, Lord Grey, imbued with a sense of responsibility for the fate of the aborigines in the interior at the hands of emigrant British subjects, gave it his support, but the annexation was only accepted on the condition that it would not constitute a further burden on the exchequer. The Orange River Sovereignty thus started its life under a stipulation which ensured that it would be deprived of the financial resources essential for success.

In Transorangia itself, the trekker section of the white population rose in rebellion, and the British resident, Warden, was turned out of Bloemfontein. Harry Smith rushed troops to the scene. The Boer forces were scattered at Boomplaats, and the rebellion collapsed, but the attitude of many of the whites to British rule remained ambivalent. Warden was left with inadequate forces and he could only hope to maintain himself by gaining the support of the white farmers.

With the annexation of the Orange River Sovereignty, the only body of emigrant British subjects still beyond the pale of British rule were those beyond the Vaal. The logic of the policy of accepting responsibility for the conduct of British subjects in the interior demanded that British sovereignty should be extended to that area also. Such a move was contemplated, but before it could be undertaken a dramatic reversal of British policy was precipitated by the collapse of Harry Smith's policies both on the eastern frontier and in the Sovereignty.

In British Kaffraria the introduction of colonial law, without provision for its adaptation to African social and legal institutions, resulted in the outlawry of such basic institutions as the payment of *lobola* cattle which legitimized marriage. The understaffed administration was forced to rely on hastily recruited and ill-trained African police who harried their own people. Smarting under their recent military defeat and a long history of grievance, the Xhosa, as in the days of Makanna, found hope in a promise of supernatural aid. A new prophet, Mlanjeni, prophesied the resurrection of past heroes to assist in the defeat of the white oppressors. In December 1850, British Kaffraria erupted in a war which was not ended until late in 1852.

[1] C. W. de Kiewiet, *British colonial policy and the South African republics 1848–1872* (London, 1929), 28–39.

In the Orange River Sovereignty, Warden was faced with the basic task of defining the limits of settlement of the white and non-white peoples. Dependent on the good will of the white settlers, he defined a border between them and the Sotho of Moshoeshoe much more advantageous to the farmers than the Sotho. As Moshoeshoe showed himself reluctant to accept this arrangement, Warden adopted the policy of divide and rule. He applied pressure on Moshoeshoe and sought to reduce his power by supporting the Rolong, Korana and Tlokwa against him. Borders were defined for these people which cut off a great deal of the territory claimed by the Sotho. Moshoeshoe's position was even more difficult than Warden's. His purpose was to preserve the kingdom, which he had built up from the remnants of many chiefdoms shattered in the course of the upheavals provoked by the invasions of the Hlubi and Ngwane. He saw clearly that the greatest threat to his people lay in the expansionist tendencies of the Boer population of Transorangia. He realized that open conflict with them would be likely to result in the ultimate defeat and break-up of his kingdom. The best insurance against the threat from the Boers of Transorangia seemed to him to lie in the protection of the British government, and it was his consistent policy to acquire and preserve this protection. He was placed in a dilemma, however, when Warden as the representative of British authority in Transorangia demanded concessions in favour of the Boers. The price which Moshoeshoe could afford to pay for peace and the continuation of British protection was limited by the need to retain the loyalty of all the diverse elements in his composite kingdom. If he were to sacrifice the interests of any section in the interests of wider political objectives, the fragile bonds of loyalty and consent which held his state together might be broken and his kingdom disintegrate. He could not afford to prevent his people from retaliating against the enemies whom Warden was supporting. As conflict between the Sotho and their African neighbours increased, Warden felt forced to intervene in support of his protégés, and set out with a very inadequate force supported by Rolong auxiliaries to humble Moshoeshoe.

At the first encounter, which took place at Viervoet hill, the Rolong were routed and Warden had to fall back on Thaba Nchu. Reinforcements were not available from the Cape, where all available forces were committed to the war on the eastern frontier, and the Sovereignty lapsed into virtual anarchy, little relieved by the arrival of a force of Zulus sent from Natal in response to Warden's urgent call for help. In his hour of victory Moshoeshoe exercised the greatest restraint and, apart from raids on Warden's African allies, and reprisals taken from the few white farmers who had joined the abortive expedition, the Sovereignty suffered relatively little. The credit of the British administration had, however, been gravely undermined. From across the Vaal, Andries Pretorius intrigued in the affairs of the Sovereignty with the hope of destroying British influence there, and some white farmers tried to make their separate peace with Moshoeshoe.

The almost simultaneous outbreak of war on the eastern frontier and in the Sovereignty greatly strengthened the hands of those groups in Britain who had long been critical of colonial expenditure and the value of having colonies at all. The missionary-philanthropic movement, discredited by Buxton's abortive Niger Expedition of 1841, was in temporary eclipse. Concern for aboriginal peoples seemed to many to be an expensive futility. It would be wiser to place faith in the white colonists, leave them free to conduct their own affairs and deal with the aborigines in their own way, thus saving large sums spent to no avail on the administration and defence of vast areas where the British government had no vital interests.[1] In this atmosphere the ultimate abandonment of the Sovereignty was accepted as a desirable object of British policy, and a two-man commission, consisting of Major William Hogge and Charles Owen, was sent out to investigate the situation.

The first major step taken by the commissioners was to buy off interference in the Sovereignty by the Boers of the Transvaal. In January 1852, they met Pretorius and a number of other Transvaal leaders at the Sand river. In spite of protests from Sovereignty Boers, who begged the Transvaalers not to abandon them by accepting the Vaal river as a political boundary, the Sand River Convention was signed. This convention marked a vital turning point in British policy. For the first time the British authorities explicitly renounced the responsibility they had heretofore consistently accepted, for the conduct of British subjects in the interior and the fate of indigenous peoples at their hands. Under the terms of the convention Britain renounced all claims to authority north of the Vaal river. The Transvaalers were to be left to deal with their African neighbours as they pleased, and the British authorities promised that the Transvaalers would be accorded free access to the Cape gunpowder market, which would be closed to their African neighbours.

The situation of the Sovereignty remained for some time in the

---

[1] De Kiewiet, *British colonial policy and the South African republics*, 40–69.

balance. As Moshoeshoe continued to practise extreme restraint, the area gradually returned to normal, but the future depended on whether it seemed likely that the Sovereignty could be maintained without substantial British expenditure. This was made clear to Cathcart, who came out to replace Harry Smith as governor and high commissioner in July 1852. In the Sovereignty the surviving commissioner, Owen (Hogge had died in the Free State in 1852), called an assembly to discover whether the white farmers would be prepared to shoulder the expenses of administration and defence in return for a measure of self-government. The assembled farmers eagerly called for an elected Volksraad, but insisted on the need for a substantial British garrison.

In October 1852 Cathcart arrived in the Sovereignty at the head of 2,500 troops and soon formed the impression that abandonment was inevitable. Before it could decently take place, however, Moshoeshoe had to be humbled, and compensation obtained for the losses of those who had supported Warden. Moshoeshoe was thus faced with an ultimatum demanding 10,000 head of cattle and 1,000 horses within three days. When he was unable to amass the total demanded in the time, Cathcart advanced towards Thaba Bosiu. On the Berea mountain, his troops became entangled in the masses of captured cattle and were forced to retreat in the face of determined Sotho counter-attacks. Moshoeshoe then sent a diplomatic message urging that the captured cattle be regarded as adequate punishment for past misdeeds. Cathcart, eager to avoid involvement in what promised to be a difficult and expensive campaign, agreed, and Moshoeshoe was left in effect victorious.

The decision to abandon the Sovereignty was then inevitable. On Cathcart's suggestion, Sir George Clerk was appointed special commissioner and sent to wind up its affairs. Brushing aside the protests of an elected assembly, Clerk managed to find a group who were prepared to take over the responsibilities of government. In February 1854 the Bloemfontein Convention was signed. Similar in essentials to the Sand River Convention, except that it did not contain a 'gunpowder clause', the Bloemfontein agreement promised the citizens of the nascent republic freedom of action north of the Orange river. The colony disclaimed any treaties with the indigenous rulers north of the Orange (except Adam Kok), and any intention of making any others that might be prejudicial to the interests of the new Free State.

The most difficult problem facing Clerk in his attempts to achieve British disengagement from the Sovereignty was the vexed question of borders between the new Free State on the one hand and Moshoeshoe and Adam Kok on the other. Realizing that any serious attempt to resolve these problems would mean postponing withdrawal indefinitely, Sir George Clerk simply left the whole matter in the air. Moshoeshoe was left with the impression that the Warden line had lapsed, but was given no indication of what the border should be, while Adam Kok, whose people were being increasingly squeezed by the pressure of white expansion, was simply left to his fate.[1]

BALKANIZATION OF THE WHITE COMMUNITIES

The movement towards reduction of imperial responsibility revealed itself also in the granting of representative institutions in the Cape. Elective municipal councils had been introduced as early as 1837. In December 1852 the long awaited grant of parliamentary institutions was made. On the insistence of the secretary of state for the colonies, the principle of legal equality embodied in the 50th Ordinance was carried over into the parliamentary franchise. British subjects of all races could vote or be voted for, subject only to economic qualifications, which in the case of the vote were deliberately set at a relatively low figure. Though the 'colour-blind' constitution did enable some non-Europeans to gain the vote, the economic qualifications in fact discriminated heavily in favour of the whites. As the overwhelming majority of non-whites were extremely poor, the whites constituted the great majority of the electors. Under the 1852 constitution, formulation of policy was still kept firmly in the hands of the governor and his officials, but the influence of settler opinion on policy had been greatly increased, and a major step taken towards handing over responsibility for the government of all races in the Cape to the representatives of the dominant white minority.

The first president of the Orange Free State, Josias Hoffman, narrowly escaped being overthrown before he could consolidate his authority. In the Transvaal, Andries Pretorius had died in 1853. His son Marthinus succeeded to the leadership of his father's following, and also to his ambition of bringing all the Boers outside British colonial frontiers within a single united republic. With the encouragement of supporters within the Free State, he rode to Winburg in 1854, hoping to precipitate an uprising. But the coup was ill-prepared and, faced with a show of firmness, he retired across the Vaal.

[1] Midgley, 'The Orange River Sovereignty', 564–7.

Hoffman was at pains to maintain good relations with Moshoeshoe. The two men were personal friends and visits were exchanged. The president's cordial relations with the Sotho king, however, provided a lever for his enemies in the Free State white community. In February 1855, the fact that Hoffman had sent a keg of gunpowder to Moshoeshoe in consideration of the salute fired on his visit to Thaba Bosiu, provided the pretext for an uprising. Hoffman resigned, to be replaced by Jacobus Boshof. With the change of president the relations between the Free State and Moshoeshoe rapidly deteriorated. Sir George Grey, who had come out to the Cape as governor and high commissioner in 1854, paid a visit to the Free State. In October 1855 he succeeded in getting the parties to agree to the Smithfield Treaty which, without definitely naming the boundary, in effect restored the Warden line.

Boshof's problems were not limited to the Sotho, however. In 1857 Marthinus Pretorius tried once more to bring about the collapse of the Free State and its fusion with the Transvaal, by a coup. He rode across the Vaal and gained the support of a substantial number of the Free Staters. Boshof, however, stood firm, and Pretorius retired only to assemble a commando and invade the Free State in force, in an attempt to stop the trial of his supporters, who had been arrested in the aftermath of the abortive coup. Boshof mounted a commando to meet him, and the two Boer forces faced each other at the Rhenoster river, while within the Transvaal a commando mounted by Pretorius's opponents in the Zoutpansberg moved down on Potchefstroom. The confrontation at the Rhenoster river ended peacefully. No shot was fired and, after the two leaders had agreed to recognize each other's independence, Pretorius rode back to deal with the situation in the Transvaal.

In the following year border tension between the Free State and the Sotho resulted in open war. A Free State commando advanced on Thaba Bosiu but failed to storm its precipitous heights. The Sotho poured into the republic, and the commando dispersed as each man hurried home to protect his farm and family. Boshof was left in an embarrassing situation and appealed both to the Cape and to the Transvaal for aid. Pretorius hastened down and offered a joint campaign against the Sotho in return for the fusion of the two Boer republics, but Sir George Grey was determined to prevent a move which would rule out a wider scheme he had been developing. He informed the Boer leaders that union of the republics would free Britain from the conditions of the conventions. At this Pretorius drew back, and Grey's mediation was accepted instead. Faced with the possibility of a union of the two Boer republics, Moshoeshoe grudgingly agreed to a border agreement, in the first Treaty of Aliwal North, which largely confirmed the Warden line but gave the Sotho a small increase in territory.

Grey had come to the Cape in 1854 from the governorship of New Zealand, where he believed he had permanently resolved the problems of relations between Maoris and settlers. He was full of confidence in settling the problems of South Africa and accustomed to being given a free hand by the home government. His first major task was to attempt yet another solution to the problem of the eastern frontier. This was to settle numbers of white settlers alongside Africans in British Kaffraria to form a thoroughly mixed settlement pattern. Close contact between the races, he believed, would lead to Africans emulating white culture and economic methods and so bring about racial harmony. His policy ignored the already severe overcrowding of the area between the Fish and the Kei, and was largely responsible for the fact that it subsequently became one of the most heavily eroded and poverty-stricken areas in South Africa.

Faced with the prospect of the loss of still more of their lands, the Xhosa were reduced to desperation and, as on two previous occasions, looked for supernatural support to save them from their oppressors. A prophetess, Nonqause, foretold that, if they would slaughter all their cattle and destroy their grain stores, the sun would rise in the west on an appointed day. Then fat cattle and abundant grain would be given to them, and their dead heroes would return aided by a mighty wind to sweep the whites into the sea. The cattle killing spread rapidly, and a major explosion seemed imminent. But on the appointed day in February 1857 the sun rose in its normal place, and the Xhosa, disillusioned and desperate, were faced with mass starvation. Grey rushed emergency food supplies to the frontier. Thousands of Xhosa saved themselves from starvation by taking employment with the whites, but thousands more succumbed. The population of the frontier areas was drastically reduced, and Grey's mixed settlement policy was accorded a breathing space.

The near explosion on the eastern frontier made Grey look to the interior and particularly to the developing tension between the Orange Free State and Moshoeshoe, for there were rumours that Moshoeshoe had a hand in the cattle killing. Grey soon formed the opinion that the divisions between the white communities in South Africa, each too weak to provide for adequate education of its own citizens or for the regular administration and policing of frontier areas, must result in endless turmoil, violence and brutality. South Africa, as he put it, seemed 'to be drifting by not very slow degrees into disorder and barbarism'.[1] The answer lay in the federation of all white groups into a single state, which would have the means to substitute regular administrative measures for periodic punitive wars and the breadth of outlook to adopt a just and humane policy towards the African peoples. Such a federation would be able to pay for its own defence and to relieve Great Britain of the greater part of its responsibilities in South Africa. These ideas, involving as they did the complete reversal of the conventions policy so recently adopted, bristling as they were with practical difficulties, and holding out possibilities of British involvement in the affairs of the interior on a scale impossible to measure, met with a chilly reception in the Colonial Office. Grey, however, unused to control by the home government, grasped at the opportunity created by the Free State's defeat to attempt a major step towards the realization of his plan. Heading off the threatened union between the Boer communities of the high veld, he encouraged the Free State to seek its salvation in union with the Cape. Then, on receipt of a query from the Colonial Office about the possibilities of federating the British colonies in South Africa, he allowed the Cape legislature to discuss a proposal from the Free State Volksraad for federation with the Cape. This was going too far, and Grey was recalled. A change of government in Britain led to his return a year later, but only on condition that the idea of federation was dropped.

The collapse of Grey's federation scheme forced the Free State back on the idea of union with their fellows across the Vaal. Deterred by Grey's threat about the consequences of republican union on the status of the conventions, M. W. Pretorius attempted to achieve his object by standing for election to the Orange Free State presidency. The two republics, while remaining formally distinct, would have the same person as president. In the atmosphere of defeatism and despair which had resulted from the conflict with Moshoeshoe, Pretorius's candidature gained enthusiastic support, and he was elected by a large majority. In the Free State one long-standing problem was solved with the departure of Adam Kok III and his Griqua community. Though some Griqua had become prosperous in the Free State, their lands had dwindled away under white pressure to such an extent that their continued existence as a community was endangered. In 1861 Sir George Grey gave Adam Kok permission to settle with his people in Nomans-

[1] Walker, *A history of southern Africa*, 271.

land. Grey hoped that the Griqua would constitute a barrier between the Sotho of Moshoeshoe and the peoples of the east coast belt. The trek began in 1861 and went via Smithfield and Hanglip. Between October 1862 and February 1863 the Griqua crossed the Drakensberg and settled in their new home, which has subsequently been known as Griqualand East. Though the Griqua suffered severe losses during their journey, their prosperity began to revive in the early 1870s. In Griqualand East a determined effort was made to build an independent republican polity. In 1867 the Griqua State even printed its own notes, though these were never put into circulation. After Cape rule was extended to Griqualand East in 1874, however, Cape liquor traders were permitted to open canteens in the area, and the Griqua began to pledge their lands as security for their growing debts. By 1878 the consciousness that they were rapidly losing their lands led to a rebellion.

Pretorius's double presidency was not a success. In the Free State he was no more able than his predecessors to resolve the problem of relations with Moshoeshoe, while in the Transvaal hard-won political unity threatened to disintegrate. In 1863 Pretorius resigned the presidency of the Orange Free State and rode back to restore the position north of the Vaal. The long struggle which had been going on since the first days of the trek to preserve the ideal of a single *maatschapij*, a united Boer polity, was at an end.

THE TRANSVAAL

In the Transvaal the white settler community, established in the aftermath of the defeat of Mzilikazi, early displayed a tendency to expand by segmentation. Economic problems, the desire to keep out of the range of possible extensions of British authority and to make contact with the sea through the Portuguese settlements, together with conflicts over leadership and constitutional principles, led to divisions. Hendrik Potgieter and his followers left the original settlement at Potchefstroom in 1845 and founded Andries Ohrigstad in the east on land given to Potgieter by the Pedi chief Sekwati. A further split then took place in the Andries Ohrigstad community. Potgieter once more moved away with his supporters and founded a new settlement in the Zoutpansberg in the extreme north of the Transvaal.

Three main centres of white population thus arose, all on the periphery of the area of the modern Transvaal, and all with the exception of Potchefstroom situated on the warmer, lower lying land initially most attractive to cattle farmers. Only gradually, with growth of population and a swing away from cattle towards sheep farming, did the higher lands in the centre of the Transvaal come to be extensively settled, thus strengthening the forces of unity and shifting the balance of power from the periphery to the centre, a process that was accentuated by the decline of the outlying north-eastern and northern settlements in the face of malaria, tsetse fly and pressure from the surrounding African peoples.[1] Andries Ohrigstad was abandoned in 1849–50, and its population moved to Lydenburg which became the new centre of the eastern settlement. Schoemansdal in the Zoutpansberg also declined after an initial boom based on ivory. In 1867 it was completely abandoned.

Geographical separation, and the absorption of each community in local conflicts with its African neighbours, dictated effective political independence, though the sense of common identity and common danger from the African majority remained strong. In 1849 a decision was taken to form a single body politic north of the Vaal river. Thereafter formal unity was preserved until 1856. A central Volksraad met fitfully, but it was rare for it to be attended by representatives of all the settler communities, and in practice each area went its own way. Conflict between the desire for unity and pressures for separation was complicated by disagreement over constitutional principles, between advocates of a strong executive and those who wished no executive authority other than the elected Volksraad. The long struggle of Andries Pretorius and his son Marthinus for political unity and an effective executive was further complicated by their continuing attachment to the idea of overall Boer unity, and their consequent involvement in the affairs of the Orange River Sovereignty and Orange Free State.

In 1855 Marthinus Pretorius achieved a major advance when he won acceptance for a new constitution (*grondwet*) providing for a regular executive in the form of an elected president. Pretoria was fixed as the capital of the boldly named South African Republic, and Pretorius was elected as its first president.[2] This development, however, precipitated the long maturing political split between Lydenburg, the centre of the north-eastern settlement, and the westerners. Differences between the two areas had by this time been complicated by religious divisions, centring on the question of whether to unite with the Cape Synod of

[1] See F. J. Potgieter, 'Die Vestiging van die Blanke in Transvaal 1837–1886', *Archives Year Book for South African History* (Cape Town, 1959).

[2] F. A. F. Wichmann, 'Die wordingsgeskiedems van die Zuid-Afrikaansche Republiek 1838–1860', *Archives Year Book for South African History* (1941), II, 147–65.

the Dutch Reformed Church or to maintain complete religious independence. In October 1856 Lydenburg formally declared itself a separate republic. Zoutpansberg also resented the growing power of Pretorius and used the opportunity of his invasion of the Free State in 1857 to menace his rear.

The enduring sense of common identity amongst the Transvaalers, however, led to a resolution of the quarrels, and in 1860 Lydenburg rejoined the South African Republic. At the same time the small white community of Utrecht, which had been founded by Boers moving out of Natal after the British occupation, and which had always been outside the limits of the 'single company', was brought into the republic. The political union of the Transvaal achieved in 1860 was almost thrown back into the melting pot by Pretorius's acceptance of the presidency of the Orange Free State. Only after his resignation from the Free State presidency in 1863 could the work of consolidation proceed.

The African population was regarded as one of the natural resources of the country,[1] and the policy adopted towards the African peoples was aimed at ensuring the exploitation of their labour while minimizing the danger to the white community. African communities which fell under the dominance of the white groups in the Transvaal were allocated areas of land, but they were not given security of tenure and were moved away when the land was needed by the expanding white farmers. Within the areas allocated to them the chiefs were left free to govern their own peoples, but they were not permitted to acquire guns, horses or wagons or to enter into alliances with one another. They were also expected to pay labour tax, that is to make labourers available in the numbers required when called upon to do so. Africans living outside the areas allocated to particular chiefs had to enter into labour contracts with white farmers, who were expected to exercise a general control over their behaviour. In practice the vast size of the country, the wide scattering of the white population, and the very rudimentary governmental institutions, made the application of any systematic policy impossible. Border areas were largely outside the rule of law, and individual whites frequently employed strong-arm methods.[2]

The process of white expansion at the expense of African peoples resulted in continuous friction, and the white communities were engaged in repeated conflicts with their African neighbours. As they lacked the resources and administrative machinery necessary for stable

[1] See Potgieter, 'Die Vestiging van die Blanke in Transvaal', 195–6.
[2] See e.g. Orpen, *Reminiscences*, I, 427.

administration, the only means of enforcing their will was by periodic commandos aimed at striking terror into the African communities.[1] In the eastern Transvaal the Pedi chief, Sekwati, after recovering from his defeat by the Ndebele, was building up a kingdom in the Lulu mountains in a rather similar way to Moshoeshoe in Lesotho. He survived a number of conflicts with the trekkers, and in 1852 narrowly escaped being overthrown by a powerful commando led by A. H. Potgieter.

In 1857 he entered into an agreement with the Lydenburg Republic, under which the Steelpoort river was recognized as the boundary of his kingdom. The final struggle between the whites and the Pedi kingdom was postponed until 1877. No major war took place between the Transvaalers and the Gaza kingdom and, although the Transvaalers gained a dubiously legal cession of a strip of territory along the Blood river from the Zulu king Mpande in 1861, the matter was not pressed to the point of war. In the Zoutpansberg, conflict with the Venda was endemic and culminated in the abandonment of Schoemansdal and most of the Zoutpansberg settlement in 1867.

It was along the western boundaries of European settlement that the most vigorous expansion took place at the expense of African peoples. In this area the Tswana chiefdoms, lacking overall political unity and barely recovered from the upheavals of the Kololo and Ndebele invasions, were attacked piecemeal. European settlement, originally bounded on the west by the Schoonspruit, steadily spread out westward to the Makwassiespruit in the south and the Marico river farther to the north. By 1870 farmers were staking out claims as far west as the Harts and Molopo rivers.[2] As they expanded westward, the Transvaalers began to touch on the preserves of the missionaries working among the Tswana tribes and to threaten the missionary road to the north. The missionaries, notably the influential Dr David Livingstone, bitterly criticized the procedures of the Transvaal whites. The Transvaalers in turn accused the missionaries of stirring up hostility amongst the African peoples, and of providing them with guns to use against the whites. They did their best to exclude those missionaries whom they regarded as hostile from the areas around their borders.

[1] One of the most notorious was the commando against Makapan which blockaded his people in a cave and killed about 3,000. M. Wilson and L. M. Thompson, eds., *The Oxford history of South Africa*, 1 (Oxford, 1969), 440. Orpen, *Reminiscences*, 1, 428–37.

[2] J. A. I. Agar-Hamilton, *The road to the north* (London, 1937), 1–88.

BASUTOLAND AND ITS ANNEXATION, 1865–71

In the Orange Free State, Pretorius was succeeded by J. H. Brand, a determined and able statesman, who succeeded in consolidating and stabilizing the republic. Brand was faced, as his predecessors had been, with the problem of the frontier between the republic and the Sotho of Moshoeshoe. With population and accompanying land hunger rising steeply in both communities, the problem admitted of no peaceful solution. The two leaders were impelled into conflict, and in 1865 the Free State declared war.

By this time the balance had shifted in favour of the Boer republic. Its white population had substantially increased since 1858. The Orange Free State enjoyed a moderate economic prosperity, and the internal political divisions of earlier times had ceased to be important. In President Brand it had a strong and able leader. Moshoeshoe on the other hand had grown old, and his sons were bickering over the antici-pated succession, adding by their mutual hostilities to the divisive forces within the composite Sotho kingdom. Lacking the firm leadership which alone could impose a thought-out strategy, the Sotho, heavily outgunned by their Boer opponents, could only fall back on defensive tactics, which allowed their enemies to attack them piecemeal. They thus threw away their only advantages, their superior numbers and the mobility provided by their possession of horses.

The Free State forces failed to capture Thaba Bosiu, but they succeeded in reducing a whole series of Sotho strongholds one by one. They followed a systematic policy of expelling the Sotho from their most fertile lands with a view to annexing them to the republic and settling them with white farmers. In March 1866 Moshoeshoe's son Molapo deserted his father's cause, and signed a separate peace with the republic under which he agreed to rule Leribe (the northern part of Lesotho) as a vassal of the republic. Moshoeshoe was forced to sue for peace to save his people from starvation. By the Treaty of Thaba Bosiu in April 1866, he agreed to the cession of the areas occupied by the Boer commandos which constituted by far the greater part of the cultivable land available to his people.

This agreement proved to be no more than a truce. No sooner had the commandos dispersed than the Sotho re-occupied their lands and began planting their crops. Two white farmers who tried to take up farms they had been allocated in the areas ceded to the Free State were murdered, and the war began again. The Free State forces wore down

Sotho resistance by systematically destroying their food supplies. Starvation was widespread, but Moshoeshoe still held out on his mountain top desperately pleading for British protection, which alone could save his people from being completely broken up. Sir Philip Wodehouse, who had succeeded Sir George Grey as governor and high commissioner in 1862, was becoming increasingly worried at the prospect of widespread anarchy and violence that must follow if the Free State carried out its intention of expelling the Sotho from their lands. He also had a strong personal sympathy for the Sotho. Moshoeshoe's cause was greatly strengthened by the outcry raised overseas as a consequence of the republic's tactically foolish action of expelling the French missionaries from the areas controlled by its commandos. Having received tentative permission to annex the Sotho kingdom to Natal if Moshoeshoe and that colony were willing, Wodehouse in 1868 exceeded his instructions by announcing the annexation of Lesotho without qualification, and by sending up the Cape police. Worn out with the long struggle, which had exhausted it almost as much as the Sotho, the Free State was in no position to offer armed resistance.

After tough bargaining, borders were settled in the second Treaty of Aliwal North in February 1869. These left the Sotho enough land to retain their corporate identity, but deprived them of substantial areas of fertile soil and ensured that in future they would have to resort to wage employment in the white controlled areas, to supplement the resources of their territory. The treaty was ratified in March 1870. In the same month old Moshoeshoe died. As the idea of annexing Lesotho to Natal had proved unpopular with Moshoeshoe and his people, as well as difficult to implement, Basutoland became a direct dependency of the crown until the Cape agreed to take over its administration in 1871.

The annexation of Basutoland was not only the first step towards a reversal of the conventions policy, and to renewed British involvement north of the Orange. It was also and more significantly the first really massive step in a new phase in the relation between whites and Africans in South Africa: the establishment of white administration over areas of African peasant occupancy, as opposed to the seizure of African lands by white farmers.[1] In this way areas of African occupancy were prevented from constituting a military threat to the white settled areas, while at the same time being preserved as labour reserves for the white dominated economy.

[1] The process could perhaps be said to have begun with Sir Harry Smith's annexation of British Kaffraria in 1847.

DIAMOND DISCOVERIES AND THE END OF AN ERA

The first step towards British involvement in affairs north of the Orange was soon followed by another. In April 1867 a solitary diamond was picked up near Hopetown in the Cape Colony. Eight months later Carl Mauch proclaimed the existence of gold at Tati, on the borders between the Ngwato and the Ndebele. The Tati gold, which initially excited great interest, soon proved a disappointment, but in 1868 substantial diamond deposits were found on the north bank of the Vaal near its junction with the Harts. In 1870 the rush to the River Diggings was under way, and later that year the discovery of still richer deposits farther to the south precipitated another rush to the Dry Diggings, which henceforth became the main centre of diamond mining.

Diamonds, and the later gold discoveries, began a transformation of South African history. A new industrial society began to grow, and the racial divisions and conflicts of the past were now transposed on to the industrial scene. Diamonds ushered in the modern period of South African history. They provided for the first time a focus of interest, much more powerful than the missionary pressures of the earlier period, for British ambitions to look to the interior, as witnessed by the alacrity with which the British seized the Diamond Fields in 1871. The lucrative new industry would bring with it a new era of railways, territorial partition, Afrikaner nationalism and British imperialism.

CHAPTER 11

TRADITION AND CHANGE IN MADAGASCAR, 1790–1870[1]

MALAGASY SOCIAL AND POLITICAL STRUCTURE

In 1790 the Malagasy people were divided into a large number of ethnic groups, and a still larger number of political units. But despite local variations there was a striking degree of uniformity in language and customs.

There were large gaps in the pattern of settlement. Ethnic groups were separated by immense empty areas of bush or forest. Hunting, fishing and gathering provided secondary resources. Agriculture depended in large measure on slash and burn techniques with the cultivation of millet, taro, bananas, yams, sweet potatoes, various beans, cassava, and mountain rice. Rice fields, constructed out of swamps or along water courses, were cultivated by means of the hoe and by trampling cattle; they provided rice in a number of areas. Zebu cattle were both work animals and visible capital, sacrificed only in religious ceremonies.

The Malagasy house was rectangular, with a steeply pitched roof, aligned along a north–south axis with a door to the west. The framework was of wood, the walls, according to area, made either of the leaf stalks of ravenala or of palm fronds, or of clay earth, the roof of leaves or thatch. Dress consisted of a loincloth and toga (*lamba*) for the men, a sheath dress for the women. Cotton and silk were woven; while on the eastern coast sheath dresses were made from interlaced reed mats. In general furniture consisted of plaited mats. Containers were of vegetable origin (gourds, bamboo, wood) or of earthenware. Each family was self-sufficient in food; for heavy work, such as embankments and house-building, they were assisted by relatives. The only specialized worker was the smith, who made tools and weapons. There was little trade, apart from a few periodic markets. Long journeys were undertaken only for the purchase of cattle and salt. There were no roads nor pack animals; loads were carried on the shoulder.

The Malagasy recognized a creator God (*Zanahary*), but sacrifices and offerings were mainly addressed to dead ancestors (*razana*) by heads of families or clans. Social life was regulated by the custom (*fomba*) of the ancestors. Magic was based largely on geomancy, of Arabic origin. Literature, which was entirely oral, was of several kinds: speeches

[1] Translated from the French by Yvonne Brett.

(*kabary*), history, tales, love poetry, songs to accompany dances; proverbs, of a practical kind, were a reflection of social solidarity, a tempered wisdom in harmony with nature.

Society was based on great families (*karazana*), which were divided into clans (*foko*), each possessing the same distant ancestor. The members owed one another mutual help and assistance in ceremonies. According to the particular area, tombs were held in common by a family, or an entire clan; it was believed that the ancestors resided there, and watched over the living. Seniority gave the power of exacting obedience. Descent was in the paternal line, or undifferentiated. The father of the family was the leader; in the hut he had a place apart, and could eject disobedient children from the group. The role of the head of the clan was chiefly religious.

Clans were divided by caste into nobles, commoners, and slaves. The latter were either men who had lost their freedom as a punishment for crime, or prisoners of war, or children of slaves. There was no inter-marriage between castes, except in certain precise circumstances. Nobles had certain privileges and taboos particular to them, but material existence varied very little.

The clan was the basic political unit. Eminent people, heads of clans, governed the community. They were the 'fathers and mothers' of their societies.

Some of the ethnic groups had no other form of social organization. In most cases, kings (*mpanjaka*), who transcended the clans, were chosen from a certain noble clan. The king was solemnly enthroned, after being designated either by his predecessor or by the chiefs of the clans of commoners. From that moment he was sacred, 'God visible', could not be killed, and alone had the right to a red parasol and to give commands. He lived in a palace – an ordinary hut somewhat larger than the others – occasionally situated in a citadel (*rova*). The heads of clans and other 'wise men' were his advisers, and made sure he respected ancestral customs, for otherwise he could be deposed. The king had a right to certain dues and forced labour services, and had at his disposal messengers and slaves.

War took place between clans, and, more frequently, between kingdoms; there were frequent periods of insecurity. Villages were built on hilltops, surrounded by thorn bushes, a palisade, or stone walls protected by a ditch. Arms included a long assegai, javelins, a round shield, catapults and cutlasses. Alliances were formed for the purposes either of war or of trade.

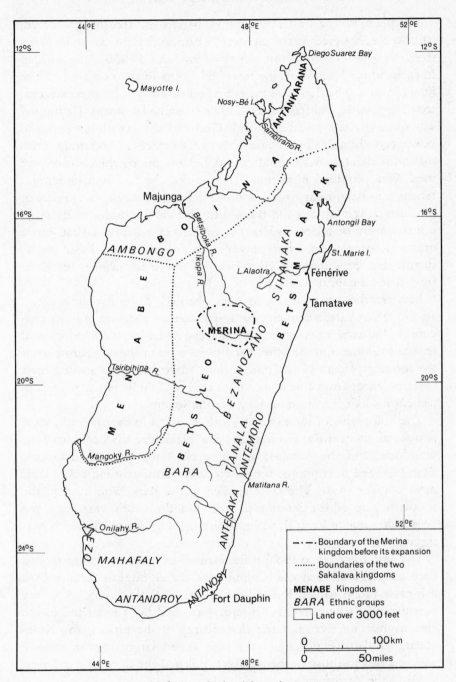

14 Madagascar in the eighteenth century

The plains to the west of the island, barren and sparsely populated, had been conquered in the eighteenth century by the Sakalava kings from the south. From this sprang two kingdoms, held by kings related to each other: Menabe in the west and Boina in the north-west. The king (or queen) held in trust the sacred relics (*dady*) of his predecessors: teeth, hair, nails, and fragments of bone contained in horns. He himself was quasi-divine, interceding with God and the ancestors. The land belonged to him. He handed out fiefs to the princes of his family. Thus the royal clan (*volamena*: gold) was dominant among the clans of free men. War provided numerous slaves, since the Sakalava undertook razzias into neighbouring territories, even as far away as the middle of the island. At Majunga the Boina had at their disposal a commercial centre run by islamized traders, the Antalaotra, natives of East Africa or the Comoros. In 1790 travellers described Queen Ravahiny as surrounded by important chiefs, dispensing strict justice, receiving from foreign countries silk fabrics and luxury goods.

Between these two large kingdoms, the fiefs of the Ambongo, situated in rather barren country, displayed a certain measure of independence. In the extreme north of the island the Antankarana kingdom paid tribute to Boina. On the other hand there were in the northern part of the interior plateau clans from various places who maintained their independence; from this comes the name of Tsimihety (he who does not cut his hair, i.e., in mourning for the sovereign).

The arid plains of the extreme south, covered in thorny bush, were populated by warlike pastoralists: the Mahafaly, divided into four kingdoms, and the Antandroy, whose clans formed confederations. Both engaged in continual reciprocal raids, cattle-rustling being their most popular sport. The same applied to the Bara, who lived in the southern part of the interior plateau. On the south-west coast the very independent Vezo lived by fishing in dug-out canoes with outriggers.

The east coast, even though fragmented by rivers and forests, had been largely unified at the beginning of the eighteenth century by a half-caste pirate named Ratsimilaho. After him, this kingdom of the Betsimisaraka (the numerous inseparables) had been restricted to the area round Fénérive. But the descendants of the pirates, the Zana-Malata (mulatto children), every year armed large dug-out canoes, which, allied to those of the Sakalava, pillaged the Comoros and even as far as the African coast.

In the south-east, the Antemoro immigrants, who had once been

Muslims, had long since founded kingdoms along the Matitana river and in neighbouring areas. They ruled over purely Malagasy peoples. They had abandoned their religion and language, but wrote Malagasy in Arabic characters on paper which they made themselves. These 'Arabo-Malagasy' manuscripts contained magic formulae and some more or less legendary historical traditions.

The Antanosy chiefs in the south-east also claimed an Islamic origin. Between the Antemoro and the Antanosy, were the Antesaka, whose numerous restive clans had been organized into several groups by chiefs of Sakalava origin.

All these peoples in the east lived from the cultivation of rice in the bush-clearings, and on forest produce. This partial dependence on the forest was especially marked amongst the peoples who lived on the slopes intermediate between the east coast and the plateau; from north to south these were the Sihanaka, the Bezanozano, and Tanala, making up small kingdoms or scattered in independent clans.

The central part of the plateau comprised in the south the four Betsileo kingdoms, in the north the four Merina kingdoms. The latter were the result of the break-up of a unified kingdom in the early part of the eighteenth century. Although they were related, the four Merina kings fought each other almost unceasingly. The Sakalava, taking advantage of these disorders, sent raiding parties into Merina territory, bringing back slaves. However, the Frenchman Mayeur, who had penetrated into Imerina (Merina land) in 1777, praised the 'intelligence and industry' of this people, whom he considered in this respect to be the superiors of those on the coast. In spite of the disorders, the population had increased greatly, owing to the cultivation of rice in the swamps surrounding the citadel town of Tananarive, the capital of one of the kingdoms. The nobles (*andriana*) ruled over the commoner clans (*hova*) and the slaves (*andevo*). The relatives of the king received fiefs (*menakely*). The villagers came together in assemblies (*fokonolona*) to enact regulations, effect works in common (notably the embankments), and to ensure order in so far as the civil wars allowed.

EUROPEAN INVOLVEMENT

Portuguese, Dutch and English undertakings had come to an end many years previously, as had the establishment of the pirates. The French had occupied Fort Dauphin from 1643 to 1674, and their influence had spread throughout the south; Madagascar had theoretically been annexed, but in fact abandoned. The French had made two more attempts to establish themselves, with Maudave at Fort Dauphin in 1768–71, and with Benyowski in the bay of Antongil in 1774–6, but both were failures.

However, the French colonization of the two Mascarene islands, Ile Bourbon (Réunion) and the Ile de France (Mauritius), had created regular commercial dealings between these islands and Madagascar. This trade extended to the whole of the east coast, but more especially to the area of Foulpointe, Fénérive, the Matitana river, and Fort Dauphin, and was concerned with rice, timber, cattle and slaves. The west coast was frequented by various nations: French, English, Portuguese and Arabs.

Local chiefs acted as intermediaries in the slave trade, for which tools, coloured beads, alcohol, iron bars, brass bangles, silver piastres and fabrics were all imported for use as gifts. Guns were much sought after. Kings and local chiefs provided themselves with guns for the wars they waged to procure slaves, who were then exchanged on the coast for more guns. This arms traffic strengthened the power of the chiefs engaged in the trade, and drove some of them to make conquests. In 1806 the number of slaves shipped from Madagascar to the Mascarenes was estimated at between 1,800 and 2,000.

Outside knowledge of the country was still largely dependent on Governor Flacourt's book, *Histoire de la grande île de Madagascar* (1658), which dealt largely with the south. The eighteenth century, however, witnessed some progress in the mapping of the coastal districts. In addition, various French traders penetrated into the interior. Mayeur traversed the north as far as Sakalava territory, and then, from a departure point on the east coast, was the first to reach Imerina in 1777. Others followed him. In 1808 one of them, Hugon, saw Andrianampoinimerina.

The wars in Europe had repercussions on the coast of Madagascar. In 1796 an English squadron destroyed the French fort of Foulpointe. In 1807 General Decaen, the governor of the Ile de France, sent Silvain Roux, a Creole trader, to found a trading post at Tamatave. Roux succeeded in provisioning the islands, but in 1810 these islands were captured by the English, who then proceeded to occupy Tamatave.

NAMPOINA AND RADAMA I: THE BEGINNINGS OF UNITY

By this time a new power had arisen in the interior of the island. About 1783, the nephew of the king of Ambohimanga (the most easterly of the four kingdoms of Imerina) had seized power with the support of the Hova clans, and had taken the name of Andrianampoinimerina (the lord at the heart of Imerina), shortened to Nampoina (the desired one). He negotiated a truce of seven years with the other kings, and this enabled him to fortify villages, have guns brought up from the coast, and make sure of political solidarity by bringing counsellors into his government.

When the respite was over, he found pretexts to declare war, and took possession of the other kingdoms, though not without difficulty. In 1796 he took Tananarive for the third time, and made it his capital. The south-western clans were only definitively conquered after four campaigns, but by 1806 Imerina was once again unified within its former boundaries.

The small neighbouring kingdoms (Imamo in the west and Vakinan-karatra in the south) were incorporated later, either through negotiations or by war. Nampoina obtained unrestricted passage to the coast across the territory of the Bezanozano. The majority of the Betsileo kingdoms submitted to being vassals. Sealed by the exchange of gifts, peace was made with the Sakalava queen of the Boina. Antemoro scribes made their way to the court. The fame of the great king travelled beyond his frontiers, even though these had been considerably extended.

As he was making his conquests, Nampoina was also organizing his state. Royal authority was strengthened. The sacred king owned the land, and the lords held their fiefs only from him, while he had the right to take them back. The clan chiefs, in particular those who had raised him to the throne, became his advisers. But the importance of the clans (*foko*) was lessened by the creation of new divisions (*toko*) on a territorial basis. The vassal kings maintained their positions under the control of envoys from Nampoina. The desert regions were peopled by soldier colonists.

Thus the role of the intermediaries was diminished. The king addressed the people directly in great *kabary* (speeches, meetings), where he made known his will in orations illustrated with metaphors and proverbs, and punctuated from time to time with questions: 'Is that right, oh people?', and the people cried: 'Yes, that is quite right.' The village *fokonolona* had the task of applying these decisions and maintaining order. They were themselves controlled by itinerant advisers. The leaders dispensed justice, which was harsh. Twelve crimes, one of which was theft, carried the death penalty. Informing was encouraged and the ordeal by poison (*tanguin*) was used in the confession of crimes. Alcohol, tobacco and hemp were banned.

The land, which in theory belonged to the king, was redistributed to each family according to its needs, 'to keep hunger from its belly'. In exchange, the king levied a tax in kind. The forest and the bush served as a place of refuge for the less fortunate. Nampoina saw to it that everyone worked; the lazy were beaten. He ordered embankments to be rebuilt, developed a system of forced labour for public works, and inaugurated competitions between the work teams of the various communities. Markets were given regulations as to weight, measure and price. Children were allowed to take leftover scraps of meat from the butchers' stalls; the poor could eat their fill of cassava in a field, provided they carried none away. From one point of view Nampoina's regime can be seen as a kind of authoritarian socialism.

For warfare the able-bodied men were recruited during those periods not prescribed for public works. They brought back numerous slaves, either as labourers for the interior, or to be sold on the coast in exchange for guns and gunpowder. Otherwise the country lived in a closed economy, increasing in prosperity and population.

. Andrianampoinimerina has been called a 'barbarian of genius'. Certainly, his genius was of a purely Malagasy nature, owing nothing to external influences – except guns. His superior intelligence and great determination, combined with his flexibility of approach and realistic methods of organization, his patience and cunning, and his fundamental contact with the people, transformed Imerina and the central plateau. He initiated the idea of central unity. At his death he bequeathed to his son Radama a final thought, which for a century was to direct the island's destiny: 'the sea is the embankment of my rice fields' (i.e. the boundary of my kingdom).

Nampoina had prepared the succession by suppressing those of his sons whom he considered least suitable, in order to reserve power for Radama. To train him for warfare, from the age of fifteen, he put him in charge of several expeditions. Nampoina himself died about 1810. He was buried at Ambohimanga, in a silver canoe. The tradition of the funerary canoe was doubtless a legacy from very remote Indonesian ancestors, come from beyond that ocean which Nampoina himself never saw.

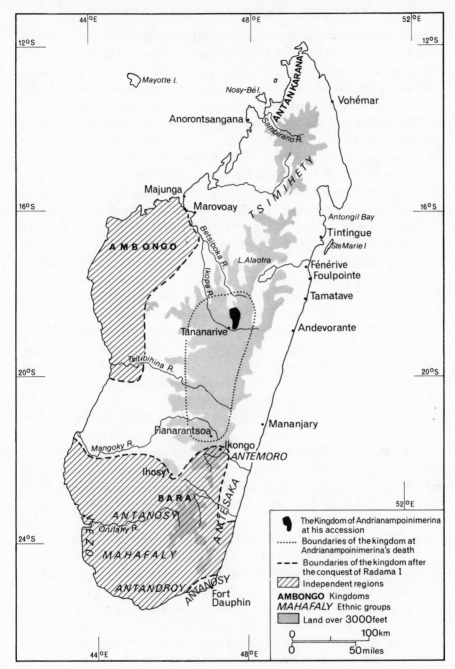

Legend:
The Kingdom of Andrianampoinimerina at his accession
.... Boundaries of the kingdom at Andrianampoinimerina's death
- - - Boundaries of the kingdom after the conquest of Radama I
///// Independent regions
AMBONGO Kingdoms
MAHAFALY Ethnic groups
Land over 3000 feet

0   100 km
0   50 miles

15   Merina expansion

The only description we have of Andrianampoinimerina's personal appearance is a phrase in Hugon, who found him ugly and like a Malay. Of Radama, on the other hand, we have portraits in European uniform: a slim and handsome man, with an olive complexion and piercing eyes. He was petulant, brilliant, authoritarian, avid for action and novelty, but he was not lacking in common sense, and, like his father, was able to take advantage of opportunities to realize his ambitions. And, moreover, circumstances were in his favour.

On the death of Nampoina, various subject peoples had rebelled. Radama vanquished them, and completed the conquest of Betsileo. In this way he made certain of being the most powerful ruler in the island.

Traders revealed this situation to the British governor of the Ile de France (Mauritius), Sir Robert Farquhar. In 1814 France had been obliged to cede this island to Britain, and had kept only its sister island, the Ile Bourbon, which lacked natural harbours. Since the treaty made no mention of Madagascar, the governor of the Ile Bourbon laid claim to the former French trading-posts: Tamatave, Foulpointe, Fénérive and Fort Dauphin. Farquhar was determined to keep them, and in addition founded an English trading-post at Port Louquez on the bay of Antongil. But the government in London, which was not anxious to be saddled with another colony, and thus alienate French opinion, ordered the evacuation of the trading-posts.

Farquhar obeyed, but resolved to prevent the French from re-establishing themselves, and to extend British influence on the 'Great Island'. While in residence in the Moluccas during the war, he had learned how to influence local rulers. In 1816 he sent a message of friendship to Radama by the intermediary of a Mauritian trader, who returned accompanied by two of the king's brothers, who were sent to be educated. A second mission concluded a commercial treaty. The third, in 1817, was entrusted to Hastie, an ex-sergeant of the Indian army; he took with him uniforms and horses, both great novelties, which delighted the king. However, Hastie's task was not easy: he had to make the king agree to the abolition of the slave trade, which, following British pressure, had been condemned by the Treaty of Vienna. But this trade was the principal export of the kingdom, and furnished a means of procuring arms. At length Radama agreed: Britain consented to indemnify him and provide him with arms; in addition she granted him the title of 'King of Madagascar'. Thus this treaty of 23 October 1817 was both an alliance and an incitement to Radama to conquer the coastlands.

But Farquhar went on leave, and his temporary replacement refused to pay the indemnity. On his return in 1820, Farquhar had great difficulty in picking up the threads again; a current expression was 'false as an Englishman'. Hastie had need of all his Scottish perseverance, and in addition made it clear that British ships would in any case be able to prevent the slave trade. On 11 October 1820 Radama imposed the new treaty, in which the previous clauses were re-established, and in addition the English agreed to accept several young people from the Merina aristocracy to be educated in England.

As early as 1817 Radama's ambition, encouraged by Farquhar, to impose his authority over the whole island as his father had intended, and to become 'the Napoleon of Madagascar', led him to campaign eastwards to gain access to the sea. The Bezanozano submitted. At Tamatave, the French half-caste Jean René, who had proclaimed himself king, became a vassal. To the west, two expeditions (1820–1) invaded the kingdom of Menabe, but the Sakalava evacuated the area; hunger, fatigue and fever killed a third of the Merina warriors, who were forced to retreat. The army in fact was merely a confused mob of able-bodied men, recruited in the dry season, undisciplined, poorly armed, living off the country. The conquest of the island required a different sort of instrument.

The reform of the military machine was accomplished by Radama with the aid of three sergeants: Hastie, the Jamaican mulatto, Brady, and Robin, a French deserter. All three were promoted to the rank of general, and assisted the king in his conquests. A smaller, more mobile army was instituted, drawing its recruits from wealthy people able to provide themselves with arms and uniforms. A tax was levied on civilians in order to feed the soldiers, who were trained in drill, discipline and shooting. A hierarchy of honours was established, rising from one honour (private soldier) to ten honours (general). This army, with an establishment of 15,000 men, supplied with modern firearms, the residue of the wars in Europe, was to triumph easily over the other Malagasy warriors, armed with assegais and the old guns of the slave trade.

In 1822 the new army underwent its first trials, in the very place where the earlier bands had failed. It advanced into Menabe, setting up military posts as permanent garrison centres. The Sakalava king suffered a limitation of his powers, and was obliged to give his daughter to Radama in marriage.

Meanwhile the French were re-asserting themselves. In 1821 Sylvain Roux had occupied the island of Ste Marie, theoretically French since

1750, and had then made the Betsimisaraka of Tintingue and other villages on the Great Island opposite swear allegiance to France.

In 1823 Radama descended on Tamatave with 13,000 soldiers. There he held a great *kabary* to which he summoned the Betsimisaraka, affirming his overlordship. His soldiers devastated the area of Tintingue. Then he advanced to the extreme north of the island, where the king, Tsialana, submitted. The following year Radama returned through the territory of the Tsimihety; he left them a limited amount of freedom, but established a military post there. The Sihanaka, entrenched in an island on lake Alaotra, held out for a time; thousands of them were taken back to Tamatave as slaves. Among other consequences of this expedition was the cessation of the periodic maritime invasions of the Comoros by the Betsimisaraka.

At the same time another Merina army, supported by Jean René and his subjects, was subjugating the eastern coast south of Tamatave. The Antemoro kings became vassals.

Immediately on his return from the north-east in 1824, Radama turned his attention to the north-west, and attacked the Sakalava kingdom of Boina. Queen Ravahiny was dead, and her grandson, Andriantsoly, had been converted to Islam, to the displeasure of a great many of his subjects. He fled before the Merina army, which reached Majunga without difficulty. The Arab governor was killed in the defence of the town, and Radama established a garrison there, under the command of his cousin Ramanetaka. Andriantsoly submitted, and ruled as a vassal at Marovoay.

The French had not opposed Radama, except with words. They retained only the Ile Ste Marie. Sylvain Roux was dead, and his successors, Blevec and Albrand, built a fort in the south of the island. There they were not attacked. On the other hand, Fort Dauphin, where the French had sent a symbolic garrison of three men under a sub-lieutenant, was taken by a Merina army of 3,000 men.

Radama's conquests had been overwhelming. Fortified Merina outposts dominated the subjected territories, and their governors imposed their will on the vassal kings. However, the coastal peoples, accustomed to independence, were not slow to exert themselves once more, owing to their dislike of paying tribute and the system of forced labour.

In 1825 the Sakalava, whom the Merina were trying to disarm, rebelled in a concerted action by the Boina and Menabe chiefs. Andriantsoly massacred a Merina garrison, but failed to take Majunga;

Ramanetaka dispersed the assailants. Andriantsoly fled to Anorontsan-gana in the north, where he regrouped his forces with the help of the Antalaotra. In 1826 a combined attack by land and sea overcame them. Andriantsoly retreated to the Comoros with many of his supporters. His sister was enthroned as vassal queen. The Merina failed to capture Ramitraho, the king of Menabe, who kept his independence in the valley of the Tsiribihina.

The Antanosy had meanwhile revolted on their own initiative, and had encircled Fort Dauphin. A new army had to be sent to subdue them. The Betsimisaraka of Tintingue attacked the Merina post at Foulpointe, but failed to take it; the Zana-Malata chiefs, descended from pirates, were taken to Tananarive and executed.

In 1827 a final expedition to the east coast, bypassing the Antemoro country, conquered the Antesaka territory, whose king was killed. The northern part of the land of the Tanala had been reduced to vassalage; a military post had been established at Ihosy among the Bara. The greater part of Bara retained its independence, along with the whole of Mahafaly and Antandroy in the extreme south. The same applied to the southern Tanala and the short stretch of coast between Antesaka and Antanosy. In the west the northern part of Menabe and Ambongo also escaped. All these were areas of wild country, difficult to penetrate, with warlike and elusive populations. However, Radama had succeeded in uniting the best part of Madagascar, more than two-thirds of the island, in a very short time. He had been, as he had hoped, the Napoleon of Madagascar.

These conquests put an end to the isolation of Imerina. Through Tamatave, and thence along forest tracks, European goods and novel-ties could reach the capital without risk of pillage. Radama, advised by Farquhar, Hastie and Robin, encouraged innovations and often im-posed them.

In the realm of ideas, the essential agents of diffusion were the British missionaries. As early as 1818 the Reverend David Jones, of the London Missionary Society (L.M.S.), spent some time in Tamatave, and in 1820 returned to settle there with his colleague Griffiths. They opened a school with only three pupils. But Radama was interested in it, and before the end of the year there were twenty-three schools with 2,300 pupils, of whom one third were girls.

The teaching medium was Malagasy. But, apart from the Antemoro dialect written in Arabic characters, the language had not previously been written down. Robin had introduced the king to the Latin alphabet; but the question was whether he would adopt French or English spelling, both of them archaic and unsatisfactory. By extreme good fortune, Jones was a supporter of the phonetic system, at that time little known. He got the principle accepted of a single letter for each sound. The king decided that Malagasy should use English consonants and French vowels, with certain modifications. This system, by its simplicity and logic, allowed a rapid increase in literacy. By 1827 more than 4,000 Malagasy could read and write. The missionaries worked on a translation of the Bible into Malagasy. The Merina dialect became the official language. The laws were posted up on the palace gate.

The number of British missionaries increased and they undertook the task of conversion to Christianity, using the *kabary* and music. Their success however owed more to novelty than to real conversion. Radama did not influence his people directly, but European opinion led him to certain decisions: the *tanguin* (ordeal by poison) on human beings was suppressed, it was forbidden to abandon children born in inauspicious circumstances, and penal immunity granted to certain families was removed. Moreover, those young people who were sent to England received there a Christian education.

Radama interested himself above all in the material progress of his people. Among the young people sent to England or Mauritius a certain number were to learn manual trades. A few European workers were attracted to Tananarive. The Scottish missionary Cameron taught the Malagasy the manufacture of unfired bricks, soap and sulphur, the tanning of skins and the use of new techniques of forging and carpentry. Louis Gros, a Frenchman, built the palace of Soanierana, made entirely of wood, of a size till then unknown, but which became widely copied. There rapidly emerged tinsmiths, carpenters, and European-style weavers and blacksmiths, stone-cutters and tanners. Horses were introduced, as was the European silkworm.

Radama had the capital cleaned, and had a roadway made to allow the town to extend downhill. European uniforms made their appearance, sometimes combined with the *lamba*. Despite protests from the women, the soldiers were forced to cut their hair.

All these innovations were limited to Tananarive and the surrounding area. Some (for instance costume) affected only the wealthy. Means of access were still difficult, and fever, as much as the distrust which Radama had inherited from his father, prevented more than a handful of Europeans from living in the country, and these were entirely subject to the king's authority.

This authority had become more marked. The regime was deviating from Nampoina's rather patriarchal system towards militarism and absolute monarchy. Radama's health, undermined by military expeditions and all kinds of abuses, in particular alcohol, was deteriorating. He died on 27 July 1828, at the age of only thirty-five. Hastie had predeceased him; Robin escaped to Réunion. What was to become of these hurried conquests, this modernization which had only just got under way, and whose main support lay in the intelligence and authority of one very exceptional man?

RANAVALONA I: A RETURN TO TRADITION

As Radama had not designated a clear successor, his wife, who was also a blood relative, seized power with the support of the principal notables, and took the name of Ranavalona (she who has been folded, kept in reserve). She had all possible rivals put to death. Ramanetaka, fearing a similar fate, fled from Majunga by sea, saying 'Life is sweet; I have saved mine.' He became king of the island of Moheli, in the Comoros.

The oligarchy, which from then on wielded power in the name of the queen, was composed largely of chiefs of the commoner clans of Ambohimanga, whose fathers had consecrated Nampoina. The principal members were Rainiharo, relatively liberal, and Rainijohary, representing the earlier traditions. Around them was grouped a ruling class, composed of Hova military leaders, with some *andriana*, all of whom held lands and monopolized slaves and commerce. This plutocratic oligarchy, wearing European dress, living in a new type of housing, surrounded by aides-de-camp, made use of forced labour and isolated itself from the people, while still remaining hostile to the Europeans, who might develop into a military threat and become commercial rivals. The queen, a prey to superstition and determined to allow no attack on her sacred office and the heritage of the ancestors, was quite prepared to support a reactionary policy. British protection was immediately terminated. The resident, Lyall, who had succeeded Hastie, was notified that the treaty was no longer valid; the queen would promise only that the slave trade would not be re-established. Lyall himself was persecuted: snakes were brought into his house, and he was accused of sacrilege. He became ill and left, half-mad.

However, the French were once again showing interest. In 1829 Charles X sent a few ships under the command of Gourbeyre to re-establish the fort of Tintingue and occupy Tamatave. But the following year, Louis-Philippe, who had just acceded, ordered Tintingue to be evacuated, so as not to alienate the English. The queen had the impression that she had vanquished Europe.

Then began the persecution of the Christians. In 1830 there were two hundred very fervent Christians in Tamatave. Even though they showed respect for the government, the queen and her court would not permit the reference either to a foreign god or to the brotherhood of man, which the Malagasy interpreted as treason towards the ancestral spirits residing in the royal 'idols' (*sampy*, bits of wood or bags of sand containing magic power favourable to the ruler), and the social order founded on the caste system and slavery.

In 1832 baptisms were prohibited. In 1835 all Malagasy peoples were forbidden to become Christians. In 1836 the missionaries were exiled, and the first Christians massacred. Persecution resumed in 1840; the martyrs were slaughtered with assegais, thrown from heights, or burned alive. In all this they displayed constancy and courage worthy of the early Church.

Protestantism seemed to have been extirpated. Catholicism had not found a foothold. A bishop who wanted to reach Tananarive had been kept in a coastal village where he had died of fever and hunger.

Meanwhile in 1836 Rainiharo had sent an ambassador to London to discuss terms for a new treaty. Palmerston claimed the right to trade freely and set up posts. The Malagasy would only permit trade with a few ports which were under the supervision of governors. The traders were soon a prey to various petty interferences. In 1845 an attempt was made to make them subject to the laws of Madagascar, including the *tanguin* and forced labour. Thereupon, they left.

The British and French governments sent ships to Tamatave, the rivals for once working together. Commander Kelly and Admiral Romain-Desfossés bombarded the town and sent landing parties to attack the fort, which put up resistance. The Anglo-French party re-embarked, leaving a score of their corpses on the beach. The heads, impaled on the shore, proved that the queen was virtually invincible. The two powers thought little more of Madagascar, having many other subjects of discord amongst themselves.

Thus in the face of European penetration Madagascar was closing its doors, as had Japan, China and Morocco. In fact the country lived in a closed economy, and had need of other countries only for firearms, gunpowder and manufactured goods to which the aristocracy had grown accustomed: clothing, sugar, and alcohol. The queen made use of a very small number of Europeans to organize trade on a limited scale, and to create industries.

Foreign trade was organized in Tamatave by the Frenchman de Lastelle, in Majunga by the American Max. They sold cattle and rice in exchange for the goods they required. Max possessed ships, and de Lastelle a sugar and rum factory.

Industry was largely the creation of another Frenchman, the Gascon Jean Laborde, who had been shipwrecked on the east coast of the island. He was a smith, who had had a good classical education, and was skilful and enterprising. In 1832 the queen employed him to make guns. He fulfilled his promises beyond all expectations, and began to manufacture all the products which were no longer arriving from Europe. He established himself at Mantasoa in the forest to the east of Tananarive, where he could find in one place wood, waterfalls and iron ore. A thousand labourers were put permanently at his disposal, and Laborde made workmen of them. An industrial township grew up with a blast furnace and machinery. Laborde manufactured guns, gunpowder, sabres, and also glass, earthenware, baked bricks, tiles, lime, cement, soap, dyes, silk, ribbons, tools, and lightning conductors. An imposing villa was put up beside the factory, with a park, a zoo and a lake; here Laborde received the queen and the court, and held festivals with music and bullfights.

Not far away, but below the escarpment, he created a centre of tropical agriculture, including an experimental garden, a plantation of sugar cane, and a factory. He introduced vanilla, fruits from Réunion, humpless cattle, Merino sheep, and the first carts. In Tananarive, on the top of the hill, he built the queen's palace, made entirely of wood, with a central column 39 metres high. Later, the Scotsman Cameron surrounded this wooden structure with a stone wall with four angle towers.

Laborde, like de Lastelle, had married locally. With a rank of fifteen honours, he was incorporated as a member of the highest aristocracy, and treated as a relative by all the important people; the new generation called him 'Father'. Entirely devoted to his adopted country, he nevertheless remained firmly French and Catholic.

Immediately after the death of Radama, Andriantsoly returned. His army threatened Majunga, but was defeated by the Merina. The Sakalava, tired of useless campaigns, and discontented under a Muslim king who favoured the Antalaotra, replaced him in 1832 by his sister Oantitsi, a vassal of Ranavalona. Her rule scarcely extended outside

Anorontsangana and its surroundings. Andriantsoly took refuge in Mayotte, where he became king.

Another Sakalava king, Tsimandroka, drove the Merina from the valley of the Sambirano. But he in his turn was driven out by the Merina, as was the king of the Antankara, Tsimiharo. These rulers took refuge on the neighbouring island of Nosy-Bé, and appealed to the sultan of Zanzibar, but in vain. They therefore made approaches to a French ship, which took them under its protection. Admiral de Hell, the governor of Réunion, ratified a convention in 1841. Mayotte also showed the French flag. Monseigneur Dalmond introduced a Catholic mission onto Nosy-Bé, in preparation for the evangelization of the Great Island. On this occasion the French used the rights of their protégés to claim a protectorate over their former territories.

Nevertheless the hurried conquest of the north-east had been consolidated. Things were quite otherwise in the west. Despite several expeditions, the Sakalava of the Tsiribihina and the Ambongo retained their independence.

The same thing applied in the south. From 1829 to 1832 four successive armies failed in their attempts to take the steep rock of the Ikongo, from which the Tanala rained down enormous stones. Their kings did however submit. On being sent to Tananarive, they were put to death. In 1850 a general revolt led by king Tsiandrofana broke out, which achieved *de facto* independence.

In the arid country of the south-west and south (Bara, Mahafaly, Antandroy), the Merina armies perished from fatigue and hunger, and their activity was limited to the establishment of border-posts.

The Antanosy, humbled but discontented, emigrated in large numbers to the west, on the river Onilahy. In 1852 the Merina post of Fort Dauphin was attacked. A French businessman, Lambert, paid court to the queen, lending her a boat to transport her troops. Fort Dauphin remained isolated.

In the same year, 1852, the Antesaka rebelled. A strong army under the command of Raharo (the son of the prime minister Rainiharo) overwhelmed the countryside, massacred the warriors, and took the women away to slavery. The Antesaka gave this catastrophe the name of *Ranobe* (the flood), or *Andriamarotola* (the lord of many bones).

Laborde, who accompanied one of these expeditions, came back appalled by the lack of order and the excesses which had been committed. The army had greatly deteriorated since the time of Radama. The wealthy no longer took part, the army being composed of worthless ruffians who plundered the people. Commanders of forts and provincial governors lived off the land and at times overstepped their powers, giving rise to revolts among the conquered peoples, who had not lost their taste for independence.

Taken as a whole, Merina rule had progressed little in extent, but had become stronger. The peoples who had been the earliest to submit, the Betsileo and the Betsimisaraka, suffered the regime passively, only reacting when they were enlisted. In 1836 the queen founded the new town of Fianarantsoa (good teaching), modelled on Tananarive, to teach the Betsileo manners. Vassal kings were sometimes invited to the court for festivals. But real unity was still remote.

In 1852 the prime minister Rainiharo died, and was replaced by his son Raharo (also called Rainivoninahitriniony). Old Rainijohary was still influential, defending the customs of the ancestors with the support of the great majority of the people. But at the court and in the town the young people, despite the discrimination against the Christians, had been won over to a certain degree of modernity in dress and ideas. Ranavalona herself had taken as her secretary Raombana, one of the young aristocrats educated in England. This gilded youth was fiercely ambitious and pinned his hopes on the accession of the queen's son, Prince Rakoto. They called him 'son of Radama', even though he had been born thirteen months after Radama's death. The queen did not lack lovers anxious either to achieve power or to consolidate their position. Rakoto showed an inclination to modernize the kingdom. Laborde had prepared him to expect much from France.

In 1855 Lambert was admitted to the court. He fascinated everyone by his commercial inventiveness; he got Rakoto to sign a secret document, asking for a French protectorate, and granting Lambert the right to form a company for the development of the resources of the island; this was the 'Lambert Charter'.

But Napoleon III, in the midst of the Crimean War, had no desire to quarrel with the British, and suggested, as he did for the Suez Canal, that they should participate in the company. He had as little success. The Reverend William Ellis, who had been sent to Tananarive, raised the matter with Rakoto, and the secret was revealed. Rainijohary alerted the queen. In 1857 sorcerers and criminals were invited to confess; more than a thousand were killed or put in chains.

Lambert returned at this difficult time. A plot was hatched with the support of a group of secret Christians (the *priants*: praying ones) to place Rakoto on the throne. Rainijohary was however informed and all the Europeans, including Laborde (whose inventions were destroyed), were banished. The Malagasy Christians were stoned, poisoned, put in chains or reduced to slavery.

The queen, now in her seventies, ill, suspicious, a prey to the darkest superstitions, lived on for three years. She died at last on 18 August 1861, having designated as her heir Rakoto, who took the name of Radama II.

REFORMS UNDER RAINILAIARIVONY

A spoilt child, without a proper education, lacking application, Radama II had immensely good qualities but little common sense. Attracted by European civilization, he wanted to possess it at once, without taking into account the reservations of his people or the danger inherent in certain innovations. In these conditions he needed a strong power-base; but he set himself to undermine it with the determination of an anarchist.

He refused to execute his adversaries, abolished the *tanguin* and the death penalty, amnestied all those already sentenced, reduced military service by three-quarters, suppressed forced labour and the customs duties (the only stable source of revenue for the regime), renounced wars, repatriated a large number of slaves, proclaimed the liberty of religion, set free the Christians who had been imprisoned, and restored their property.

The Christian missionaries returned in strength, the Protestants with Ellis, but Catholics as well. Laborde was named French consul. The Lambert Charter was confirmed: the company to be created was given a monopoly of mining, the right to acquire land, to mint money, and to do 'anything it judged to be in the interests of the country', giving in exchange 10 per cent of the profits. In 1862 treaties were signed with France and England instituting the right to establish posts and guaranteeing freedom of movement. An Englishman, Caldwell, obtained a charter less extravagant than Lambert's, but even less precise.

Difficulties soon arose. Ellis fought the influence of France. The oligarchy would not allow the economy to be taken over by the Europeans. The prime minister, Raharo, and his brother the commander of the army, Rainilaiarivony, chiefs of northern clans traditionally associated with the government, were unfavourably disposed towards Radama, who surrounded himself with favourites (*menamaso*) from other parts of Imerina. When an epidemic causing convulsions broke out, this was seen as a result of the anger of the ancestors.

Radama, unconscious of the danger, took it into his head to advocate duelling, a European novelty. Raharo and his brother had the unprotected palace surrounded; the *menamaso* were massacred, then the king (whose sacred blood could not be shed) was strangled (11 May 1863). His wife was proclaimed queen under the name of Rasoherina (the chrysalis). In fact, what then began was the dictatorship of the prime minister.

Raharo made use of the opportunity to revoke the Lambert Charter. But his brutality alienated the queen, who replaced him by Rainilaiarivony on 14 July 1864.

The new prime minister was thirty-six years old. He belonged to the modernizing generation, but his prudence, brilliant intelligence and taste for and practice of authority never made him attempt the impossible. In this way he succeeded in ruling his country until the French conquest of 1895, in the name of three queens: Rasoherina, Ranavalona II, and Ranavalona III, who succeeded each other and each of whom he married.

First it was necessary to frustrate the plots of his rivals; he exiled his brother and old Rainijohary. In 1868 Rasoherina died; the prime minister replaced her with a cousin who became Ranavalona II. New treaties were signed with Britain, the United States and France. The Lambert Charter was publicly burnt. Laborde had avoided a complete break with France.

Nevertheless the prime minister felt the need for some external support. The queen, a good pupil of the Protestants, was pressing him in their favour. The Protestant party was getting larger, and threatened to become dangerous. Rainilaiarivony decided to draw it under his influence, counting on the fact that at the same time this would guarantee British support.

At the coronation on 3 September 1868, the 'idols' were replaced by the Bible. On 21 February 1869, the queen and prime minister were converted and underwent a Christian form of marriage. He had to repudiate his existing wife, who had borne him sixteen children, and whom he had been able to keep until then by virtue of polygamy. The 'idols' were sent to be burnt. The number of Protestants increased rapidly. The officials had churches built, and ordered the people they administered to go to them. This was the 'church labour service'. Catholics were persecuted. The prime minister restrained these excesses. He created a palace church to control the missions, but friction continued between them.

Reforms followed with the aim of modernizing government organization and by introducing a certain number of new regulations inspired by Christianity or European practice, changing the customs of the country. As early as 1868 the Code of 101 Articles was promulgated, slightly moderating the harshness of the penal laws.

The army was somewhat improved; regular exercises were reintroduced; the grades were revised; arms were bought or manufactured locally.

By 1870 reform had merely begun. But the major step, the Christianization of the ruling class, had been taken and began to spread gradually. Among the masses Christianity was only superficial, and they still remained deeply attached to the cult of the ancestors.

From this traditional point of view, the queen, even though a Christian, was still a sacred being, the emblem of the nation. Everyone bowed down before her, and her special chant was intoned whenever she passed by beneath her red parasol. Her annual bath (*fandroana*) was the rite which marked the birth of a new year and made nature fruitful. It was in her name that the prime minister governed and presented the new laws to the people, to be ritually acclaimed. The oligarchy of the Hova chiefs, together with a few *andriana*, occupied positions of importance, directed commerce, increased its lands and the number of its slaves.

The clans and the *fokonolona* still existed, as did the feudatories, but they were strictly controlled by the prime minister and his officials. These officials levied only a small proportion of the taxes for themselves, but lived off the country, especially outside Imerina. The governors and commanders of these outer provinces, supported by Merina forts and garrisons, had at their command native chiefs, vassal kings, or heads of clans, responsible for the maintenance of order and the dispensing of justice at the lowest level. It was a well-constructed colonial system, tyrannical at times, but on the whole adaptable to diverse circumstances, and not interfering with traditional customs. The Betsileo were under a separate code.

The taxes were diverse also. The Betsileo gave mats, the Sihanaka wood and fish. Capitation and land tax were moderate. The most important source of revenue was customs duty at a rate of 10 per cent *ad valorem*. The treasury was very small; but officials were unpaid, and the system of forced labour was sufficient for public works. In Imerina the presence of the court made the forced labour system very onerous. Artisans were conscripted for indefinite periods.

The economy was still based on the production of the family unit. On the east coast Creole colonists (from Réunion and Mauritius) introduced coffee and vanilla. The government granted vast concessions, especially for forestry and mines. Crafts developed in Imerina, among them carpentry, brick-making, iron-work, lace making, and the manufacture of candles, and straw hats.

Periodic markets in Imerina and Betsileo grew much more numerous. Imports from abroad were still few: clothes and furniture for the oligarchy, and cheap canvas, printed cloths, cast iron pots and rum. Live cattle and rice were exported to the Mascarenes, raffia and wax to Europe. The chief ports were Tamatave, Majunga and Mananjary.

There were neither roads nor bridges. The path from Tamatave to Tananarive was the one most used by porters; the average load was 40 kilos and the journey took six days. There was no local currency; the Spanish piastre or the five franc piece were used, cut into small pieces.

A large part of the island was still uninhabited; the population was concentrated mainly in the eastern coastal regions or the valleys of the interior. It was estimated in 1828 that Imerina had 750,000 inhabitants. For the island as a whole, a figure of two million has been suggested, but without any serious foundation. The population of Tananarive is said to have numbered 75,000, of whom two-thirds were slaves. Tamatave was a large village, while the other centres were merely groups of villages surrounding a Merina fort.

Imerina had spread westward and southward as a result of colonization or the flight from forced labour. The hill of Tananarive was still crowned by the large wooden houses of the aristocracy, but brick houses were making their appearance, and huts of daub covered in red clay crowded together in the lower quarters near the rice fields. These were continually extended further and further into the swamps in order to feed a growing population. The winding, slippery paths became torrents when it rained.

The Betsileo were completely subjugated; the vassalized kings had become merely the agents of the government. Pacification made possible the extension of the rice fields, but the edges of the rice fields were plundered from time to time by Sakalava or Bara warriors. The Bezanozano and Sihanaka lands were also peaceful, and were gradually infiltrated by Merina colonizers.

After the massacre of the Zana Malata, the Betsimisaraka had been subjected to virtually direct rule. At Tamatave lighters were unloading on the beaches: there could be found there numerous *bourjanes* (porters) who conducted the trade with the interior.

Antankarana in the extreme north was still sparsely populated, and, even so, only on the coast. The magnificent roadstead of Diego Suarez was hardly used.

The small islands, Sainte Marie, Nosy-Bé and its neighbours, remained French colonies, and cultivated cloves, sugar and vanilla.

The Sakalava kingdoms had suffered various fates. Boina was occupied by Merina military posts, especially along the Betsiboka river and on the coast; in the interior Sakalava heads of cantons were in charge of the country under the authority of Merina governors. Majunga was populated by Antalaotra, in Arab-style houses. Ambongo and the north of Menabe (Tsiribihina) were still independent. The south of Menabe was held by two lines of Merina forts. The interior zone east of the coastal plain and west of the plateau was virtually a desert.

The extreme south (Bara, Mahafaly, Antandroy, and Antanosy emigrants) was independent; only the north of Bara territory had a Merina post at Ihosy. In 1873 a Merina army turned nearby marauding tribes into vassals, although this was ineffective in practice.

In the south-east the Antanosy were unruly; the Antesaka had been crushed in 1852. Between them and the forest zone, the peoples remained untouched.

FOREIGN AND MISSIONARY INFLUENCES

The London Missionary Society, which had sent out its first missionaries under Radama I, quickly reinstated itself under Radama II, and made rapid progress under Ellis's direction. In 1867 there were 27,000 Christians, particularly evident among the aristocracy and young people. The conversion of the queen and the prime minister strengthened the movement. In one year 16,000 new Christians were baptized. In addition to the L.M.S. there were also the Anglicans (1864), the Norwegian Lutherans (1866), and the Quakers (1867). At first restricted to Imerina, christianization spread to Betsileo and several places on the east coast.

The Catholics, who had arrived under Radama II, encountered difficulties after the conversion of the queen, and had to fall back for converts mainly on slaves and Betsileo. However, the daughter-in-law of the prime minister, Victoire Rasoamanarivo, was a fervent Catholic and effectively protected her co-religionists.

The schools, which had 4,000 pupils before their suppression by Ranavalona I, were reopened in 1862. By 1875 there were 30,000 pupils in the Protestant missions alone. In 1862 the L.M.S. founded a teacher training school, and in 1868 a secondary college. In 1864 it had founded a hospital. The Catholics, with fewer resources, set up schools and dispensaries. The modernizing movement was mainly concentrated in Imerina. The evolution of the Merina tended to separate them from the other, less favoured peoples, and to produce confusion in the minds of the most advanced intellectuals.

Knowledge of Madagascar had made great strides. The pacification of the greater part of the island had made travel easier for scholars. The most notable was Alfred Grandidier, who from 1864 to 1870 travelled the length and breadth of the island, drew reconnaissance maps, and worked out a triangulation of Imerina; he revealed the real structure of the island, and began the publication of a monumental work, *Histoire physique, naturelle et politique de Madagascar*, which was to include all the sciences. Some missionaries ventured into little-known regions, others compiled dictionaries. Ellis left useful volumes on the history and life of the island at the time of his travels. In 1875 Sibree founded the scientific journal, *Antananarivo Annual*. Father Callet collected the oral traditions of the Merina kingdom.

The number of foreigners amounted to a few hundreds. Indians were trading on the west coast. The first Chinese arrived in 1862. Tamatave was a Creole town, with a few import–export houses. The other Europeans were mainly missionaries: English, French, Norwegian, American.

The French government had not officially repudiated the theoretical annexation of the island decreed by Louis XIV. In 1862 it had only recognized Radama II as king of Madagascar with the proviso that the 'rights of France' should be taken into account. Two pressure groups were trying to make these rights a reality: first, the Catholics, who complained of persecution by the Protestants; secondly, the Réunionese, who, feeling restricted in their own small island, dreamed of spreading into the vast land nearby. The opening of the Suez Canal in 1869 had conferred a new importance on the Indian Ocean. In the mid-1870s France was still making good her losses after the war of 1870, but was soon to throw herself into expansion. A motive for intervention was provided by the protectorate in Sakalava territory granted to the kings who had fled to Nosy-Bé. The death of Laborde in 1878, and the problem of finding a successor, afforded another pretext. Laborde himself, an old man who had lost credit with both sides, had tried to find a means of conciliation. After his death, imperialism, which at that time was being unleashed throughout the world, also reached Madagascar.

CHAPTER 12

AFRICANS OVERSEAS,
1790–1870[1]

THE EROSION OF SLAVERY

Africa, like Europe, is a continent which has exported millions of colonists, who through their labours and initiative created the 'New World' of North and South America, with all that implies for the shape of the modern world. The African emigrants, almost without exception, were taken from Africa by force, and colonized America and the Caribbean as slave labourers. Thus, whilst helping to create the New World by their labour, the historical legacy of African immigration to the American hemisphere has left deep and bitter social, economic and political problems which are still far from solution. The period 1790–1870 represents a great watershed in this historical movement of world significance. It is not, perhaps, a theme of Africa's domestic history, but none the less one which, through its effects on the relationships of 'white' and 'black' races and their attitudes to one another, has constantly had the effect of directly influencing the development of African, as well as European and American history.

The essential feature of the period under review is that it witnessed a revolutionary transformation in the legal and civil status of Africans and people of African descent[2] living overseas. In 1770, although there

[1] To attempt a comprehensive survey of the role of Africans throughout the world would be impossible in the space available here. In this chapter emphasis has been placed on Brazil, the Caribbean and the United States of America, because these were areas from which people of African descent were to make their presence felt in African history through re-emigration to Africa, movements which were concerned with Africa, and ultimately in pan-African ideas and ideologies. Though large numbers of African slaves were imported to mainland Hispanic America, they and their descendants played little or no role in the history of Africa thereafter.

[2] The authors of this chapter face serious difficulties of terminology in describing the various groups which emerged out of the African migration to the New World. These problems are technical, in that it is important at times to describe precisely that a person was of full African descent, or part-white, etc., when these considerations affected his political and social behaviour, as they did, in different ways, in Brazil or the USA, but at the same time precise terms, such as 'mulatto', are considered offensive in some, but not all, societies. Some terms which are considered insulting in one society are actually demanded in another. For example many Africans would find it insulting to be referred to as 'blacks'; they are not black but brown, and in any case see no particular reason, other than gratuitous insult, why attention should be drawn to their pigmentation, and why they should not be called simply 'Africans'. In North America, however, especially in recent years, people of African descent resent the term 'Negro', find that of 'coloured' patronizing, and actually demand

were significant groups of free 'people of colour' in North and South America, the Caribbean, and Britain, they were small in number, and emancipated by individual acts, as part of no movement hostile to slavery as such. In general in 1770 white people felt it to be acceptable and normal that the status of black men outside Africa should be that of slavery. By 1790 the position had begun to change, as the result of new attitudes of enlightenment among whites in Europe and America and the activities of free Afro-Americans. In 1772 Chief Justice Mansfield of England delivered his famous judgement in which he declared that he could find no positive law of England sanctioning slavery, thus emancipating the black population of England. In the ensuing two decades, slavery withered away under the impact of more enlightened attitudes, and of economic conditions which were increasingly irrelevant to slavery in the northern areas of British North America. The American revolution cracked the strength of slavery both by the ideological implications of its revolutionary propaganda, and by British policies of encouraging Negro support for the loyalist cause.

The French Revolution caused an even greater ferment in the Caribbean, provoking the first permanently successful Negro revolution in St Domingue in 1791, and the proclamation of the Republic of Haiti in 1804. In 1807 the British made the slave trade illegal for British subjects, and after 1815 forced similar laws on the weaker European powers by financial bribery or bullying diplomacy, increasingly creating a European moral climate in which slavery and the slave trade were held up as objects of moral detestation. By 1800 slavery in British North America was a defunct institution, no longer upheld by the courts, in the remaining British colonies of Upper and Lower Canada, Nova Scotia and New Brunswick. In the Act of 1833 slavery was abolished throughout the British Empire, where the main effect was felt in the British islands of the Caribbean. The French, faltering after

to be called 'blacks'. But this is not universal; Nova Scotians of an older generation for example find the term 'black' positively offensive.

The word 'Negro' has sometimes been used in this chapter, often simply to avoid the literary boredom of constantly repeating the only really accurate term 'persons of African or part-African descent'. It might be argued that 'Afro-American' is a better term, but this too is cumbersome, and seems to indicate a closeness to African culture which is often not present, and thus it can be misleading. It too, however, has been used where its use seemed accurate.

The term 'free coloured' has been used throughout this chapter in a precise way to indicate persons of part-African descent who were legally not slaves.

The authors hope that their readers, whether Africans, blacks, Negroes, mulattoes, mestizos, Afro-Americans or the pink-skinned, will be offended by none of these terms, but will read them in the spirit with which they were written, which is that the courage and achievements of all men deserve the respect of those who come after.

the great revolution of 1789, and hesitating again in 1830, finally swept the institution away in 1848. Meanwhile revolutions in Latin America paved the way for steady erosion of slavery in the newly founded nations there: Mexico abolished slavery in 1829, Bolivia in 1831, Uruguay in 1842, Colombia in 1851, Argentina in 1853, Venezuela in 1854, and Peru in 1855. In the United States the question of slavery, raised in the Revolution, became a major issue in the development of the new nation, and a central issue of regional rivalries. Though not itself the only cause of the Civil War of 1861–5, slavery in the United States was destroyed as a byproduct of the war between North and South. Thus by 1870 the situation of 1790 had been almost totally reversed: it was now normal for people of African descent living overseas to be legally freemen. Support for the idea of preserving Negro slavery was regarded as reactionary and immoral. In 1870 Brazil and Cuba remained as places where slavery was strong and effective, but few people of the time expected the institution to last long; Cuba was to abolish slavery in 1886, Brazil in 1888.

Such a bald chronicle of the legal history of slavery, though important in historical perspective, is primarily (though not completely) an account of political decisions made by a white power structure, and tells us little of the Afro-Americans or Afro-Caribbeans themselves. Moreover the history of the legal abolition of the slave trade and slavery gives an impression of inexorable 'progress' throughout the period, whereas in fact, whilst slavery as an economic system was in decline in the British and French Caribbean, and in Spanish America, Canada and the northern USA, it was profitably expanding in boom fashion in the south-western United States, Brazil, and Cuba. Thus, changes in the movement and condition of black people overseas were very complex; vast new areas in Brazil and the south-western United States were colonized in the nineteenth century by slaves working the plantation system of forced labour, and the total numbers of Afro-Americans expanded at its fastest rate both by fresh imports of slaves from Africa, and by natural reproduction. When after 1850 the trans-Atlantic slave trade virtually ceased from West Africa, great new internal slave trades developed in America, with certain areas, such as the 'border' states in the USA, acting as breeders of new slaves for expansion in new areas.

AFRICANS IN ASIA AND EUROPE

By 1790 the African diaspora was a well-established phenomenon. Africans had been taken forcibly to alien societies from very ancient times, and were absorbed into the classical societies of the ancient Mediterranean, where the enslavement of whites was more common than that of blacks. The commerce of the Red Sea and the Indian Ocean had long seen East Africans as an article of trade, and the conquests of Islam in North Africa extended the lines of the slave trade across the Sahara. Throughout the period 1790–1870 trans-Saharan traders of Egypt and North Africa and the Swahili-Arab traders of East Africa provided African slaves for the Islamic world. North Africa, Persia, Arabia, and even Turkey and India, absorbed a steady though not massive influx of Africans over many centuries down to the middle of the nineteenth century. This movement, however, did not produce black communities socially separated from the other societies of the Middle East. Though they absorbed them initially as slaves the Islamic countries rarely used Africans as agricultural labourers or treated them as pure chattels. The most dreadful fate awaiting the African in these areas was castration for use as a eunuch. Others were put to domestic servitude where they might marry, embrace Islam and their offspring be absorbed by the local culture. African women were mainly desired for their beauty, and as concubines donated African genes to the local human stock. Thus the legacy of the slave trade in the Middle East was mainly a darkening of skin pigmentation, with very little cultural influence on the area.

African immigration to Europe was similar in its lack of profound social effects. The Portuguese had imported slaves for agricultural and domestic work in Portugal in the fifteenth century, before the discovery of America, but within a century the Africans had inter-married with the Portuguese and disappeared as a separate recognizable group. Of more significance was the small, and separate black population which emerged in Britain in the eighteenth century. These immigrants, with very few exceptions, entered as slaves; a few directly from West Africa, but most came from the West Indies as domestic slaves brought back by retiring planters. Those who remained in service were on the whole well treated and well regarded, and manumission was common. These freed blacks naturally gravitated to the towns and seaports for employment, and created small, interesting pockets of black Englishmen in London, Cardiff, Bristol and Liverpool, which were reinforced by newcomers from the ranks of the slaves after Mansfield's judgement of 1772. It was from these 'black poor' that the first settlers were recruited for Sierra Leone.

Eighteenth-century England also saw the first articulate impact upon European thought by Africans educated in the European culture. Ignatius Sancho's letters were collected and published after his death by his British friends,[1] whilst Ottobah Cugoano published a work concerned to demonstrate the wickedness of the slave trade and to combat ideas of the inferiority of the 'Negro race'.[2] One of the most interesting 'British' Africans was the Ibo, Oloudah Equiano, known in Britain as Gustavus Vassa, a slave who had purchased his freedom in the West Indies and emigrated to Britain, where he presented a petition to Parliament in 1790. The year before he had published an autobiographical work, in two volumes, *The interesting narrative of the life of Oloudah Equiano, or Gustavus Vassa*, which ran into eight editions in five years. There were other isolated examples of Africans in Europe who made their way in the society of the time to become 'gentlemen', and who thus helped to confuse the general stereotype of the Negro as being naturally of the lower classes.

AFRICANS IN SOUTH AMERICA

African emigration to Asia and Europe, though a fascinating topic well worthy of greater investigation, cannot be regarded as of great significance in world history: it is otherwise with the massive impact of Africans on the history of the Americas. The slave trade represented one of the largest emigration movements in history, surpassed in scale only by that of Europeans to America. By 1700 some 1½ million Africans had been landed alive in the Americas, another 6 million were brought in the eighteenth century, and nearly 2 million more before the slave trade died away in the second half of the nineteenth century. The imported slaves, however, created by reproduction whole new expanding populations of Spanish-, Portuguese-, English-, and French-speaking blacks. In the United States the slave population alone rose from 700,000 in 1790, to 2 million by 1830, and 4 million by 1860, by which time there were an additional half-million black freemen. In Brazil there were 1½ million African slaves as early as 1798, and free

[1] *Letters of the late Ignatius Sancho, an African, in two volumes to which are prefixed memoirs of his life* (London, 1781).
[2] O. Cugoano, *Thoughts and sentiments on the wicked traffic of the slavery and the commerce of the human species, humbly submitted to the inhabitants of Great Britain* . . . etc. (London, 1787).

blacks made up the total to 2 millions; by 1847 Brazil had 4½ million Afro-Brazilians, of whom over 3 million were slaves. By the mid-nineteenth century there were some 2 million people of African descent in the British and French Caribbean islands, and perhaps about the same number scattered over Central and South America excluding Brazil. After emancipation statistics revealing racial origins are difficult to come by, especially for South America where inter-marriage was common, but it may be estimated that in 1870 the Americas contained some 20 million people of African descent, and millions of others with some African ancestry.

Though the Afro-American populations had been entirely created by the slave trade, and their initial history in America was that of a slave caste, there were real and important variations in the conditions under which they suffered, which have profoundly affected them and the histories of the countries to which they were brought. Recently historians have paid considerable attention to the comparative study of slavery in North and South America and the Caribbean, and several of them have argued that in Latin America slaves were treated with far more flexibility and humanity than in the United States of America. Several factors have been stressed to support this argument; cultural differences between the Spanish and Portuguese on the one hand and the English on the other, differing legal concepts of slavery, differences between Catholic and Protestant attitudes, and different colonial institutions.

The fundamental difference, however, was that the Iberians, even when enslaving Africans, did not deny their essential humanity and regarded slaves as *persons*, whilst in the northern Anglo-Saxon colonies the black slave came to be regarded, both socially and in law, as a *thing*, a piece of property no different from farm animals. These different attitudes arose, somewhat ironically, from the fact that, whereas slavery had died out in northern Europe, in Portugal and Spain slavery had persisted throughout the medieval period, and Church and State had from the thirteenth century built up restraining influences upon masters in the interests of royal and ecclesiastical authority, but in the process had facilitated voluntary manumission of slaves and the inter-marriage of slaves and freemen. Though the Spanish did not issue a 'slave code' of laws for their American colonies until 1789, the pre-amble to the code stressed that it was merely a summary of 'ancient laws' and conformed to actual practice in America.[1] The code in

[1] Frank Tannenbaum, *Slave and citizen* (New York, 1947).

particular favoured the practice of manumission, and established procedures whereby the slave could compel his master to free him if he were able to offer money to buy his own freedom. No doubt, this was not easy in practice, and a determined master could make sure his slaves earned no cash to buy their freedom; nevertheless in Cuba and Mexico, and in Portuguese Brazil, many slaves achieved freedom that way. In Cuba slaves could even have the price of their freedom fixed by the courts, and pay for themselves by a series of instalments, moving from the master's house after paying the first instalment.

Manumission of slaves by masters was everywhere in Latin America regarded as a noble deed of honour, bringing praise from society and the Church, and supported by the law. Numerous social customs existed which continued to swell the ranks of free Negroes and people of mixed race. Slaves would be freed to celebrate the birth of a son to the master, or the marriage of his daughter, or a slave would be freed for a brave deed, or even for work well done. Slave women would seek free godfathers for their children, in the hope that they would buy their godchildren's freedom.

The presence of slave craftsmen, and numerous Catholic holidays, also made it possible for slaves to work in their own time to accumulate money to buy freedom. The Catholic Church constantly pressed the masters to bring slaves to church, and formal Catholic marriage was regarded as necessary for slaves. Church marriage gave solidity to slave families and prevented masters from selling partners separately, while church membership gave opportunity for co-operation among slaves, even to the extent of pooling resources to buy freedom.[1]

Other historians have regarded as a romantic myth the view that slaves were better treated in Spanish- and Portuguese-speaking America. There is much evidence to indicate that masters in Brazil and Spanish America were adept at evading the provisions of the law, which, as a ruling caste, they themselves could often administer or influence. Equally, the great plantation owners or mine owners had little to fear from the admonitions of the Church. A chronicle of cruelties, sadism and barbarities practised by masters against their African slaves would be no more difficult to assemble for Brazil or Cuba than it would be for Jamaica or Virginia, and the contents would be sickeningly similar.[2]

---

[1] José H. Rodrigues, *Brazil and Africa* (Berkeley, 1965), 59.

[2] For examples of historians who are sceptical of the better treatment of slaves in Latin America, see Charles R. Boxer, *Race relations in the Portuguese colonial empire, 1415–1825* (London, 1963); Marvin Harris, *Patterns of race in the Americas* (New York, 1964); David B. Davis, *The problem of slavery in Western culture* (New York, 1966).

However cruel, the evidence nevertheless indicates that, in contrast to the United States, the social climate of Latin America undoubtedly favoured manumission and the creation of a free Afro-American population. In Cuba, where slavery was not abolished until 1886, 213,000 blacks, or 39 per cent of the Afro-Cuban population, were freemen in 1860.[1] The process is most dramatically illustrated in Brazil, which appeared to manumit its slave population almost as rapidly as it absorbed vast numbers of new Africans in the nineteenth-century slave trade. By 1818 there were already 585,000 freedmen and nearly 2 million slaves. By 1872, one-half of the Afro-Brazilian population had been freed by voluntary manumission. When the slave trade to Brazil virtually ceased in the 1860s, the slave population therefore dwindled rapidly, and at emancipation in 1888 there were only 728,000 slaves left to free.[2]

Just as significant as the factor of constant manumission in Brazil was the development there of miscegenation between Europeans and Africans, to produce people of mixed Afro-European genes, who in Portuguese are called mestizos. In Brazil in the nineteenth century this process of racial intermixture was on such an extensive scale that by 1872 mestizos formed the largest single classification (42·18 per cent).[3] Miscegenation in Brazil was a phenomenon of the slave system itself, and it was African women, through illicit sexual relations with the slave masters, who gave birth to the mestizo population. The process was not a result of more liberal attitudes to race relations in Brazil, for masters did not marry their slaves, but made concubines of them. Church and State succeeded in preventing inter-marriage with Africans in a series of extensive laws establishing white racial supremacy in the eighteenth and early nineteenth centuries. Concubinage with African women was also prohibited by the Church and the law, but ineffectively. The development of miscegenation is full of fascinating historical paradoxes and consequences: in order to preserve white supremacy in a society based on black slavery, racial inter-marriage was forbidden, but white masters could not resist the sexual attractiveness of slave women and their accessibility. The result was the production of the mestizo group, acceptable to both black and white, growing larger and larger outside the slave system, and naturally unconcerned about the finer distinctions

[1] Herbert S. Klein, *Slavery in the Americas: a comparative study of Cuba and Virginia* (Chicago, 1967). He compares Virginia, with the same black population, only 11 per cent free.

[2] Figures from John H. Franklin, *From slavery to freedom* (New York, 1967), 120. For greater detail see Rodrigues, *Brazil and Africa*, 72–9.

[3] Rodrigues, *Brazil and Africa*, 73. Whites formed 38·14 per cent and Negroes 19·86 per cent. The Indian population of Brazil was by this time insignificant.

of race and colour. Though racial prejudices continued among whites and in politics, the sheer weight of numbers of the mestizo class outside the slave system was beginning to break up racial stereotypes by the early nineteenth century. In 1834 the French ambassador could write 'in Brazil today it would be very difficult to limit the place of persons of colour . . . be convinced that no situation is inaccessible to men of colour'.[1] By a most curious irony one of his successors was the Comte de Gobineau, one of the originators of European racialist doctrines in the nineteenth century,[2] who served as French ambassador to Brazil during 1869 and 1870. As a believer in European racial superiority, Gobineau was shocked by what he observed:

if the Emperor was a pure Aryan, or almost, Brazilians on the contrary are not only mulattoes but mulattoes of the lowest category. A completely mulatto population, vitiated in blood and spirit. No Brazilian is pure-blooded, but the combinations of marriages between whites, Indians and Negroes are so multiplied that the shades of flesh are innumerable, and all this has produced the saddest kind of degeneration, in both lower and upper classes.[3]

The steady growth of the mestizo population in Brazil acted as a safety valve which prevented the growth of deep racial bitterness in the country, and allowed political, social, and economic disputes and divisions to spill over colour lines so that conflict of classes became more important in Brazilian history than clashes of colour. But in the same way issues which did deeply affect Afro-Brazilians, and especially the slaves, such as the movement to abolish slavery itself, did not excite the mestizo population in the same way as they fired black freemen suffering the humiliations of a racialist society in the USA. Here the nature of Brazilian political history must also be taken into account, for Brazil achieved its independence in a gradualist manner following the flight of the court and Crown from Portugal in 1808, until the creation of a separate empire under Don Pedro, the son of the Portuguese king, in 1822. This shielded Brazil from the impact of French and American revolutionary ideas which swept the rest of Latin America at this time; whilst the 'Anglo-Saxon' anti-slavery sentiments of the Protestant evangelical movement could make no impact on a solidly orthodox Catholic regime.[4]

[1] Comte de St Priest to French Foreign Minister, 17 June 1834, quoted in Rodrigues, *Brazil and Africa*, 71.
[2] Comte de Gobineau, *Essai sur l'inégalité des races humaines* (Paris, 1855).
[3] G. Readers, *Le Comte Gobineau au Brésil* (Paris, 1934), 32, 51, 52, quoted in Rodrigues, *Brazil and Africa*, 80–1.
[4] Indeed it can be argued that British pressures upon Brazil to abolish slave trading did much to stimulate Brazilian nationalism. The British demanded a Brazilian promise in 1826

But if Afro-Brazilian slaves did not find inspiration and leadership among the free mestizos, they were quite capable, given the right conditions, of furnishing it themselves. Here again Brazil presents contrasts with the 'Anglo-Saxon' slave populations. Slave rebellions in Brazil were very common, often of formidable proportions, effectively led by slave leaders, sometimes regionally successful for long periods of time, and were often well organized with realizable goals. These rebellions frequently displayed strongly 'African' inspiration, by reviving African forms of leadership, social organization, religious observances and cultural forms among the rebels.

Before the nineteenth century these movements generally began as fugitive slave settlements, called *quilombos*, many of which lasted but a year or two. A few, however, grew and maintained their autonomy for many years, creating institutions of government on African lines, such as the *quilombo* of Minas Gerais (1712–19) and Carlota, in Mato Grosso, which lasted from 1770 to 1795. The outstanding *quilombo*, however, was the 'Republic' of Palmares, in Pernambuco, which maintained an independent existence and developed as an African state inside Brazil from the 1590s until its conquest by the Portuguese in 1694. It withstood numerous Portuguese attacks and developed a fascinating constitution with an elected king, the *ganga-zumba*, who distributed office and patronage much in the manner of a central African king.[1]

In the nineteenth century *quilombos* could no longer be maintained effectively, and movements among African slaves took on the form of insurrections of a revolutionary kind, or armed revolts designed to force slave owners to ameliorate conditions. These movements generally showed important African influences, and leadership came from groups which would have been influential at home in Africa. In Bahia there were nine revolts between 1807 and 1835 in which Muslim leaders were outstanding. Yoruba and Hausa stressed their 'tribal' identities, and the Yoruba *ogboni* society re-appeared openly. Some of these revolts even aimed at a return to Africa. Many of the leaders of

that the slave trade would be abolished in three years, as the price for British recognition of Brazil's independence. This the Brazilians evaded. After 1845 the British navy began seizing Brazilian slave ships and even entered Brazilian harbours to destroy them, and these actions were bitterly resented in Brazil. Between 1850 and 1853 the Brazilians enacted legislation abolishing the slave trade, but did so without consultation with Britain. Once the slave trade was abolished, British influence in Brazil declined sharply, and Brazil escaped from what had, in the 1820s, been almost an informal British control. See A. K. Manchester, *British pre-eminence in Brazil: its rise and decline* (Durham, NC, 1933).

[1] See R. K. Kent, 'Palmares: an African state in Brazil', *Journal of African History*, 1965, 6, 2, 161–75. The footnotes to this article contain an excellent bibliography of Brazilian works dealing with Palmares and slave revolts in the colonial period.

these movements were remarkable individuals who acquired an almost legendary character in Brazil for their brilliant tactics, gallant actions, and warlike ferocity – in marked contrast to the rather pathetic rebel leaders among US slave revolts.[1]

The survival of a spirited sense of African identity, as expressed in these revolts, is almost unique to Brazil. Two main factors help to explain it. The first is the nature of Brazilian society, the fact that slaves were not predominantly chattels working the land, but had opportunities to become craftsmen, skilled workers, and even petty traders, to join religious societies and become practising Catholic Christians, to raise families, and 'remain human'. Another important factor, however, was the composition of the slave population itself. As the Dutch in the seventeenth century, and the English in the eighteenth, increasingly dominated the slave trade, the Portuguese, who remained the suppliers of Brazil's new slaves, found themselves increasingly restricted to fewer African slave exporting centres. With the British navy's abolitionist blockade in the nineteenth century, 'Portuguese' (in fact, increasingly Brazilian) slave traders became confined to only two major slave-trading centres: the area from Lagos to Whydah on the coast of Dahomey, and the Portuguese colony of Angola.[2] Thus, though the Portuguese and Brazilians, like all the slaving nations, attempted not to allow too many slaves of the same language group to predominate in any one area, their ability to do so was much more restricted than that of the English or Dutch slavers. Thus Hausa, Fulani and Yoruba often retained a consciousness of their origins, whilst the slaves from Angola were all of the Bantu linguistic group. Some Brazilian writers have even claimed that Brazilian Negroes are 'superior', in that the Hausa and Fulani elements brought an infusion of 'Hamitic blood'.[3] In the opinion of slave owners, Bantu from Angola were preferred as more submissive, friendly and easily converted to Christianity; slaves of Dahomeyan origin were regarded with suspicion as less resigned to their fate, whilst Muslims and the Hausa gained a reputation as the instigators of revolts.[4]

The strength of 'African-ness' among Brazilian Negroes was shown also in non-violent ways, which have perhaps had more permanent effects on Brazilian life and culture Their impact on the composition of

[1] A. Ramos, *The Negro in Brazil* (New York, 1945), 24–53.
[2] At times Mozambique provided a slave supply for Brazil.
[3] G. Freyre, *Casa Grande & Senzala* (Rio de Janeiro, 1958), 333.
[4] J. H. Rodrigues, 'The influence of Africa on Brazil and of Brazil on Africa', *Journal of African History*, 1962, **3**, 1, 52–6.

the Brazilian population has already been examined; massive misce-genation through African women naturally affected the atmosphere of ordinary life. The use of kola nuts as a ritual stimulant associated with Yoruba gods and the guinea fowl as a food are but two of dozens of typically African items in the Brazilian diet. The traditional dress of women, especially in Bahia, is developed from West African fashions. Dozens of Bantu, Hausa and Yoruba words have become part of Brazilian Portuguese (though its grammar remained unaffected), and linguists believe that the soft way of speaking Portuguese, so different from the guttural and hard tones used in Portugal, is the result of African pronunciations. Brazilian folklore and music are strongly influenced by the African forms and heritage, whilst African religious beliefs and cults persisted and became merged with Catholic practices and the cult of saints.[1]

That Brazilians in the nineteenth century should have been active in the African continent need come as no surprise: Brazil's dependence on the slave trade and her maintenance of the institution of slavery for so long was reason enough for this, and explains the very strong, and perhaps dominant, influence of Brazilians upon the development of Angola. At the same time, among Afro-Brazilians the sense of identity with Africa did create a desire to return 'home', and a significant minority did so. By the 1880s there were 3,000 Brazilians in Lagos alone, where most of the returned 'Brazilians' were of Yoruba origin.[2] It was they who spread the Brazilian Indian technique of making cassava non-poisonous and edible, and it is to them that Lagos owes its 'Brazilian' styles of architecture. The returned 'Brazilians', however, in marked contrast to their English-speaking counterparts in Liberia, Sierra Leone and other parts of West Africa,[3] brought back with them no revolutionary or reforming zeal or desire to change Africa along 'modern' lines. Indeed their acceptance of the slave trade and tradi-tional African society allowed them to win positions of strong influence in states like Dahomey. Brazilians like Francesco Felix De Souza, by

---

[1] It should perhaps be pointed out that the comments made throughout this chapter on the nature of Brazilian society refer to the nineteenth century, the period covered by this volume. With the abolition of slavery in 1888 Brazil suffered an acute labour shortage, which was overcome by large-scale immigration of Europeans, predominantly Italians and Portuguese. Over 1½ million immigrants from Europe entered Brazil in the ten years after 1888. Ironically, therefore, the abolition of slavery somewhat stiffened the colour line in Brazil, which turned in the twentieth century to 'white ideals'.

[2] Sir Harry Johnston (*The Negro in the New World* (New York, 1916), 98) estimated 4,000 Brazilians in Lagos and Whydah in 1872. Maloney to C.O., 20 July 1887, gives over 3,300 by 1881 in Lagos (P.R.O., C.O. 147/59).

[3] See chapter 5, 'Freed slave colonies in West Africa'.

developing the slave trade in Whydah in the 1820s and 1830s, won ready acceptance in the political and social life of Dahomey. King Ghezo appointed De Souza *chacha* of Whydah, in full charge, answerable only to the king, of European trading matters in the port. In the 1840s, Domingo Martinez became the leader of the Afro-Brazilian community on the west coast of Africa, interfering in the politics of Lagos and Porto Novo, maintaining large houses in Whydah and Porto Novo, palm oil estates and a cattle ranch in Dahomey. When the British navy in the 1850s began to do severe damage to the slave trade, Martinez tried to diversify his commercial and economic activities, and turned over to palm oil to maintain his position, but lost influence with the rulers of Dahomey. In fact he died in a fit of rage in 1864, on hearing the news that the king of Dahomey had given permission for French traders to set up in direct competition.[1] Brazilians did not return to Africa to regenerate the continent; they came to make their fortunes in trade and to settle among Africans. The Brazilians remained Roman Catholic in religion, continued to use Portuguese as a language, and strove to acquire 'European' material comforts. They considered themselves descendants of Africans, and often maintained a sense of being of Yoruba, or Fon or Ewe origin, but nevertheless maintained a superior attitude towards the 'natives', whilst Africans considered them to be a species of 'European'.[2]

AFRICANS IN THE CARIBBEAN

The West Indian Islands had been the cradle of the slave trade from West Africa, and it was in the Caribbean that Africans were subjected to the most brutal and ruthless exploitation of all the slave plantation systems. The root cause of this was the emergence after 1640 of sugar as the single dominating crop of the islands, and the discovery that Africans, already skilled and experienced in agricultural labour in the tropics, were superior workers, even as unwilling slaves under the lash, to the native Indians or European indentured labourers. As sugar worked by African slaves created larger and larger profits, bigger plantations developed, and in the seventeenth century the more modest white settlers left the British islands like Barbados to settle in Virginia.

[1] David A. Ross, 'The career of Domingo Martinez in the Bight of Benin, 1833–64', *Journal of African History*, 1965, **6**, 1, 79–90. See also J. Hargreaves, *Prelude to the partition of West Africa* (London, 1963), 111–13, and P. Verger, *Bahia and the west coast trade 1549–1851*) (Ibadan, 1964), for discussions of Brazilian trade in West Africa.

[2] Ross, 'Domingo Martinez', 83.

Thereafter the West Indies developed a unique social structure, in which the whites remained a tiny minority in a sea of African slaves. By the latter half of the eighteenth century, in rich sugar islands like English Jamaica or French St Domingue, African slaves outnumbered whites ten to one,[1] in British Barbados slaves outnumbered whites about four to one, and in French Martinique and Guadeloupe the ratio was six to one. Such ratios were unknown on the mainland of North or South America, where slaves were never a majority of the population, and large white populations who possessed no slaves gave variety and solidity to the economy and social structure. Outnumbered so severely, the West Indian planters lived in constant and justified terror of slave revolts, which they allayed by draconian punishments and discipline. As the supply of new slaves was furnished by English, Dutch, and French slave-trading ships, new slave cargoes landed were of such varied origins that they had no common African language, and they could be further distributed among 'seasoned' and 'docile' slaves through the island plantations. In these circumstances hardly anything of traditional African languages, culture or religious beliefs could survive, and the slaves rapidly lost their sense of African identity.[2]

Indeed it is probably incorrect to speak at this time of West Indian 'society', for the true nature of the organization of the West Indies was simply that the islands functioned as vast forced labour camps which subordinated all considerations to the production of larger quantities of sugar. Even for the white planters the ultimate ambition, if not always realized, was to retire wealthy and to settle in England or France. The slave owners and their 'overseers' were not subjected, before 1800, to any effective controls from England or France, nor were there any other local impediments such as the Church, royal officials, or a morality of non-slave-holding whites or free mestizos, to check the planters' vested interest in treating slaves merely as farm animals. Thus organized marriage was unknown in the British islands; it would have impeded the planters' control over slaves, especially

[1] By mid-eighteenth century Jamaica had 280,000 slaves and only 25,000 whites; in 1791 St Domingue had 425,000 slaves and 40,000 whites (R. Augier and D. Hall *et al.*, *The making of the West Indies* (London, 1960), 110–11).

[2] In British and French islands, religious cults, popularly called 'voodoo', emerged among the black peoples, and attempts have been made to show that these have African origins. But is it impossible to link 'voodoo' practices with African cults in any precise way, such as is possible, for example, in Brazil, where cults of specific African deities, such as the Yoruba god Shango, survived. As neither the British Protestants nor the French Catholics made serious efforts to convert slaves to Christianity until the end of the eighteenth century, 'voodoo' may more acceptably be regarded as simply a creation by the slaves of a set of religious and magical beliefs appropriate to their desperate circumstances.

when he wished to sell children or women to other owners. Similar motives made the planters most reluctant to see their slaves become Christian in religion.

The Spanish island of Cuba was an exception to the general picture, and as already noted earlier, shows features reminiscent of Brazil. This could be ascribed to the Iberians in their attitude towards slaves, especially the legal and moral insistence, buttressed by the Catholic church, that slaves were human and not analogous to property in animals. Moreover the Spanish had no significant African slave-trading bases, and relied on the Portuguese for their supply, and thus a greater African 'identity' could be retained by the slaves drawn from limited areas of Africa. However, perhaps too much should not be made of these factors; the French in St Domingue, Martinique and Guadeloupe were 'Latins' and Roman Catholic, but their islands did not display the features of Cuba. At root Cuba's differences were economic. Sugar did not begin to dominate the Cuban scene until the nineteenth century; as late as 1774 Cuba's white population of 96,000 outnumbered the 44,000 African slaves by more than two to one, and the white population continued to grow. By 1827 there were 311,000 whites and still they outnumbered the slaves, of whom there were 286,000.[1] As sugar took hold on the island, the Spanish authorities, with the support of the whites, made deliberate efforts to encourage white immigration, so that slaves slightly outnumbered whites only in the decade of the 1840s.[2]

An outstanding demographic difference between Cuba and the other Caribbean islands was the growth of a population, as in Brazil, of freed and free Negroes and people of mixed race, from 31,000 in 1774 to 106,000 in 1827. In the British and French islands the number of free Negroes or 'coloureds' remained very small before emancipation, in the ratio of 5 to every 100 slaves, or even less. The figures were the result of a general hostility to the idea of manumission of slaves among the British and French planters, who, even though they produced children by miscegenation with slave women, preferred to keep such 'coloureds' either as domestic house servants, or to ship them away to England or France out of the way. Those that did move into the small free coloured communities were, unlike the Brazilian mestizos, members of a tiny minority which felt threatened both by the black slaves, whom they often abused and by whom they were hated, and the white

[1] J. E. Fagg, *Cuba, Haiti and the Dominican Republic* (New Jersey, 1965), 25, 30, 31.
[2] Klein, *Slavery in the Americas*, 202, table 2.

oligarchy, which regarded them as an embarrassing illogicality. The free coloured thus adopted a *laager* mentality, constantly attempting to win and define privileges for themselves, but little interested in the plight of the slaves.

The Africans and their descendants in the French and British islands thus existed in what must seem a hopeless and completely demoralized position, with all their cultural, social and religious African background systematically destroyed, but replaced with no alternative social organization higher than that of convicts in a prison system. In such circumstances there could be no great revolutionary outbreaks or heroic leaders such as had occurred in Brazil. Nevertheless violent resistance by slaves was constant. In eighteenth-century Jamaica, riots or rebellions occurred on an average every five years, and in two of these, the Maroon wars of 1738 and 1795, small communities of ex-slaves actually established their independence in the interior mountain districts. Slaves born in Africa played a crucial part in leading these movements, and the abolition of the slave trade by the British in 1807 ironically brought a temporary end to rebellions, as no new Africans came in to Jamaica to provide leadership.[1] Such rebellions, however, though frequent, were in general poorly organized, lacked realistic goals and objectives, were characterized by violence and nihilism, and were constantly suppressed by cruel and savage punishments.

At the end of the eighteenth century two movements from Europe began to affect the Caribbean scene; both were essentially movements of ideas, and their effect was to present the Afro-Caribbean slaves with hope of constructive freedom in their hitherto hopeless situation. These were the French Revolution of 1789, and the Protestant evangelical revival in Britain.

The French Revolution had the more immediate and apparently far-reaching effects. A revolution for 'Liberty, Equality and Fraternity' clearly faced some awkward anomalies once the new French governments after 1789 were brought face to face with the slave colonies of the French West Indies. Only the extremist radicals such as the *Amis des Noirs*, however, were ready to consider eradicating slavery itself; the issue which precipitated the most formidable of all slave rebellions was that of suffrage and civil rights, not for the slaves, but for the free 'mulattoes'. A decree of the French Constituent Assembly of 8 March 1790 gave voting rights to the free coloureds, who the whites in St

[1] Mary Reckord, 'The Jamaica slave rebellion of 1831', *Past and Present*, July 1968, **40**, 108.

Domingue protested were 'a bastard and degenerate race'.[1] The St Domingue whites, in counter-revolutionary mood, alienated the free coloureds, who rallied to the colonial officials attempting to carry out instructions from Paris. It was in this situation of serious racial tension that the black slave majority rose in revolt in August 1791. There ensued a savage and bloody carnage of the utmost confusion, complicated by changes of alliances, the intervention of nearby Spanish forces and a British invasion in 1793, from which at last the blacks found a brilliant leader in Toussaint L'Ouverture, who, in uneasy alliance with the mulatto leader André Rigaud, emerged as master of the French part of the island in 1797, in co-operation with the remnants of French colonial authority. Toussaint had been catapulted from the status of a furtively literate house-slave to that of leader of the first black-ruled state with a population consisting almost entirely of slaves. He tried to compromise with France, now increasingly dominated by Napoleon Bonaparte, to rebuild the country on a basis of quasi-autonomy within the French colonial empire. In 1795 Spain ceded its part of the island, San Domingo, to France, and Toussaint occupied this area in 1801.

Napoleon had risen to power in France with the support of the propertied classes, as the man of order who would restore stability and consolidate the revolution. He was by temperament unwilling to accept an ex-slave Negro rival in St Domingue; his wife Josephine was a Martinique-born white whose sympathies were with the St Domingue sugar planters, and his supporters among the Girondiste bourgeoisie had investments and trading connections with St Domingue. Moreover, Napoleon planned to rebuild France's American colonial empire, and control of St Domingue was essential if he was to keep Louisiana. In January 1802 Napoleon ordered General Leclerc's expedition to reconquer the country, capture Toussaint L'Ouverture by fair means or foul, and re-establish slavery and the sugar economy.

At first it appeared that Leclerc's expedition would succeed. After the first French military successes, most of Toussaint's generals defected, and he himself retired to a plantation he had carved out for himself, ready to hand over power. Toussaint was now the victim of treachery: Leclerc lured him to the French headquarters with the promise of a safe conduct only to arrest him and ship him off to France, where he died in prison in 1803.

[1] C. L. R. James, *The Black Jacobins, Toussaint L'Ouverture and the San Domingo revolution* (New York, 1938), 72.

This action was a serious error of judgement, for it rallied the black population to desperate resistance through guerrilla tactics, which the French found no effective way to combat. The French troops were badly hit by yellow fever, and 50,000 perished. On 1 January 1804 Dessalines, Toussaint's successor, declared the independence of the new Republic of Haiti, the first colony of Latin America to cut its ties with the old world, but symbolically much more important, the first Negro-ruled state outside Africa. Independence was confirmed shortly afterwards by the defeat of the remaining French forces under General Ferrand. One year later all the whites, some of whom had returned at the invitation of the Dessalines government, were massacred. Thereafter the young black state was isolated by the great powers, all of whom had slave-holding territories, for fear the Haitian example should prove infectious.

Thus Haiti, born in blood, fire and treachery, placed under international quarantine for several decades and cut off from the modernizing influences of the very European revolutionary ideas which had spawned its birth, relapsed into economic decline and political chaos. Dessalines, who had proclaimed himself emperor, was assassinated, and Haiti became divided between Henri Christophe and Alexandre Pétion, the former claiming the emperorship, whilst Pétion, a mulatto educated in France, ruled the southern part of the country on more 'liberal' lines. It was Pétion who gave Haiti its first success in exporting revolution. Pétion had already befriended and given refuge to a number of Spanish American colonial patriots; in 1815 the greatest of these, Simon Bolivar, defeated by Spanish forces in Venezuela, took refuge in southern Haiti. Pétion agreed to support Bolivar's little army discreetly with money, provisions and arms in return for a pledge that Bolivar, himself a slave owner in Venezuela, would abolish slavery there after winning independence from Spain. In December 1816 Bolivar sailed for South America and launched the movement which was to overturn the Spanish colonial system on the mainland. He was as good as his word, and slavery was ended in his revolutionary state of Gran Colombia. But when Bolivar wished to invite Haiti to the first Pan-American Conference in Panama in 1824, he had to give way to pressure from the USA, and Haiti was left out.

After the deaths of Christophe and Pétion, Haiti was reunified in 1824 by J. P. Boyer, who also brought San Domingo under Haitian control. In 1859 a revolution brought to an end the rule of Haitian emperors, but instability continued, with bitter and violent racial struggles between the mulatto ruling class, which clung to French traditions and dominated political life, and the mass of blacks, who formed 95 per cent of the population. Despite attempts from time to time to revive slavery under forms of serfdom or forced labour, the sugar industry, which before the revolution had been the most profitable and productive in the Caribbean, collapsed, and the black masses had perforce to revert to a subsistence agriculture. Some writers have argued that Haiti 'relapsed' into a society which was basically African.[1] Neither modern nor contemporary Africans would have recognized it as such. No African language re-emerged, the mulattoes and northern blacks cultivating French, the blacks in the south a French *patois*. Though communal forms of agriculture did emerge, and the ex-slaves clung fiercely to their land rights, these were not specific revivals of any particular African ideas of land use, but simply efforts to deal with pressing needs for subsistence. The Roman Catholic religion, often in modified forms, remained that of the masses and the ruling class, which went hand in hand with widespread practice of *vodun*, the 'voodoo' magical cults, which had their roots in African religion, but now assumed specifically Haitian forms.[2]

Although the Haitian revolution was in fact a disastrous failure for the Haitian blacks and their aspirations, it nevertheless had great symbolic importance for Afro-Americans, especially those remaining in a slave status, or in conditions of discrimination against free coloureds, in the other West Indian islands and the USA. Such people remembered little and could learn nothing of Africa itself, or of real African independent states of the early nineteenth century, so that Haiti assumed an obsessive importance, as apparently the only country where black people managed their own affairs. It was this feeling which underlay the disastrous attempts by black people from the USA to emigrate to Haiti.[3] Not surprisingly, as Haiti was itself an independent state, there was no disposition on the part of Haitian blacks to return to Africa, and Haitians played no part in the nineteenth-century history of the African continent.

Slavery was disrupted on the other French West Indian islands after the French Revolution, but without the spectacular results of Haiti. In 1792 Jacobin commissioners arrived in Guadeloupe and Martinique, and their attempts to take control, with the support of free coloureds,

---

[1] E.g. G. Pendle, *A history of Latin America* (Harmondsworth, 1963), 118.

[2] James G. Leyburn's *The Haitian people* (New Haven, rev. ed. 1966), contains a useful analysis of *vodun* in chapter VII, 131–74. Leyburn accepts the view that *vodun* is Dahomeyan in origin.　　　　　　　　　　　[3] See below, pp. 450–1.

and embark on emancipation, were too much for the French planters, who turned to the British for help rather than submit. The revolutionary wars between France and England were also fought out in the West Indies, and the French at first appealed to slave populations to rise up for France and liberty. Though the British, with their control of sea power, regained the whip hand by 1801, the slave populations in all the islands had received a taste of the heady ideas of political and civil liberty, albeit in the crudest forms.

With Napoleon's rise to power, however, the slaves could no longer look to a revolutionary France for liberation. With French Caribbean possessions restored in the Peace of Amiens in 1801, Napoleon was bent on restoring the old regime and slavery, and his governor successfully did so in Guadeloupe, overthrowing the free coloureds who had seized power during the war.

Ironically it was the British, internationally still the bulwark of conservative forces, whose policies increasingly shifted into an anti-slavery stance. This is not the place to interpret the complicated question of British motives; from the viewpoint of the slaves, however, perceptible changes in British attitudes could be observed after 1800. The planter interest had been weakened by the American revolution, as the new United States took into itself a substantial section of the British slave holding interests, and the rise of free trading ideas and British industrial growth weakened the importance of the West Indian planter as a consumer of British luxury goods. But the most direct impact on the slaves came from the introduction of evangelical Protestant Christianity. In Jamaica the Baptist faith was introduced by two American loyalist Negroes who had fled from the United States after 1783; the movement spread, and in 1814 Baptist missionaries came from England. The Methodists also began intensive activity among the slaves. Neither group intended to subvert slavery, but preached quiescence and rewards for the obedient in heaven, but the very presence of such men, unconnected as they were with the slavery interests, alarmed the planters; missionaries were persecuted and their chapels attacked by whites, which in turn pushed the free coloureds, and the British government, into some sympathy with the missionaries. In 1823 the British government began imposing protective legislation for free coloureds, and for slaves, in the face of a mounting campaign for outright abolition in Britain. News of these developments gradually percolated through to the slaves, often garbled hearsay received at third or fourth hand from political discussions heard by domestic slaves at the master's table. These stirrings began to fan the spark of disaffection among the blacks.

In British Guiana a slave rebellion erupted in 1823, in which the rebels demanded immediate emancipation. In its suppression a hundred blacks were killed, and the local white missionary was jailed on suspicion of being involved in the revolt, and died in prison shortly afterwards. The most formidable rebellion, however, occurred in Jamaica in 1831. As in Haiti, it appears to have been touched off by inflammatory talk from the planters, who now feared British abolition of slavery in the near future, talked of armed revolt with assistance from the USA and schemed for independence. It was probably not seriously intended, as the whites were too few to defy Britain, but their mood induced in the slaves the belief that 'they are soon to be free, and are anxiously waiting till King William sends them their free paper'.[1] The conviction then began to grow that the king of England had in fact already granted all slaves in the British empire their freedom, but that the facts were being concealed by the planters: thus British troops would not fight against the slaves if they claimed their legal rights; some slaves even believed that the king would send them arms and ammunition. Leadership arose from the Protestant religious groups among the slaves, and the rebellion was planned at secret prayer meetings, where military commands were allotted, and 'regiments' organized. The revolt erupted, as planned, at Christmas 1831, and swept the western part of Jamaica. It was savagely suppressed, and followed by swift courts-martial and many indiscriminate hangings. Nevertheless the Jamaica rebellion did have an effect in hastening emancipation, for white missionaries were blamed by the planters for the revolt, persecuted and stopped from preaching. Some of them went to England to protest, where they were caught up in the abolition debate, and made a strong impact on parliamentary opinion. Their argument that further delay in emancipation might provoke more rebellions was one which stiffened the British government's resolve to act.[2]

The period from 1834 to 1848 saw legal and civic freedom extended to the slave populations of the British and French Caribbean.[3] From

---

[1] Quoted in Mary Reckord, 'The Jamaica slave rebellion', 111.

[2] See Mary Reckord, 'The Jamaica slave rebellion', which analyses the rebellion with depth and perception, and upon which the above account is based.

[3] The British emancipation act was passed in 1833, and freed the slaves from 1834. Until 1838 the ex-slaves remained obliged to give labour to the planters under a system of apprenticeship. The effective French movement was a decade behind; the French Society for the Abolition of Slavery was formed only in 1834, and although amelioration policies were followed after 1833, abolition was not enacted until 1848.

the point of view of people of African descent, emancipation was both a liberation and a disappointment, for abolition by itself was a doctrinaire measure which gave little thought to the social and economic problems arising from abolition, except to assume that somehow the plantation system and sugar production had to be maintained. The ex-slaves wished above all to be free of the plantation, and working there for wages was not 'liberation' for them. Thus, where there was empty land, the ex-slaves moved on to it as squatters and developed as a peasantry, using the land much as their ancestors had done in Africa. Elsewhere they thirsted for education as a route into work or professions which carried respect and human dignity. Where land was fully divided among the plantations, however, the Negroes could do little but remain a rural, but now wage-earning, proletariat.

Among the masses there was little depth of feeling for Africa, and no disposition to return there. In the British islands, however, significant groups of literate, educated and religious West Indians showed an active interest in West Africa. Their attitudes were quite different from those of the Brazilians. West Indians did not identify themselves with Africa as such, or with particular areas of Africa, but felt more a sense of racial identity with Africans, and when they returned to Africa did so with ideas of 'redeeming' Africa, or 'vindicating the Negro', by showing that he was as capable as the white man of spreading 'Christianity, commerce and civilization'. The British in Sierra Leone played an important part in making return to Africa seem both desirable and feasible to some English-speaking West Indians. Freetown became known as a place where educated blacks might rise to positions of wealth and dignity in trade, in the clergy and even in the colonial service and the professions of medicine and law. After the abolition of slavery, the British tried to provide wage labour for the planters by settling Africans liberated from slave ships captured by the Royal Navy; 36,000 such came over a thirty-year period. One third of these returned to Africa, mainly through Sierra Leone. They thus developed the routes for a return to Africa, and provided a source of information on conditions there. After 1840, individual English-speaking West Indians began to settle all along the West African coast. Several reached positions of responsibility in the British colonial service.[1] West Indians were active as traders or trading agents on the Niger in the years after 1860, and could be found as clergy or missionary helpers in many of the Protestant

[1] See the article by Abiosey Nichol, 'West Indians in Africa', *Sierra Leone Studies*, new series, no. 13, 1960, 14ff.

missions. Hope Waddell's mission in Calabar was largely staffed by West Indian agency in its early years. In addition troops of the British West India Regiment were frequently employed in West African wars before 1900, and many of them became familiar with west coast towns like Freetown, Accra or Lagos.

West Indian immigrants in West Africa did not identify their interests with those of the African states or societies, and by most Africans they were regarded as a species of Englishmen. But they did find much community of interest and aspiration with the educated Africans, the 'creole' community of Freetown, and the African clergy, and they were generally active and sympathetic to the efforts of educated Africans to resist racial discrimination and seek participation in political and religious life. This tradition laid the foundation for the roles which prominent West Indians like E. W. Blyden and later George Padmore were to play in the ideology and politics of African nationalism.

AFRICANS IN THE UNITED STATES OF AMERICA

The history of people of African descent in the area which became the United States is one of unique complexity. In Brazil and Latin America blacks and mestizos were and continue to be absorbed and integrated into society; in the Caribbean emancipation, colonial rule and de-colonization has made 'black power' a reality in societies where whites are an insignificant numerical minority. In the United States social integration and biological absorption of the blacks is still a distant goal which many whites and blacks reject, whilst 'black power' must of necessity be something less than the literal sovereignty possessed by the black people of African or Caribbean states.

When African slaves were introduced into the southern colonies of British North America in the seventeenth century for the purpose of cultivating the staple tobacco crop, it was natural that the same attitudes towards the slave as obtained in the English West Indian colonies should be displayed; the slave was regarded legally and morally as a piece of property analogous to a farm animal. As in the West Indies, neither the British imperial system nor the churches concerned themselves with controlling the master's power over or use of slaves.[1] The savage and brutal exploitation of the African's labour thus became as

---

[1] The Quakers and their Pennsylvania settlement are an exception to this generalization, but as their economy was not based on slavery and located in the north, their attitudes had little or no effect on the southern plantation system until the USA was convulsed by the slavery issue in the nineteenth century.

characteristic of the plantations in British North America as it was in the Caribbean.

The social setting, however, was quite different. The United States was a white man's country, and the slave population remained always a small percentage of the population, even though until 1865 the USA had the largest number of slaves of all the American states.[1] Nevertheless the presence of a large majority of white settlers not directly involved in slave-holding did little to temper the institution of slavery in the south. Instead the United States developed its own peculiar regional situation. The northern colonies had traditionally been settled by white families working the land themselves without much capital. Though slaves were not uncommon in the seventeenth century in the northern colonies, they were not used in large numbers as terrorized plantation labour, and with the growing diversification of the northern economy, and its industrialization in the nineteenth century, slavery died out there by 1830. The United States was a federal country with a weak constitution, and before 1860 it appeared to many, even in the north, that each region must be allowed its own 'peculiar institutions' if the federation were to survive and develop.

While slavery died away in the north, in the south it underwent a phenomenal expansion after the invention of the cotton gin in 1791. Vast areas of land in the deep south were put under cotton cultivation, and each decade saw the system pushed westwards into the south-western region where new slave-holding states were carved out. With cotton cultivation, the classic slave plantation, employing hundreds and sometimes thousands of slaves under the lash, emerged, as ruthless and brutal as the West Indian sugar plantations. The need to force the slaves to work, to preserve the institution, and the fear of slave revolts, became basic considerations of the southern way of life.

As in the British West Indies, manumission of slaves and individual acts by masters to free their slaves were disliked and often prevented by laws passed in the colonial period. In the north, however, especially after independence, this feeling died away, and the slaves were freed to become a depressed element of the working classes in the towns. In the south, with the nineteenth century expansion of slavery, manumission continued to be discouraged by the white society, and by the laws of

[1] In 1790 there were 700,000 slaves and 59,000 free coloureds, forming 19 per cent of the population. Though the slave population rose to 2 million in 1830, 3.2 million in 1850 and 4 million in 1860, it was declining as a percentage of total population, while the whites increased rapidly by free immigration. By 1950 Negroes formed only 10 per cent of the US population.

the states. In 1790 there were only 59,000 free 'Negroes' (many were in fact of mixed blood), of whom 27,000 were in the north. There was thus less than one free coloured to every ten slaves, a proportion as low as that in the West Indies. This small free population rose sharply from 1790 to 1810 as slavery died in the northern states, but thereafter as cotton expanded in the south it ceased to expand significantly as a percentage of the slave, or of the total white, populations. Nevertheless, though an insignificant percentage of the total population, the free coloured population was of great historical importance. In absolute numbers it grew by natural increase and the slow influx of manumissions to over 300,000 persons by 1830, and nearly half a million in 1860, divided about equally between north and south.

In the slave regimes of the south the free coloured population could be allowed no scope for intellectual or political activity; thus the freer spirits fled to the more liberal climate of the free north. Escaping slaves also made for the north, so that it is not remarkable that the free Negroes and mulattoes in the north should have become the most articulate and politically active representatives of Negro thought, and succeeded in forming modern organizations of their own, expressing aspirations independent of the white majority. Had the free Negroes in the north become absorbed completely into white economic and social life, this might not have happened; in particular mulattoes elsewhere, as has been seen, could easily adopt an indifferent attitude to black slaves. The north, however, though it had turned its back on slavery, was still deeply imbued with the concept of Negroes as an 'inferior race' and was especially opposed to inter-marriage between white and black. Discrimination against free coloureds thus cemented their feeling of kinship with the oppressed black slaves.

Though there was thus a certain solidarity among people of complete or partial African descent in the USA, there were important differences of status, linked to skin colour, which created a system of social stratification among Afro-Americans. Miscegenation, generally illegal, between white masters and 'the Sable Venus' had produced the mulatto population. The mulattoes stood a much greater chance of achieving freedom by manumission, or of buying their freedom after working for some time in a semi-autonomous status as domestic servants or town artisans, and they formed the backbone of the free coloured population in both north and south. However, laws against manumission limited this process; in 1860 there were 400,000 mulatto slaves in the south, one in ten of the total slave population. The mulatto slaves, however, were generally employed as house-slaves or craftsmen, their conditions greatly more comfortable than those of the field slaves, and opportunities for religious activity and learning to read and write were much greater. They thus formed an élite group among the slaves, but one which was often divided between loyalty to race and loyalty to the white master-father.

The mulattoes, especially the free group in the north, thus became the intellectual and political élite of the Afro-Americans. Despite discrimination against them, their lives were easier than that of the pure-bred Africans, and the more successful they were the more their inclinations lay towards integration into the country and the society of their white fathers or grandfathers. They therefore felt little drawn to Africa, either emotionally or physically, and it was only under the stress of severe segregation and discrimination of the worst kind with no prospect of speedy or real redress that the coloured élite was willing to contemplate emigration or a return to Africa.

The masses of pure African descent were, before emancipation, entirely subjected to plantation slavery in the south, and felt its cruelty and brutality much more directly than any other group. Their ranks had for centuries been refilled with slaves coming directly from Africa, and it was on the plantations that African customs survived best,[1] and among them the readiness to flee the land of their sorrows and return to 'Heav'n', 'Jerusalem' or 'Mother Africa' was much greater.[2] Men

[1] The extent to which African culture survived in the USA is a controversial one, upon which scholars have disagreed violently. It is interesting that the Africanist, Melville J. Herskovits, a white man, devoted much of his scholarly career to the proposition that African cultural survivals formed an important part of Negro life in some areas of the USA. His arguments were expressed most fully in *The myth of the Negro past* (New York, 1941). The Afro-American scholar E. Franklin Frazier, in works such as *The Negro family* (New York, 1939), *The Negro in the United States* (New York, 1957) and *The Negro Church in America* (New York, 1963) passionately denied the 'Africanness' of the American Negro. The truth would seem to lie at both extremes, and recent scholars such as R. Bastide (*Les Amériques noires, Les civilisations africaines dans le Nouveau Monde* (Paris, 1966), especially 29–50) would seem to suggest a synthesis of these ideas which shows that African culture survived, especially in certain areas such as the islands of the eastern seaboard of the southern states, sometimes to a remarkable degree, but that the passage of time, the cessation of slave imports, and the impact of emancipation and industrialization weakened the survivals steadily, so that by the twentieth century they became insignificant in the total culture of Afro-Americans. In recent times, Afro-Americans have 'revived' their African cultural 'heritage' by artificial means, introducing African dress, names, and even learning Swahili (which is hardly a language of their West African ancestors!); but this movement represents not a survival of African culture, but the impact of modern post-colonial African independence, and the feeling of dignity and self-respect which it can give to people of African descent.

[2] For the way these sentiments are revealed in slave songs, one of the few means of self-expression open to the slaves, see Miles M. Fisher, *Negro slave songs in the United States* (Ithaca, NY, 1953).

of pure African descent were the most responsive whenever the 'back to Africa' cry was uttered, and the prominent exponents of re-emigration to Africa were all full blooded 'Negroes', proud of this fact, and they often cultivated a racialist contempt of mulattoes.

We may now examine the various responses to their depressed condition which the descendants of Africans could and did make in the United States, and it will be noted that each alternative was bound to have a subtly different appeal for each of the social groups just discussed. There were four main ways in which the slave system and racial discrimination against free Negroes could be resisted. These were, first, rebellion; second, individual or group escapes to more liberal areas; third, emigration to a country outside the USA or back to Africa; and, fourth, political activity and organization designed to bring about a change of the system within the USA itself.

Rebellion could have little appeal for the northern freemen, and not much for those in the south who were free. Nevertheless, rebellions could at times attract individual free, or house-slave, leaders. The slave uprising, however, was endemic among the black slaves in the southern plantation system, and fear of it a constant horror among the whites.[1] Such revolts, however, were hopeless. The best that could be achieved was the creation of bandit groups in the unsettled back country similar to the Jamaican Maroons. Heavily outnumbered by the white population and generally ill-led, the slave rebellions created only bloodshed and disaster, followed by cruel repression.

It could be otherwise when slaves seized the opportunity of civil war or internal disorder among the whites, or times of foreign war or threat to the USA during and after independence. Here slaves often behaved with considerable political shrewdness[2] and, during major upheavals such as the war of independence, the war of 1812 against Britain, and the civil war between north and south from 1860 to 1865, large numbers of slaves effectively liberated themselves by military action. In such conditions Afro-Americans in general always seem to have followed the principle that whoever was opposed to the slave owners of the south was to be supported by the Negroes, slave and free, as an agency for liberation, even though there might be little evidence to show that

[1] There is not space here to give illustrations of these revolts; they have been documented in detail, decade by decade, in Herbert Aptheker's *American Negro slave revolts* (New York, 1964).

[2] Aptheker, *American Negro slave revolts*, chapter IV, gives dozens of detailed examples showing how slave unrest and rebellions occurred at times of frontier and Indian wars, rivalry with adjacent Spanish and French territories, civil unrest between white rival groups, and at times of white political agitation.

ideologically the south's enemy was in favour of slave emancipation. Somewhat surprisingly this principle worked in practice.

The phenomenon can be shown rather startlingly in the role played by Afro-Americans in the revolt of the thirteen colonies against the British. The American revolution was undoubtedly a progressive, and for its time even a radical movement, with its strong element of democratic and liberal constitutional and political ideology. There was much in the ringing oratory and slogans of the radicals to appeal to both slave and free Afro-Americans, and the revolutionary truth, proclaimed as 'self-evident' in the Declaration of Independence, that 'all men are created equal' was completely subversive of slavery and racial discrimination. Much of the idealistic thinking and speechifying of the revolutionaries, particularly during the fighting, suggested that slavery and the slave trade would be swept away in time by the revolution; thus Patrick Henry, a Virginia slaveholder himself, declaimed 'I will not, I can not justify it . . . I believe a time will come when an opportunity will be offered to abolish this lamentable evil . . . It is a debt we owe to the purity of our religion.'[1] In 1774 the Continental Congress declared the slave trade one of the wrongs to be righted by defiance of the British, and some northern states during the war against Britain prohibited importation of slaves and abolished slavery within their borders. Even Virginia passed laws during the revolution to encourage manumission of slaves.

It might be expected, therefore, that Afro-Americans in the northern colonies rebelling against Britain should accept the general revolutionary values that Britain was the reactionary enemy, the rebellious colonies the progressive liberalizing force. Many indeed did so. The first 'American' killed by British troops in Boston was in fact a Negro, Crispus Attucks. Negroes fought on the revolutionary side at Lexington, Concord, and Bunker Hill. In all some 5,000 Negroes, almost entirely from the northern colonies, fought against the British. American Negro historians have traditionally stressed this participation, in order to show that their race was part of the 'patriotic' force which founded the nation.

In reality, however, the evidence indicates overwhelmingly that when Afro-Americans chose to take sides in the war, they chose the British side. This was especially the case in the south, where 65,000 slaves, over 10 per cent of the slave population, fled to the British lines during the

---

[1] Quoted in M. Savelle and R. Middlekauf, *A history of colonial America* (rev. ed., New York, 1964), 579.

war. This process was not simply one of blind escape, for in 1775 the British invited Negroes to join their army as free men. From the Afro-American point of view, joining the British was an act of rebellion against their American masters. When the British lost the war of independence, they evacuated not only their white 'Tory' supporters among the colonists, but also the 'black loyalists', some 20,000 in all, some of whom were still the slaves of white loyalist masters, the others the freed men with the British army or other service.[1]

In the evacuation these people were scattered to several quarters. Most of those who were still slaves were taken to the Bahamas or the West Indian islands; in Jamaica it was free black loyalists who introduced the Baptist faith among the slaves there. Some few dozen free blacks emigrated to England, whilst a whole corps of black soldiers who had fought with the Brunswick contingent on the British side settled in Germany. The most important group of the free Negroes, however, settled in Canada, and it was from this group that the first 'back to Africa' movement came to fruition.[2]

The black loyalists who came north to the still-British colony of Nova Scotia were, like their white counterparts, promised land and assistance to establish themselves as settlers. But the whites of substantial means received the priority, the blacks had to wait months or years for their land grants, and when these came, the land allotted was often of poor quality, rocky or heavily forested, and remote from transport. A substantial group of the black settlers began to feel that they were being cheated by local white influence, and resolved to send a representative to Britain to seek redress. They chose Thomas Peters, a runaway slave who had joined the British army in 1776, had been twice wounded, and had risen to sergeant's rank. In London Peters did secure an inquiry into his grievances, but also was taken up by the anti-slavery group which had founded the Sierra Leone Company, whose settlement at Freetown was languishing for lack of able black colonists. The result was a mission by John Clarkson, Thomas Clarkson's brother, to Halifax, Nova Scotia in October 1791, and by January 1792 Clarkson had embarked 1,190 souls for Freetown. The Nova Scotian

[1] Many Negroes who fled from the southern plantations during the war did not necessarily join the British army, but melted into the freer climate of the northern states, to swell the ranks of the free coloured. Numbers were also killed fighting on the British side, or captured and executed as runaway slaves by the Americans. Thus the 20,000 who left with the British is far less than the 65,000 who fled from the south, and included a 'hard core' of Afro-Americans, nearly all runaway slaves from the south, who were determined to run no risk of re-enslavement in the independent USA.

[2] Benjamin Quarles, *The Negro in the American revolution* (Chapel Hill, 1961), is a fascinating study of this theme, on which the above paragraphs are mainly based.

blacks were in fact the group which established Sierra Leone as a viable colony, and laid the foundation of the 'creole' class there.[1]

Thus, seen from an Afro-American viewpoint, the American revolution was an opportunity created by the divisions within white ranks to escape the plantation, join the enemies of the slave-owning aristocracy and, failing to overthrow them, to emigrate elsewhere. In the Nova Scotia example, continued racial discrimination in the economic and social sphere led a substantial group to return to Africa, despite their newly won free legal status.

The American civil war between the northern and southern states from 1860 to 1865 was the most cataclysmic of all the struggles within white society in the USA, and it produced a complete upheaval in the position of the Negro. It did not begin as a crusade by the northerners against southern plantation slavery, however, but was compounded of many factors, political, constitutional, social and economic, too numerous and complex to be analysed here. As in the revolution, however, the Afro-Americans appear instinctively to have thrown their weight from the first on the northern side, the side whose victory must disrupt plantation slavery. The story of Negro participation in the civil war is a large and complex one, but the overall picture is clear: 178,000 negro soldiers fought on the northern side, and the majority of these came from the south and were of slave origin. From the secessionist states 93,000 were recruited, and 40,000 from the border (slave-holding) states which remained within the Union, whilst only 52,000 came from the north. The majority therefore were in fact slave rebels against the Confederate States, fighting not for their own freedom, but for the overthrow of the slave owners.[2] With their blood, and the political support of white abolitionists, they created the situation which made the decision to abolish slavery in the United States an inevitable one, taken before the war was over.

In the above account of Negro participation in America's civil wars it has been argued that, for Afro-Americans, and especially the enlisted slave runaways, participation offered a fruitful opportunity for constructive rebellion. In the civil war there seems to have been equal participation among southern slaves and northern free, between blacks

---

[1] James Walker, *The Black Loyalists: the search for a promised land in Nova Scotia and Sierra Leone, 1783–1870* (London, 1976) is the authoritative study of the Negro in Nova Scotia before 1792, the reasons which led some Negroes to emigrate and others to stay, and the role of the 'Nova Scotians' in the early history of Sierra Leone.

[2] For a full study of the Negro soldiers in the civil war, see Dudley T. Cornish, *The sable arm: Negro troops in the Union army, 1861–1865* (New York, 1956).

and mulattoes.[1] Other less spectacular means of resisting and protesting against the slave system and discrimination must now be examined: escape, emigration, and political activity.

Escape from slavery was something which most slaves contemplated; but to check the impulse, the southern states built up savage codes of punishment for runaways, including lashings, bodily mutilations, and even hanging. In the USA, however, the federal constitution meant that the northern states could develop different laws, or refuse to enforce existing laws to hand back slaves to their owners. Moreover, farther north in Canada,[2] where slavery had died early, slave-holding became positively illegal after 1834, and the British-oriented colonists had no interest in maintaining the integrity of US institutions such as slavery. The 'underground railway', a clandestine system of routes from the south, through the northern states, ending in southern Ontario and freedom under the British flag, was developed. The phenomenon was unique to the United States; no other slave-holding country ever developed organized escape routes for slaves, and the nearest analogy to the institution is the system of escape routes operated by European, anti-Nazi resistance movements in World War II for hiding and moving Jews, prisoners of war and concentration camp escapees. The underground railroad was essentially the work of the white and free coloured abolitionists and their Canadian sympathizers. It had great symbolic importance for the slaves as a ray of hope, for the free coloureds as a commitment to active work against the slave system, and as a story it has the dramatic quality fitting its theme. Historically, however, its role has been exaggerated. Very few slaves, as a proportion of the whole, ever used it. Its main importance was in some of the rare and gifted individuals whom it did liberate, such as Frederick Douglass, the great Negro abolitionist. In Canada it resulted in the creation of a small but significant Negro population in southern Ontario, who developed their own newspapers, schools and churches, as well as attempting several communal experiments designed to prove the Negro's capacity for hard work, achievement and self-government. A

[1] The larger numbers of blacks and southern slaves in the Union army is accountable to the much larger population of Negroes in the south. *Pro rata* a larger proportion of northern Negroes and mulattoes joined, but of course their opportunities of doing so were much greater.

[2] The Dominion of Canada was not, of course, formed until 1867. Canada is used throughout this chapter to indicate the geographical area of modern Canada. Similarly modern Provinces, such as Ontario, are referred to before they came into existence, as these names are more familiar than the historic names such as 'Canada East' or 'Upper Canada', which do not appear on modern maps.

good number of these people returned to the USA during and after the civil war.

Emigration outside the USA, except through escape to Canada, was not an alternative open to the slave population of the south before 1865. It was, however, an option which the free coloured people had to consider. In general it did not fill them with enthusiasm, except in times of acute stress and discrimination, for their aim was full and free integration into American society, and not flight or a return to Africa. Africa seems to have been more tempting to people of pure African descent, those more recently freed from slavery, and those lacking employment or land, as in the Nova Scotian settlement in Freetown.

In 1816 the American Colonization Society (ACS) was founded with the aim of resettling free US Negroes in Africa, and it began by sending colonists to Sierra Leone. Essentially, however, this was a white con- trolled movement, with mixed motives. Its northern membership had much the same aims as the British Sierra Leone Company; and these had the support of some free Negroes who sought to 'vindicate' the capacities of the Negro and 'redeem Africa'. Equally, however, the ACS received support from some southern whites who were anxious to export free coloured and free blacks, because they destroyed the tidiness of the equation between white skin colour and freedom, black and slavery. This was particularly the feeling in the 'border states' between north and south, where slavery as an economic system was in decline and where cotton could not be grown. When after 1821 the ACS began the Liberia settlement, not enough free Negroes volun- teered to go; and several slave owners in the border states set their slaves free as emigrants to Liberia, some feeling this was a humanitarian action, that it disposed of slaves who were becoming unprofitable and still had to be fed and housed, and that it was preferable to releasing slaves as freemen among the American population. Owners in the deep south, where cotton was booming, scorned this attitude and were opposed to the Liberia project.[1]

The free coloured, especially the more politically aware and articulate groups, were bitterly opposed to the Liberia project, which they saw as an attempt to weaken black strivings for freedom within the USA. Behind this opposition was fear that if Liberia were a success, it might lead to compulsory deportation of free Negroes to 'solve the Negro problem'. The Liberia project made the free Negroes draw nearer to

[1] For a more detailed analysis see P. J. Staudenraus, *The African colonization movement, 1816–1865* (New York, 1961).

the slaves as allies, and concentrate more intensely on the abolitionist cause. 'Africa' came to be less appealing to them as a consequence: 'without art, without science, without a proper knowledge of government, to cast into the *savage wilds of Africa* the *free people of color*, seems to us the circuitous route through which they must return to perpetual bondage.'[1] Free Negro opposition to Liberia, continued with fresh vigour after 1830, had significant effects. It persuaded important members of the white abolitionist and anti-slavery movement, such as William Lloyd Garrison, Gerrit Smith and the brothers Arthur and Lewis Tappan, to change their positions and drop their support for African colonization. In doing so they swung the anti-slavery forces increasingly to focus on the domestic scene in the USA, and opened the new and decisive phase of their movement which ended with emancipation in 1863.

Nevertheless Liberia did come to acquire a certain ideological importance, particularly after the appointment of its first black governor in 1841, with the subsequent establishment of the independent Republic of Liberia in 1847 and the removal of ACS control. The fact that opposition from the deep south prevented recognition of Liberia by the USA until 1862, long after Britain and France had established diplomatic relations with Monrovia, tempered the previous abolitionist suspicion of the new country. Edward W. Blyden, the West Indian whose frustrations at being refused university entrance in the USA led him to emigrate to Liberia in 1850, did much to create a favourable image of Liberia by his eloquence with word and pen during subsequent visits to the USA.[2]

Another potential magnet for emigration by free Negroes was Haiti, which hardly appeared to be tainted by slave owners' participation in its founding. In 1824, after the reunification of northern and southern Haiti, President J. P. Boyer invited Afro-Americans from the USA to come and settle, in a bid to try to introduce educated and skilled people to the state. It is significant that the politically active free coloured in the USA responded positively, in marked contrast to the opposition to Liberia which they were mounting at this time. A 'Society for Promot-

---

[1] H. Aptheker, *Documentary history of the Negro people in the United States*, 2 vols. New York, 1964), I, 70.

[2] E.g. Blyden's *Liberia's offering: the call of providence to the descendants of Africa in America*, etc., addresses given to congregations in Negro churches in New York, Philadelphia, Baltimore and smaller cities during the summer of 1862 (New York, 1862). Blyden carried on this advocacy in later years, visiting the USA eleven times between 1872 and 1888. He later became somewhat disillusioned with Liberia. For a detailed analysis of his views, see Hollis R. Lynch, *Edward Wilmot Blyden: Pan-Negro patriot, 1832–1912* (London, 1967), especially 10–31 and 32–53.

ing the Emigration of Free Persons of Color to Haiti' was founded, with Richard Allen, first bishop of the African Methodist Episcopal Church and a leader of the opposition to Liberia, as its president.[1] By 1825 nearly 2,000 people had emigrated to Haiti, many of them members of Allen's church. But disillusion followed, as graft was revealed in the emigration society, and differences of culture, language and religion brought friction with the Haitians. Boyer began to feel that too many 'Americans' would threaten his position, and the emigrants began returning to the USA. A generation later, in 1860 and 1861, the troubled first two years of the civil war, there was a renewed wave of voluntary emigration to Haiti, again involving about 2,000 souls, and failing for the same reasons as in 1825. In the following year President Lincoln, still uncommitted to domestic abolition of slavery, began to contemplate large-scale emigration of Negroes to Haiti or central America as an alternative to emancipation. On 14 August 1862 he met leaders of the Negro community at the White House, only to find that Frederick Douglass, the most prominent of the Negro abolitionists, was as opposed to Haitian emigration as he had earlier been to the Liberia project. It was only when the contractor whom Lincoln had entrusted with the emigration scheme turned out to be a swindler that the idea was dropped, and with it the stage was set for the complex political decisions which led to the emancipation proclamation of 1863.[2]

It will be noted that Sierra Leone, Haiti or Liberia were none of them genuinely 'African states', and only one emigration scheme proposed a 'return' of Afro-Americans to traditional African society ruled by native-born Africans. This was the scheme put forward by Martin J. Delany in 1859 for Afro-American settlement in Yorubaland, which was unique in many ways and foreshadowed later ideas of pan-Africanism.

Delany was a remarkable man. Born a 'full-blooded Negro' in Charleston, his mother taught him to read and write, which forced the family to move north, as literacy was illegal in South Carolina for free Negroes at that time. In the north he worked with Frederick Douglass and in a cover organization for the 'underground railroad' in Pittsburgh. He studied medicine at Harvard, and later was to become the first Negro to be commissioned with field rank as an army doctor by President Lincoln. He appears to have first formulated the idea of a

[1] On Allen, see below, p. 453.
[2] For details of the 1860–2 schemes for Haitian emigration, see James McPherson, *The struggle for equality: abolitionists and the Negro in the civil war and reconstruction* (Princeton, 1964), 77–99 and John H. Franklin, *The emancipation proclamation* (New York, 1963).

return to Africa during the winter of 1831/2, after the expulsion of his family from the south, and also just after the futile slave rebellion of Nat Turner. By 1850 Delany was a convinced emigrationist, and had a certain following, though he disguised his preference for Africa, which he nevertheless referred to always as his 'Fatherland'. At the Negro Convention held in Cincinnati, Ohio, in 1852, Delany and his followers demanded a vote on the principle of emigration, but lost four to one in the plenary session. Delany and his group seceded to form the 'National Emigration Convention of Colored Men', which met in Cleveland, Ohio in 1854, with Delany as president, and approved his report which, however, did not openly advocate Africa as the goal of emigration. This was revealed, however, in a secret session of the convention. It was then decided to explore the chances of emigration to Haiti and West Africa.

Delany and Robert Campbell, an Afro-West Indian, then set out in 1859 for West Africa. They visited Liberia first, where Delany saw in the proposal for a Liberian University 'a grand stride in the march of African regeneration and Negro Nationality',[1] and then proceeded via Lagos up country to the Egba capital at Abeokuta. There they met Samuel Ajayi Crowther, the Yoruba Anglican clergyman who was later to become the bishop of the Niger,[2] who acted as interpreter in securing the signature of the *alake* of Abeokuta to a treaty in December 1859, granting land to Afro-American immigrants who came to settle.

The scheme never came to fruition, as the American civil war intervened to absorb the energies of Delany and free American Negroes. Nevertheless the scheme is of great interest. Robert Campbell did in fact settle in Lagos, where he edited a periodical, The *Anglo-African Magazine*. Delany, however, possessed a greater vision, and his schemes were shot through with political and ideological content of a pan-African kind. He was one of the first to use the slogan 'Africa for the Africans',[3] and unlike most Afro-Americans he believed that traditional Africa had much to teach them. 'I have determined to leave to my children the inheritance of a country, the possession of territorial domain, the blessings of a national education and the indisputable right of self-government' aptly summarized his *credo*.[4]

[1] Quoted in G. Shepperson, 'Notes on Negro American influences on the emergence of African nationalism', *Journal of African History*, 1960, 1, 2, 301.
[2] For the significance of Crowther's career, see J. F. Ajayi, *Christian missions in Nigeria, 1841–1891* (London, 1965), especially 196ff. and 206ff.
[3] Shepperson, 'Negro American influences', 301.
[4] The words are from Delany's *Official report of the Niger exploration party* (New York, 1961), 55.

The civil war, emancipation, and the 'reconstruction' period which followed the North's victory, put an end to emigration schemes and pushed the activities of politically conscious Afro-Americans firmly on to the political plane. Emancipation itself was a political act, and reconstruction at first appeared to offer solid hope that the future of all Americans of African descent would lie not merely in legal freedom, but even in civil, social and economic integration. The hopes of those, mainly free mulattoes, who had from the 1790s firmly insisted on political and intellectual activity for integration within the USA, seemed at last triumphant.

The history of the political activities of the free Negroes in the USA has striking parallels with the history of modern political awareness in West Africa. In both cases the political awakening was the result of work by literate and educated groups, which began in the religious sphere. The early centres for these developments in the USA were the cities of Philadelphia and Boston. In the closing years of the eighteenth century in Philadelphia, a group of free coloureds reacted against discrimination in their Methodist church by withdrawing from it and founding, under the leadership of two local preachers, Richard Allen and Absolom Jones, the 'Free African Society'. Similar organizations, half prayer-meeting, half benevolent society, sprang up shortly afterwards in other eastern cities of the north. In Philadelphia a formal 'Bethel Church' developed in 1794, and in 1816 the same Richard Allen brought several of such Negro churches together as the 'African Methodist Episcopal Church' (AME). Because of personal and often petty rivalries, the local Afro-American churches in the New York area organized themselves separately in 1820 under the leadership of James Varick as the 'African Methodist Episcopal Zion Church' (AMEZ).

The AME and the AMEZ, though in permanent dissension and rivalry, were the first modern and comprehensive organizations of Afro-Americans in the New World to have lasting impact. They were the schools of Afro-Americans; in the literal sense, beginning schools for elementary education, and moving later in the nineteenth century to found the early Negro colleges and universities, but in the political sense becoming the training grounds in which Afro-Americans could manage the financial and administrative affairs of the churches and develop the arts of public speaking and pamphleteering. Their clergy and bishops inevitably soon stepped across the indefinable frontier between religion and politics; they were the first to demand the principle of civic equality regardless of skin colour, and they were the backbone of the agitation against the Liberia project through the 'Negro Convention' movement, the first openly political organization of Afro-Americans. Intellectually they created a whole tradition of Negro thought, denying racialist theories of man's origins and capabilities, and seeking to vindicate the Afro-American and the African through African history.

In Boston Negro stirring began in a more clearly political and social way. In 1787 Prince Hall, a light-skinned mulatto from Barbados, received a charter from the Grand Lodge of Freemasons in London for the establishment in Boston of the 'Free African Lodge', and thus began a long, and still largely mysterious, history of Negro freemasonry.[1] In the same year Prince Hall led a petition of free Afro-Americans to the Massachusetts Legislature asking for equal access for their community to school facilities. The petition was rejected, and twelve years later Hall opened the first school for Negro children in his own house.[2]

The frequent use of the word 'African' in the naming of these early organizations and churches might suggest that the coloured freemen had a deep sense of their African roots. Such an interpretation, however, is probably romantic. Benevolent whites at this time, such as the Quakers and abolitionists, frequently referred to Afro-Americans as 'Africans' as a polite term, feeling that 'Negro' was too closely associated with the slave status. Thus it was natural that free Afro-Americans, experiencing the first rebuffs of white society and seeking to form their own organizations, should have used the word 'African', always qualified by 'free', to stress their status. As has been seen, in later years when emigration to Africa was a proposed 'solution' to 'the Negro problem', these organizations staunchly emphasized their American attachments and their demands to be integrated into the society of the USA.

The early organization of independent churches, societies, and Masonic Lodges, the protests against African colonization in Boston, Philadelphia and New York, helped to galvanize the free coloured of the North, and soon led to more purely secular and political activity. Having rejected 'back to Africa' as a solution to their problems, and still being rejected by the white society, free blacks and mulattoes naturally focused increasingly on the slavery issue, seeing abolition as the major Negro political goal. In 1827 John Russwurm and Samuel

[1] See H. van B. Voorhis, *Negro masonry in the United States* (New York, 1940).
[2] Aptheker, *Documentary History*, 19.

Cornish launched the first Negro newspaper, *Freedom's Journal*, naturally an organ of the freemen, but one which constantly attacked the evils of slavery. In 1829 David Walker, a Boston clothier and agent for the new newspaper, produced a bitter pamphlet, *Walker's Appeal*, to the 'coloured citizens' of the world, denouncing the treatment of non-whites, slave and free, in the USA. It caused consternation in the south and led to repressive legislation there against 'seditious literature'.

In 1830 the Philadelphia Bethel church saw the first of what were to become regular National Negro Conventions in which the secular and political condition of Negroes, free and slave, were the centre of discussion and debate. Regularly the conventions attacked the Liberia concept and African colonization, deplored segregation, and demanded that Negroes organize, establish educational institutions and practise temperance and economy. Around this central core, Negroes throughout the north established state organizations, educational societies, clubs and moral reform groups, which developed new Negro leadership, and threw a large strength behind the white-organized anti-slavery movement, gathering support after the formation of the Anti-Slavery Society in 1833.

In the 1840s and 1850s American Negroes even began bidding for foreign help. Frederick Douglass and several others toured Britain, speaking to packed audiences of their own humiliations in the USA, and experiencing the heady wine of lionization by mid-Victorian liberal society, often to return home to suffer almost immediate further humiliation.[1] These efforts were not without some results, for the Emancipation Proclamation, when it came in 1863, was particularly motivated by the need to appeal to the British and French peoples to make it more difficult for their governments to recognize the Confederacy.[2]

From the 1840s to the civil war, the northern free Negroes were increasingly overshadowed by the growing strength of the white abolitionist movement led by W. L. Garrison. Nevertheless Negroes were an important element in the abolitionist movement; Garrison himself pointed out in 1834 that three-quarters of the subscribers to the

[1] E.g. W. W. Brown in the *Liberator*, 22 July 1853, recounted how back in Philadelphia after a European tour he was refused a place on an omnibus – 'The omnibuses of Paris, Edinburgh, Glasgow and Liverpool, had stopped to take me up, but what mattered that?' Quoted in Leon F. Litwack, *North of slavery: the Negro in the free states, 1790–1860* (Chicago, 1961), 239. Litwack's book is a mine of information on free Negro political activities, and much of the above three paragraphs is culled from this source.

[2] Elbert D. Smith, in *The death of slavery: the United States, 1837–65* (Chicago, 1967), 190, goes so far as to describe the Proclamation simply as 'designed to strengthen the pro-North spirit of the British and French peoples'.

Liberator were non-whites. When the abolitionist movement became seriously divided on issues of strategy and tactics in the 1840s and 1850s, non-whites divided too, and sat on the executive boards of both the rival anti-slavery societies.

The defeat of the confederacy and the end of the civil war in 1865 ushered in the period which was to be the most exciting yet for Africa's descendants in the USA – reconstruction. This was in many ways the most daring period of US history. Not only had the southern slaves been freed, the north now emancipated them fully into citizenship, with the ultimate civil right of the franchise and the right to hold public office. For a time it looked as if the south would experience the first success of the idea of racial partnership and integration, for the Negro proved himself neither vindictive nor incompetent, nor even a real threat, for he did not organize to dominate and control southern politics. The experience, however, turned sour. The northern politicians who had enfranchised the Negro had done so mainly to assure Republican control; when, by the mid-1870s, they no longer needed black votes and could have their economic interests protected by resurgent southern whites, the Negro was abandoned. The north, imbued with *laissez faire* economic principles, made no efforts to plan an economic place for the emancipated slaves, and semi-feudal 'share-cropping', with Negroes tied to the landowners, developed in the rural south. The southern whites were gradually allowed to resume political control and 'solve' southern problems, first by intimidating the Negro away from the polls and political office by terrorist means such as the Klu Klux Klan, later by the sanctions of the states' post-reconstruction legislation.[1] Gradually it became clear that reconstruction had been a false

[1] The traditional picture of the reconstruction, which used to be standard in American historiography, was that reconstruction was a disastrous failure explainable by the (perhaps understandable) incompetence of the Negro, the influx of rapaciously corrupt 'carpet-baggers' from the north, and the influence of the 'scalawags' (i.e. southern whites who co-operated with the northerners), who between them ushered in a reign of corruption, job-bery, incompetence and economic ruin, terminated in the end only by the resurgence of more 'responsible' southern control. Modern historical research by white and non-white scholars has, in the opinion of these authors, quite demolished this interpretation. They have shown that Negroes did not in fact dominate the state governments or political parties, or the courts, and that many of them were well educated and highly competent, some were graduates of northern white or European universities – one had even gone through Eton with the scions of the English aristocracy (J. J. Wright, appointed judge of South Carolina's Supreme Court during reconstruction). The 'carpetbaggers', though no doubt including many unscrupulous men, were not all such; many were dedicated and idealist ex-Union army officers, filled with admiration for the bravery of their former Negro comrades, who wished to build up a new society in the south. The 'scalawags' were probably the worst maligned, for many of them were ex-slave-owners agonizingly attempting to come to terms with the revolution imposed on their way of life. For these revisionist views of reconstruc-

dawn, and that those of African descent would not enter the 'melting pot' experienced by the children of German, Italian, Polish, Russian or Irish immigrants, but would remain for many more decades a sub-community of the American social fabric.

tion, see John Hope Franklin, *Reconstruction after the civil war* (Chicago, 1961); Kenneth M. Stampp, *The era of reconstruction* (New York, 1965); C. Vann Woodward, *The strange career of Jim Crow* (2nd rev. ed., New York, 1966).

CHAPTER 13

CHANGING EUROPEAN ATTITUDES
TO AFRICA

THE EUROPEAN PRESENCE IN AFRICA

The history of every continent is the product of a complex amalgam of forces, some of internal, others of external origin. In Africa, where the technique of literacy was introduced to most indigenous communities only in comparatively recent times, the exploits of outsiders are far more richly documented than those of local people. Thus there exists a bias tending to overstress the importance of external influences inherent in most of the written material available to the student of the African past, a bias that needs constantly to be corrected by an imaginative awareness of the achievements of African societies in developing their own varied and elaborate cultures. Obviously modern Africa has been profoundly affected by the techniques, the institutions and the ideas introduced by men and women of European origin; but in historical terms the impact of Europe must be regarded as a relatively recent development, to be measured in most parts of the continent in terms not of centuries, but merely of decades. When this comparatively brief involvement with Europe is set against the long span of intercourse with Asia, it becomes clear that Africa, at least until the end of the eighteenth century, was far more deeply affected by the greater of her two continental neighbours.

For it was from Asia that there had come, probably as early as the sixth millennium BC, the revolutionary techniques of cereal cultivation and of pastoralism. Later innovations of Asian origin, each capable of exercising a profound influence on the lives of those who adopted them, included the craft of iron-working, the camel, the banana, the largest of the yams and a variety of other food-crops. From Asia, too, Africa had received the complex culture of Islam, a culture so powerfully attractive that it could transform the thoughts and actions of its converts. Carried first by victorious Arab armies across the breadth of North Africa, borne later by enterprising Muslim merchants and teachers along the trade routes of the Sahara, the Red Sea and the Indian Ocean, Islam had become by the end of the eighteenth century the dominant culture, not only of Egypt and the Maghrib, but also of the Sudanic belt, the Horn of Africa and of the East African coast. Here in an expanse of territory

458

covering much of the northern part of the continent, an Asian Muslim traveller of the 1790s would have found many communities of his co-religionists, men whose view of the world was not so greatly different from his own.

In contrast to the immense influence of Asia, the total European impact on Africa up to the end of the eighteenth century appears as relatively slight and superficial. The ruins of splendid cities such as Cyrene, Leptis Magna or Timgad stood as memorials to an age when men of Greek and Roman stock had ruled in North Africa, but the Arab invasions of the seventh century had shattered the superstructure of cultural unity that spanned the Mediterranean in the days of Macedonian, Roman or Byzantine greatness, and the living cultures of the peoples of the region contained few traits inherited directly from this distant age of European hegemony. In 1790 the European presence in the Muslim states of North Africa was limited to a handful of consuls, a few small communities of merchants and a number of Christian slaves and adventurers in Muslim service.

With western Africa, European contacts dated back no further than the fifteenth century. Here, along 5,000 kilometres of littoral stretching from Senegal to Angola, the trading-posts established by the Portuguese, the Dutch, the Danes, the French and the English had brought to many African communities their first direct contact with a wider world, and introduced them to a considerable range of material innovations, including new food-crops – notably maize and cassava (manioc) – of American origin, cotton-goods from the Indies and flintlock muskets and other articles of European manufacture. But the trade developed along the coasts of western Africa had from an early date come to be largely dependent on the export of slaves; thus it affected African communities in contradictory ways. To some, notably to those polities of seventeenth-century foundation, Asante, Dahomey and the trading states of the Niger delta, it brought a considerable increase in power and wealth; to others, including the older kingdoms of Kongo and Ndongo and many smaller polities, the slave trade was the direct cause of desolation and decline. Disastrous, too, for many of the trading communities of the East African coast had been the century and a half of Portuguese hegemony, a period that saw the destruction of many of the commercial ties that had previously bound the peripheral lands of the Indian Ocean so fruitfully together. No less destructive for many of the 'Bushmen' and 'Hottentot' communities occupying the southern extremity of the continent had been the advance, begun in the latter half of the seventeenth century, of the Dutch colonists from their base at Cape Town. Some of the peoples of Madagascar had also suffered at European hands: the abortive French attempt, drawn out over several decades in the mid-seventeenth century, to establish a colony on the east coast of the great island had been accompanied by much disruption and loss of life.

Certainly by 1790 Europe had made some impact on Africa. Yet set against the vast bulk of the entire continent, the areas affected by the direct action of Europeans were relatively small. And though European activities in Africa had been, through the development of the slave trade, of major importance in the establishment of lucrative planta-tion colonies in the New World, the total European stake in the continent was still relatively modest. Indeed in 1790 there cannot have been more than 25,000 Europeans resident in the entire conti-nent.[1] By way of comparison one may note that the Portuguese island of Madeira, uninhabited when first discovered by medieval navigators, had acquired by 1768 a European population numbering no less than 64,000.

Between 1790 and 1875 the steady expansion of European activities, and the growing assurance of European power, transformed the nature of the European presence in Africa. In medieval times the technologies and the political structures to be found in parts of Africa were not so vastly different from those existing in many parts of Europe. Now, as the gap between the two continents widened, Europeans began to adopt new attitudes towards peoples of alien culture whose way of life seemed increasingly different from their own. To be properly understood, these new intellectual currents in the European consciousness, these shifts of thought and emotion, need to be viewed against a backcloth that depicts the outline of European activities in Africa during these years and at the same time conveys an impression of the mighty changes taking place within Europe itself.

Briefly, it may be said that in 1790 the supremacy of Europe over the other continents of the Old World was far from assured; by 1875 Europeans had some justification for assuming themselves to be – or at least to be in the process of becoming – 'the lords of human kind'. The extraordinary advance in European technology, making possible sustained economic growth at a rate unprecedented in past human

---

[1] In 1790 by far the greatest concentration of European residents in Africa was to be found in the Dutch Colony of the Cape, whose white population was put at 21,746 in 1798. In 1787 there were only 52 Frenchmen resident in Egypt; at this time France carried on a more substantial trade with Egypt than any other European power.

experience, provided the base for this truly revolutionary development. In 1790 European armies were still dependent on the muzzle-loading flintlock musket; by 1875 they were being equipped with the breech-loading rifle and the machine-gun. In 1790 the despatch rider, the mail coach, the sailing ship and the canal barge provided the most efficient means of communication or transport; by 1875 the major powers of Europe had at their disposal the railway train, the iron-clad steamship and the telegraph. In 1790 large-scale factory industry was in its infancy; in 1875 a growing proportion of the labour force of Britain, France and Germany was finding employment in an ever-widening range of manufacturing industries.

These advances in technology formed part of a complex of changes which in their totality were to have a profound effect on Europe's approach to Africa. The population of Europe increased more rapidly than it had ever done before: in Britain the population was nearly trebled between 1800 and 1880, and substantial advances were recorded for most other European countries.[1] This rise in population took place at a time when European migration to other continents – including a small but steady movement across the Mediterranean to Algeria, Tunis and Egypt – was running at an unprecedented level. This growth in population was accompanied, though in varying degrees in different parts of Europe, by increasing wealth. Larger populations with more money to spend meant a steady growth in demand for the products of other continents, products that included the cotton of Egypt, the palm oil of West Africa, the ivory of tropical Africa and the wool of South Africa. Increasing wealth had other consequences. It produced a new class of investors, some of whom were prepared to lend money to foreign governments. Thus between 1863 and 1876 the Khedive Ismā'īl of Egypt was able to raise foreign loans to the value of £90 million. Newly established missionary and scientific societies experienced a notable rise in the volume of donations and subscriptions. The annual revenue of the Anglican Church Missionary Society, for example, rose from £30,000 in 1830 to £150,000 in 1875, while the Royal Geographical Society, a major patron of British exploration in Africa, received an average income of close on £8,000 in the years 1871–5 compared with an average of less than £1,000 in the years 1848–53. Most important consequence of all, the metropolitan govern-

---

[1] Great Britain: 10·5 m. in 1800; 26·1 m. in 1870. France: 28·3 m. in 1800; 37·7 m. in 1870. Germany: 24·8 m. in 1816; 41·1 m. in 1870. Italy: 17·2 m. in 1800; 26·8 m. in 1880. Spain: 10·5 m. in 1800; 16·2 m. in 1870. (Source: Colin Clark, *Population growth and land use* (London, 1967), 106–7, table III. 14.)

ments of Britain and France now found themselves with sufficient financial resources at their disposal to enable them to engage in enterprises – for the British the diplomatic and naval campaign against the slave trade, intermittent frontier wars in South Africa and costly expeditions in Ethiopia (1868) and against Asante (1874); for the French a long-drawn-out struggle in Algeria and a vigorous military policy in Senegal – all involving expenditure of a costliness that would have seemed quite prohibitive two or three generations earlier.

Increasing wealth combined with a more efficient technology to make possible a wider diffusion of knowledge. The nineteenth century in Europe was marked by a massive proliferation of the printed word. From the penny tracts of missionary societies, from paragraphs of news in daily papers, from lengthy articles in encyclopaedias and learned journals, from the spate of books produced by travellers and explorers, Europeans could pick up fragments of information about Africa of a kind that would never have come their way a century earlier. And these fragments could often now be supplemented by the accounts of friends and relatives with first-hand experience of African countries – soldiers returning to French villages with stories of campaigning in Algeria, well-to-do young men amusing London drawing-rooms with tales of travel in Egypt, missionaries home on leave sermonizing about their work among the heathen, traders or naval officers reminiscing about days in Lagos or Zanzibar. Thus, though there must still have been many areas of total ignorance, knowledge of a kind about Africa percolated more widely than ever before.

Finally it should be remembered that Europeans were experiencing during these years major changes in the political pattern of their own continent. The superstructure of Ottoman rule was visibly crumbling, and an Asian people, once capable of terrorizing central Europe with their armies and scourging the western Mediterranean with their fleets, found themselves the subject of contemptuous reference and patronizing discussion. Meanwhile from the multitude of petty polities among which so many of the German- and Italian-speaking peoples had been for so long divided, there emerged by the 1870s two powerful new states. Gradually throughout much of Europe the old peasant isolation was breaking down, as men began moving in increasing numbers to the towns or found themselves subjected to periods of compulsory military service. At the same time, certain sections of the public in some European countries were coming to display a more vociferous pride in their respective nationhoods. These developments, though internal to

Europe, are not irrelevant to Africa. The ideas and emotions Europeans derived from contemplating their own societies – their pride, their confidence, their arrogance – served to tint the filters, often the power-fully distorting filters, through which they observed other parts of the world. At all times the attitudes of Europeans towards Africa can be fully understood only if they are seen as part of a wider intellectual system, a total world view.

Some of the events in which Europeans were involved in Africa between 1790 and 1875 were of a quality so dramatic that they were well calculated to impress themselves on the consciousness of con-temporaries. Bonaparte's expedition to Egypt in 1798, the French capture of Algiers in 1830, followed by the slow conquest of the remainder of the country, the Great Trek of the South African Boers, the British navy's fight against the slave trade, the exploits of European explorers, the spectacular British expeditions in Ethiopia and against Asante – events such as these pandered strongly to national or racial pride, and so were ideally suited to contribute to that selective amalgam of anecdote and legend that constituted most contemporaries' notion of history. A more prosaic approach is needed if one is to discern the broad lines along which the European presence in Africa developed during this period. One must point first to the great increase in the number of Europeans with a stake in Africa, then to the steady expan-sion in the frontiers of European activity, and finally to the widening range of European interests in the continent.

The most substantial increases in the European population of Africa took place in the northern and southern extremities of the continent. In Morocco the number of European residents rose from less than 200 in 1820 to 2,820 in 1877, in Tunis from 8,000 in 1834 to 15,000 in 1870, in Egypt from 14,500 in 1834 to 71,000 in 1871. Most spectacular of all these North African developments was the transformation of Algeria. In the first decade of the nineteenth century Christian slaves, most of them taken by Algerian corsairs in attacks on European shipping and numbering about 1,000, constituted by far the largest element in the European population of the country. By 1875, after two generations of French rule, Algeria had a European population of 279,000 to which should be added an army of occupation of 60,000 men. Although by 1875 people from many different parts of Europe were to be found in the countries of North Africa, the majority of immigrants came from the Mediterranean lands. Thus Greeks formed the largest element in the European population of Egypt, Italians and Maltese of Tunis, Spaniards of Morocco and western Algeria, while many of the French settlers were drawn from Corsica and Provence.

In South Africa the European population of the Dutch colony at the Cape was put at just under 22,000 in 1798. By 1875 there were 300,000 Europeans in South Africa: 237,000 in the Cape Colony, 18,000 in Natal, 30,000 in the Transvaal and 15,000 in the Orange Free State. Two substantial movements by settlers from England, to the eastern Cape in 1820 and to Natal in the 1850s, helped the rapidly multiplying Dutch or Boer population to produce in seventy years this fourteen-fold increase in the white population of South Africa. The only other areas of permanent white settlement in Africa were to be found in the Portuguese territories of Angola and Mozambique. In 1845 Angola had less than 2,000 whites, Mozambique probably even less, and little increase can have taken place in the course of the next thirty years.

In tropical Africa European communities were still very modest. The European population of St Louis, capital of Senegal and largest European settlement in West Africa, was put at 177 in the early 1850s, while Sierra Leone, the largest British colony in tropical Africa, contained no more than 125 whites in 1870. Elsewhere on the west coast and in the East African dominions of the sultan of Zanzibar, European communities were even more diminutive. Of the islands that come within the ambit of Africa, the Mascarenes contained the most substantial European populations. By 1875 there were more than 50,000 whites in French Réunion and more than 10,000 in British Mauritius.[1] All in all, the European population of Africa and its adjoining islands had risen from about 32,000 in 1790 to close on three-quarters of a million by 1875.

A development even more striking to contemporaries than this growth in European populations in Africa was the phenomenal expansion of the frontiers of European activity. Steadily the pioneers – explorers, missionaries, bush-traders, elephant hunters, soldiers and settlers – moved into the interior. In 1875 there were still many blanks on European maps, still a large number of African communities entirely unaffected by the European presence. But the area of European ignorance – and with it the area of African freedom from European intervention – was steadily shrinking year by year. In 1790 it would have been scarcely credible to imagine European missionaries preaching the gospel on the upper Nile or in the interior of Madagascar, European

---

[1] The European population of Mauritius was put at 8,135 in 1830, the last occasion on which Europeans were enumerated separately.

traders carrying on a flourishing business on the lower Niger, European settlers comfortably established far beyond the Orange river, European soldiers victoriously campaigning on the borders of the Sahara, amid the forests of Asante or among the mountains of Ethiopia – yet by 1875 all these things had come to pass.

In 1790 most Europeans resident in Africa – with the important exception of the Dutch frontiersmen, the *trekboers*, of the Cape – were primarily interested in trade. In 1875 the search for commercial opportunity still remained a major motive in attracting individual Europeans to Africa, whether they were Spanish or Sicilian smugglers in the ports of North Africa, 'palm oil ruffians' in the trading states of the Oil rivers or diamond dealers in the new boom town of Kimberley. But by 1875 most European communities in Africa had become very much more diverse in their range of occupations. The European traveller inspired by scientific curiosity was a rarity in eighteenth-century Africa; by the second half of the nineteenth century, the professional explorer was established as one of the categories of Europeans to be found in Africa. In 1790 Africa contained a handful of European missionaries, but their influence was almost negligible; by 1875 European priests and lay-workers were established in almost every part of Africa with which Europeans maintained regular intercourse, and some mission stations had developed into major centres of political and even more markedly of cultural influence. In the eighteenth century Europe had maintained diplomatic relations only with the states of North Africa; by 1875 not only had the system of consular representation in North Africa been enlarged, but some European countries had found it necessary to establish new consular posts in East and West Africa, the Sudan and Ethiopia.

Naturally it was in the major areas of European settlement that the greatest diversification of population took place. In contrast to the meagrely staffed trading-posts of the eighteenth-century European colonies, nineteenth-century Africa contained a number of elaborate official establishments. Particularly noticeable was the presence of the military. Between the disastrous defeats suffered by Portuguese expeditions on the Zambezi and in Morocco in the 1570s, and the French invasion of Egypt in 1798, Europeans had been involved in no major military campaigns in Africa. But the nineteenth century brought the French army experience of the rigours of campaigning and the tedium of garrison duty in Egypt, Algeria and Senegal, while between 1800 and 1875 British regiments acquired battle-honours in Egypt, South Africa,

West Africa and Ethiopia. In South Africa and in Algeria the officials and the soldiers were outnumbered by two other groups, the settlers, whose acquisition of landed property gave them the most tangible of stakes in Africa, and the men of varied occupations who thronged the major colonial towns. This latter group contained a leavening of professional men – doctors and teachers, lawyers and journalists, bankers and shipping agents – together with a large number of the more humbly employed – clerks, shop-keepers, café proprietors, builders and market-gardeners. A European urban population also grew up in certain North African cities, Tangier, Tunis, Cairo and Alexandria, where the special privileges associated with the system of 'Capitulations' allowed the local European communities a good deal of autonomy.

One other feature of the expanding and diversifying European population of Africa needs to be noted – the increasing proportion of women. Inevitably in the pioneering stage of European communities in Africa, men predominated. The European population of Algiers, for example, contained, in 1839, 7,000 men and only 2,800 women. (The French authorities attempted to achieve a better balance by encouraging prostitutes to transfer their business from metropolitan cities to the colonial capital.[1]) But the number of European women prepared to live in Africa increased rapidly. Thus by 1870 the European community of Natal, though still possessing something of a pioneering flavour, had achieved an almost equal balance of the sexes, and even in the 'White Man's Grave' of Sierra Leone there were 26 European women to 99 men.[2]

This radical transformation of the European presence in Africa was accompanied by the founding in Europe of new institutions with an orientation towards Africa. Both the British and the French governments considered it expedient to establish special departments or sub-departments of state to deal with colonial affairs. The civil servants who staffed these new offices rarely possessed first-hand experience of Africa, but they were well placed to acquire a mass of information relating to the intricate problems of colonial government and so to exercise a considerable influence on the shaping of policy. A notable proliferation in the number of Christian missionary societies, both of Protestant and of Catholic foundation, took place in the decades after 1790; most of these new societies were eager to establish contact with Africa. The

[1] Charles-André Julien, *Histoire de l'Algérie contemporaine: la conquête et les débuts de la colonisation (1827–1871)* (Paris, 1964), 158.
[2] *Statistical tables relating to the colonial and other possessions of the United Kingdom: Part XIV. 1868–1869–1870* (London, 1875), 330, 377.

intellectual life of nineteenth-century Europe was characterized by the foundation of learned societies dedicated to the promotion of research in particular disciplines; those concerned with geography, ethnography or anthropology took a special interest in Africa. Finally there appeared in the last years of this period a number of bodies, of which the London-based Royal Colonial Institute may serve as an example, founded with avowedly expansionist aims.

Any study of European attitudes to Africa must, then, be set against a highly complex pattern of events, the product of a steady increase in the force of the European presence and of a constant expansion in the forms of European involvement. Valid generalizations about European attitudes are extremely hard to make, when Europeans of so many nationalities – Greeks, Italians, Spaniards, Portuguese, Frenchmen, Englishmen, Germans and Afrikaners of Dutch descent, to mention only the most prominent – following so wide a range of professions, were involved in so many different African environments. Can one find anything in common – beyond a certain sense of cultural superiority over the 'natives' – in the attitudes of a Greek trader in Egypt, a French army officer in Algeria, an English missionary in Sierra Leone and a Boer farmer in the Transvaal? Individuals such as these fall into the category of 'men on the spot', Europeans whose reactions were shaped at least in part by the vagaries of first-hand experience. But any study of European attitudes must also bear in mind two other groups: that small, select body of opinion-makers – the politicians, the senior civil servants, the businessmen, the journalists, the academics, the missionary statesmen – who had acquired an interest in Africa, though often without ever having had the opportunity to set foot on African soil, and who made frequent reference to the continent in their speeches and their writings; and beyond them the wide mass of the general public, in whose minds Africa tended to be reduced to a few crude disparate but powerful images.

Clearly this is a subject where there is much scope for further research through the multiplication of detailed studies – a number of which have indeed already appeared – devoted to the response of particular European groups to particular African environments over fairly limited periods of time. In the present chapter one can do no more than provide an introductory analysis of the most significant currents in the evolution of European attitudes in a period of rapid change.

CURIOSITY, SCHOLARSHIP AND ROMANCE

In 1788 there was published in London a brochure setting out the 'Plan' of the recently founded 'Association for Promoting the Discovery of the Interior Parts of Africa'. The anonymous author of this remarkable document – it was in fact written by Henry Beaufoy, first secretary of the new Association – began by pointing out that 'at least a third of the habitable surface of the globe', including 'almost the whole of Africa', was at the present time 'unvisited and unknown'. Such ignorance, he continued, 'must be considered as a degree of reproach upon the present age', and

sensible of this stigma, and desirous of rescuing the age from a charge of ignorance, which, in other respects, belongs so little to its character, a few individuals, strongly impressed with a conviction of the practicality and utility of thus enlarging the fund of human knowledge, have formed the plan of an Association for promoting the discovery of the interior parts of Africa.[1]

'A conviction of the practicality and utility of . . . enlarging the fund of human knowledge' – here, expressed in the rotund jargon of its age, was an attitude of mind that can be traced along a constantly ramifying stream of scholarly activity from the late eighteenth century to the present day.

The most spectacular results achieved by this vigorous mood of precise inquiry lay in the field of geographical research. One has only to compare the maps of Africa available in the 1870s with those produced in the 1780s to become aware of the advance that had taken place. By 1875 the two most engrossing mysteries of African geography – the courses of the Niger and of the Nile – had been solved, and while there were still many blanks on the map, notably in the area of the Congo basin, a vast amount of detailed information had been acquired relating to every region of the continent.

For their own countrymen, the exploits of the explorers who brought back this information constituted one of the epics of the age, a dramatic manifestation of European courage, initiative and resource. Viewed from an African angle, many of the journeys of exploration appear more prosaic – the crossing of the Sahara, for example, was a feat accomplished by hundreds of African travellers every year. But both sides may find common ground today in admiring the passionate energy displayed by the greatest of the European travellers in collecting

[1] Robin Hallet, ed., *Records of the African Association 1788–1831* (London, 1964), 42, 45.

material. Thus James Bruce brought back from Ethiopia a collection that included historical manuscripts, vocabularies, drawings of plants and animals, together with much ethnographical, geographical and meteorological information, most of which was presented to the world in the massive volumes of his *Travels to discover the source of the Nile* (1790). Mungo Park showed himself, in his account of the Mandingo of the western Sudan, to be possessed of that spirit of enlightened curiosity, at once sympathetic and objective, that inspires the work of the best of modern social anthropologists. Heinrich Barth, in the course of his five years of residence and travel in the countries between Bornu and Timbuktu, laid the foundations for scholarly research by Europeans into the history of the Sudanic belt of West Africa. Richard Burton, possibly the most widely travelled man of his generation, proved himself both an outstanding linguist and an extremely acute, if patronizing, observer of alien cultures. David Livingstone revealed in his writings a remarkably wide-ranging intellect, sane and generous in its humanity, lofty in its speculations and vigorous in its concern for scientific inquiry. Men such as these were, of course, outstanding figures; but one might mention many other Europeans – missionaries, administrators, diplomatic agents, as well as professional explorers – who made substantial contributions to Europe's expanding knowledge of Africa.

Some travellers went to Africa on their own initiative, some Europeans resident in Africa made scholarly research the occupation of their leisure hours. But much of the best work was sponsored either by metropolitan or colonial governments, or by learned societies in Europe. Thus between 1805 and 1830 the British government financed a series of expeditions which did much, through the enterprise of Park, Denham and Clapperton, the Lander brothers and others, to reveal the interior of West Africa. Less spectacular, but in its contribution to the growth of knowledge no less important, was the patronage accorded by French governments to scholars first in Egypt, then in Algeria. The French army that invaded Egypt in 1798 was accompanied by a specially formed Commission of the Arts and Sciences. Between them the 167 *savants* of the Commission covered every field of contemporary knowledge. The product of their labour – the massively documented and superbly illustrated volumes of the *Description de l'Égypte* – remain to this day one of the outstanding monuments of European scholarship in an African setting. Forty years later, when the French were grappling with the problem of Algeria, the government of Louis-Philippe established a commission to undertake the 'scientific exploration' of the country.

The thirty-nine volumes published between 1844 and 1867 ranged from works on zoology, botany and geology to detailed studies of Kabylia and of the trade routes of southern Algeria.

Some of the material brought back by contemporary Africanists – particularly that relating to plants and animals – could be incorporated in already established fields of study. More exact information about the varied peoples and cultures of Africa made possible the emergence of the new disciplines of anthropology and ethnography. There were notable advances in other fields of scholarship of relevance to Africa. In 1822 the young French scholar, J. F. Champollion, succeeded in cracking the code of the hieroglyphs, an achievement that at last made possible the reconstruction of the past of ancient Egypt, laid the foundations for the rigorous new discipline of Egyptology, and greatly stimulated the detailed study of the magnificent archaeological sites of the Nile valley. Islamic studies provided another subject to which valuable contributions were made by scholars working in an African setting. Particularly valuable was the work of French Arabists in publishing and translating some of the great works of medieval Islam, including the history of Ibn Khaldūn and the travels of Ibn Baṭṭūṭa. Some progress was also made in the formidable task of studying and classifying the languages of sub-Saharan Africa. The work of all these scholars laid the foundations for a sane appreciation of African achievement. As S. W. Koelle pointed out in his *African native literature* (1854), the collection made by him of 'proverbs, tales, fables and historical fragments' in the Kanuri language

introduces the reader, to some extent, into the inward world of Negro mind and Negro thoughts, and this is a question of paramount importance, so long as there are any who either flatly negative the question, or, at least, consider it still open, 'whether the Negroes are a genuine portion of mankind or not'.[1]

There must always be something of a gap between the ideas of the European student of Africa, especially when his mind has been fertilized by a wide range of first-hand impressions, and the conceptions of a remote continent current among other Europeans, however highly educated the latter may feel themselves to be. Since classical times a few clichés had dominated conventional thought about Africa. Old tags such as *ex Africa semper aliquid novi* or Horace's line, *leonum arida nutrix*, provided sophisticated Europeans with a substitute for knowledge. Africa was a 'burning and savage territory', its inhabitants 'the most

[1] S. W. Koelle, *African native literature* (London, 1854), vi.

ignorant and unpolished people in the world'. The growth of detailed knowledge might serve to purge Africa of those monsters with which, from classical times, the European imagination had delighted to populate the continent; it could not strip Africa of its strangeness, its 'mystery'.

Indeed this sense of mystery was heightened by one of the currents of early nineteenth-century European sensibility. The Romantic vision exaggerated the strangeness of the alien, even as the romantic temperament sought to rise above the flatness of normality, by stimulating and intensifying emotions. Thus John Leyden, a remarkable young Scotsman and author of one of the first studies of African exploration, found, in the words of his friend, Walter Scott, much in the history of Africa 'to enchant an imagination that loved to dwell upon the grand, the marvellous, the romantic and even the horrible'.[1] In a typical passage of his journal, John Lander, a man with considerable literary ambitions, described one of the wooded valleys of western Yorubaland through which he and his brother passed as being 'more wild, romantic and picturesque than can be conceived'.[2] A generation later another young English traveller, Winwood Reade, called Africa 'that land of adventure and romance', and in so doing spoke for many of his contemporaries.

This romantic view merged with the cult of the exotic, a cult particularly vigorously practised when Europeans made their first contact with the Muslim world, 'the realm of minaret and muezzin, bashaw and bulbul, camel and veil and palm', as a modern writer with a nice choice of the conventional images has described it.[3] Literary-minded Europeans of the early nineteenth century relished the sensation of viewing the outward spectacle of the alien societies of Egypt and the Maghrib through the beguiling filters provided by the *Arabian nights* or the Old Testament. 'Most of the people look like a living Bible', exclaimed Heinrich Röntgen, a young German traveller, on arriving in Morocco in 1809.[4] And Théophile Gautier, the eminent French writer, described himself walking through the labyrinth of streets of old Algiers 'as in a dream, not knowing if we were awake or asleep', so 'mysterious', so 'fantastic' seemed the surroundings.[5] This search for a greater intensity of experience could transform even the wretchedness

[1] John Leyden, *Poems and ballads*, with a memoir by Walter Scott (Kelso, 1858), 14.

[2] Richard and John Lander, *The Niger journal*, ed. Robin Hallett (London, 1965), 58.

[3] V. G. Kiernan, *The lords of human kind: European attitudes towards the outside world in the imperial age* (London, 1969), 131.

[4] Quoted by Robin Hallett, *The penetration of Africa: European enterprise and exploration particularly in northern and western Africa up to 1830*, vol. 1, to 1815 (London, 1965), 382.

[5] Théophile Gautier, *Loin de Paris* (Paris, 1865), 36.

of a defeated people. Thus the painter, Eugène Fromentin, on his first visit to Algeria in 1846, wrote of 'the true Arabs in rags and full of vermin, with their wretched scabby donkeys and their mangy camels', but saw them set against 'splendid horizons' and noted the 'grandeur of their gesture', the 'beauty in the folds of all these rags'.[1] An astringent corrective to Fromentin's elegant, lacquered vision was provided by Alphonse Daudet in his short novel, *Tartarin de Tarascon*, in which his absurd hero sets out on a lion-hunt in Algeria, a country where, as Daudet saw it in the 1860s, 'the old Oriental perfumes are replaced by a strong blend of absinthe and the barracks'.[2]

It is always hard to appreciate the basic normality of peoples and places, which by virtue solely of their difference seem extraordinary or strange. Though one can point to a wide range of similarities, the landscapes, the peoples, the fauna and the flora of Africa are in some respects strikingly different from those of Europe, and it was natural for the writers of brief literary accounts to stress these differences. Moreover the contrasts between an apparently 'stagnant' Africa and a rapidly 'progressing' Europe were becoming more evident with every year that passed. In 1875 the time was not far off when Europeans could look to Africa with its 'wide open spaces' and its 'simple', 'primitive' peoples for something their own continent appeared to have lost. Certainly there was a strain of generosity in the romantic approach to Africa, but it was a far more vulnerable attitude than the cool but not unsympathetic appraisal of African reality made by the scholarly observer, and it offered no convincing intellectual opposition to those crude notions based on seemingly elaborate theories of race and culture that came to be accepted by an increasing number of Europeans in the course of the nineteenth century.

THEORIES OF RACE AND CULTURE: 'THE NEGRO'S PLACE IN NATURE'

Medieval Europeans had lived in a narrow world, their geographical horizons largely bounded by the crescent of powerful Muslim states that stretched from Persia to Morocco. A break-through came with the voyages of discovery of the fifteenth century. From the sixteenth century on, the printed narratives of travellers, steadily mounting in

---

[1] Eugène Fromentin, *Une année dans le Sahel*, with an introduction by L. Morel (Oxford, 1911), xxviii–xxix.

[2] Alphonse Daudet, *The prodigious adventures of Tartarin de Tarascon*, English translation (London, 1896), 210.

volume, made Europeans increasingly aware of the extraordinary variety of humanity, of the existence of peoples differing greatly in their physical characteristics from the European norm, and of societies sharply distinguished one from another by their culture. This mass of new information came to present inquiring minds with two formidable tasks: it was necessary first to devise an intellectual system capable of embracing this enlarged vision of humanity, then, having identified the differences of physical type and culture that clearly existed, to provide some explanation of the way in which these variations had come about.

In considering the theories about race and culture put forward in the eighteenth and nineteenth centuries, the modern reader needs to bear in mind that the material which served to stimulate these speculations contained, when judged by the standards of modern scientific inquiry, a great many flaws. The first contacts between peoples of different culture cannot be expected to produce really satisfactory descriptions of anything but externals. Neither side knows the other's language; thus neither side is in a position to explore the complexities of the other's society nor the intricacies of its system of ideas. Accounts must be based on visual impressions, and visual impressions are of their nature selective and therefore subjective. Inevitably the nature of the relationship established between the two sides affects the way one describes the other: the European missionary, for example, is likely to show scant sympathy for those who reject or revile his teaching. Moreover it appears to be a natural human tendency to sum up the 'character' of a people in moral terms. Not that Europeans always agreed in their summaries of the character of an alien people. Thus the Hottentots (Khoi) were regarded, in van Riebeeck's notorious phrase, as 'black stinking dogs' by most of the Dutch settlers at the Cape. A German traveller, on the other hand, who came to the Cape to make astronomical observations in 1705, reported that the Hottentots were 'not so stupid, irrational and inhuman as they have been represented among us', praised their hospitality, their sense of justice and their 'most beautiful Simplicity of Manner', but conceded that they were, 'both in Body and Mind, the laziest People under the Sun'.[1]

Confronted as he constantly was with such contradictory material, the European theorist found himself free to select those 'facts' that accorded best with his own preconceptions. By the late eighteenth century there was enough material available on those African peoples

[1] Peter Kolben, *The present state of the Cape of Good Hope*, translated from the German (London, 1731), I, 37, 165, 299, 366, 46.

with whom Europeans had been in fairly regular contact for more than two centuries, to allow Europeans with an interest in the problems of race and culture to put forward a number of different theories. Inevitably, these theories have not stood the test of later inquiry, for their authors were trapped within the limitations of their age and forced to rely on imperfect material. Nevertheless, however crude these theories may seem to the present generation, for the historian they possess a double significance: for a considerable period they helped to shape European actions in their contact with peoples of alien culture; at the same time they served to stimulate a mood of inquiry that contributed to the evolution of the modern discipline of anthropology.

The most striking fact about the population of Africa was the predominance of dark-skinned people of a physical type quite unlike anything to be found in Europe or in Asia. Were these black men really members of the same human species as white people? The Bible traced all men back to a common ancestor, but as early as 1520 the Swiss medical writer Paracelsus had incurred the wrath of the Church by arguing in favour of a different origin for Negroes. It was not, however, until the latter half of the eighteenth century that there developed a really vigorous debate about Negro origins, with the monogenists ascribing a common origin to all humanity, and their opponents, the polygenists, asserting that Negroes were members of a different species.

Two powerful currents of thought – the humanitarianism of English Evangelicals and the enlightened rationalism of French *philosophes* – served to support eighteenth-century monogenism. Evangelicals found in the Christian Gospel an irrefutable argument: 'God that made the world . . . hath made of one blood all nations of men' (Acts xvii, 24–6). *Philosophes* took their stand on the challenging assertion of Descartes: 'le bons sens est la chose du monde la mieux partagée . . . La puissance de bien juger . . . est naturellement égale à tous les hommes.' Given the right opportunities, to the Evangelicals all men could be saved; to the *philosophes* and to later generations of liberal thinkers, all men were capable of developing into completely rational human beings. The polygenists countered these arguments by pointing to the 'realities' of the situation as they saw it. Thus Edward Long, an Englishman who had spent several years in the West Indies observing only Negro slaves, could nevertheless lay claim to a far greater measure of first-hand experience of the Negro character than the armchair philosophers of Europe. Long asserted in his *History of Jamaica* (1774), one of the most influential books of the age, that Africans were 'brutish, ignorant, idle, crafty, treacherous, bloody, thievish, mistrustful and superstitious people', 'void of genius . . . and almost incapable of making any progress in civility or science', that these characteristics were to be found throughout the 'vast regions' of Negro Africa and that Negroes should be regarded as a separate species intermediate between Europeans and similar species and 'orang-outangs'.[1]

The idea accepted by all polygenists, that black men were in some way intermediate between white men and apes, accorded well with long-established notions of the 'brutish' nature of savage people. It also fitted in with a more sophisticated concept – the theory, lucidly defined by Charles White in his *Account of the regular graduations in man* (1799), that 'from men down to the smallest reptiles . . . there exhibits to our view an immense chain of beings, endowed with various degrees of intelligence and active powers, suited to their situation in the general system'.[2] Travellers provided polygenists with enough material to 'prove' the mental inferiority of Negroes. Meanwhile developments in the science of anatomy seemed to define more exactly the physical differences between Africans and Europeans. Thus in the 1840s the American anatomist, S. G. Morton, set about measuring 'cranial capacity' by filling skulls with white pepper seeds. His researches 'proved' that Caucasians had a considerably larger brain than Negroes. Henceforward writers on race felt they were justified in using such terms as 'large-brained Europeans' and 'small-brained savages', until at length the fallacies in Morton's theory – his crude system of measurement, his inadequate sampling, his mistaken correlation of size of brain with intelligence – were exposed. Research such as that carried on by Morton provided the 'scientific physical facts' on which James Hunt, the most combative of mid-nineteenth-century polygenists and the founder in 1863 of the Anthropological Society of London, based his theory of the innate differences between Negroes and Europeans, contrasting his own seemingly solid intellectual foundations with the 'vague general assertions' of his monogenist opponents.[3]

The polygenists found, then, an easy solution to the problem of physical and cultural variations: Negroes represented a different species of humanity and could not reasonably be regarded as capable of the same achievements as Europeans. Monogenists, on the other hand, with their stress on the essential unity of mankind, were forced to

[1] Edward Long, *The history of Jamaica* (London, 1774), II, 353–6.
[2] Charles White, *An account of the regular graduations in man and in different animals and vegetables* (London, 1799), 1.
[3] *The Anthropological Record*, 1863, I, 390.

develop a more elaborate system of ideas. It was widely accepted among late eighteenth-century European intellectuals that human history could be described in terms of progression through the stages of 'Savagery', 'Barbarism' and 'Civilization'. Clearly Negro Africans, with their modest technology and their small-scale polities, fell into the categories of 'savages' or 'barbarians'. Naturalists were inclined to consider the black skin of the Negroes as being in some way a product of the hot climate in which they lived. Could there not also be some connection between this climate and the state of Negro society? In that seminal work, *De l'esprit des lois* (1748), Montesquieu had forcefully restated an old-established notion when he declared that the cool climate of temperate lands made northerners naturally more vigorous in body and mind than southerners. This hypothesis tallied well with the theory that the exuberant vegetation of tropical latitudes enabled men to gain an easy living, and thus encouraged them to become 'lazy', and deprived them of the incentive to develop the arts and industries of 'Civilization'.

Not all eighteenth-century thinkers were prepared to accept the rigid determinism implicit in an excessive stress on the influences of the natural environment. African 'backwardness' – a concept with both moral and material implications – could not be denied, but might it not rather be due, so many English humanitarians asked themselves, to the peculiar character of African institutions? Thus the author of the article 'Negro' in the 1797 edition of the *Encyclopaedia Britannica* began, in a manner reminiscent of Long, by listing the 'vices' that 'seem to be the portion of this unhappy race'. But he went on to point out, through a judicious use of quotations, that Negro vices had in fact been exaggerated and that the moral failings of black people should be ascribed to the fact that 'the majority of negroes groan under the cruellest slavery'.[1] This was a point of view that commended itself strongly to the English abolitionists, for whom the Atlantic slave trade came to provide the main cause of the 'degradation' of Africa. 'Degradation' was a concept to be developed further by the missionaries of the early nineteenth century. 'You can have no idea from any wretchedness you see in this country in what a sad condition the Heathen live', declared the writer of a pamphlet put out by the Anglican Church Missionary Society in 1816, and he went on to describe how the Bulom of Sierra Leone offered sacrifices to a cannon-ball.[2] 'The natives of West Africa

[1] *Encyclopaedia Britannica* (Edinburgh, 1797), XII, 794.
[2] Church Missionary Society, *Missionary Papers*, 1816, no. 2.

live in the greatest ignorance and superstition'.[1] Statements such as these, commonplace in the missionary literature of the time, implied that the real cause of African backwardness lay in the people's deluded system of ideas. But in the Christian view, even the most 'degraded' were capable of 'redemption'.

Any discussion about 'Negro' capacity inevitably brought with it the danger of confusing race (in the narrow sense of physical type) and culture. Even so eminent a scholar as J. C. Prichard failed to avoid this pitfall. Prichard was the leading English ethnologist of the first half of the nineteenth century, a man of great learning, a humanitarian and a convinced monogenist. The range of his knowledge made him vividly aware of the difficulties involved in classifying people according to physical type. Nevertheless, after 'reviewing the descriptions of all the races' of West Africa, he felt he could 'observe a relation between their physical character and their moral condition'. He argued that

Tribes having what is termed the Negro character in the most striking degree are the least civilized. The Pepels, Bisagos, Ibos, who are in the greatest degree remarkable for deformed countenances, projecting jaws, flat foreheads and for other Negro peculiarities, are the most savage and morally degraded of the natives hitherto described. The converse of this remark is applicable to all the most civilized races. The Fulahs, Mandingos, and some of the Dahomes and Inta [i.e. Akan] nations have, as far as form is concerned, nearly European countenances and a corresponding configuration of the head.[2]

Thus the ideas of monogenists and polygenists converged in a common assumption that physical type appeared to have some bearing on culture. From 1850 onwards 'race', a term comparatively rarely used in the late eighteenth century, occurred ever more frequently in discussions on African and indeed on global themes, and developed into a concept that provided an easy explanation of the two most remarkable phenomena of the age, the unprecedented rate of European technological development, and the equally unprecedented rate at which white people were expanding into every corner of the globe. 'Race', declared Robert Knox in the introduction to his *Races of man* (1862), 'is everything: literature, science, art – in a word, civilization, depends on it.'[3]'Look all over the globe,' he wrote in another passage, 'it is always the same; the dark races stand still, the fair progress . . . There must be a physical and, consequently, a psychological inferiority in the

[1] Church Missionary Society, *Missionary Papers*, 1818, no. 4.
[2] J. S. Prichard, *Researches into the natural history of mankind*, 3rd ed., II (London, 1836), 97.
[3] Robert Knox, *The races of man* (London, 1862), v.

dark races generally.'[1] Knox was a trained anatomist who earned his living as a popular lecturer. Skilled at putting forward his ideas with straightforward vigour, he could also invest them with an air of 'scientific' credibility. The mystical aura that surrounded his concept of race made it all the more difficult for his contemporaries to perceive the basic absurdity of his arguments.

There was another theme in Knox's racist philosophy of considerable significance for the future – that of racial conflict. In Knox's view antagonism between race and race was one of the basic factors of human history, but it was not until 'the Saxon race began to migrate over the earth, to establish free colonies, as they are called – free to the white man and their own race – dens of horror and of cruelty to the coloured', that racial conflict appeared in its 'terrible form'.[2] Knox's views were obviously profoundly influenced by his personal experience of South Africa, where as a young man he had spent a few years as an army doctor. He spoke of the Bantu as 'a bold and noble race of men, fighting . . . for all that men hold dear', described the European in South Africa as displaying 'all that piratical energy that stamps him as the prince of filibusters' and predicted gloomily that 'the Saxon . . . pushing northwards [from South Africa] will take possession of the entire continent'.[3]

The theory of racial conflict was provided with a more elaborate intellectual basis when the followers of Charles Darwin started to draw analogies between the relationships that Darwin had described among the lower species of the animal world on the one hand, and the interaction of human societies on the other. 'It will be the common and widely spread species,' Darwin predicted in the concluding chapter of *The origin of species* (1859), 'belonging to the larger and dominant groups within each class, which will ultimately prevail and procreate new and dominant species.'[4] And in *The descent of man* (1871) he himself applied his theories of 'the struggle for existence' and 'the survival of the fittest' to the relationship between different societies. 'Extinction follows chiefly from the competition of tribe with tribe and race with race. When civilized nations come into contact with barbarians, the struggle is short.'[5] The experience of the Bushmen of South Africa, and of small aboriginal populations in other continents, provided a measure of support for this theory. Some Europeans were pre-

[1] *Ibid.* 222, 224.   [2] *Ibid.* 546.   [3] *Ibid.* 548, 546, 552.
[4] Charles Darwin, *The origin of species by means of natural selection*, Everyman ed. (London, 1934), 462.
[5] Charles Darwin, *The descent of man* (London, 1871), I, 238.

pared to go even further, to carry the theory to its logical conclusion by suggesting that the entire 'Negro race' was threatened with extinction.[1]

Even Darwin may be accused on occasion of loose thinking, but his approach to phenomena of a biological nature was guided by a rigorous discipline that was entirely salutary in its consequences. The intellectual foundations on which both monogenists and polygenists had erected their respective theories were completely demolished by the evidence Darwin brought forward in *The origin of species*. Monogenists were shown that the biblical view of creation, which most of them had accepted in quite literal terms, was not compatible with scientific truth. At the same time, the polygenists were discomforted to learn that detailed research provided no evidence to justify the division of mankind into different species. Darwin made use of the term 'race', but he was clearly critical of the hard-and-fast distinctions current in contemporary classifications of mankind. Races, he pointed out, 'graduate into each other, so that it is hardly possible to discover clear distinctive characters between them'.[2] This scholarly caution was not however an intellectual characteristic of the Social Darwinists, that section of Darwin's followers who applied evolutionary theories to the study of human society.

At the heart of the evolutionist theory lay the concept of progress, a concept strikingly dynamic when contrasted with the earlier notion of a rigid 'chain of being', yet flexible and capacious enough to provide former monogenists and polygenists with new arguments to maintain their deeply entrenched views on the capability of different 'races'. Many Christians came to equate 'progress' with an acceptance of Christianity. If the Negro could be 'saved', then clearly he could also 'progress'. On the other hand, 'progress' also seemed to imply the existence of a social hierarchy. History was regarded as a ladder up which all societies were climbing, but on which some societies had reached a higher rung and were advancing at a faster rate than others. So simplistic a notion of the complex process of historical change served most effectively to bolster up the complacency and self-satisfaction of those who felt justified in claiming that their society had 'advanced furthest'. 'Talk of the improvement of the breed,' exclaimed an English politician, Sir Charles Adderley, in 1864, 'why, the race we ourselves represent . . . the old Anglo-Saxon race, are the best breed in

---

[1] See, for example, the extraordinary peroration contained in the concluding paragraphs of W. Winwood Reade's *Savage Africa* (London, 1863), 587.

[2] Darwin, *Descent of man*, I, 226.

the whole world.'[1] By an obvious corollary, such a notion served to produce a greater measure of disdain for those who could now be described as 'lower' or 'inferior' races. 'Savages' could be regarded as the 'contemporary ancestors' of Europeans, occupying a stage which 'civilized' peoples had left behind many centuries ago. Alternatively, by means of a false analogy between the development of human personality from infancy to maturity and that of human society from primitive savagery to civilization, the members of 'inferior races' could be described as 'children' – a concept that fitted in well with a current anatomical theory, the exponents of which argued that the development of the brain of the Negro 'never goes beyond that developed in the Caucasian in boyhood'.[2]

There were yet other currents in nineteenth-century European thought that contributed to the formation of a body of opinion peculiarly unappreciative of the real achievements of tropical African peoples. There could, for example, be no proper understanding of African sculpture. As Bernard Smith has pointed out in his study of European reactions to the cultures of the peoples of the South Pacific, 'in a century which treasured realism in the visual arts more than any other, idols which failed to resemble things with any accuracy were held up for special scorn and ridicule'.[3] Aesthetic revulsion at the outward form of ritual objects made it impossible to penetrate sympathetically to the inner meaning of the cult concerned. 'What sort of deities must they be,' exclaimed a missionary preacher in 1818, 'of which images so ridiculously fantastic, so monstrously uncouth, so frightfully distorted as many heathen idols are, are yet considered by their worshippers as the appropriate and worldly representatives?'[4]

Even observers who showed themselves capable of a more sympathetic approach could not escape from these aesthetic preconceptions. Thus Winwood Reade, writing in 1863, pointed out that 'fetishes' were to be regarded as 'symbols', that 'in all countries the illiterate are alike superstitious' and that 'the mythology of the Negroes resembles that of the Greeks and Romans'. In the context of the times these were shrewd and perceptive remarks, but Reade could not really divest

[1] Quoted by Matthew Arnold in his essay, 'The function of criticism in the present time', first published in 1864.

[2] Robert Dunn, 'Some observations on the physiological differences which exist among the typical races of man', Transactions of the Ethnological Society of London, 1865, n.s. 3, 22.

[3] B. Smith, European vision and the South Pacific, 1768–1850 (Oxford, 1962), 245.

[4] 'The contemplation of heathen idolatry an excitement to missionary zeal', an account of a sermon by Rev. M. Wardlow, Missionary Sketches, no. III, October 1818, quoted by Smith, European vision, 245–6.

himself of the straightjacket imposed by a classical education. 'Paganism, to please,' he concluded, 'must be clothed with flowers, as it was in Athens and in Rome. Here its grotesque and uncouth nakedness inspires disgust, so soon as curiosity is sated.'[1]

On the varied forms of political organization to be found among the peoples of sub-Saharan Africa, there existed by the 1860s a considerable amount of descriptive material: notable accounts included those written by Bowdich on the Asante, by Burton on Dahomey and by Casalis on the Sotho. But the structure of African polities did not fit in with the forms of political organization familiar to Europeans, and those who attempted to generalize about African politics fell back on crude and highly misleading simplifications. 'Government among the Negroes', wrote a leading English ethnologist in 1866, 'is in the rudest form of a despotism the most absolute and unrestrained . . . No Negro people has ever had the capacity to build up an empire or monarchy of any extent or durability.'[2] As for those societies organized in the form of what a modern historian would describe as 'stateless polities', their condition was even more 'degraded', their inhabitants being – in the words of another authority – 'usually idle, turbulent, quarrelsome and licentious'.[3]

'The common form description of an African,' wrote an Englishman deeply versed in the contemporary literature,

is that he is cruel, dirty, superstitious, selfish, a cannibal and addicted to fetishism, human sacrifices, sorcery and slave-dealing, besides being a drunkard, a polygamist, a neglecter of domestic ties, a liar and a cheat.[4]

This was a view of African capacity no less harsh than that expressed by Edward Long a century earlier, but far more difficult to combat. Apparently based on a greater measure of circumstantial evidence, it fitted in well with the general ideas of some of the most vigorous thinkers of the age. The spread of this highly infectious attitude of censorious moral superiority can be most clearly traced in the writings of European travellers. Richard Hill has made the point well in his study of European literature on the Sudan, contrasting the 'modest, tolerant, observant' approach of early nineteenth-century travellers with the changed 'tone' that appeared about 1870:

[1] W. Winwood Reade, *Savage Africa* (London, 1863), 538.
[2] John Crawfurd, 'On the physical and mental characteristics of the Negro', *Transactions of the Ethnological Society of London*, 1866, n.s. 4, 216–17.
[3] Hugh Murray, *The African continent: a narrative of discovery and adventure* (London, 1853), 450.
[4] R. N. Cust, *A sketch of the modern languages of Africa* (London, 1883), 457.

The newer men from the West have given up wearing Turkush *nizam* dress and come clothed in outlandish modifications of European garb. They no longer feed off the country but bring instead stores with them. They also bring a new mental attitude; it is as though they have been subjected to the influence of a new ideology at home.[1]

In 1790 the English abolitionists publicized their cause by distributing a plaque designed by Josiah Wedgwood showing a chained Negro in a suppliant posture and inscribed with the words, 'Am I not a man and a brother?' By 1875 the general public in Britain – and, through the rapid diffusion of ideas, in other parts of Europe – was being vigorously conditioned to accept as a realistic portrayal of the varied populations of sub-Saharan Africa that extraordinary image of the objects of 'the white man's burden', those 'new-caught, sullen peoples, half-devil and half-child'.

REACTIONS TO ISLAM

Racial theories about the Negro could not of course be applied to every part of the continent. In North Africa Europeans were in contact with peoples of a physical type not greatly different from their own. The population of North Africa contained many different elements, but most North Africans were Muslims – a fact that gave a measure of unity to the region and allowed Europeans to put forward wide-ranging generalizations. Thus the varying European reactions to Islam represent an important strand in the complex skein of European attitudes to Africa.

Long-held prejudices develop deep roots. For centuries Western Christendom had regarded the ideology of Islam with abhorrence and the power of Muslim peoples with apprehension. For centuries European commentators on Islam had adopted the bitter tone of polemic, denouncing the central figure of the Muslim faith as impostor, sensualist, arch-intriguer and man of blood. The decline of Turkish power that set in during the eighteenth century freed Europe from its fear of Islam. At the same time improved facilities for travel in the lands of the Ottoman Empire made it easier for Europeans to experience at first hand the Muslim way of life. Thus, gradually, through the work of European scholars specializing in the field of Muslim studies, the foundations for a better informed, a more rational, tolerant and

[1] R. L. Hill, 'Historical writing on the Sudan since 1820', in B. Lewis and P. M. Holt, eds., *Historians of the Middle East* (London, 1962), 389.

sympathetic approach to Islam came to be laid. But the crude concepts of medieval polemic lingered on. Indeed, they received a new lease of life when the upsurge of Christian missionary ardour, so militant, so dogmatic, so narrow-minded in many of its manifestations, led to the revival of an aggressive hostility to Islam in certain sections of the European public.

In 1829 Godfrey Higgins, an Englishman with an interest in the history of religion, was moved to produce a short work on Islam as a counterblast to what he termed 'the disgusting trash which has been written respecting the character and conduct of Mohamed by the Christian priests'.[1] No doubt, Higgins had in mind works such as the anonymous life of Muhammad published in London in 1799, in which the prophet was described as 'a sink of iniquity, lust and ambition' and the Koran as a 'motley jumble of inconsistencies', while the impassioned author had ended his long tirade with the assertion that

nothing but the conquest of Mahometan countries, by which the sentiments of men may be freed from their fetters, will ever see the destruction of that system of blasphemy and iniquity by which they are at present enslaved.[2]

At the opposite pole to this aggressive attitude lies an appreciation of the inner spirituality of Islam. Certainly there were some Europeans – men and women with generous, sympathetic and inquiring minds enriched by the experience of long residence in Muslim countries – who succeeded in achieving a deep understanding of an alien culture. But to most Europeans – even if they possessed some knowledge of the East – one can probably apply the remark made by Lucie Duff Gordon about the English in Egypt in the 1860s that 'the difference of manners is a sort of impassable gulf'.[3] It was easy in these circumstances for intellectually minded Europeans, whether their cast of mind was Christian or rational and agnostic, to dismiss Islam as a 'false' religion. But Islam's offence was not confined to matters of doctrine. It could be denounced as a religion that sanctioned slavery and tolerated the horrors of the slave trade, that encouraged sensuality in men and inflicted on women the degrading seclusion of the harem, that promoted the rule of despots and stimulated in their subjects an irrational hatred of all out-

[1] Godfrey Higgins, *An apology for the life and character of the celebrated prophet of Arabia called Mohamed, or the Illustrious* (London, 1829), 5.

[2] Anon., *The life of Mahomet: or, the history of the imposture which was begun, carried on, and finally established by him in Arabia, and which has subjugated a larger portion of the globe, than the religion of Jesus has set at liberty* (London, 1799), 143, 147, 115.

[3] Lady Duff Gordon, *Letters from Egypt (1862–1869)*, edited by Gordon Waterfield (London, 1969), 120.

siders. 'The fanaticism of a brutalizing religion':[1] the phrase of the British politician, Richard Cobden, sums up this farrago of prejudice and half-truth.

The developing mood of racial arrogance, and the increasing acceptance of evolutionary theories of historical change, intensified European contempt for Islam. Muslim fatalism was an attitude of mind deeply antipathetic to the ebullient, all-conquering individualists of the West. The European observer had only to examine the condition of Muslim countries to convince himself that Islam, in contrast to Christianity, was essentially an 'unprogressive' religion. 'A state of universal barbarism'[2] was Volney's comment on Egypt in the 1780s. Half a century later the modernizing schemes of Muḥammad 'Alī put Egypt in a somewhat different category, at least in the opinion of the more sympathetic observers, but a remark similar to Volney's could easily have been applied in the mid-nineteenth century to the other Muslim states of North Africa. One wonders how many contemporary Europeans would have been prepared to question Robert Knox's ignorant and arrogant assertion that 'the Oriental races have made no progress since the time of Alexander the Great'.[3]

Viewed from western Europe, Muslim societies appeared, then, as backward and barbarous. But when the European observer shifted his position and looked northwards from Black Africa, Islam appeared in a quite different perspective. In comparison with the smaller polities of Guinea or of the equatorial regions, the great Muslim states of the western Sudan described in such vivid detail by Denham, Clapperton and Barth, took on the guise of more or less 'civilized' communities, their inhabitants being regarded, in the words of Hugh Murray, as 'more advanced in all the arts and improvements of life' and as displaying 'a character more amiable, manners more dignified and polished and moral conduct more correct'.[4] In some parts of the continent, particularly in West Africa, it was evident that Islam was still a proselytizing religion. This was a development those rival proselytizers, the Christian missionaries and their supporters, could hardly be expected to applaud. But in the latter half of the nineteenth century a few European observers were prepared to argue that Islam was a religion better adapted than Christianity to act as a 'civilizing agent' in Black Africa. The most eloquent English advocate of this

[1] Quoted by Norman Daniel, *Islam, Europe and Empire* (Edinburgh, 1966), 546. Cobden visited Egypt in 1836.
[2] C. F. Volney, *Travels through Syria and Egypt*, translated from the French (Dublin, 1793), 129.   [3] Knox, *Races of man*, 599.   [4] Murray, *The African continent*, 450.

highly controversial notion was the young freelance traveller, Winwood Reade, who first visited West Africa in the early 1860s, and saw in the Casamance area of Senegambia African 'pagans' and Muslims living side by side.

The first are drunkards, gamblers, swine: as diseased in body as debased in mind. The latter are practical Christians ... sober; truthful; constant in their devotions; strictly honest; they treat kindly those who are below them; they do their duty to their neighbours.[1]

It was hardly surprising to find that a good many Europeans working in tropical Africa began to develop a bias in favour of those African peoples most affected by the culture of Islam. Muslim societies possessed a structure much more easily comprehensible to Europeans than the complex polities of 'pagan' Africa, and their ruling groups displayed in their personal behaviour a decorum or a panache, both of which were highly pleasing to the aesthetic sense of many Europeans. Of course the Muslim African could not be regarded as the equal of the Christian European, but it was coming to be recognized that he was far 'superior' to the 'savage' – and preferable, too, in the opinion of some Europeans, to the 'trousered nigger', the product of the mission schools of the coast.[2]

THE 'NEGLECTED ESTATE':
EUROPEAN ATTITUDES TO THE NATURAL RESOURCES
OF AFRICA

If it was difficult for nineteenth-century Europeans to achieve a proper understanding of the peoples and cultures of Africa, it was even harder for them to reach a balanced view of African resources, for they themselves had still to develop the techniques required in making an accurate assessment of an area's potentialities. Guesses and impressions served as an unsatisfactory substitute for detailed knowledge and tended to encourage the extremes of optimism or of pessimism.

From classical times Europeans had inherited the concept of a 'Torrid Zone'. This zone was regarded as covering much of the interior of the continent, 'the Midland Parts' being, in the words of one late eighteenth-century geographer, 'for a long while believed inaccessible and uninhabitable by reason of their intolerable Heat'.[3]

---

[1] Reade *Savage Africa*, 584–5.
[2] Cf. R. F. Burton's remark, 'the Christian converts of Sierra Leone, male and female, are the most demoralized race I know in Africa', *Journal of the Anthropological Institute*, 1865, 3, ccv.   [3] Edward Bowen, quoted by Hallett, *Penetration of Africa*, 42.

This concept of African barrenness lingered on. In 1847 the writer of a school geography could summarize his impressions of Africa with the remark that 'being in general extremely hot and arid, the soil and climate are in many places unfit for the residence of men'.[1] And as late as 1873 a leader-writer in *The Times* could remark that 'it is not long since Central Africa was regarded as nothing better than a region of torrid deserts or pestiferous swamps'.[2]

On the other hand the exuberant vegetation of tropical Africa called forth images of a very different kind, and seemed to hold out the promise of vast resources of natural wealth still untouched. 'It cannot be denied,' wrote the author of the article on Africa in the 1797 edition of the *Encyclopaedia Britannica*, 'that were the country well cultivated, it would be extremely fertile: and would produce in great abundance, not only the necessities, but also the luxuries of life.'[3] Almost half a century later a contributor to the *Edinburgh Review* took up the same theme, when he spoke of Africa as 'a vast neglected estate' and referred to the continent's 'inexhaustible fertility'.[4] The accounts of mid-nineteenth-century explorers helped to confirm this optimistic view of the continent's resources: in 1879 the writer of a general work on Africa could speak of the interior as containing

millions of square miles of rich and fertile lands, some of which are open and park-like in their appearance; and others covered with extensive forests of valuable timber, where the sound of the woodman's axe has never yet been heard, and which only require the culture of the husbandman to make them produce an ample return for his labour.[5]

These grandiose hypotheses of African fecundity were bolstered up by the no less enthusiastic observations made by commentators with a propagandist interest in particular areas. Thus, at an early stage in the French involvement in Algeria, the advocates of a policy of vigorous colonization suggested that the country could become a producer of tropical crops on a scale comparable to that of the lost West Indian island of St Domingue, or harked back to an age long past when North Africa had been the granary of Rome. In much the same spirit, at once euphoric and uncritical, the small group of influential Englishmen who, from the 1790s on, favoured vigorous attempts to penetrate the interior of West Africa, pointed to the enticing opportunities for

[1] J.W.C., *Progressive geography for children* (London, 1847), 39.
[2] *The Times*, 9 December 1873, quoted by Richard Gray, *A history of the southern Sudan, 1839–1889* (London, 1961), 172.
[3] *Encyclopaedia Britannica* (Edinburgh, 1797), I, 225.
[4] *Edinburgh Review*, 1841, **72**, 457.
[5] An Old Resident, *Africa past and present* (London, 1879), 128.

enrichment that awaited the first Europeans to establish a direct commercial intercourse with the apparently flourishing and populous states of the Sudanic belt, while promoters of emigration from Britain to Natal in the late 1840s spoke of a 'land covered with luxuriant vegetation and capable of producing the best sea-island cotton in the world', and 'emphasized the contrast with the "arid sandy plains" of Australia and the dense undergrowth of parts of North America'.[1]

These visions of tropical bonanzas were clouded by the harsh realities of the African environment, by the threat of drought, locusts, disease and any of the other plagues with which Africa was afflicted. The lethal fevers of the tropics were the most fearsome of the natural hazards experienced by Europeans; they were not confined to the notorious Guinea coast, where the horrific phrase, 'the white man's grave', came into use in the 1820s, but were also encountered in East Africa, in the Mascarenes and in the marshy coastal plains of Algeria. Anti-colonial groups both in Britain and in France inevitably used reports of heavy mortality among white men as a powerful argument in favour of the abandonment of costly colonial establishments. But if one makes the exception of the collapse of such minor schemes as the unofficial British attempt to colonize Bulama island off Guinea Bissau, in the early 1790s, the period saw no major retreat by Europeans in any part of the continent. Indeed by 1875, though the cause of the dreaded malaria remained as mysterious as ever, the growing use of quinine as a prophylactic was providing Europeans with a means of overcoming the most formidable of all the natural obstacles in their path. Clearly the confidence of nineteenth-century Europeans in their ability to master any natural environment has not in the long run proved unreasonable, nor has their belief in the vast potential wealth of Africa remained unjustified. By 1875 the discovery of diamonds in South Africa had provided a striking indication of the entirely unexpected riches to be found in Africa, and given new meaning to the wise remark made by Samuel Purchas more than two hundred years earlier: 'And yet may Africa have a Prerogative in Rarities, and some seeming Incredibilities be true.'[2]

[1] A. F. Hattersley, *The British settlement of Natal* (Cambridge, 1960), 146.
[2] Samuel Purchas, quoted by E. W. Bovill, *The golden trade of the Moors*, 2nd rev. ed. (London, 1968), 119.

'CIVILIZING MISSIONS'

Barbarism or savageism is the effect of ages of debasement and vice ... [Savages] possess neither courage, patriotism, natural affection, honour, nor honesty. They have no stimulus for any mental improvement.

The world is rolling on to the golden age. The inmates of our workhouses have more comforts than rich chieftains in Africa have; they have soap, clean linen, glass windows, and chimneys ... Intelligence is communicated instantaneously, and travellers are conveyed on the ocean and in the land with a celerity which our forefathers could not comprehend and which Africans now consider fabulous.[1]

Here, in two passages, taken from the private journals of David Livingstone, is a particularly vigorous expression of the two major currents of thought that served to shape the European concept of a 'civilizing mission' – a conviction of absolute moral superiority over African peoples and a consciousness of power, power that could be used to transform any environment no matter how alien. Increasing, as the nineteenth century advanced, Europeans working in Africa acquired this sense of superiority and power and drew from it a justification for their actions.

The notion of a 'civilizing mission' was a flexible one; it meant different things to different men and it could be employed in a wide range of situations. Thus, when in 1798 the French launched their conquistadorial attack on Egypt, they talked of restoring the country to its former grandeur and of liberating the Egyptian people from the oppressive rule of the Mamluks. In 1816 the British bombardment of Algiers, an action intended to force the dey to release all his Christian slaves, was described by the admiral in command of the attacking fleet as 'an issue between a handful of Britons in the noble cause of Christianity and a horde of fanatics'.[2] In 1847, after the French had been engaged for years in fighting a particularly brutal and savage war of conquest in Algeria, an apologist could describe French actions as fulfilling

une magnifique mission providentielle, mission d'ordre et de paix, dans des contrées qui jadis s'enrichissaient par le pillage et s'honoraient de leurs cruautés; mission de civilisation parmi des peuplades douées d'une vive intelligence, qu'il suffit d'éclairer et de guider; mission religieuse sur un sol que notre religion a arrosé du sang de nos martyrs.[3]

[1] I. Schapera, ed., *Livingstone's private journals, 1851–1853* (London, 1960), 253, 167–8.
[2] P.R.O., Admiralty 1/434. Exmouth to Croker, 28 August 1816.
[3] X. Marmier, *Lettres sur l'Algérie* (Paris, 1847), 81, quoted by Daniel, *Islam, Europe and Empire*, 331.

Clearly a 'civilizing mission' could easily be confused with an imperial destiny. But the urge to 'civilize', and a desire to achieve political domination, need not necessarily go together. The barbarian may be urged, encouraged, even bribed to amend his ways and to set out on the steep path that leads to a 'higher stage of humanity'. Thus another aspect of the growing sense of European superiority was revealed in an ever increasing readiness to give advice. Once he had made contact with Europeans, no independent ruler from the Ottoman sultan to the chief of some petty Bantu tribe could escape being told what he should do 'to improve the lot of his people'. To many con- temporaries it seemed that 'the introduction of the European element' brought with it, as a British consul wrote of Tunis in the mid-nine- teenth century, 'the germs of a nascent civilization'.[1]

Of course much of the advice given by Europeans, especially when it turned on the introduction of new techniques or sought to explain the intricacies of international diplomacy, was extremely useful to its recipients. But often the European adviser spoke *de haut en bas*; however generous, however altruistic he might feel himself to be, he patronized and therefore he ran the risk of humiliating. Yet, when one thinks of Edward Lane or Lucie Duff Gordon and their circle of Arab friends in Egypt, of the explorer Hugh Clapperton and the genial relationships he established with many of the great men in the countries through which he passed on his two expeditions to Sokoto, or of the veteran mission- ary, Robert Moffat, and the deep affection which developed between him and the formidable Ndebele chief, Mzilikazi, one sees that the barriers imposed by alien cultures were not insurmountable, and that there were always some Europeans who were brought, partly by the nature of their occupation, but even more by the prompting of their temperament, into such close contact with Africans that they were able to establish the warm bonds of personal friendship.

'Civilization' is a word that does not appear to have come into use either in England or in France before the latter half of the eighteenth century. During the nineteenth century it developed into a concept that seemed to have a universalistic ring about it. In fact, as defined by most Europeans, it meant no more than that complex of ideas, institutions, and techniques with which a particular group of Europeans were familiar in their own culture. With a dynamic people, so blinkered a vision could lead to that attitude which Matthew Arnold detected in his fellow-Englishmen, 'of wishing to improve everything but them-

[1] Sir Robert Wood in 1871, quoted by Daniel, *Islam, Europe and Empire*, 356.

selves off the face of the earth'.[1] Sometimes a more limited meaning was applied to 'civilization': it involved no more than the introduction of new methods of production and communication, a process that would now be termed 'modernization' or 'development'. To evangelically minded Christians this was far too narrow a view of civilization: as the members of the Aborigines Protection Society proclaimed in their constitution, 'the complete Civilization and the real Happiness of Man can never be secured by anything less than the diffusion of Christian Principles'.[2] However defined, the introduction of 'civilization' to Africa was bound to involve considerable changes in the cultures of African peoples. By what means, nineteenth-century Europeans had to ask themselves, was this process to be carried through? To phrase the question in the terms of contemporary jargon, how were 'savages' to be 'civilized'?

The 'civilizing' of Africa was an issue first raised – at least in England – during the early debates on the abolition of the slave trade. Many influential Englishmen were seized with a sense of guilt and horror when they came to recognize the extent of their compatriots' participation in a loathsome form of commerce. They were eager to find means of promoting the 'civilization and happiness of Africa'. But their knowledge of African realities was inevitably limited and their concentration on the slave trade, which they regarded as the basic cause of African 'degradation', led them to take too simplistic a view of the complex problems of African development. Thus, by stressing what seemed to them the paramount importance of 'legitimate commerce', they glossed too easily over the difficulties faced by African producers in shifting from one type of economy to another.

By the middle of the nineteenth century, many liberal-minded Europeans had come to accept what might be termed the litany of the C's – Commerce, Christianity, Civilization, Colonization – as providing the most effective recipe for the transformation of Africa. The benefits of commerce for peoples 'hitherto in a quiescent, indolent, uncultivated state' were eloquently expounded by John Stuart Mill:

The opening of a foreign trade, by making them acquainted with new objects ... sometimes makes a sort of industrial revolution in a country whose resources were previously undeveloped for want of energy and ambition in the people: inducing those who were satisfied with scant comforts and little

---

[1] Matthew Arnold, 'On the study of Celtic literature', in *Lectures and essays in criticism*, ed. R. H. Super (Ann Arbor, 1962), 297–8.

[2] Aborigines Protection Society, *Constitution* (1837), 7, quoted by George R. Mellor, *British imperial trusteeship, 1783–1850* (London, 1951), 257.

work, to work harder for the gratification of their new tastes, and even to save and accumulate capital, for the still more complete satisfaction of those tastes at a future time.

Even greater, in Mill's opinion, were the 'intellectual and moral' advantages of a developing commerce:

It is hardly possible to overrate the value, in the present low state of human improvement, of placing human beings in contact with persons dissimilar to themselves, and with modes of thought and action unlike those with which they are familiar . . . Commercial adventurers from advanced countries have usually been the first civilizers of barbarians. Commerce . . . is one of the primary sources of progress . . . rapidly rendering war obsolete, by strengthening and multiplying the personal interests which are in opposition to it.[1]

The blessings conferred by Christianity on peoples hitherto shrouded in the 'darkness' of 'paganism' were self-evident to any orthodox Christian. Civilization could be equated with the introduction of some of the artefacts and techniques of contemporary Europe together with the appropriate modes of conduct. As for colonization, it could be interpreted either as the establishment of European political control over well-defined areas or as the introduction of European settlers. Clearly the method chosen depended on the nature of the environment. But both types of colonization could produce the same advantages: an increase in security made possible by the ending of incessant local wars, greater opportunities for the development of legitimate commerce, the creation of political and social structures favourable to the work of Christian missionaries.

These theories were put to the test of practical action in two remarkable attempts to establish model European-dominated communities in the interior of Africa. The first, inspired by the ideas of Sir Thomas Fowell Buxton, Wilberforce's successor as leader of the English humanitarians and founder of the African Civilization Society, took the form of an elaborately organized British expedition up the Niger in 1841. The second, undertaken twenty years later in response to an appeal from David Livingstone, aimed to establish 'centres of Christianity and civilization for the promotion of true religion, agriculture and lawful commerce'[2] in the Malawi area, and was undertaken by missionaries and lay workers of the newly founded Universities Mission to Central Africa. Both attempts ended in total failure, thus

[1] John Stuart Mill, *Principles of political economy*, 6th ed. (London, 1865), II, 122.
[2] H. Goodwin, *A memoir of Bishop Mackenzie* (Cambridge, 1864), 188, quoted by Roland Oliver, *The missionary factor in East Africa* (London, 1952), 13.

illustrating the enormous difficulties faced by those who sought the 'deliverance' of Africa, and making it easy for contemporary critics to point out the flaws in their arguments. But, in spite of these reverses, it is clear that the idealism of those who advocated a more dynamic approach to Africa was based on a great deal of good sense. A later generation may not share their moral certainties, but cannot deny their general thesis that the European trader, the European missionary and the European settler represented powerful agents of change, through whose labours the culture of many African peoples was bound to be powerfully affected.

STRATEGIC CONSIDERATIONS: THE IMPERIAL VIEW OF AFRICA

To European statesmen concerned with the grand problems of imperial strategy, Africa took on the appearance not of a continent of fascinating variety, nor of a challenging field for 'civilizing missions', but rather of a relatively simple configuration on a world map, some parts of which, by virtue solely of their geographical position, were of particular interest. Ever since the latter half of the fifteenth century, the trading-posts established on the coasts and islands of Africa had been involved in the conflicts between rival European powers. But it was not until the last decade of the eighteenth century that certain African territories came to be seen by politicians in Britain and in France as areas of major strategic importance. Two inter-related developments, neither of which had anything to do with Africa, placed the continent in this new perspective. In Asia the British were finding their stake in India increasingly profitable and were therefore prepared to accept a steady expansion of their responsibilities. In Europe the outbreak of the Revolutionary war in 1793 served to intensify the already bitter sense of rivalry between Britain and France. In these circumstances the sea routes skirting Africa and leading to the East became for the British arteries vital for the maintenance of their country's economic prosperity and for the French obvious targets in time of war.

As early as 1781, the directors of the British East India Company had pointed out that 'the Power possessing the Cape of Good Hope has the key to and from the East Indies'.[1] In 1795 the British took over the Cape from the Dutch, and so made sure that this 'key' was firmly

[1] Quoted by Gerald S. Graham, *Great Britain in the Indian Ocean: a study of maritime enterprise, 1810–1850* (London, 1968), 24.

in their hands. But British supremacy in the Indian Ocean could still be threatened by the French base at Mauritius. So successful, indeed, were French privateers from Port Louis in their attacks on the ships of the East India Company, that the British found themselves forced in 1810 to undertake the conquest of the island-group of the Mascarenes by means of a hazardous amphibious operation. Egypt was the third African territory the strategic significance of which was clearly brought out during the long Anglo-French conflict. Bonaparte's expedition of 1798, seen with alarm as a deliberate French move against India, taught British statesmen that they must always keep a careful watch on a country of whose existence they had previously scarcely been aware. When peace was concluded in 1815, the British made sure that the Cape and Mauritius remained in their possession. As for Egypt, British statesmen developed a line of policy clearly defined by Lord Palmerston in 1857:

What we wish about Egypt is that it should continue to be attached to the Turkish Empire, which is a security against it belonging to any European Power. We want to trade with Egypt and to travel through Egypt, but we do not want the burden of governing Egypt.[1]

A similar policy came to be applied to two other North African countries – Morocco and Tunis. Morocco overlooked the important British base at Gibraltar, while Tunis lay at the narrowest point in the central Mediterranean. Even before the opening of the Suez Canal in 1869, the British were making increasing use of Egypt as a staging post for passengers and mails to and from India. Should either Morocco or Tunis be occupied by a potentially hostile European power, the British reckoned that their route through the Mediterranean to India would be seriously threatened. In these circumstances the native governments of the Moroccan sultan and the Tunisian bey must be protected against the encroachments of their European neighbours, France and Spain. Similarly, in the Red Sea the British were prepared to support Egyptian expansion, seeing that it served to fill a vacuum which might otherwise have attracted a European power. But it was impossible for the British completely to exclude, through their policy of negative imperialism, a competitor so vigorous as France. Indeed with every decade of the nineteenth century, the number of areas of potential Anglo-French friction steadily increased. 'Even the most barren islands of the Indian Ocean', a modern historian has noted of the period up to 1850, 'were getting tangled in European rivalries.'[2]

---

[1] Quoted by the Earl of Cromer, *Modern Egypt* (London, 1911), 71.
[2] Graham, *Great Britain in the Indian Ocean*, 80.

An expanding foreign trade was an essential ingredient of British power, and advances in British industry made possible commercial expansion on an unprecedented scale. The protection of British merchants and the creation of new commercial opportunities could thus be regarded as important aspects of overall British strategy. British trade with Africa expanded steadily during the nineteenth century, as British merchants developed an interest in the novel commodities offered by their old customers in West and South Africa, found new openings such as that presented by Zanzibar, and broke into the markets of Egypt and Morocco from which they had been virtually excluded by local restrictions during the eighteenth century. But by the 1870s trade with African countries made up little more than 5 per cent of total British commerce. To Victorian Britain, Africa was in commercial terms the least important of the continents.

France was the only other European power to make a major impact on Africa in this period. With the conquest of Algeria, the expansion in Senegal under Faidherbe, the establishment of close links with Egypt, and the growth of a vigorous settler population in Réunion, the French stake in Africa increased no less substantially than that of the British. But the reasons for French interest were different. Commerce was less important, though French investors in Tunis and in Egypt were developing into powerful imperialist lobbies; humanitarian arguments were heard less frequently in Paris than in London; questions of grand strategy hardly arose. It was prestige that provided the most cogent argument for empire. As for the other European nations soon to participate vigorously in the 'scramble' for African territories, Germany, Italy, Portugal and Belgium, already before 1875 the writings and speeches of small groups of outward-looking individuals, some already occupying positions of influence and authority, gave some indication of the outburst of vigorous activity soon to come.

The European conquest of Africa reached its climax in the colonial wars and the diplomatic bargaining of the 'age of imperialism' in the last decades of the nineteenth century. But it was a movement that had begun very much earlier: 1798, the date of the French attack on Egypt, might be suggested as a starting-point. Long before the 1880s and the 1890s, one can detect the emergence of those moods – the racial arrogance, the conviction of a 'civilizing mission', the awareness of technological superiority, the vision of natural resources waiting to be developed by the industry and expertise of Europe, the intense suspicion of fellow-European rivals – that are usually regarded as peculiarly characteristic of the high noon of European imperialism. Yet to think of the development of European attitudes to Africa in the first three-quarters of the nineteenth century as a steady crescendo towards an imperial climax is to adopt too simple a view of a highly complex process. Whenever a group of Europeans spoke up in favour of some vigorous initiative in an African context, they invariably provoked argument and controversy. The passionate debates in Britain over the abolition of the slave trade, or in France over policy towards Algeria, provide obvious examples of this process. But in fact every possible line of European action in Africa could arouse dissension and stimulate discussion: were colonial establishments really worth the money they cost to maintain? could parts of Africa really be said to offer profitable fields for commercial enterprise? could Europeans really 'civilize' Africans? There were many Europeans who would have returned a negative answer to all these questions. Before 1875 only a small group of enthusiasts would have replied with the vigorous affirmatives required of budding imperialists.

And yet a majority of his contemporaries would probably have agreed with the English army officer who wrote in 1837, after completing a journey up the Red Sea:

It seems to me a law of nature that the civilized nations shall conquer and possess the countries in a state of barbarism and by such means, however unjustifiable it may appear at first, extend the blessings of knowledge, industry and commerce among people hitherto sunk in the most gloomy depth of superstitious ignorance.[1]

The unshakeable self-confidence of such a statement, so jarring to late twentieth-century ears, is an essential characteristic of the mood of the more vigorously expansionist sections of European society. The sentiment itself was not a new one: Europeans settled in the New World had long been accustomed to speak in such terms when describing their relations with the indigenous peoples of the Americas. The novelty lay in the application of such a sentiment to Africa. Before 1790, Africa had truly been something of a 'dark continent' to Europe. By the 1870s that newly-coined phrase – popularized by H. M. Stanley's

---

[1] Quoted by Thomas E. Marston, *Brtiain's imperial role in the Red Sea area, 1800–1878* (Hamden, Conn., 1961), 476, from a report by Captain James Mackenzie contained in P.R.O., F.O. 78/3185.

narrative of his journey down the Congo, *Through the dark continent* (1878) – was already something of a misnomer. For Europeans now had at their disposal a greater mass of information about Africa than ever before, their interests in the continent had grown more diversified and more widely diffused, and the tide of their activities, often abrasive, sometimes invigorating in its impact on African societies, was steadily, inexorably rising.

BIBLIOGRAPHICAL ESSAYS

I. EGYPT AND THE NILE VALLEY

The primary source-materials for this period of Egyptian history are abundant, but by no means fully or systematically exploited. The Egyptian archives in Cairo form a massive corpus from the time of Muḥammad 'Alī Pasha onwards, although at present problems of accessibility and administration limit their use. Some idea of their nature and scope is given by Jean Deny, *Sommaire des archives turques du Caire* (Cairo, 1930); and by Helen Anne B. Rivlin, *The Dār al-Wathā'iq in 'Ābdīn Palace at Cairo as a source for the study of the modernization of Egypt in the nineteenth century* (Leiden, 1970). The Ottoman archives relating to Egypt in this period are in the Başbakanlık Arşivi, Topkapı Sarayı Arşivi and Hariciye Arşivi in Istanbul. Their range is indicated in three articles in P. M. Holt, ed., *Political and social change in modern Egypt* (London, 1968), 28–58, by Stanford J. Shaw, 'Turkish source-materials for Egyptian history', Şinasi Altundağ, 'Ottoman archival materials on nineteenth-century Egyptian history', and Hasan Adalı, 'Documents pertaining to the Egyptian Question in the Yıldız Collection of the *Başbakanlık Arşivi*, Istanbul'. The archives of the Egyptian administration in the Sudan were destroyed or lost during the Mahdia, and nothing of them now remains at Khartoum. The archives of Britain, France and other European powers are an important source of information, and extensive selections, relating principally to the time of Muḥammad 'Alī Pasha were published by the Société Royale de Géographie d'Égypte under the auspices of King Fu'ād I (1922–36). The papers of statesmen, officials and others supplement the state archives, from which they are not always clearly distinguishable. Two articles in Holt (1968), 59–75, provide some guidance in this field: H. S. Deighton, 'Some English sources for the study of modern Egyptian history', and Ahmed Abdel Rahim Mustafa, 'The Hekekyan Papers'.

The last Egyptian exponent of traditional historiography, al-Jabartī, died in 1825 or 1826. His chronicle, *'Ajā'ib al-āthār fi'l-tarājim wa'l-akhbār* (Būlāq, 1297 [1880]) and other editions, covers the French occupation and subsequent developments down to 1236/1821. There is a poor French translation by Chefik Mansour and others, *Merveilles biographiques et historiques* (Cairo, 1888–96). Al-Jabartī also wrote a separate chronicle of the French occupation, *Muzhir al-taqdīs bi-dhahāb dawlat al-Faransīs*, edited by Muḥammad ʿAṭā as *Yawmiyyāt al-Jabartī* (Cairo, n.d., 2 vols.); and by Ḥasan Muḥammad Jawhar and ʿUmar al-Dasūqī under the original title ([Cairo], 1389/1969). There is an old French translation by Alexandre Cardin, *Journal d'Abdurrahman Gabarti pendant l'occupation française en Égypte* (Alexandria, 1835; Paris, 1838). On al-Jabartī, see David Ayalon, 'The historian al-Jabartī and his background', *Bulletin of the School of Oriental and African Studies*, 1960, **23**, 2, 217–49. Another account of the French occupation by a contemporary Syrian Christian has been edited and translated into French by Gaston Wiet as Nicolas Turc, *Chronique d'Égypte, 1798–1804/Mudhakkirāt Niqūlā Turk* (Cairo, 1950). Traditional in form, being modelled on a fifteenth-century prototype by al-Maqrīzī, is the encyclopaedic topographical work by ʿAlī Mubārak, *al-Khiṭaṭ al-tawfīqiyya al-jadīda* (Būlāq, 1304–5/1886–9). A mine of information on many aspects of Egypt at the end of the period, it is described and analysed by Gabriel Baer, ''Alī Mubārak's *Khiṭaṭ* as a source for the history of modern Egypt', in Holt (1968), 13–27; also available in Baer (see below) (1969). The continuators of the Funj Chronicle bring the history of the Egyptian Sudan down to various dates. The recension edited by al-Shāṭir Buṣaylī ʿAbd al-Jalīl, *Makhṭūṭat Kātib al-Shūna* [Cairo, c. 1961], goes to 1253/ 1837, while that by Makkī Shibayka [Mekki Shibeika], *Taʾrīkh mulūk al-Sūdān* (Khartoum, 1947), ends with the year 1288/1871–2. This is also the terminal date of the recension translated by H. A. MacMichael, *A history of the Arabs in the Sudan* (Cambridge, 1922; repr. London, 1967), II, 354–430.

The accounts of European travellers and residents in Egypt are less important for this than for an earlier period, but exception must be made of E. W. Lane, *The manners and customs of the modern Egyptians* first published in London in 1836, many numerous later editions. It is a classic account of traditional Egyptian society. Other writings are discussed by H. S. Deighton, 'The impact of Egypt on Britain: a study of public opinion', in Holt (1968), 231–48, while Jean-Marie Carré, *Voyageurs et écrivains français en Égypte*, 2nd ed. Cairo, 1956, 2 vols., is a useful guide to French writers. The deficiency of source-materials on the Egyptian Sudan renders travellers' accounts particularly valuable. There are useful data in Hill (1959), 174–7 (see below). Two manuscript journals there mentioned and relating to the years 1822–41 have now been published by Richard Hill, *On the frontiers of Islam* (Oxford, 1970).

There is no detailed and up to date history of Egypt in this period, but short general accounts are given in P. M. Holt, *Egypt and the Fertile Crescent, 1516–1922* (London, 1966); and P. J. Vatikiotis, *The modern history of Egypt* (London, 1969). More detailed treatment, with a nationalist bias, is given in a series by 'Abd al-Raḥmān al-Rāfiʿī, *Taʾrīkh al-ḥaraka al-qawmiyya wa-taṭawwur niẓām al-ḥukm fī Miṣr* (Cairo, 1348/1929, 2 vols.); *ʿAṣr Muḥammad ʿAlī*, 3rd ed. (Cairo, 1370/1951); *ʿAṣr Ismāʿīl* (Cairo, 1355/1937, 2 vols.). For the Sudan, Richard Hill, *Egypt in the Sudan, 1820–1881* (London, 1959), describes the main developments, while the consequences of the break-through to the Equatorial Nile and the Baḥr al-Ghazāl are studied in Richard Gray, *A history of the southern Sudan, 1839–1889* (London, 1961). Naʿūm Shuqayr, *Taʾrīkh al-Sūdān* (Cairo, [1903]), although old, is still useful.

On special aspects of Egyptian history in this period, there has been a good deal of published work, much of it of high quality. The standard account of the French occupation is C. de la Jonquière, *L'expédition en Égypte, 1798–1801* (Paris, 1899–1907, 5 vols.). The career of Muḥammad ʿAlī is described (mainly from European archival sources) by Henry Dodwell, *The founder of modern Egypt* (Cambridge, 1931, repr. Cambridge, 1967); this may be supplemented by Shafik Ghorbal, *The beginnings of the Eastern Question and the rise of Mehemet Ali* (London, 1929). There is a voluminous and detailed, but incomplete study of the reign of Ismāʿīl, based largely on Egyptian archives, by Georges Douin, *Histoire du règne du Khédive Ismaïl* (Rome, 1933–4, Cairo, 1936–41). The appearance of overt and subversive political groupings is examined by Jacob M. Landau in *Parliaments and parties in Egypt* (Tel Aviv, 1953; New York, 1954); and in 'Prolegomena to a study of secret societies in Egypt', *Middle Eastern Studies*, 1965, I, 2, 1–52. An important study of the modernization of Egypt under Muḥammad ʿAlī, much wider than the title implies, is Helen Anne B. Rivlin, *The agricultural policy of Muḥammad ʿAlī in Egypt* (Cambridge, Mass., 1961). A basic subject is treated by Gabriel Baer, *A history of landownership in modern Egypt, 1800–1950* (London, 1962); the same author's *Studies in the social history of modern Egypt* (Chicago, 1969) covers a wider range of important topics. David S. Landes, *Bankers and pashas* (London, 1958), throws light on the problem of khedivial indebtedness. There are several articles relevant to this period in Holt (1968). The best introduction to the changing intellectual climate is Albert Hourani, *Arabic thought in the liberal age, 1798–1939* (London, 1962, repr. London, 1970), while J. Heyworth-Dunne, *An introduction to the history of education in modern*

Egypt (London, 1939, repr. London, 1968) is a cultural history of wider range than the title suggests.

The abundant periodical literature on the period is listed in J. D. Pearson, *Index Islamicus, 1906–1955* and its *Supplements* (Cambridge, 1958). Indispensable guides to the published material on the Sudan are R. L. Hill, *A bibliography of the Anglo-Egyptian Sudan from the earliest times to 1937* (London, 1939); Abdel Rahman el Nasri, *A bibliography of the Sudan 1935–1958* (London, 1962); and Yūsuf Asʿad Dāghir, *Al- Uṣul al-ʿarabiyya li'l-dirāsāt al-sūdāniyya* ([Beirut], 1968). There are relevant articles in the *Encyclopaedia of Islam*, 2nd ed. (Leiden and London, in progress).

2. ETHIOPIA AND THE HORN
Documentary materials

There is a great wealth of source-material for the nineteenth-century history of Ethiopia and the Horn. Its utilization, however, presents several problems. Firstly, the documentary sources are widely scattered and sparsely published. In Ethiopia itself there are no organized central archives open to scholars. The earliest government papers preserved in the archives of the Ministry of Pen seem to be from the Menelik period (post-1889), while the archives of the emperors Tewodros and Yohannes were presumably lost at Magdala and Metemma respectively. Occasional documents and small collections can be found in churches and monasteries as well as in the hands of private persons, but the work of tracing these documents for the purpose of historical research has only just begun. The foreign government archives of greatest importance for the period before 1885 are the Egyptian National Archives (E.N.A., also known as Abdin Archives), the Archives du Ministère des Affaires Étrangères (A.E.), Paris, and the Public Record Office (P.R.O.) and the India Office Library (I.O.), London, but the Belgian, Italian, Austrian, German and Turkish archives also provide documents on Ethiopia and the Horn.

The Ethiopian materials at the E.N.A. include a series of very valuable original letters from Ethiopian rulers in *Carton 19 Bahr Berra* as well as many documents (including such originals) scattered throughout the cartons and files of *Soudan* (in Arabic), *Soudan et Abyssinie*, *Soudan et Afrique Orientale*, *Soudan Général*, etc. (in French). Much information is also to be gained by referring to the registers of supreme orders, dispatches, telegrams, etc., but the items on Ethiopia and the Horn are not always easy to locate. In the French foreign office archives, the Ethiopian and Somali materials are largely concentrated in *Mémoires et Documents, Afrique, Abyssinie* and *Mer Rouge*, respectively, and *Correspondance politique, Égypte, Massouah*. The *Abyssinia* series of original correspondence at the P.R.O., F.O.1, contains 31 volumes up to 1885, and the *Turkey* series, F.O. 78, has much additional material, particularly on the Somali coast. The coverage in the Foreign Office Confidential Print varies, but the material is easier to handle than in the original correspondence; there are separate series covering *Abyssinia*, F.O. 401, and the *Somali Coast*, F.O. 403. In the I.O., the Aden archives are of particular value. It was only the British government that published significant collections of documents on its relations with Ethiopia. Of the French materials nothing was published at the time and only stray documents were later included in the *Documents diplomatiques français 1871–1914*. The Italian parliamentary papers (*Libri Verdi*) become important only towards the end of the period dealt with here, and the same is true of the documentary volumes of *L'Italia in Africa* edited by Carlo Giglio. The lengthy extracts from the documents of the E.N.A. provided by G. Douin in *Histoire du règne du Khédive Ismaïl* (Rome and Cairo, 1933–41) are very valuable although they have quite naturally been selected to present the Egyptian side of the story.

The second problem in connection with the documentary sources is linguistic. Letters and agreements were at the time translated from Amharic into Arabic (for Egypt) and from Amharic and Arabic into European languages. Once these often incorrect and sometimes deliberately falsified translations had been presented, the originals were ignored. Not only did the politicians of the time refuse to consider the Amharic versions and seemingly remain ignorant of the discrepancies; historians have by and large taken the same line. They have in other words allowed themselves to be misled by these secondary texts in the same way as European governments were repeatedly misled at the time about the positions, plans and requests of the rulers of Ethiopia. This situation will hopefully be corrected by the forthcoming publication in the original languages of the correspondence of Ethiopian rulers and other important documents such as treaties.

The most important collections of documents outside the government archives are found at the British Museum (for instance, the papers of Henry Salt and Charles Gordon) and the Bibliothèque Nationale, Paris (the d'Abbadie collections), and in the archives of the Church Missionary Society, the Congrégation de la Mission, Paris, 'Propaganda Fide', Rome, the Basel Mission, the Swedish Evangelical Mission, Stockholm, etc.

Published narratives and memoirs by Europeans

The value of the numerous published reports, narratives and memoirs (as well as of most of the archival materials) obviously varies tremendously with the knowledge and personalities of the authors, the character of their involvement with Ethiopia, their opportunities of observing the events and their motives for writing about them. Much still needs to be done on the background of the individual Europeans, as well as on comparative analyses of the descriptions of political, social, religious and economic conditions provided by men like H. Salt, N. Pearce, E. Rüppell, E. Combes and M. Tamisier, Samuel Gobat, J. L. Krapf, Giuseppe Sapeto, Antoine and Arnauld d'Abbadie, Th. Lefebvre, P. V. Ferret and J. G. Galinier, C. F. X. Rochet d'Héricourt, W. C. Harris, C. J. Cruttenden, C. C. von der Decken, Richard Burton, C. T. Beke, Th. von Heuglin, Cardinal Massaia, W. Plowden, H. Stern, G. Lejean, H. Blanc, H. Rassam, and W. Munzinger, to mention a cross-section of fairly well-known names from the first three-quarters of the century. There was a considerable amount of plagiarizing (for instance, the Frenchman Bardel copying Plowden's out-dated reports and dispatching them to his own government), and a few 'travellers' appear who had never left their desks in Europe, such as É. Jonveaux and F. H. Apel.

Ethiopian chronicles and oral history

The political and military history of the Ethiopian state, in particular, is dealt with in a number of chronicles, in the Ge'ez language and mostly anonymous for the first half of the century, thereafter in Amharic as well as Ge'ez and with named or at least identifiable authors. Chronicles for the last decades of the *Zamana Mesafent* originating in the Gondar area have been published by Conti Rossini and Weld Blundell. For the reign of Tewodros, there are three distinct published chronicles: Zeneb's, Welde Maryam's and an anonymous one published by L. Fusella. Less has been published for the early reign of Yohannes, in fact only a very brief chronicle in Ge'ez, 'Histoire du régne de Iohannes IV, roi d'Éthiopie (1868–1889)', in *Revue sémitique* (1913). Though Shoa and Menelik are at the centre of the story, Gebre Sellassie's published chronicle of the reign of Menelik also provides some information for the reigns of the preceding emperors.

A number of important but unpublished manuscripts exist in European collections, for instance the chronicles by Lemlem and

Zeyohannis in the Collection Mondon-Vidailhet of the Bibliothèque Nationale. Much more can certainly be brought to light by the systematic inventory of manuscripts in Ethiopian churches and in private hands in the country. Interesting works that have become known to historians in the last few years include manuscripts of *Tarike Nagast* which carry the narrative through the nineteenth century, sometimes with clearly regional emphasis, such as the manuscript of Tekle Iyesus (Gojjam) and some of the manuscripts of Gebre Mika'el Gurmu (Tigre and Eritrea), now available at the Institute of Ethiopian Studies in Addis Ababa. New manuscript materials on Harar are also coming to light. The most pressing task at present is probably to speed up the recording of more of the oral history of the Galla, Somali and other ethnic groups, whose history is much less known and all too often ignored because of the relative scarcity of information compared with the wealth of source material on the central institutions and areas of the Ethiopian state.

·Secondary literature

The general works on Ethiopian history by Sir E. A. Wallis Budge, J.-B. Coulbeaux, G. K. Rein, Tekle Ṣadiq Mekuriya and others have in recent years been supplemented by more detailed and scholarly publications on various aspects of the history of the last century. The *Zamana Mesafent* has been dealt with by M. Abir in *Ethiopia: the Era of the princes* (London, 1968) and by D. Crummey in *Priests and politicians: Protestant and Catholic missions in Ethiopia 1830–1868* (Oxford, 1972), which also covers the reign of Tewodros. The emphasis of Abir is on economic-political, of Crummey on religious-diplomatic developments. *King of Kings Tewodros of Ethiopia* by S. Rubenson attempts to explain the personality and policies of this ruler in terms of his political and family background rather than his dealings with Europeans. The economic history of the period is covered by R. Pankhurst in *Economic history of Ethiopia 1800–1935* (Addis Ababa, 1968). The British, French and Italian policies and contacts with the area have been dealt with by T. E. Marston, *Britain's imperial role in the Red Sea area 1800–1878* (Hamden, 1961), G. Malécot, *Les voyageurs français et les relations entre la France et l'Abyssinie de 1835 à 1870* (Paris, 1972) and C. Giglio, *L'Italia in Africa. Etiopia-Mar Rosso (1857–1885)* (Rome, 1959–72), respectively. For the Somali coast the best study is I. M. Lewis, *The modern history of Somaliland* (London, 1965).

3. THE MAGHRIB

Some of the problems of studying the history of North Africa in this period of the nineteenth century have been discussed in Douglas Johnson, 'Algeria: some problems of modern history', *Journal of African History*, 1964, **5**, 2, 221–42 and, with particular reference to the pre-colonial period and its interpretation, by M. Brett, 'Problems in the interpretation of the history of the Maghrib', *Journal of African History*, 1972, **13**, 3, 489–506. There is further discussion, together with a bibliography, in Lucette Valensi, *Le Maghreb avant la prise d'Alger* (Questions d'histoire no. 10, Paris, 1969), although this does not include Tripolitania. Bibliographies are to be found in R. L. Playfair and Brown, *Bibliography of Morocco* (1892), R. L. Playfair, *A bibliography of Algeria* (1889 and 1898), and H. S. Ashbee, *A bibliography of Tunisia* (1889). More recent bibliographies are to be found in Ch. André Julien, *Histoire de l'Algérie contemporaine*, vol. I, *La conquête et les débuts de la colonisation 1827–1871* (Paris, 1964); J.-L. Miège, *Le Maroc et l'Europe 1830–1894*, vol. I (Paris, 1961); and in a more limited sense in J. Ganiage, *Les origines du protectorat français en Tunisie, 1861–1881* (Paris, 1959). On Tripoli, one should consult R. L. Playfair, 'Bibliography of the Barbary States, Part I. Tripoli and the Cyrenaica', Royal Geographical Society, *Supplementary papers*, vol. II (1899); E. E. Evans-Pritchard, 'A select bibliography of writings on Cyrenaica', *African Studies*, September 1945 and September 1946; and the unpublished thesis by K. Folayan, 'Tripoli during the reign of Yusuf Pasha Qaramanli' (Ph.D., London, 1970).

It is natural that the main concentration of studies should have been on Algeria, its conquest and colonization, and that it should have been the work of French scholars. Thus the period of Turkish rule is described by Colombe in the collective work, *Initiation à l'Algérie* (Paris, 1957), and by Prenant, in Y. Lacoste, A. Nouschi and A. Prenant, *Algérie, passé et présent* (Paris, 1960); the problem of the population of Algeria about 1830 is surveyed by X. Yacono, in 'Peut-on évaluer la population de l'Algérie vers 1830?', *Revue africaine*, 1954, 277–307; an evaluation of Algeria at the time of the conquest is to be found in Marcel Emerit, 'L'état intellectuel et moral de l'Algérie en 1830', *Revue d'histoire moderne et contemporaine*, July–September 1954, 201–12; the actual details of the conquest of Algiers can be studied in G. Esquer, *Les commencements d'un empire. La prise d'Alger (1830)* (Paris, 1923). For studies which, whilst examining the evidence for the history of the pre-1830 period, emphasize French colonization, there are a number of detailed works which concentrate on particular regions. Thus there is R. Tinthoin, *Colonisation et évolution des genres de vie dans la région ouest d'Oran de 1830 à 1885* (Oran, 1947); J. Franc, *Le chef-d'œuvre colonial de la France en Algérie: la colonisation de la Mitidja* (Paris, 1928); P. Boyer, *L'évolution de l'Algérie médiane (ancien département d'Alger) de 1830 à 1956* (Paris, 1960); X. Yacono, *La colonisation des plaines du Chélif* (Algiers, 1955, 2 vols.); A. Nouschi, *Enquête sur le niveau de vie des populations rurales constantinoises, de la conquête jusqu'en 1919* (Paris, 1961). Other historians have taken particular periods in history, such as the resistance usually associated with 'Abd al-Qādir, which can be studied in M. Emerit, *L'Algérie à l'époque d'Abd el-Kader* (Paris, 1951), or in R. Germain, *La politique indigène de Bugeaud* (Paris, 1955). Particularly interesting themes are investigated by Yvonne Turin, *Affrontements culturels dans l'Algérie coloniale* (Paris, 1971) and H. Isnard, *La vigne en Algérie*, vol. 1 (Gap, 1947). The effects of the Franco-Prussian war and the rising associated with the name of al-Muqrānī have recently been studied by Ch. R. Ageron, *Les Algériens musulmans et la France 1871–1910* (Paris, 1968, 2 vols.).

There is no comparable body of literature for the other North African territories. A number of excellent works survey Morocco, Algeria, and Tunisia together, and place the nineteenth century in a longer perspective of history. Thus E. Albertini, G. Marçais and G. Yver, *L'Afrique du nord française dans l'histoire* (Paris, 1937), and a work by a geographer, J. Despois, *L'Afrique du Nord* (Paris, 1949). A study of colonization which extends to Libya is E. de Leone, *La colonizzazione dell'Africa del Nord* (Padua, 1957–60, 2 vols.). An even more general treatment is to be found in Jamil M. Abun-Nasr, *A history of the Maghrib* (1971), which contains a bibliography in Arabic as well as in English and French. Two English books of a general nature are S. H. Roberts, *The history of French colonial policy 1870–1925* (London, 1929) and H. I. Priestley, *France overseas: a study of modern imperialism* (New York, 1938).

For Morocco, vols. II and III of J. L. Miège, *Le Maroc et l'Europe* (Paris, 1961 and 1962), deal with the nineteenth century. For Tunisia see Ganiage (1959) and F. Arnoulet, 'La pénétration intellectuelle en Tunisie avant le protectorat', *Revue africaine*, 1954, 140–80. For some European contacts with Tripoli see A. A. Boahen, *Britain, the Sahara and the western Sudan 1788–1861* (London, 1964).

4. THE NINETEENTH-CENTURY JIHADS IN WEST AFRICA

The jihad in Hausaland

The source material, both in Arabic and Hausa, for the jihad in Hausa-land is substantial, although only a small proportion of it has been translated into European languages. A comprehensive list of the Arabic sources with information as to their present whereabouts will be found in the bibliography of M. Last, *The Sokoto caliphate* (London, 1967). A shorter list, consisting of the most important and more easily accessible Arabic sources, will be found in M. Hiskett, *The sword of truth* (New York, 1973), 'Arabic sources'. A 'List of Hausa poems', being a select list of published and unpublished Hausa sources, will be found in the same work.

The basic Arabic sources for the jihad in Hausaland are certainly the following:

1. *Infāq al-maisūr* of Sultan Muḥammad Bello. The first part of this substantial work is a biographical dictionary, which gives accounts of the lives of *'ulamā'* of the various kingdoms of the western Sudan from approximately the end of the fifteenth century down to the author's own day. There follows an account of the Shehu Usuman dan Fodio's period of peripatetic missionary work, then of the campaigns of the jihad, of the setting up of the Fulani caliphate of Sokoto, of the 'Bornu correspondence', the Shehu's writings, his children, his helpers and other incidental matters.

An unsatisfactory Arabic text, compiled under difficult wartime conditions, was published by C. E. J. Whitting (London, 1951). A more reliable Arabic text, prepared by Abubakar Gummi, was published in Cairo in 1964. The only translation in a European language is F. J. Arnett's *The rise of the Sokoto Fulani* (Kano, 1922), which is part para-phrase, part translation. It is unreliable in detail but adequate for general purposes.

2. *Tazyīn al-waraqāt* of 'Abdullāh b. Muḥammad. This is also a substantial work and is divided into two parts. The first part deals in considerable detail with the Shehu Usuman's period of itinerant missionary work before the jihad and with the events leading up to the jihad. The second part describes the campaigns of the jihad, particularly those in which the author himself took part. A critical edition of the Arabic text, together with an English translation, has been published by Hiskett (Ibadan, 1963).

3. *Iḥyā al-sunna* of 'Uthmān b. Fūdī (Usuman dan Fodio). This long

work is mainly of theological interest, and is essential for an under-standing of the doctrinal basis of the jihad in Hausaland. A short description of its form, content and significance will be found in Hiskett (1973), pp. 52–3. A critical edition of the Arabic text with an introduction in English has been prepared by I. A. S. Balogun (1967). An Arabic edition was also published in Cairo in 1962, but has not been seen by the present author. No translation in a European language exists, as far as he knows.

4. *Bayān wujūb al-hijra ʿalā al-ʿibād* of ʿUthmān b. Fūdī. A long work, which is basically a doctrinal and legal justification of the jihad in Hausaland, and a theoretical exposition of Islamic constitutional theory with special reference to the setting up of the Sokoto caliphate. It is briefly described in Hiskett (1973), pp. 119–20. A critical edition of the Arabic text with an Introduction and English translation has been prepared by F. H. El-Masri (1968).

For publication details of shorter but important works, such as ʿAbdullāh b. Muḥammad's *Idāʿ al-nusūkh*, which describes the education of Shehu Usuman dan Fodio, the *Kitāb al-farq* of the *shehu*, which succinctly sets out the legal and moral basis of his constitutional theory, and other works, see Hiskett (1973), Bibliography, section B, under Bivar, Hamet, Hiskett and Martin.

Among secondary critical studies by present-day scholars, the basic works are Last (1967), Hiskett (1973), H. A. S. Johnston, *The Fulani Empire of Sokoto* (London, 1967), and R. A. Adeleye, *Power and diplomacy in Northern Nigeria 1804–1906* (London, 1971).

The Masina jihad

The Arabic sources relating to the jihad in Masina are considerable, but almost entirely unpublished. They are preserved, for the most part, in local collections and libraries in West Africa, and are therefore not easily accessible to research workers outside West Africa. It is not practical to list them in this brief bibliographical essay: nor is it necessary, because they are listed comprehensively in W. A. Brown's Ph.D. thesis, pp. 243f., 'Arabic sources'. This thesis is available in several university libraries in USA and a xerox copy is held by the Library of the School of Oriental and African Studies of London University. The consider-able corpus of contemporary French accounts of the empire of Masina, which are of course primary sources, is also listed in the same work (pp. 248f).

Undoubtedly the most comprehensive study of the Masina jihad is still that of Amadou Hampaté Ba and Jacques Daget, *L'Empire peul du Masina*, vol. 1 (Paris, 1962), but its account is factual rather than critical. W. A. Brown's Ph.D. thesis is a valuable and more analytical study, but one which relies somewhat uncritically on oral traditions.

The jihad of al-Ḥājj 'Umar b. Sa'īd

The history of the jihad of al-Ḥājj 'Umar is better supported by accessible primary sources than is that of the jihad in Masina, but much less well than that of the jihad in Hausaland.

Twenty-one works in Arabic are attributed to al-Ḥājj 'Umar by John R. Willis in his Ph.D. thesis (1970) and are listed in that work with information as to their whereabouts. As far as I know, only two have been published.

1. *Rimāḥ ḥizb al-raḥīm 'alā nuḥūr ḥizb al-rajīm*. This substantial text has been published in an undated edition in Cairo, in the margin of the *Jawāhir al-ma'ānī* of 'Alī Ḥarāzim b. al-'Arabī. It is not a commentary on this later work, as has sometimes been suggested. The *Rimāḥ* is mainly of theological importance and, as Willis has shown, is essential for an understanding of al-Ḥājj 'Umar's doctrinal attitudes. It is also an important source for the study of Tijāni doctrines and contains a good deal of incidental information which throws light on the chronology of al-Ḥajj 'Umar's career. Unfortunately, no translation of this important work exists in a European language.

2. *Kitāb fī mā waqa'a baina shaikh 'Umar wa Aḥmad b. Aḥmad b. Aḥmad Lūbbū*. A work by this title is attributed to al-Ḥājj 'Umar by Willis (1970), who states that a version of it has been published in an Egyptian edition under the title *Al-Ḥājj 'Umar al-Fūtī sulṭān al-dawla al-Tijāniyya bi-gharb afriqiyya shai' min jihādihi wa ta'rīkh ḥayātihi*. This work has not been seen by the author of this chapter.

The other major Arabic works relating to al-Ḥājj 'Umar's jihad are unpublished at the present time, as far as is known. Students of this jihad are advised to consult Willis (1970) for further information.

Of Western scholarly writings Willis (1970) is certainly the most comprehensive, particularly as regards the sources and nature of al-Ḥājj 'Umar's doctrines. Also useful is B. Olatunji Ọlọruntimẹhin, *The Segu Tukolor Empire, 1848–1893* (1972). See also articles by B. G. Martin and Willis, and the early study by Jules Salenc in the Bibliography to this volume. Information on al-Ḥājj 'Umar's relations with the French will be found in M. E. Mage's *Voyage dans le Soudan occidentale* (Paris, 1868) and in official French archives listed by Willis (1970). Finally, a major work probably to be entitled 'Studies in West African history' is being prepared under the editorship of Willis, and contains a chapter on al-Ḥājj 'Umar as well as other chapters relating to the period of the jihads in West Africa. It is expected that this work will shortly be published in London.

5. FREED SLAVE COLONIES IN WEST AFRICA

The two basic sources for the history of Sierra Leone in this period are Christopher Fyfe, *A history of Sierra Leone* (London, 1962), and *Sierra Leone inheritance* (London, 1964), a book of documents. They should be supplemented by John Peterson, *Province of freedom: a history of Sierra Leone, 1787–1870* (London, 1969), a historical study of the Sierra Leone recaptive community; by Stiv Jakobsson, *Am I not a man and a brother?* (Uppsala, 1972), which concentrates on the Christian missions; by Arthur Porter, *Creoledom* (London, 1963), a sociological study of the development of Freetown society; and by N. A. Cox-George, *Finance and Development in West Africa: the Sierra Leone experience* (London, 1961), a pioneer survey of economic history. Every work on West African economic history published before 1973 needs to be reconsidered in the light of A. G. Hopkins's epoch-making *An economic history of West Africa* (London, 1973).

E. Ade Ijagbemi's doctoral thesis 'A history of the Temne in the nineteenth century' (University of Edinburgh, 1968), rewritten as *Rivalry and diplomacy on the Rokel: a history of Sierra Leone, 1816–87* (forthcoming), and his articles, 'The Rokel river and the development of inland trade in Sierra Leone', *Odu*, 1970, **3**, 45–70, 'The Freetown colony and the development of legitimate trade in the adjoining territories', *Journal of the Historical Society of Nigeria*, 1970, **5**, 2, 243–56, and 'The Kossoh war, 1838–41', *Journal of the Historical Society of Nigeria*, 1971, **5**, 4, 549–64, cover the same period of Sierra Leone history from the standpoint of the Temne.

J. M. Gray, *A history of the Gambia* (Cambridge, 1940), though written from a strictly European standpoint, remains the best published source for the history of the Gambia at this period. Florence K. Mahoney's unpublished doctoral thesis, 'Government and opinion in the Gambia, 1816–1901' (University of London, 1963), gives a more Gambia-centred account.

An outline history of the Sierra Leone Creole diaspora in Yorubaland may be found in Jean H. Kopytoff, *A preface to modern Nigeria: the 'Sierra Leoneans' in Yoruba, 1830–1890* (Madison, 1965). It should be supplemented by J. F. Ade Ajayi, *Christian missions in Nigeria 1841–91* (London, 1965), and two books by E. A. Ayandele, *The missionary impact on modern Nigeria, 1842–1914* (London, 1966), and his biography of Bishop James Johnson, *Holy Johnson* (London, 1970). Ayandele's *The educated elite in the Nigerian society* (Ibadan, 1974) is a devastating critique of Creole influence in Nigeria.

C. H. Huberich, *The political and legislative history of Liberia* (New York, 1947) is still the most authoritative printed source for the early history of Liberia. P. J. Staudenraus, *The African colonization movement 1816–65* (New York, 1961) also provides detailed information on the early period, as do Svend E. Holsoe, 'A study of relations between settlers and indigenous peoples in Western Liberia, 1821–47', *African Historical Studies*, 1971, 4, 2, 331–62, and Tom W. Schick, 'A quantitative analysis of Liberian colonization from 1820 to 1843', *Journal of African History*, 1971, 12, 1, 45–60. Penelope Campbell, *Maryland in Africa* (Chicago, 1971) outlines the history of the Maryland settlement from an American standpoint. Abayomi Karnga, *History of Liberia* (Liverpool, 1926) is a brief pioneer survey by a Liberian historian.

French colonial policy in West Africa during the mid-nineteenth century is analysed in Bernard Schnapper, *La politique et le commerce français dans le Golfe de Guinée de 1838 à 1871* (Paris, 1961). Hubert Deschamps, 'Quinze ans de Gabon: les débuts de l'établissement français, 1839–1853', *Revue française d'Outre-Mer*, 1963, 50, 283–345, and 1965, 52, 92–126, and Guy Lasserre, *Libreville: la ville et sa région* (Paris, 1958), give information on the Libreville settlement.

6. WEST AFRICA IN THE ANTI-SLAVE TRADE ERA

Nineteenth-century West Africa has been a major focus of scholarly research. There are, however, very few general syntheses. Probably the best survey is to be found in Hargreaves (1963). Hopkins (1973) generally, and chapter 4 in particular, provides a significant analysis of the economic data. In contrast to the emphasis here on the continuities of the nineteenth century with the past, Hopkins stresses the revolutionary nature of the European impact on the West African economy. Apart from such syntheses, one depends on collaborative works such as the collection of social anthropological essays on West African kingdoms in the nineteenth century edited by Forde and Kaberry (1967) or volume II of *A history of West Africa* edited by Ajayi and Crowder (1974) containing ten chapters by different specialist authors on the nineteenth century before the European conquest.

On the internal history of different pre-colonial West African polities in this period, there are the chapters in Ajayi and Crowder (1974) and several monographs of which only a sample can be referred to here. On Bornu, Brenner (1973); on Hausaland and the Sokoto caliphate, Last (1967) and Adelẹyẹ (1971); on Yorubaland, Ajayi and Smith (1964) and Akintoye (1971); on Benin, Ryder (1969); on the Niger delta, Dike (1956) and Jones (1963); on the Asante and Fante states, Boahen (1974); on Masina, Hampaté Ba and Daget (1962) and Brown (1968); on the Tukulor empire, Ọlọruntimẹhin (1972); on Senegambia, Wane (1969) and Barry (1972). The emphasis of scholars so far has been largely on the history of political institutions, structures of centralized states, major rulers, military and religious leaders. There are some very conspicuous gaps. Non-Muslim peoples on the fringes of the Bornu and the Fulani emirates in Hausaland are receiving initial studies in doctoral theses; there are at the moment few surveys or syntheses published. The same is true of Iboland in the nineteenth century. Ross (1967) on Dahomey needs to be brought up to date and published. The Ewe in the nineteenth century have received little attention. There is as yet no adequate study published on Liberia, either of the Americo-Liberian settlers or of the indigenous states and peoples. The hinterland of the Ivory Coast and Guinea outside the Dyula empire of Samori has been neglected.

Islam and Christianity as religious factors have been stressed, but in comparison traditional religions have received little attention. There is emphasis on Islam as the main, if not exclusive force in the rise of new polities throughout the Western Sudan. The histories of Hausaland and Bornu, Masina and the Tukulor empire cited above are seen largely as a history of Islam, Muslim leaders and Islamic ideas in these states. Christianity on the other hand – see Groves (1957), Ajayi (1965), Peterson (1969) – is more easily discernible as only one factor, along with European trade and politics, operating within European enclaves on the fringes of traditional states along the coast and in the forest areas. However, apart from the factor of religious change, other aspects of social history have so far in comparison tended to be neglected. The work of al-Naqar (1972) on the pilgrimage is of special interest. The history of education, changing concepts of law, morality and the family are potentially fruitful fields. That is why published accounts of nineteenth-century European travellers remain valuable, even though none rivals Barth (1860) in the ability of the traveller to observe thoroughly and perceptively, and record accurately. Such travellers' accounts and oral tradition remain some of our best sources on the institution of domestic slavery, which loomed so large in the nineteenth century, but has as yet received little study in depth by scholars.

Apart from the work of Christian missionaries already referred to, European trading and expansionist activities along the coast have received much scholarly attention. This theme looms large in studies of the coastal states referred to above. In addition, Lloyd (1949) and Mannix and Cowley (1962) discuss the Atlantic slave trade and the naval struggle to end it. Staudenraus (1961) discusses the American colonization movement that led to the foundation of Liberia, while Fyfe (1962) discusses Sierra Leone from all aspects. Hardy (1921) remains a good study of early French efforts at colonization on the Senegal in the nineteenth century.

The slave trade and the struggle to end it and replace it with 'legitimate' trade have featured prominently in innumerable studies of European activities and Euro-African relationships in West Africa. Yet the slave trade, abolition and legitimate trade remain very controversial subjects, because data are scarce and few detailed economic studies have so far been attempted for the pre-colonial nineteenth century. Abolition has been described as a 'distorted theme'. This is perhaps because the slave trade is usually studied without a basic framework of the economic history of West Africa. Hopkins (1973) has made a bold start in trying to establish this framework. But his is a pioneer effort. He has attempted to make a survey of West African economic history in one volume. But the detailed study of different localities, different epochs, different commodities, etc., on which a synthesis can be based is only just being undertaken, e.g. Polanyi (1966), Meillassoux (1971). In the absence of enough of such studies, generalization is difficult. At any rate, it seems more satisfactory to explain nineteenth-century economic phenomena in the context of the political power structure, than vice versa.

7. THE FOREST AND THE SAVANNA OF CENTRAL AFRICA

Historical research in Central Africa has lagged far behind the work done in eastern Africa, and even further behind that done in western Africa. Although nine university-type institutions of higher education were established in the region during the 1960s, not much was done to encourage historical research till about 1970. Until then, historical investigation was sponsored either by local research institutes which mostly specialized in anthropology, or by foreign universities, whose scholars were often restricted in the type of evidence to which they had access. Scholars in both these traditions have tended to neglect the nineteenth century and to concentrate on the three popular topics of sixteenth-century Kongo, early colonial exploitation, and mid-twentieth-century political upheavals. There is, nevertheless, a wealth of nineteenth-century primary data waiting to be worked over. Most accessible, and often very rewarding, is the travel literature of men such as Burton, Du Chaillu (Gabon), Peschel-Loesche (Loango), Bastian (Kongo), Monteiro (Angola), Magyar (Ovimbundu), Pogge (Lunda), Livingstone, Silva Pôrto, Bateman (Kasai), Cameron, Schweinfurth, Wissman, Gamitto (Kazembe), few of whose diaries, with the striking exception of the last one, have been adequately republished or annotated.

The second major category of published evidence derives from ethnographic works of the twentieth century. The writers show varying degrees of historical interest, but even those with quite a limited time-scale can give useful insights into societies as they survived into the colonial period. Others give deliberate and extensive reference to the oral traditions and historical charters of the people they study. Many ethnographic studies have been the work of missionaries or colonial administrators, stationed for years at a time in societies which they tried to understand. Other, more recent, works have been the products of fully trained anthropologists. These scholars include Childs (Ovimbundu), Estermann (south-west Angola), White (north-west Zambia), Soret (French Congo), Laman (Kongo), Raponda-Walker (Gabon), Moeller (north-east Zaïre), Vansina (Kuba), Verhulpen (Luba), Colson (Tonga), Van der Kerken (Mongo), Duysters (Lunda).

The third major category of historical data available in Central Africa is archival material. As yet these archives have been but superficially used. There is, however, a well-established scholarly tradition which has led to the publication, and in some cases microfilming, of selected documents with a greater or lesser degree of historical assessment and comment. The best-known collections are those of Paiva-Manso (Kongo), Jadin (Kongo), Albuquerque Felner (southern Angola), Brásio (Holy Ghost Mission), Oliveira (Angola) and Bontinck (Congo Independent State). There remain, however, enormous quantities of nineteenth-century archival materials, particularly concerning local government in the proto-colonial communities of Angola, which have barely been touched. For the third quarter of the nineteenth century, the mission archives are of great importance, and the records of both old slave-trading houses and new legitimate trading-houses are in some cases still extant.

The fourth source of raw evidence is the oral information preserved by each community. It is even more abundant than the almost virgin archives, yet it has been even less studied. Some of the pioneering work on oral history, and indeed the premier methodological guide, were produced by Jan Vansina in Zaïre, but there has been only a most limited follow-up to his efforts. The major disincentive to this kind of field work has been the more than usually perturbed politics of most Central African countries in the 1960s.

Finally one must consider the products of modern research. In the bibliography of his magisterial *Kingdoms of the savanna* (Madison), drawn up in 1963–4, Vansina listed some 550 entries, of which less than a dozen articles, pamphlets or chapters could be described as original historical research relating to the period from 1790 to 1870. Since then important new research has been undertaken, and several major studies appeared after this chapter was drafted. Leading works, only some of which were taken into account in revising the text, include Joseph C. Miller, 'Kasanje', in F. W. Heimer, *Social change in Angola* (Munich, 1973), K. D. Patterson, *The northern Gabon coast to 1875* (Oxford, 1975), Pierre Kalck, *Histoire de la République centrafricaine* (Paris, 1974), J. L. Vellut (Lunda, 1972), A. D. Roberts (Bemba, 1973), Mutumba Mainga (Lozi, 1973), Phyllis Martin (Loango, 1972), Jan Vansina (Teke-Tyo, 1973). The earlier secondary sources included Auguste Verbeken (Msiri, 1956), Roger Anstey (British trade, 1962), Hubert Deschamps (Gabon, 1965), Pierre Alexandre (the Fang, 1965), Éric de Dampierre (Bangassou, 1967), Joseph C. Miller (Chokwe, 1970), Georges Mazenot (French Congo, 1970).

8. EAST AFRICA: THE EXPANSION OF COMMERCE

Oral traditions and chronicles

The main documentation for East African history before 1870 comes from oral traditions, and every historian of the period is nowadays expected to contribute to its collection. Unfortunately few researchers have been able to make their collections available. Notable exceptions include G. S. Were's *Western Kenya historical texts* (Nairobi, 1967),

A. Coupez, *Textes historiques du Rwanda*, and R. M. Maxon's 'Gusii historical texts' in the West Virginia University Library. In the meantime we are dependent for indigenous sources upon the chronicles.

The Swahili chronicles of the coast such as those of Pate, Mombasa, Lamu, those collected by Velten *c.* 1900, Abdallah bin Hemedi's *Kilindi*, and Razik's *History of the Imams and Seyyids of Oman*, 1871, have been analysed and criticized for some time. Important chronicles appear in G. S. P. Freeman-Grenville's *The East African coast: select documents* (Oxford, 1962).

The interlacustrine region also possesses a rich store of chronicles. Three major ones have been published in European languages: A. Coupez and T. Kamanzi, *Récits historiques du Rwanda* . . . (Tervuren, 1962), Apolo Kaggwa's *Basekabaka*, edited by M. Kiwanuka as *The kings of Buganda* (Nairobi, 1971) and J. W. Nyakatura's *Abakama*, edited by G. Uzoigwe as *The anatomy of an African kingdom* (New York, 1973). A. Kagwa's *Empisa (Customs)* (Kampala, 1905), *Ebika (Clans)* (Kampala, 1908), and *Nsenene* (Kampala, n.d.), are also important, as is Nyakatura's *Aspects of Bunyoro customs and traditions* (Nairobi, 1970). There are many other chronicles in the vernacular languages, such as Nsimbi and Kabuga on Buganda, Lubogo on Busoga, Lwamgira on Kiziba, Bikunya on Bunyoro, Karabanga on Toro, Katate and Kamugungunu on Nkore, Mugenyi and Rwakishana on Mpororo, Kagame on Rwanda, Osogo on the Baluya, Ngologoza on Kigezi, Anywar, Malandra and Okech on Acholi, Ogwah on Lango, Ekadu on Kumam, Mayegu on the Bamasaba, and Kabeya on Mirambo.

The coast

Unpublished sources for the history of Zanzibar and the coast in the nineteenth century include the British Foreign Office records (F.O. 84), the secretariat archives in Zanzibar, and the Kirk papers. Published material includes the British and Foreign State Papers from 1839, the three volumes of Guillain's *Documents sur l'histoire, la géographie et le commerce de l'Afrique orientale* (Paris, 1857) relating to French activities, Burton's book on Zanzibar published in 1872, the Rigby report on the Zanzibari dominions of 1861, and *Selections from the records of the Bombay Government*, 1856. The amount of conventional documentary material has led to a flow of secondary works on Zanzibar: F. B. Pearce, *The island metropolis of eastern Africa* (London, 1920), W. H. Ingrams, *The dialects of the Zanzibar sultanate* (London, 1924), and *Zanzibar: its history and its people* (London, 1931), R. H. Crofton, *The old consulate at Zanzibar* (London, 1935), L. M. Russell, ed., *General Rigby, Zanzibar and the slave trade* (London, 1935), R. Coupland's *East Africa and its invaders* (Oxford, 1938) and *The exploitation of East Africa* (1939), L. W. Hollingsworth, *Zanzibar under the Foreign Office* (London, 1953), J. E. E. Craster, *Pemba: the spice island of Zanzibar* (London, 1913), J. S. Kirkman, *The Arab city of Gedi: excavations at the Great Mosque* (London, 1954), J. M. Gray, *The British in Mombasa 1824–1826* (London, 1957), A. H. J. Prins, *The Swahili-speaking peoples of Zanzibar and the East African coast* (London, 1961), and the best history of Zanzibar to the death of Sayyid Sa'īd Gray's *History of Zanzibar* (London, 1962).

Travellers' accounts

The Oxford *History of East Africa*, vol. 1 (1963) has a comprehensive listing of travel accounts and publications relating to them. Travellers within the central region, and the date of publication of their major works include: Burton (1860), Speke (1863), Grant (1864), Livingstone (1874), Stanley (1872, 1878 and 1890) and Hore (1892). For the Masai, Christie's *Cholera epidemics* (1876) and Thomson's *Through Masai land* (1885) are particularly useful. For the northern regions, Baker (1867 and 1874), Thomson (1881), Schweinfurth (1873), Cassati (1891 and 1898), Stuhlmann (1894) and Von Höhnel (1894) are the most cited. In Rwanda and Burundi, Baumann (1894), Duke Adolphus Frederick's *In the heart of Africa* (1910) and R. Kandt's *Caput Nili* (1919) are outstanding. Care must be taken to separate what the traveller observed from his interpretation of it, what he is reporting directly from the people concerned as against the report of one people about another. J. L. Krapf's *Travels, researches and missionary labours* (London, 1860) set an early, but seldom equalled, model of careful observation.

The travellers are often quoted for the oral traditions which they recorded. Some historians are inclined to the view that these accounts have greater accuracy than later chronicles by African authors because they were less contaminated by political considerations. This suggests that there were few political considerations in the nineteenth century, and must be balanced against the casual method of collection and the biases through which travellers often filtered the information gathered from Africans. Reliance upon these accounts can have the effect of delaying further collection of oral traditions in some areas, and of prolonging the preoccupations of historians with issues of major concern to aliens.

Historiography

In general colonial writers did not show great interest in East African history before the colonial period. In the interlacustrine region there was some concern about origins, and, following Speke and the White Fathers, the concept of Hamitic origins figured in the works of Roscoe, J. Gorju's *Entre le Victoria* . . . (Rennes, 1920) and *Face au royaume hamite du Ruanda: le royaume frère de l'Urundi* (Brussels, 1938) and Pagès's *Un royaume Hamite: le Ruanda* (Brussels, 1933). According to such theories the Bahima-Batutsi were of Ethiopian type, and they or their institutions had spread from western Uganda to most chiefly peoples, such as those in the Ntemi area of Tanzania. Even as late as 1957, J. C. D. Lawrance in *The Iteso* (London) was urging colonial consideration for the Iteso because they were partly Hamitic. R. B. Fisher's *Twilight tales of the black Baganda* (London, 1911) are useful to the historian as coming directly from known African sources.

'Ethnography was king' during much of the colonial period, and most ethnographers paid some attention to history. Roscoe was probably the most prolific author, with five books between 1911 and 1924. Other writers include Rehse on Kiziba (1910), Driberg on the Lango (1923), de Lacger on Rwanda (1940), Bourgeois on Rwanda and Burundi (1953–8), Bösch (1930) and Blohm (1831–3) on the Nyamwezi, Claus on the Gogo (1911), Nigmann on the Hehe (1908) and the Culwicks on the Bena (1935). Just as the Kenya area was poorly served by chronicles and travellers' accounts, Europeans in Kenya were preoccupied in the colonial period with the settler society of whites, but books which might be noted include Hollis on the Masai (1905) and Nandi (1909), Lindblom on the Kamba (1920), Boyes (1911) and Cagnolo (1933) on the Kikuyu. The Tanzanian area possesses one source unequalled in any other East African country, the Tanganyika 'District Books' – especially in their sections on 'Tribal history and records' – begun in 1923, and added to in later years. The ethnographic preoccupations of the colonial period culminated with the publication in the 1950s of the *Ethnographic survey of Africa*. It is unfortunate for historians that such work seems now out of fashion. Probably the most valuable contributions of the colonial period were the *Uganda Journal* and *Tanganyika Notes and Records* which contain many historical articles often of unique value for particular peoples.

The 1950s and early 1960s was a transition period from colonial preoccupations and set the stage for modern East African historiography. The new trend was marked by the frequent use of the word 'history' in the titles of works such as Lambert on the Kikuyu (1950), d'Arianoff's *Histoire des Bagesera* (1952), Southall's 'Alur tradition and its historical significance' (1954), Oliver's 'Traditional histories' (1955), Cory's *History of Bukoba* (1958), as well as by the historical concerns of D. A. Low, Southall's *Alur society* (1953), Crazzolara's *The Lwoo* (1950–4) and Stahl's *Chagga* (1964). From these beginnings, and especially for the Ugandan area, have come such newer and useful works as H. F. Morris's *A history of Ankole* (Kampala, 1962), A. R. Dunbar's *A history of Bunyoro-Kitara* (Nairobi, 1965), Karugire's *Nkore* (1971), D. W. Cohen's *The historical tradition of Busoga: Mukama and Kintu* (Oxford, 1972), M. S. M. Kiwanuka's *Buganda* (1971) and *A history of Kigezi* edited by Denoon (1972). The publication of the *Oxford History of East Africa*, vol. I, edited by R. Oliver and G. Mathew, in 1963 may be regarded as a summation of the new historical scholarship of the transition period, helping to lead into the modern outburst of historical writing.

The modern period of historiography opened with the publication in 1967 of B. A. Ogot's *History of the Southern Luo* (Nairobi), a work based almost entirely on his own collection of oral traditions from a non-centralized society with no important published chronicles or travellers' accounts. Ogot's work was based on collation and analysis of 'mass tradition', which opened up the possibility to historians of moving outside the traditional centralized states, with their specialist institutions for preserving historical evidence.

With the foundation of universities in Nairobi and Dar es Salaam, new historical advances were made, most dramatically in Tanzania, where the long-standing preoccupation with the coast was abandoned for a thrust into the interior, often in group projects such as I. Katoke's 'Lake kingdoms'. In 1968 three important works appeared, Kimambo's *A political history of the Pare* (Nairobi, 1969), *Tanzania before 1900*, edited by A. Roberts (Nairobi, 1968) and *A history of Tanzania*, edited by I. N. Kimambo and A. J. Temu (Nairobi, 1969). The Historical Association of Tanzania also began publishing historical pamphlets. In Rwanda historians moved to greater critical analysis of royal traditions, and to consider non-royal sources in more detail. The new trend was led by J. Vansina's *L'évolution du royaume Rwanda* (Brussels, 1961) and continued by L. de Heusch, *Le Rwanda et la civilisation interlacustre* (Brussels, 1966), J. J. Maquet, *The premise of inequality in Rwanda* (London, 1961), and M. d'Hertefelt, *Les clans du Rwanda ancien* (Tervuren, 1971).

Kenya has never had a definite focus in historiography, partly because of disparity of research interests; no other country in East Africa has been as prolific as Kenya in its output of journals, monographs and books. In addition to Ogot's work noted above special attention should be given to G. S. Were, *A history of the Abaluyia of western Kenya* (Nairobi, 1967), and *Zamani* (1968), edited by Ogot and Kieran. Scholars should also consult *Ngano*, the *Transafrican Journal of History*, the *Hadith* series and the *Kenya Historical Review*.

9. THE NGUNI OUTBURST

The importance of this subject was recognized early in the development of South African historiography by George McCall Theal, who for all his strongly pro-settler attitude paid serious attention to the activities of African peoples as a significant element in the history of South Africa. Thereafter, preoccupation with the activities and conflicts of the two white 'races', itself a reflection of the racial status structure of South African society, led to the activities of African peoples being relegated to a very subordinate role in historical works.

Such serious study of the history of African societies and the nature of African polities as was undertaken was the province of the compiler of traditions and the social anthropologist rather than the professional historian. To these we are indebted for such great compilations of tradition as D. F. Ellenberger's and J. C. Macgregor's *History of the Basuto, ancient and modern* (London, 1912), A. T. Bryant's *Olden times in Zululand and Natal* (Cape Town, 1965), and J. H. Soga's *The south-eastern Bantu* (Johannesburg, 1930) which, in spite of all the work that has been undertaken since, remain key sources of traditional evidence, much of which has subsequently been forgotten or distorted by more recent developments.

To the social anthropologists we owe such fundamental works of socio-political analysis as I. Schapera's *Government and politics in tribal societies* (London, 1965) and his more specific studies of the Tswana, M. Gluckman's analysis of the Zulu kingdom in Fortes and Evans-Pritchard's *African political systems* (London, 1940), J. Barnes's outstanding study of the Ngoni kingdom of Mpezeni, *Politics in a changing society* (London, 1954), and A. J. Hughes's *Kin, caste and nation among the Rhodesian Ndebele* (Manchester, 1956), to mention just a few of what remain classic studies in spite of subsequently perceived new perspectives and interpretations.

In recent years the revolution in African historiography, which has taken place with the waning of the colonial era and the emergence of independent African nations, has drawn attention to the significance of the history of African peoples and this has begun to spread to the study of South African history. The place accorded to the study of African societies in the *Oxford History of South Africa* is perhaps an expression of this. Omer-Cooper's *Zulu aftermath*, published in 1966, has been followed by a great deal of further work, much of it by scholars from the University of California, Los Angeles, and the School of Oriental and African Studies, London. M. Legassick has studied the Griqua and W. Lye has analysed the *Difaqane* in the Sotho/Tswana area, while Alan Smith has worked on the history of the peoples of southern Mozambique. In 1968 papers bringing together much of the current work in this general area were presented to a conference at the University of Zambia, sponsored by the University of California, Los Angeles. A number of these were subsequently published under the editorship of Leonard Thompson in *African societies in southern Africa* (London, 1969).

In 1967 Gerhard Liesegang produced the first serious study of the Gaza kingdom, using Portuguese documentation, *Beiträge zur Geschichte des Reiches der Gaza Ngoni im südlichen Moçambique*.

Work is currently being undertaken by students from the School of Oriental and African Studies, London, on the genesis of the process of state formation among the Northern Nguni peoples, the history of the Sotho and Swazi kingdoms, of African polities between the eastern frontier of the Cape colony and Natal, and of the Griqua states. Other scholars are attempting to deepen our historical knowledge and understanding of the Ngoni kingdoms in Malawi, Zambia and Tanzania.

Apart from the studies being undertaken of peoples who played an active role in the upheavals of the Nguni outburst, our knowledge of the whole complex process is being further illuminated by new work on peoples who felt the impact of the disturbances. Among such studies are A. Roberts's work on the Bemba, M. Bull's study of the Lozi kingdom, H. Langworthy's examination of the Chewa kingdom of Undi, and T. Tlou's study of the Tswana of Lake Ngami. The general area with which this chapter is concerned is thus one of intense research activity at the present time. Much more, however, still remains to be undertaken. The student of any of the facets of this wide ranging subject will find fascinating questions still unexplored and relatively abundant material at his disposal. The dramatic process of political change, migration and state formation is so relatively recent that, in addition to the compilations of tradition already made or in the process of being collected, much still remains unrecorded in the living traditions of the people involved. Furthermore it took place at a time when Europeans were beginning to penetrate the heart of the African continent, with the result that some of the crucial phases of the process were observed by European witnesses, like the English traders who settled in Natal during the reign of Shaka, or the missionary Moffat, who became the close friend of Mzilikazi. The researcher thus has the rare advantage in pre-colonial African history of being able to compare and interrelate the evidence of oral tradition with the written testimony of contemporary European observers. Much of this written evidence, notably in the Orange Free State and Transvaal archives, in the records of the German occupation of Tanganyika, and in the papers of Andrew Smith and others in the Killie Campbell collection in Natal, is still far from adequately exploited.

10. COLONIAL SOUTH AFRICA AND ITS FRONTIERS

The history of white settlement and expansion in South Africa in the nineteenth century is incomparably the best documented field of study for this period in African history.

In addition to the rich published and unpublished record material of the metropolitan government, there are those of Cape Colony, Natal and the trekker republics. This huge volume of official material, much of it available in printed compilations, can be supplemented by information published in the contemporary Dutch and English language newspapers, and by the journals, diaries and letters of trekkers, English settlers, traders and missionaries. The views of outside observers can be gleaned from the accounts of temporary visitors, travellers and explorers.

Not only is the subject heavily documented, it has also been much studied. The interested reader has at his disposal the voluminous works of George McCall Theal which, however out of date in interpretation and irritating for their lack of references, remain classics of South African historiography. There is also the voluminous study by George Cory covering the period down to 1853, *The rise of South Africa* (Cape Town, 1956). An encyclopaedic compendium of factual material is available in E. Walker's *A history of southern Africa* (London, 1965). There is the sixth volume of the *Cambridge history of the British Empire*, and now the two-volume *Oxford history of South Africa*. Such general works are supplemented by a wide range of studies of more limited scope in both English and Afrikaans. Among the more significant of these germane to the subject of this chapter are W. M. Macmillan's *Bantu, Boer and Briton* (Oxford, 1963), S. D. Neumark's *Economic influences on the South African frontier* (Stanford, 1957), MacCrone's classic study of the early development of racial stratification and attitudes, *Race attitudes in South Africa* (London, 1937). Also invaluable for the period leading up to the Great Trek is Van der Merwe's *Die noordwaartse beweging van die Boere voor die Groot Trek* (The Hague, 1937). On the Great Trek itself, E. Walker's *The Great Trek* (London, 1934) remains the best overall study, while the period between the Great Trek and the British occupation of the Transvaal is the subject of two of the greatest works of South African historiography, De Kiewiet's *British colonial policy and the South African republics* (London, 1929) and his *The imperial factor in South Africa* (Cambridge, 1937). On the expansion of the Transvaal settlement into the Tswana area, J. A. I. Agar-Hamilton's *The road to the north* (London, 1937) is unrivalled. For Natal we have the works of Hattersley and more recently Brookes and Webb, *A history of Natal* (Pietermaritzburg). A large series of detailed monographs is to be found in the volumes of the *Archives Yearbook for South African History*. Amongst these are some valuable monographs in Afrikaans dealing with the early settlement and development of the Transvaal, an area as yet very inadequately covered in English works on South African history.

In spite of the preoccupation of South African historiography with the activities of the white groups, and in spite of the great volume of published works on the subject, however, there is a sense in which the study of the subject of white expansion and settlement in South Africa can be said to have hardly begun. With very few exceptions the studies which have been made of this topic have not been informed by the new perspectives, by the concern for social and economic analysis, which have illuminated the recent historiography of Britain and Europe and of Africa north of the Zambezi. So far as these approaches have been applied to South African history in recent years it has been mainly to the history of the African peoples that this has been done. Paradoxically in spite of the relative neglect which the history of these societies has suffered until recently, in comparison with that of the whites, we now probably know more about the inner dynamics of the Zulu and Sotho kingdoms than of South African white polities. Such topics as the relationship between kinship and neighbourhood groupings, and the pattern of political power and segmentation in the Transvaal Boer community, for example, are still untouched. In the same way the study of white expansion and settlement in relation to patterns of land tenure and utilization, and the complex interaction of white and African initiatives, is only in its infancy. Looked at from these points of view, the subject matter covered by this chapter constitutes a field wide open for further research and one abundantly stocked with the documentary resources on which such inquiries could be based.

11. TRADITION AND CHANGE IN MADAGASCAR, 1790–1870

The primary source-materials for the 1790 to 1870 period of Malagasy history are both numerous and rich, but they have never been fully utilized by researchers. The Archives Royales section of the Archives de la République Malgache in Tananarive contains a large amount of material dating back to the reign of the Merina monarch Radama I (r. 1810–28), and access to the classified holdings is not difficult for accredited scholars. There is no comprehensive guide to each of the individual documentary series, though one is presently being compiled by the archival staff. Until such time as it is ready, Jean Valette, *Les archives de Madagascar* (Abbeville, 1962), must serve in its place. Of particular importance for the history of Madagascar are the writings of Raombana, a Malagasy educated in England by the London Missionary Society. Raombana's works, written in English and later translated into French, consist of a history of the kingdom of Imerina and its sovereigns, as well as a personal journal. They are housed in the archives of the Académie Malgache in Tananarive. Robert Lyall, British representative at the Merina court, was present at a time when both monarchs and attitudes were changing, and he kept a brief but important account of his stay in the island between 1828 and 1829. His original journal is in the British Museum, while a copy is in the Mauritius archives. The archives of the London Missionary Society contain considerable material on the social, economic, and political, as well as the religious history of the island from 1818, the year when Christianity was introduced. Two Anglican missionary societies, the Church Missionary Society and the Society for the Propagation of the Gospel in Foreign Parts, began work on the island in 1864, and thus their holdings for this period are not extensive. The Quaker Friends' Foreign Missions Association also entered Imerina in the 1860s, but in 1922 most of the records up to 1917 were destroyed by fire. The archives of Great Britain and France also serve as important sources of information on Madagascar before 1870.

The works of foreign travellers and residents provide valuable material on all aspects of life in Madagascar. Two early travellers to the island were B. F. Leguével de Lacombe and M. Guillain. Lacombe's *Voyage à Madagascar et aux Comores, 1823 à 1830* (Paris, 1840), is a rather imaginative work, while Guillain's *Documents sur l'histoire, la géographie et le commerce de la partie occidentale de Madagascar* (Paris, 1845) serves as an important source of information for the west coast and Sakalava country. Ida Pfeiffer, the world traveller, came to Madagascar in 1857, and later published a description of the island in an account entitled *The last travels of Ida Pfeiffer* (London, 1881). Another account of the island was produced by A. Vinson, author of *Voyage à Madagascar* (Paris, 1865). The first explorer to describe Madagascar in detail, however, was Alfred Grandidier (1836–1921). A scholar with rather catholic tastes, Grandidier devoted his life to gathering information for his massive *Histoire physique, naturelle et politique de Madagascar*, 38 vols. (Paris and Tananarive, 1875–1958). His work was continued by his son Guillaume Grandidier (1873–1957). Some insight into life in Madagascar during the reign of Queen Ranavalona I (r. 1828–61) may be gained from a reading of J. J. Freeman and D. Johns, *A narrative of the persecutions of the Christians in Madagascar* (London, 1840), and the Reverend William Ellis, *Three visits to Madagascar* (London, 1858). Another work by Ellis, *Madagascar revisited* (London, 1867), deals with the island under Radama II (r. 1861–3) and Rasoherina (r. 1863–8). A number of his missionary companions also wrote on Madagascar, but the most valuable pieces were produced by the Reverend James Sibree. An acute observer of local life, Sibree was the author of *Madagascar and its people* (London, 1870), and *The great African island: chapters on Madagascar* (London, 1880). Both continue to serve as basic works for the period.

One of the earliest histories of the island was William Ellis's *History of Madagascar* (London, 1838), but the principal work is that of the Reverend François Callet, *Tantara ny Andriana eto Madagaiskara*, 3 vols. (Antananarivo, 1872, 1875, 1883), later translated as *Histoire des rois*, 4 vols. (Tananarive, 1953–8). Victor Malzac, *Histoire du royaume hova depuis ses origines jusqu'à sa fin* (Paris, 1912), was a summary of the former work, written from the standpoint of the dominant Merina peoples. Guillaume Grandidier, *Histoire physique, naturelle et politique de Madagascar*, vol. v, tomes I–III (Paris and Tananarive, 1942–58), is still a useful series, and was considered the standard work on Madagascar until Hubert Deschamps published his *Histoire de Madagascar* (Paris,

1960). In 1966 Édouard Ralaimihoatra introduced his own *Histoire de Madagascar* (Tananarive). Deschamps, a former colonial administrator who served in Madagascar, deals with the history of the island in the succinct style of a European historian. Ralaimihoatra on the other hand employs a more traditional style of historiography, and places more emphasis on the pre-colonial period and the non-Merina peoples.

A body of literature on special aspects of Malagasy history began to appear in the 1860s. Many missionaries gathered material on the various ethnic groups in the island, and some useful articles appeared in the *Antananarivo Annual*. A comprehensive and in-depth study is Alfred Grandidier's *Ethnographie de Madagascar*, Paris, 1875–1928, which is a part of his *Histoire physique, naturelle et politique de Madagascar*. After he began to publish the results of his research, a flurry of articles on the ethnography of the peoples of Madagascar began to appear in various learned journals, especially the *Bulletin de l'Académie Malgache*. Useful works on Malagasy ethnography are the Reverend P. Dubois, *Monographie des Betsileo* (Paris, 1938), Hubert Deschamps, *Les migrations intérieures passées et presentes à Madagascar* (Paris, 1959), and Raymond Decary's two studies, *La mort et les coutumes funéraires à Madagascar* (Paris, 1962), and *Mœurs et coutumes des Malgaches* (Paris, 1951). Richard Andriamanjato, *Le Tsiny et le Tody dans la pensée malgache* (Paris, 1957), and Jorgen Rudd, *Taboo: a study of Malagasy customs and beliefs* (London and Oslo, 1960), are both basic for an understanding of traditional Malagasy religion. Biographies of prominent Malagasy from this period are few. G. S. Chapus and G. Mondain published a study of the most important nineteenth-century prime minister entitled *Rainilaiarivony: un homme d'état Malgache* (Paris, 1953), but the main work of Chapus is *Quatre-vingt ans d'influence européenne en Imerina*. Jean Valette's *Études sur le règne de Radama I* (Tananarive, 1962), while not a biography as such, reveals more about the first modernizing monarch than any previous work. R. Delval, *Radama II: prince de la renaissance malgache, 1861–63* (Paris, 1972), is an extensive study which sheds new light on the short, but important, reign of this young monarch. The economic history of the island has been sadly neglected, and to date only Dan A. Segre, 'Madagascar: an example of indigenous modernization of a traditional society in the nineteenth century', *St Anthony's Papers*, no. 21 (Oxford, 1969), and Phares M. Mutibwa, 'Patterns of trade and economic development in nineteenth century Madagascar', *Transafrican Journal of History*, **2** (1972),1, have shed any light on this subject. Religious history, on the other hand, has received wide coverage, and missionary monographs are numerous. On the Roman Catholic side the most informative work was that of Père Adrien Boudou, author of *Les Jésuites à Madagascar au XIXe siècle*, 2 vols. (Paris, 1940–2). The best accounts of the work of the British Protestant missions before 1870 were written by the Reverend Charles Jukes, *Country work in Madagascar* (London, 1870), and the Reverend James Sibree, *The Madagascar mission* (London, 1907). Malagasy diplomatic relations with Great Britain and France are explored in depth in Phares M. Mutibwa, *The Malagasy and the Europeans* (London, 1974).

There is an abundance of periodical literature on Madagascar for the years before 1870, and those articles which appeared in the *Bulletin de l'Académie Malgache* between 1902 and 1967 may be found in a classified alphabetical index published by that institution in 1969. A valuable guide to all published material on Madagascar is Guillaume Grandidier's exhaustive *Bibliographie de Madagascar* (Paris, 1905, 1906, 1935, 1957). Another particularly useful research tool for Malagasy history is Régis Rajemisa Raolison, *Dictionnaire historique et géographique de Madagascar* (Fianarantsoa, 1966).

12. AFRICANS OVERSEAS, 1790–1870
Documentary sources

For most of this period, the vast majority of blacks in the United States were enslaved in the southern portion of the country. Few blacks left written records, but a small number of archival collections do exist, which contain materials of great richness and utility for reconstructing part of the history of black Americans. Two of the most important of these collections grew out of efforts made by northern philanthropic organizations and a federal government agency to educate, protect, and provide material assistance for freed slaves during and after the Civil War. Although these materials speak most directly of the slave and free black experience during the 1860s, they can, if used carefully, shed light on critical areas of slave life and race relations for the late ante-bellum period as well.

The most important and larger of these collections is the archive of the Bureau of Refugees, Freedmen, and Abandoned Lands, located in the National Archives, Washington, D.C., under the heading of record group 105. The Bureau was created by Congress in March 1865 to assist emancipated blacks and loyal whites, to supervise the care of abandoned and confiscated lands, and to adjudicate racial disputes. It sent hundreds of agents throughout the South, who collected information on the material, educational, religious, and labour conditions among southern blacks and whites. Thousands of letters and petitions from southern whites and blacks are scattered through this huge collection. A sizeable portion of the Bureau's records have been microfilmed and are available through the National Archives. The second collection is the American Missionary Association's record group. Located at Dillard University in New Orleans, this collection consists of letters and reports on educational and religious matters and on the condition of the freed blacks, written by hundreds of black and white teachers and ministers who served in the South during and after the war. The dozen or more magazines published by freedmen's aid societies in the North at this time supplement the archival record. The university libraries at Harvard and Cornell own the most extensive collections of these publications.

Writings by blacks during this period

The Frederick Douglass Papers (Washington, D.C.) are the largest and most important of black manuscript collections. Philip S. Foner, ed., *The life and writings of Frederick Douglass*, 4 vols. (New York, 1951–5) includes virtually all of Douglass's most important writings. Douglass's autobiographical works (1855 and 1884) should be consulted. Scores of fugitive slave narratives were published before the Civil War. The bibliography in George P. Rawick, *From Sundown to Sunup* (Westport, Conn., 1972), lists the extant slave narratives. Some of the best of the slave narratives have been reprinted in Gilbert Osofsky, ed., *Puttin' on ole massa* (New York, 1969).

Among the most important of the ante-bellum tracts written by blacks are those by David Walker (1830), which called for violent resistance against slavery, and Martin R. Delany (1852), which proposed black emigration from the United States to Central America as a solution to the black man's problems.

Republished selections of primary documents on Afro-American history were relatively rare until quite recently. Carter G. Woodson, a black historian who pioneered the study of Negro history, edited two very useful collections of black writings (1925 and 1926). Herbert Aptheker (1951) added another helpful collection. The broadening interest in Afro-American history during the past decade spawned a host of new documentary collections. Some of the more interesting volumes include: Thomas R. Frazier (1970), Leslie H. Fishel, Jr and Benjamin Quarles (1970), Maxwell Whiteman (1971), Gilbert Osofsky (1967), John H. Bracey, August Meier, and Elliott Rudwick (1970), and Philip S. Foner (1972).

Black oral history

In the 1920s researchers from Southern University in Louisiana and Fisk University in Tennessee, both black institutions, interviewed hundreds of former slaves about their experiences as bondsmen. The Social Science Institute at Fisk University published these interviews as 'God struck me dead' (Nashville, 1945) and 'Unwritten history of slavery' (Nashville, 1945). A far more extensive interviewing campaign, which sought out the stories of 2,000 former slaves, was undertaken in the mid-1930s. The resulting collection, called The Slave Narrative Collection of the Federal Writers' Project of the Works Project Administration, was housed in the Rare Books Division of the Library of Congress for many years. Recently, the Fisk collections and the Slave Narratives were published as *The American slave: a composite autobiography* (Westport, Conn., 1971–2) under the general editorship of George P. Rawick. Rawick (1972) stands as volume one of the series. It is a helpful guide to the narratives themselves and an excellent monograph on slave society. Among the many books which have reprinted selected portions of the slave narratives, the following stand out: Arna Bontemps (1969), Benjamin Botkin (1945), and Norman R. Yetman (1970). These testimonies by former slaves, it should be emphasized, are critically important for Afro-American history, a field that must rely for the most part upon white sources.

Secondary literature

The secondary literature on blacks in the New World is vast and growing rapidly. Only a tiny fraction of the important work is discussed here. Emphasis has been placed on the more recent works, in part because they indicate the directions that Afro-American studies are presently taking, and in part because they contain the most up to date bibliographies. Four general histories of blacks in the United States, which are particularly valuable, are: John Hope Franklin (1967), August Meier and Elliott Rudwick (1970), Lerone Bennett Jr (1969), and

Benjamin Quarles (1964). Two major sociological studies of the biracial history of the United States are Gunnar Myrdal (1944) and E. Franklin Frazier (1957). An important and controversial thesis about African survivals in the New World has been advanced by Melville J. Hersko-vits (1941). Herskovits's most ardent critic has been E. Franklin Frazier (1964), who repeats these criticisms in several other works. Four of the better anthologies of reprinted essays in Afro-American history, which quickly introduce the student to much of the significant litera-ture, are: Melvin Drimmer (1968), Eric Foner (1970), August Meier and Elliott Rudwick (1969), and Nathan I. Huggins, Martin Kilson, and Daniel M. Fox (1971).

The controversy over the nature of American slavery has raged for decades. The chief spokesman for the benign interpretation of the slave regime was Ulrich B. Phillips (1918 and 1929). Kenneth M. Stampp, Phillips's chief antagonist, argued that slavery was an oppressive system founded upon the naked and violent exploitation of black slaves. Eugene D. Genovese (1965) borrowed and expanded upon Phillips's concept of plantation slavery as a way of life, but rejected his racial biases. Richard C. Wade (1964) is the standard survey of urban slavery. Wade's thesis, that urban conditions eroded the disciplines necessary for slavery and persuaded many masters to withdraw their slaves from the city, was questioned by Robert S. Starobin (1970) and directly refuted by Robert W. Fogel and Stanley L. Engerman (1974), a work which, by arguing that slavery was an efficient and profitable system, challenged most of the existing interpretations of American slavery.

Not all blacks in the United States before the Civil War were slaves. The standard work on Northern free Negroes, Leon F. Litwack, *North of slavery: the Negro in the free states, 1790–1860* (Chicago, 1961), demon-strates that they suffered discrimination. Eugene H. Berwanger (1967) and Eric Foner (1970) expand many of the points that Litwack put forth. The most comprehensive study of the southern free Negro class is Ira Berlin, *Slaves without masters: the free Negro in the ante-bellum South* (New York, 1974). More narrowly designed but of great use are John Hope Franklin (1943) and Luther P. Jackson (1942). The best studies of the Negro's role in the abolitionist movement are Benjamin Quarles (1969) and Howard H. Bell (1969). Other important books on the abolition movement include: Aileen Kraditor (1960), Louis Filler (1960), and James M. McPherson (1964). That blacks actively agitated against slavery in the North and took up arms against the Confederacy has been amply demonstrated in Benjamin Quarles (1953), James M.

McPherson (1969), Dudley T. Cornish (1956), and Thomas Wentworth Higginson (1869).

The best study of the colonization movement, which sought to remove blacks, particularly free Negroes, from the United States, is P. J. Staudenraus, *The African colonization movement, 1816–65* (New York, 1961). Carter G. Woodson's early study of the black church (1945) is still very useful. Black religious life is analysed in Leonard Haynes (1953). Two recent works which have imaginatively studied white racial attitudes are Winthrop D. Jordan (1968) and George M. Fredrickson (1971).

The debate over the role of the freed slaves after the war has been heated and intense. During the first decades of the twentieth century, William A. Dunning and his students, who dominated the field, openly questioned the Negroes' fitness for freedom and citizenship, criticized the Radical Republicans, and lionized the defeated Confederates. Several black historians challenged the Dunning school, but had little impact in reshaping popular notions about the reconstruction period. Chief among these black historians was W. E. B. DuBois, whose *Black reconstruction* (New York, 1935) is a treasury of provocative, insightful interpretations. Other important studies by black historians include: Alrutheus A. Taylor (1926), Vernon L. Wharton (1947), and Horace M. Bond (1939). Modern scholars have completely revised the Dunning school's interpretations. Among the best general surveys of the reconstruction period are: Kenneth M. Stampp (1965), John Hope Franklin (1961), and Rembert W. Patrick (1967). Two more specialized studies of superior quality are Willie Lee Rose (1964) and Joel Williamson (1965).

American historians had, in their studies of slavery, developed an enormous literature on the system of enslavement and on the whites who owned the slaves, but had, until quite recently, discovered little about the lives of the slaves. This imbalance is currently being redressed, and much of the credit for this investigation into the nature of slave life and culture must go to Stanley M. Elkins, *Slavery: a problem in American institutional life* (Chicago, 1959). Elkins argued that slavery in the United States was a uniquely closed institution that fostered infantilism among its victims. The Sambo figure, he continued, appeared only in the United States and was a product of the total control that masters wielded over their slaves. Praised and criticized by a host of scholars, *Slavery* stands as a landmark in the historiography of American slave studies; it is a mark of its enormous influence that most scholars now working on slavery feel obliged to agree or disagree with Elkins. Much of the best commentary on Elkins's thesis appears in Ann Lane (1971). Elkins's claim that the Sambo image was historically valid challenged historians to study seriously the nature of slave personality and culture. Lawrence W. Levine (1971) used slave songs to recreate an important facet of the slaves' culture. Several essays in Eugene D. Genovese (1968) explore new paths to discovering the slave past which have led to *Roll Jordan Roll* (New York, 1974), Genovese's brilliant study of the slave world. Other important studies of slave life include: Gerald W. Mullin (1972), and John W. Blassingame (1972). A work that promises to be of seminal importance in Afro-American studies is Herbert G. Gutman (1974–5).

Elkins did more than reintroduce the slave to slavery studies; he popularized the comparative method for studying slavery in his attempt to argue for the uniqueness of the American slavery system. Elkins employed and extended a thesis propounded by Frank Tannenbaum (1947), which held that Latin American slavery, because of religious and legal traditions and due to the influence of the Roman Catholic Church, was more open and gave more explicit recognition to the slaves' basic humanity than did the slavery system in the North where these traditions and that institution were absent. The Tannenbaum–Elkins thesis received important support for the Latin American side of the comparison from Gilberto Freyre's magnificent study (1946) of Brazilian slavery. Herbert S. Klein's economic analysis of two New World slave regimes (1967) added new backing to that thesis. Among the most persuasive critics of the Tannenbaum–Elkins thesis are: David Brion Davis (1966), Marvin Harris (1964) and Carl Degler (1971). Charles R. Boxer (1963) and Franklin W. Knight (1970) raise doubts about the humaneness of Latin American slavery. An interesting analysis of New World slaveries is Eric Williams (1944). Two anthologies of printed articles introduce the student to the major disputes in comparative slavery studies: Allen Weinstein and Frank O. Gatell (1968), and Laura Foner and Eugene D. Genovese (1969). An essential reference work for comparative study is Philip D. Curtin (1969). For a suggestive essay on the implications of Curtin's work, see 'Southern slaves in the world of Thomas Malthus', in C. Vann Woodward (1971).

The best volume on blacks in Canada is Robin W. Winks (1971). The literature on blacks in Latin America and the Caribbean is enormous, and only a small sampling from it can be mentioned here. Immensely readable and exciting are Gilberto Freyre (1963) and C. L. R. James

(1963). Ramiro Suerra y Sanchez (1964) gives an outstanding study of blacks and whites in Cuba. H. Orlando Patterson (1967) analyses slave life in Jamaica, and L. E. Braithwaite (1971) deals particularly with the social life of blacks in plantation society. Other important works on blacks in the New World include: Donald Wood (1968), Philip D. Curtin (1955), D. G. Hall (1971), Douglas Hall (1971) and Magnus Mörner (1967).

A number of outstanding bibliographies of Afro-American history can be consulted by students seeking a far more extensive survey of the literature. Monroe N. Work (1928) was the most complete guide at the time it was published. More recent publications include: Erwin K. Welsch (1965), Dorothy B. Porter (1970) and finally, James M. McPherson *et al.* (1971) which ranges far beyond history and beyond the boundaries of the United States.

13. CHANGING EUROPEAN ATTITUDES TO AFRICA

For the student of European attitudes to Africa everything written by Europeans about the continent has a certain relevance. This means, then, that he finds himself confronted with a fund of primary material intriguing in its variety but daunting in its mass. It will not be enough for him to look at the obvious sources, the narratives of explorers, the records of missionaries, the speeches of politicians. He must cast his net wider to draw in other publications, school text-books, encyclopaedias, popular novels, the proceedings of learned societies. Some of this material is the work of those who can speak from first-hand experience, but much of it, he will soon discover, has been produced by writers who have never set foot in the continent. This difference between first-hand and second-hand experience provides a useful line of classification. On the one side can be placed the descriptive works of the explorers and the correspondence and reports – material still largely unpublished – of European missionaries, traders and administrators; on the other, the products of armchair geographers and ethnologists, metropolitan politicians and philanthropists, romantic poets, pedagogues and philosophers. Wherever possible, this material should be subdivided according to the particular aspect of the continent with which each individual work is concerned: its geography, vegetation, natural products, the culture of its peoples, their social structure, political institutions, religion, language, art, economy and so on. Ideally, one should go still further and group the material according to its country of origin. At this point, however, the student of European attitudes will begin to realize that his knowledge suffers from serious limitations. Though he may talk about 'Europe', all his most easily accessible material will be drawn from a very limited number of countries – notably Britain, France, Germany and the United States. What did Russians or Spaniards, Greeks or Poles, Norwegians or Italians think about Africa in the nineteenth century? Not being able to answer such a question, one may go on to press the bounds of one's ignorance still further. What did Africa look like to English working men or French peasants? Most conventional sources are the product of members of the better educated and more highly privileged sections of society. There is no justification for assuming total ignorance and indifference among the underprivileged. Stories about Africa must have spread verbally from French soldiers who had fought in Egypt or Algeria, or English sailors who had served in the anti-slavery squadron. What effect did these have on the imagination of contemporaries? A diligent combing of the cheap fiction of the day might produce some interesting indications. Clearly, then, the subject of European attitudes to Africa is one that still provides ample opportunity for research.

Anyone approaching the subject for the first time would do well to begin by digesting two seminal secondary works, Philip D. Curtin, *The image of Africa* (London, 1965) and H. A. C. Cairns, *Prelude to imperialism* (London, 1965). Curtin's study is exclusively concerned with West Africa. Cairns's work is defined in its subtitle as a study of 'British reactions to central African society, 1840–1890'. Both books are based on rich documentation.

The period 1790–1870 saw a spectacular increase in Europe's knowledge of African geography. This is precisely illustrated in the cartography of the age; for reproductions of contemporary maps see Prince Yusuf Kamal, *Monumenta cartographica Africae et Aegypti*, 14 vols. (Cairo, 1926–39), and R. V. Tooley, *Collector's guide to the maps of the African continent and southern Africa* (London, 1969). Another way of observing the expansion of knowledge is to study the articles on Africa in successive issues of contemporary encyclopaedias. (The *Encyclopaedia Britannica* went through nine editions between 1768 and 1889; for a guide to other contemporary works of reference see the article 'Encyclopaedia' in the *Encyclopaedia Britannica*, 11th ed.) Contemporary works of geography relating to Africa include J. MacQueen, *A geographical survey of Africa* (London, 1840); H. Murray, *The African continent*

(London, 1853); C. Ritter, *Die Erdkunde* (Berlin, 1822); and Malte-Brun, *Géographie universelle*, 8 vols. (Paris, 1812–29).

The writers of these general works on African geography drew their material from the accounts produced by European explorers. Most of the major works of the period are now available in facsimile reprints, but comparatively few have been subjected to the scholarly editing their importance as source material requires. Among the works which have been so edited are the narratives and correspondence of Hornemann, Denham, Clapperton and Laing in E. W. Bovill, ed., *Missions to the Niger*, 4 vols. (Hakluyt Society, London, 1966); two works by Richard F. Burton, *First footsteps in East Africa*, edited by Gordon Waterfield (London, 1966), and *A mission to Gelele, king of Dahome*, edited by C. W. Newbury (London, 1965); and *Livingstone's private journals* (London, 1960) and *Livingstone: family letters, 1841–56* (London, 1959), both edited by I. Schapera. Livingstone's three major published works, on the other hand, have still to be given full editorial treatment, and the same must be said of the works of Bruce, Park, Barth, Speke and Stanley, to mention only the best-known African explorers. By the mid-nineteenth century a number of African territories – Egypt, Algeria, the west coast, the Cape – were sufficiently well known for those who wrote about them to be described as travellers rather than as explorers. Works that come into this category include C. F. Volney, *Travels through Syria and Egypt* (Dublin, 1793); W. W. Reade, *Savage Africa* (London, 1863), an account of travels in western Africa; Th. Gautier, *Loin de Paris* (Paris, 1865); and Lady Lucie Duff Gordon, *Letters from the Cape*, edited by D. Fairbridge (London, 1927), and *Letters from Egypt (1862–1869)*, edited by Gordon Waterfield (London, 1969). The two most massive descriptive works of the period were both produced in France. *Description de l'Égypte*, 9 vols. of text and 10 vols. of plates (Paris, 1809–28), was based on the work of the galaxy of scholars who accompanied Napoleon Bonaparte to Egypt in 1798. The intellectual tradition established by these French orientalists found expression a generation later in *Exploration scientifique de l'Algérie* (Paris, 1844–67, 39 vols.).

The published work of individual travellers and explorers may be supplemented by articles appearing in the geographical journals of the age. The earliest of these appeared towards the end of the eighteenth century: see, for example, the German *Allgemeine Geographische Ephemeriden* (Weimar, from 1798). The French Société de Géographie produced its regular *Bulletin* (Paris) from 1822, the Royal Geographical Society its *Journal* (London) from 1832. Particularly important from the mid-nineteenth century was *Dr. A. Petermanns Mitteilungen aus Justus Perthes' Geographischer Anstalt* (Gotha, from 1855). To the student of European attitudes the reports and accounts of meetings to be found in some of these periodicals are as instructive as the narratives of individual explorers.

Secondary works on European exploration include J. N. L. Baker, *History of geographical discovery and exploration*, new edition (London, 1937); Robin Hallett, *The penetration of Africa*, vol. 1 (London, 1965), a study of European interest in the interior of northern and western Africa up to 1815; A. A. Boahen, *Britain, the Sahara and the western Sudan, 1788–1861* (London, 1964); and R. I. Rotberg, ed., *Africa and its explorers* (London, 1970), a symposium containing studies of the 'Motives, methods and impact' of nine nineteenth-century explorers. For studies of particular societies concerned with exploration see Robin Hallett, ed., *Records of the African Association, 1788–1831* (London, 1964) and C. R. Markham, *The first fifty years' work of the Royal Geographical Society* (London, 1881). T. W. Freeman, *100 years of geography* (London, 1967), and R. C. Dickinson and O. J. R. Howarth, *The making of geography* (Oxford, 1933), provide useful overall accounts of the development of geography as a science.

European interest in African ethnology tended to concentrate on that highly generalized figure, the 'Negro'. European opinions about the 'Negro' must be placed in the context of gradually evolving ideas about 'race'; at the same time they must be seen as contributing to the emergence of a distinct science of ethnology. The general development of ethnology and anthropology is well set out in Mervin Harris, *The rise of anthropological theory* (London, 1969). Curtin (1965) and Cairns (1965) contain much relevant material on this aspect of European attitudes. On the evolution of ideas about 'race' there is a particularly lucid account in T. F. Gosset, *Race: the history of an idea in America* (Dallas, 1963). Winthrop D. Jordan, *White over Black* (Chapel Hill, 1968), is primarily concerned to explore the development of white American attitudes towards black people in the seventeenth and eighteenth centuries, but it also examines the stereotyped images of the 'Negro' prevalent in sixteenth-century England, images that survived in the popular imagination well into the nineteenth century. Nineteenth-century European attitudes are explored in V. G. Kiernan, *The lords of human kind* (London, 1969), and in Christine Bolt, *Victorian attitudes to race* (London, 1971). Among contemporary works particularly interesting for their discussion of 'the Negro's place in nature' are the following: Edward Long, *History of Jamaica* (London, 1774); T. Bendyshe, ed., *The anthropological treatises of Johann Friedrich Blumenbach* (London, 1865); Charles White, *An account of the regular graduations in man* (London, 1799); J. S. Prichard, *Physical history of mankind* (London, 1836) and *Natural history of man* (London, 1843); R. Knox, *The races of man* (London, 1850); James Hunt, 'On the Negro's place in nature', *Memoirs read before the Anthropological Society of London* (London, 1863–4); see also the article 'Negro' in contemporary encyclopaedias. Also to be consulted are the journals of the various anthropological or ethnological societies of the period: Anthropological Society of London, *The Anthropological Review* (1863–70), *Memoirs* (1863–60); Ethnological Society of London, *Journal* (1848–56), *Transactions* (1861–9); [Royal] Anthropological Institute, *Journal* (from 1871); Société d'Anthropologie, *Bulletin* (from 1860); Société d'Ethnographie, *Annuaire* (from 1862), *Revue* (from 1869). (For a comprehensive list of learned societies established in the eighteenth and nineteenth centuries, see *Encyclopaedia Britannica*, 11th ed., article 'Societies, learned'.)

Studies which discuss certain aspects of the literary presentation of 'Black Africa' include W. Sypher, *Guinea's captive kings: British anti-slavery literature of the XVIIIth century* (Chapel Hill, 1942); H. Baudet, *Paradise upon earth: Europe's image of non-European man* (London, 1965); H. N. Fairchild, *The noble savage* (New York, 1928). The extensive literature produced by French writers in Egypt is vividly presented in J. M. Carré, *Voyageurs et écrivains français en Égypte* (Cairo, 1932, 2 vols.). C. A. Julien, *Histoire de l'Algérie contemporaine* (Paris, 1964) contains much material drawn from contemporary French writers on Algeria. For European writing on the Sudan, see R. L. Hill, 'Historical writing on the Sudan since 1820' in B. Lewis and P. M. Holt, eds., *Historians of the Middle East* (London, 1962); for West Africa, Curtin (1965); for eastern and central Africa, Cairns (1965). Many aspects of the European vision of Africa – the way Europeans thought about African political systems, for example – remain unexplored and would well repay study. Another subject which needs to be researched is the European iconography of Africa: B. Smith, *European vision and the South Pacific, 1768–1850* (Oxford, 1962), would serve here as a stimulus and a model.

One aspect of African culture which came, largely as a result of the work of European missionaries, to receive increasing attention during the nineteenth century was that of language. Important contemporary works include S. W. Koelle, *Polyglotta Africana* (London, 1852), and

R. N. Cust, *A sketch of the modern languages of Africa* (London, 1883). See also Edwin Ardener, ed., *Social anthropology and language* (London, 1971).

On European attitudes to Islam there are two invaluable studies by Norman Daniel, *Islam and the West: the making of an image* (Edinburgh, 1960), and *Islam, Europe and Empire* (Edinburgh, 1966). European attitudes to Islam are also discussed by Carré (1932), Julien (1964), Cairns (1965) and Kiernan (1969).

Any study of the European concept of a 'civilizing mission' should pay particular attention to the development of the humanitarian movement, with special reference to the campaign against the slave trade. The two most important contemporary works are Thomas Clarkson, *History of the rise, progress and accomplishment of the abolition of the slave trade by the British Parliament* (London, 1808, 2 vols.), and Thomas Fowell Buxton, *The African slave trade and its remedy* (London, 1841). Peter C. Hogg's 'classified and annotated bibliography of books, pamphlets and periodical articles' on *The African slave trade and its suppression* (London, 1973) provides a comprehensive guide to contemporary material. Particularly valuable are the sections on 'abolitionist societies and conferences', 'the history of abolition literature' and 'imaginative literature'. For the British abolitionist movement, the most useful introductory work is Sir Reginald Coupland, *The British anti-slavery movement* (London, 1933), a work that has been vigorously criticized by Eric Williams, *Capitalism and slavery* (Chapel Hill, 1944). For a criticism of Williams's thesis see R. T. Anstey, 'Capitalism and slavery: a critique', *Economic History Review*, 1968, **21**.

Another important aspect of Europe's 'civilizing mission' is to be found in the development of Christian missionary enterprise. There is as yet no comprehensive bibliographical guide to the vast mass of contemporary missionary publications, the published reports of missionary societies, the magazines, the sermons, and the Sunday-school tracts, but use should be made of the bibliographical references in the works by Curtin (1965) and Cairns (1965). Recent studies of nineteenth-century missionary activity in Africa include C. P. Groves, *The planting of Christianity in Africa*, vol. I, to 1840 (London, 1948), vol. II, 1840–78 (London, 1953); Roland Oliver, *The missionary factor in East Africa* (London, 1952); J. F. A. Ajayi, *Christian missions in Nigeria* (London, 1965); and Geoffrey Moorhouse, *The missionaries* (London, 1973).

Any study of European attitudes to Africa must study the gradual emergence of imperialist ideas. For British imperialism, the most comprehensive bibliography is that contained in the *Cambridge history of the British Empire*, vol. II, *The new Empire, 1783–1870* (Cambridge, 1940). See also R. W. Winks, ed., *The historiography of the British Empire–Commonwealth* (Durham, NC, 1966). On the contemporary literature of French imperialism, see R. Lebel, *Histoire de la littérature coloniale en France* (Paris, 1931). Ronald Robinson, John Gallagher and Alice Denny, *Africa and the Victorians* (London, 1961), a richly documented study of the 'official mind' of British imperialism, traces the development of British imperialist thinking about Africa from the middle of the nineteenth century. Other relevant studies are C. A. Bodelsen, *Studies in mid-Victorian imperialism*, 2nd ed. (London, 1960), and G. R. Mellor, *British imperial trusteeship, 1783–1850* (London, 1951). The number of detailed studies which trace the growth of British interest in particular parts of Africa is steadily increasing. Works which come into this category include E. C. Martin, *The British West African settlements, 1750–1821* (London, 1927); Reginald Coupland, *East Africa and its invaders* (Oxford, 1938) and *The exploitation of East Africa, 1856–1890* (London, 1939); K. O. Dike, *Trade and politics in the Niger delta* (Oxford, 1956); Boahen (1964); John Marlowe, *Anglo-Egyptian relations, 1800–1953* (London, 1954). Collections of official documents include G. E. Metcalfe, *Great Britain and Ghana: documents of Ghana history, 1807–1957* (University of Ghana, 1964); C. W. Newbury, *British policy towards West Africa: selected documents, 1786–1874* (Oxford, 1965); and G. M. Theal, *Records of the Cape Colony from 1793 to 1826* (London, 1897–1905, 36 vols.). On the development of French imperial ideas there are a number of general works: H. Deschamps, *Les méthodes et les doctrines coloniales de la France du XVIe siècle à nos jours* (Paris, 1953); H. Blet, *Histoire de la colonisation française* (Paris, 1946–50, 3 vols.); J. Saintoyant, *La colonisation française sous l'ancien régime* (Paris, 1929, 2 vols.), *La colonisation française pendant la Révolution, 1789–1799* (Paris, 1930, 2 vols.); *La colonisation française pendant la période napoléonienne, 1799–1815* (Paris, 1931); G. Hanotaux and A. Martineau, eds., *Histoire des colonies françaises et de l'expansion française dans le monde* (Paris, 1930–4, 6 vols.). Detailed studies of French enterprise in various parts of Africa include Julien (1964); Ganiage (1959); G. Hardy, *La mise en valeur du Sénégal de 1817 à 1854* (Paris, 1921); S. Howe, *The drama of Madagascar* (London, 1938). On Portuguese relations with Africa in this period, the two most useful works in English are James Duffy, *Portuguese Africa* (London, 1959), and R. J. Hammond, *Portugal in Africa, 1815–1910* (Stanford, 1966).

BIBLIOGRAPHY

GENERAL

The following bibliographic and reference works are of value to the study of the period covered by this volume as a whole. Space permits only a very selective list, which does not claim to be comprehensive.

The most complete guide to the literature of African studies is P. Duignan's *Guide to research and reference works on Sub-Saharan Africa* (Stanford, 1971). This can be supplemented for works published since 1971 by the periodical, edited by J. D. Pearson, *International African bibliography: current books, articles and papers in African studies* (London, 1971–).

Ajayi, J. F. A. and Crowder, M. eds. *History of West Africa*, 2 vols. London, 1971–4.

Anene, J. C. and Brown, G. N. eds. *Africa in the nineteenth and twentieth centuries*. Ibadan, 1971.

Ardener, E. ed. *Social anthropology and language*. London, 1971.

Barth, H. *Travels and discoveries in North and Central Africa*, 5 vols. (English edition). London, 1857.

Blet, H. *Histoire de la colonisation française*, 3 vols. Paris, 1946–50.

Brunschwig, H. *L'avènement de l'Afrique noire*. Paris, 1963.

Cambridge History of the British Empire, vol. II, ed. J. H. Rose *et al.* Cambridge, 1940.

Cornevin, R. *Histoire des peuples de l'Afrique noire*. Paris, 1960.

Curtin, P. D. *African History*. New York, 1964.

Curtin, P. D. *The image of Africa: British ideas and action 1780–1850*. London, 1965.

Curtin, P. D. *The Atlantic slave trade: a census*. Madison, 1969.

Davidson, B. *Black Mother*. London, 1961.

Douglas, M. and Kaberry, P. M. eds. *Man in Africa*. London, 1969.

Encyclopaedia of Islam, 5 vols. Leiden, 1913–32. 2nd edn in progress since 1954.

Ethnographic survey of Africa. International African Institute, London, 1950– .

Fage, J. D. *An atlas of African history*. London, 1966.

Fortes, M. and Evans-Pritchard, E. E. *African political systems*. London, 1940.

Garling, A. *Bibliography of African bibliographies*. Cambridge, 1968.

Guides to material for West African history in European archives (series). London, 1962– .

Hallett, R. *Africa to 1875*. Ann Arbor, 1970.

Hanotaux, G. and Martineau, A. eds. *Histoire des colonies françaises et de l'expansion française dans le monde*, 6 vols. Paris, 1930–4.

Hogg, P. C. *Bibliography of the African slave trade and its suppression*. London, 1973.

Hopkins, A. G. *An economic history of West Africa*. London, 1973.

International Council on Archives. *Guide to the sources on African history outside of Africa* (series). Zug, 1970– .

Kamal, Y. *Monumenta cartographica*, 14 vols. Cairo, 1926–39.

Ki-Zerbo, J. *Histoire de l'Afrique noire*. Paris, 1972.

Koelle, S. W. *Polyglotta Africana*. London, 1852.

McEwan, P. J. M. ed. *Readings in African history*, vol. II, *Nineteenth-century Africa*. Oxford, 1968.

Oliver, R. and Atmore, A. *Africa since 1800*. 2nd ed. Cambridge, 1972.

Oliver, R. and Mathew, G. *History of East Africa*, vol. I. Oxford, 1968.

Pearson, J. D. *Index Islamicus* and *Supplements*. Cambridge, 1958.

Pearson, J. D. ed. *A guide to documents and manuscripts in the British Isles relating to Africa*. London, 1970.

Rotberg, R. I. *A political history of tropical Africa*. New York, 1965.

Rotberg, R. I. *Africa and its explorers*. London, 1970.

Shepperson, G. A. 'Africa, the Victorians and imperialism', in *The theory of imperialism and the European partition of Africa*. Edinburgh, 1967.

Thompson, L. M. and Wilson, M. *The Oxford history of South Africa*, vol. I. Oxford, 1969.

Winks, R. W. ed. *The historiography of the British Empire and Commonwealth*. Durham, NC, 1966.

I. EGYPT AND THE NILE VALLEY

'Abd al-Raḥmān al-Rafi'ī. *Ta'rīkh al-ḥaraka al-qawmiyya wa-taṭawwur niẓām al-ḥukm fī Miṣr*, 2 vols. Cairo, 1929.

'Abd al-Raḥmān al-Rafi'ī. *'Aṣr Ismā'il*, 2 vols. Cairo, 1937.

'Abd al-Raḥmān al-Rafi'ī. *'Aṣr Muḥammad 'Ali*. 3rd ed. Cairo, 1951.

Abu-Lughod, Ibrahim. *Arab rediscovery of Europe – a study in cultural encounters* (Oriental Studies Series, no. 22). Princeton, 1963.

'Ali Mubārak. *Al-Khiṭāṭ al-tawfīqiyya al-jadīda*. Bulāq, 1886–9.

Allen, B. M. *Gordon and the Sudan*. London, 1931.

Ayalon, D. 'The historian al-Jabartī and his background', *Bulletin of the School of Oriental and Africa Studies*, 1960, **23**, 2, 217–49.

Baer, G. *A history of landownership in modern Egypt, 1800–1950* (Middle Eastern Monographs, 4). London, 1962.

Baer, G. *Egyptian guilds in modern times* (Oriental Notes and Studies, no. 8). Jerusalem, Israel Oriental Society, 1964.

Baer, G. *Studies in the social history of modern Egypt*. Chicago, Center for Middle Eastern Studies, 1969.

Baker, S. W. *Ismailia*. London, 1874. 2 vols.

Brinton, J. Y. *The mixed courts of Egypt*, rev. ed. New Haven, 1968.

Browne, W. G. *Travels in Africa, Egypt, and Syria from the year 1792 to 1798*. London, 1799.

Burckhardt, J. L. *Travels in Nubia*. London, 1819.

Carré, J.-M. *Voyageurs et écrivains français en Égypte*, 2 vols. 2nd ed. Cairo, 1956.

Clot, A. B. *Aperçu général sur l'Égypte*. Brussels, 1840. 2 vols.

Combe, E., Bainville, J. and Driault, E., *L'Égypte ottomane. L'expédition française en Égypte et le règne de Mohamed Aly (1517–1849)* (Précis de l'histoire d'Égypte, III). Cairo, 1933.

Crabitès, P. *Americans in the Egyptian army.* London, 1938.

Deny, J. *Sommaire des archives Turques du Caire.* Cairo, 1930.

Dodwell, H. H. *The founder of modern Egypt: a study of Muhammad 'Ali.* Cambridge, 1931. Reprinted, Cambridge, 1967.

Douin, G. *Histoire du règne du Khédive Ismaïl.* Rome, 1933–8. 4 vols.

Funj Chronicle, ed. al-Shāṭir Busayli 'Abd al-Jalīl as *Makhṭūṭat Kātib al-Shūna.* Cairo, c. 1961.

Funj Chronicle, ed. Makkī Shibayka (Mekki Shibeika) as *Ta'rīkh mūlūk al-Sūdān.* Khartoum, 1947.

Funj Chronicle, trans. H. A. MacMichael as *A history of the Arabs in the Sudan.* Cambridge, 1922; reprinted London, 1967.

Gendzier, I. L. *The practical visions of Ya'qub Sanu'* (Harvard Middle Eastern Monographs, xv). Cambridge, Mass., Center for Middle Eastern Studies of Harvard University, 1966.

Gray, R. *A history of the southern Sudan, 1839–1889.* Oxford, 1961.

Herrold, J. C., *Bonaparte in Egypt.* London, 1963.

Heyworth-Dunne, J. *An introduction to the history of education in modern Egypt.* London, [1939]. Reprinted, London, 1968.

Hill, R. L. *A bibliography of the Anglo-Egyptian Sudan from the earliest times to 1937.* London, 1939.

Hill, R. L. *Egypt in the Sudan, 1820–1881* (Middle East Monographs). London, Royal Institute of International Affairs, 1959.

Hill, R. L. *A biographical dictionary of the Sudan,* 2nd ed. of *A biographical dictionary of the Anglo-Egyptian Sudan.* London, 1967.

Hill, R. L. *On the frontiers of Islam.* Oxford, 1970.

Holt, P. M. *A modern history of the Sudan from the Funj Sultanate to the present day,* 2nd ed. London, 1963.

Holt, P. M. *Egypt and the Fertile Crescent, 1516–1922.* London, 1966.

Holt, P. M. ed. *Political and social change in modern Egypt.* London, 1968.

Holt, P. M. 'Modernization and reaction in the nineteenth-century Sudan', in Polk, W. R. and Chambers, R. L. eds., *Beginnings of modernization in the Middle East* (Chicago, Center for Middle Eastern Studies, 1968), pp. 401–15.

Hourani, A. *Arabic thought in the liberal age, 1798–1939.* London, Royal Institute of International Affairs, 1962. Reprinted, London, 1970.

al-Jabartī. *'Ajā'ib al-āthār fi'l-tarājim wa'l-akhbār.* Būlāq, 1880. Trans. Chefik Mansour *et al.* as *Merveilles biographiques et historiques.* Cairo, 1888–96.

al-Jabartī. *Muẓhūr al-taqdīs bi-dhahāb dawlat al-Tāvansīs,* ed. Muhammad 'Ata as *Yawmiyyāt al-Jabartī,* 2 vols. Cairo, n.d. Also ed. Ḥasan Muḥammad Jawhar and 'Umar al-Dasūqī. Cairo, 1969. Trans. A. Cardin as *Journal d'Abdurrahman Gabarti....* Alexandria, 1835; Paris 1838.

Keddie, N. R. *An Islamic response to imperialism – political and religious writings of Sayyid Jamāl ad-Dīn al-Afghānī'.* Berkeley and Los Angeles, 1968.

La Jonquière, C. de. *L'expédition en Égypte, 1798–1801*. Paris, 1899–1907. 5 vols.

Landau, J. M. *Parliaments and parties in Egypt*. Tel Aviv, 1953; New York, 1954.

Landau, J. M. 'Prolegomena to a study of secret societies in modern Egypt', *Middle Eastern Studies*, 1965, I, 2, 135–86.

Landau, J. M. 'The beginnings of modernization in education: the Jewish community in Egypt as a case study', in Polk, W. R. and Chambers, R. L. eds. *Beginnings of modernization in the Middle East* (Chicago, Center for Middle Eastern Studies, 1968), pp. 299–312.

Landes, D. S. *Bankers and pashas*. London, 1958.

Lane, E. W. *The manners and customs of the modern Egyptians*. London, 1836 (many later eds.).

Lewis, B. and Holt, P. M. *Historians of the Middle East*. London, 1962.

Marlowe, J. *Anglo-Egyptian relations, 1800–1953*. London, 1954.

Marlowe, J. *The making of the Suez Canal*. London, 1964.

Marsot, Afaf Lutfi al-Sayyid. 'The beginnings of modernization among the rectors of al-Azhar, 1798–1879', in Polk, W. R. and Chambers, R. L. eds., *Beginnings of modernization in the Middle East* (Chicago, Center for Middle Eastern Studies, 1968), pp. 267–80.

Murray, T. D. and White, A. S. *Sir Samuel Baker: a memoir*. London, 1895.

el Nasri, A. R. *A bibliography of the Sudan, 1938–58*. London, 1962.

Na'ūm Shuqayr. *Ta'rīkh al-Sūdān*. Cairo, 1903.

Rivlin, H. A. B. *The agricultural policy of Muhammad 'Alī in Egypt* (Harvard Middle Eastern Studies, 4). Cambridge, Mass., 1961.

Rivlin, M. A. B. *The Dār al-Wathā'iq*. Leiden, 1970.

Sammarco, A. *Les règnes de 'Abbas, de Sa'id et d'Isma'il, 1848–1879* (Précis de l'histoire d'Égypte, IV). Rome, 1935.

Shafik Ghorbal. *The beginnings of the Eastern Question and the rise of Mehemet Ali*. London, 1928.

el Shayyal, G. el-Din. *A history of Egyptian historiography in the nineteenth century* (Faculty of Arts Publication, no. 15). Alexandria, 1962.

Steppat, F., 'National education projects in Egypt before the British occupation', in Polk, W. R. and Chambers, R. L. eds., *Beginnings of modernization in the Middle East* (Chicago, Center for Middle Eastern Studies, 1968), pp. 281–97.

Trimingham, J. S. *Islam in the Sudan*. London, 1949.

Turc, Nicolas. *Mudhakkirāt Nigūlā Turk*, ed. G. Wiet. Cairo, 1950. Trans. as *Chronique d'Égypte. . .*

Vatikiotis, P. J. *The modern history of Egypt* (Asia–Africa Series of Modern Histories, ed. Bernard Lewis). London, 1969.

Yūsuf As'ad Dāghir. *Al-Uṣul al-'arabiyya li'l-dirāsāt al-sūdāniyya*. (Beīrut), 1968.

2. ETHIOPIA AND THE HORN

Abbadie, A. d'. *Douze ans dans la Haute-Éthiopie.* Paris, 1868.

Abir, M. 'The emergence and consolidation of the monarchies of Enarea and Jimma in the first half of the nineteenth century', *Journal of African History*, 1965, **6**, 2, 205–19.

Abir, M. 'The origins of the Ethiopian–Egyptian border problem in the nineteenth century', *Journal of African History*, 1967, **8**, 3, 443–61.

Abir, M. *Ethiopia: the era of the princes.* London, 1968.

Basset, R. ed. *Les apocryphes éthiopiens, XI, Fekkaré Iyasous.* Paris, 1909.

Beke, C. T. *Abyssinia.* London, 1840.

Beke, C. T. *Sources of the Nile.* London, 1860.

Bibliothèque Nationale, Paris. MS Collection Mondon-Vidailhet.

Blanc, H. *A narrative of captivity in Abyssinia.* London, 1868.

Bruce, J. *Travels to discover the source of the Nile.* London, 1790. Reprinted Edinburgh, 1964.

Budge, Sir E. A. T. W. *A history of Ethiopia.* London, 1928.

Burton, Sir Richard F. *First footsteps in East Africa or, an exploration of Harar.* London, 1856.

Cairo, Abdin Archives. Soudan, Carton 5.

Chaine, M. ed. 'Histoire du règne de Iohannes IV, roi d'Éthiopie (1868–1889)', *Revue sémitique*, 1913, **21**.

Combes, E. and Tamisier, M. *Voyage en Abyssinie.* Paris, 1838.

Conti Rossini, C. ed. 'La cronaca reale abissina dall'anno 1800 all'anno 1840', *Rendiconti della Reale Accademia dei Lincei*, Serie 5, 1916, **25**, 779–923.

Coulbeaux, J.-B. *Histoire politique et religieuse de l'Abyssinie.* Paris, 1929.

Coursac, J. de. *Le règne de Yohannès – depuis son avènement jusqu'à ses victoires sur l'armée égyptienne* (Romans, 1926).

Crummey, D. 'Tewodros as reformer and modernizer', *Journal of African History*, 1969, **10**, 3, 457–69.

Crummey, D. *Priests and politicians.* Oxford, 1972

Cruttenden, C. J. *Memoir on Edoor tribes . . .* Bombay, 1848.

Decken, C. C. von der. *Reisen in Ost-Afrika.* Leipzig and Heidelberg, 1869–79.

Douin, G. *Histoire du règne du Khédive Ismaïl. L'Empire Africain.* Cairo, 1936–51.

Dye, W. M. *Moslem Egypt and Christian Abyssinia.* New York, 1880.

Ferret, P. U. and Galinier, J. G. *Voyage en Abyssinie.* Paris, 1847.

France, Archives. Ministère des Affaires Étrangères. 1. Mémoires et Documents, Afrique, Abyssinie, Mer Rouge. 2. Correspondance politique, Égypte, Massouah.

Fusella, L. ed. *Yaṭē Tēwodros tarik* (Testi, 3). Rome, 1959.

Gebre Sellassie, *Chronique du règne de Ménélik II, roi des rois d'Éthiopie.* Paris, 1930–1.

Giglio, C. ed. *L'Italia in Africa.* Rome, 1959–72.

Gobat, S. *Journal of a three years' residence in Abyssinia.* London, 1834.

Great Britain, Parliamentary Papers. *Correspondence respecting Abyssinia, 1846–1868* (1867–8, Accounts and papers 33, LXXII). London, 1868.

Great Britain. Public Record Office. 1. Foreign Office 1, Abyssinia. 2. Foreign Office 95, Royal Letters.

Harris, W. C. *The highlands of Aethiopia*, 2nd ed. London, 1844.

Heuglin, M. Th. von. *Reise nach Abyssinien*. Jena, 1868.

Hill, G. B. *Colonel Gordon in Central Africa 1874–1879*, 4th ed. London, 1885.

Holland, T. J. and Hozier, H. M. *Record of the expedition to Abyssinia*. London, 1870.

Krapf, J. L. *Travels, researches, and missionary labours during an eighteen years' residence in eastern Africa*. London, 1860.

Lefebvre, Th. *Voyage en Abyssinie*. Paris, 1847.

Lejean, G. *Théodore II, le nouvel empire d'Abyssinie et les intérêts français dans le sud de la Mer Rouge*. Paris, 1865.

Lewis, H. S. *A Galla monarchy*. Madison, 1965.

Lewis, H. S. 'The origins of the Galla and Somali', *Journal of African History*, 1966, **7**, 27–46.

Lewis, I. M. *The modern history of Somaliland* (Asia–Africa Series of Modern Histories). London, 1965.

Longrigg, S. H. *A short history of Eritrea*. Oxford, 1945.

Loring, W. W. *A confederate soldier in Egypt*. New York, 1884.

Malécot, G. *Les voyageurs français et les relations entre la France et l'Abyssinie*. Paris, 1972.

Markham, C. R. *A history of the Abyssinian expedition*. London, 1869.

Massaia, G. *I miei trentacinque anni di missione nell'alta Etiopia*. Rome, 1921–30.

Mathew, D. *Ethiopia, the study of a polity, 1540–1935*. London, 1947.

Munzinger, J. A. W. *Ostafrikanische Studien*. Schaffhausen, 1864.

Pankhurst, R. K. P. *Economic history of Ethiopia 1800–1935*. Addis Ababa, 1968.

Pearce, N. *Life and adventures . . . in Abyssinia*. London, 1831.

Plowden, W. C. *Travels in Abyssinia and the Galla country*. London, 1868.

Rassam, H. *Narrative of the British mission to Theodore, king of Abyssinia*. London, 1869.

Rein, G. K. *Abessinia, ein Landeskunde nach Reisen und Studien*. Berlin, 1918.

Rochet d'Hericourt, C. E. X. *Second voyage sur les deux rives de la Mer Rouge*. Paris, 1846.

Rubenson, S. 'The Adwa peace treaty of 1884', *Proceedings of the Third International Conference of Ethiopian Studies*, **1**. Addis Ababa, 1969.

Rubenson, S. *King of Kings Tewodros of Ethiopia*. Addis Ababa, 1966.

Rüppell, W. P. E. S. *Reise in Abyssinien*. Frankfurt am Main, 1838, 1840.

Russel, S. *Une mission en Abyssinie et dans la Mer Rouge, 23 oct. 1859–7 mai 1860*. Paris, 1884.

Sapeto, Giuseppe. *Viaggio e missione . . . dell' Abissinia*. Rome, 1857.

Stern, H. A. *Wanderings among the Falashas in Abyssinia*. London, 1862.

Trimingham, J. S. *Islam in Ethiopia*. London, 1952.

Weld Blundell, H. *Royal chronicle of Abyssinia*. Cambridge, 1922.

Welde Maryam. *Chronique de Théodros II, roi des rois d'Éthiopie.* Publ. by C. Mondon-Vidailhet, Paris, n.d.

[Zeneb], *Yetewodros Tarik* (The chronicle of King Theodore of Abyssinia), ed. and publ. by Enno Littmann. Princeton, 1902. Translated by Martino Mario Moreno, 'La cronaca di re Teodoro attribuita al dabtarā "Zaneb"', *Rass. St. Etiop.*, 1942, **2**, 143–80.

3. THE MAGHRIB

Abun-Nasr, J. M., *A history of the Maghrib.* London, 1971; 2nd ed. 1975.

Ageron, C. R. *Les Algériens musulmans et la France, 1871–1919* (Publications de la Faculté des Lettres et Sciences Humaines de Paris-Sorbonne, Série Recherches, 44 & 45. Paris, 1968. 2 vols.

Albertini, E. and others. *L'Afrique du nord française dans l'histoire.* Paris, 1937.

Arnoulet, F. 'La pénétration intellectuelle en Tunisie avant le protectorat', *Revue Africaine*, 1954, **98**, 140–80.

Ashbee, H. S. *A bibliography of Tunisia.* London, 1889.

Boahen, A. A. *Britain, the Sahara and the Western Sudan.* London, 1964.

Bovill, E. W. *The golden trade of the Moors.* 2nd rev. ed. London, 1968.

Boyer, P. *L'évolution de l'Algérie médiane, ancien département d'Alger de 1830 à 1956.* Paris, 1960.

Brett, M. 'Problems in the interpretation of the history of the Maghrib in the light of some recent publications', *Journal of African history*, 1972, **13**, 3, 489–506.

Colombe, M. 'Contribution à l'étude du recrutement de l'Odjaq d'Alger dans les dernières années de l'histoire de la Régence', *Revue africaine*, 1943, **87**, 396/397, 166–83.

Colombe, M. *Initiation à l'Algérie.* Paris, 1957.

Cossé Brissac, P. de. *Les rapports de la France et du Maroc pendant la conquête de l'Algérie, 1830–1847.* Paris, 1931.

Despois, J., *L'Afrique du Nord* (L'Afrique Blanche Française, 1). Paris, 1949.

Emerit, M. *Les Saint-Simoniens en Algérie.* Paris, 1941.

Emerit, M. 'Les méthodes coloniales de la France sous le Second Empire', *Revue africaine*, 1943, **87**, 396/397, 184–218.

Emerit, M. *L'Algérie à l'époque d'Abd-el-Kader.* Paris, 1951.

Emerit, M., 'L'état intellectuel et moral de l'Algérie en 1830', *Revue d'histoire moderne et contemporaine*, 1954, new series **1**, 3, 199–212.

Esquer, G. *Les commencements d'un empire: la prise d'Alger (1830).* Paris, 1923.

Evans-Pritchard, E. E. 'A select bibliography of writings on Cyrenaica', *African studies*, 1945, **4**, 3, 146–50; 1946, **5**, 3, 189–94.

Folayan, K. 'Tripoli during the reign of Yusuf Pasha Qaramanli'. Ph.D. thesis, University of London, 1970.

Franc, J. *Le chef d'œuvre colonial de la France en Algérie: la colonisation de la Mitidja.* Paris, 1928.

Ganiage, J. *Les origines du Protectorat français en Tunisie, 1861–1881* (Publications de l'Institut des Hautes Études de Tunis). Paris, 1959.

Germain, R. *La politique indigène de Bugeaud.* Paris, 1955.

Isnard, H., 'Le Sahel d'Alger en 1830', *Revue africaine*, 1937, **81**, 372/373, 587–96.

Isnard, H. *La réorganisation de la propriété rurale dans la Mitidja*. Algiers, 1950.

Isnard, H. *La vigne en Algérie: étude géographique*, 1. Gap, 1951.

Johnson, D. 'Algeria: some problems of modern history', *Journal of African history*, 1964, **5**, 2, 221–42.

Julien, C.-A. *Histoire de l'Algérie contemporaine*, 1. Paris, 1964.

Lacoste, Y. and others. *L'Algérie passée et présente*. Paris, 1960.

Leone, E. de. *La colonizzazione dell'Africa del Nord*. Padua, 1957–60. 2 vols.

Miège, J.-L. *Le Maroc et l'Europe 1830–1894*. Paris, 1961–3. 4 vols.

Nouschi, A. *Enquête sur le niveau de vie des populations rurales constantinoises, de la conquête jusqu'en 1919*. Paris, 1961.

Playfair, R. L. *Handbook to the Mediterranean*, 2nd ed. London, 1882.

Playfair, R. L. *et al. The bibliography of the Barbary states 1888–1898*. Reprinted London, 1971. Bibliographies of Morocco, Tunisia, Algeria, Tripoli and Cyrenaica by Playfair, Ashbee and Brown.

Priestley, H. I. *France overseas* . . . New York, 1938.

Roberts, S. H. *A history of French colonial policy*. London, 1929.

Tinthoin, R. *Colonisation et évolution des genres de vie dans la région ouest d'Oran de 1830 à 1885*. Oran, 1947.

Turin, Y. *Affrontements culturels dans l'Algérie coloniale: écoles, médecines, religion, 1830–1880*. Paris, 1971.

Valensi, L. *Le Maghreb avant la prise d'Alger, 1790–1830* (Questions d'histoire, no. 10). Paris, 1969.

Yacono, X., 'Peut-on évaluer la population de l'Algérie vers 1830?', *Revue africaine*, 1954, **98**, 438/439, 277–307.

Yacono, X. *La colonisation des plaines du Chélif*. Algiers, 1955–6. 2 vols.

4. THE NINETEENTH-CENTURY JIHADS IN WEST AFRICA

Abun-Nasr, J. M. *The Tijaniyya, a Sufi order in the modern world* (Middle Eastern Monographs, 7). London, Royal Institute of International Affairs, 1965.

Adeleye, R. A. *et al. 'Sifofin Shehu*: an autobiography and character study of 'Uthmān b. Fūdī in verse', *Research Bulletin of the Centre of Arabic Documentation*, 1966, **2**, 1, 1–36.

Adeleye, R. A. *Power and diplomacy in Northern Nigeria, 1804–1906* (Ibadan History Series, ed. K. Onwuka Dike). London, 1971.

Arnett, E. J. *The rise of the Sokoto Fulani*. Kano, 1922. Containing an English version of *Infāq al-maisūr* of Muḥammad Bello and 'History of Sokoto'.

Balogun, I. A. B. 'Critical edition of the *Iḥyā al-sunna wa ikhmād al-bid'a* of 'Uthmān b. Fūdī, popularly known as Usuman dan Fodio'. Ph.D. thesis, University of London, 1967.

Balogun, S. A. 'Gwandu emirates in the nineteenth century with special reference to political relations: 1817–1903'. Ph.D. thesis, University of Ibadan, 1970.

Barth, H. *Travels and discoveries in northern and central Africa*. 2nd ed., I–V. London, 1857.

Bivar, A. D. H., 'The *Wathīqat Ahl al-Sūdān*: a manifesto of the Fulani *Jihād*', *Journal of African History*, 1961, **2**, 2, 235–43.

Bivar, A. D. H. and Hiskett, M. 'The Arabic literature of Nigeria to 1804: a provisional account', *Bulletin of the School of Oriental and African Studies*, 1962, **25**, 1, 104–48.

Bivar, A. D. H., *Nigerian panoply*. Lagos, 1964.

Brown, W. A. 'The growth of Islam: toward a chronology for the caliphate of Hamdullahi (Masina)', *Cahiers d'études africaines*, 1968, **31**, 428–34.

Brown, W. A. 'The caliphate of Hamdallahi ca. 1818–1864'. Ph.D. thesis, University of Wisconsin, 1969.

Burdon, J. A. *Northern Nigeria: historical notes on certain tribes and emirates*. London, 1909.

Caillié, R. *Journal d'un voyage à Tembouctou et à Jenné dans l'Afrique centrale*, I–III. Paris, 1830.

Clapperton, H. *Journal of a second expedition into the interior of Africa*. London, 1829.

Crowder, M. *West African resistance*. London, 1971.

Crowder, M. *Revolt in Bussa: a study of British 'Native Administration' in Nigerian Borgu, 1902–1935*. London, 1973.

Delafosse, M. E. F. *Haut-Sénégal-Niger*, I–III. Paris, 1912.

Denham, D., Clapperton, H. and Oudney, W. *Narrative of travels and discoveries in northern and central Africa*. London, 1826.

Dubois, F. *Tombouctou la mystérieuse*. Paris, 1896.

El-Masri, F. H., 'The life of Shehu Usuman dan Fodio before the jihād', *Journal of the Historical Society of Nigeria*, 1963, **2**, 4, 435–48.

El-Masri, F. H. 'A critical edition of Dan Fodio's *Bayān wujūb al-hijra 'alā 'l-'ibād* with introduction, English translation and commentary'. Ph.D. thesis, University of Ibadan, 1968.

Fisher, H. J. 'Jamil Abun-Nasr, *The Tijaniyya* (London, 1965)'. Review, *Bulletin of the School of Oriental and African Studies*, 1967, **30**, 1, 230–2.

Fisher, H. J. 'The early life and pilgrimage of al-Ḥājj Muḥammad al-Amīn the Soninke (d. 1887)', *Journal of African History*, 1970, **11**, 1, 51–69.

Greenberg, J. H. *The influence of Islam on a Sudanese religion*. New York, 1946.

Gummi, A. *Infāq 'l-maisūr*. Cairo, 1964.

al-Ḥājj 'Umar b. Sa'īd al-Fūtī al-Ṭūrī al-Kadawī, *Kitāb fī mā waqa'a baina shaikh 'Umar wa Aḥmad b. Aḥmad b. Aḥmad Lūbbū*, attributed to al-Ḥājj 'Umar by J. R. Willis (Ph.D. thesis, 1970) and said to be published in Egypt under the title *Al-Ḥājj 'Umar al-Fūtī sultān al-dawla al-Tijāniyya bi-gharb afriqiyya shai' min jihādihi wa ta'rīkh ḥayātihi*. Not seen.

al-Ḥājj 'Umar b. Sa'īd al-Fūtī al-Ṭūrī al-Kadawī, *Rimāḥ ḥizb al-raḥīm 'alā nuḥūr ḥizb al-rajīm*. Cairo, n.d.

Hampate-Ba, A. and Daget, J. *L'empire peul du Macina*, I, 1818–53; II, 1853–93. Paris, 1962.

Hiskett, M. 'Material relating to the state of learning among the Fulani before their *jihād*', *Bulletin of the School of Oriental and African Studies*, 1957, **19**, 3, 550–78.

Hiskett, M. 'Kitāb al-farq: a work on the Habe kingdoms attributed to 'Uthmān dan Fodio', *Bulletin of the School of Oriental and African Studies,* 1960, **23**, 558–79.

Hiskett, M. 'An Islamic tradition of reform in the Western Sudan from the sixteenth to the eighteenth century', *Bulletin of the School of Oriental and African Studies,* 1962, **25**, 3, 577–96.

Hiskett, M., 'Hausa Islamic verse: its sources and development prior to 1920', Ph.D. thesis, University of London, 1969.

Hiskett, M. 'The "Song of the Shehu's Miracles": a Hausa hagiography from Sokoto', *African Language Studies,* 1971, **12**.

Hiskett, M. *The sword of truth: the life and times of the Shehu Usuman Dan Fodio.* New York, 1973. The bibliography contains details of the works of 'Uthmān dan Fodio and 'Abdullāh b. Muḥammad.

Hiskett, M. ed. and tr., *Tazyīn al-waraqāt of 'Abdullāh b. Muḥammad.* Ibadan, 1963.

Hodgkin, T. "Uthmān dan Fodio', *Nigeria Magazine,* 1960, Special Independence Issue, pp. 75–82.

Hogben, S. J. and Kirk-Greene, A. H. M. *The emirates of Northern Nigeria.* London, 1966.

Huizinga, J. *The waning of the Middle Ages,* tr. F. Hopman. Harmondsworth, 1972.

Johnston, H. A. S. *The Fulani Empire of Sokoto* (West African History Series, ed. G. S. Graham). London, 1967.

Kanya-Forstner, A. S. 'Mali-Tukulor', in Crowder, M. ed., *West African resistance: the military response to colonial occupation* (London, 1971), pp. 53–79.

Keddie, N. ed. *Scholars, saints and Sufis.* Berkeley, 1971.

Last, M. 'A note on attitudes to the supernatural in the Sokoto *jihād*', *Journal of the Historical Society of Nigeria,* 1967, **4**, 1, 3–13.

Last, M. *The Sokoto caliphate* (Ibadan History Series, ed. K. Onwuka Dike). London, 1967.

Last, M. and al-Hajj, M. A. 'Attempts at defining a Muslim in nineteenth-century Hausaland and Bornu', *Journal of the Historical Society of Nigeria,* 1965, **3**, 2, 231–49.

le Chatelier, A. *L'Islam dans l'Afrique Occidentale.* Paris, 1899.

Levtzion, N. *Muslims and chiefs in West Africa.* London, 1968.

Lugard, Lady Flora Louisa. *A tropical dependency.* London, 1905.

Mage, A. E. *Voyage dans le Soudan occidental.* Paris, 1868.

Martin, B. G. 'A Mahdist document from Futa Jallon', *Bulletin de l'I.F.A.N.,* 1963, **25**, ser. B., 1–2, 47–65.

Martin, B. G., 'Unbelief in the Western Sudan: 'Uthmān dan Fodio's "Ta'līm al-ikhwān"', *Middle East Studies,* 1967, **4**, 1.

Martin, B. G., 'Notes sur l'origine de la Ṭarīqa des Tiğāniyya et sur les débuts d'al-Ḥāǧǧ 'Umar', *Revue des études islamiques,* 1969, **37**, 2, 267–90.

Marty, P., *Études sur l'Islam et les tribus du Soudan,* I–IV. Paris, 1920–1.

Mischlich, A. and Lippert, J. *Beiträge zur Geschichte der Haussastaaten.* Berlin, 1903. Contains the 'Hausa Chronicle'.

Monteil, C. *Les Bambara du Ségou et du Kaarta*. Paris, 1924.

Muḥammad, A. al-Hajj. 'The thirteenth century in Muslim eschatology: Mahdist expectations in the Sokoto caliphate', *Research Bulletin of the Centre of Arabic Documentation*, 1967, **3**, 2, 100–15.

Muḥammad Bello, Sultan of Sokoto, *Infāk al Maisūr*, ed. C. E. J. Whitting. London, 1951.

Olderogge, D. A. 'Feodalism v Zapadnom Sudane v 16–19 vv.', *Sovetskaya Etnografiya*, 1957, **4**, 91–102.

Oloruntimehin, B. O. *The Segu Tukulor Empire, 1848–1893*. London, 1972.

Palgrave, W. G. *Essays on eastern questions*. London, 1872.

Palmer, H. R. *Sudanese memoirs*, III. Lagos, 1928. Contains the 'Kano Chronicle'.

Robinson, C. H. *Mohammedanism: has it any future?* London, 1897.

Saint-Martin, Y., 'L'artillerie d'El-Hadj Omar et d'Ahmadou', *Bulletin de l'I.F.A.N.*, 1965, **27**, ser. B., 3–4, 560–72.

Salenc, J. 'La vie d'Al-Hadj Omar', *Bulletin du comité d'études historiques et scientifiques de l'Afrique occidentale française*, 1918, **1**.

Smith, H. F. C., 'The islamic revolutions of the nineteenth century', *Journal of the Historical Society of Nigeria*, 1961, **2**, 2, 169–85.

Smith, M. G., 'Historical and cultural conditions of political corruption among the Hausa', *Comparative Studies in Society and History*, 1964, **6**, 2, 164–94.

Tauxier, L. *Le noir du Soudan. Pays Mossi et Gourounsi*. Paris, 1912.

Tauxier, L. *Histoire des Bambara*. Paris, 1942.

Trimingham, J. S. *A history of Islam in West Africa*. London, 1962.

Trimingham, J. S. *The influence of Islam upon Africa*. Beirut, 1968.

'Uthmān b. Fūdī. *Bayān wujūb al-hijra 'alā al-'ibād*, ed. and trans. F. H. El-Masri. 1968.

Waldman, M. R. 'The Fulani *jihad*: a reassessment', *Journal of African History*, 1965, **3**.

Wilks, I., 'The transmission of islamic learning in the Western Sudan', in *Literacy in traditional societies*, ed. J. Goody. Cambridge, 1968.

Willis, J. R. 'Jamil M. Abun-Nasr, *The Tijaniyya, a Sufi order in the modern world*. Review, *Research Bulletin of the Centre of Arabic Documentation*, 1965, **2**, 1, 39–48.

Willis, J. R. '*Jihād Fī Sabīl Allāh* – its doctrinal basis in Islam and some aspects of its evolution in nineteenth-century West Africa', *Journal of African History*, 1967, **8**, 3, 395–415.

Willis, J. R. 'The nineteenth-century revivalist movements in the western Sudan: literary themes, sources and influences'. Unpublished paper presented at the School of Oriental and African Studies Seminar 'Islamic influences on the literary cultures of Africa', March 1968.

Willis, J. R. 'Al-Ḥājj 'Umar Sa'īd al-Fūtī al Tūrī (c. 1794–1864) and the doctrinal basis of his islamic reformist movement in the Western Sudan'. Ph.D. thesis, University of London, 1970.

Willis, J. R. ed. *Studies in West African history*. Forthcoming.

5. FREED SLAVE COLONIES IN WEST AFRICA

Ayandele, E. A. *The missionary impact on modern Nigeria*. London, 1966.

Ayandele, E. A. *Holy Johnson*. London, 1970.

Ayandele, E. A. *The educated elite in Nigerian society*. Forthcoming.

Bethell, L. 'The Mixed Commissions for the suppression of the trans-atlantic slave trade in the nineteenth century', *Journal of African History*, 1966, **7**, 1, 79–93.

Blyden, E. W. *A voice from bleeding Africa on behalf of her exiled children*. Liberia, 1856.

Blyden, E. W. *Christianity, Islam and the Negro race*. London, 1887. Reprinted Edinburgh 1968.

Burke, Edmund. 'A sketch of the Negro Code', in *Works*. London, 1829.

Buxton, T. F. *The African slave trade and its remedy*. London, 1840. Reprinted 1967, 1968.

Campbell, P. *Maryland in Africa*. Chicago, 1971.

Clarke, R. *Sierra Leone*. London, n.d. [1843].

Clercq, A. and J. *Recueil de traités de la France*, IV. Paris, 1865.

Cox-George, N. A. *Finance and development in West Africa: the Sierra Leone Experience*. London, 1961.

Curtin, P. D. *The image of Africa*. Madison, 1964.

Davidson, B. *Black mother*. London, 1961.

Davis, D. B. *The problem of slavery in western culture*. Ithaca, 1966.

Deschamps, H. 'Quinze ans de Gabon: les débuts de l'établissment français, 1839–1853', *Revue française d'histoire d'Outre-Mer*, 1963, **50**, 283–345 and 1965, **52**, 92–126. This article includes a note on archival resources and a bibliography.

Dorjahn, V. R. and Fyfe, C. 'Landlord and stranger', *Journal of African History*, 1962, **3**, 3, 391–7.

Falconbridge, A. M. *Two voyages to Sierra Leone*. London, 1794. Reprinted 1794, 1802, 1968.

Fox, E. L. *The American Colonization Society*. Baltimore, 1919.

Fyfe, C. A. *A history of Sierra Leone*. London, 1962. Pages 621–39 are a guide to manuscript and printed sources.

Fyfe, C. *Sierra Leone inheritance*. London, 1964.

Fyfe, C. 'Opposition to the slave trade as a preliminary to the European partition of Africa', in *The theory of imperialism and the European partition of Africa* (Edinburgh, Centre of African Studies, University of Edinburgh, 1967).

Gautier, R. P. 'Étude historique sur les Mpongwe', *Mémoires de l'Institut d'Études Centrafricaines*, 1950, **3**, 66–8.

Gray, J. M. *A history of the Gambia*. Cambridge, 1940. Reprinted London, 1966.

Gurley, R. R. *Life of Jehudi Ashmun, late Colonial Agent in Liberia*. Washington, 1835.

Hair, P. E. H. 'A bibliographical guide to Sierra Leone 1650–1800', *Sierra Leone Studies* (new series), 1960, **13**, 41–9.

Hair, P. E. H. 'A check-list of British Parliamentary Papers on Sierra Leone', *Sierra Leone Studies* (new series), 1966, **19**, 146–50.

Hair, P. E. H. 'Africanism: the Freetown contribution', *Journal of Modern African Studies*, 1967, **5**, 4, 521–39.

Hargreaves, J. D. *A life of Sir Samuel Lewis*. London, 1958.

Hargreaves, J. D. 'African colonization in the nineteenth century: Liberia and Sierra Leone', *Sierra Leone Studies* (new series), 1962, **16**, 189–203.

Holden, E. *Blyden of Liberia*. New York, 1966.

Holsoe, S. 'A study of relations between settlers and indigenous peoples in Western Liberia, 1821–41', *African Historical Studies*, 1971, **4**, 2, 331–62.

Horton, J. A. B. *West African countries and peoples*. London, 1868.

Howell, T. B. *A complete collection of state trials 1771–77*. London, 1814.

Huberich, C. H. *The political and legislative history of Liberia*. New York, 1947.

Ifemesia, C. C. 'The "civilizing" mission of 1841', *Journal of the Historical Society of Nigeria*, 1962, **2**, 3, 291–310.

Ijagbemi, E. A. 'A history of the Temne in the nineteenth century'. Ph.D. thesis, University of Edinburgh, 1968.

Ijagbemi, E. Ade. 'The Rokal river and the development of inland trade in Sierra Leone', *Odu*, 1970.

Ijagbemi, E. Ade. 'The Freetown colony and the development of legitimate trade', *Journal of the Historical Society of Nigeria*, 1970.

Ijagbemi, E. Ade. 'The Kossoh war', *Journal of the Historical Society of Nigeria*, 1971.

Jakobsson, S. *Am I not a man and a brother?* Uppsala, 1972.

Jones, A. B. 'The struggle for political and cultural unification in Liberia 1847–1930'. Ph.D. thesis, Northwestern University, 1962.

Karnga, A. *History of Liberia*. Liverpool, 1926.

Kopytoff, J. H. *A preface to modern Nigeria: the 'Sierra Leonians' in Yoruba, 1830–1890*. Madison, 1965.

Lasserre, G. *Libreville: la ville et sa région*. Paris, 1958.

Latrobe, J. H. *Maryland in Liberia*. Baltimore, 1885.

Luke, H. C. *A bibliography of Sierra Leone*. London, 1925.

Lynch, H. R. *Edward Wilmot Blyden: Pan-Negro patriot 1832–1912*. London, 1967.

Lynch, W. F. *Report of Commander W. F. Lynch, in relation to his mission to the coast of Africa*. Washington, 1853.

Mahoney, F. K. 'Government and opinion in the Gambia 1816–1901'. Ph.D. thesis, University of London, 1963.

Mahoney, F. K. 'African leadership in Bathurst in the nineteenth century', *Tarikh*, 1968, **2**, 2, 25–38.

Mayer, B. *Captain Canot, or twenty years of an African slaver*. New York, 1854.

Melville, E. H. *A residence at Sierra Leone*, by a Lady (Mrs E. H. Melville). London, 1849.

Ord, H. W. and others. *Markets and marketing in West Africa*. Edinburgh, Centre of African Studies, University of Edinburgh, 1966.

Peterson, J. 'The enlightenment and the founding of Freetown', in Fyfe, C. and Jones, E., *Freetown: a symposium*. London, 1968.

Peterson, J. *Province of freedom: a history of Sierra Leone 1787–1870*. London, 1969.

Porter, A. T. *Creoledom*. London, 1963.

Schick, T. W. 'A quantitative analysis of Liberian colonization', *Journal of African History*, 1971, **12**, 1, 45–60.

Schnapper, B. *La politique et le commerce français dans le Golfe de Guinée de 1838 à 1871*. Paris, 1961.

Sierra Leone Bulletin of Religion. Freetown, 1958–.

Sierra Leone Studies. Old series, Freetown, 1918–39; new series, Hertford, 1953–63, Freetown, 1966– .

Solomon, M. D. and D'Azevedo, W. L. *A general bibliography of the Republic of Liberia*. Evanston, 1962.

Staudenraus, P. J. *The African colonization movement 1816–65*. New York, 1961.

Williams, E. E. *Capitalism and slavery*. Chapel Hill, 1944.

Principal Manuscript Sources

Public Record Office, London – series C.O. 267–272 (Sierra Leone), C.O. 87 (Gambia), C.O. 82 (Fernando Po), F.O. 84 (slave trade), F.O. 47 (Liberia).
Church Missionary Society Archives.
Methodist Missionary Society Archives.
Liberian National Archives, Monrovia.
Papers of the American Colonization Society, Library of Congress, Washington, D.C.

6. WEST AFRICA IN THE ANTI-SLAVE TRADE ERA

Adelẹyẹ, R. A. *Power and diplomacy in Northern Nigeria*. London, 1971.

Ajayi, J. F. A. 'The British occupation of Lagos 1851–61: a critical review', *Nigeria Magazine*, 1961, **69**, 96–105.

Ajayi, J. F. A. 'The development of secondary grammar school education in Nigeria', *Journal of the Historical Society of Nigeria*, 1963, **2**, 4, 517–35.

Ajayi, J. F. A. *Christian missions in Nigeria (1841–91): the making of a new elite*. London, 1965.

Ajayi, J. F. A. 'The aftermath of the fall of Old Oyo', in Ajayi, J. F. A. and Crowder, M., eds. *A history of West Africa*, II. London, 1974.

Ajayi, J. F. A. and Smith, R. S. *Yoruba warfare in the nineteenth century*. Cambridge, 1964.

Akintoye, S. A. *Revolution and power politics in Yorubaland, 1840–1893*. London, 1971.

Asiegbu, J. U. J. *Slavery and the politics of liberation, 1787–1861: a study of liberated African emigration and British anti-slavery policy*. New York, 1969.

Awẹ, B. A., 'The Ajele system: a study of Ibadan imperialism in the nineteenth century', *Journal of the Historical Society of Nigeria*, 1964, **3**, 1, 47–60.

Ayandele, E. A. 'Observations on some social and economic aspects of slavery in pre-colonial Northern Nigeria', *Journal of Economic and Social Studies*, 1967, **9**, 3.

Barry, B. *Le royaume du Waalo: le Sénégal avant la conquête*. Paris, 1972.

Barth, H. *Travels and discoveries in North and Central Africa*. London, 1967. Reprint.

Boahen, A. A. 'Asante and Fante in the nineteenth century', in Ajayi, J. F. A. and Crowder, M. eds., *A history of West Africa*, II. London, 1974.

Bouche, D. *Les villages de liberté en Afrique Noire françaises, 1887–1910*. Paris, 1968.

Brenner, L. *The Shehus of Kukawa: a history of the al-Kanemi dynasty of Bornu*. London, 1973.

Brooks, G. E. *The Kru mariner in the nineteenth century: an historical compendium*. Newark, USA, 1972.

Brown, W. A. 'Towards a chronology for the caliphate of Hamdullahi (Masina)', *Cahiers d'études africaines*, 1968, **8**, 3, 428–34.

Burton, R. F. *A mission to Gelele, king of Dahome*, ed. C. W. Newbury. London, 1965.

Buxton, T. F. *The African slave trade and its remedy*. Reprint. London, 1967.

Dike, K. O. *Trade and politics in the Niger delta*. Oxford, 1956.

Fage, J. D. *A history of West Africa: an introductory survey*. Cambridge, 1969.

Fage, J. D. 'Slavery and the slave trade in the context of West African history', *Journal of African History*, 1969, **10**, 3, 393–404.

Forde, C. D. and Kaberry, P. M. *West African kingdoms in the nineteenth century*. Oxford, 1967.

Fyfe, C., *A history of Sierra Leone*. London, 1969.

Graham, J. D. 'The slave trade, depopulation and human sacrifice in Benin history', *Cahiers d'études africaines*, 1965, **5**, 2, 217–34.

Griffeth, R. R. 'Dyula recruitment techniques in the West Volta region: an example of pre-colonial state formation processes in West Africa'. African History Colloquium on West African State Formation, UCLA, 1972.

Groves, C. P. *The planting of Christianity in Africa*, III. London, 1957.

Hampate-Ba, A. and Daget, J. *L'empire peul du Macina*. Paris, 1962.

Hardy, G. *La mise en valeur du Sénégal de 1817 à 1854*. Paris, 1921.

Hargreaves, J. D. *Prelude to the partition of West Africa*. London, 1963.

Hargreaves, J. D. *West Africa: the former French states*. Englewood Cliffs, N.J., 1967.

Hargreaves, J. D. (ed.). *France and West Africa: an anthology of historical documents*. London, 1969.

Hopkins, A. G. 'Economic imperialism in West Africa: Lagos 1882–92', *Economic History Review*, 1968, **21**.

Horton, R. 'From fishing village to city state: a social history of New Calabar', in Douglas, M. and Kaberry, P. M., eds., *Man in Africa*. London, 1969.

Ifemesia, C. C. 'British enterprise on the Niger'. Ph.D. thesis, University of London, 1959.

Johnson, G. W. *The emergence of black politics in Senegal*. Stanford, 1971.

Jones, G. I. *The trading states of the oil rivers: a study of political development in eastern Nigeria*. London, 1963.

Kersaint-Gilly, F. de. 'Essai sur l'évolution de l'esclavage en Afrique Occidentale Française: son dernier stade au Soudan Français', *Bulletin du Comité d'Études Historiques et Scientifiques de l'Afrique Occidentale Française*, 1924, 7.

Klein, M. A. *Islam and imperialism in Senegal*. Stanford, 1968.

Klein, M. A. 'The Moslem revolution in nineteenth century Senegambia', in McCall, D. F., Bennett, N. R. and Butler, J., eds., *Western African history* (Boston University Papers on Africa, IV). London, 1969.

Last, M. *The Sokoto caliphate*. London, 1967.

Levtzion, N. *Muslims and chiefs in West Africa*. Oxford, 1968.

Lloyd, C. *The navy and the slave trade*. London, 1949.

McCall, D. F., Bennett, N. R. and Butler, J. eds. *Western African history*. London, 1969.

Mannix, D. P. and Cowley, M. *Black cargoes*. New York, 1962.

Meillassoux, C. *The development of indigenous trade and markets in West Africa*. London, 1971.

Metcalfe, G. E. *Great Britain and Ghana: documents of Ghana history, 1807–1957*. University of Ghana, 1964.

Nair, K. K. *Politics and society in Old Calabar*. London, 1972.

al-Naqar, 'Umar. *The pilgrimage tradition in West Africa: an historical study with special reference to the nineteenth century*. Khartoum, 1972.

N'Diaye, F. 'La colonie du Sénégal au temps de Brière de l'Isle (1876–1881)', *Bulletin de l'Institut Fondamental d'Afrique Noire*, series B, 1968, 30, 2.

Newbury, C. W. *British policy towards West Africa: select documents (1786–1874)*. Oxford, 1971.

Oloruntimehin, B. O. 'The impact of the abolition movement on the social and political development of West Africa in the nineteenth and twentieth centuries', *African Notes*, 1971, 7, 1, 33–58.

Oloruntimehin, B. O. *The Segu Tukulor empire*. London, 1972.

Olusanya, G. O. 'The freed slaves' homes: an unknown aspect of Northern Nigerian social history', *Journal of the Historical Society of Nigeria*, 1966, 3, 3, 523–38.

Pasquier, R. 'À propos de l'émancipation des esclaves au Sénégal en 1848', *Revue française d'histoire d'Outre-Mer*, 1967, 54, 194–7.

Peterson, J. *Province of freedom: a history of Sierra Leone, 1787–1870*. London, 1969.

Polanyi, K. 'The economy as instituted process', in Polanyi, K., Arensberg, C. M. and Pearson, H. W., eds., *Trade and markets in the early empires*. Glencoe, Illinois, 1957.

Polanyi, K. *Dahomey and the slave trade: an analysis of an archaic economy*. Seattle, 1966.

Ross, D. A. 'The career of Domingo Martinez in the Bight of Benin, 1833–64', *Journal of African History*, 1965, **6**, 1, 79–90.

Ross, D. A. 'The autonomous kingdom of Dahomey, 1818–94'. Ph.D. thesis, University of London, 1967.

Ross, D. A. 'The first Chacha of Whydah: Francisco Felix de Souza', *Odu: University of Ife Journal of African Studies*, n.s., 1969, **2**, 19–28.

Rodney, W. 'Jihad and social revolution in Futa Djallon in the eighteenth century', *Journal of the Historical Society of Nigeria*, 1968, **4**, 2, 269–84.

Ryder, A. F. C. *Benin and the Europeans, 1485–1897*. London, 1969.

Sidibé, M. 'Coutoumier du cercle de Kita (Soudan Français – A.O.F.)', *Bulletin du Comité d'Études Historiques et Scientifiques de l'A.O.F.*, 1935, **15**.

Staudenraus, P. J. *The African colonization movement, 1816–65*. New York, 1961.

Stewart, C. C. and Stewart, E. K. *Islam and social order in Mauritania: a case study from the nineteenth century*. Oxford, 1973.

Suret-Canale, J. 'La Guinée dans le système coloniale', *Présence africaine*, 1960, **29**, 9–44.

Trimingham, J. A. *A history of Islam in West Africa*. London, 1962.

Ukwu, U. I. 'The development of trade and marketing in Iboland', *Journal of the Historical Society of Nigeria*, 1967, **3**, 4, 647–62.

University of Edinburgh. Centre of African Studies, *The transatlantic slave trade from West Africa*. Edinburgh, 1965.

Wane, Y. *Les Toucouleurs du Fouta Tooro*. Dakar, Institut Fondamental d'Afrique Noire, 1969.

Wilks, I. 'Ashanti government', in Forde, C. D. and Kaberry, P. M., eds., *West African kingdoms in the nineteenth century*. London, 1967.

Zuccarelli, F. 'Le régime des engagés à temps au Sénégal 1817–48', *Cahiers d'études africaines*, 1962, **2**, 3, 420–61.

7. THE FOREST AND THE SAVANNA OF CENTRAL AFRICA

Alexandre, P. 'Proto-histoire du groupe Beti-Bulu-Fang: essai de synthèse provisoire', *Cahiers d'études africaines*, 1965, **5**, 4 (20), 503–60.

Almeida, F. J. M. de Lacerda e. *Travessia da Africa*. Lisbon, 1936.

Anstey, R. T. *Britain and the Congo in the nineteenth century*. London, 1962.

Bastian, A. *Deutsche Expedition an der Loango Küste*. Jena, 1874.

Bateman, C. S. L. *The first ascent of the Kasai*. London, 1889.

Bouchaud, J. *La côte du Cameroun dans l'histoire et la cartographie des origines à l'annexion allemande (1884)* (Mémoires de l'Institut Français d'Afrique Noire, 5). Douala, 1952.

Brásio, A. *Angola* (Spiritalia Monumenta Historica, Series Africana). Pittsburgh and Louvain, 1966–71. 5 vols.

Brunschwig, H. *Brazza explorateur: l'Ogooue, 1875–1879* (Documents pour servir à l'histoire de l'Afrique équatoriale française, 2e série, 1). Paris, École Pratique des Hautes Études, 1966.

Childs, G. M. *Umbundu kinship and character*. London, International African Institute and Witwatersrand University Press, 1949.

Colson, E. *Social organisation of the Gwembe Tonga*. Manchester, 1960.

Colson, E. *Plateau Tonga of Northern Rhodesia: social and religious studies.* Manchester, 1962.

Corrêa, E. A. da Silva. *História de Angola* (Collecção dos Classicos da Expansão Portuguesa no Mundo, E). Lisbon, 1937.

Cunnison, I. 'Kazembe and the Portuguese', *Journal of African History*, 1961, 2, 1, 61–76.

Dampierre, E. de. *Un ancien royaume Bandia du Haut-Oubangui* (Recherches en Sciences Humaines, 24). Paris, 1967.

Deschamps, H. *Quinze ans de Gabon: les débuts de l'établissement français, 1839–1853.* Paris, 1965.

Du Chaillu, P. B. *Explorations and adventures in equatorial Africa.* London, 1861.

Du Chaillu, P. B. *Journey to Ashango-land.* London, 1867.

Duysters, L. 'Histoire des Aluunda', *Problèmes d'Afrique centrale*, 1958, 12, 40, 75–81.

Estermann, C. *Etnografia do sudoeste de Angola* (Memórias, 4, 5, 30). Lisbon, 1956–61. 3 vols.

Felner, A. A. *Angola: apontamentos sôbre a colonização dos planaltos e litoral do Sul de Angola.* Lisbon, 1940. 3 vols.

Flint, E. 'Trade and politics in Barotseland during the Kololo period', *Journal of African History*, 1970, 11, 1, 71–86.

Gamitto, A. C. P. *King Kazembe*, tr. I. Cunnison. Lisbon, 1960. 2 vols.

Graça, J. R. 'Viagem feita de Loanda', *Annães do Conselho Ultramarino*, 1855.

Gray, R. and Birmingham, D. *Pre-colonial African trade.* London, 1970.

Kalck, P. *Histoire de la république centrafricaine.* Paris, 1974.

Laman, K. E. *The Kongo.* Uppsala, 1953–68.

Lima, J. J. Lopes de, 'Ensaio sôbre a statistica d'Angola e Benguella e suas dependencias na costa occidental d'Africa ao sul do Equador', in his *Ensaios sôbre a statistica das possessões portuguezas*, III. Lisbon, 1846.

Livingstone, D. *Missionary travels and researches in South Africa.* London, 1857.

Lovett-Cameron, V. *Across Africa.* London, 1877.

Mainga, M. *Bulozi under the Luyana kings.* London, 1973.

Martin, P. M. *The external trade of the Loango coast, 1576–1870* (Oxford Studies in African Affairs). London, 1972.

Mazenot, G. *La Likouala-Mossaka: histoire de la pénétration du Haut Congo, 1878–1920* (Monde d'Outre-Mer, 1ère série, Études XXIX. Paris, 1970.

Miller, J. C. 'Cokwe trade and conquest in the nineteenth century', in Gray, R. and Birmingham, D., *Pre-colonial African trade* (London, 1970), pp. 174–201.

Miller, J. C. 'Kasanje', in Heimer, W. F., *Social change in Angola.* Munich, 1973.

Miller, J. C. *Kings and kinsmen.* Oxford, 1976.

Miracle, M. 'Plateau Tonga entrepreneurs in historical inter-regional trade', *Rhodes-Livingstone Journal*, 1959, 26, 34–50.

Moeller, A. *Les grandes lignes des migrations des Bantous de la Province Orientale du Congo Belge* (Mémoires de l'Institut Royal Colonial Belge, VI). Brussels, 1936.

Monteiro, J. J. *Angola and the river Congo.* London, 1875. 2 vols.

Oliveira, M. A. Fernandes de. *Angolana (documentação sôbre Angola), 1783–1883,* I. Luanda and Lisbon, 1968.

Patterson, K. D. *The northern Gabon coast to 1875.* Oxford, 1975.

Pechuel-Loesche, E. *Die Loango Expedition.* Leipzig, 1888–1907.

Petermann, A. 'Ladislaus Magyar's Erforschung von Inner-Afrika', in *Petermann's Mitteilungen.* Gotha, 1860.

Pogge, P. *Im Reiche des Muata Jamwo* (Beiträge zur Entdeckungsgeschichte Afrika's, Drittes Heft). Berlin, 1880.

Pôrto, A. F. da Silva. *A travessia do continente africano.* Lisbon, 1938.

Pôrto, A. F. da Silva. *Viagens e apontamentos de um Portuense em Africa.* Lisbon, 1942.

Roberts, A. D. 'Tippu Tip, Livingstone and the chronology of Kazembe', *Azania,* 1967, **2,** 115–31.

Roberts, A. D. 'Pre-colonial trade in Zambia', *African social research,* 1970, **10,** 715–46.

Roberts, A. D. *A history of the Bemba: political growth and change in northeastern Zambia before 1900.* London, 1973.

Schweinfurth, G. *The heart of Africa.* London, 1873. 2 vols.

Soret, M. *Les Kongo nord-occidentaux.* Paris, 1959.

Stanley, H. M. *Through the dark continent.* London, 1878.

Sutherland-Harris, N. 'Zambian trade with Zumbo in the eighteenth century', in Gray, R. and Birmingham, D., *Pre-colonial African trade* (London, 1970), pp. 231–42.

van der Kerken, G. *L'ethnie mongo* (Mémoires de l'Institut Royal Colonial Belge, XIII, 1). Brussels, 1944. 2 vols.

Vansina, J. *Les tribus Ba-Kuba et les peuplades apparentées* (Annales; Sciences de l'Homme, Monographies Ethnographiques, 1; Tervuren, Musée Royal du Congo Belge, 1954).

Vansina, J. *Introduction à l'ethnographie du Congo.* Kinshasa, 1966.

Vansina, J. *Kingdoms of the savanna.* Madison, 1966.

Vansina, J. *The Tio kingdom of the middle Congo, 1880–1892.* London, 1973.

Vellut, J.-L. 'Relations internationales du Moyen-Kwango et de l'Angola dans la deuxième moitié du XVIIIe s.', *Études d'histoire africaine,* 1970, **1,** 75–135.

Vellut, J.-L. 'Notes sur le Lunda et la frontière luso-africaine (1700–1900)', *Études d'histoire africaine,* 1972, **3,** 61–166.

Verbeken, A. *Msiri, roi du Garenganze.* Brussels, 1956.

Verbeken, A. and Walraet, M. *La première traversée du Katanga en 1806* (Mémoires de l'Institut Royal Colonial Belge: Série Historique, XXX, 2). Brussels, 1953.

Verhulpen, E. *Baluba et Balubaïsés du Katanga.* Antwerp, 1936.

Walker, A. R. *Notes d'histoire du Gabon.* Montpelier, 1960.

Walker, A. R. *Rites et croyances des peuples du Gabon.* Paris, 1962.

White, C. M. N. *Rhodes-Livingstone papers* (on Luvale). Manchester, 1959–62.
Wilson, A. 'Long distance trade and the Luba Lomami empire', *Journal of African History*, 1972, **13**, 4, 575–89.
Wissman, H. von. *In Innern Afrikas*. Leipzig, 1891.
Wissman, H. von. *Second journey through Equatorial Africa*. London, 1891.
Wright, M. and Lary, P. 'Swahili settlements in northern Zambia and Malawi', *African Historical Studies*, 1971, **4**, 3, 547–73.

8. EAST AFRICA: THE EXPANSION OF COMMERCE

Abdallah bin Hemedi 'l Ajjemy. *Habari za Wakilindi*, ed. J. W. F. Allen. East African Literature Bureau, 1962. English edition, 1963.
Adefuye, A. 'Political history of the Paluo, 1400–1911'. Ph.D. thesis, University of Ibadan, 1973.
Arianoff, A. d'. *Histoire des Bagesera*. Brussels, 1952.
Baker, Sir S. W. *The Albert N'yanza*. London, 1867.
Baker, Sir S. W. *Ismailia*. London, 1874.
Baumann, O. *Durch Masailand zur Nilquelle*. Berlin, 1894.
Bennett, N. R. *Mirambo of Tanzania 1840?–1884*. New York, 1971.
Blohm, W. A. *Die Nyamwezi*, 3 parts. Hamburg, 1931–3.
Bösch, Fr. *Les Banyamwezi*. Munster, 1930.
Bourgeois, R. *Banyarwanda et Burundi*, 3 vols. Brussels, 1954–7.
Boyes, J. *John Boyes, king of the Wa-kikuyu*. London, 1911.
Burton, R. F. *The lake regions of Central Africa*. Reprint. New York, 1960.
Burton, R. F. *Zanzibar, city, island and coast*. London, 1872.
Casati, G. *Ten years in Equatoria*. London, 1891 and 1898.
Christie, J. *Cholera epidemics in East Africa*. London, 1896.
Claus, H. *Die Wagogo*. Berlin, 1911.
Cohen, D. W. *The historical tradition of Busoga*. Oxford, 1972
Cory, H. *History of Bukoba*. Dar es Salaam, 1958.
Coupez, A. and Kamanzi, T. *Récits historiques du Rwanda* . . . Tervuren, 1962.
Coupland, R. *East Africa and its invaders: from the earliest times to the death of Seyyid Said in 1856*. Oxford, 1938.
Coupland, R. *The exploitation of East Africa*. London, 1939.
Craster, J. E. E. *Pemba, the Spice island of Zanzibar*. London, 1913.
Crazzolara, J. P. *The Lwoo*. Verona, 1950–4.
Crofton, R. H. *The old consulate at Zanzibar*. London, 1935.
Culwick, A. T. and E. M. *Ubena of the rivers*. London, 1935.
Denoon, D. *A history of Uganda*, II. Nairobi, forthcoming.
Driberg, J. H. *The Lango*. London, 1923.
Dunbar, A. R. *A history of Bunyoro-Kitara*. Nairobi, 1965.
Fisher, R. B. *Twilight tales of the black Baganda*. London, 1913.
Freeman-Grenville, G. S. P. *The East African coast*. Oxford, 1962.
Gorju, J. *Entre la Victoria*... Rennes, 1920.
Gorju, J. *Face au royaume hamite du Ruanda: le royaume frère de l'Urundi*. Brussels, 1938.
Grant, J. A. *A walk across Africa*. Edinburgh, 1864.

Gray, Sir John M. *The British in Mombasa*. London, 1957.

Gray, Sir John M. *History of Zanzibar from the Middle Ages to 1856*. London, 1962.

Gray, R. and Birmingham, D. eds. *Pre-colonial African trade: essays on trade in central and eastern Africa before 1900*. London, 1970.

Guillain, M. *Documents sur l'histoire, la géographie et le commerce de l'Afrique orientale*. Paris, 1857.

Hartwig, G. W. 'The Victoria Nyanza as a trade route in the nineteenth century', *Journal of African History*, 1970, **11**, 4, 535–52.

Hertefelt, M. d'. *Les clans du Rwanda ancien*. Tervuren, 1971.

Heusch, L. de. *Le Rwanda et la civilisation interlacustre*. Brussels, 1966.

Höhnel, L. von. *Discovery of Lakes Rudolph and Stephanie*. London, 1894.

Hollingsworth, L. W. *Zanzibar under the Foreign Office*. London, 1953.

Hollis, A. C. *The Masai*. Oxford, 1905.

Hollis, A. C. *The Nandi*. Oxford, 1909.

Hore, E. C. *Tanganyika: eleven years in Central Africa*. London, 1892.

Ingrams, W. H. *The dialects of the Zanzibar sultanate*. London, 1924.

Ingrams, W. H. *Zanzibar: its history and its people*. London, 1931.

Ishumi, A. G. M. 'The kingdom of Kiziba', *Journal of World History*, 1971, **13**, 4, 714–35.

Kagwa, A. *Empisa (Customs)*. Kampala, 1905.

Kagwa, A. *Ebika (Clans)*. Kampala, 1908.

Kagwa, A. *Nsenene*. Kampala, n.d.

Kagwa, A. *Basekabaka*, ed. M. S. M. Kiwanuka, as *The kings of Buganda*. Nairobi, 1971.

Kandt, R. *Caput Nili*. Berlin, 1919.

Karugire, S. R. *A history of the kingdom of Nkore in western Uganda to 1896*. Oxford, 1971.

Katoke, I. K. 'Karagwe: a pre-colonial state', *Journal of World History*, 1971, **13**, 3, 515–41.

Kimambo, I. N. *A political history of the Pare*. Nairobi, 1969.

Kimambo, I. N. and Temu, A. J. eds. *A history of Tanzania*. Nairobi, 1969.

Kirkman, J. S. *The Arab city of Gedi: excavations at the Great Mosque*. London, 1954.

Kiwanuka, M. S. M. *A history of Buganda*. London, 1971.

Krapf, J. L. *Travels, researches and missionary labours . . . in eastern Africa*. London, 1860.

Lambert, H. E. *Kikuyu*. Cape Town, 1950.

Lindblom, K. G. *The Akamba*. Uppsala, 1920.

Livingstone, D. *Last journals*. London, 1874.

Low, D. A. *Religion and society in Buganda 1875–1900*. Kampala, 1957.

Lugard, F. D. *The rise of our East African empire*. London, 1893.

Lwamgira, F. X. *Amakuru ga Kiziba*. 2nd ed. Tabora, 1949. Trans. E. R. Kamuhangire as *The history of Kiziba*.

Maquet, J. J. *The premise of inequality in Rwanda*. London, 1961.

Mecklenburg-Schwerin, A. R. von. *In the heart of Africa*. London, 1910.

Morris, H. F. *A history of Ankole*. Kampala, 1962.

Muriuki, G. *A history of the Kikuyu 1500–1900*. Nairobi, 1974.

Nigmann, E. *Die Wahehe*. Berlin, 1908.

Nyakatura, J. W. *Aspects of Bunyoro customs and traditions*. Nairobi, 1970.

Nyakatura, J. W. *Abakama*, ed. G. Uzoigwe as *The anatomy of an African kingdom*. New York, 1973.

Ogot, B. A. ed. *Hadith I: proceedings of the annual conference of the Historical Association of Kenya*. Nairobi, 1968.

Ogot, B. A. ed. *Hadith II: proceedings of the annual conference of the Historical Association of Kenya*. Nairobi, 1970.

Ogot, B. A. and Kieran, J. A. eds. *Zamani: a survey of East African history*. Nairobi, 1968.

Ogot, B. A. *History of the Southern Luo*. Nairobi, 1967.

Oliver, R. *The missionary factor in East Africa*. London, 1952.

Oliver, R. 'Traditional histories of Buganda, Bunyoro and Ankole', *Journal of the Royal Anthropological Institute*, 1955, **85**, 111–17.

Onyangoku-Odongo, J. and Webster, J. B. *The Central Luo during the Aconya*. Forthcoming.

Pagès, F. *Un royaume Hamite: le Ruanda*. Brussels, 1933.

Pearce, F. B. *The island metropolis of eastern Africa*. London, 1920.

Prins, A. H. J. *The Swahili-speaking peoples of Zanzibar and the East African coast*. London, 1961.

Redmond, P. M. 'Political history of the Songea Ngoni'. Ph.D. thesis, University of London, 1972.

Rehse, H. *Kiziba*. Stuttgart, 1910.

Roberts, A. D. ed. *Tanzania before 1900*. Nairobi, 1968.

Roscoe, J. *The Baganda*. London, 1911.

Roscoe, J. *The Northern Bantu*. Cambridge, 1915.

Roscoe, J. *The Bakitara*. Cambridge, 1923.

Roscoe, J. *The Banyankole*. Cambridge, 1923.

Roscoe, J. *The Bagesu*. Cambridge, 1924.

Russell, L. M. ed. *General Rigby, Zanzibar and the slave trade*. London, 1935. Includes General Rigby's Report as appendix II.

Sassoon, H. 'The collection of metalwork from the kingdom of Karagwe and its relationship to the insignia of neighbouring territories'. D. Phil. thesis, University of Oxford, 1971.

Schweinfurth, G. *The heart of Africa*. English ed., London, 1873.

Shorter, A. *Chiefship in western Tanzania*. Oxford, 1972.

Southall, A. W. 'Alur tradition and its historical significance', *Uganda Journal*, 1954, **18**, 2, 137–65.

Southall, A. W. *Alur society*. Cambridge, 1956.

Speke, J. H. *Journal of the discovery of the sources of the Nile*. London, 1863.

Stahl, K. M. *The Chagga*. The Hague, 1964.

Stanley, H. M. *In darkest Africa*. London, 1870.

Stuhlmann, F. *Mit Emin Pascha ins Herz von Afrika*. Berlin, 1894.

Sutton, J. E. G. *The East Africa coast: an historical and archaeological review* (Historical Association of Tanzania Paper no. 1). Nairobi, 1966.

Swann, A. J. *Fighting the slave-hunters in Central Africa*. London, 1910.

Thomson, J. *To the Central African Lakes and back*. London, 1881.

Thomson, J. *Through Masailand*. London, 1885.

Unomah, A. 'Economic expansion and political change in Unyanyembe, c. 1840–1900'. Ph.D. thesis, University of Ibadan, 1973.

Vansina, J. *L'évolution du royaume Ruanda*. Brussels, 1962.

Webster, J. B. *et al. The Iteso during the Asonya*. Nairobi, 1974.

Were, G. S. *A history of the Abaluyia of western Kenya*. Nairobi, 1967.

9. THE NGUNI OUTBURST

Abraham, D. P. 'The principality of Maungwe: its history and traditions', *Nada*, 1951, **28**, 56–83.

Alberti, L. *Description physique et historique des Caffres*. Amsterdam, 1811.

Alberto, M. S. 'Os Angones os ultimos povos invasores da Angónia Portugesa', *Moçambique*, July–September 1941, **27**.

Andersson, K. J. *Lake Ngami*. London, 1856.

Arbousset, T. and Daumas, F. *Narrative of an exploratory tour of the north east of the Colony of the Cape of Good Hope*. Cape Town, 1846. Facsimile reprint, Cape Town, 1968.

Ashton, H. *The Basuto*. London, 1952.

Ayliff, J. and Whiteside, J. *History of the Abambo*. Facsimile reprint of 1912 edition, Cape Town, 1962.

Backhouse, J. *A narrative of a visit to the Mauritius and South Africa*. London, 1844.

Bain, A. G. *Journals of Andrew Geddes Bain*, ed. M. H. Lister (Van Riebeeck Society). Cape Town, 1949.

Barnes, J. A. 'Some aspects of political development among the Fort Jameson Ngoni', *African Studies*, 1948, **7**, 2–3, 99–109.

Barnes, J. A. *Marriage in a changing society* (Rhodes-Livingstone Papers, no. xx). Cape Town, 1951.

Barnes, J. A. *Politics in a changing society* (London, 1954).

Baxter, T. W. 'The Angoni rebellion and Mpeseni', *Northern Rhodesia Journal*, 1950, **I**, 2, 14–24.

Baxter, T. W. 'More about Mpeseni', *Northern Rhodesia Journal*, 1955, **2**, 6, 46–52.

Becker, P. *Path of blood*. London, 1962.

Beemer, H. 'The development of the military organization in Swaziland', *Africa*, 1937, **10**, 1, 55–74.

Binns, C. T. *The last Zulu king*. London, 1963.

Boxer, C. R. ed. *The tragic history of the sea 1589–1622*. Cambridge, 1959.

Broadbent, S. *A narrative of the first introduction of Christianity amongst the Barolong tribe*. London, 1865.

Brown, R. 'The Ndebele succession crisis, 1868–1877', in *Historians in Tropical Africa* (Proceedings of the Leverhulme History Conference, 1960, cyclostyled). Salisbury, 1962.

Bryant, A. T. *Olden times in Zululand and Natal*. London, 1929. Facsimile reprint, Cape Town, 1965.

Bryant, A. T. *The Zulu people*. Pietermaritzburg, 1949.

Bryant, A. T. *A history of the Zulu and neighbouring tribes* (Cape Town, 1964).

Burton, R. F. *The lake regions of Central Africa*. London, 1860. 2 vols.

Burton, R. F. *Lacerda's journey to Cazembe in 1798*. London, 1873.

Campbell, J. *Travels in South-Africa . . . narrative of a second journey. . . .* London, 1822. 2 vols.

Casalis, E. *The Basutos*. London, 1861. Facsimile reprint, Cape Town, 1965.

Chase, J. C. 'Substance of the journal of two trading travellers and of the communications of a missionary', *South African Quarterly Journal*, 1829, 1.

Chibambo, Y. M. *My Ngoni of Nyasaland*. London, 1942.

Colson, E. F. and Gluckman, M. eds. *Seven tribes of British Central Africa*. London, 1951.

Cook, P. A. W. 'History and Izibongo of the Swazi chiefs', *Bantu Studies*, 1931, 5, 181–201.

Crawshay, R. 'A journey in the Angoni country', *Geographical Journal*, 1894, 3, 1, 59–60.

Davis, C. S. 'The Amandebele habitat', *Nada*, 1934, 13, 74–9.

Decle, L. *Three years in savage Africa*. London, 1898.

Doyle, D. 'A journey through Gazaland', *Proceedings of the Royal Geographical Society*, 1891, new series, 13, 10, 588–91.

Ebner, E. *History of the Wangoni* (cyclostyled). Songea, 1959.

Ellenberger, D. F. and Macgregor, J. C. *History of the Basuto, ancient and modern*. London, 1912.

Elmslie, W. A. *Among the wild Ngoni*. Edinburgh, 1899.

Erskine, St V. W. 'Journey of exploration to the mouth of the river Limpopo', *Journal of the Royal Geographical Society*, 1869, 39, 233–76.

Foá, É. *Du Cap au Lac Nyassa*. Paris, 1897.

Fraser, D. *Winning a primitive people*. London, 1914.

Fraser, D. *The autobiography of an African*. London, 1925.

Fynn, H. F. *The diary of Henry Francis Fynn*, ed. J. Stuart and D. M. Malcolm. Pietermaritzburg, 1950.

Gardiner, A. F. *Narrative of a journey to the Zoolu country*. London, 1836.

Genthe, H. 'A trip to Mpezeni's', *British Central Africa Gazette*, 1897, 4, 13.

Gluckman, M. 'The kingdom of the Zulu', in Fortes, M. and Evans Pritchard, E. E. eds., *African political systems*. London, 1940.

Gluckman, M. 'Analysis of a social situation in modern Zululand' (Rhodes-Livingstone Papers, no. XXVIII). Manchester, 1958. Reprinted from *Bantu Studies*, 14, 1940.

Gluckman, M. 'The Lozi', in Colson, E. and Gluckman, M. eds., *Seven tribes of British Central Africa*. London, 1951.

Gulliver, P. A. 'A history of the Songea Ngoni', *Tanganyika Notes and Records*, 1955, 41, 16–30.

Hall, R. de Z. 'Angoni raids in the Rufiji District', *Tanganyika Notes and Records*, 1949, 27, 74–5.

Hammond-Tooke, W. D. *Bhaca society: a people of the Transkeian uplands, South Africa.* Cape Town, 1962.

Harris, W. C. *The wild sports of Southern Africa.* London, 1839.

Harvey, R. J. 'Mirambo, "the Napoleon of Central Africa"', *Tanganyika Notes and Records,* 1950, **28,** 10–28.

Hatchell, G. W. 'The Angoni of Tanganyika territory', *Man,* 1935, **35,** 70–87, 69–71.

Hlazo, T. J. 'The naming of the hill "Intaba Yezinduna", Matabeleland', *Nada,* 1934, **12,** 72–3.

Hodgson, A. G. O. 'Notes on the Achewa and Angoni of the Dowa District of the Nyasaland Protectorate', *Journal of the Royal Anthropological Institute,* 1933, **63,** 123–64.

Holden, W. C. *The past and future of the Kaffir races.* London, 1866.

Hole, H. M. *Lobengula.* London, 1929.

Hole, H. M. *The passing of the black kings.* London, 1932.

How, M. 'An alibi for Mantatisi', *African Studies,* 1954, **13,** 2, 65–76.

Hughes, A. J. B. *Kin, caste and nation among the Rhodesian Ndebele* (Rhodes-Livingstone Papers, no. xxv). Manchester, 1956.

Hunt, D. R. 'An account of the Bapedi', *Bantu Studies,* 1937, **5,** 275–326.

Hunter, M. (afterwards Wilson, M.). *Reaction to conquest.* London, 1961.

Isaacman, A. F. *Mozambique: the africanisation of a European institution: the Zambezi Prazos 1750–1902.* Madison, 1972.

Isaacs, N. *Travels and adventures in eastern Africa,* ed. L. Herrman (Van Riebeeck Society). Cape Town, 1936. 2 vols.

Johnston, K. 'Native routes in East Africa from Dar-es-Salaam towards Lake Nyassa', *Proceedings of the Royal Geographical Society,* 1879, new series, **I,** 7, 417–22.

Jones, N. (Mhlagazanhlansi). *My friend Kumalo.* Salisbury, 1945.

Kay, S. *Travels and researches in Caffraria.* London, 1833.

Kerr, W. M. *The far interior.* London, 1886. 2 vols.

Kollman, P. *The Victoria Nyanza.* London, 1899.

Kotzé, D. J. ed. *Letters of the American missionaries, 1835–1838* (Van Riebeeck Society). Cape Town, 1950.

Kuper, H. *An African aristocracy.* London, 1947.

Kuper, H. *The Swazi* (Ethnographic Survey of Africa, ed. D. Forde; Southern Africa, pt. I). London, International African Institute, 1952.

Kuper, H., Hughes, A. J. B. and Van Velsen, J. *The Shona and Ndebele of Southern Rhodesia* (Ethnographic Survey of Africa, ed. D. Forde; Southern Africa, pt. IV). London, International African Institute, 1951.

Lagden, Sir G. *The Basutos.* London, 1909. 2 vols.

Lancaster, D. G. 'Tentative chronology of the Ngoni', *Journal of the Royal Anthropological Institute,* 1937, **67,** 77–90.

Lane-Poole, E. H. L. 'The date of the crossing of the Zambesi by the Ngoni', *Journal of the African Society,* 1930, **29,** 290–2.

Langworthy, H. W. *Zambia before 1890.* London, 1972.

Laws, R. *Reminiscences of Livingstonia.* Edinburgh, 1934.

Legassick, M. C. 'The Griqua, the Sotho-Tswana and the missionaries . . .'. Ph.D. Thesis, University of California, Los Angeles, 1969.

Lewis, D. G. 'Lobengula's regiments: recruiting and Lobola', *Nada*, 1956, **33.**

Lewis, D. G. 'The battle of Zwangendaba', *Nada*, 1956, **13.**

Liengme, G. 'Un potentat Africain: Goungounyane et son règne', *Bulletin de la Société Neuchâteloise de Géographie*, 1901, **13.**

Liesegang, G. J. *Beiträge zur Geschichte des Reiches der Gaza Nguni im südlichen Moçambique 1820–1895.* Bromberg, 1967.

Liesegang, G. J. 'Dingane's attack on Lourenço Marques in 1833', *Journal of African History*, 1969, **10**, 4, 565–79.

Livingstone, D. *Family letters, 1841–56*, ed. I. Schapera. London, 1959. 2 vols.

Livingstone, D. *Livingstone's missionary correspondence, 1841–56.* London, 1961.

Livingstone, D. *Livingstone's private journals.* Berkeley, 1960.

Livingstone, D. *The last journals of David Livingstone*, ed. H. Waller. London, 1874.

Livingstone, D. *Missionary travels and researches in South Africa.* London, 1857.

Livingstone, D. & C. *Narrative of an expedition to the Zambesi and its tributaries.* London, 1865.

Livingstone, W. P. *Laws of Livingstonia.* London, 1921.

Livingstone, W. P. *A prince of missionaries.* London, [1931].

Lye, W. F. 'The Difaqane; the Mfecane in the southern Sotho area, 1822–24', *Journal of African History*, 1967, **8**, 1, 107–31.

Lye, W. F. 'The Ndebele kingdom south of the Limpopo river', *Journal of African History*, 1969, **10**, 1, 87–104.

Lye, W. F. 'The Sotho wars in the interior of South Africa 1822–1837'. Ph.D. thesis, University of California, Los Angeles, 1969.

Macgregor, J. C. *Basuto traditions.* Cape Town, 1905. Facsimile reprint, University of Cape Town Library, Cape Town, 1957.

Mackenzie, J. *Ten years north of the Orange river.* Edinburgh, 1871.

Mainga, M. *Bulozi under the Luyana kings.* London, 1973.

Maples, C. *Journals and papers of Chauncy Maples*, ed. E. Maples. London, 1899.

Marwick, B. A. *The Swazi.* Cambridge, 1940.

Mhlanga, W. (1) 'The story of Ngwaqazi', (2) 'The history of the Amatshangana', *Nada*, 1948, **25**, 70–3.

Moffat, R. *Missionary labours and scenes in southern Africa.* London, 1842.

Moffat, R. *Matabele journals*, ed. J. P. R. Wallis. London, 1945.

Moffat, R. and Moffat, M. *Apprenticeship at Kuruman*, ed. I. Schapera. London, 1951.

Moir, F. L. M. *After Livingstone.* London, [1923].

Montez, C. 'As invasões dos Mangunis e dos Machanganas', *Moçambique*, 1937, **9–10.**

Moodie, D. C. F. *The history of the battles and adventures of the British, the Boers and the Zulus.* Cape Town, 1888.

Morris, D. R. *The washing of the spears: a history of the rise of the Zulu nation under Shaka and its fall in the Zulu War of 1879.* New York, 1965.

Msebenzi, G. *History of Matiwane and the Amangwane tribe*, ed. N. J. van Warmelo (Union of South Africa, Dept. of Native Affairs, Ethnological Publications, VII). Pretoria, 1938.

Murray, A. C. *Nyasaland en mijne ondervindingen aldaar*. Amsterdam, 1897.

Omer-Cooper, J. D. *The Zulu aftermath*. London, 1966.

Oswell, W. E. *William Cotton Oswell, hunter and explorer*. London, 1900. 2 vols.

Owen, F. *The diary of the Rev. Francis Owen*, ed. G. E. Cory (Van Riebeeck Society). Cape Town, 1926.

Owen, W. F. *Narrative of voyages to explore the shores of Africa, Arabia and Madagascar*. London, 1833. 2 vols.

Philip, J. In *Letters of the American missionaries 1835–1838*. (Van Riebeeck Society). Cape Town, 1950.

Philip, J. *Researches in southern Africa*. London, 1828.

Posselt, F. W. T. 'Mzilikazi: the rise of the Amandebele', *Proceedings and Transactions of the Rhodesian Scientific Association*, 1919, **18**, 1.

Rangeley, W. H. J. 'Mtwalo', *Nyasaland Journal*, 1952, **1**.

Rangeley, W. H. J. 'The Makololo of Dr Livingstone', *Nyasaland Journal*, 1959, **12**, 1.

Ranger, T. O. *Revolt in Southern Rhodesia, 1896–97*. London, 1967.

Read, M. 'Tradition and prestige among the Ngoni', *Africa*, 1936, **9**, 4, 453–84.

Read, M. 'Songs of the Ngoni people', *Bantu Studies*, 1937, **11**, 1–35.

Read, M. 'The moral code of the Ngoni and their former military state', *Africa*, 1938, **11**, 1, 1–24.

Read, M. *The Ngoni of Nyasaland*. London, 1956.

Ritter, E. *Shaka Zulu*. London, 1955.

Samuelson, R. C. A. *Long long ago*. Durban, 1929.

Sanders, P. B. 'Sekonyela and Moshweshwe: failure and success in the aftermath of the Difaqane', *Journal of African History*, 1969, **10**, 3, 439–55.

Schapera, I. *Ditirafalo tsa merafe ya Batswana*. Lovedale, 1940.

Schapera, I. *The ethnic composition of Tswana tribes*. London, 1952.

Schapera, I. *The Tswana* (Ethnographic Survey of Africa, ed. D. Forde; Southern Africa, pt. III). London, International Africa Institute, 1953.

Schapera, I. *Government and politics in tribal societies*. London, 1956.

Schapera, I. ed. *The Khoisan peoples of South Africa*. London, 1930.

Schapera, I. ed. *The Bantu-speaking tribes of South Africa*, 4th ed. London, 1953.

Shaw, W. *Memoirs of Mrs Anne Hodgson*. London, 1836.

Shaw, W. *The story of my mission in south-eastern Africa*. London, 1860.

Sillery, A. *Sechele*. Oxford, 1954.

Slaski, J. *Peoples of the Lower Luapula valley* (Ethnographic Survey of Africa, ed. D. Forde; East Central Africa, pt. II). London, International African Institute, 1951.

Smith, A. *The diary of Dr. Andrew Smith* (Van Riebeeck Society). Cape Town, 1939. 2 vols.

Smith, A. *Andrew Smith and Natal*, ed. P. R. Kirby (Van Riebeeck Society). Cape Town, 1955.

Smith, E. W. *The life and times of Daniel Lindley*. London, 1949.

Smith, E. W. 'Sebetwane and the Makololo', *African Studies*, 1956, **15**, 2.

Smith, K. W. 'The fall of the BaPedi of the North-Eastern Transvaal', *Journal of African History*, 1969, **10**, 2, 237–52.

Soga, J. H. *The south-eastern Bantu.* Johannesburg, 1930.

Speke, J. H. *Journal of the discovery of the source of the Nile.* London, 1863.

Stanley, H. M. *How I found Livingstone.* New York, 1872.

Stanley, H. M. *Through the dark continent.* New York, 1878.

Steedman, A. *Wanderings and adventures in the interior of Southern Africa.* London, 1835. 2 vols.

Stevenson-Hamilton, J. *The low-veld: its wild life and its people.* London, 1929.

Stow, G. W. *The native races of South Africa.* London, 1905. Facsimile reprint, Cape Town, 1964.

Summers, R. 'The military doctrine of the Matabele', *Nada*, 1955, **32**, 7–15.

Swann, A. J. *Fighting the slave-hunters in Central Africa.* London, 1910.

Tabler, E. C., *The far interior.* Cape Town, 1955.

Taylor, G. A. 'The Matabele head ring (Isidhlodhlo) and some fragments of history', *Nada*, 1925, **3**, 37–42 (reprinted in 1939, **16**).

Tew, M. *Peoples of the Lake Nyasa region* (Ethnographic Survey of Africa, ed. D. Forde; East Central Africa, pt. i). London, International African Institute, 1950.

Thompson, L. M. ed. *African societies in southern Africa.* London, 1969.

Thomson, J. *To the Central African lakes and back.* London, 1881. 2 vols.

Thornton, R. W. *The origin and history of the Basuto pony.* Marika, 1936.

Tylden, G. *The rise of the Basuto.* Cape Town, 1950.

Van Warmelo, N. J. *A preliminary survey of the Bantu tribes of South Africa* (Union of South Africa, Dept. of Native Affairs, Ethnological Publications, v). Pretoria, 1935.

Van Warmelo, N. J. ed. *History of Matuvane and the Amangwane tribe.* Pretoria, 1938.

Walton, J. 'Village of the paramount chiefs of Basutoland: I Butha Buthe', *Lesotho*, 1959, **1**, 15–21.

Walton, J. 'Villages of the paramount chiefs of Basutoland: II Thaba Bosiu, the mountain fortress of Chief Moshesh', *Lesotho*, 1960, **2**, 11–19.

Warhurst, P. R. *Anglo-Portuguese relations in South-Central Africa 1890–1900.* London, 1962.

Wheeler, D. L. 'Gungunyane the Negotiator: a study in African diplomacy', *Journal of African History*, 1968, **9**, 4, 585–602.

Whiteley, W. *The Bemba and related peoples of Northern Rhodesia* (Ethnographic survey of Africa, ed. D. Forde; East Central Africa, pt. ii). London, International African Institute, 1951.

Wiese, C. 'Expedição portugueza a M'Pesene', *Boletim da Sociedade de Geographia de Lisboa* 1891, **10** and 1892, **11**.

Wilkerson, G. J. *The Matabele nation.* Manuscript in Central African Archives.

Wilson, G. H. *History of the Universities Mission to Central Africa.* London, U.M.C.A., 1936.

Wilson, M. 'The early history of the Transkei and Ciskei', *African Studies*, 1959, **18**, 4, 167–79.

Winterbottom, J. M. 'A note on the Angoni paramountcy', *Man*, 1937, **37**, 126–7, 155–73.

Woods, G. G. B. 'Matabele history and customs', *Nada*, 1929, **7**, 43–9.

Woods, G. G. B. 'Extracts from customs and history: Amandebele', *Nada*, 1931, **9**, 16–23.

Young, E. D. *Nyassa*. London, 1877.

Young, T. C. *Notes on the history of the Tumbuka-Kamanga peoples*. London, 1932.

Young, T. C. 'Tribal intermixture in Northern Nyasaland', *Journal of the Royal Anthropological Institute*, 1933, **63**, 1–18.

10. COLONIAL SOUTH AFRICA AND ITS FRONTIERS

Agar-Hamilton, J. A. I. *The native policy of the Voortrekkers: an essay on the history of the interior of South Africa, 1836–1858*. Cape Town, 1928.

Agar-Hamilton, J. A. I. *The road to the north*. London, 1937.

Arnot, D. and Orpen, F. H. S. *The land question of Griqualand West*. Cape Town, 1875.

Attree, E. M. 'The Closer Union Movement between the Orange Free State, South African Republic and Cape Colony (1838–1863)', *Archives Year Book for South African History*, 1949, 1.

Aylward, A. *The Transvaal of today*. Edinburgh, 1881.

Baines, T. *The gold regions of south eastern Africa*. London, 1877.

Barnard, Lady Anne, *South Africa a century ago: letters written from the Cape of Good Hope 1797–1801*. Cape Town, 1901.

Barnard, B. J. ''n Lewensbeskrywing van Majoor Henry Douglas Warden', *Archives Year Book for South African History*, 1948, 1, 313–485.

Bell, K. N. and Morrell, W. P. *Select documents on British colonial policy, 1830–60*. Oxford, 1928.

Bennie, J. *An account of a journey into Transorangia and the Potchefstroom-Winburg Trekker Republic in 1843*, ed. D. Williams. Cape Town, 1956.

Bird, J. *The annals of Natal*. Pietermaritzburg, 1888. 2 vols.

Boyce, W. B. *Notes on South African affairs from 1834 to 1838*. Graham's Town, 1838.

Brookes, E. H. *The history of native policy in South Africa from 1830 to the present day*. Cape Town, 1924.

Brookes, E. H. and Webb, C. de B. *A history of Natal*. Pietermaritzburg, 1965.

Burchell, W. J. *Travels in the interior of southern Africa* (reprint of 1822–4), ed. I. Schapera. London, 1953. 2 vols.

Campbell, W. B. 'The South African frontier, 1865–1885: a study in expansion', *Archives Year Book for South African History*, 1. Cape Town, 1959.

Cathcart, G. *Correspondence of Lieut.-General the Hon. Sir George Cathcart, K.C.B., relative to his military operations in Kaffraria* (reprint of 1856 ed.). New York, 1969.

Chapman, J. *Travels in the interior of South Africa*. London, 1868. 2 vols.

Chase, J. C. *Natal papers*. Graham's Town, 1843. 2 vols.

Cloete, H. *The history of the Great Boer Trek*, ed. W. Broderick-Cloete. Cape Town, 1899.

Collins, W. W. *Free Statia: reminiscences of a lifetime in the Orange Free State*, 2nd ed. Cape Town, 1965.

Cory, Sir George E. *The rise of South Africa* (reprint of 1910 ed.) Cape Town, 1965. 6 vols.

De Kiewiet, C. W. *British colonial policy and the South African republics, 1848–1872* (Imperial Studies, 3). London, 1929.

De Kiewiet, C. W. *The imperial factor in South Africa*. Cambridge, 1937.

De Kiewiet, C. W. *A history of South Africa, social and economic*. Oxford, 1941.

Delegorgue, A. *Voyage dans l'Afrique australe, notamment dans le territoire de Natal, dans celui des Cafres Amazoulous et Makatisses, et jusqu'au tropique du Capricorne, exécuté durant les anneés 1838, 1839, 1840, 1841, 1842, 1843 et 1844*. Paris, 1847. 2 vols.

De Vaal, J. B. 'Die Rol van João Albasini in die Geskiedenis van die Transvaal', *Archives Year Book for South African History*. 1. Cape Town, 1953.

Dicke, B. H. 'The Northern Transvaal Voortrekkers', *Archives Year Book for South African History*, 1941, 4, 1.

Duly, L. C. 'The failure of British land policy at the Cape, 1812–28', *Journal of African History*, 1965, 6, 3, 357–71.

Du Plessis, A. J. 'Die Republiek Natalia', *Archives Year Book for South African History*, 1942, 5, 1, 101–238.

Du Plessis, J. A. *A history of Christian missions in South Africa* (facsimile reprint of 1911 ed.). Cape Town, 1965.

Du Toit, A. E. 'The Cape Frontier', *Archives Year Book for South African History*, 1. Cape Town, 1954.

Eybers, G. von Welfling ed. *Select constitutional documents illustrating South African History, 1795–1910*. London, 1918.

Foster, W. *British rule in South Africa*. Cape Town, 1868.

Fryer, A. K. 'The government of the Cape of Good Hope, 1825–1854: the age of imperial reform', *Archives Year Book for South African History*, 1. Cape Town, 1964.

Fuller, C. *Louis Trigardt's trek across the Drakensberg, 1837–38*, ed. L. Fouché (Van Riebeeck Society, 13). Cape Town, 1932.

Furneaux, R. *The Zulu war*. London, 1963.

Gailey, H. H., Jr. 'John Philip's role in Hottentot emancipation', *Journal of African History*, 1962, 3, 3, 419–34.

Galbraith, J. S. 'The "turbulent frontier" as a factor in British expansion', *Comparative Studies in Society and History*, 1960, 2, 2, 150–68.

Galbraith, J. S. *Reluctant empire*. Berkeley, 1963.

Godlonton, R. *A narrative of the irruption of the Kaffir hordes into the eastern province of the Cape of Good Hope, 1834–35*. Graham's Town, 1836.

Godlonton, R. *Case of the colonists of the eastern frontier of the Cape of Good Hope, in reference to the Kaffir wars of 1835–6 and 1846*. Graham's Town, 1846.

Godlonton, R. and Irving, E. *Narrative of the Kaffir war* (reprint of 1851 ed.). Cape Town, 1962.

Goodfellow, C. F. *Great Britain and South African Confederation 1870–1881*. Cape Town, 1966.

Grobbelaar, J. J. G. 'Die Vrystaatse Republiek en die Basoetoe-Vraagstuk', *Archives Year Book for South African History*, 11. Cape Town, 1939.

Halford, S. J. *The Griquas of Griqualand*. Cape Town, 1941.

Hattersley, A. F. *More annals of Natal*. London, 1936.

Hattersley, A. F. *Later annals of Natal*. London, 1938.

Hattersley, A. F. *Portrait of a colony: the story of Natal*. Cambridge, 1940.

Hattersley, A. F. *The British settlement of Natal: a study in imperial migration*. Cambridge, 1950.

Hockly, H. E. *The story of the British settlers of 1820 in South Africa*, 2nd ed. Cape Town, 1957.

Holden, W. C. *History of the Colony of Natal* (reprint of 1855 ed., Africana Collectanea, 4). Cape Town, 1963.

Kirk, A. 'Progress and decline in the Kat River Settlement, 1829–1854', *Journal of African History*, 1973, **14**, 3, 411–28.

Leibbrandt, H. C. V. ed. *The rebellion of 1815, generally known as Slachters Nek*. Cape Town, 1902.

Lewin, J. 'Dr. John Philip and liberalism', *Race Relations Journal*, 1960, **27**, 2, 82–90.

Leyds, W. J. *The first annexation of the Transvaal*. London, 1906.

Lichtenstein, M. H. C. *Travels in southern Africa*. Van Riebeeck Society, 10 and 11. Cape Town, 1928–30. 2 vols.

Lindley, A. F. *Adamantia, the truth about the South African diamond fields*. London, 1873.

McCracken, J. L. *The Cape parliament, 1854–1910*. Oxford, 1967.

MacCrone, I. D. *Race attitudes in South Africa*. London, 1937.

Macmillan, W. M. *The Cape Colour question*. London, 1927.

Macmillan, W. M. *Bantu, Boer and Briton*, revised and enlarged 1929 ed. Oxford, 1963.

Macquarrie, J. W. ed. *The reminiscences of Sir Walter Stanford* (Van Riebeeck Society, 39), I. Cape Town, 1958.

Malan, J. H. *Die Opkoms van 'n Republiek*. Bloemfontein, 1929.

Marais, J. S. *Maynier and the first Boer republics*. Cape Town, 1944.

Marquard, L. *The peoples and policies of South Africa*, 4th ed. Cape Town, 1969.

Martineau, J. *The life and correspondence of Sir Bartle Frere*. London, 1895. 2 vols.

Mentzel, O. F. *A geographical and topographical description of the Cape of Good Hope*, ed. H. T. Mandelbrote (Van Riebeeck Society, 25), III. Cape Town, 1944.

Midgley, J. F. 'The Orange river sovereignty (1848–1854)', *Archives Year Book for South African History*, 11, v–xxiv, 1–594. Cape Town, 1949.

Molteno, P. A. *The life and times of Sir John Charles Molteno*. London, 1900. 2 vols.

Moodie, D. *The Record, or a series of official papers relative to the condition and treatment of the native tribes of South Africa* (photostatic reprint). Amsterdam, 1960.

Muller, C. F. J. *Waarom die Groot Trek geslaag het* (communication of the University of South Africa, B. 12). Pretoria, 1960.

Nathan, M. *The Voortrekkers of South Africa.* London, 1937.

Neumark, S. D. *Economic influences on the South African frontier, 1652–1836.* Stanford, 1957.

Orpen, J. M. *Reminiscences of life in South Africa from 1846 to the present day.* 2nd ed. Cape Town, 1946.

Orpen, J. M. *History of the Basutus of South Africa.* 1857. Facsimile reprint, Cape Town, 1955.

Payton, C. A. *The diamond diggings of South Africa.* London, 1872.

Pelzer, A. N. *Geskiedenis van die Suid-Afrikaanse Republiek.* Cape Town, 1958.

Philip, J. *Researches in South Africa.* London, 1828. 2 vols.

Phillips, T. *1820 settler, his letters,* ed. A. Keppel-Jones. Pietermaritzburg, 1960.

Potgieter, F. J. 'Die Vestiging van die Blanke in Transvaal 1837–86', *Archives Year Book for South African History*, II. Cape Town, 1959.

Preller, G. S. *Voortrekkermense.* Cape Town, 1920–5. 4 vols.

Preller, G. S. ed. *Voortrekker wetgewing: notule van die Natalse Volksraad, 1839–1845.* Pretoria, 1924.

Pringle, T. *Narrative of a residence in South Africa.* London, 1835.

Rutherford, J. *Sir George Grey, K.C.B., 1812–1898.* London, 1961.

Schoeman, A. E. *Coenraad de Buys: the first Transvaler.* Pretoria, 1938.

Scholtz, G. D. *Die Konstitutie en Staatinstellings van die Oranje Vrijstaat, 1854–1872.* Amsterdam, 1937.

Scholtz, J. du P. *Die Afrikaner en sy taal, 1806–1875,* 2nd ed. Cape Town, 1965.

Smith, H. G. W. *The autobiography of . . . Sir Harry Smith,* ed. G. C. Moore Smith. London, 1903. 2 vols.

Smith, K. W. 'The fall of the Bapedi of the north-eastern Transvaal', *Journal of African History*, 1969, **10**, 2, 237–52.

Stockenstrom, Sir Andries. *Narrative of transactions connected with the Kafir war of 1846 and 1847; embracing correspondence between Sir P. Maitland, Lieutenant-Colonel M. Johnstone, Sir A. Stockenstrom, and others.* Grahamstown, 1848.

Stockenstrom, Sir Andries. *The autobiography of . . . Sir Andries Stockenstrom,* ed. C. W. Hutton (reprint of 1887 ed.). Cape Town, 1964. 2 vols.

Theal, G. M., *Basutoland records,* 1883. Facsimile reprint. Cape Town, 1964. 4 vols.

Theal, G. M. *The Republic of Natal.* Cape Town, 1886.

Theal, G. M. *History of South Africa.* London, 1892–1919. 11 vols.

Theal, G. M. *Records of the Cape Colony.* London, 1897–1905. 36 vols.

Theal, G. M. *Documents relating to the Kaffir War of 1835.* London, 1912.

Trapido, S. 'The origins of the Cape franchise qualification of 1853', *Journal of African History*, 1964, **5**, 1, 37–54.

Uys, C. J. *In the era of Shepstone.* Lovedale, 1933.

Van der Merwe, P. J. *Die noordwaartse beweging van die Boere voor die Groot Trek, 1770–1842.* The Hague, 1937.

Van der Merwe, P. J. *Die Trekboer in die geskiedenis van Kaapkolonie, 1657–1842.* Cape Town, 1938.

Van Jaarsveld, F. A. 'Die Veldkornet en sy aandeel in die opbou van die Suid-Afrikaanse Republiek tot 1870', *Archives Year Book for South African History,* 1950, **13**, 2.

Van Jaarsveld, F. A. *Die Tydgenootlike Beoordeling van die Groot Trek, 1836–1842* (communications of the University of South Africa, C. 36). Pretoria, 1962.

Van Ryneveld, H. B. ed. *Willem Stephanus van Ryneveld* (Van Riebeeck Society). Cape Town, 1942.

Walker, E. *The frontier tradition in South Africa.* Oxford, 1930.

Walker, E. *The Great Trek,* 4th ed. London, 1960.

Walker, E. *A history of southern Africa.* Rev. ed. London, 1965.

Walker, E. ed. *South Africa,* in *The Cambridge history of the British Empire,* VIII. 2nd ed. Cambridge, 1963.

Welsh, D. *The roots of segregation: native policy in colonial Natal, 1845–1910.* Cape Town, 1971.

Wichmann, F. A. F. 'Die Wordingsgeskiedenis van die Zuid-Afrikaansche Republiek 1838–1860', *Archives Year Book for South African History,* II, v–xii, 1–255. Cape Town, 1941.

Wilmot, Count A. *The life and times of Sir Richard Southey.* London, 1904.

11. TRADITION AND CHANGE IN MADAGASCAR, 1790–1870

Andriamanjato, R. *Le Tsiny et le Tody dans la pensée malgache.* Paris, 1957.

Archives, 'Les archives de Madagascar', *Bulletin de Madagascar,* 1958, **150**, 973–4.

Association des Géographes de Madagascar, *Atlas de Madagascar.* Tananarive, 1969.

Ayache, S. ed. *Annales de Raombana.* Tananarive, n.d. Madagascar in the first half of the nineteenth century.

Ayache, S. ed. *Histoires de Raombana.* Tananarive, n.d. Madagascar in the first half of the nineteenth century.

Bloch, M. 'Notes sur l'organisation sociale de l'Imerina avant le règne de Radama I', *Annales de l'Université de Madagascar,* 7, 119–32.

Boudou, A. *Les Jésuites à Madagascar au XIXe siècle.* Paris, 1940–2. 2 vols.

Callet, F. *Tantara ny Andriana eto Madagaskara.* Antananarivo, 1872–83. 3 vols. [Incomplete French translation, Tananarive, 1953–8.] A fundamental work for the history of Imerina, including Merina oral traditions.

Chapus, G. S. *Quatre-vingt ans d'influences européennes en Imerina.* Tananarive, 1925. A history of the European influence on the indigenous civilization.

Chapus, G. S. and Mondain, G. *Rainilaiarivony: un homme d'état Malgache.* Paris, 1953.

Cousins, W. E. ed. *Ten years' review of mission work in Madagascar, 1861–1870.* Antananarivo, 1870.

Decary, R. *La mort et les coutumes funéraires à Madagascar.* Paris, 1962.

Decary, R. *Mœurs et coutumes des Malgaches.* Paris, 1951.

Delval, R. *Radama II: prince de la renaissance malgache.* Paris, 1972.

Deschamps, H. *Les Antaisaka.* Tananarive, 1938.

Deschamps, H. *Les migrations interieures passées et presentes à Madagascar.* Paris, 1959.

Deschamps, H. *Histoire de Madagascar.* Paris, 1972.

Dubois, H. M. *Monographie des Betsileo.* Paris, 1938.

Duignan, P. *Madagascar (the Malagasy Republic): a list of materials in the African collections of Stanford University and the Hoover Institution.* Stanford, 1962.

Du Maine, 'Voyages au pays d'Ankay', in *Annales des voyages.* 1810.

Ellis, W. *History of Madagascar.* London, 1838. 2 vols.

Ellis, W. *Three visits to Madagascar.* London, 1858.

Ellis, W. *Madagascar revisited.* London, 1867.

Freeman, J. J. and Johns, D. *A narrative of the persecutions of the Christians in Madagascar.* London, 1840.

Grandidier, A. and G. *Ethnographie de Madagascar.* Paris, 1908–28.

Grandidier, G. *Bibliographie de Madagascar.* Paris, 1905, 1906, 1935, 1957.

Grandidier, G. *Histoire physique, naturelle et politique de Madagascar.* Paris, 1952–8. History of the Merina and of several other peoples, with numerous notes.

Guillain, M. *Documents sur l'histoire, la géographie et le commerce de la partie occidentale de Madagascar.* Paris, 1845.

Howe, S. *The drama of Madagascar.* London, 1938.

Jukes, Rev. C. *Country work in Madagascar.* London, 1870.

Julien, G. *Institutions politiques et sociales de Madagascar.* Paris, 1908.

Leguével de Lacombe, B. F. *Voyage à Madagascar et aux Comores, 1823 à 1830.* Paris, 1840.

Malzac, V. P. *Histoire du royaume hova.* Tananarive, 1912. A résumé of the work by Callet [see above].

Mayeur, V. P. 'Voyage au pays d'Ancore (1777)', *Bulletin de l'Académie Malgache,* 1912–13.

Mayeur, V. P. 'Voyage au pays de Séclaves (1774)', *Bulletin de l'Académie Malgache,* 1912–13.

Moss, C. F. A. 'A brief account of Radama II', *Antananarivo Annual,* 1900, 24, 486–9.

Munthe, L. *La Bible à Madagascar.* Oslo, 1969.

Mutibwa, P. M. 'Patterns of trade and economic development in nineteenth century Madagascar', *Transafrican Journal of History,* 1972, 2, 1, 33–63.

Mutibwa, P. M. *The Malagasy and the Europeans: Madagascar's foreign relations, 1861–1895.* Ibadan History Series. Ibadan, 1974.

Pfeiffer, I. *The last travels of Ida Pfeiffer.* London, 1881.

Rajemisa-Raolison, R. *Dictionnaire historique et géographique de Madagascar.* Fianarantsoa, 1966.

Ralaimihoatra, E. *Histoire de Madagascar.* Tananarive, 1966.

Rochon, A. M. de. *Voyage à Madagascar et aux Indes Orientales.* Paris, 1791.

Rudd, J. *Takoo: a study of Malagasy customs and beliefs.* London and Oslo, 1960.

Segu, D. A. 'Madagascar: an example of indigenous modernisation of a traditional society in the nineteenth century', *Saint Antony's Papers*, Oxford, 1969, **21**, 67–91.

Sibree, J. *Madagascar and its people*. London, 1870.

Sibree, J. *The great African island: chapters on Madagascar*. London, 1880.

Sibree, J. 'A quarter-century of change and progress: Antananarivo and Madagascar twenty-five years ago', *Antananarivo Annual*, 1888, **12**, 397–420.

Sibree, J. *The Madagascar mission*. London, 1907.

Sibree, J. *Fifty years in Madagascar*. London, 1924.

Standing, H. F. 'The tribal divisions of the Hova Malagasy', *Antananarivo Annual*, 1887, **11**, 354–63.

Thorne, J. C. 'Elementary education in Madagascar', *Antananarivo Annual*, 1885–8, **10**, 27–40.

Valette, J. *Les archives de Madagascar*. Abbeville, 1962.

Valette, J. *Études sur le règne de Radama I*. Tananarive, 1962.

Valette, J. 'Madagascar', in Deschamps, H. ed., *Histoire générale de l'Afrique noire*, II (Paris, 1971), 325–56.

Vinson, A. *Voyage à Madagascar*. Paris, 1865.

12. AFRICANS OVERSEAS, 1790–1870

Aptheker, H. ed. *A documentary history of the Negro people in the United States*. New York, 1951, 2nd ed. 1964.

Aptheker, H. *American Negro slave revolts*. New York, 1964.

Augier, R. and Hall, D. *et al*. *The making of the British West Indies*. London, 1960.

Bastide, R. *Les Amériques noires*. . .Paris, 1967.

Bell, H. H. *A survey of the Negro Convention Movement, 1830–1861*. New York, 1969.

Bennett, L., Jr. *Before the Mayflower: a history of black America*. 4th ed. rev. Chicago, 1969.

Berlin, I. *Slaves without masters: the free Negro in the ante-bellum South*. New York, 1974.

Berwanger, E. H. *The frontier against slavery: Western anti-Negro prejudice and the slavery extension controversy*. Urbana, Ill., 1967.

Blassingame, J. W. *The slave community: plantation life in the ante-bellum South*. New York, 1972.

Blyden, E. W. *Liberia's offering*. . .New York, 1862.

Bond, H. M. *Negro education in Alabama: a study in cotton and steel*. Washington, 1939.

Bontemps, A. ed. *Great slave narratives*. Boston, 1969.

Botkin, B. ed. *Lay my burden down*. Chicago, 1945.

Boxer, C. R. *Race relations in the Portuguese colonial empire, 1415–1825*. London, 1963.

Bracey, J. H., Meier, A. and Rudwick, E. eds. *The Afro-American: selected documents*. Boston, 1970. 2 vols.

Braithwaite, L. E. *The development of Creole society in Jamaica*. Oxford, 1971.

Cornish, D. T. *The sable arm: Negro troops in the Union army, 1861–1865*. New York, 1956.

Cromer, Earl of. *Modern Egypt*. London, 1911.

Curtin, P. D. *Two Jamaicas*. Cambridge, 1955.

Davis, D. B. *The problem of slavery in Western culture*. Ithaca, N.Y., 1966.

Degler, C. *Neither black nor white: slavery and race relations in Brazil and the United States*. New York, 1971.

Delany, M. J. *The conditions, elevation, emigration and destiny of the colored people of the United States*. Philadelphia, 1852.

Delany, M. J. *Official report of the Niger exploration party*. Reprint, New York, 1961.

Douglass, Frederick. *My bondage and my freedom*. New York, 1855.

Douglass, Frederick. *The life and times of Frederick Douglass*. Hartford, Conn., 1884.

Drimmer, M. ed. *Black history: a reappraisal*. Garden City, N.Y., 1968.

DuBois, W. E. B. *Black reconstruction*. New York, 1935.

Elkins, S. M. *Slavery: a problem in American institutional life*. Chicago, 1959.

Fagg, J. E. *Cuba, Haiti and the Dominican Republic*. New Jersey, 1965.

Filler, L. *The crusade against slavery. 1830–1860*. New York, 1960.

Fishel, L. H., Jr and Quarles, B. eds. *The black American: a documentary history*. Glenview, Ill., 1970.

Fogel, R. W. and Engerman, S. L. *Time on the cross: the economics of American Negro slavery*. Boston, 1974. 2 vols.

Foner, E. *Free soil, free labor, free men: the ideology of the Republican Party before the Civil War*. New York, 1970.

Foner, E. ed. *America's black past: a reader in Afro-American history*. New York, 1970.

Foner, L. and Genovese, E. D. eds. *Slavery in the New World: a reader in comparative history*. Englewood Cliffs, N.J., 1960.

Foner, P. S. ed. *The life and writings of Frederick Douglass*. New York, 1951–5. 4 vols.

Foner, P. S. ed. *The voice of black America: major speeches by Negroes in the United States, 1797–1971*. New York, 1972.

Franklin, J. H. *The free Negro in North Carolina, 1790–1860*. Chapel Hill, N.C., 1943.

Franklin, J. H. *Reconstruction after the Civil War*. Chicago, 1961.

Franklin, J. H. *The emancipation proclamation*. New York, 1963.

Franklin, J. H. *From slavery to freedom: a history of Negro Americans*. 3rd ed. rev. New York, 1967.

Frazier, E. F. *The Negro family*. New York, 1939.

Frazier, E. F. *The Negro in the United States*. New York, 1957.

Frazier, E. F. *The Negro Church in America*. New York, 1963 and Liverpool, 1964.

Frazier, T. R. ed. *Afro-American history: primary sources*. New York, 1970.

Frederickson, G. M. *The black image in the white mind: the debate on Afro-American character and destiny, 1817–1914*. New York, 1971.

Freyre, G. *The master and the slaves*. New York, 1946.

Freyre, G. *The mansions and the shanties: the making of modern Brazil*. New York, 1963.

Genovese, E. D. *The political economy of slavery*. New York, 1965.

Genovese, E. D. *In red and black: Marxian explorations in Southern and Afro-American history*. New York, 1968.

Genovese, E. D. *Roll Jordan roll: the world the slaves made*. New York, 1974.

Gutman, H. G. *The many children of Adam and Evelin: a social history of the Afro-American family during and after enslavement, 1750–1930*.

Hall, D. G. *Five of the Leewards, 1834–1870*. Barbados, 1971.

Hall, D. G. *Free Jamaica*. Barbados, 1971.

Harris, M. *Patterns of race in the America's*. New York, 1964.

Haynes, L. *The negro community within American Protestantism, 1619–1844*. Boston, 1953.

Herskovits, M. J. *The myth of the Negro past*. New York, 1941.

Higginson, T. W. *Army life in a black regiment*. Boston, 1869.

Huggins, N. I., Kilson, M. and Fox, D. M. eds. *Key issues in the Afro-American experience*. New York, 1971. 2 vols.

Jackson, L. P. *Free Negro labor and property holding in Virginia, 1830–1860*. New York, 1942.

James, C. L. R. *The black Jacobins: Toussaint L'Ouverture and the San Domingo revolution*. New York, 1938. Reprinted 1963.

Johnston, Sir H. *The Negro in the New World*. New York, 1916.

Jordan, W. D. *White over black: American attitudes towards the Negro, 1550–1812*. Chapel Hill, N.C., 1968.

Kent, R. K. 'Palmares, an African state in Brazil', *Journal of African History*, 1965, **62**, 161–75.

Klein, H. S. *Slavery in the Americas: a comparative study of Cuba and Virginia*. Chicago, 1967.

Knight, F. W. *Slave society in Cuba during the nineteenth century*. Madison, Wis., 1970.

Kraditor, A. *Means and ends in American abolitionism: Garrison and his critics on strategy and tactics, 1834–1860*. New York, 1960.

Lane, A. ed. *The debate over slavery: Stanley Elkins and his critics*. Urbana, Ill., 1971.

Levine, L. W. 'Slave songs and slave consciousness: an exploration in neglected sources', in Hareven, T. K. ed., *Anonymous Americans: explorations in nineteenth-century social history*. Englewood Cliffs, N.J., 1971.

Leyburn, J. G. *The Haitian people*. Rev. ed. New Haven, 1966.

Litwack, L. F. *North of slavery: the Negro in the free states, 1790–1860*. Chicago, 1961.

McPherson, J. M. *The struggle for equality: abolitionists and the Negro in the Civil War and reconstruction*. Princeton, 1964.

McPherson, J. M. *The Negro's Civil War*. New York, 1969.

McPherson, J. M. *et al. Blacks in America: bibliographical essays*. Garden City, N.Y., 1971.

Manchester, A. K. *British pre-eminence in Brazil*. . . Durham, N.C., 1933.

Meier, A. and Rudwick, E. *From plantation to ghetto*. 2nd ed. rev. New York, 1970.

Meier, A. and Rudwick, E. eds. *The making of black America*. New York, 1969. 2 vols.

Mullin, G. W. *Flight and rebellion: slave resistance in eighteenth-century Virginia*. New York, 1972.

Mörner, M. *Race mixture in the history of Latin America*. Boston, 1967.

Myrdal, G. *An American dilemma*. New York, 1944. 2 vols.

Nichol, A. 'West Indians in Africa', *Sierra Leone Studies*, 1960, new series, **13**, 14ff.

Osofsky, G. ed. *The burden of race: a documentary history of Negro–white relations in America*. New York, 1967.

Osofsky, G. ed. *Puttin' on ole massa: the slave narratives of Henry Bibb, William Wells Brown and Solomon Northup*. New York, 1969.

Patterson, H. O. *The sociology of slavery*. London, 1967.

Patrick, R. W. *The reconstruction of the nation*. New York, 1967.

Pendle, G. *A history of Latin America*. London, 1963.

Phillips, U. B. *American Negro slavery*. New York, 1918.

Phillips, U. B. *Life and labor in the old South*. Boston, 1929.

Pooter, D. B. comp. *The Negro in the United States: a selected bibliography*. Washington, 1970.

Quarles, B. *The Negro in the Civil War*. Boston, 1953.

Quarles, B. *The Negro in the American revolution*. Chapel Hill, 1961.

Quarles, B. *The Negro in the making of America*. New York, 1964.

Quarles, B. *Black abolitionists*. New York, 1969.

Ramos, A. *The Negro in Brazil*. New York, 1945.

Rawick, G. P. *From sundown to sunup: the making of the black community*. Westport, Conn., 1972.

Rawick, G. P. ed. *The American slave: a composite autobiography*. Westport, Conn., 1971–2. 19 vols.

Reckord, M. 'The Jamaican slave rebellion of 1831', *Past and Present*, July 1968, **40**, 108.

Rodrigues, J. H. 'The influence of Africa on Brazil and of Brazil on Africa', *Journal of African History*, 1962, **3**, 1, 52–6.

Rodrigues, J. H. *Brazil and Africa*. Berkeley, 1965.

Rose, W. L. *Rehearsal for reconstruction*. Indianapolis, 1964.

Ross, D. A. 'The career of Domingo Martinez in the Bight of Benin, 1833–64', *Journal of African History*, 1965, **6**, 1, 79–90.

Savelle, M. and Middlekauf, R. *A history of colonial America*. Rev. ed. New York, 1964.

Shepperson, G. 'Notes on Negro American influences on the emergence of African nationalism', *Journal of African History*, 1960, **1**, 2, 301.

Smith, E. D. *The death of slavery*. Chicago, 1967.

Stampp, K. M. *The era of reconstruction, 1865–1877*. New York, 1965.

Starobin, R. S. *Industrial slavery in the old South*. New York, 1970.

Staudenraus, P. J. *The African Colonization Movement, 1816–1865*. New York, 1961.

Suerra y Sanchez, R. *Sugar and society in the Caribbean*. New Haven, Conn., 1964.

Tannenbaum, F. *Slave and citizen*. New York, 1947.

Taylor, A. A. *The Negro in the reconstruction of Virginia*. Washington, 1926.

Verger, P. *Bahia and the west coast trade 1549–1851*. Ibadan, 1964.

Voorhis, M. Van B. *Negro masonry in the United States*. New York, 1940.

Wade, R. C. *Slavery in the cities: the South, 1820–1860*. New York, 1964.

Walker, D. *Walker's appeal*, in four articles. Boston, 1830.

Walker, J. *The Black Loyalists: the search for a promised land in Nova Scotia and Sierra Leone, 1783–1870*. London, 1976.

Weinstein, A. and Gattell, F. O. eds. *American Negro slavery: a modern reader*. New York, 1968.

Welsch, E. K. *The Negro on the United States: a research guide*. Bloomington, Ind., 1965.

Wharton, V. L. *The Negro in Mississippi, 1865–1890*. Chapel Hill, N.C., 1947.

Whiteman, M. ed. *Afro-American history series*. Wilmington, Del., 1971. 10 vols.

Williams, E. *Capitalism and slavery*. Chapel Hill, N.C., 1944, 2nd impr. London, 1964.

Williamson, J. *After slavery: the Negro in South Carolina during reconstruction, 1861–1877*. Chapel Hill, N.C., 1965.

Winks, R. W. *The blacks in Canada: a history*. New Haven, Conn., 1971.

Wood, D. *Trinidad in transition*. Oxford, 1968.

Woodson, C. G. *Negro orators and their orations*. Washington, 1925.

Woodson, C. G. *The mind of the Negro as reflected in letters written during the crisis, 1800–1860*. Washington, 1926.

Woodson, C. G. *The history of the Negro Church*. 2nd ed. Washington, 1945.

Woodward, C. Vann. *The strange career of Jim Crow*. 2nd ed. rev. New York, 1960.

Woodward, C. Vann. *American counterpoint: slavery and racism in the North–South dialogue*. Boston, 1971.

Work, M. N. *A bibliography of the Negro in the United States: a research guide*. Bloomington, Ind., 1965.

Yetman, N. R. ed. *Voices from slavery*. New York, 1970.

13. CHANGING EUROPEAN ATTITUDES TO AFRICA

Africa Past and Present. London, 1879.

Alazard, J. and others. *Histoire et historiens de l'Algérie (1830–1930)*. Paris, 1931.

Anstey, R. T. 'Capitalism and slavery: a critique', *Economic History Review*, 1968, **21**, 307–20.

The Anthropological Record (London). 1863, **I**, 390.

Arnold, M. *Lectures and essays in criticism*, ed. R. H. Super. Ann Arbor, 1962.

Baudet, H. *Paradise upon earth*. London, 1965.

Bodelsen, C. A. *Studies in mid-Victorian imperialism*. London, 1960.

Bolt, C. *Victorian attitudes to race*. London, 1971.

Bovill, E. W. *The Niger explored*. London, 1968.

C., J. W., *Progressive geography for children*. London, 1847.

Cairns, H. A. C. *Prelude to imperialism: British reactions to central African society, 1840–1890*. London, 1965.

Coupland, Sir Reginald. *The British anti-slavery movement*. London, 1933.

Crawfurd, J. 'On the physical and mental characteristics of the Negro', *Transactions of the Ethnological Society*, 1866, new series, **4**.

Curtin, P. D. *The image of Africa: British ideas and action, 1780–1850*. London, 1965.

Cust, R. N. *A sketch of the modern languages of Africa*. London, 1883.

Daniel, N. *Islam and the West: the making of an image*. Edinburgh, 1960.

Daniel, N. *Islam, Europe and Empire*. Edinburgh, 1966.

Darwin, C. *The descent of man*. London, 1871. 2 vols.

Daudet, A. *The prodigious adventures of Tartarin de Tarascon* (English translation). London, 1896.

Deschamps, H. *Les méthodes et les doctrines coloniales de la France (du XVIe siècle à nos jours)*. Paris, 1953.

Duff Gordon, Lady Lucie. *Letters from the Cape*, ed. D. Fairbridge. London, 1927.

Duff Gordon, Lady Lucie. *Letters from Egypt (1862–1869)*, centenary ed. by Gordon Waterfield. London, 1969.

Duffy, J. *Portuguese Africa*. London, 1959.

Dunn, R. 'Some observations on the physiological differences which exist among the typical races of man', *Transactions of the Ethnological Society of London*, 1865, new series, **3**, 9–25.

Encyclopaedia Britannica, 3rd ed. Edinburgh, 1797.

Exploration scientifique de l'Algérie pendant les années 1840, 1841, 1842. Paris, 1844–67. 39 vols.

Fairchild, H. N. *The noble savage*. New York, 1928.

Fromentin, E. *Une année dans le Sahel*, with an introduction by L. Morel. Oxford, 1911.

Fück, J. W. 'Islam as a historical problem in European historiography since 1800', in Lewis, B. and Holt, P. M. eds., *Historians of the Middle East*. London, 1962.

Ganiage, J. *Les origines du protectorat français en Tunisie (1861–1881)*. Paris, 1959.

Gautier, Th. *Loin de Paris*. Paris, 1865.

Glanville, S. R. K. *The growth and nature of Egyptology*. Cambridge, 1947.

Gobineau, J. A. de. *Essai sur l'inégalité des races humaines*. Paris, 1853–5. 4 vols.

Gosset, T. F. *Race: the history of an idea in America*. Dallas, 1963.

Graham, G. S. *Great Britain in the Indian Ocean: a study of maritime enterprise, 1810–1850*. London, 1968.

Groves, C. P. *The planting of Christianity in Africa*, i–iv. London, 1948–58.

Hallett, R. *The penetration of Africa: European enterprise and exploration principally in Northern and Western Africa up to 1830*, i. London, 1965.

Hallett, R. ed. *Records of the African Association 1788–1831.* London, 1964.

Hammond, R. J. *Portugal in Africa.* Stanford, 1966.

Hattersley, A. F. *The British settlement of Natal.* Cambridge, 1960.

Helly, D. O. '"Informed" opinion on tropical Africa in Great Britain, 1860–1890', *African Affairs*, 1969, **68**, 272, 195–217.

Higgins, G. *An apology for the life and character of the celebrated Prophet of Arabia called Mohamed, or the Illustrious.* London, 1829.

Hill, R. L. 'Historical writing on the Sudan since 1820', in Lewis, B. and Holt, P. M. eds., *Historians of the Middle East.* London, 1962.

Howe, S. *The drama of Madagascar.* London, 1938.

Jomard, E. F. ed. *Description de l'Égypte.* Paris, 1809–28, 20 vols. (9 vols. text; 11 vols. plates). 2nd ed. Paris, 1821–9. 24 vols.

Julien, C. A. *Histoire de l'Algérie contemporaine: la conquête et les débuts de la colonisation (1827–1871).* Paris, 1964.

Kiernan, V. G. *The lords of human kind: European attitudes towards the outside world in the imperial age.* London, 1969.

Knorr, K. E. *British colonial theories, 1570–1850*, new ed. London, 1963.

Knox, R. *The races of man*, 1st ed. London, 1850. 2nd ed. with supplementary chapters, London, 1862.

Koelle, S. W. *African native literature.* London, 1854.

Kolb, P. *The present state of the Cape of Good Hope*, tr. from the German. London, 1731. 2 vols.

Lander, R. and J. *The Niger journal*, ed. R. Hallett. London, 1965.

Lebel, R. *Histoire de la littérature coloniale en France.* Paris, 1931.

Leyden, J. *Poems and ballads, with a memoir by Walter Scott.* Kelso, 1858.

The life of Mahomet: or, the history of the imposture which was begun, carried on and finally established by him in Arabia, and which has subjugated a larger portion of the globe, than the religion of Jesus has set at liberty. London, 1799.

Long, E. 'Thoughts on the Negroes of Africa in general', in his *The history of Jamaica*, II, 351–84. London, 1774.

MacCrone, I. D. *Race attitudes in South Africa: historical, experimental and psychological studies.* London, 1937.

MacQueen, J. *A geographical survey of Africa.* London, 1840.

Madden, A. F. 'The attitude of the Evangelicals to the Empire and imperial problems (1820–1850)'. D.Phil. thesis, University of Oxford, 1950.

Marston, T. E. *Britain's imperial role in the Red Sea area, 1800–1878.* Hamden, Conn., 1961.

Martin, E. C. *The British West African settlements.* London, 1927.

Masson, P. *Histoire des établissements et du commerce français dans l'Afrique Barbaresque (1560–1793).* Paris, 1903.

Masson, P. *L'histoire du commerce français dans le Levant au XVIIIe siècle.* Paris, 1911.

Mellor, G. R. *British imperial trusteeship 1783–1850.* London, 1951.

Miège, J. L. *Le Maroc et l'Europe (1830–1894)*, I–IV. Paris, 1961.

Mill, J. S. *The principles of political economy*, 6th ed. London, 1865. 2 vols.

Missionary papers, 1816, no. 2; 1818, no. 9.

Moorhouse, G. *The missionaries.* London, 1973.

Murray, H. *The African continent: a narrative of discovery and adventure*. London, 1853.

Newbury, C. W. *British policy towards West Africa: selected documents, 1786–1874*. Oxford, 1965.

Park, M. *Travels in Africa*. London, 1954.

Prichard, J. S. *Researches into the physical history of mankind*, 3rd ed. London, 1836–47. 5 vols.

Reade, W. W. *Savage Africa*. London, 1863.

Robinson, R. and Gallagher, J. with Denny, A. *Africa and the Victorians: the official mind of imperialism*. London, 1961.

Schapera, I. ed. *Livingstone's private journals, 1851–1853*. London, 1960.

Smith, B. *European vision and the South Pacific, 1768–1850*. Oxford, 1962.

Sypher, W. *Guinea's captive kings: British anti-slavery literature of the XVIIIth century*. Chapel Hill, N.C., 1942.

Volney, C. F. *Travels through Syria and Egypt*, translated from the French. Dublin, 1793.

White, C. *An account of the regular graduations in man and in different animals and vegetables*. London, 1799.

Wilson, M. and Thompson, L. eds. *The Oxford history of South Africa*, 1. Oxford, 1969.

INDEX

Page numbers in italics indicate substantive references

Saker, Alfred 257
Sakka 85
Salama, *abba, abuna*, 62, 63, 64, 67, 68, 76
Salenc, J. 508
al-Ṣāliḥiyya, battle of 16
Salīm Qabūdān 33, 38
Salla festival 148
salt: deposits, mines 8, 55, 65, 82, 86, 94,
    240, 241, 247, 249, 251, 268, 287, 288,
    289, 294; lakes 289, 291, 292, 294, 295;
    trade 55, 64, 245, 249, 256, 262, 263,
    393; tribute 227, 233, 242
Salt, Henry 501, 502
Samba 251
Sambirano r. 410
Sambo (Hadejia) 138
'Sambo' 530, 531
Samory 165, 204, 511
sampy ('idols') 408
San ('Bushmen') 319, 353 and n., 355, 363,
    364, 439, 478
Sanaga region 259
Sancho, Ignatius 422 and n.
San Domingo 435
Sand r. 370, 380; Sand River Convention
    380
Sandile, chief 376
Sanga people 246
Sangu 277, 279, 280
Sanna Abba Jifar *see* Abba Jifar
Sanua, James (Ya'qūb Ṣanū') 48
Sanusiyya brotherhood 124
São João Baptista (ship) 323n.
São Salvador 261
São Tomé 268
Sapeto, Giuseppe 502
Sardinia 103
sarakuna (royals and courtiers) 138
Sarmento, Alfredo de 261
'Saro' (returned recaptives) 188
Sa'ūd (House of) 23; Sa'ūdī 24
Savelle, M. and Middlekauf, R. 445n.
Say (Lower Nubia) 14
Sayyid Bargash 306, 307
Sayyid Sa'īd b. Sulṭān 2, *273–6*, 298, 303,
    306, 310
'scalawags' 456n.
Schapera, I. 488n., 534
Schick, T. W. 510
Schmaltz, Julien 211
Schnapper, B. 197n., 198n., 510
Schoemansdal 387, 389
School of Oriental and African Studies 520
schools 116, 187, 193, 194, 217, 405, 416,
    453, 454; koranic 204
Schoonspruit 389
Schweinfurth, G. 266n., 513, 516

Scott, Sir Walter 471
Scottish Presbyterian mission 216
'scramble for Africa' 1, 9, 196, 199, 494
Sebagadis, *dejazmach* 60, 61
Sebetwane 341, 342
secession (Boer) 352, 366, 367
Sega Lijoch see Sost ledet
segments, territorial 327–8, 330
Segre, D. A. 525
Segregation 374
Segu 152, 153, 157, 159, 202, 203, 204
Sekeletu 234, 342
Sekonyela 338, 370
Seku Ahmadu *see* Aḥmad b. Muḥammad of
    Masina
Sekwati 386, 389
*Selections from the Records of the Bombay
    Government* 515
Selim III, Sultan 14, 19, 22
Semakokiro, *kabaka* 291
Semboja 286, 287, 313, 314
Semhar 64, 65, 89
Sena 349
Senegal 155, 156n., 164, 184, 186, 214, 215,
    219, 462, 464, 465, 494, 512; communes
    219, 221; valley 10, 158, 160, 181, 206,
    211, 218
Senegambia 129, 130, 131, 202, 204, 209, 485
Sennar 14, 15, 24; province 27
Senzangakone 326
Seqota 82
Sera'e 95
serfs 102, 137, 227, 228, 436
settlement: Arab 9, *270–2*, 306; European
    1, 10, 92, 104, 111, 117, 180, 521; freed
    slave 9, *170–199*
Seyfu 74
Sfax 103
Shādhiliyya 14, 137
Shafīk Ghorbal 499
Shaka 6, *326–35*, 337, 338, 340, 343
Shakini 283
Shambaa 280, 284, 287, 302, 304, 313, 314
Shango cult 431n.
Shanqualla 97
shī'a 29, 138, 139, 146, 148, 149, 153, 154
Sharīf Pasha 48
Sharp, Granville 171, 174, 175, 176, 182,
    190
Shaw, S. J. 497
Shāyqiyya 15, 24, 30
shea butter 212, 213
Shebele r. 56
sheep farming 387, 409
shehu see Usuman de Fodio
Shehu Ahmadu *see* Aḥmad b. Muḥammad
    of Masina

Smyrna 99
Sneeuwbergen 353
Soanierana (palace) 406
soap 406, 409
Sobat 33, 38, 42
Sobhuza 6, 323, 325, 326, 333
social change *298–306*; social reform 148; socio-economic system 213, 214
'Social Darwinists' 479
Société d'Anthropologie 536
Société d'Ethnographie 536
Société de Géographie 534
Société Royale de Géographie d'Egypte 497
Society for the abolition of slavery (French) 438n.
Society of African Missions (Catholic) 216
Society for the Propagation of the Gospel 523
sofa (converts) 158, 159
Sofala 271, 349
Soga people 294, 295
Soga, J. H. 519
Sokoto (city) 131, 135, 141, 168, 489
Sokoto caliphate 6, 7, 9, 137, 142, 150, 153, 154, 157, 160, 202, 506, 511
soldiers 101, 118, 158, 183, 184, 340, 341, 399, *400–12*, 464; *see also* cavalry
Solomonic descent, dynasty 58, 67, 71, 72
Somali, Somaliland, Somali coast 1, 44, 56, 57, 86, 87, 88, 501, 503
Somapunga 334
Somerset, James 171 and n.
Songea 278, 279, 350
Songhay 5, 7, 128, 129, 146, 153, 202
Songye 249, 251
Soninke 160n.
Soret, M. 513
sorghum 289
Sorogo 262
Sost Ledet (=*Sega Lijoch*) 62, 64, 67
Sotho 5, 6, 322, 323, 325, 331n., 338, 339–41, 351, 376, 379, 381, 383–4, 386, 390, 481, 520, 522
Sotho-Kololo 233; Sotho-Tswana 319, 321, 323, 343, 345
Souk-Ahras 118
Sousse 103
South Africa 1, 3, 10, *319–92*, 463, 464, 465, 478
South African Republic 387, 388
Southall 518
South Carolina 451
south-eastern Africa 241
southern Africa 2, 3, 5, 7, 222, *319–92*
Southern Baptist Convention 216
southern Central Africa 222, 229, *241–9*

South Pacific 480
South West Africa (Namibia) 319
Souza, Francesco Feliz de, *chacha* 429–30
Souza Machado, Saturnino de 263
sovereignty 170, 175, 184, 191, 192, 197, 198, 199, 209
Spain, Spanish 111, 122, 123, 125, 189, 208, 210, 222, 423, 434, 435, 463, 465, 467, 493
Spanish America 418n., 420, 423–4
spears (as trade goods, tribute) 228, 249, 266, 280, 288; *see also* under weapons
Speke, J. H. 42, 291, 297, 516, 517, 534
spelling 406
spirit possession 304
Stahl 518
Stampp, K. M. 457n., 529, 530
Stanley, H. M. 265, 297, and n., 496, 516, 534
Stanley Falls 265
Starobin, R. S. 529
state building 7, 203, 321–2, 340, 349
stateless peoples, societies 267, 279, 481
status groups 345, 349
Staudenraus, P. J. 190n., 499n., 510, 512, 530
Stavenisse (ship) 334n.
Steelpoort r. 322, 344, 389
Steenkamp, A. 366n.
Stella, Father 89–90, 92
Stephenson, Robert 34
Stern, H. 79, 502
Stockenstroom, Andries 365, 367, 376
stockmen 210
Stockton, Lieut. R. F. 191, 192
stone cutters, masons 406
strategy, imperial 492–6
straw hats 415
Stuhlmann, F. 284, 516
Suakin 15, 28, 44
subsistence economy, self-sufficiency 102, 230, 241, 261, 262, 436
succession system 251, 316; struggles, disputes 311, 341, 342
Sudan, Nilotic 5, 13, 22, 24, 25–6, 28, 29, 30, 33, 42–4, 481–2, 497–500
Sudan, Western 153, 155, 156, 202, 469
Sudanic belt 458, 487
Suerra y Sanchez, R. 532
Suez 34, 35; Suez canal 35, 40, 41, 44, 411, 417, 493
sufi orders 14, 47, 126, 129, 137, 150, 152, 154, 156, 161, 162, 166, 169; sufi litany 136
sugar 105, 180, 208, 210, 231, 240, 375, 408, 409, 416, 430–1, 432, 434, 436, 441; sugar cane 297, 409
Sukuma 280
Sulaymān (son of al-Zubayr) 45